THE THIRD REICH FROM ORIGINAL SOURCES

THE NUREMBERG TRIALS

THE COMPLETE PROCEEDINGS

Vol 4 : Individual Responsibilty of the Defendants

7th-19th January 1946

Edited and introduced by Bob Carruthers

CODA
BOOKS LTD

This edition published in Great Britain in 2011 by
Coda Books Ltd, The Barn, Cutlers Farm Business Centre, Edstone,
Wootton Wawen, Henley in Arden, Warwickshire, B95 6DJ
www.codahistory.com

Copyright © 2011 Coda Books Ltd

All rights reserved. No part of this publication may be reproduced or transmitted in any form or by any means, electronic or mechanical, including photocopy, recording, or any information storage and retrieval system, without permission in writing from the publisher.

A CIP catalogue record for this book is available from the British Library

ISBN 978 1 908538 81 9

Originally published as
"The Trial of German Major War Criminals
Proceedings of the International Military Tribunal Sitting at Nuremberg, Germany"
under the authority of
H.M. Attorney-General by His Majesty's Stationery Office
London : 1946

CONTENTS

Introduction 4

Twenty-Eighth Day: Monday, January 7th, 1946 8

Twenty-Ninth Day: Tuesday, January 8th, 1946 54

Thirtieth Day: Wednesday, January 9th, 1946 102

Thirty-First Day: Thursday, January 10th, 1946 148

Thirty-Second Day: Friday, January 11th, 1946 195

Thirty-Third Day: Monday, January 14th, 1946 241

Thirty-Fourth Day: Tuesday, January 15th, 1946 264

Thirty-Fifth Day: Wednesday, January 16th, 1946 310

Thirty-Sixth Day: Thursday, January 17th, 1946 361

Thirty-Seventh Day: Friday, January 18th, 1946 407

Thirty-Eighth Day: Saturday, January 19th, 1946 448

About Coda Books 470

Introduction

The trial of the German major war criminals is better known to posterity as the Nuremberg Trials. This was a revolutionary new form of justice which was without parallel in the history of warfare.

In the wake of six years of savagery, inhumanity and turmoil it was sensed that a series of summary executions would not bring closure to the years of violence which had seen unheralded scenes of brutality as civilian populations were targeted for bombardment on a scale never before witnessed.

In 1945, faced with the stark evidence of the appalling crimes against humanity committed by the Nazi regime, there was an understandable clamour, particularly from the Soviet camp, for a series of quick summary executions to draw the line under the past and allow the world to get back to civilised behaviour. Given the scale of the crimes and the gruesome evidence emerging from Dachau, Auschwitz and Bergen-Belsen, it was certainly difficult to argue against making a rapid example of men like Hermann Göring, the father of the Gestapo.

Fortunately clearer heads prevailed and it was felt necessary to create some form of judicial process which would mark the transition back from barbarism to the rule of law. However there was then no such thing as an international court and there was no precedent for the legal trial of defeated belligerents. The plan for the "Trial of European War Criminals" was therefore drafted by Secretary of War Henry L. Stimson and the War Department. Following Roosevelt's death in April 1945, the new president, Harry S. Truman, gave strong approval for a judicial process. After a series of negotiations between Britain, the US, the Soviet Union and France, details of the trial were finally agreed. The trials were to commence on 20th November 1945, in the Bavarian city of Nuremberg.

At the meetings in Potsdam (1945), the three major wartime powers, the United Kingdom, the United States, and the Union of Soviet Socialist Republics finally agreed on the principles of punishment for those responsible for war crimes during World War II. France was also awarded a place on the tribunal.

The legal basis for the trial was established by the London Charter, issued on August 8th, 1945, which restricted the trial to "punishment of the major war criminals of the European Axis countries". Some 200 German war crimes defendants were ultimately tried at Nuremberg, and 1,600 others were tried under the traditional channels of military justice. The legal basis for the jurisdiction of the court was that defined by the Instrument of Surrender of Germany. Political authority for Germany had been transferred to the Allied Control Council which, having sovereign power over Germany, could choose to punish violations of international law and the laws of war. Because the court was limited to violations of the laws of war, it did not have jurisdiction over crimes that took place before the outbreak of war on September 3rd, 1939.

Leipzig, Munich and Luxembourg were briefly considered as the location for the trial. The Soviet Union had wanted the trials to take place in Berlin, as the capital city of the 'fascist conspirators', but Nuremberg was chosen as the site for the trials for two specific reasons: firstly because the Palace of Justice was spacious and largely undamaged (one of the few civic buildings that had remained largely intact through extensive Allied bombing), and secondly that a large prison was also part of the complex.

Nuremberg was also considered the ceremonial birthplace of the Nazi Party, and hosted annual rallies. It was thus considered a fitting place to mark the Party's symbolic demise.

As a compromise with the Soviet Union, it was agreed that while the location of the trial would be Nuremberg, Berlin would be the official home of the Tribunal authorities. It was also agreed that France would become the permanent seat of the IMT and that the first trial (several were planned) would take place in Nuremberg.

Each of the four countries provided one judge and an alternate, as well as a prosecutor.

- Major General Iona Nikitchenko (Soviet main)
- Lieutenant Colonel Alexander Volchkov (Soviet alternate)
- Colonel Sir Geoffrey Lawrence (British main and president)
- Sir Norman Birkett (British alternate)
- Francis Biddle (American main)
- John J. Parker (American alternate)
- Professor Henri Donnedieu de Vabres (French main)
- Robert Falco (French alternate)
- The chief prosecutors were as follows
- Attorney General Sir Hartley Shawcross (United Kingdom)
- Supreme Court Justice Robert H. Jackson (United States)
- Lieutenant-General Roman Andreyevich Rudenko (Soviet Union)
- François de Menthon (France)

Assisting Jackson was the lawyer Telford Taylor, Thomas J. Dodd and a young US Army interpreter named Richard Sonnenfeldt. Assisting Shawcross were Major Sir David Maxwell-Fyfe and Sir John Wheeler-Bennett. Mervyn Griffith-Jones, later to become famous as the chief prosecutor in the Lady Chatterley's Lover obscenity trial, was also on Shawcross's team. Shawcross also recruited a young barrister, Anthony Marreco, who was the son of a friend of his, to help the British team with the heavy workload. Assisting de Menthon was Auguste Champetier de Ribes.

The International Military Tribunal was opened on October 18th, 1945, in the Palace of Justice in Nuremberg. The first session was presided over by the Soviet judge, Nikitchenko. The prosecution entered indictments against 24 major war criminals and six criminal organizations – the leadership of the Nazi party, the Schutzstaffel (SS) and Sicherheitsdienst (SD), the Gestapo, the Sturmabteilung (SA) and the "General Staff and High Command," comprising several categories of senior military officers.

The Defendants were Hermann Wilhelm Goering, Rudolf Hess, Joachim von Ribbentrop, Robert Ley, Wilhelm Keitel, Ernst Kaltenbrunner, Alfred Rosenberg, Hans Frank, Wilhelm Frick, Julius Streicher, Walter Funk, Hjalmar Schacht, Gustav Krupp von Bohlen und Halbach, Karl Doenitz, Erich Raeder, Baldur von Schirach, Fritz Sauckel, Alfred Jodl, Martin Bormann, Franz von Papen, Artur Seyss-Inquart, Albert Speer, Constantin von Neurath and Hans Fritzsche

The indictments were for:
- Participation in a common plan or conspiracy for the accomplishment of a crime against peace
- Planning, initiating and waging wars of aggression and other crimes against peace
- War crimes
- Crimes against humanity

Under the circumstances the Proceedings of the International Military Tribunal just about passes muster as an exercise in establishing a platform from which to dispense a reasonably balanced form of justice. There was, of course, the questionable involvement of Stalin's legal team and it was ironic that his crimes against peace and humanity matched, if not surpassed those of Adolf Hitler. Ribbentrop and Molotov between them had secretly carved up Poland and in so doing had certainly been guilty of crimes against peace, planning war. Stalin had also waged an aggressive was against Finland and had annexed the Baltic States. Had Stalin been on trial his own actions would have condemned him to a guilty verdict on all four counts, but history is always written by the victors, and Stalin's crimes were airbrushed out of history in order that his team could sit in judgement as if nothing untoward had ever happened.

It has been asked many times were the trials fair. In strict legal terms they certainly were not. Declaring the instruments of the Nazi state to be illegal was illogical and unreasonable, but this was certainly no Stalinist show trial with a guilty verdict and a hangman's noose already awaiting the defendants. Under the circumstances the court was incredibly well balanced as was evidenced by the fact that three of the Defendants were acquitted and others received comparatively light sentences. Of the twenty-four accused only twelve received death sentences.

Ultimately the process had its flaws but it did provide a civilised alternative to Stalin's suggestion that 50,000 to 100,000 German officers should be executed without trial, and it was to serve as a forerunner for the International Court now located at the Hague.

This is the fourth volume in the complete proceedings of the Nuremberg trial of the German major war criminals before the International Military Tribunal sitting at Nuremberg, Germany.

Taken from the original court transcript this volume covers the proceedings from 7th-19th January 1946 and represents an essential primary source for scholars and general readers alike. The transcripts are complete and contain the whole of the proceedings as taken from the original court documents.

This volume presents the case against the individual responsibility of the defendants and includes the official Nazi policy towards captured POWs, partisans and victims of the U-boat attacks, forced labour camps and the suppression of the Church as originally published under the authority of H.M. Attorney-General by His Majesty's Stationery Office London in 1946.

It includes the testimony of Dr Franz Blaha, a Czech prisoner at Dachau concentration camp who performed hundreds of autopsies on the victims of medical experiments, Karl-Heinz Moehle, a U-boat commander and Erich von dem Bach-Zelewski, an SS-Obergruppenführer.

Dr. Franz Blaha was himself was experimented upon, but when his medical background was discovered, was forced to perform hundreds of autopsies on the victims of medical experiments.

Karl-Heinz Moehle was a successful U-boat commander, who sank 21 Allied ships from September 1939 until retiring from front line service in June 1941. He was sentenced to five years imprisonment for implementing Donitz's War Order No. 154 to those under his command. War Order No. 154 forbade U-boat commanders to rescue any survivors from the sea: "No attempt of any kind must be made at rescuing crews of ships sunk, and this includes picking up persons in the water and putting them in lifeboats, righting capsized lifeboats, and handing over food and water. These are absolutely forbidden."

Erich von dem Bach-Zelewski was an SS-Obergruppenführer and was responsible for the murder of 35,000 civilians in Riga and more than 200,000 in Belarus and eastern Poland. In 1943, he received command of anti-partisan operations in Belarus and adjoining parts of Russia, including the Warsaw uprising. In exchange for his testimony against his superiors at Nuremberg, he never faced trial, nor was he extradited to Poland or the USSR. In 1951, von dem Bach-Zelewski was finally sentenced to 10 years in a labor camp for the murder of political opponents in the early 1930s; however, he did not serve time until 1958, when he was convicted of killing Anton von Hohberg und Buchwald, an SS officer, during the Night of the Long Knives, and was sentenced to four and a half years imprisonment. In 1961, he was sentenced to an additional 10 years in home custody for the murder of 10 German Communists in the early 1930s. None of the sentences referred to his role in Poland, in the East and his participation in the Holocaust, although he openly denounced himself as a mass murderer. He died in a Munich prison on 8 March 1972.

Bob Carruthers

Twenty-Eighth Day:
Monday, January 7th, 1946

COLONEL TELFORD TAYLOR: May it please the Court, Sir, when the Court rose on Friday I had completed that part of the presentation on Counts 1 and 2. I now turn to that part of the Indictment which charges that the General Staff and High Command Group had a major responsibility for the War Crimes and Crimes against Humanity involved in the execution of the Common Plan or Conspiracy set forth in Counts 3 and 4 of the Indictment. For the purposes of brevity I shall refer to these crimes simply as War Crimes.

The presentation of the documents under this part of the case should take all or the better part of the morning session. At the conclusion of that, I propose to call a single witness, one witness, Erich von dem Bach-Zelewski, whose testimony on direct examination should not exceed 25 or 30 minutes. After that, I shall take possibly 10 minutes to conclude, and that will be the entire presentation.

On this part of the case I propose to show that members of the General Staff and High Command Group, including the defendants who are members of the Group, ordered and directed the commission of War Crimes, and thereby participated in the commission of War Crimes in their official capacity as members of the Group. I also propose to show, in certain instances, the actual commission of War Crimes by members of the German armed forces as a result of these orders, or as a result of other orders and arrangements made by members of the General Staff and High Command Group which controlled the German armed forces. However, I do not propose to make a full showing of War Crimes committed by the German armed forces. The full presentation of the evidence under Counts 3 and 4 will be made pursuant to agreement among the Chief Prosecutors, by the French and Soviet delegations, and a substantial amount of the evidence to be presented by them will be relevant to the charges against the General Staff and High Command Group.

We will at this time show the Tribunal that the General Staff and High Command became wedded to a policy of terror. In some cases, the evidence of this policy is in documentary form, and we will present the papers which were signed by, initialled by and circulated among the members of the Group. In other instances, where the actual crimes were committed by other than members of the German armed forces, where, for example, prisoners of war were handed over to and mistreated by the S.S. or S.D., we will show that in those cases members of this group were well aware that they were assisting in the commission of War Crimes. We will show that many crimes committed by the S.S. and S.D. were committed with the knowledge and necessary support of the General Staff and High Command Group.

The first matter which I will take up relates to the killing, in violation of International Law and the rules of war, of Allied Commandos, Paratroopers, and members of military missions, and the first document to which I wish to refer is 498-PS, which will be Exhibit USA 501.

This story starts with the order embodied in that document, which is an order issued by Hitler on 18th October, 1942, and which Mr. Storey has already mentioned in the presentation of charges against the Sicherheitsdienst. The order begins with a recital that Allied Commandos were using methods of warfare alleged to be outside the scope of the Geneva Convention, and thereafter proceeds to specify the methods of warfare which German troops should use against Allied Commandos, and the disposition which should be made of captured Commandos.

This order is one of the two basic documents in the story. I will read it in full:-

"1. For some time our enemies have been using, in their warfare, methods which are outside the International Geneva Conventions. Especially brutal and treacherous is the behaviour of the so-called Commandos, who, as is established, are partially recruited even from freed criminals in enemy countries. From captured orders it is divulged that they are directed not only to shackle prisoners, but also to kill defenceless prisoners on the spot at the moment in which they believe that the latter, as prisoners, represent a burden in the further pursuit of their purposes, or could otherwise be a hindrance. Finally, orders have been found in which the killing of prisoners has been demanded in principle.

2. For this reason it was already announced, in an addendum to the Armed Forces report of 7th October, 1942, that in the future, Germany in the face of these sabotage troops of the British and their accomplices, will resort to the same procedure, that is, that they will be ruthlessly mowed down by the German troops in combat, wherever they may appear.

3. I, therefore order:

From now on all enemies on so-called Commando missions in Europe or Africa, challenged by German troops, even if they are to all appearances soldiers in uniform or demolition troops, whether armed or unarmed, in battle or in flight, are to be slaughtered to the last man. It does not make any difference whether they are landed from ships and airplanes for their actions, or whether they are dropped by parachute. Even if these individuals, when found, should apparently be prepared to give themselves up, no pardon is to be granted them on principle. In each individual case full information is to be sent to the O.K.W. for publication in the Report of the Military Forces.

4. If individual members of such Commandos, such as agents, saboteurs, etc., fall into the hands of the military forces by some other means, through the police in occupied territories, for instance, they are to be handed over immediately to the S.D. Any imprisonment under military guard, in P.W. stockades, for instance, etc., is strictly prohibited, even if this is only intended for a short time.

This order does not apply to the treatment of any soldiers who, in the course of normal hostilities, large- scale offensive actions, landing operations and airborne operations, are captured in open battle or give themselves up. Nor does this order apply to enemy soldiers falling into our hands after battles at sea, or to enemy soldiers trying to save their lives by parachute after air battles.

6. I will hold responsible under Military Law, for failing to carry out this order, all commanders and officers who either have neglected their duty of instructing the troops about this order, or acted against this order when it was to be executed."

It is signed, by Adolf Hitler, and the Tribunal will note that this order was issued by O.K.W. in 12 copies, and the distribution shown on the second page included [Page 3] the three Supreme Commands, Army, Sea, and Air, and the principal Field Commands.

Now, the same day Hitler issued a supplementary order, this is, Document 503-PS, which will be Exhibit USA 542. This was issued for the purpose of explaining the reasons why the basic order was issued. In this explanation, Hitler gave a rather different set of reasons for the issuance of the order and pointed out that Allied Commando operations had been extraordinarily successful in the destruction of rear communications, intimidating labourers and destroying important war plants in occupied areas. This is the other basic document, and while I need not read it in full, I would like to read substantial excerpts, starting with the first paragraph at the top of the page:

"Added to the decree concerning the destruction of terror and sabotage troops" - then in parentheses was a cross reference to the order which I have just read - a supplementary order of the Fuehrer is enclosed.

"This order is intended for commanders only and must not, under any circumstances, fall into enemy hands.

The further distribution is to be limited accordingly by the receiving bureaux.

The bureaux named in the distribution list are held responsible for the return and destruction of all distributed copies of this order and copies made thereof."

It is signed, "The Chief of the High Command of the Armed Forces, by order of Jodl."

Thereafter follows a distribution list and then the supplementary order itself, signed by Hitler. I will start reading the first two paragraphs of the supplementary order which appear at the bottom of Page 1 of the translation:

"I have been compelled to issue strict orders for the destruction of enemy sabotage troops and to declare non- compliance with these orders severely punishable. I deem it necessary to announce to the competent commanding officers and commanders the reasons for this decree.

As in no previous war, a method of destruction of communications behind the front; intimidation of the populace working for Germany; as well as the destruction of war-important industrial plants in territories occupied by us, has been developed in this war."

I propose to pass to the bottom of Page 2, the last two paragraphs on Page 2 of the translation:

"The consequences of these activities are of extraordinary weight. I do not know whether each commander and officer is cognisant of the fact that the destruction of one single electric power plant, for instance, can deprive the Luftwaffe of many thousand tons of aluminium, thereby eliminating the construction of countless aircraft that will be missed in the fight at the front, and so contributing to serious damage of the homeland as well as to bloody losses of the fighting soldiers.

Yet this form of war is completely without danger to the adversary, for, since he lands his sabotage troops in uniform but at the same time supplies them with civilian clothes, they can, according to need, appear as soldiers or civilians. While they themselves have orders ruthlessly to remove any German soldiers or even natives who get in their way, they run no danger of suffering really serious losses in their operations, since at the worst, if they are caught, they can immediately surrender in the belief that they will theoretically fall under the provisions of the Geneva Convention. There is no doubt, however, that this is a misuse in the worst form of the Geneva agreements, especially since part of these elements are even criminals, freed from prisons, who can rehabilitate themselves through these activities.

England and America will therefore always be able to find volunteers for this kind of warfare, as long as they can truthfully assure them that there is no danger of loss of life for them. At worst, all they have to do is successfully to commit their attacks on people, traffic installations, or other installations, and upon being encountered by the enemy, to capitulate.

If the German conduct of war is not to suffer grievous damage through such methods, it must be made clear to the adversary that all sabotage troops will be exterminated, without exception, to the last man.

This means that their chance of saving their lives is nil. Under no circumstances can it be permitted, therefore, that a dynamite, sabotage, or terrorist unit simply allows itself to be captured, expecting to be treated according to the rules of the Geneva Convention. It must, under all circumstances, be ruthlessly exterminated.

The report on this subject appearing in the Armed Forces communique will briefly and laconically state that a sabotage, terror or destruction unit has been encountered and exterminated to the last man.

I therefore expect the officers commanding armies, as well as individual commanders, not only to realise the necessity of taking such measures, but to carry out this order with all energy. Officers and non-commissioned officers who fail through some weakness are to be reported without fail or, if the circumstances require, it, e.g., if danger is imminent, to be at once made strictly accountable. The homeland, as well as the fighting soldier at the front, has the right to expect that the essentials of nourishment as well as the supply of war-important weapons and ammunition remains secure.

These are the reasons for the issuance of this decree.

If it should become necessary, for reasons of interrogation, initially to spare one or two men, then they are to be shot immediately after such interrogation."

Your Lordship, the next is Document C-179 which will be Exhibit USA 543. As this document shows, ten days later, on 28th October, 1942, and while the defendant Raeder was Commander-in-Chief of the German Navy, the Naval War Staff in Berlin transmitted its copy of the basic order of 18th October to the lower naval commands. The copy distributed by the Navy and the covering: memorandum from the Naval War Staff show clearly the secrecy which surrounded the dissemination of this order, and I read the first sheet of this. document only, the cover sheet:

"Enclosed please find a Fuehrer Order regarding annihilation of terror and sabotage units. This order must not be distributed in writing by flotilla leaders, section commanders or officers of this rank. After verbal notification to subordinate sections, the above officers must hand this order over to the next higher section, which is responsible for its withdrawal and destruction."

Passing over to Page 3 of this document, at the very end, we find a similar admonition in the notice for distribution, at the very end of the document. I read:

"These instructions are not to be distributed over and above the battalions and the corresponding staffs of the other services. After notification those copies, distributed over and above the regimental and corresponding staffs of the other services, must be withdrawn and destroyed."

The next document, your Lordship, is C-178, which becomes Exhibit USA 544. This document is dated 11th February, 1943, which was twelve days after the defendant Donitz had become Commander-in-Chief of the German Navy. On that day, this memorandum was circulated within the Naval War Staff in order to clear up certain misunderstandings as to the scope of the basic order of 18th October, 1942. This document, of which I will read the first four paragraphs, indicates why the earlier order had been treated as such a secret matter, and also directs that all naval commanders and officers who failed to carry out the order, or to instruct their units concerning the order, would run the risk of serious court martial penalties. I will read the first four paragraphs only:

> "From the notice given by the Naval War Staff on 1st February, 1943, it has been discovered that the competent departments of the General Staff of the Army, as well as those of the Air Force Operations Staff, have a wrong conception regarding the treatment of saboteurs. A telephone inquiry at the Naval War Staff proved that this naval authority was not correctly informed either."

In view of this situation, reference is made to paragraph 6 of the Fuehrer Order of 18th October, 1942 - and then a cross-reference - "according to which all commanders and officers who have neglected their duty in instructing their units about the order referring to treatment of saboteurs are threatened with punishment by court martial.

The first Fuehrer Order concerning this matter of 18th October, 1942, was given the protection of Top Secret merely because it stated therein (1) that according to the Fuehrer's views, the spreading of military sabotage organisations in the East and West may have tremendous consequences for our whole conduct of the war and (2) that the shooting of uniformed prisoners acting on military orders must be carried out even after they have surrendered voluntarily and asked for pardon.

On the other hand, the annihilation of sabotage units in battle is not at all to be kept secret, but, on the contrary, to be currently published in the O.K.W. reports. The purpose of these measures - to act as a deterrent - will not be achieved if those taking part in enemy Commando operations do not learn that certain death, and not safe imprisonment awaits them. As the saboteurs are to be annihilated immediately unless their statements are first needed for military reasons, it is necessary that not only all members of the armed forces must receive instructions that these types of saboteurs, even if they are in uniform, are to be annihilated, but also all departments of the Home Staff, dealing with this kind of questions, must be informed of the course of action which has been ordered."

I will call the Tribunal's attention to the two reasons given in that quotation for keeping secret from the public, knowledge of the fact that uniformed prisoners would be shot, even after they had surrendered and asked for pardon. This shows a clear awareness that that was in direct contravention of The Hague and Geneva Conventions.

THE PRESIDENT: Colonel Taylor, did you read the paragraph beginning, "Practical difficulties ..."?

COLONEL TAYLOR: No, your Honour. I will read that.

THE PRESIDENT: I think you should.

COLONEL TAYLOR:

> "Practical difficulties may develop because of the definition of the term 'Sabotage Units.' The annihilation and destruction, according to paragraph 5 of the Fuehrer Order of 18th October, do not apply to troops participating in large-scale landing operations and large-scale air-borne operations. The criterion is to be found in that, in the latter case, an open battle takes place, whereas, for instance, ten or more people who land by sea or air, or drop by parachute not to fight an open battle but to destroy either a factory, a bridge or a railway installation, would fall into the category of those who must be annihilated."

The next document, your Honour, is 508-PS, which will be Exhibit USA 545. Now, the Hitler Order of 18th October, 1942, was actually carried out in a number of instances, of which we have the documentary proof for several. Document 508-PS shows that during the night of l9th-20th November, 1942, a British freight glider crashed near Egersund, in Norway. The glider carried a British Commando Unit of 17 men, of whom three were apparently killed in the crash. All were in British uniform. Fourteen survivors were executed in accordance with the Hitler Order, the evening of 20th November. In proof of this I will read certain extracts from 508-PS, beginning on Page 1 of the translation, the paragraph numbered (1):

"(1) Following supplementary report is made about landing of a British freight glider at Egersund in the night of -"

It reads 11th November in the translation, but I believe in the original it was 20th November; that is a typographical error.

"(a) No firing on the part of the German defence.
(b) The towing plane (Wellington) has crashed after touching the ground; 7-man crew dead. The attached freight glider also crashed; of the 17-man crew 14 alive. Indisputably a sabotage force. Fuehrer Order has been carried out."

I pass to Page 3 of the translation, on which page appear two teletype messages. I wish to read the first two paragraphs at the top of that page.

"On 20th November, 1942, at 5.50 an enemy plane was found 15 km. N.E. of Egersund. It is a British aircraft (towed glider) made of wood, without engine. Of the 17- member crew three are dead, six are severely, the others slightly wounded.

All wore English khaki uniforms without sleeve-insignia. Furthermore, following items were found: 8 knapsacks, tents, skis and radiosender, exact number is unknown. The glider carried rifles, light machine guns and machine pistols, number unknown. At present the prisoners are with the battalion in Egersund."

Passing to the second teletype message, the first paragraph:

"Beside the 17-member crew extensive sabotage material and work equipment were found. Therefore the sabotage purpose was absolutely proved. The 280th Infantry Division ordered the execution according to the Fuehrer Order. The execution was carried out toward the evening of 20th November. Some of the prisoners wore blue ski- suits under their khaki uniforms which had no insignia on the sleeves. During a short interrogation the survivors have revealed nothing but their names, ranks and serial numbers."

I pass to the last paragraph of that teletype, at the foot of Page 3 of the translation:

"In connection with the shooting of the members of the crew, the Armed Forces Commander of Norway has issued an order to the district commanders, according to which the interrogations by G-2" - that was Ic in the German - "and by B.D.S." - police - "are important before the execution of the Fuehrer Order; in case of paragraph No. 4 of the Fuehrer Order the prisoners are to be handed over to the B.D.S."

Your Lordship, the next document is 512-PS, Exhibit USA 546. This document recites three specific instances where the Hitler Order was carried out in Norway, and especially emphasises the desirability of taking individual Commandos prisoner for interrogation. I read from Document 512-PS, dated 13th December, 1942:

"According to the last sentence of the Fuehrer Order of 18th October, individual saboteurs can be spared for the time being in order to keep them for interrogation. The importance of this measure was proved in the cases of the Glomfjord, 2-man torpedo Drontheirn, and glider plane Stavanger, where interrogations resulted in valuable knowledge of enemy intentions. Since in the case of Egersund the saboteur was liquidated immediately and no clues were found, therefore Armed Forces Commander refers to the above mentioned last sentence of the Fuehrer Order calling for liquidation only after a short interrogation."

One final document from the Norwegian theatre of war is relevant.

THE PRESIDENT: Colonel Taylor, what does "R.K." in the last paragraph mean? The first words of the last paragraph?

COLONEL TAYLOR: Red Cross, Rotes Kreuz.

THE PRESIDENT: So they had a protest from the Red Cross?

COLONEL TAYLOR: Yes, Sir.

THE PRESIDENT: And "B.D.S."?

COLONEL TAYLOR: That is "Befehlshaber der Sicherheitspolizei (Sipo)."

Document 526-PS, which is Exhibit USA 502, dated 10th May, 1943, Colonel Storey has already brought to the Tribunal's attention in connection with the presentation against the Sicherheitsdienst.

I will first read the opening sentences:

"On the 30th March, 1943, in Toftefjord (degree of latitude 70), an enemy cutter was sighted. Cutter was blown up by enemy.

Crew: 2 dead and 10 taken prisoners.

Cutter sent from Scalloway (Shetland Isles) by the Norwegian Navy.

Armament: 2 Colt machine guns; 2 mounted machine guns. Also a small transmitting set. There were likewise found on board: 4 tripods for mounting machine guns, 6 sub- m achine guns and 1,000 kilos of high explosives.

Cutter's Commander: Lt. Eskeland, of the Royal Norwegian Navy."

Passing to the word "Purposes":

Purpose: "Construction of an organisation for the sabotaging of strong-points, battery positions, staff and troop billets and bridges.

Assigner of Mission in London: Norwegian Major Munthe.

Fuehrer Order executed by Sicherheitsdienst (Security Service).

Wehrmacht Report of 6th April announces the following about it:

" 'In Northern Norway an enemy sabotage unit was engaged and destroyed on approaching the coast.'"

Now, shifting to the Italian theatre of war, I call the Court's attention to Document 509-PS, which will be Exhibit USA 547. This document is dated 7th November, 1943, and is a telegram from the Supreme Commander in Italy to O.K.W., and it shows that on 2nd November, 1943, three British Commandos, taken prisoner near Pescara in Italy, were given "special treatment" - (sonderbehandelt), which, as the Court knows from previous evidence in the case, meant death. What happened to the nine remaining prisoners of war in the hospital, we do not know.

I have one more document from the Italian theatre of war, 2610-PS, Exhibit USA 548. This specifically shows the carrying out of Hitler orders. It consists of an affidavit, dated 7th November, 1945, by Frederick W. Roche, a Major in the Army of the United States. Major Roche was the Judge Advocate of an American Military Commission which tried General Anton Dostler, formerly Commander of the 75th German Army Corps, for the unlawful execution of fifteen members of the United States armed forces. I will read from this affidavit:

"Frederick W. Roche, being duly sworn, deposes and says:
I am a Major in the, Army of the United States.
I was the Judge Advocate of the Military Commission which tried Anton Dostler for ordering the execution of the group of fifteen United States Army personnel who comprised the 'Ginny Mission.' This Military Commission, consisting of five officers, was appointed by command of General McNarney, by Special Orders No. 269, dated 26th September, 1945, Headquarters, Mediterranean theatre of Operations, United States Army, A.P.O. 512.
The Military Commission met at Rome, Italy, on 8th October, 1945, and proceeded with the trial of the case of the United States v. Anton Dostler. The trial of this case lasted four days and the findings and sentence were announced on the morning of 12th October, 1945. The charge and specification in this case are as follows:
Charge: Violation of the Law of War.
Specification: In that Anton Dostler, then General, commanding military forces for the German Reich, a belligerent enemy nation, to wit the 75th Army Corps, did on or about 24th March, 1944, in the vicinity of La Spezia, Italy, contrary to the law of war, order to be shot summarily a group of United States Army personnel consisting of two officers and thirteen enlisted men who had then recently been captured by forces under General Dostler, which order was carried into execution on or about 26th March, 1944, resulting in the death of the said fifteen members of the Army of the United States" - and a list of names follows.
I was present throughout the entire proceeding. I heard all the testimony and I am familiar with the records in this case. The facts developed in this proceeding are as follows: On the night of 22nd March, 1944, two officers and thirteen enlisted men of the 2677th Special Reconnaissance Battalion of the Army of the United States, disembarked from some United States Navy Boats and landed on the Italian coast near Stazione di Framura. All fifteen men were members of the army of the United States and were in the military service of the United States. When they landed on the Italian coast they were all properly dressed in the field uniform of the United States Army and they carried no civilian clothes. Their mission was to demolish a railroad tunnel on the main line between La Spezia and Genoa. That rail line was being used by the German forces to supply their fighting forces on the Cassino and Anzio Beachhead fronts. The entire group was captured on the morning of 24th March, 1944, by a patrol consisting of Fascist soldiers and a group of members of the German Army. All fifteen men were placed under interrogation in La Spezia and they were held in custody until the morning of 26th March, 1944, when they were all executed by a firing squad. These men were never tried nor were they brought before any court or given any hearing; they were shot by order of Anton Dostler, then General Commanding the 75th German Army Corps.
Anton Dostler took the stand in this case and testified, by way of defence, that he ordered the fifteen American soldiers to be shot pursuant to the Hitler Order of 18th October, 1942, on Commando Operations, which provided that Commandos were to be shot and not taken prisoners of war, even after they had been interrogated. He also testified that he would have been subject to court- martial proceedings if he did not obey the Hitler Order."
The following is a true copy of the findings and sentence in the case of the United

States against Anton Dostler, as these findings and sentence appear in the original record of the trial and as they were announced in open court at Rome, Italy, on 12th October, 1945:

"Findings: General Dostler, as President of this Commission it is my duty to inform you that the Commission, in closed session and upon secret written ballot, at least two-thirds of all the members of the Commission concurring, finds you of the specification and of the charge: Guilty.

Sentence: And again in closed session and upon secret written ballot, at least two-thirds of all the members of the Commission concurring, sentences you: to be shot to death by musketry."

Now the order of 18th October, 1942, remained in force, so far as we know, until the end of the war. I wish to offer Document 506-PS, which will be Exhibit USA 549. This document is dated 22nd June, 1944. It is initialled by Warlimont and in it the O.K.W. made it clear that the Hitler Order was to be applied even in cases where the Commando operation was undertaken by only one person. I will read the single paragraph of the order:

"The Operations Staff agrees with the view taken in the letter of the Army Group Judge to the Supreme Commander Southwest of 20th May, 1944. The Fuehrer Order is to be applied even if the enemy employs only one person for a task. Therefore, it does not make any difference if several persons or a single person take part in a Commando Operation. The reason for the special treatment of participants in a Commando Operation is that such operations do not correspond to the German concept of usage and customs of (land) warfare."

The Allied landing in Norway early in June, 1944, in the course of which large-scale airborne operations took place, raised among the Germans the question as to how far the Hitler Order would be applied in Normandy, and in France behind the German lines. I direct the Court's attention to Document 531-PS, which will be Exhibit USA 550. The memorandum is dated 23rd June, 1944, and is signed by Warlimont. Warlimont's memorandum starts by quoting a teletype from the Supreme Command in the West, inquiring what should be done about applying the Hitler Order to Airborne Troops and Commandos.

I would like to read a small part of the teletype from the beginning:

"Supreme Command West reports by teletype message, Top Secret, 23rd June, 1944:

The treatment of enemy Commando Groups has so far been carried out according to the order referred to." (If I may interpolate here, the order referred to is shown in the cross-reference to the Fuehrer Order of 13th October, 1942.)

"With the large-scale landing achieved, a new situation has arisen. The order referred to directs, in paragraph 5, that enemy soldiers who are taken prisoner in open combat or surrender within the limits of normal combat operations (such as large-scale landing operations and undertakings) are not to be treated according to paragraphs 3 and 4. It must be established in a form easily understood by the troops how far the concept 'within the limits of normal combat operations' is to be extended."

Then I pass down to sub-paragraph D and read the first sentence of that sub-paragraph.

THE PRESIDENT: I think you ought to read the latter part of "C."

COLONEL TAYLOR: Your Honour, I think it is all summarised in the one sentence.

THE PRESIDENT: The last sentence is the one that I mean.

COLONEL TAYLOR: "Considerable reprisals against our own prisoners must be expected if its contents become known."

Then, continuing with "D":

"The application of number 5 for all enemy soldiers in uniform penetrating from the outside into the occupied Western Areas, is held by the Supreme Command West to be the most correct and clearest solution."

Accordingly, as it is there shown, the Supreme Command in the West directed that paragraph 5, which is the paragraph under which the orders for execution are not to be applied, should be utilised in the West.

At the foot of the page is the position taken by the Armed Forces Operational Staff, the recommendation they were making:

"1. The Commando Order remains basically in effect, even after the enemy landing in the West.

2. Number 5 of the Order is to be clarified to the effect that the Order is not valid for those enemy soldiers in uniform, who are captured in open combat in the immediate combat area of the beachhead by our troops committed there, or who surrender. Our troops committed in the immediate, combat area means the divisions fighting on the front line, as well as reserves up to and including Corps Headquarters.

3. Furthermore, in doubtful cases, enemy personnel who have fallen into our hands alive are to be turned over to the S.D., upon whom it is incumbent to determine whether the Commando Order is to be applied or not.

4. Supreme Command West is to see to it that all units committed in its zone are orally acquainted in a suitable manner with the Order concerning the treatment of members of Commando undertakings of 18th October, 1942, together with the above explanation."

The final document on this episode, or inquiry, is Exhibit USA 551, and this is the actual Order of 25th June, 1944, constituting O.K.W.'s reply to the inquiry from the Supreme Command West, signed by Keitel, initialled by Warlimont and Jodl. I will read this, beginning with:

"Subject: Treatment of Commando Participants.

1. Even after the landing of Anglo-Americans in France, the order of the Fuehrer on the destruction of terror and sabotage units of 18th October, 1942, remains fully in force.

Enemy soldiers in uniform in the immediate combat area of the bridgehead, that is, in the area of the divisions fighting in the most forward lines, as well as of the reserves up to the Corps Commands, according to number 5 of the basic order of 18th October, 1942, remain exempted.

2. All members of terror and sabotage units, found outside the immediate combat area, including fundamentally all parachutists, are to be killed in combat. In special cases, they are to be turned over to the S.D.

3. All troops, committed outside the combat area of Normandy, are to be informed, briefly and succinctly, according to the directives issued for it, about the duty to destroy enemy terror and sabotage units.

4. Supreme Commander West will report immediately each day, how many saboteurs have been liquidated in this manner. This applies especially also to undertakings by the military commanders. The number is to be published

daily in the Armed Forces Communique to exercise a frightening effect, as had already been done towards previous Commando undertakings in the same manner."

Your Lordship, there is just one further development in connection with this order, this basic order, and that was in July, 1944. The question was then raised within the German High Command as to whether the order should be applied to members of foreign military missions, with special regard to the British, American and Soviet Military Missions which were co-operating with Allied Forces in South- eastern Europe, notably in Yugoslavia. A long document signed by Warlimont, which is 1279-PS, and becomes Exhibit USA 552, embodies the discussions which were held at O.K.W. I think I need not read from this document, and merely wish to point out that the Armed Forces Operational Staff recommended, that the order should be applied to these military missions, and drew up a draft to this effect. I would, however, like to read Document 537-PS, which becomes Exhibit USA 553. This is the order which actually resulted from these discussions. It is dated 30th July, 1944. I will read it in full:

"Subject: Treatment of members of foreign 'Military Missions,' captured together with Partisans.

In the areas of the High Command South-east and South- west, members of foreign so-called 'Military Missions' (Anglo-American as well as Soviet-Russian), captured in the course of the struggle against Partisans, shall not receive the treatment as specified in the special orders regarding the treatment of captured Partisans. Therefore, they are not to be treated as prisoners of war but in conformity with the Fuehrer's order concerning the elimination of terror and sabotage troops of 18th October, 1942.

This order shall not be transmitted to other units of the Armed Forces via the High Commands and equivalent staffs, and is to be destroyed after being made known.

The Chief of the High Command of the Wehrmacht, Keitel."

Pursuant to this order, approximately fifteen members of an Allied Military Mission to Slovakia were executed in January, 1945, as is shown by Document L-51, which is already in the record as Exhibit USA 521, and which has been read in full by Lieutenant Harris. I will not read it again.

This concludes the presentation of documents with respect to the order of the 18th October, 1942, and its subsequent enforcement and application. I can pass from here to another subject.

THE PRESIDENT: We will adjourn for ten minutes now.

(A recess was taken.)

COL. TAYLOR: Your Lordship, the order I have just been discussing operated chiefly in the Western theatre of war. This was natural, since Germany occupied almost the entire Western coast of Europe from 1940 until the last year of the war, and during that period land fighting in Western Europe was largely limited to Commando Operations.

I want to pass now to the Eastern front, where there was large-scale land fighting in Poland and the Soviet Union, from 1941 on. Here the German forces were fighting among a hostile population and had to face extensive Partisan activities behind their lines. I propose to show here that the activities of the German Armed Forces against Partisans and against other elements of the population became a vehicle for carrying out Nazi political and racial policies, and a vehicle for the massacre of Jews, and numerous segments of the Slav population which were regarded by the Nazis as undesirable. I will show that it was the policy of the German Armed Forces to behave with the utmost severity to the civilian population of the occupied territories, and that its military operations, particularly against Partisans, were so conducted as to advance the Nazi policies to which I have referred.

I will show that they supported, assisted and acted in co-operation with the S.S. groups to which reference has been made in the presentation by Major Farr and Colonel Storey.

I do not plan to make a full or even partial showing of War Crimes on the Eastern front. That will be done by the Soviet delegation. Nor do I plan to retrace the ground covered by Colonel Storey and Major Farr during their presentation of the evidence against the S.S., S.D. and Gestapo, except to the extent necessary to clarify the relations between these organisations and the German Armed Forces, and to demonstrate their close collaboration in the occupied territories of Eastern Europe.

The first document to which I will make reference is Document C-50, which will be Exhibit USA 554, and it will show that these policies of severity were determined upon and made official even before the invasion of the Soviet Union took place. This document consists of an order by Hitler, dated 13th May, 1941, and two covering transmittal sheets of subsequent date. I ask the Tribunal to note, on Page 4 of the translation, that the order is signed by Keitel, the Chief of the Supreme Command of the Armed Forces, and also to note the distribution, which appears at the foot of the second sheet, showing the distribution to the principal staff sections. The order itself begins on the third page, and that is where I propose to read. The document is entitled "Order concerning the exercise of martial jurisdiction and procedure in the area 'Barbarossa' and special military measures."

"The application of martial law aims, in the first place, at maintaining discipline.

The fact that the operational areas in the East are so far-flung, the battle strategy which this necessitates, and the peculiar qualities of the enemy, confront the courts martial with problems which, being short-staffed, they cannot solve while hostilities are in progress, and until some degree of pacification has been achieved in the conquered areas, unless jurisdiction is confined, in the first instance, to its main task.

This is possible only if the troops take ruthless action themselves, against any threat from the enemy population.

For these reasons I herewith issue the following order effective for the area 'Barbarossa' (Area of Operations, Army Rear Area, and Area of Political Administration):

I. Treatment of offences committed by Enemy Civilians.

1. Until further notice the military courts and the courts martial will not be competent for crimes committed by enemy civilians.

2. Guerrillas should be disposed of ruthlessly by the military, whether they are fighting or in flight.

3. Likewise all other attacks by enemy civilians on the Armed Forces its members and employees, are to be suppressed at once by the military, using the most extreme methods, until the assailants are destroyed.

4. Where such measures have been neglected or were not at first possible, persons suspected of criminal action will be brought at once before an officer. This officer will decide whether they are to be shot.

On the orders of an officer with the powers of, at least, a Battalion Commander, collective drastic measures will be taken without delay against localities from which cunning or malicious attacks are made on the Armed

Forces, if circumstances do not permit of a quick identification of individual offenders.

5. It is expressly forbidden to keep suspects in custody in order to hand them over to the courts after the reinstatement of civil courts.

6. The Commanders-in-Chief of the Army Groups may, by agreement with the competent Naval and Air Force Commanders, reintroduce military jurisdiction for civilians, in areas which are sufficiently pacified.

For the area of the Political Administration this order will be given by the Chief of the Supreme Command of the Armed Forces.

II. Treatment of offence committed against inhabitants by members of the Wehrmacht and its employees.

1. With regard to offences committed against enemy civilians by members of the Wehrmacht and its employees, prosecution is not obligatory, even where the act is at the same time a military crime or offence.

2. When judging such offences, it must be borne in mind, whatever the circumstances, that the collapse of Germany in 1918, the subsequent sufferings of the German people and the fight against National Socialism which cost the blood of innumerable supporters of the movement, were caused primarily by Bolshevik influence and that no German has forgotten this fact.

3. Therefore, the judicial authority will decide in such cases whether disciplinary action is indicated, or whether legal proceedings are necessary. In the case of offences against inhabitants it will order a court martial only if maintenance of discipline or security of the forces call for such a measure. This applies, for instance, to serious offences originating in lack of self-control in sexual matters, or in a criminal disposition, and to those offences which indicate that the troops are threatening to get out of hand. Offences which have resulted in senseless destruction of billets or supplies or other captured material, to the disadvantage of our forces, should as a rule be judged no less severely.

The order to institute proceedings requires in every single case the signature of the judicial authority.

4. Extreme caution is indicated in assessing the credibility of statements made by enemy civilians.

III. Responsibility of Military Commanders within their sphere of competence: Military Commanders are personally responsible for seeing that:

1. Every commissioned officer of the units under their command is instructed promptly and in the most emphatic manner on principles set out under (1) above.

2. Their legal advisers are notified promptly of these instructions and of verbal information in which the political intentions of the High Command were explained to Commanders-in-Chief.

3. Only those court sentences are confirmed which are in accordance with the political intentions of the High Command.

IV. Security.

Once the camouflage is lifted, this decree will be treated as 'Most Secret.'"

Your Lordship, the next document will be C-148, Exhibit USA 555. Less than three months after the invasion of the Soviet Union, the instructions which I have just read were amplified and made even more drastic. Document C-148 is an order dated 16th

September, 1941, signed by Keitel, and widely distributed, as is shown on the second sheet where the distribution is listed. This order is of general application in all theatres of war, but from its contents it is clearly of primary importance for the Eastern Front. I read, beginning at the start of the order:

"Subject: Communist Insurrection in occupied territories.

1. Since the beginning of the campaign against Soviet Russia, Communist insurrection movements have broken out everywhere in the area occupied by Germany. The type of action taken is growing from propaganda measures and attacks on individual members of the Armed Forces, to open rebellion and widespread guerrilla warfare.

It can be seen that this is a mass movement centrally directed by Moscow, which is also responsible for the apparently trivial isolated incidents in areas which otherwise have been quiet up to now.

In view of the many political and economic crises in the occupied areas, it must, moreover, be anticipated that nationalist and other circles will make full use of this opportunity of making difficulties for the German occupying forces, by associating themselves with the Communist insurrection.

This creates an increasing danger to the German war effort, which shows itself chiefly in general insecurity for the occupying troops, and has already led to the withdrawal of forces to the main centres of disturbance.

2. The measures taken up to now, to deal with this general Communist insurrection movement, have proved inadequate. The Fuehrer has now given orders that we take action everywhere with the most drastic means, in order to crush the movement in the shortest possible time.

Only this course, which has always been followed successfully throughout the history of the extension of influence of great peoples, can restore order.

3. Action taken in this matter should be in accordance with the following general directions:

(a) It should be inferred, in every case of resistance to the German occupying forces, no matter what the individual circumstances, that it is of Communist origin.

(b) In order to nip these machinations in the bud, the most drastic measures should be taken immediately and on the first indication, so that the authority of the occupying forces may be maintained, and further spreading, prevented. In this connection it should be remembered that a human life, in the countries concerned, frequently counts for nothing, and a deterrent effect can be attained only by unusual severity. The death penalty for fifty to one hundred Communists should generally be regarded in these cases as suitable atonement for the death of one German soldier. The way in which sentences are carried out should still further increase the deterrent effect.

The reserve course of action, that of imposing relatively lenient penalties, and of being content, for deterrent purposes, with the threat of more severe measures, does not accord with these principles and should not be followed."

Your Lordship, the next exhibit will be USA 556, and it has been given the number D-411. It is also Exhibit UK 81. It is the last document in Document Book 2. This is a set of documents which includes a directive dated 10th October, 1941, by Field Marshal von Reichenau, who was the Commander-in-Chief (Oberbefehlshaber) of the German 6th Army, then operating on the Eastern Front. Reichenau, who died in 1942, was therefore a member of the group as defined in the Indictment, and here is what he had to say. I begin reading at Page 5 of the translation:

"Subject: Conduct of Troops in Eastern Territories.

Regarding the conduct of troops towards the Bolshevistic System, vague ideas are still prevalent in many cases. The most essential aim of the war against the Jewish-Bolshevistic system is a complete destruction of their means of power and the elimination of Asiatic influence from the European culture. In this connection the troops are facing tasks which exceed the one-sided routine of soldiering. The soldier in the Eastern Territories is not merely a fighter according to the rules of the art of war, but also a bearer of ruthless national ideology and the avenger of bestialities which have been inflicted upon German and racially related nations.

Therefore, the soldier must have full understanding of the necessity for a severe but just revenge on subhuman Jewry. The Army has to aim at another purpose, that is, the annihilation of revolts in the Hinterland, which, as experience proves, have always been caused by Jews.

The combating of the enemy behind the front line is still not being taken seriously enough. Treacherous, cruel Partisans and unnatural women are still being made prisoners of war, and guerrilla fighters dressed partly in uniforms or plain clothes, and vagabonds, are still being treated as proper soldiers and sent to prisoner-of-war camps. In fact, captured Russian officers even talk mockingly about Soviet agents moving openly about the roads and very often eating at German field kitchens. Such an attitude of the troops can only be explained by complete thoughtlessness, so it is now high time for the commanders to clarify the meaning of the present struggle.

The feeding from our army kitchens of the natives and of prisoners of war who are not working for the armed forces is an humanitarian act just as much misunderstood as is the giving of cigarettes and bread. Things which the people at home can spare under great sacrifices and things which are being brought by the Command to the Front under great difficulties, should not be given to the enemy by the soldier, not even if they originate from booty. They are an important part of our supply.

When retreating, the Soviet troops have often set buildings on fire. The troops should be interested in extinguishing fires only as far as it is necessary to secure sufficient numbers of billets. Otherwise, the disappearance of symbols of the former Bolshevistic rule, even in the form of buildings, is part of the struggle of destruction. Neither historic nor artistic considerations are of any importance in the Eastern Territories.

The command issues the necessary directives for the securing of raw materials and plants essential for war economy. The complete disarming of the civil population in the rear of the fighting troops is imperative, considering the long and vulnerable lines of communication. Where possible, captured weapons and ammunition should be stored and guarded. Should this be impossible because of the situation, the weapons and ammunition must be rendered useless. If isolated Partisans are found, using firearms in the rear of the Army, drastic measures are to be taken. These measures will be extended to that part of the male population who were in a position to hinder or report the attacks. The indifference of numerous allegedly anti-Soviet elements, which originates from a 'wait-and-see' attitude, must give way to a clear decision for active collaboration. If not, no one can complain about being judged and treated as members of the Soviet system.

The fear of the German counter-measures must be stronger than the threats of the wandering Bolshevistic remnants. Being far from all political considerations of the future the soldier has to fulfil two tasks:

    1. Complete annihilation of the false Bolshevistic doctrine of the Soviet State and its Armed Forces.

    2. The pitiless extermination of foreign treachery and cruelty, and thus the protection of the lives of military personnel in Russia.

This is the only way to fulfil our historic task to liberate the German people once and for ever from the Asiatic-Jewish danger.

(Signed) von Reichenau,
Commander-in-Chief."

The Tribunal will note the sheet immediately preceding Reichenau's order. That is sheet number 4 of the translation, which is a memorandum dated 28th October, 1941. It shows that Reichenau's order met with Hitler's approval and was thereafter circulated by order of the Commander-in- Chief of the German Army.

The Tribunal will also note from the first sheet, the very top sheet of the several following, that Reichenau's order was thereafter circulated down to divisional level, and was received by the 12th German Infantry Division on 27th November, 1941.

These being the directives and policies prescribed by the German military leaders, it is no wonder that the Wehrmacht joined in the monstrous behaviour and activities of the S.S. and S.D. on the Eastern Front.

Colonel Storey described to the Tribunal the formation by the Sipo and S.D. of units known as Einsatzgruppen, which were sent out to operate in and behind the operational areas on the Eastern Front, in order to combat Partisans and to cleanse and pacify the civilian population. Major Farr and Colonel Storey both presented to the Tribunal a large amount of evidence showing the manner in which these units operated.

I want to refer back briefly to a few of these documents in order to trace the participation of the Armed Forces in those circumstances.

Colonel Storey read at length from Document 3012-PS, which is Exhibit USA 190, dated 19th March, 1943. It is a directive from the Commanding Officer of one of these groups. This directive praised and justified such activities as the shooting of Hungarian Jews, the shooting of children and the total burning of villages, and directed that in order not to obstruct the procuring of slave labour for the German armament industry, "as a rule no more children will be shot."

Major Farr read from Document R-102, which is Exhibit USA 470, a report covering the Work of the Einsatzgruppen in the German occupied territories of the Soviet Union during the month of October, 1941. This report states cynically on Page 4: "Spontaneous demonstrations against Jewry followed by pogroms on the part of the population against the remaining Jews have not been recorded, on account of the lack of adequate investigation."

It shows as clearly as the human eye can see that "pacification" and "anti-Partisan activities" became mere code words for the extermination of Jews just as much as "Weserubung " was the code word for the invasion of Norway and Denmark.

We have seen from the documents quoted a few moments ago that the German Army received some similar policies and directives. It only remains to show that in the field the army and the S.S. worked hand in glove.

The Tribunal will recall the document quoted by Major Walsh, 1061-PS, already in evidence as Exhibit USA 275, It describes the destruction of the Warsaw Ghetto, and at this time I merely want to call attention to one paragraph appearing at Page 6 of the translation, the third paragraph from the bottom of the page, where the author of the document stresses the close co-operation between the S.S. and the Army. Quoting:

"The longer the resistance lasted, the tougher the men of the Waffen S.S., Police and Wehrmacht became; they fulfilled their duty indefatigably in faithful comradeship, and stood together as models and examples of soldiers. Their duty hours often lasted from early morning until late at night. At night, search patrols with rags wound round their feet remained at the heels of the Jews and gave them no respite. Not infrequently they caught and killed Jews who used the night hours for supplementing their stores from abandoned dug-outs and for contacting neighbouring groups or exchanging news with them."

To the same general effect is Document R-135, Exhibit USA 289, which is a report dated 5th June, 1943, by the German General Commissioner for Minsk. Major Farr read from this report, describing an anti-Partisan operation in which 4,500 enemies were killed, 5,000 suspected Partisans and 59 Germans. The co-operation by the German Army is shown in the following excerpt, and I will begin reading at the bottom of Page 3 of the translation:

"The figures mentioned above indicate that again a heavy destruction of the population must be expected. If only 492 rifles are taken from 4,500 enemy dead, this discrepancy shows that among these enemy dead were numerous peasants from the country. The battalion Dirlewanger especially has a reputation for destroying many human lives. Among the 5,000 people suspected of belonging to bands, there were numerous women and children.

By order of the Chief of anti-Partisan units, S.S. Obergruppenfuehrer von dem Bach, units of the Armed Forces have also participated in the operation. S.S. Standartenfuehrer Kunze was in command of the Armed Forces detachments, among whom there were also 90 members from my office and from the District Commissariat of Minsk. Our men returned from the operation yesterday without losses."

I need not read the rest of that. The next paragraph shows again the participation of the Armed Forces personnel.

The S.S. Obergruppenfuehrer von dem Bach, referred to in this quotation, will be a witness later in the day, and in this connection I want to call the Court's attention to Document 1919-PS, Exhibit USA 170, which is Himmler's speech on 4th October, 1943 to a gathering of S.S. Generals at Posen. In this speech, Himmler mentioned the appointment of von dem Bach to be chief of all anti-Partisan units, and I would like to read one paragraph from Page 3 of the document merely for purposes of identification of the Witness.

"Chief of the anti-Partisan Units:

In the meantime I have also set up the department of the Chief of the anti-Partisan units. Our comrade S.S. Obergruppenfuehrer von dem Bach is chief of the anti-Partisan units. I considered it necessary for the Reichsfuehrer S.S. to be in authoritative command in all these battles, for I am convinced that we are best in a position to take action in this struggle, which is decidedly a political one. Except where the units which had been supplied and which we had formed for this purpose were taken from us to fill in gaps at the front, we have been very successful."

There is one further document which has already been introduced, from which I wish read new material. That is L- 180, which is already in evidence as Exhibit USA 276. It is the report of Einsatzgruppe A, covering the period up to 15th October. 1941. I think the excerpts which I will read will make clear beyond doubt the participation of the German military leaders and Armed Forces in the activities of these Einsatzgruppen. I read first from Page 2 of the translation, the top of the page:

"Einsatz Group A, after preparing their vehicles for action, proceeded to their area of concentration as ordered on 23rd June, 1941, the second day of the campaign in the East. Army Group North, consisting of the 16th and 18th Armies and Panzer-Group 4, had left the day before. Our task was to establish hurriedly personal contact with the Commanders of the Armies and with the Commander of the Army of the Rear Area. It must be stressed from the beginning that co-operation with the Armed Forces was generally good; in some cases, for instance, with Panzer-Group 4, under Colonel General Hoeppner, it was very close and almost cordial. Misunderstandings which cropped up with some authorities in the first days, were cleared up mainly through personal discussions."

This ends that particular extract. I read next a series of extracts, of which the first is at the bottom of Page 2:

"Similarly, native anti-Semitic forces were induced to start pogroms against Jews during the first hours after the occupation, though this inducement proved to be very difficult. According to orders, the Security Police was determined to solve the Jewish question with all possible means and most decisively. But it was desirable that the Security Police should not put in an immediate appearance, at least in the beginning, since the extraordinarily harsh measures were apt to stir even German circles. It had to be shown to the world that the native population itself took the initiative, by way of natural reaction against the suppression by Jews during several decades, and against the terror exercised by the Communists during the preceding period."

Next I pass to Page 4 of the translation, about half-way down the page, the middle of the first complete paragraph:

"After the failure of purely military activities, such as the placing of sentries and combing through the newly occupied territories with whole divisions, even the Armed Forces bad to look out for new methods. The Einsatz Group undertook to search for new methods. Soon, therefore, the Armed Forces adopted the experiences of the Security Police and their methods of combating the Partisans. For details I refer to the numerous reports concerning the struggle against the Partisans."

I pass next to Page 6 under "Instigation of Self-Cleansing Actions":

"Considering that the population of the Baltic countries had suffered very heavily under the government of Bolshevism and Jewry while they were incorporated in the U.S.S.R., it was to be expected that after the liberation from that foreign government, they (that is, the population themselves) would render harmless most of the enemies left behind after the retreat of the Red Army. It was the duty of the Security Police to set in motion these self-cleansing movements, and to direct them into the correct channels in order to accomplish the purpose of the cleansing operations as quickly as possible. It was no less important, in view of the future, to establish the unshakeable and provable fact that the liberated populations themselves took the most severe measures against the Bolshevist and Jewish enemy quite on their own, so that the direction by German authorities could not be found out.

In Lithuania this was achieved for the first time by Partisan activities in Kowno. To our surprise it was not easy at first to set in motion an extensive pogrom against Jews. Klimatis, the leader of the Partisan unit mentioned above, who was used for this purpose primarily, succeeded in starting a pogrom on the basis of advice given to him by a small advance detachment acting in Kowno, and in such a way that no German order or German instigation was noticed from the outside. During the first pogrom, in the night from 25th to 26th June, the Lithuanian Partisans did away with more than 1,500 Jews, set fire to several synagogues or destroyed them by other means, and burned down a Jewish dwelling district consisting of about 60 houses. During the following nights about 2,300 Jews were made harmless in a similar way. In other parts of Lithuania similar actions followed the example of Kowno, though smaller and extending only to the Communists who had been left behind.

These self-cleansing actions went smoothly because the Army authorities, who had been informed, showed understanding for this procedure. From the beginning it was obvious that only the first days after the occupation would offer the opportunity for carrying out pogroms. After the disarmament of the Partisans the self- cleansing action of necessity came to an end."

I pass to Page 10 of the translation, toward the bottom under "Other Jobs of the Security Police":

"Occasionally the conditions prevailing in the lunatic asylums necessitated operations of the security Police."

Passing to the next paragraph:

"Sometimes authorities of the Armed Forces asked us to clean out in a similar way other institutions which were wanted as billets. However, as interests of the Security Police did not require any intervention, it was left to the authorities of the Armed Forces to take the necessary action with their own troops."

I pass on to Page 17 of the translation, the paragraph at the top of the page: "But it was decided - "

THE PRESIDENT: Colonel Taylor, did you read paragraph 5 (1) on Page 10?

COLONEL TAYLOR: 5 (1) on Page 10? I read the first passage, your Honour. If you would like it in full

THE PRESIDENT: I think perhaps you might go to the end of it.

COLONEL TAYLOR:

"Occasionally the conditions prevailing in the lunatic asylums necessitated operations of the Security Police. Many institutions had been robbed by the retreating Russians of their whole food supply. Often the guard and nursing personnel had fled. The inmates of several institutions broke out and became a danger to the general security; therefore, in Aglona (Lithuania), 544 lunatics, in Mariampol (Lithuania), 109 lunatics, and in Magutowo, near Luga, 95 lunatics were liquidated."

Passing back to Page 17, the first paragraph on that page:

"When it was decided to extend the German operations to Leningrad and also to extend the activities of Einsatz Group A to this town, I gave orders on 18th July, 1941, to parts of Einsatz Commands 2 and 3 and to the Staff of the Group, to advance to Novosselje, in order to prepare these activities and to be able to advance as early as possible into the area around Leningrad and into the city itself. The advance of the forces of Einsatz Group A, which were intended to be used for Leningrad, was effected in agreement with and on the express wish of Panzer-Group 4."

The final quotation from this document is Page 18, last paragraph:

"Einsatz Commands of Einsatz Group A of the Security Police participated from the beginning in the fight against the nuisance created by Partisans. Close collaboration with the Armed Forces and the exchange of experiences which were collected in the fight against Partisans, brought about a thorough knowledge of the origin, organisation, strength, equipment and system used by the Red Partisans as time went on."

Now, in the light of these documents, I would like to turn to some of the remaining affidavits which are before the Tribunal in Document Book 1. These affidavits have been furnished by responsible officials in both the Wehrmacht and the S.S., and fill in much of the background for the documents.

Affidavit number 12 is an affidavit by Schellenberg, which, in view of the fact that its contents have been covered in Schellenberg's and Ohlendorf's testimony, I do not propose to read. It covers much of the same ground, and I see no reason to take the time of the Tribunal by reading it. I should like to have it considered, subject to the usual rule that Schellenberg can be questioned on any of these matters by the defence. The affidavit itself is available in French and Russian as well as in English, and in German for the defence, so I will pass over that one.

I turn to Affidavit number 13, which will be Exhibit USA 558. Schellenberg's affidavit will be 557. This is an affidavit by Wilhelm Scheidt, a retired captain of the German army, who worked in the War History Section of the O.K.W. from 1941 to 1945. It sheds considerable light on the relations between. the Wehrmacht and the S.S. at the top with respect to anti-Partisan warfare I will read this affidavit:

"I, Wilhelm Scheidt, belonged to the War History Section of the O.K.W. from the year 1941 to 1945. Concerning the question of Partisan Warfare I state that I remember the following from my knowledge of the documents of the Operations Staff of the O.K.W., as well as from my conversations in the Fuehrer's headquarters with Generalmajor Walter Scherff, whom the Fuehrer had appointed to compile the history of the War.

Counter-Partisan warfare was originally a responsibility of Reichsfuehrer S.S. Heinrich Himmler, who sent police forces to handle this matter.

In the years 1942 and 1943, however, counter-Partisan warfare developed to such an extent that the Operations Staff of the O.K.W. had to give it special attention. It proved necessary to conduct extensive operations against the Partisans with Wehrmacht troops in Russian, as well as Jugoslavian territory. Partisan operations for a long while threatened to cut off the lines of communication and transport routes that were necessary to support the German Wehrmacht. For instance, a monthly report concerning the attacks on the railroad lines in occupied Russia revealed that in, the Russian area alone from 800 to 1,000 attacks occurred each month during that period, causing among other things, the loss of from 200 to 300 locomotives.

It was well known that Partisan warfare was conducted with cruelty on both sides. It was well known that reprisals were inflicted on hostages and communities whose inhabitants were suspected of being Partisans or of supporting them. It is beyond question that these facts must have been known to the leading officers in the Operations Staff of the O.K.W. and in the Army's General Staff. It was further well known that Hitler believed that the only successful method of conducting counter-Partisan warfare was to employ cruel punishments as deterrents.

I remember that at the time of the Polish revolt in Warsaw, S.S.-Gruppenfuehrer Fegelein reported to Generaloberst Guderian and Jodl about the atrocities of the Russian S.S.-Brigade Kaminski, which fought on the German side."

Now, the foreign documents and the testimony of Ohlendorf and Schellenberg relate to the arrangements which were made between the O.K.W., O.K.H., and Himmler's headquarters with respect to anti-Partisan warfare. They show conclusively that these arrangements were made jointly, and that the High Command of the Armed Forces was not only fully aware of, but was an active participant in these plans.

Turning now to the field, I would like to read three statements by General Hans Rottiger, which will be Affidavits numbers 15 and 16, Exhibits USA 559 and 560. General Rottiger attained the rank of General of Panzer Troops, the equivalent of a Lieutenant-General in the American Army, and was Chief of Staff of the German Fourth Army, and later of Army Group Centre on the Eastern front, during the period of which he speaks.

The first statement is as follows:

"As Chief of Staff of the Fourth Army from May, 1942 to June, 1943, to which was later added the area of the Ninth Army, I often had occasion to concern myself officially with anti-Partisan warfare. During these operations the troops received orders from the highest authority, as, for example, even the O.K.H., to use the harshest methods. These operations were carried out by troops of the Army Group and of the Army, as, for example, security battalions.

At the beginning, in accordance with orders which were issued through official channels, only a few prisoners were taken. In accordance with orders, Jews, political Commissars and Agents were delivered up to the S.D.

The number of enemy dead mentioned in official reports was very high in comparison with our own losses. From the documents which have been shown to me I have now come to realise that the order from the highest authorities for the harshest conduct of the anti- Partisan war can only have been intended to make possible a ruthless liquidation of Jews and other undesirable elements, by using for this purpose the military struggle of the Army against the Partisans."

The second statement:

Supplementary to my above declaration, I declare: "As I stated orally on 28th November, my then Commander-in- Chief of the Fourth Army instructed his troops may times not to wage war against the Partisans more severely than was required at the time by the position. This struggle should only be pushed to the annihilation of the enemy after all attempts to bring about a surrender failed. Apart from humanitarian reasons we necessarily had an interest in taking prisoners, since very many of them could very well be used as members of native volunteer units against the Partisans.

Alongside the necessary active combating of Partisans, there was propaganda directed at the Partisans, and also at the population, with the object of causing them by peaceful means, to give up Partisan activities. For instance, in this way the women too were continually urged to get their men back from the forests or to keep them by other means from joining the Partisans, and this propaganda had good results. In the spring of 1943 the area of the Fourth Army was as good as cleared of Partisans. Only on its boundaries, and then only from time to time, were Partisans in evidence, when they crossed into the area of the Fourth Army from neighbouring areas. The Army was obliged for this reason, on the orders of the Army Group, to give up security forces to the neighbouring army to the South."

The third statement by Rottiger, number 16:

"During my period of service in 1942-43 as Chief of Staff of the Fourth Army of the Central Army Group, S.D. units were attached in the beginning, apparently for the purpose of counter-intelligence activity in frontline areas. It was clear that these S.D. units were causing great disturbances among the local civilian population, with the result that my commanding officer asked the Commander-in-Chief of the Army Group, Field Marshal von Kluge, to order the S.D. units to clear out of the frontline areas. This was done immediately. The reason for this, first and foremost, was that the excesses of the S.D. units, in the form of execution of Jews and other persons, assumed such proportions as to threaten the security of the Army in its combat areas, because of the infuriated civilian populace. Although, in general, the special tasks of the S.D. units were well known and appeared to be carried out with the knowledge of the highest military authorities, we opposed these methods as far as possible, because of the danger which existed for our troops."

I would like now to offer one final document, the last document, 1786-PS, which will be Exhibit USA 561. This is an extract from the War Diary of the Deputy Chief of the Armed Forces Operational Staff, dated 14th March, 1943. I propose to read the last two paragraphs, which deal with the problem of shipping of suspected Partisans to concentration camps in Germany.

The Tribunal will see, from the extracts which I will read, that the Army was chiefly concerned with maintaining sufficiently severe treatment for suspected Partisans without, at the same time, obstructing the procurement of labour from the occupied territories.

I will read the last two paragraphs:

"The General Quartermaster, together with the Economic Staff, has proposed that the deportees should be sent either to prison camps or to training centres in their own area, and that deportation to Germany should take place only when the deportees are on probation and in less serious cases.

In view of the Armed Forces Operations Staff, this proposal does not take sufficient account of the severity required, and leads to a comparison with the treatment meted out to the 'peaceful population' which has been called upon to work. He recommends, therefore, transportation to concentration camps in Germany which have already been introduced by the Reichsfuehrer S.S. for his sphere, and which he is prepared to introduce for the Armed Forces in the case of an extension to the province of the latter. The High Command of the Armed Forces therefore orders: that Partisan helpers and suspects who are not to be executed, should be handed over to the competent Higher S.S. and Police Leader, and that the difference between 'punitive work' and 'work in Germany' is to be made clear to the population."

Finally, I would like to offer a group of four affidavits which show that the anti-Partisan activities on the Eastern front were under the command of and supported by the Wehrmacht, and that the nature of these activities was fully known to the Wehrmacht.

The first of these is Affidavit No. 17, Exhibit USA 562, by Ernst Rode, who was an

S.S. Brigadefuehrer and Major General of the Police, and was a member of Himmler's personal Command Staff from 1943 to 1945:

"I, Ernst Rode, was formerly Chief of the Command Staff of the Reichsfuehrer S.S., having taken over this position in the spring of 1943, as successor to former S.S. Obergruppenfuehrer Kurt Knoblauch. My last rank was Generalmajor of Police and of the Waffen S.S. My function was to furnish the forces necessary for anti- Partisan warfare to the higher S.S. and police leaders, and to guarantee the support of Army Forces. This took place through personal discussions with the leading officers of the Operations Staff of the O.K.W. and O.K.H., namely, with General Warlimont, General von Buttlar, Generaloberst Guderian, Generaloberst Zeitzler, General Heusinger, later General Wenk, Colonel Graf Kielmannsegg and, later, Colonel von Bonin. Since anti- Partisan warfare also was under the sole command of the respective Army Commander-in-Chief in operational areas - for instance, in the Central Army Group under Field Marshal Kluge and later Busch - and since police troops for the most part could not be spared from the Reich Commissariats, the direction of this warfare lay almost always entirely in the hands of the Army. In the same way orders were issued not by Himmler but by the O.K.H. S.S. and police troops transferred to operational areas from the Reich Commissariats to support the Army Groups were likewise under the latter's command. Such transfers often resulted in harm to anti-Partisan warfare in the Reich Commissariats. According to a specific agreement between Himmler and the O.K.H., the direction of individual operations lay in the hands of the troop leader who commanded the largest troop contingent. It was therefore possible that an Army General could have S.S. and Police under him, and, on the other hand, that army troops could be placed under a General of the S.S. and Police. Anti-Partisan warfare in operational areas could never be ordered by Himmler. I could merely request the O.K.H. to order it, until 1944, mostly through the intervention of Generalquartiermeister Wagner, or through State Secretary Ganzenmuller. The O.K.H. then issued corresponding orders to the army groups concerned, for compliance.

The severity and cruelty with which the intrinsically diabolical Partisan warfare was conducted by the Russians had already resulted in Draconian laws being issued by Hitler to deal with it. These orders, which were passed on to the troops through the O.K.W. and O.K.H., were equally applicable to army troops as well as to those of the S.S. and Police. There was absolutely no difference in the manner in which these two components carried on this warfare. Army soldiers were exactly as embittered against the enemy as were those of the S.S. and Police.

As a result of this embitterment orders were ruthlessly carried out by both components, a thing which was also quite in keeping with Hitler's desires or intentions. As proof of this, an order of the O.K.W. and O.K.H. can be adduced which directed that all captured Partisans, for instance, Jews, agents and political Commissars, should without delay be handed over by the troops to the S.D. for special treatment. This order also contained the provision that in anti-Partisan warfare no prisoners except the above-named be taken. That anti-Partisan warfare was carried on by army troops mercilessly and to every extreme, I know as the result of discussions with army troop leaders, for instance with General Herzog, Commander of the 38th Army Corps, and with his Chief of Staff, Colonel Pamberg, in the General Staff, both of whom support my opinion. Today it is clear to me that anti-Partisan warfare gradually became an excuse for the systematic annihilation of Jewry and Slavism."

Your Lordship, I am told that I misread and said "Hitler" instead of "Himmler."

I next wish to offer another and shorter statement by Rode, which shows that the S.D.-Einsatzgruppen were under Wehrmacht command. This is Affidavit number 18, Exhibit USA 563:

> "As far as I know, the S.D. Combat Groups with the individual Army Groups were completely subordinate to them, that is to say tactically as well as in every other way. The Commanders-in-Chief were therefore thoroughly cognisant of the missions and operational methods of these units. They clearly approved of these missions and operational methods, for apparently they never opposed them. The fact that prisoners, such as Jews, Agents and Commissars who were handed over to the S.D., underwent the same cruel death as victims of so-called purifications, is a proof that the executions had their approval. This also corresponded with what the highest political and military authorities wanted. Frequent mention of these methods were naturally made in my presence at the O.K.W. and O.K.H., and they were condemned by most S.S. and police officers, just as they were condemned by most army officers. On such occasions I always pointed out that it would have been quite within the scope of the authority of the Commanders-in-Chief of Army Groups to oppose such methods. I am of the firm conviction that an energetic and unified protest by all Field Marshals would have resulted in a change of these missions and methods. If they should ever assert that they would then have been succeeded by even more ruthless Commanders-in-Chief, this, in my opinion, would be a foolish and even cowardly dodge."

I would like next to read the final affidavit, number 24, in Document Book 1.

THE PRESIDENT: Colonel Taylor, unless you are going to conclude this particular part, I think we had better adjourn now.

COLONEL TAYLOR: I will conclude with two affidavits, your Honour, but it will take probably ten minutes.

THE PRESIDENT: Very well, if that will conclude it, go on.

COLONEL TAYLOR: It will conclude it. Firstly, Affidavit number 24, which becomes Exhibit USA 565. This is by Colonel Bogislav von Bonin, who, at the beginning of the Russian Campaign, was a staff officer with the 17th Panzer Division:

> "At the beginning of the Russian campaign I was the first General Staff Officer of the 17th Panzer Division, which had the mission of driving across the Bug, north of Brest-Litovsk. Shortly before the beginning of the attack my division received, through channels, from the O.K.W. a written order of the Fuehrer. This order directed that Russian Commissars be shot upon capture, without judicial process, immediately and ruthlessly. This order extended to all units of the Eastern Army. Although the order was supposed to be relayed to companies, the Commanding General of the 37th Panzer Corps - General of Panzer Troops Lemelsen - forbade its being passed on to the troops because it appeared unacceptable to him from military and moral points of view."

That brings us to the final affidavit, number 20, Exhibit USA 564, which is by Adolf Hesinger.

THE PRESIDENT: What was the number?

COLONEL TAYLOR: It is number 20, your Honour, Exhibit USA 564, by Adolf Hesinger, Generalleutnant in the German Army, and from 1940 to 1944 Chief of the Operations Section at O.K.H. I read:

"1. From the beginning of the war in 1939 until autumn 1940 I was I-a of the Operations Section of the O.K.H., and from autumn 1940 until 20th July, 1944, I was Chief of that Section.

When Hitler took over Supreme Command of the Army, he gave to the Chief of the General Staff of the Army the function of advising him on all operational matters in the Russian theatre.

This made the Chief of the General Staff of the Army responsible for all matters in the operational areas in the East, while the O.K.W. was responsible for all matters outside the operational areas, for instance all troops - security units, S.S. units, Police - stationed in the Reich Commissariats.

All Police and S.S. units in the Reich Commissariats were also subordinate to the Reichsfuehrer S.S. When it was necessary to transfer such units into operational areas, this had to be done by order of the Chief of the O.K.W. On the other hand, corresponding transfers from the front to the rear were ordered by the O.K.W. with the concurrence of the Chief of the General Staff of the Army.

The High S.S. and Police leaders normally had command of operations against Partisans. If stronger army units were committed together with the S.S. and Police units within operational areas, a High Commander of the Army could be designated commander of the operation.

During anti-Partisan operations within operational areas all forces committed for these operations were under the command of the respective Commander-in-Chief of the Army Group.

2. Directives as to the manner and methods of carrying on counter-Partisan operations were issued by the O.K.W. - Keitel - to the O.K.H. upon orders from Hitler and after consultation with Himmler. The O.K.H. was responsible merely for the transmission of these orders to Army Groups, for instance, such orders as those concerning the treatment to be accorded to Commissars and Communists, those concerning the manner of prosecuting, by courts martial, army personnel who had committed offences against the population, as well as those establishing the basic principles governing reprisals against the inhabitants.

3. The detailed working out of all matters involving the treatment of the local populace, as well as anti- Partisan warfare in operational areas, in pursuance of orders from the O.K.W., was the responsibility of the Generalquartiermeister (Quartermaster-General) of the O.K.H.

4. It had always been my personal opinion that the treatment of the civilian population and the methods of anti-Partisan warfare in operational areas presented the highest political and military leaders with a welcomed opportunity of carrying out their plans, namely, the systematic extermination of Slavism and Jewry. Entirely independent of this, I always regarded these cruel methods as military insanity, because they only helped to make combat against the enemy unnecessarily more difficult."

THE PRESIDENT: We will adjourn until a quarter past two.

(A recess was taken until 14.25 hours.)

COLONEL TAYLOR: Will your Lordship swear the witness?

THE PRESIDENT: What is his name?
COLONEL TAYLOR: Erich von dem Bach-Zelewski.
BY THE PRESIDENT:
Q. What is your name?
A. Erich von dem Bach-Zelewski.

Q. Will you take this oath? "I swear by God the Almighty and Omniscient that I will speak the pure truth and will withhold and add nothing."

(The witness repeated the oath.)

BY COLONEL TAYLOR:

Q. May I remind the witness to speak very slowly and to keep his answers as short as possible?
Can you hear me?
A. Yes.
Q. Were you a member of the S.S.?
A. Yes.
Q. What was the last rank you held in the S.S.?
A. S.S. Obergruppenfuehrer and General der Waffen S.S.
Q. Did you serve in the 1914 to 1918 war?
A. Yes. I was at the front from 1914 to 1918, was twice wounded and received the Iron Cross, first and second class.
Q. Did you remain in the army after the end of the last war?
A. Yes, I stayed in the 100,000 men army.
Q. How long did you remain in the army?
A. Till 1924, when I applied for my discharge.
Q. Did your military activities then stop?
A. No, I was Battalion Leader in the Border Defence, and until the campaign against Poland I did my exercises with the Wehrmacht.
Q. Did you join the Nazi Party?
A. Yes.
Q. In what year?
A. In the year 1930.
Q. What branch of the party did you join?
A. The "Allgemeine S.S."
Q. What were your activities in the S.S. prior to the outbreak of the war?
A. I was with the General S.S. and the S.S. Border Defence in the districts of Schneidemuhl and Frankfurt on the Oder, and from 1934 I was Oberabschnittsfuehrer in East Prussia and afterwards in Silesia.
Q. Were you a member of the Reichstag during this period?
A. Yes, I was a member of the Reichstag from 1932 right up to the end.
Q. Did you take any active part during this war before the campaign against the Soviet Union?
A. No, not before the campaign against Russia.
Q. What was your rank at the beginning of the war?
A. At the beginning of the war I was S.S. Group Leader and Lieutenant-General.
Q. And when were you promoted?
A. I was promoted on the 9th November, 1941, to S.S. Obergruppenfuehrer and General of the Waffen S.S.

Q. What was your position after the beginning of the campaign against the Soviet Union?

A. Would you kindly repeat the question; it was not quite clear.

Q. What was your position, your function, at the beginning of the war against the Soviet Union?

A. At the beginning of the campaign against Russia I was a member of the Higher S.S. and I was at the Rear Zone of the Army Group Centre.

Q. Was there a similar S.S. official in the Rear Zone of each Army Group?

A. Yes, in every Army Group, North, Middle and South, there was, at that time, a Higher S.S. and Police Leader.

Q. Who was the Commander-in-Chief of Army Group Centre?

A. The Commander-in-Chief of Army Group Centre was, in the beginning, General Field-Marshal von Beck, and later General Field-Marshal Kluge.

Q. Who was the Armed Forces Commander in the Rear Zone of Army Group Centre?

A. General of the Infantry, von Schenkendorff.

Q. Was he directly subordinate to the Commander-in-Chief of the Army Group?

A. Yes.

Q. Who was your immediate superior in the S.S.?

A. Heinrich Himmler.

Q. And who was your immediate superior in the Rear Zone of the Army?

A. General von Schenkendorff.

Q. What was your principal task as Higher S.S. and Police Leader in Central Russia?

A. My principal activities lay in the struggle against the Partisans.

Q. Are you generally familiar with the operations of the so-called Einsatzgruppen of the S.D.?

A. Yes.

Q. Did these units play any important part in large-scale anti-Russian operations?

A. No.

Q. What was the principal task of the Einsatzgruppen?

A. The principal task of the Einsatzgruppen of the S.D. was the annihilation of the Jews, Gypsies and Political Commissars.

Q. Then what forces were used for large-scale anti-Partisan operations?

A. For anti-Partisan activities, formations of the Waffen S.S., of the Order Police and above all, of the Wehrmacht were used.

Q. Please describe the nature of these regular army units that were used for anti-Partisan operations.

A. The units of the Wehrmacht constituted, in the first place, the Security Divisions introduced in the rear zone, behind the battle front. Further, there were the so-called Regional Defence Units which, naturally, came under the orders of the Military District Commanders. Further, we had Wehrmacht formations, introduced for the air defence of certain installations, such as railways and landing grounds and for the protection of other military objectives. Moreover, as from 1942 or 1943, so-called "Alarm Units" were introduced, composed of formations in the rear, i.e., from administrative formations.

Q. Until when did you remain Higher S.S. and Police Leader for Central Russia?

A. Subject to certain interruptions, when I was sent to the front, I was Higher

Police Leader for Central Russia - excepting a period when I was very ill, and was absent for about six months - up to the end of 1942, when I was appointed Chief of the Units for combating the Partisans.

Q. Was this position, of Chief of anti-Partisan Units, created specially for you?
A. Yes.

Q. To whom were you directly subordinate in this new capacity?
A. Heinrich Himmler.

Q. Were your functions in this new capacity restricted to any particular part of the Eastern front?
A. No. My sphere of action comprised the entire Eastern zone.

Q. What was the general nature of your duties as Chief of the anti-Partisan Units?
A. First of all, I had to establish, at Himmler's headquarters, a central office to which all notices were sent in connection with Partisans. Here these notices were studied and then forwarded to the competent authorities.

Q. In the course of your duties, did you confer with the Commanders of Army Groups and Armies of the Eastern front?
A. With the Commanders-in-Chief of Army Groups, but not of the Armies, and with the District Commanders of the Wehrmacht.

Q. Did you consult these Commanders with respect to methods to be employed in anti-Partisan warfare?
A. Yes.

Q. Will you name some of the Commanders with whom you personally conferred?
A. I cannot give you a complete list, but I will endeavour to quote from memory: Wehrmacht Commander Ostland; General of Cavalry Bromer; General Field Marshal Kuechler; Commander-in-Chief of the Army Group North; Commander-in-Chief of the Army Group Centre, Klugge; and later Busch; the Wehrmacht Commander-in-Chief of the Ukraine; General of the Luftwaffe Kitzinger; General Field Marshal Freiherr von Weichs, the Commander-in-Chief in Serbia at Belgrade; and Kugler, Commander-in-Chief of the Trieste Area.

Q. What proportion of Wehrmacht troops as compared to Police and S.S. troops was employed in anti-Partisan operations?
A. Since the number of the troops of the Police and of the S.S. was a very small one, anti-Partisan operations were mainly undertaken by Wehrmacht formations.

Q. Were anti-Partisan troops usually commanded by Wehrmacht officers or by officers of the S.S.?
A. This varied. It depended mostly on the individual area; in the operational areas it was always the Wehrmacht, but orders existed to the effect that whatever the formation, be it Wehrmacht, S.S. or Police, the formation which had the most troops had to lead.

Q. Did the highest Military Leaders issue instructions that anti-Partisan operations were to be conducted with severity?
A. Yes.

Q. Did the highest Military Authorities issue any detailed instructions concerning the methods to be used in anti-Partisan warfare?
A. No.

Q. What was the result, in the occupied territories, of this lack of detailed directives from above?
A. Since orders proved insufficient, a wild state of anarchy resulted in all anti-

Partisan operations.

Q. In your opinion, were the measures taken in anti-Partisan operations far more severe than the circumstances warranted, or were they not?

A. Since there were no definite orders and since the Lower Command was forced to act independently, many undertakings were executed according to the character of the officer in command and to the quality of the troops. These, naturally, varied very considerably. I am of opinion that operations on numerous occasions, not only failed in their purpose, but they very often overshot their mark.

Q. Did these measures result in the unnecessary killing of large numbers of the civilian population?

A. Yes.

Q. Did you report these excessive measures to the commanders of the Army Groups and other Wehrmacht officers with whom you collaborated?

A. These measures were generally known. There was no necessity to make any special report, since every operation was directly reported in each individual case and in its every detail, and was known to every responsible leader.

Q. Were any effective steps taken by the highest military authorities or by any commanders of Army Groups to suppress these excesses?

A. I remember that General von Schenkendorff, in particular, made numerous reports in this connection. He discussed them with me, and later we both forwarded them through our service channels.

Q. Did these reports by General von Schenkendorff have any effect?

A. No.

Q. Why not?

A. Quartermaster General Wagner certainly attempted to effect a change by imposing on the troops a more rigid line of conduct, but he did not succeed in his purpose.

Q. Was an order ever issued, and that by the Highest Authorities, that German soldiers who had committed offences against the civilian population were not to be punished in the military courts?

A. Yes, a similar order was given.

Q. Did this order prove an obstacle to correcting the excesses of the troops?

A. Yes, in my opinion this order prevented the only possible way of dealing with the excesses, since you can educate the soldiery only if you wield disciplinary powers, if you have jurisdiction over the troops and are able to do something to check the excesses.

Q. What decorations did you win during the War?

A. In this war I received the Clusters to the Iron Cross I and II, the German Cross in gold and the Knight's Cross to the Iron Cross.

COLONEL TAYLOR: Your Lordship, the witness is available for examination by others.

THE PRESIDENT: Does the Soviet prosecutor wish to ask any questions?

COLONEL POKROVSKY: If you will permit me, I wish to ask a series of questions:

(Direct examination by Colonel Pokrovsky.)

Q. Which forces of the Police and S.S. were at your disposal in 1941 and 1942, when you were Chief Leader of the Police and S.S. in the Rear Zone of the Central Army Group?

A. There were directly under my command, in 1941, one Police Regiment of the Regular Police, and occasionally, for about two or three months at a time, one S.S. Cavalry Brigade.
Q. Was the Einsatzgruppe B, headed by Nebe, under your command?
A. No.
Q. Did you or did you not receive Nebe's reports?
A. Not directly, but I saw to it that they reached me eventually.
Q. What do you know of the activities of Einsatzgruppe B?
A. Einsatzgruppe B was in Smolensky, where it operated exactly like all the other Einsatz Groups. We heard everywhere, in conversations, that the Jews were being rounded up and sent to the ghettos.
Q. Did you report to the Commands of the Operational Groups, on the activities of Einsatzgruppe B?
A. I learned about their activities directly through Schenkendorff, who was at the head of Army Group Centre.
Q. Did you know of the order issued by the Commander of the Sixth Army, General Reichenau, regarding the Partisan Movement?
A. Would you be good enough to repeat the name; was it General von Reichenau?
Q. Yes.
A. Yes, I know about that. I think it was in 1941, although it might have been in 1942; there was an order by General von Reichenau which was sent to all the Wehrmacht Commanders, and in this order he opposed the actions taken against the Jews and Partisans.
Q. In 1943 or later were there, under your command, units or companies specially selected to combat the Partisan Movement?
A. In 1943, as Chief of the anti-Partisan Movement, I had no particular authority or command, since I was Head of the Central Office, but I did lead some operations whenever the authority of two commanders overlapped.
Q. Do you know anything about the existence of a special brigade consisting of smugglers, poachers and persons released from prison?
A. Of all the troops considered suitable for anti-Partisan struggle in the beginning of 1942, one battalion, under the command of Dirlewanger was introduced into the Army Group Centre, and this battalion was gradually strengthened by the addition of reserve units until it reached the proportions, first of a regiment and, later, of a brigade. This "Dirlewanger Brigade" consisted for the greater part of previously convicted criminals, officially of so-called poachers, although there were, amongst them, authentic criminals convicted of burglary, murder, etc.
Q. How do you explain the fact that the German Army Command so willingly strengthened and increased its forces by adding to them from the ranks of criminals and directing these criminals specifically against the Partisans?
A. I am of the opinion that this step was closely connected with a speech made by Heinrich Himmler, at the beginning of 1941 prior to the campaign against Russia, when he spoke at the Weselburg of the purpose of the Russian campaign, which was, he said, to decimate the Slav population by thirty million, and that in order to achieve this purpose units of inferior calibre would have to be introduced.
Q. Have I understood you correctly when I say that the calibre of the human element, introduced by the commanders to fight the Partisans, had been given careful, prior consideration? Had they received precise instructions how to treat the population and how to act against the Partisans? I am now referring to the proposed

and officially sanctioned extermination of the populace.

A. I share your opinion that this purpose was a decisive factor in the selection of certain commanders and of some quite definite formations.

Q. By what means and by what measures were Wehrmacht units brought into fight the Partisans? Were they specially recruited or were they introduced from time to time, according to some particular plan?

A. There was apparently no absolutely definite plan, but so-called large-scale operations were initiated at headquarters, planned and executed. Anti-Partisan fighting, however, was mostly of a spontaneous nature, since every lower commander was obliged to keep his own area free from Partisans, which means that he acted on his own initiative.

Q. You have shown that in very many cases generals and officers of the Wehrmacht personally headed the operations against the Partisans. Can you give us some concrete facts and the names of some of the generals and officers?

A. I do not fully understand the purpose of the question. The names of commanders?

Q. You have told us that, in the course of certain operations during the struggle against the Partisans, officers and generals of the Wehrmacht conducted operations, and I now ask you if you can name some of the officers and generals?

A. I did not quite understand. Names? The idea is still not quite clear. Oh Yes! You mean the surnames of the generals. Partly. I remember General von Hartmann, in Central Russia. He either commanded a large-scale anti-Partisan operation or else led it in his capacity of highest ranking senior officer. I also remember General (Full General) Reinhardt; he had important Partisan groups in his rear zone. I should like to add that there was not a single general in the rear zone who had not participated in the struggle against the Partisans. I cannot, of course, bear in mind who had and who had not participated, but if I hear the names mentioned, I might remember if he had taken part in the anti-Partisan warfare or not.

Q. Could you tell us what undertaking had been commanded by General Ackmann?

A. No. I cannot remember that.

Q. Were there any general orders relating to prisoners of war, the civilian population or the Partisan Movement?

A. Unfortunately, there were no general instructions whatsoever to hand, which clearly stated how the Partisans or the population were to be treated. That was the complaint I made, namely, that no instructions had been issued concerning the treatment of the Partisans or even who was to be considered as a Partisan at all. When anything ever happened to the German Wehrmacht, orders were invariably missing to tell us clearly what was to be done by way of reprisals.

Q. Am I to understand that in the absence of direct orders, commanders were given a clear field and had the right to declare any person they liked a Partisan and treat him accordingly?

A. He certainly could and had to decide independently. No precise control was possible in individual cases, but the activities of all the troops introduced were constantly visible to the High Command, since in individual reports those counter-measures were scrupulously listed. This means that the number of Partisans killed in combat, the number of Partisans shot, of Partisan suspects shot, as well as the number of our own losses, had to be carefully reported. Equally careful reports had to be made on the amount of captured booty in the form of weapons, so that each leader could clearly realise how an operation worked out in practice.

Q. That means that each commander decided for himself whether there was any reason to suspect a man and to execute him?

A. Yes.

Q. Do you know of any order prescribing the seizure of hostages and the burning of villages as a reprisal for abetting the Partisans?

A. No. I do not think that such orders were ever issued, and it is precisely this lack of orders that I deplore. It should, for instance, have been definitely stated how many people were to be executed for the killing of one, or of ten German soldiers.

Q. Am I to understand that if certain commanders burned villages as a punitive measure against the local population, they the commanders, would be acting on their own initiative?

A. Yes. These steps would be taken by a commander on his own initiative. His superior officers could do nothing about it, since orders emanating from the highest authorities definitely stated that if any damage were inflicted on the civilian population, no disciplinary or juridical measures could be taken.

Q. And can we assume that the same applied to the seizure of hostages?

A. Well, I consider that the question of hostages did not arise at all in the anti-Partisan struggle. In any case, I believe that the "Hostage System" was reserved exclusively for the Western Front. The term "hostage" was unknown in anti-Partisan warfare.

Q. Do you know anything about the forcible abduction and deportation to Germany of minors between 14 and 18 years of age?

A. I do not remember that in detail, but I do know that, when I was appointed Chief of anti-Partisan warfare, I welcomed the issue of an order that in future, during this struggle, Partisans and Partisan suspects would no longer be shot when arrested, but shipped to the Reich to work in the Sauckel organisation.

Q. If I understood you correctly, you replied to the question by my colleague, the American prosecutor, by saying that the struggle against the Partisan Movement was a pretext for destroying the Slav and Jewish population?

A. Yes.

Q. Was the Wehrmacht Command aware of the methods adopted for fighting the Partisan Movement and for destroying the Jewish population?

A. The methods were generally known, certainly by the military leaders. I do not, of course, know whether they were aware of the plan mentioned by Himmler.

Q. Did you personally take part in any conferences with generals of the Wehrmacht, during which the methods of anti- Partisan warfare were clearly and plainly discussed.

A. The methods of this warfare were discussed in detail and provided for, but at these discussions it was not mentioned that so-and-so many persons were to be shot. That is not at all how the matter should be understood.

Q. You have told us that the Germans intended to destroy the Slav population in order to reduce the number of Slavs to 30 million. Where did you get this figure and this order?

A. I wish to make an amendment: not to reduce to 30 million, but by 30 million. Himmler mentioned this in his speech at the Weselburg.

Q. Do you confirm the fact that actually all the measures carried out by the German commanders and by the Wehrmacht in the occupied Russian territories were directed to the sole purpose of reducing the number of Slavs and Jews by 30 million?

A. The meaning is not quite clear to me. Did the Wehrmacht know that the Slav population was to be diminished by 30 million? The sense is not clear. Would you kindly repeat the question?

Q. I have asked: Can you actually and truthfully confirm that the measures taken by the Wehrmacht Command, in the District Administrative Areas then occupied by the Germans, were directed to the purpose of diminishing the Slavs and Jews by 30 million? Do you now understand the sentence?

A. I am of opinion that this method would have definitely led to the extermination of 30 million, had it been continued and had conditions not been changed by the eventual development of the situation.

COLONEL POKROVSKY: I have no further questions to put to the witness.

THE PRESIDENT: Has the defence any questions?

CROSS-EXAMINATION BY DR. EXNER (Counsel for the General Staff of the O.K.W.):

Q. Witness, you said you were Chief of anti-Partisan Operations?

A. Chief of the anti-Partisan Combat Units.

Q. If such chaotic conditions really did exist, why did you not alter the system?

A. Because I was never given the requisite authoritative powers.

Q. Why?

A. Because I was never given authoritative powers. I could not command, I had no disciplinary powers, and I was not an appointing authority.

Q. Did you make a report on existing conditions to your superior officer?

A. Every day. I had a permanent staff at Himmler's Headquarters.

Q. Did you suggest any changes?

A. Persistently.

Q. And why were these changes never realised?

A. I think I have already expressed myself quite clearly; I was of the opinion that these changes were not desired.

Q. You also, as you have previously informed us, reported to your superior authorities on the number of enemy dead, wounded and prisoners after each operation. Tell me; what, approximately, was the proportion of enemy prisoners to the enemy dead?

A. The figures varied from case to case. You cannot cram both feet into the same shoe. It was a fact that prisoners far outnumbered the dead, although this certainly was not the case in the years when orders were given that no prisoners should be taken.

Q. The system was harsher at first, you say, and milder later on?

A. Yes, it was milder in a way, since now we received definite orders where the prisoners were to be deported and to whom they were to be handed.

Q. Can you name orders which you received from any military authorities directed to or aiming at the annihilation of 30 million Slavs?

A. I have already answered the question when I stated that no such orders were ever issued in writing.

Q. Do you know that the reports which you submitted to Himmler concerning the actions you had carried out were re-submitted by Himmler directly to the Fuehrer?

A. May I be rather more explicit in replying? At first I had a permanent staff at Himmler's headquarters. My Chief of Staff was there permanently when I was at the front. Between the Wehrmacht offices, i.e. O.K.W., O.K.H. and my own staff, there was a constant interchange of reports. It was not as if reports on Partisan activities always reached me in the first instance, since areas existed which were under the direct supervision of the O.K.H. This means that the Wehrmacht reported just as freely to us as we reported to the Wehrmacht. After these reports had been collected by my staff from day to day, they were passed up to Himmler, who forwarded them on again.

Q. To whom?

A. The Chiefs of the Wehrmacht. They have already confirmed to me, in captivity, that these reports reached them.

Q. Did Jews participate in the Partisan Groups?

A. It was undeniable that in individual Partisan Groups Jews did participate, commensurate in number to the number of the Jewish population.

Q. In individual groups? Was it not more in the nature of an exception?

A. Yes, it was definitely in the nature of an exception.

Q. I do not therefore quite understand why actions taken against the Partisans should lead to the extermination of the Jews.

A. I did not say that. We have been talking about the question of the Einsatz groups.

Q. Tell me, do you know the Dirlewanger Regiment? Do you remember that?

A. That is the Dirlewanger Brigade, as I explained to the prosecutor a short time ago.

Q. Was that Brigade at any time under your command?

A. Yes, in 1941.

Q. Was it a formation of the Army or of the S.S.?

A. No. It was not a formation of the Waffen S.S.; it was provided by the General S.S., i.e., Amt. Berger.

Q. Can you tell me who was present at Himmler's speech?

A. There were about 12 S.S. Gruppenfuehrer present.

Q. Were any officers of the Wehrmacht present?

A. No.

DOCTOR EXNER: Thank you very much.

BY PROFESSOR DOCTOR KRAUS (Counsel for defendant Schacht):

Q. On the 18th of August, 1935, you were present, in Konigsberg, when the former President of the Reichsbank, Schacht, made a speech at the "Ostmesse" (Eastern Fair)?

A. Yes.

Q. What was your profession at that time?

A. I was Oberabschnittsfuehrer.

Q. Were you present at the speech in your professional capacity?

A. Yes, as Oberabschnittsfuehrer of the S.S.

Q. You suddenly left the room in the middle of the speech as a protest?

A. Yes, in the middle of the speech I left the room.

Q. As a protest?

A. That is so.

Q. Then you did not agree with the speech?

A. I did not leave on account of the speech but as a protest against the contents of the speech.

Q. May I ask, why you protested?

A. It is a well-known fact that I had, in East Prussia, conducted a violent campaign against the then Gauleiter Koch, which led to his suspension. Koch and I were so bitterly opposed to each other that I could not understand why Reichsminister Schacht should pay compliments to this man, this man whom I knew to be corrupt, and, God knows, this is scarcely a reason for complimenting any one.

Q. I still do not understand. Were you protesting against Schacht or against Koch?

A. I think Herr Schacht must have known that this was a protest against Koch. In any case I had the matter explained to him later on, and finally we reached an agreement through mediators.

Q. Witness, you have said that a change came into the treatment of the Partisans. You said it was ordered, that these Partisans were to be placed at the disposal of the Labour Service. Where did this order originate?

A. I cannot tell you that in detail, I only know that Sauckel himself travelled in the Eastern zone, made long speeches and said it would be best if Partisan prisoners were placed at the disposal of the Labour Services.

Q. I asked where this order originated. Did it originate with Himmler or, as you have said, with the Sauckel Organisation?

A. No. Not the Sauckel Organisation, who could never issue orders in connection with the Partisans. I presume that Sauckel himself instigated the orders but that they originated with Himmler or the O.K.W. I no longer know.

Q. What do you know of the existence of the Sauckel Organisation? What did it consist of?

A. It was generally known that this organisation existed for the purpose of introducing manpower into the Reich for work in the armament industry.

Q. I did not refer to it in the sense of a definite organisation; that is not what I meant. I apologise. This was merely a *lapsus lingua*.

Then you did not know that Sauckel had an organisation of his own and that this organisation controlled the entire impressment of labour and the entire administrative machine?

A. No, I know nothing at all about it.

THE PRESIDENT: I want the attention of the defendant's counsel. What I want to say is that unless counsel and the witnesses speak slowly (is that coming through? Can you hear me now?) and make adequate pauses between the questions and the answers, it is impossible for the interpreters to interpret properly, and the only result is that the questions and answers do not come through to the Tribunal, nor do the defendants' counsel get the benefit of the true meaning of the answers which have been given in the examination-in-chief, and everything that you may think you gain by rapidity of cross-examination, you lose by the inadequacy of the translation. I will repeat, that you should pause at the end of your sentences and at the end of your questions, so as to give the interpreter's voice time to come through.

BY DR. STAHMER (Counsel for defendant Goering):

Q. Witness, you have said that from 1942 onwards you were Chief of the anti-Partisan Groups. As such, it was your duty to fight the Partisans in the East?

A. Yes, that is true, to fight the Partisans.

Q. Now, did you say that there was a certain lack of clarity as to what should be understood by the term "Partisan"; the concept of "Partisan" had been nebulous during the entire period. Is that correct?

A. In the essential meaning, yes. In my opinion a distinction should have been drawn between Partisan and Partisan suspects. Troops did not always understand this distinction. A Partisan was a man carefully selected and trained by the enemy. He was also very well armed. I always insisted that special emphasis be laid on this concept and that it should not be said indiscriminately, if fire opened from a wood, a house or a village, that everyone present was a Partisan. This idea does not apply, since Partisans wanted to disappear rapidly after a successful action; they relied on the element of surprise.

Q. Now, what did you do in a positive way in order to clarify this concept of "Partisan"?

A. As I have previously said, ever since 1941, even before I was Chief of the anti-Partisan Forces, not only I but also General Schenkendorff, handed in a continuous number of memos suggesting how to combat these gangs. For instance, we submitted such memos repeatedly to the Central Army Group; we organised schools on the Partisan fighting in Russia. Schenkendorff and I, together, worked out a series of regulations on Partisan fighting. These were never published. Immediately after I was appointed Chief of the anti-Partisan Forces, that is, in the beginning of 1943, my staff took up its work and prepared another series of regulations for Partisan fighting. It was, however, some months before these regulations were finally published, in 1944, when it was really already too late.

Q. Who published these regulations?

A. These regulations were published as a Wehrmacht regulation in 1944.

Q. What were their contents?

A. They were entitled "Bandenbekampfungsvorschrift" (Regulations for the Fighting of Partisans).

Q. What were their contents?

A. They referred to Partisan warfare, to reconnaissance, both small- and large-scale reconnaissance, and to methods of carrying on the fight and so forth.

Q. These regulations appeared not earlier than 1944. Having to conduct the fight against Partisans in the entire East, was it not your duty to inform your forces how they should behave?

A. First of all I had no authority to issue commands. I have already said so. I could only make suggestions. Secondly, there were never any definite anti-Partisan forces. Any kind of formations might be assigned to this job according to circumstances. It is wrong to assume that I had troops whose only purpose was the fighting of Partisans. I should like to emphasise that the document appointing me Chief of the anti-Partisan forces stated: Authorised to fight the Partisans is only either the Higher S.S. or Police Officer, or the competent Wehrmacht commander. I myself, in that regulation, simply had the character of an Inspector, in spite of my continuous request for authority to issue commands.

THE PRESIDENT: You must go slowly and you must pause between your sentences.

Q. As General of the Waffen S.S. you must have had power to issue commands?

A. I only had authority to issue commands when I conducted an undertaking personally.

Q. But you were appointed for the fighting of Partisans and therefore you must have had combat units?

A. No, I had no such units.

Q. But then with what did you conduct your fight against the Partisans?

A. According to circumstances, I went to the respective Commander-in-Chief and discussed with him the problem at stake, and requested the necessary troops, unless they were given to me, as it often happened, by the O.K.W. or the O.K.H. directly.

Q. You requested troops. Those troops assigned to you were under your command therefore?

A. As I said before, only when I personally conducted the undertaking. Either the respective General of the Wehrmacht or, in the field of Civil government, the Higher S.S. Police Leader were in command. It was expressly noted in the regulations for the fighting of Partisans that I could only request authority to issue commands where the competence of the Higher S.S. Police Leaders or of two Wehrmacht Commanders overlapped, thus making necessary a Higher Command for the handling of the difficulties.

Q. Did you ever conduct an action personally?

A. I did so in the year 1943.

Q. In what way?

A. This undertaking took place in the autumn of 1943, in the region of Idrizza Polotsk. I first flew to the Central Army Group and talked these matters over with my then chief, General Krebs. Then I went on to the Army Group North, and discussed the same matters with Field Marshal Kuchler. Kuchler had concentrated all the troops of the S.S. Police or of the rear areas in a so-called corps under the command of Jacklin. The same thing had been done by the Central Army Group; a corps had been set up under the command of the Higher Police Officer in the Group. I was in charge of them and had, as liaison officer, Colonel von Mellentin from the O.K.H. Then I conducted the enterprise personally. In the meantime, the front had been broken through in the Nebe Sector and I came to the independent decision to turn against the Red Army where it had broken through; thus I was with my unit in the first line.

Q. You said a little while ago that you had been decorated with the Knight's Cross. Did you receive this decoration for this undertaking?

A. No, as I said before, I was already in the year 1941 in the front line service. Again and again I was with fighting units. In 1941 in front of Moscow, in 1942 at Veliki-Luki and later at the uprising in Warsaw. From 1944 on I led an S.S. Corps.

Q. Did you not know that you were particularly praised by Hitler and Himmler, mainly for your ruthless and efficient fighting of Partisans?

A. No, I received no decoration for my fighting of Partisans. I received all my decorations when in the Wehrmacht, and for my services at the front line.

Q. Was the Brigade Dirlewanger an S.S. Brigade?

A. The Brigade Dirlewanger did not belong to the Waffen S.S. It was an organisation which at best could be classified as Allgemeine S.S. With respect to supplies it was not placed under the Waffen S. S. but under the " Amt Berger."

Q. Was the Commander of the Brigade Dirlewanger a member of the S.S.?

A. Yes.

Q. Did you yourself suggest that criminals should be organised and used for the fighting of Partisans?

A. No.

DR. THOMA (Counsel for defendant Rosenberg):

Q. Witness, do you know that the Civil Government in White Ruthenia often protested against the manner in which the anti-Partisan activities were carried on?

A. Yes.

Q. The Civil Authority was subordinate to the Reich Kommissar, and he in turn was subordinate to Rosenberg who was Minister for the Occupied Eastern Territories?

A. Yes.

Q. If I understood you correctly, you objected to the way in which the fight against Partisans was carried on, a way which involved many innocent people, and was not in agreement with Reichsfuehrer S.S. Himmler's orders?

A. Yes.

Q. How can you reconcile it with your conscience to organise Einsatz Groups although you were in charge of the anti- Partisan warfare?

THE PRESIDENT: The question had not come through then on the interpreter's voice before you began to answer. You must give greater pauses between the question and answer.

Q. How did you reconcile it with your conscience to remain an inspector of the anti-Partisan forces?

A. I did not reconcile that with my conscience. But I actually strove to obtain this position because, in the years 1941 and 1942 I saw, as did Schenkendorff, that things could not continue as they were. General Schenkendorff, my immediate superior, recommended me for the position.

Q. But you knew that you could achieve nothing with these suggestions?

A. No, I could not know that. I did not know at that time what I know to-day.

Q. At any rate, you did not achieve anything?

A. That is not my fault. My opinion is that if someone else had been in that position, many more misfortunes would have occurred.

Q. Do you believe that Himmler's speech, in which he demanded the extermination of thirty million Slavs, expressed only his personal opinion, or do you consider that it was part of the National Socialist attitude towards life?

A. To-day I am of the opinion that this was the logical consequence of our attitude towards life.

Q. To-day?

A. To-day.

Q. What was your own opinion at that time?

A. It is difficult for a German to arrive at this conclusion. It took me a long time.

Q. Then how is it that a few days ago a witness appeared in this Tribunal, namely Oblendorf, who admitted that the Einsatz Group murdered ninety thousand people, and informed the Court that this did not harmonise with the National Socialist ideology?

A. I am of the opinion that if, for decades, a doctrine is preached to the effect that the Slav race is an inferior race, and Jews not even human at all, then such an explosion is inevitable.

Q. Nevertheless the fact remains that, together with whatever attitude you may have bad at the time, you also had a conscience?

A. To-day also, and that is the reason why I am here.

THE PRESIDENT: Dr. Exner, are you cross-examining on behalf of some other defendant, or what?

DR. EXNER (Counsel for defendant Jodl): I should like to ask two questions, which my client considered important and which he put to me during the recess.

THE PRESIDENT: You have already cross-examined, have you not?

DR. EXNER: Yes, but I now have three new questions. We were not able to prepare ourselves for this cross-examination.

THE PRESIDENT: Very well. Go on.

FURTHER CROSS-EXAMINATION BY DR. EXNER

Q. Witness, you said an order was issued in the year 1944 regarding the Partisan warfare. During the recess, I read in the document book provided us by the prosecution, under 1786- PS, and there I found a regulation mentioned regarding Partisan warfare, of 27th November, 1942. Do you know anything about this?

A. No.

Q. But it must exist, since it is mentioned to me here. Do you not know about it?

A. No.

Q. Please tell me whether you know of a Russian regulation regarding Partisans?

A. Yes.

Q. Could you tell us something of the contents of this regulation?

A. I can no longer recall.

Q. Do you know where this regulation is to be found?

A. No.

DR. EXNER: Thank you.

THE TRIBUNAL (Mr. Biddle): One moment! Do you know how many members of the Wehrmacht were used at any one time in this anti-Partisan activity? What was the largest number of the troops?

THE WITNESS: Large undertakings were involved, that is to say, undertakings of the strength of one division upwards. I believe that the largest number might have been as much as three divisions.

THE TRIBUNAL (Mr. Biddle): I mean all the troops on the Eastern Front, at any one time used in these anti-Partisan activities?

THE WITNESS: I cannot answer that, because these troops were never under my direction at one time, they were there with individual operations simultaneously and continually; large and small operations. Reports of these activities came in every day.

THE TRIBUNAL (Mr. Biddle): Do you know how many Einsatz groups were used?

THE WITNESS: I know of three, one for each Army Group.

THE PRESIDENT: Do you want to re-examine?

COLONEL TAYLOR: No, Sir.

THE PRESIDENT: Then the witness may go.

(The witness withdrew.)

COLONEL TAYLOR: Your Lordship, that concludes the evidence under Counts 3 and 4 of the Indictment and I have only a few more words by way of general conclusion.

I ask the Tribunal to bear in mind that the German High Command is not an evanescent thing, the creature of a decade of unrest, or a school of thought or tradition which is shattered and utterly discredited. The German High Command and military tradition have in the past achieved victory and survived defeat. They have met with triumph and disaster, and they have survived through a singular durability.

An eminent American statesman and diplomat, Mr. Sumner Welles, has written, and I quote from his book "The Time for Decision," Page 261:

"... that the authority to which the German people have so often and so disastrously responded was not in reality the German Emperor of yesterday, or the Hitler of today, but the German General Staff. Whether their ostensible ruler is the Kaiser, or Hindenburg, or Adolf Hitler, the continuing loyalty of the bulk of the population is given to that military force controlled and guided by the German General Staff."

I think that this emphasises the historical importance of the decision which this Tribunal is called upon to make. But we are not now indicting the German General Staff at the bar of history, but on specific charges of Crimes against International Law and the dictates of the conscience of mankind, as embodied in the Charter, which governs this Court.

The picture we have seen is that of a group of men with great power for good or ill, who chose the latter; who deliberately set out to arm Germany to the point where the German will could be imposed on the rest of the world, and who gladly joined with the most evil forces at work in Germany. "Hitler produced the results which all of us warmly desired," we are told by Blomberg and Blaskowitz, and that is obviously the truth. The converse is no less clear; the military leaders furnished Hitler with the means and might which were necessary to his survival, to say nothing of the accomplishment of those purposes which seemed to us so ludicrously impossible in 1932 and so fearfully imminent in 1942.

I have said that the German militarists were inept as well as persistent. Helpless as Hitler would have been without them, he succeeded in mastering them. The Generals and the Nazis were allies in 1933. But it was not enough for the Nazis that the Generals should be voluntary allies; Hitler wanted them permanently and completely under his control. Devoid of political skill or principle, the Generals lacked the mentality or morality to resist. On the day of the death of President Hindenburg in August, 1934, the German officers swore a new oath. Their previous oath had been to the Fatherland; now it was to a man, Adolf Hitler. It was not until a year later that the Nazi emblem became part of their uniform, and the Nazi flag their standard. By a clever process of infiltration into key positions, Hitler seized control of the entire military machine.

We will no doubt hear the Generals ask what they could have done about it. We will hear that they were helpless, and that to protect their jobs and families and lives, they had to follow Hitler's decisions. No doubt this became true, but the Generals were a key factor in Hitler's rise to complete power and a partner in his criminal aggressive designs. It is always difficult and dangerous to withdraw from a criminal conspiracy. Never has it been suggested that a conspirator may claim mercy on the ground that his fellow conspirators threatened him with harm, should he withdraw from the plot.

In many respects the spectacle which the German General Staff and High Command group presents today, is the most degrading of all the groups and organisations before this court. They are the bearers of a tradition, the bearers of a tradition not devoid of valour and honour; they emerge from this war stained both by criminality and ineptitude. Attracted by the militaristic and aggressive Nazi policies, the German Generals found themselves drawn into adventures of a scope they had not foreseen. From crimes in which almost all of them participated willingly and approvingly, were born others in which they participated partly because they were too ineffective to alter the governing Nazi policies, and partly because they had to continue collaboration to save their own skins.

Having joined the partnership, the General Staff and the High Command group planned and carried through manifold acts of aggression which turned Europe into a charnel-house, and caused the Armed Forces to be used for foul practices, foully executed, of terror, pillage and wholesale slaughter. Let no one be heard to say that the military uniform shall be their cloak, or that they may find sanctuary by pleading membership in the profession to which they are an eternal disgrace.

COLONEL STOREY: If the Tribunal please, the next subject will be the presentation of supplemental evidence concerning the persecution of the Churches, as presented by Colonel Wheeler.

COLONEL LEONARD WHEELER, JR.: The material now to be submitted comprises, first, supplemental proof on the suppression of the churches within Germany - the Evangelical Churches, the Catholic Church and the Bibelforscher, or Bible Researchers; and second, acts of suppression in the annexed and occupied territories - Austria, Czechoslovakia and Poland. A large part of this proof will be from the official files of the Vatican.

I now submit to the Court United States trial brief "H"- Supplemental" on "Suppression of the Christian Churches in Germany and in the Occupied Territories," and Document Book "H-Supplemental," containing English translations of all the documents referred to in the supplemental brief, or to be referred to in my oral presentation. I shall take up first the supplemental proof on the suppression of the Churches in Germany.

Hitler announced, in March, 1933, a distinction in his policy toward politics and morals, on the one hand, and religion on the other. I offer in evidence Document 3387-PS, Exhibit USA 565. It is a speech by Hitler to the Reichstag on 23rd March, 1933, quoted in the "Volkischer Beobachter," 24th March, 1933, Page one, column 5, of the German newspaper. I quote from this speech:

"Inasmuch as the Government is determined to carry out a political and moral purge of our public life, it thereby creates and guarantees the foundation of a true and religious life. The Government sees in both Christian denominations the most important factors for the maintenance of our Folkdom. It will respect agreements concluded between them and the other States. It expects, however, that its participation shall meet with the same respect as it has afforded to all the other responsible denominations. But it will never permit that membership in any one denomination, or the fact of belonging to any one race, should be considered as a free pass for the commission or toleration of crime. The Government will devote itself to the maintenance of sincere good- fellowship between Church and State."

Toward the Evangelical Churches, the Nazi conspirators proceeded at first with caution, and an appearance of legality. They set up a new constitution of the German Evangelical Church, which introduced the innovation of a single Lutheran Reich-Bishop, who assumed all the administrative functions of the old agencies of the Churches. I refer to Document 3422-PS, the decree concerning the Constitution of the German Evangelical Church, dated 14th July, 1933, appearing in the Reichsgesetzblatt, 1933, Part I, Page 471, and request that the Court take judicial notice of it.

It is too well known to require documentation that the new Reich-Bishop, Bishop Muller, heeded the voice of his Nazi masters. One of his first steps was to manoeuvre the Evangelical Youth Association into the Hitler Jugend under the defendant von Schirach, in December, 1933. I refer to Document 1458-APS, already in evidence as part of Document Book "D" Transcript for 23rd November. It is an excerpt from von Schirach's book, "The Hitler Youth, Idea and Formation."

By 1935 it had become evident that more than persuasion by the Reich-Bishop was necessary. Consequently the Nazi conspirators promulgated a number of public laws which, under innocent sounding titles, gradually wove a tight net of State control over all the affairs of the Evangelical Churches. We ask that the Court take judicial notice of these laws published in the Reichsgesetzblatt. These may be briefly summarised as follows:

3434-PS, Law concerning Procedure for Decisions in Legal Affairs of the Evangelical Church, dated 26th June, 1935, signed by Hitler and Frick, appearing in 1935 in Reichsgesetzblatt, Part 1, Page 774. This gave the Reich Ministry of the Interior - the defendant Frick - when question was raised in a civil lawsuit, sole authority to determine the validity of measures taken in the Evangelical State Church, or in the German Evangelical Church since 1st May, 1933.

3435-PS, First Ordinance for Execution of the Law concerning Procedure for Decisions in Legal Affairs of the Evangelical Church, dated 3rd July, 1935, appearing in 1935 Reichsgesetzblatt, Part 1, Page 851. This implemented the earlier law, by setting up an Office for Decisions with three members appointed by the Reich Minister of the Interior.

3466-PS, Decree to Unite the Competences of Reich and Prussia in Church Affairs, dated 16th July, 1935, signed by Hitler, published in 1935 Reichsgesetzblatt, Part 1, Page 1029. This transferred to "Reich Minister without Portfolio Kerrl" the Church Affairs hitherto handled by the Reich and Prussian Ministries of the Interior and for Science, Education and Training of the Population.

3436-PS, Law for the Safeguarding of the German Evangelical Church, dated 24th September, 1935, published in the 1935 Reichsgesetzblatt, Part 1, Page 1178, signed by Hitler and the Minister for Church Affairs, Dr. Kerrl. This empowered the Reich Minister of Church Affairs to issue ordinances with binding legal force.

3437-PS, Fifth Decree for Execution of the Law for the Safeguarding of the German Evangelical Church, dated 2nd December, 1935, published in 1935 Reichsgesetzblatt, Part 1, Page 13 70. This prohibited "Organs of Church Leadership" in the Evangelical Churches from filling pastorates, engaging clerical assistants, examining and ordaining candidates of the State Churches, visitation, publishing of the banns, and collection and administration of church dues and assessments.

This series of laws culminated on 26th June, 1937, in 3439- PS, the Fifteenth Decree for the Execution of the Law for Security of the German Evangelical Church, dated 25th June, 1937, published in 1937 Reichsgesetzblatt, Part 1, Page 697. By Decree for the Execution of the Law for Security of the German Evangelical Church dated 25th June, 1937, published in 1937 Reichsgesetzblatt, Part 1, Page 697, the Reich Minister for Church Affairs (Kerrl) established a Finance Department for the churches to supervise the administration of church property, the budget, and the use of budget funds, and to regulate salaries and allowances of officials, clergy and employees. Thus, before the outbreak of the war, the Nazi conspirators had the Evangelical Churches tied hand and foot physically and administratively, if not spiritually.

Against the Catholic Church with its international organisation the Nazi conspirators launched a most vigorous and drastic attack again, at first cloaked under a mantle of co-operation and legality. A concordat signed by the defendant von Papen, one of the foremost Catholic laymen in Germany, was concluded between the Reich Government and the Vatican on 20th July, 1933. It is printed in the 1933 Reichsgesetzblatt, Part 11, Pages 679 and 680, and contained in Document 3280-A-PS, and I will ask the Court to take judicial notice of it. I quote Article I:

"The German Reich guarantees freedom of profession and public practice of the Catholic religion. it acknowledges the right of the Catholic Church, within the limit of those laws which are applicable to all, to manage and regulate her own affairs independently and, within the framework of her own competence, to publish laws and ordinances binding on her members."

Other articles which, being matters of common knowledge, I assume need not be read into the record, formulated basic principles such as freedom of the Catholic Press, of Catholic education, and of Catholic charitable, professional and other organisations.

The proposal for the Concordat came from the Reich, and not from the Vatican. I refer to Document 3268-PS, Exhibit USA 356, excerpts from the Allocution of Pope Pius XII to the Sacred College on 2nd June, 1945, already read into evidence. I quote from Page I of the English mimeographed excerpt, Page I of the German translation, third paragraph, which has not previously been read:

"In Spring, 1933, the German Government asked the Holy See to conclude a Concordat with the Reich."

Relying upon the Nazis' assurances, particularly upon Hitler's speech of 23rd March, 1933, above quoted-Document 3387-PS-the Catholic hierarchy revoked its previous opposition against Catholics becoming members of the National Socialist Party. I offer in evidence Document 3389- PS, Exhibit USA 566, a Pastoral Letter, dated 23rd March, 1933, from the Bishop of Cologne, and I quote from the "Volkischer Beobachter" of 29th March, 1933, Page 2, columns 2 and 3:

"The official announcement by the Archbishop of Cologne, Cardinal Schulte, on behalf of the Bishops' Conference at Fulda, 28th March, 1933.

The Lord Bishops of the Dioceses of Germany, in their dutiful anxiety to keep the Catholic faith pure and to protect the untouchable aims and rights of the Catholic Church, have adopted, for weighty reasons during the last years, an oppositional attitude towards the National Socialist Movement, through prohibitions and warnings, which were to be in effect as long and as far as these reasons remained valid."

It must now be recognised that official and solemn declarations have been issued by the Highest Representative of the Reich Government who at the same time is the authoritative leader of that movement - which acknowledged the inviolability of the teachings of the Catholic Faith and the full value of the legal pacts concluded with the various German States (Laender) and the Church.

Without lifting the condemnation of certain religious and ethical errors implied in our previous measures, the Episcopate now believes it can entertain the confidence that those prescribed general prohibitions and warnings may not be regarded as necessary any more."

The Catholic Centre Party, yielding to those assurances and to pressure was dissolved on 5th July, 1933. I refer to Document 2403-PS already in evidence as part of U.S.A. Document Book "B," an excerpt from documents of German politics, an official Nazi publication, a document of which the Court can take judicial notice; and I quote from the last five lines of Page 1 of the English translation, appearing on Page 55 of the original German text, which states: I quote:

"Also the parties of German Catholicism, which were supposed to be most deeply rooted, had to bow to the law of the New Order. On 4th July, 1933, the Bavarian People's Party (Document 27) and on 5th July, 1933, the Centre Party (Document 29) published an announcement of their dissolution."

In spite of these evidences of confidence and co-operation or submission on the part of the Catholics, the Nazi conspirators almost immediately commenced a series of violations of the Concordat. I offer in evidence Document 3476-PS, Exhibit USA

567, this being the Papal Encyclical, "Mit Brennender Sorge," in German, by Pope Pius XI, on 14th March, 1937, and ask the Tribunal to take judicial notice of all of it. On Page 2, paragraph 2 of the German original, which is now in evidence. It was secretly reproduced at Fulda, from copies smuggled into Germany from Rome, and read defiantly from pulpits all over Germany. I quote:

> "It discloses intrigues which from the beginning had no other aim than a war of extermination. In the furrows in which he had laboured to sow the seeds of true peace, others - like the enemy in the Holy Scripture (Matthew xiii. 25) - sowed the tares of suspicion, discord, hatred, calumny, of secret and open fundamental hostility to Christ and His Church, fed from a thousand different sources and making use of every available means. On them and on them alone and on their silent and vocal protectors rests the responsibility that now, on the horizon of Germany, there is to be seen not the rainbow of peace but the threatening storm clouds of destructive religious wars.
>
> Anyone who had any sense of truth left in his mind and even a shadow of a feeling of justice left in his heart will have to admit that, in the difficult and eventful years which followed the Concordat, every word and every action of ours was governed by loyalty to the terms of the agreement; but also he will have to recognise with surprise and deep disgust that the unwritten law of the other party has been arbitrary misinterpretation of agreements, evasions of agreements, distortion of the meaning of agreements and, finally, more or less open violation of agreements."

DR. ALFRED SEIDL (Counsel for defendant Frank): The United States Prosecution has previously declared that a certain part of the, material now under consideration, which is to be presented in the matter of the opposition to the Church, has been made available by the Vatican. The defendant Hans Frank directed a written memorandum to me, containing a question I do not wish to withhold from the Tribunal, namely:

(1) Is the Vatican a signatory to the Charter of the International Military Tribunal?

(2) Did the Vatican deliver the material in an accusatory capacity?

(3) Has the Vatican, acting as a co-prosecutor, identified itself with the principles of these proceedings?

The defendant, Hans Frank, justified these questions by stating that his further allegiance to the Roman Catholic Church depends on the reply to these questions.

THE PRESIDENT: I think it desirable that the Tribunal should clearly understand your objections. The first question that you ask is: Is the Vatican a Signatory to the Charter? Is that correct?

DR. SEIDL: Yes.

THE PRESIDENT: What was your second question?

DR. SEIDL: The second question is: Whether the Vatican submitted the material here present as a co-prosecutor?

THE PRESIDENT: And your third question?

DR. SEIDL: The third question is - and it is addressed directly to the prosecution - whether the Vatican has recognised, as prosecutor, the principles upon which the Trial is being conducted?

THE PRESIDENT: Whether the Vatican recognises the principles upon which the Trial is being conducted? Will you repeat the question?

DR. SEIDL: The last question?

THE PRESIDENT: Yes.

DR. SEIDL: It reads: Has the Vatican acquainted itself with the material now being submitted at this Trial and does the Vatican, as co-prosecutor, share the principles upon which the Trial is being conducted? And, as a reason for his questions, the defendant Hans Frank states that his further allegiance to the Roman Catholic Church depends on the answers to these questions.

THE PRESIDENT: In the opinion of the Tribunal, the observations which have just been made by counsel on behalf of the defendant Frank are entirely irrelevant and any motion, which they are so intended to support, is denied. The prosecution will therefore continue.

COLONEL WHEELER: I now offer in evidence the first of a number of documents which the Vatican has supplied to the prosecution in this case from its own files, and which authoritatively state the acts of suppression of the Church by the Nazi conspirators. This first Vatican document, which deals in part with acts of suppression within Germany, is Document 3261-PS, Exhibit USA 568, a verbal note of the Secretariat of State of His Holiness the Pope to the German Embassy, dated 18th January, 1942, I read the certificate accompanying this document:

"The Vatican, 13th November, 1945.

I, Domenico Tardini, Secretary of Extraordinary Ecclesiastical Affairs, hereby certify that the attached document, consisting of nine printed pages and entitled:

Verbal note of the Secretariat of State of His Holiness, to the German Embassy (18th January, 1942) (pp. 3-11) is a true and correct translation into the English language from the Italian language of a carbon copy of a document now in the possession of the Secretariat of State of His Holiness, the original of which was despatched to the German Embassy.

(Signed) Domenico Tardini."

The paper in the document books, your Honours, is a mimeographed copy of the same printed document which we received from the Vatican. We did not have enough printed documents to put them in the document books.

On Page 2 of the English mimeographed text is this verbal note, paragraphs 3 and 4, appearing on Page 2 of the German translation. The Papal Secretary of State describes: I quote:

"Measures and acts which gravely violate the rights of the Church, being contrary not only to the existing Concordats but to the principles of International Law ratified by the Second Hague Conference - "

THE PRESIDENT: Did you say you were reading the third paragraph?

COLONEL WHEELER: Yes, your Honour. It is the third paragraph on Page 2. It starts in the middle of that paragraph, with the last word on the 7th line.

THE PRESIDENT: It is very difficult for us to find it if you do not tell us, it being in the middle of the paragraph.

COLONEL WHEELER: I'm sorry, Sir. " - and often-and this is much more grave - to the very fundamental principles of Divine Law both natural and positive."

The next paragraph specifies these measures. I quote:

"Let it suffice to recall in this connection, among other things, the changing of the Catholic State elementary schools into un-denominational schools; the permanent or temporary closing of many minor seminaries, of not a few major seminaries and of some theological faculties; the suppression of almost all the private schools and of numerous Catholic boarding schools and colleges; the repudiation, decided unilaterally, of financial obligations which the State, municipalities, etc. had towards the Church; the increasing difficulties put in the way of the activity of the religious Orders and Congregations in the spiritual, cultural and social field, and above all, the suppression of abbeys, monasteries, convents and religious houses in such great numbers that one is led to infer a deliberate intention of rendering impossible the very existence of the Orders and Congregations in Germany."

The Nazis did not overlook other sects or denominations in their efforts to suppress Christian religion in Germany. They persecuted the "Bibelforscher" or Bible Research -

THE PRESIDENT: Perhaps, as you are going into another Church, it would be better to break off until to-morrow morning.

(The Tribunal adjourned until 10.00 hours, on 8th January, 1946.)

Twenty-Ninth Day: Tuesday, January 8th, 1946

COLONEL WHEELER: The Nazis did not overlook other sects or denominations in their efforts to suppress Christian religion in Germany. They persecuted the "Bibelforscher" or Bible research workers as well. There has already been introduced and read into evidence Document D-84, Exhibit USA 236, showing that members of this sect were not only prosecuted in the courts, but also seized and sent to concentration camps, even after serving or remitting of their judicial sentences.

In Document 2928-PS, Exhibit USA 239, included in U.S.A. Document Book A, further evidence of persecution of "Bibelforscher" appears.

THE PRESIDENT: I think you are going a little bit fast. We are not going to refer to D-84?

COLONEL WHEELER: I am not going to read from it, sir.

THE PRESIDENT: Then you go to 2928-PS?

COLONEL WHEELER: 2928-PS; it is in the document book, sir.

THE PRESIDENT: Are you going to read from there?

COLONEL WHEELER: I was going to read a few lines from that.

THE PRESIDENT: Very well.

COLONEL WHEELER: This document is an affidavit by Matthias Lex, Vice-President of the National Union of Shoemakers. In describing his experience in Dachau concentration camp he says, and I quote from the third page of his affidavit: ...

"I include in the political prisoners the Bible-researchers (Bibelforscher) whose number I estimate at over 150."

I want to read further from the last line of that page and the next few lines of the next page:

"The following groups were kept entirely isolated: The members of the so-called 'Punishment-Companies' (Strafkompanien) who were in a concentration camp for a second time, and after about 1937 also the 'Bibelforscher.' Members of the 'Punishment-Companies' were such prisoners as had committed disciplinary or slight offences against the camp regulations. The following groups lived separately but could mix with the other groups during the day, either while working or while strolling through the camp: Political prisoners, Jews, Anti-Socials, Gypsies, Felons, Homosexuals, and, before 1937, also the Bible-researchers."

I refer also to Document 1531-PS - this is not in the document book - Exhibit USA 248, which is already in evidence. This was an order by the R.S.H.A., in 1942, authorising third-degree methods against Jehovah's Witnesses. That was read by Colonel Storey.

I now turn to acts of suppression in the annexed and occupied territories. In Austria, Bishop Rusch of Innsbruck has written an illuminating report on this subject. I offer this sworn statement in evidence-Document 3278-PS, Exhibit USA 569. This is a report on the fighting of National Socialism in the Apostolic Administration of Innsbruck- Feldkirch, of Tyrol and Vorarlberg. In this the Bishop declares, and I start on the first page of the English text and of the German translation:

"After having seized power, National Socialism immediately showed a tendency to exclude the Church from publicity."

The expression "Publicity" - this was written in English by the Bishop - evidently means "public activities." I continue to quote:

"At Corpus Christi, in 1939, the customary solemn procession was forbidden. In the summer of the same year all ecclesiastical schools and kindergartens were disbanded. Daily newspaper and weekly reviews of "Christian Thinking" were likewise removed. In the same years all kinds of ecclesiastical organisations, especially youth organisations, such as Boy Scouts, were disbanded, and all activity forbidden.

The effect of these prohibitions came soon: the clergy took opposition against them, they could not do otherwise. Then a great wave of priest arresting followed. About a fifth of them were eventually arrested. Reasons for arrests were:

1. The "Pulpit prohibition' - when Party actions were mentioned or criticised even in the humblest manner.

2. The practice of taking care of young people. A specially heavy prohibition was instituted in November, 1939. Children's or youth's mass or services were forbidden. Religion or faith lessons were not allowed to be given in the Church except lessons of preparing for first communion or confirmation. Teaching of religion at school was very often forbidden without any reason.

Priests, because of their conscience, could not fall in with this public proscription and this explained the great number of their arrests. Finally, they were arrested on account of their charitable work. It was, for instance, forbidden to give anything to foreigners or prisoners. A priest was arrested because he gave a cup of coffee and some bread to two hungry Dutchmen. This charitable act was seen to favour elements foreign to the race.

In 1939 and 1940 a new activity began. Cloisters and abbeys were seized and disbanded, and many churches belonging to them closed. Among these, two nunneries were disbanded: the cloister of the Dominican Sisters of Kludenz and that of the 'Perpetual Adoration' of Innsbruck. In the latter the Sisters were dragged, one by one, out of the cloister by the Gestapo. In the same way ecclesiastical property such as Association-Houses, Parish and Youth Homes were seized. A list of these closed churches, disbanded cloisters and ecclesiastical institutions is attached.

Despite all these measures the results were not satisfactory, and so priests were then not only arrested, but also deported to concentration camps. Eight priests of Tyrol and Vorarlberg have been imprisoned, among them the Provicar Monsignore Dr. Charles Lampert. One died there on account of the ill-treatment, the others returned. Provicar Lampert was released but required to remain in Stettin, where later he was re-arrested, and was executed in November, 1944, after having been condemned to death by secret proceedings."

There is attached to this report a three-and-a-half page list entitled: "List of churches, nunneries, monasteries and ecclesiastical objects of Tyrol and Vorarlberg, seized, that is, confiscated, and of the institutions, confessional schools, etc., disbanded." Unless the Tribunal requires it, I shall not read these names.

I offer in evidence Document 3274-PS, Exhibit USA 570, received from Cardinal

Innitzer of Vienna and authenticated by him. This is the first joint Pastoral Letter of the Archbishops and Bishops of Austria after liberation, dated 17th October, 1945. I quote from Page 1, second paragraph of the English and German texts, which sums up the Nazi conspirators' campaign in Austria:

"A war which has raged terribly and horribly, like none other in past epochs of the history of humanity, is at an end. At an end also is an intellectual battle, the goal of which was the destruction of Christianity and the church among our people; a campaign of lies and treachery against truth and love, against divine and human rights, and against International Law."

I quote further from the fourth and following paragraphs:

"Direct hostility to the church was revealed in regulations against orders and monasteries, Catholic schools and institutions, against religious foundations and activities, against the buildings of ecclesiastical houses and institutions; without the least rights to defend themselves they were declared enemies of both people and State and their existence destroyed.

Religious instruction and education of children and youth were purposely limited, frequently entirely prevented. They encouraged in every manner all efforts hostile to religion and the church and thus sought to rob the children and youth of our people of their most valuable treasure of holy faith and of true morality born of the Spirit of God. Unfortunately, the attempt succeeded in innumerable cases to the permanent damage of young people.

Spiritual care of souls in churches and ecclesiastical houses, in hospitals and other institutions was seriously obstructed. It was made ineffectual in the Armed Forces and in the Labour Service, in the sending of youth to the country and, beyond that, even in individual families and among numerous persons, to say nothing of the prohibition of spiritual ministration to people of another nationality and of other races.

How often was the divine service as such, also sermons, folk missions, communion days, retreats, processions, pilgrimages, limited for the most impossible reasons and made entirely impossible.

Catholic literature, newspapers, periodicals, church papers, religious writings were stopped, books and libraries destroyed.

What an injustice occurred in the dissolution of many Catholic societies, in the destruction of numerous church activities.

Individual Catholic and Christian believers, whose religious confession was allegedly free, were spied upon, criticised on account of their belief, and scorned on account of their Christian activity. How many local officials, teachers, public and private employees, labourers, businessmen and artisans, indeed, even peasants were put under pressure and terror. Many lost their jobs, some were pensioned off, others dismissed without pension, demoted, deprived of their real professional activity. Often enough such people as remained loyal to their convictions were discriminated against, condemned to hunger or tortured in concentration camps. Christianity and the Church were continually scorned and exposed to hatred.

The apostasy movement found every assistance. Every opportunity was used to induce many to withdraw from the Church."

In assessing responsibility for these acts of suppression in Austria, the Court will recall that the defendant, von Schirach, was Gauleiter of Vienna from 1940 to 1945.

I now come to the acts of suppression in Czechoslovakia, where, the Court will recollect, the defendant, von Neurath, was Reich Protector for Bohemia and Moravia from 1939 to 1943 and was succeeded by the defendant Frick. These acts have been summarised in an official Czech Government report. I refer to Document 998-PS, Exhibit USA 91, already in evidence. These are excerpts not previously read or referred to from the "Czech Official Report for the Prosecution and Trial of the German Major War Criminals by the International Military Tribunal established according to the Agreement of the Four Great Powers of 8th August, 1945." Since this is an official Government document or report of one of the United Nations, I ask that the Tribunal take judicial notice of it under Article 21 of the Charter and I suggest that I be permitted to summarise rather than read it.

It describes the maltreatment of Catholic priests-four hundred and eighty-seven of whom were sent to concentration camps as hostages-dissolution of religious orders, suppression of religious instruction in Czech schools, suppression of Catholic weekly and monthly publications, dissolution of the Catholic gymnastic organisation of 800,000 members, and seizure of Catholic Church property. It describes the entire prohibition of the Czechoslovak National Church and confiscation of all its property in Slovakia and its crippling in Bohemia. The report describes the severe restriction on freedom of preaching b the Protestants, and the persecution and imprisonment and execution of ministers, and the suppression of Protestant Church youth organisations and theological schools, and shows the complete subordination and, later, the dissolution of the Greek Orthodox Church. It states that all Evangelical education was handed over to the civil authorities, and that many Evangelical teachers lost their employment.

The repressive measures adopted by the Nazi conspirators in Poland against the Christian Church were even more drastic and sweeping.

The Vatican documents now to be introduced describe persecutions of the Catholic Church in Poland in three areas: first, the Incorporated Territories, especially the Warthegau; second, the Government General; and third, the Incorporated Eastern Territories.

The Court will recall that the incorporated territories comprised territories adjacent to the old Reich, chiefly the Reich District Wartheland or Warthegau, which included particularly the cities of Poznan and Lodz and the Reich district Danzig, West Prussia.

The occupied Polish territories which were organised into the Government General comprised the remainder of Poland, seized by the German forces in 1939 and extending to the new boundary with the Soviets, formed at that time. This included Warsaw and Cracow. After the Nazis attacked the Union of Soviet Socialist Republics in June, 1941, the parts of old Poland lying farther to the East, and then overrun, were included in the so-called Occupied Eastern Territories.

For the purpose of tying in the defendants' responsibility for the persecutions occurring in their respective areas, the Court will bear in mind that the defendant Frick was the official chiefly responsible for the reorganisation of the Eastern territories. The defendant Frank was head of the Government General from 1939 to 1945. The defendant Seyss-Inquart was Deputy Governor General there from 1939 to 1940, and the defendant Rosenberg was Reich Minister for the Occupied Eastern Territories from 17th July, 1941, to the end.

I now offer in evidence Document 3263-PS, Exhibit USA 571, headed "Memorandum of the Secretariat of State to the German Embassy regarding the Religious Situation in the 'Warthegau,' 8th October, 1942." This document bears a certificate of authenticity from the Vatican signed by the Papal Secretary of Extraordinary Ecclesiastical Affairs corresponding to that accompanying Document 3261-PS, read in evidence a few minutes ago. Unless, the Court requires otherwise, I suggest that it is not necessary to read each of these certificates, which are all similar. I quote from Document 3263-PS, the first paragraph:

"For quite a long time the religious situation in the region called 'Warthegau' has given cause for very grave and ever-increasing anxiety. There, in fact, the Episcopate has been little by little almost completely eliminated; the secular and regular clergy have been reduced to proportions that are absolutely inadequate, because they have been in large part deported and exiled; the education of clerics has been forbidden; the Catholic education of youth is meeting with the greatest opposition; the nuns have been dispersed; insurmountable obstacles have been put in the way of affording people the help of religion; very many churches have been closed; Catholic intellectual and charitable institutions have been destroyed; ecclesiastical property has been seized."

On 2nd March, 1943, the Cardinal Secretary of State addressed to the defendant von Ribbentrop, Foreign Minister of the Reich, a note setting forth in detail the persecution of bishops, priests and other ecclesiastics and the suppression of the exercise of religion in the occupied Polish provinces. This document is so explicit and so authoritative that it deserves extensive quotation. I accordingly offer it in evidence, Document 3264-PS, Exhibit USA 572. It is headed: "A Note of His Eminence the Cardinal Secretary of State to the Foreign Minister of the Reich about the Religious Situation in the 'Warthegau' and in the Other Polish Provinces Subject to Germany." It bears a Vatican certificate of authenticity like that of Document 3261-PS. It is signed "L. Card. Maglione," meaning "Luigi Cardinal." I quote from this note, starting with Page 1, the third paragraph of the English mimeographed text and of the German translation:

"The place where, above all, the religious situation, because of its unusual gravity, calls for special consideration is the territory called the 'Reichsgau Wartheland.'

Six bishops resided in that region in August, 1939; now there is left but one. In fact, the Bishop of Lodz (Litzmannstadt) and his Auxiliary were, in the course of the year 1941, first confined in a small district of the diocese and then expelled and exiled in the Government General.

Another bishop, Mgr. Michael Kozal, Auxiliary and Vicar General of Wladislavia, was arrested in the autumn of 1939, detained for some time in a prison in the city and later in a religious house in Lad, and finally was transferred to the concentration camp at Dachau.

Since His Eminence the Cardinal Archbishop of Gniezno and Poznan and the Bishop of Wladislavia, who had gone away during the period of military operations, were not allowed to return to their sees, the only bishop who now remains in the 'Warthegau' is His Excellency Mgr. Valentina Dymck, Auxiliary of Poznan; and he, at least up to November, 1942, was interned in his own house."

I pass now to Page 2, fourth paragraph of the English text, the fifth paragraph of the German text:

"If the lot of their Excellencies the Bishops has been a source of anxiety for the Holy See, the condition of an immense number of priests and members of religious orders has caused it, and still causes it, no less grief.

In the territory now called 'Warthegau' more than two thousand priests exercised their ministry before the war; they are now reduced to a very small number.

According to accounts received from various quarters by the Holy See, in the first months of the military occupation not a few members of the secular clergy were shot or otherwise put to death, while others-some hundreds-were imprisoned or treated in an unseemly manner, being forced into employments unbecoming their state, and exposed to scorn and derision.

Then, while numbers of ecclesiastics were exiled or constrained in some other way to take refuge in the Government General, many others were transferred to concentration camps. At the beginning of October, 1941, the priests from the dioceses of the 'Warthegau' detained in Dachau already numbered several hundreds; but their number increased considerably in that month, following a sharp intensification of police measures, which culminated in the imprisonment and deportation of further hundreds of ecclesiastics. Entire 'Kreise' (districts) remained thus completely deprived of clergy. In the city of Poznan itself the spiritual care of some 200,000 Catholics remained in the hands of not more than four priests.

No less painful was the fate reserved for the regular clergy. Many members of religious orders were shot or otherwise killed; the great majority of the others were imprisoned, deported or expelled.

In the same way far-reaching measures were taken against the institutions preparing candidates for the ecclesiastical state. The diocesan seminaries of Gniezno and Poznan, of Wladislavia and of Lodz were closed. The seminary in Poznan for the training of priests destined to work among Polish Catholics was also closed.

The noviciates and houses of instruction of the religious orders and congregations were closed.

Not even the nuns were able to continue their charitable activities without molestation. For them was set up a special concentration camp at Bojanowo, where towards the middle of 1941 about four hundred sisters were interned and employed in manual labour. To a representation of the Holy See made through the Apostolic Nunciature in Berlin your Reich Ministry for Foreign Affairs replied, in the Memorandum Pol. III, 1886 of 23rd September of the same year, that it was only a question of a temporary measure, taken with the consent of the Reichstatthalter for Wartheland, in order to supply the lack of housing for Polish Catholic sisters. In the same memorandum it was admitted that as a result of reorganisation of charitable institutions many Catholic sisters were without employment.

But, in spite of the fact that this measure was declared to be temporary, it is certain that towards the end of 1942 some hundreds of nuns were still interned at Bojanowo. It is established that for some time the nuns were deprived even of spiritual help.

Likewise in the matter of education and religious instruction of youth no attention was paid in the 'Warthegau' to the rights of the Catholic Church.

All the Catholic schools were suppressed."

I turn now to Page 4 ...

THE PRESIDENT: Who was the Foreign Minister of the Reich at the time that document was sent?

COLONEL WHEELER: It was the defendant von Ribbentrop.

I turn to Page 4, the tenth paragraph of the English text, Page 5, fourth paragraph of the German text:

"The use of the Polish language in sacred functions, and even in the

Sacrament of Penance, was forbidden. Moreover - and this is a matter worthy of special mention and is at variance with the natural law and with the dispositions accepted by the legal systems of all nations - for the celebration of marriage between Poles the minimum age limit was fixed at 28 years for men and 25 years for women.

Catholic action was so badly hit as to be completely destroyed. The National Institute, which was at the head of the whole Catholic Action Movement in Poland, was suppressed; as a result all the associations belonging to it, which were flourishing, as well as all Catholic cultural, charity and social service institutions, were abolished.

In the whole of the 'Warthegau' there is no longer any Catholic Press, and not even a Catholic bookshop.

Grave measures were repeatedly taken with regard to ecclesiastical property.

Many of the churches closed to public worship were turned over to profane uses. From such an insult not even the cathedrals of Gniezno, Poznan, Wladislavia and Lodz were spared. Episcopal residences were confiscated, the real estate belonging to the seminaries, convents, diocesan museums, libraries and church funds were confiscated or sequestered."

I pass now to the third full paragraph on Page 5, a two-line paragraph:-

"Even before ecclesiastical property was affected, the allowances to the clergy had been abolished."

Now, reading from Page 6, the fourth full paragraph of the English text:

"The administrative regulations published by the Statthalter's office for the application of the Ordinance of 13th September, 1941, made the situation of the Catholics in that region still more difficult.

For example, on 19th November, 1931, came a decree of the Reichs-statthalter by which, among other things, it was set forth that, as from the previous 13th September, the property of the former juridical persons of the Roman Catholic Church should pass over to the 'Romisch- Katholische Kirche deutscher Nationalitat im Reichsgau Wartheland' in so far as, on the request of the above- mentioned 'Religionsgesellschaft' such property shall be recognised by the Reichsstatthalter as 'non-Polish property.' In virtue of this decree practically all the goods of the Catholic Church in the 'Warthegau' were lost."

Now I pass to Page 7, the second full paragraph:-

"If we pass from the 'Warthegau' to the other territories in the East, we unfortunately find there, too, acts and measures against the rights of the Church and of the Catholic faithful, though they vary in gravity and extension from one place to another.

In the provinces which were declared annexed to the German Reich and joined up with the Gaue of East Prussia, of Danzig-West Prussia, and of Upper Silesia, the situation is very like that described above in regard to seminaries, the use of the Polish mother- tongue in sacred functions, charitable works, associations of Catholic Action, the separation of the faithful according to nationality. There, too, one must deplore the closing of churches to public worship, the exile, deportation, the violent death of not a few of the clergy (reduced by two-thirds in the diocese of Culma and by at least a third in the diocese of Katowice), the suppression of religious instruction in the schools, and above all the complete suppression in fact of the Episcopate. Actually, after the Bishop of Culma, who had left during the military operations, had been refused permission to return to his diocese, there followed - in February, 1941 - the expulsion of the Bishop of Plock and his Auxiliary, who both died later in captivity; the Bishop, the venerable octogenarian Mgr. Julian Anthony Nowowiejski, died at Dzialdowo on 28th May, 1941, and the Auxiliary, Mgr. Leo Wetmanski, 'in a transit camp' on 10th October of the same year.

In the territory called the Government General, as in the Polish provinces which had been occupied by Soviet troops in the period between September, 1939, and June, 1941, the religious situation is such as to cause the Holy See lively apprehension and serious preoccupation. Without pausing to describe the treatment meted out in many cases to the clergy (priests imprisoned, deported and even put to death), the confiscation of ecclesiastical property, the closing of churches, the suppression even of associations and publications of simply and exclusively religious character, the closing of the Catholic secondary and higher schools and of the Catholic University of Lublin, let it suffice to recall two series of specially grave measures: those which affect the seminaries and those which weigh on the Episcopate.

When the buildings of the various seminaries had been completely or in part occupied, the intention for some time (November, 1940-February, 1941) was to reduce these institutions for the training of priests to two - those of Cracow and Sandomir; then the others were permitted to reopen, but only on condition that no new students were admitted, which in practice inevitably means that all these institutions will soon be closed."

I omit one paragraph here.

"Mention has several times been made of ecclesiastics deported or confined in concentration camps. The majority of them were transferred to the Altreich, where their number already exceeds a thousand."

THE PRESIDENT: What was the "Altreich"?

COLONEL WHEELER: The Altreich is the Old Reich of Germany.

THE PRESIDENT: Yes.

COLONEL WHEELER:

"When the Holy See asked that they should be liberated and permitted to emigrate to neutral countries of Europe or America (1940), the petition was refused; it was only promised that they should all be collected in the concentration camp at Dachau, that they should be excused too hard labour, and that some should be permitted to say mass, which the others could hear.

The treatment of the ecclesiastics interned at Dachau, which, for a certain time, in 1941, was, in fact, somewhat mitigated, grew worse again at the end of that year. Particularly sorrowful were the announcements which for many months, in 1942, came from that camp of the frequent deaths of priests, even of some young priests among them."

I pass by two paragraphs:

"Polish Catholics are not allowed to contract marriage in the territory of the Altreich; just as requests for religious instruction or instruction in preparation for Confession and Holy Communion for the children of these workers are, in principle, not accepted."

What happened to complaints - even from the Vatican - as to religious affairs in the overrun territories is disclosed in Document 3266-PS, Exhibit USA 573, which I now offer in evidence. This is a letter from the Cardinal Archbishop of Breslau to the Papal Secretary of State, dated 7th December, 1942. It bears a Vatican authentication similar to those already read.

This letter lays at the door of the Party Chancellery the responsibility for determining the policy and exercising final authority on religious questions in the occupied territories. I quote from Page 1, the first paragraph of this letter, and remind the Court that the defendant Bormann was at that time Chief of the Nazi Party Chancellery and that the defendant Kaltenbrunner was the Chief of the Reichssicherheitshauptamt, the R.S.H.A. I quote from Document 3266-PS, beginning with the sixth line:

> "About some of the gravest injuries inflicted on the Church I not only protested on each occasion as the individual incident occurred, but I also made a most formal protest about them in globo in a document which, as spokesman of the Hierarchy, I sent to the supreme Ruler of the State and to the Ministries of the Reich on 10th December, 1941. Not a word by way of answer has been sent to us.
>
> Your Eminence knows very well that the greatest difficulty in the way of opening negotiations comes from the overruling authority which the National Socialist Party Chancellery exercises in relation to the chancellery of the Reich and to the single Reich Ministries. This 'Parteikanzlei' directs the course to be followed by the State, whereas the Ministries and the Chancellery of the Reich are obliged and compelled to adjust their decrees to these directions. Besides, there is the fact that the Supreme Office for the Security of the Reich, called the 'Reichssicherheitshauptamt' enjoys an authority which precludes all legal action and all appeals.
>
> Under it are the Secret Offices for Public Security, called 'Geheime Staatspolizei' (a title shortened usually to 'Gestapo'), of which there is one for each province. Against the decrees of this Central Office and of the Secret Offices there is no appeal through the Courts, and no complaint made to the Ministries has any effect. Not infrequently the councillors of the ministries suggest that they have not been able to do as they would wish to because of the opposition of these Party offices. As far as the executive power is concerned, the organisation called the S.S., that is, 'Die Schutzstaffeln der Partei,' is in practice supreme.
>
> On a number of very grave and fundamental issues we have also presented our complaints to the Supreme Leader of the Reich, the Fuehrer. Either no answer is given, or it is apparently edited by the above-mentioned Party Chancellery, which does not consider itself bound by the Concordat made with the Holy See."

I now offer in evidence Document number 3279-PS, Exhibit USA 574. This is an excerpt from Charge number 17 against the defendant Hans Frank, Governor General of Poland, entitled "Maltreatment and Persecution of the Catholic Clergy in the Western Provinces," submitted by the Polish Government under the terms of Article 21 of the Four-Power Agreement of 2nd August, 1945. This gives further figures indicating the extent of the persecution of priests. I quote:

> "The extract attached hereto and dealing with the 'General Conditions and Results of the Persecution' is taken from the text of Charge 17, Page 5, paragraph IV, of the Polish Government against the defendants named in the Indictment before the International Military Tribunal, subject: , Maltreatment and Persecution of the Catholic Clergy in the Incorporated Western Provinces of Poland.' It is a true translation into English of the original Polish.
>
> It is submitted herewith to the International Military Tribunal in accordance

with Article 21 of the Charter of the Court.

Signed: Dr. Tadeuez Cyprian, Polish Deputy Representative on the United Nations War Crimes Commission in London, signing on behalf of the Polish Government and of the Main Commission for Investigation of German War Crimes in Poland, whose seal I hereby attach."

THE PRESIDENT: I do not think you need read such certificates as that.

COLONEL WHEELER: This is the only one, Sir, that I have. I now read from this extract:

"General Conditions and Results of the Persecution:

11. The general situation of the clergy in the Archdiocese of Poznan in the beginning of April, 1940, is summarised in the following words of Cardinal Hlond's second report:

> 5 priests shot; 27 priests confined in harsh concentration camps at Stutthof and in other camps; 190 priests in prison or in concentration camps at Bruczkov, Chlodowo, Gerusski, Kazimierz, Buskupi, Lad, Lublin and Puszczykovo; 35 priests seriously ill in consequence of ill treatment; 122 parishes left entirely without priests.

12. In the diocese of Chelmno, where about 650 priests were installed before the War, only 3 per cent. were allowed to stay, the other 97 per cent. were imprisoned, executed or put into concentration camps.

13. By January, 1941, about 700 priests were killed, 3,000 were in prison or concentration camps."

I refer also to Document 3268-A-PS, Exhibit USA 356, excerpts from the Allocution of Pope Pius XII to the Sacred College, 2nd June, 1945, which has already been introduced into evidence and read from extensively. I shall not read from it again. This document gives some very revealing figures concerning the priests and lay brothers confined in the concentration camp at Dachau.

The Tribunal will recall, from the previous reading of this document, the imprisonment of 2,800 priests and lay brothers in Dachau alone from 1940 to 1945, of whom all but about 800 were dead by April, 1945, including an Auxiliary Bishop.

This document presents a forceful summary of the principal steps in the struggle of the Nazi conspirators against the Catholic Church.

To sum up, the Prosecution submits that the evidence presented to the Court proves that the attempted suppression of the Christian Churches in Germany, Austria, Czechoslovakia, and Poland was an integral part of the defendants' conspiracy to eliminate internal opposition, and otherwise to prepare for and wage aggressive war and shows the same conspiratorial pattern as their other War Crimes and Crimes against Humanity.

COLONEL STOREY: If the Tribunal please, before we present the subject of individual defendants, by agreement with our British colleagues, Major Elwyn Jones will now present a brief subject entitled "Aggression as a Basic Nazi Idea." Major Elwyn Jones.

MAJOR ELWYN JONES: May it please the Tribunal, it is now my duty to draw to the Tribunal's attention a document which became the statement of faith of these defendants. I refer to Hitler's "Mein Kampf." It is perhaps appropriate that this should be considered at this stage of the trial just before the prosecution presents to the Tribunal the evidence against the individual defendants under Counts 1 and 2 of the Indictment, for this book, "Mein Kampf," gave to the defendants adequate foreknowledge of the unlawful aims of the Nazi leadership. It was not only Hitler's political testament; by adoption it became theirs.

This book "Mein Kampf" might be described as the blueprint of Nazi aggression. Its whole tenor and content enforce the prosecution's submission that the Nazi pursuit of aggressive designs was no mere accident arising out of the immediate political situation in Europe and the world which existed during the period of Nazi power. "Mein Kampf" establishes unequivocally that the use of aggressive war to serve their aims in foreign policy was part of the very creed of the Nazi Party.

A great German philosopher has said that "ideas have hands and feet." It became the deliberate aim of these defendants to see to it that the ideas, doctrines and policies of "Mein Kampf" should become the active faith and guide for action of the German nation, and particularly of its malleable youth.

As my American colleagues have already submitted to the Tribunal, from 1933 to 1939 an extensive indoctrination in the ideas of "Mein Kampf" was pursued in the schools and universities of Germany, as well as in the Hitler Youth under the direction of the defendant Baldur von Schirach and in the S.A. and S.S. and amongst the German population as a whole by the agency of the defendant Rosenberg.

A copy of this book "Mein Kampf" was officially presented to all newly-married couples in Germany, and I now hand to the Tribunal such a wedding present from the Nazis to the newly- weds of Germany and for the purposes of the record it will be Exhibit GB 128. The Tribunal will see that the dedication on the fly-leaf of that copy reads: "To the newly-married couple, Friedrich Rosebroek and Else geborene Zum Beck, with best wishes for a happy and blessed marriage. Presented by the Communal Administration on the occasion of their marriage on the 14th of November, 1940, for the Mayor, the Registrar."

The Tribunal will see, at the bottom of the page opposite to the contents page, that that edition of "Mein Kampf," which was the 1940 edition, brought the number of copies published to 6,250,000. This was the scale upon which this book was distributed. It was blasphemously called "The Bible of the German people."

As a result of the efforts of the defendants and their confederates, this book poisoned a generation and distorted the outlook of a whole people.

As the S.S. General von dem Bach-Zelewski indicated yesterday, if you preach for years, as long as ten years, that the Slav peoples are inferior races and that the Jews are subhuman, then it must logically follow that the killing of millions of these human beings is accepted as a natural phenomenon.

From "Mein Kampf" the way leads directly to the furnaces of Auschwitz and the gas chambers of Maidanek.

What the commandments of "Mein Kampf " were I shall seek to indicate to the Tribunal by quotations from the book, which are set out in the extracts which I trust are now before the Tribunal. These extracts are set out in the order in which I shall, with the Tribunal's permission, refer to them.

Now these quotations fall into two main categories. The first category is that of the general expression of Hitler's belief in the necessity of force as the means of solving international problems. The second category is that of Hitler's more explicit declarations on the policy which Germany must pursue.

Most of the quotations in the second category come from the last three chapters, 13, 14, and 15 of Part II of "Mein Kampf," in which Hitler's views on foreign policy were expounded. The significance of that fact will be realised if the Tribunal looks at the German edition of "Mein Kampf." The Tribunal will observe that Part II was first published in 1927, that is to say, less than two years after the Locarno Pact and within a few months of Germany's entry into the League of Nations. The date of the publication of these passages, therefore, brands them as a repudiation of the policy of international co-operation embarked upon by Stresemann, and as a deliberate defiance of the attempt to establish, through the League of Nations, the rule of law in international affairs.

First I place before the Tribunal some quotations showing the general views held by Hitler and accepted and developed by the defendants about war and aggression generally. The first quotation, from Page 556 of "Mein Kampf," reads:

"The soil on which we now live was not a gift bestowed by Heaven on our forefathers. But they had to conquer it by risking their lives. So also in the future our people will not obtain territory and therewith the means of existence as a favour from any other people, but will have to win it by the power of a triumphant sword."

On Page 145 Hitler revealed his own personal attitude to war. Of the years of peace before 1914 he wrote:

"Thus I used to think it an ill-deserved stroke of bad luck that I had arrived too late on this terrestrial globe, and I felt chagrined at the idea that my life would have to run its course along peaceful and orderly lines.

As a boy I was anything but a pacifist and all attempts to make me so proved futile."

Generally Hitler wrote of war in this way. On Page 162 we find:

"In regard to the part played by humane feeling, Moltke stated that in time of war the essential thing is to get a decision as quickly as possible and that the most ruthless methods of fighting are at the same time the most humane. When people attempt to answer this reasoning by high-brow talk about aesthetics, etc., only one answer can be given. It is that the vital questions involved in the struggle of a nation for its existence must not be subordinated to any aesthetic consideration."

How faithfully these precepts of ruthlessness were followed by the defendants, the prosecution will prove in the course of this trial.

Hitler's assumption of an inevitable law of struggle for survival is linked up in Chapter 11 of Book 1 of "Mein Kampf," with the doctrine of Aryan superiority over other races and the right of Germans, by virtue of this superiority, to dominate and use other peoples as instruments for their own ends. The whole of Chapter 11 of this book is dedicated to this master race theory, and, indeed, many of the later speeches of Hitler, his addresses to his generals, etc., were mainly repetitive of that chapter.

If the Court will look at the extract from Page 256, it reads as follows:

"Had it not been possible for them to employ members of the inferior race which they conquered, the Aryans would never have been in a position to take the first steps on the road which led them to a later type of culture; just as, without the help of certain suitable animals which they were able to tame, they would never have come to the invention of mechanical power, which has subsequently enabled them to do without these beasts.

For the establishment of superior types of civilisation the members of inferior races formed one of the most essential prerequisites."

And in a later passage, at Page 344, Hitler applies these general ideas to Germany:

"If in its historical development the German people had possessed the unity of herd instinct by which other people have so much benefited, then the German Reich would probably be mistress of the globe to-day. World history would have taken another course, and in this case no man can tell if what many blinded pacifists hope to attain by petitioning, whining and crying may not have been reached in this way: namely, a peace which would not be based upon the waving of olive branches by tearful misery-mongering of pacifist old women, but a peace that would be guaranteed by the triumphant sword of a people endowed with the power to master the world and administer it in the service of a higher civilisation."

In these passages which I have quoted, the Tribunal will have noticed Hitler's love of war and scorn of those whom he described as pacifists. The underlying message of the whole of this book, a message which appears again and again, is, first, that the struggle for existence requires the organisation and use of force; secondly, that the Aryan- German is superior to other races and has the right to conquer and rule them; and thirdly, that all doctrines which preach peaceable solutions of international problems represent a disastrous weakness in the nation that adopts them.

Implicit in the whole of the argument is a fundamental and arrogant denial of the possibility of any rule of law in international affairs.

It is in the light of the general doctrines of "Mein Kampf" that I invite the Tribunal to consider the more definite passages in which Hitler deals with specific problems of German foreign policy.

The very first page of the book contains a remarkable forecast of Nazi policy. It reads - Page 1, column 1:

"German-Austria must be restored to the great German Motherland; and not, indeed, on any grounds of economic calculation whatsoever. No, no. Even if the union were a matter of economic indifference, and even if it were to be disadvantageous from the economic standpoint, still it ought to take place. People of the same blood should be in the same Reich. The German people will have no right to engage in a colonial policy until they shall have brought all their children together in one State. When the territory of the Reich embraces all the Germans and finds itself unable to assure them a livelihood, only then can the moral right arise from the need of the people, to acquire foreign territory. The plough is then the sword; and the tears of war will produce the daily bread for the generations to come."

Hitler, in this book, also roundly declares that the mere restoration of Germany's frontiers as they were in 1914 would be wholly insufficient for his purposes. At Page 553 he writes:

"In regard to this point I should like to make the following statement: To demand that the 1914 frontiers should be restored, is a glaring political absurdity, that is fraught with such consequences as to make the claim itself appear criminal. The confines of the Reich as they existed in 1914 were thoroughly illogical because they were not really complete, in the sense of including all the members of the German nation. Nor were they reasonable, in view of the geographical exigencies of military defence. They were not the consequences of a political plan which had been well considered and carried out, but they were temporary frontiers established in virtue of a political struggle that had not been brought to a finish; and, indeed, they were partly the chance result of circumstances."

In further elaboration of Nazi policy Hitler does not merely denounce the Treaty of Versailles; he desires to see a Germany which is a world Power with territory sufficient for a future German people, of a magnitude which he does not define.

In the next quotation, from Page 554, the first sentence reads: "For the future of the German nation the 1914 frontiers are of no significance." And in the third paragraph the Court sees:

"We National Socialists must stick firmly to the aim that we have set for our foreign policy, namely, that the German people must be assured the territorial area which is necessary for it to exist on this earth. And only in such action as is, undertaken to secure those ends can it be lawful, in the eyes of God and our German posterity, to allow the blood of our people to be shed once again; before God, because we are sent into this world with the commission to struggle for our daily bread, as creatures to whom nothing is donated and who must be able to win and hold their position as lords of the earth only through their own intelligence and courage.

And this justification must be established also before our German posterity, on the grounds that for each one who has shed his blood the life of a thousand others will be guaranteed to posterity. The territory on which one day our German peasants will be able to bring forth and nourish their sturdy sons will justify the blood of the sons of the peasants that has to be shed to-day. And the statesmen who have decreed this sacrifice may be persecuted by their contemporaries, but posterity will absolve them from all guilt for having demanded this offering from their people."

Then, the next quotation; Hitler writes, at Page 557:

"Germany will either become a world power or will not continue to exist at all. But, in order to become a world power, it needs that territorial magnitude which gives it the necessary importance to-day and assures the existence of its citizens."

And, finally, he writes:

"We must take our stand on the principles already mentioned in regard to foreign policy, namely, the necessity of bringing our territorial area into just proportion with the number of our population. From the past we can learn only one lesson, and this is that the aim which is to be pursued in our political conduct must be twofold, namely: (1) the acquisition of territory as the objective of our foreign policy; and (2) the establishment of a new and uniform foundation as the objective of our political activities at home, in accordance with our doctrines of nationhood."

Now these passages from "Mein Kampf" raise the question: Where did Hitler expect to find the increased territory beyond the 1941 boundaries of Germany? To this Hitler's answer is sufficiently explicit. Reviewing the history of the German Empire from 1871 to 1918, he wrote, in an early passage of "Mein Kampf," at Page 132:

"Therefore, the only possibility which Germany had of carrying a sound territorial policy into effect was that of acquiring new territory in Europe itself. Colonies cannot serve this purpose so long as they are not suited for settlement by Europeans on a large scale. In the nineteenth century it was no longer possible to acquire such colonies by peaceful means. Therefore, any attempt at such a colonial expansion would have meant an enormous military struggle. Consequently it would have been more practical to undertake that military struggle for new territory in Europe rather than to wage war for the acquisition of possessions abroad.

Such a decision naturally demanded that the nation's undivided energies should be devoted to it. A policy of that kind, which requires for its fulfilment every ounce of available energy on the part of everybody concerned, cannot be carried into effect by half measures or in a hesitant manner. The political leadership of the German Empire should then have been directed exclusively to this goal. No political step should have been taken in response to considerations other than this task and the means of accomplishing it. Germany should have been alive to the fact that such a goal could have been reached only by war, and the prospect of war should have been faced with calm and collected determination.

The whole system of alliances should have been envisaged and valued from that standpoint."

And, then, this is the vital sentence:

"If new territory were to be acquired in Europe, it must have been mainly at Russia's cost, and once again the new German Empire should have set out on its march along the same road as was formerly trodden by the Teutonic Knights, this time to acquire soil for the German plough by means of the German sword and thus provide the nation with its daily bread."

To this programme of expansion in the East Hitler returned again at the end of "Mein Kampf." After discussing the insufficiency of Germany's pre-war frontiers, he again points the path to the East and declares that the "Drang nach Osten," the drive to the East, must be resumed; and he writes:

"Therefore we National Socialists have purposely drawn a pen through the line of conduct followed by pre-war Germany in foreign policy. We put an end to the perpetual Germanic march towards the South and West of Europe and turn our eyes towards the lands of the East. We finally put a stop to the colonial and trade policy of pre-war times and pass over to the territorial policy of the future.

But when we speak of new territory in Europe to-day we must principally think of Russia and the border states subject to her."

Now Hitler was shrewd enough to see that his aggressive designs in the East might be endangered by a defensive alliance between Russia, France and England. His foreign policy, as outlined in "Mein Kampf," was to detach England and Italy from France and Russia, and to change the attitude of Germany towards France, from the defensive to the offensive.

The final quotation from "Mein Kampf" comes from Page 570:

"As long as the eternal conflict between France and Germany is waged only in the form of a German defence against a French attack, that conflict can never be decided, and from century to century Germany will lose one position after another. If we study the changes that have taken place, from the twelfth century up to our day, in the frontiers within which the German language is spoken, we can hardly hope for a successful issue to result from the acceptance and development of a line of conduct which has hitherto been so detrimental for us.

Only when the Germans have taken all this fully into account will they cease allowing the national will-to- live to wear itself out in merely passive defence and rally together for a last decisive contest with France. And in this contest the essential objective of the German nation will be fought for. Only then will it be possible to put an end to the eternal Franco-German conflict which has hitherto proved so sterile.

Of course it is here presumed that Germany sees in the suppression of France nothing more than a means which will make it possible for our people finally to expand in another quarter. To-day there are eighty million Germans in Europe. And our foreign policy will be recognised as rightly conducted only when, after barely a hundred years, there will be 250 million Germans living on this Continent, not packed together as the coolies in the factories of another Continent, but as tillers of the soil and workers whose labour will be a mutual assurance for their existence."

I submit, therefore, that, quite apart from the evidence already submitted to the Tribunal, the evidence of "Mein Kampf," taken in conjunction with the facts of Nazi Germany's subsequent behaviour towards other countries, goes to show that from the very first moment that they attained power, and, indeed, long before that time, Hitler and his confederates, the defendants, were engaged in planning and preparing aggressive war as is alleged against them in this Indictment.

Events have proved, in the blood and misery of millions of men, women and children, that "Mein Kampf" was no mere literary exercise to be treated with easy indifference, as unfortunately it was treated before the war by those who were imperilled, but was the expression of a fanatical faith in force and fraud as the means to Nazi domination in Europe, if not in the whole world. The Prosecution's submission is that, accepting and propagating the jungle philosophy of "Mein Kampf," the Nazi confederates who are indicted here deliberately pushed our civilisation over the precipice of war.

THE PRESIDENT: The Tribunal will now adjourn for ten minutes.

(A recess was taken.)

SIR DAVID MAXWELL FYFE: May it please the Tribunal, the next stage of the prosecution is the presentation of the cases against the individual defendants under the Counts 1 and 2 of the Indictment. Before that is begun the Chief Prosecutors for the United States and Great Britain wish, with the permission of the Tribunal, to make four points perfectly clear.

The object of this part of the case is to collect for the benefit, first, of the members of the Tribunal and, secondly, of the defence counsel concerned, the evidence against each defendant under Counts 1 and 2 which has been presented by the American and British delegations. Otherwise it would be easy among the many documents already before the Court to miss relevant pieces of evidence which the Tribunal might wish to consider and to which the defendants may wish to make a reply.

This does not mean that the case against these defendants has in any way ended. Vital and important parts of the case remain concerning the actual atrocities, both war crimes and crimes against humanity. The evidence in regard to these will shortly be presented by the French delegation and the delegation of the Union of Soviet Socialist Republics, and when the massive documentation of these crimes is placed before the Court, the French and Soviet delegations will have the opportunity of relating them to the individual defendants in the dock.

It has been the desire of all the Chief Prosecutors to delimit as clearly as possible the evidence under the respective Counts of the Indictment. The documents in evidence, however, were not written with a view to this trial, and therefore many of them inevitably deal with offences under more than one Count. It is by reason of this alone that some overlapping and repetition necessarily exists.

Similarly, it may occur that, as the French and Soviet cases are developed, documents may come to light which bear on the Common Plan or the Initiation of Wars of Aggression, or on other material connected with Counts 1 and 2. The American and British delegations will welcome any addition to the evidence on these parts of the case which such documents may provide and will gladly receive such reinforcement from their French and Soviet colleagues.

With this explanation, and I am very grateful to the Tribunal for allowing me to make it, I call on my friend Mr. Albrecht to commence this part of the case.

DR. THOMA (Counsel for defendant Rosenberg): Colonel Wheeler in his prosecution speech talked about the Church and persecution in the Eastern Territory, and the Reich Minister for the Occupied Eastern Territories, the defendant Rosenberg, was mentioned and held responsible. I have, however, neither in the speech of the prosecutor nor in the document book, found proof that such persecution of the Church also took place in those territories administered by Rosenberg. I wish rather to direct the attention of the Tribunal to Document 1517-PS, in which there is a note for the files signed by Rosenberg in regard to a conversation dealing with questions of the East. This document contains the following statement made by Rosenberg: "The Fuehrer agrees with Rosenberg's Edict of Tolerance."

THE PRESIDENT: Am I to understand that you are making a motion at this stage?

DR. THOMA: I have a request to make to the prosecution: that, if possible, its charge against Rosenberg be subsequently substantiated.

THE PRESIDENT: Is your point that this Document 1517-PS has not yet been in, or what is your point?

DR. THOMA: To my knowledge this document has already been submitted in connection with Hitler's opinion that the crimes should be cleaned up completely. But in my present request I am concerned with the fact that the prosecution stated that just as the Government General and Warthegau and in the Eastern countries, so in the areas administered by the defendant Rosenberg, persecution of the Church actually took place. The prosecution has presented evidence for the first three points, but as far as the last point is concerned, I have heard no such evidence in the document book or in the personal presentation made by the prosecution.

THE PRESIDENT: Well, you must understand that the Tribunal are not at this stage accepting everything that has been said by the prosecution. You will have full opportunity when you present the case on behalf of the defendant Rosenberg to present any document which may be relevant and to comment upon any documents which have been cited by the prosecution and to make any argument that you think right; but this is not the appropriate time to make any such argument. We are still considering the case for the prosecution, and you will have full opportunity hereafter. Do you understand?

DR. THOMA: Then I ask the High Tribunal to consider my present explanation as nothing but a statement of fact.

THE PRESIDENT: We will do so, but it is not convenient that counsel for the defence shall intervene with statements of this sort; otherwise each one of the defendants' counsel might be doing it all the time. We must ask you therefore to withhold such statements until your time comes to answer the case for the prosecution.

MR. ALBRECHT: May it please the Tribunal, I have been charged by the Chief of Counsel for the United States with the duty of pointing out, on the basis of evidence already admitted and of additional evidence that will be offered, the individual responsibility of some of these defendants for the crimes specified in Counts 1 and 2 of the Indictment.

When these defendants chose to abandon everything that had been recognised as good in German life and affirmatively participated in the work of achieving the objectives of the Party, we submit that they well knew what National Socialism stood for. They knew of the programme announced. by the Nazi Party and they also had knowledge of Nazi methods. The official N.S.D.A.P. programme with its 25 points was open and notorious. Announced and published to the world in 1920, it was published and republished and referred to throughout the years. The Nazis made no secret of their intentions to make the Party programme the fundamental law of the German State. The Nazis made no secret of their intentions generally. For all to read there was "Mein Kampf," the product of the warped brain of the Fuehrer, and there were the prolific writings and utterances of many other leaders who rose to prominence, some of whom are not sitting in the defendants' box. And Hitler himself had announced that the Nazis would use force if necessary to achieve their purposes.

Among these conspirators there were those who, like the defendants Hess, Rosenberg and Goering, were associated with Hitler since the very inception of the conspiracy. These men were among the original planners. They were the men who subsequently set the pace and cast the mould for the future. But there were also other conspirators (the balance of the defendants in the dock fit into this category), who - voluntarily - joined the conspiracy later.

While these men may be characterised perhaps as cruel, callous or inhuman, they certainly may not be called dull or stupid. They knew, and had had the opportunity to observe, the manifestations of Nazi violence and Nazi methods as the pattern of the Swastika developed. They knew the nature of what they were getting into. Therefore they must be presumed to have had the desire to participate (and participate they did) voluntarily, and so we submit that it may not validly be inferred that they did not join the stream of the conspiracy with their eyes open, scienter, as the conspiracy gathered momentum and developed into a rushing torrent.

Much evidence has already been admitted by the Tribunal of the overt acts of these defendants, as well as of their fellow conspirators. We shall make no effort at this time to present an exhaustive recital of all crimes planned or initiated by these defendants for which they must bear full responsibility beyond peradventure. The world already knows more of the evil deeds of these men and of their co-conspirators than the prosecution could possibly hope to establish within the reasonable limits of time and of men's patience. At this point we shall attempt to focus attention merely to illustrative criminal conduct of the individual conspirators.

There is, we submit, an advantage in proceeding, as we propose to, with the permission of the Tribunal, to show in outline the extent to which these defendants have become implicated in the serious charges against them. In the case of many of them, a recital of their crimes will relate to their planning of several of the categories of crimes described in Counts 1 and 2 of the Indictment. We shall draw these various threads together and show, as I have said, the outline of the completed proof, as it were, within Count 1 of the Indictment, against the individual conspirators.

Thus, on behalf of the United States, I shall begin by showing how some of these defendants fit into the broad stream of the Common Plan or Conspiracy to Wage Aggressive War and the extent of their individual responsibility for their acts in pursuance of that conspiracy.

First of all, we mention the late defendant Robert Ley who, by recourse to self-destruction, has escaped all punishment for his participation in the conspiracy.

Next we mention Gustav Krupp von Bohlen und Halbach, the action against whom has been severed from this proceeding.

Nevertheless, it should be noted that documentary proof has been offered and will be offered in support of the allegations of the Indictment that implicate both Ley and Krupp as co-conspirators, for whose crimes the remaining defendants also must accept responsibility.

Next we consider the defendant Fritz Sauckel. The case against Sauckel has been completely stated and supported by a wealth of damning evidence by my learned colleague Mr. Dodd in his presentation of the case on slave labour. We submit that it is unnecessary to add anything further to the case against Sauckel to demonstrate how completely he filled his place in the stream of the conspiracy.

The next defendant to be considered is Albert Speer. Like his fellow-conspirator Sauckel, Speer is deeply implicated as a member of the conspiracy and much of the case against him has been presented by Mr. Dodd in the case on slave labour. But, unlike Sauckel, Speer's criminal activity went substantially beyond the realm of slave labour. His was one of the master minds in the plan for the systematic robbery and spoliation of the lands overrun by the German war machine. Documentary proof of Speer's participation in the spoliation practices in the countries of Western Europe, as well as in the Occupied Eastern Territories will be presented subsequently by our learned colleagues, the Chief Prosecutor representing the Soviet Union and the Chief French Prosecutor, under the remaining Counts of the Indictment. This is essentially the case that proves Speer to have been a member of the conspiracy.

There is, however, one additional Exhibit that I would like to offer into evidence at this time. It was received only a few days ago from the Ministerial Document Centre at Kassel and it is a dossier maintained on the defendant Speer in the offices of the Reichsfuehrer S.S. I offer this file as Exhibit USA 575. It is our Document 3568, and I shall read from the dossier.

I shall read from the letter dated the 25th July, 1942, from the second paragraph: "Reich Minister Speer was enrolled as an S.S. man on the personal staff of the Reichsfuehrer S.S. under S.S. No. 46104, with effect from the 20th July, 1942, by order of the Reichsfuehrer S.S." - and I think that is all I need to read from that letter. But I should like to call the Tribunal's attention to the annexed document, which is a questionnaire, and right at the beginning of it it is related that Albert Speer had been in the S.S. since the autumn of 1932, and his membership number in the Party was 474481.

I next mentioned the defendant Ernst Kaltenbrunner, whose case has been completely presented in connection with the presentation on the Gestapo and the S.D. as Criminal Organisations. We submit that further proof is not needed to prove how completely this enemy of his own fatherland, Austria, had been carried along in the stream of the conspiracy.

We pass then to the case of, perhaps, the most important conspirator on trial before this Tribunal; the Number Two Nazi, the Nazi who stood next to the Fuehrer himself; the Nazi who was in some respects even more dangerous than the Fuehrer and other leading Party leaders.

We say that he was more dangerous because, unlike many leading Nazis, including Hitler, who were morally and socially on the fringes of society before the Nazi Party rode to success in 1933, this conspirator was known to come of substantial family which had furnished officers to the army and important civil servants to the country in the past. Moreover, he was possessed of substantial appearance, an ingratiating manner, a certain affability. But all of these facets of character were but deceptions, because they helped to conceal the man's core of steel, his vindictiveness, his cruelty, his lust for self- adornment, self-glorification and power.

This man, was most dangerous, furthermore, because the outward characteristics to which I have called attention, and which he has to some extent demonstrated here in the presence of the Tribunal, were useful in deceiving the representatives of foreign states who, in their concern, sought to learn from him the true intentions of the Nazi State which, by its repeated floutings of its international commitments, had so seriously disturbed the tranquillity of the world since 1933.

And I think that the record should show how throughout the earlier stages of this trial, that is, before the nature of the documentary evidence offered by the

Prosecution became too grim and almost implausible, much of the benevolence of this conspirator, his ever-ready smile and ingratiating manner, were daily in evidence in this chamber. His ready affirmation, by a pleasant nod for all to see, of the correctness of statements made or the contents of documents offered by counsel, his chiding shake of the head when he disagreed with such facts were commonplace.

THE PRESIDENT: I do not think the Tribunal is interested in this, Mr. Albrecht.

MR. ALBRECHT: I shall pass on, then, with the presentation, with the permission of the Tribunal, and I shall give an account of certain facts already established by the documents in evidence; and with the permission of the Tribunal I shall not, unless it is so wished, refer to the exhibit numbers or citations of most of the old evidence that I shall allude to. These are all set forth in the Trial Brief that has already been distributed.

Against the background of this factual account, into which we have drawn the main threads of the case already presented that show the complicity of the defendant Goering, we shall offer certain additional documentary evidence which we believe necessary to demonstrate his connection and responsibility for certain phases of the conspiracy.

I should have said before, if your Honours please, that there have been distributed and are now before you three volumes of document books bearing the letters "DD," which contain substantially all the documents, new as well as old, bearing on the individual responsibility of this defendant.

We shall first deal with the individual responsibility of this conspirator for Crimes against Peace. These crimes include Goering's participation in the acquisition and consolidation of power in Germany, the economic and military preparations for war and the waging of aggressive war.

For more than two decades Goering's activities extended over nearly every phase of the conspiracy. He was one of the conspirators associated with Hitler from the very beginning. A member of the Party since 1922, he participated in the Munich "Putsch" of November, 1923, at the head of the S.A., a Nazi organisation shown to have been committed to the use of violence.

He fled the country after the Putsch in order to escape arrest. After his return he became more than a commander of street fighters. He was designated Hitler's first political assistant. A measure of the man may be gleaned from an exhibit already in evidence, namely, Gritzbach's official biography of Goering, in which are recorded his dealings with the Bruning Government, his attempts to break down the barrier around President von Hindenburg, and his coup as Reichstag President in September, 1932, in procuring a vote of no confidence against the von Papen Government just before the Reichstag was dissolved.

His writings show him not to be backward in taking credit for his efforts to advance the cause of the Party. Full credit has also been accorded him by Hitler, and Goering has boasted that no title and no decoration could make him so proud as the designation given to him by the German people, and I quote, "the most faithful paladin of our Fuehrer." That short quotation, may it please the Court, comes from our Exhibit USA 233, our Document 2324-PS.

With the advent of the Nazis to power in January, 1933, Goering became Acting Minister of the Interior and Prime Minister of Prussia. In these capacities he proceeded promptly to establish a regime of terror in Prussia designed to suppress all opposition to the Nazi programme.

His chief tool in that connection was the Prussian Police, which remained under his jurisdiction until 1936. As early as February, 1933, he directed the entire police force to render unqualified assistance to the para-military organisations supporting the new government, such as the S.A. and the S.S., and to crush all political opponents with fire-arms, if necessary, and regardless of the consequences. The Tribunal will take judicial notice of the Directives of the 10th and 17th of February, 1933, which are cited on Page 7 of our brief and which appear in that collection of decrees known as the "Ministerialblatt fur dis Preussische Innere Verwaltung" of 1933.

Goering has frequently and proudly acknowledged his personal responsibility for the crimes committed pursuant to orders of this character, and I recall his words which he uttered before thousands of his fellow Germans:

" ... each bullet which leaves the barrel of a police pistol now, is my bullet. If one calls this murder, then I have murdered; I ordered all this, I back it up. I assume the responsibility and I am not afraid to do so."

That quotation, may it please the Tribunal, comes from our Exhibit USA 233, already in evidence, Document 2324-PS.

Soon after he became Prime Minister of Prussia, in pursuance of the conspiracy, Goering began to develop the Gestapo or Secret State Police, the details of which organisation of terror were presented to the Court by my learned colleague, Colonel Storey. As early as the 26th April, 1933, he signed the first law officially establishing the Gestapo in Prussia; and, pursuant to a decree which he signed, he named himself Prime Minister, Chief of the Prussian Secret State Police.

Goering was undoubtedly an efficient conspirator. He was impatient to consolidate the power of the Party at home. Already by the spring of 1933 the concentration camps had been established in Prussia. Men and women, so-called "Marxists" and other political opponents, taken into custody by the Gestapo, were thrown into concentration camps without trial. Goering said, "Against the enemies of the State we must proceed ruthlessly." That statement appears in our Document 2324-PS, which is already in evidence as Exhibit USA 233.

The range of political terrorism under his leadership was almost limitless. A glance at a few of his police directives in those early days will indicate the extent and thoroughness with which every dissident voice was silenced. I ask the Tribunal to take judicial notice of some of these decrees in the same collection I mentioned a short while ago, entitled the "Ministerialblatt fur die Preussische Innere Verwaltung," and we have cited these decrees on Pages 9 and 10 of our brief. These include:

A directive of the 22nd June, 1933, which required all officials to watch the statements of civil servants and to denounce to Goering those who made critical remarks. The failure to make such reports was to be regarded as proof of hostile attitude. Then there was the directive of the 23rd June, 1933, which suppressed all activities of the Social Democratic Party, including meetings and the party press, and ordered the confiscation of its property. There was the directive of the 30th June, 1933, which directed the Gestapo authorities to report to the Labour Trustees on the political attitude of the workers. There was the directive of the 15th January,1934, which ordered the Gestapo and the frontier police to keep track of emigres, particularly political emigres and Jews residing in neighbouring countries, and to arrest them and put them in concentration camps if they returned to Germany.

The essential ruthlessness of Goering is further illustrated by a well-known bloody episode. After the elimination of the forces of the opposition, the Nazis felt it necessary to dispose of non-conformists within their own ranks. This they accomplished in what has become known as the Roehm purge of the 30th June, 1934. The defendant Frick, a chief conspirator in his own right, stated in that connection, in an affidavit, that many people were murdered who had nothing to do with the internal S.A. revolt, but who were "just not liked very well."

Goering's role in this sordid affair was related less than two weeks after the event by Hitler in a speech to the Reichstag, and I would like to offer in evidence as Exhibit USA 576 our Document 3442-PS, in which is contained the speech of Hitler made on the 13th July, 1934, in the Reichstag. It is published in "Das Archiv," Vol. 4-6, at Page 505. I quote:

"Meanwhile Minister President Goering had already received my instructions that in case of a purge he was to take analogous measures at once in Berlin and in Prussia. With an iron fist he beat down the attack on the National Socialist State before it could develop."

With the accession of the Nazis to power Goering at once assumed a number of the highest and most influential positions in the Reich also. The proof already presented on the composition and functions of the Reich Cabinet and of the offices he held shows him to have been, in fact, the most important executive of the Nazi State.

A member of the Reichstag since 1928 and its President since 1932, he was a member of the Cabinet from the beginning as Reich Minister without Portfolio. Shortly thereafter he received the portfolio as Reich Minister for Air. When, in an early meeting, the Cabinet discussed the pending Enabling Act, which gave the Cabinet plenary powers of legislation, he offered the suggestion that the required two-thirds majority might be obtained simply by refusing admittance to Social Democratic delegates. I offer in evidence, as Exhibit USA 578, our Document 2962-PS, which contains the minutes of that meeting. If your Honours will note, that meeting was held on the 15th of March, 1933, and there were present, besides the defendant Goering, the defendants von Papen, von Neurath, Frick and Funk. I read from Page 6 of that document:

"Reich Minister Goering expressed his conviction that the Enabling Act would be passed with the necessary two-thirds majority. Possibly a majority could be obtained by banishing several Social Democrats from the hall. Possibly the Social Democrats would even refrain from voting on the Enabling Act."

In 1935, with the unmasking of a secret Luftwaffe, Goering became its commander-in-chief. He sat as a member and the Fuehrer's Deputy on the Reich Defence Council, established by the secret law of the 21st of May, 1933. The purpose of that Council was, as stated by the defendant Frick in an affidavit, that is, in evidence:

"To plan preparations and decrees in case of war, which later on were published by the Ministerial Council for the Defence of the Reich."

His assumption of ever greater responsibility seemed limitless. In 1936 he was made Plenipotentiary for the Four Year Plan, whereby he acquired plenary legislative and administrative powers over all German economic life. In 1938 he became a member of the Secret Cabinet Council, which had been established to act as "an advisory board in the direction of foreign policy."

The Ministerial Council for the Defence of the Reich, created in 1939, took over, in effect, all of the legislative powers of the Cabinet which had not been reserved otherwise, and Goering became its chairman.

His efficient and ruthless services were recognised by Hitler in 1939, when he designated Goering as his successor, as heir apparent to the "New Order."

In April, 1936, Goering was appointed Co-ordinator for Raw Materials and Foreign Exchange and empowered to supervise all State and Party activities in these fields. I offer in support of that fact, as Exhibit USA 577, our Document 2827-PS, which is an excerpt from Ruhle, "Das Dritte Reich." I read from the fourth paragraph of the excerpt, if your Honour please, which is an excerpt from a decree signed by Hitler, and it reads, as follows:

"Minister President General Goering will take the measures necessary for the accomplishment of the tasks given to him and has the authority to issue decrees and general administrative directives. He, for this purpose, is authorised to question and issue directives to all authorities, including the highest Reich authorities, and all agencies of the Party, its formations and attached organisations."

In this capacity Goering convened the War Minister, the defendant Schacht, as Minister of Economics and President of the Reichsbank, and the Finance Minister for the Reich and the State of Prussia, to discuss inter-agency problems connected with war mobilisation. At a meeting of this group on the 12th May, 1936, when the question of the prohibitive cost of synthetic raw material substitutes arose, Goering decided:

"If we have war to-morrow we must help ourselves by substitutes. Then money will not play any role at all. If that is the case, then we must be ready to create the prerequisites for that in peace time."

A few days later, on the 27th May, 1936, at a meeting of the same group Goering opposed any limitations dictated by orthodox financial policies. He said that "all measures are to be considered from the standpoint of an assured waging of war."

The well-known Four Year Plan was proclaimed by Hitler at the 1936 Nuremberg Party Day. Goering was appointed Plenipotentiary in charge of the programme which was intended to achieve national self-sufficiency. Furthermore Goering commented in 1936 that his chief task as Plenipotentiary was "to put the whole economy on a war footing within four years." I would like to offer into evidence, as Exhibit USA 579, our Document EC-409, so that I may direct the Tribunal's attention to a memorandum, dated the 30th December, 1936, of the Defence Division of the Wehrmacht, entitled " Memorandum on the Four Year Plan and Preparation of the War Economy," and in the third paragraph of the translation, or at Page 2, in the middle of paragraph number 3 in the German original, there is the statement registered in the protocol, in the memorandum, that:

"Minister President General Goering, as Commissioner for the Four Year Plan, by authority of the Fuehrer and Reich Chancellor, granted 18th October, 1936.

As regards the war economy, Minister President General Goering sees it as his task 'within four years to put the entire economy in a state of readiness for war.'"

The exhibit from which I have just read is of interest because of another document that has just been brought to the attention of the prosecution. It is a note for the files, dated 2nd December, 1936, written in longhand on the letterhead of "Minister President General Goering," and is in the handwriting of Colonel Bodanschatz, Goering's Chief 'of Staff. I offer this memorandum as Exhibit USA 580. It is our Document 3474-PS, and I direct the Tribunal's attention to the fact that the date of this document is the 2nd December, 1936. That was a conference, apparently, at which all the chief officers and generals of the Air Force, the German Air Force, met. Besides the defendant Goering, there were General Milch, General Kesselring, Rudel, Stumpf, Christiansen, and all the top commanders of the Air Force, and I read:

"World Press excited about the landing of 5,000 German volunteers in Spain.
Official complaint by Great Britain; she gets in touch with France.

Italy suggests that Germany and Italy send, each, one division ground troops to Spain. It is, however, necessary that Italy, as interested Mediterranean power, issue a political declaration first. A decision can be expected only after a few days.

The general situation is very serious. Russia wants the war. England rearms speedily. Command therefore: beginning to-day 'hochste Einsatzbereitschaft.'"

Apparently the translator did not see fit to translate that word, which means the "highest degree of readiness" - regardless of financial difficulties. Goering takes over full responsibility.

"Peace until 1941 is desirable. However, we cannot know whether there will be implications before. We are already in a state of war. It is only that no shot is being fired so far."

THE PRESIDENT: Perhaps that would be a convenient time to break off.

(A recess was taken until 14.00 hours.)

MR. ALBRECHT: May it please the Tribunal, two important conferences which have already been referred to by the prosecution show clearly how the defendant Goering inspired and directed the preparation of the German economy for aggressive war. On the 8th July, 1938, he addressed a number of the leading German aircraft producers. He stated that war with Czechoslovakia was imminent and boasted that the German Air Force was already superior in quality and quantity to the English. He said that "if Germany wins the war, she will be the greatest power in the world, dominating the world market, and Germany will be a rich nation. For this goal, risks must be taken." That quotation, may it please the Court, is taken from Document R-140, Exhibit USA 160.

A few weeks after the Munich Agreement, on the 14th October, 1938, at another conference held in Goering's office, he made the statement that Hitler had instructed him to organise a gigantic armament programme which would make insignificant all previous achievements. He indicated that he had been ordered to build as rapidly as possible an Air Force five times as large, to increase the speed of Army and Navy rearmament, and to concentrate on offensive weapons, principally heavy artillery and heavy tanks; and at that meeting he proposed a specific programme designed to accomplish those ends. That is a short summary of facts which appear in Exhibit USA 123, already in evidence, our Document 1301-PS.

In his dual role as Reich Air Minister and Commander-in- Chief of the German Air Force it was Goering's function to develop the Luftwaffe to practical war strength. As early as the 10th March, 1935, in an interview with the correspondent of the London Daily Mail, the mask of hypocrisy was removed and Goering frankly announced to the world that he was in the process of building a true military Air Force.

Two months later, in a speech to one thousand Air Force officers, Goering spoke in a still bolder vein. I offer in evidence from Exhibit USA 437, our Document 3441-PS, which is Goering's "Reden und Aufsdtze," another excerpt that has not yet been read in evidence, from Page 242. Goering said:

"I repeat: I intend to create a Luftwaffe which, if the hour should strike, shall burst upon the foe like a chorus of revenge. The enemy must have the feeling of being lost already even before having fought ...."

In the same year, on the 16th March, 1935, he signed his name to the Conscription Law, which provided for compulsory military service and constituted an act of defiance on the part of Nazi Germany in violation of the Versailles Treaty. The Tribunal will take judicial notice of that decree, which is our Document 1654-PS, from which I shall not read, with the permission of the Tribunal, the Law for the Organisation of the Armed Forces; it is cited in 1935 Reichsgesetzblatt, Part 1, Page 369.

As is demonstrated by the affidavit of Ambassador Nessersmith already in evidence, Goering's statements during this period left no doubt in the minds of Allied diplomats that Germany was engaged in full mobilisation of her air power for an impending war.

Goering was, in fact, the central figure in German preparation for military aggression. In German economic development, too, he held the key positions throughout the pre-war period. Although he held no official position in the field of foreign affairs, history records that, as the No. 2 Nazi, he was prominent in all major phases of Nazi aggression between 1937 and 1941.

In the Austrian affair Goering was the prompter and director of the diplomatic "tragicomedy" enacted before a shocked but silent world.

The Tribunal is familiar with Goering's complicity in the aggression against Austria. However, some additional documents have just come to our notice which show that he not only participated actively, but may even have been in direct charge of the German plan to bring about the Austrian Anschluss. I will offer the first of these documents, Document 3473-PS, as Exhibit USA 581. I shall not read from that exhibit, if your Honours please, but I would like to call the attention of the Tribunal to a letter addressed to Goering from Keppler, who was one of his agents. It is dated the 6th January, 1938. From its context it would seem that a valid inference can be drawn that Goering was already active in the Austrian matter in 1937. Our prior evidence brought him into the picture much later. The prosecution believes it to be of great significance, as it shows that the defendant Seyss-Inquart actually had Goering's mandate to carry out the orders of the Nazi conspirators in Vienna. The document itself will be read and discussed in the presentation of the case showing the individual responsibility of the defendant Seyss-Inquart; and I shall not take the time of the Tribunal at present.

The second document I wish to introduce is Exhibit USA 582, our Document 3472-PS. This exhibit would seem to show that the conspirators attempted to create the impression that the Anschluss, when it took place, was achieved by "legal" means. The command apparently was given to the members of the N.S.D.A.P. in Austria to keep "hands off" in order to permit the devilry to be worked out by the official Reich agencies, i.e., through the defendant Goering and, presumably, the defendant von Papen, by direct contact with the Austrian officials.

I read from that document:

"Yesterday information reached me to the effect that Landesleiter Leopold" - and may I interrupt for a moment to point out that the word "Landesleiter" is the title of the Leader of the Nazi community in Austria - "also on his part has started negotiations with Chancellor Schuschnigg. Thereupon I have asked the Foreign Office to investigate the truth of this information and, in case it is true, to take care that such negotiations be not held because they would merely disturb the proceedings of the other negotiations.

Just now I got word from the Foreign Office that they had received a report from the embassy in Vienna confirming the facts. I therefore would like to know whether it would not be more appropriate to forbid Landesleiter Leopold and the other members of the country's leadership to negotiate with Chancellor Schuschnigg or with any Austrian Government authorities, as to the execution of the pact of the 11th July, 1936 unless it is done after contacting and in agreement with the authorities in charge in the Reich."

Now below, if I may call the attention of the Tribunal to the note that appears in this letter. It is typewritten in blue, and, while the translator has not indicated the initial below that note, it is a large "G"; and I have no doubt that this note was written by the defendant Goering. It reads:

"Agreed, Minister Hess or Herr Bormann can give this order best! Keppler ought to ask therefore by telephone!"

If I may direct your attention to the upper right corner, there is another note in pencil, "Transmitted to Herr Keppler on the 11th February, 1938, by Miss Cest," and it is signed with initial "G," which, in this case, however, we are quite sure is the initial of Miss Grundmann, one of Goering's secretaries.

The third document I offer as Exhibit USA 583 - our Document 3471-PS. The first letter of this exhibit is written by the same Keppler to the same Bodenschatz mentioned a short while ago, but who is now a General. I shall not read from this exhibit, with the permission of the Tribunal, but I shall briefly summarise it. This letter and the annexes show that Leopold, the Nazi Landesleiter in Austria, was apparently not completely amenable to the orders given by Berlin, and that he pursued his own methods for accomplishing an Anschluss. The second annex to this letter, addressed to Keppler, who appears from it to have been an S.S. Obergruppenfuehrer, shows that prominent Nazis had declared themselves in favour of a Major Klaussner to succeed Leopold as Landesleiter; and I would like to call the Tribunal's attention to the fact that in the left margin of the covering letter appear some red crayon marks in the characteristic colour employed on several occasions, to our knowledge, by Goering; and they would seem to show that Goering personally had seen those documents and that General Bodenschatz had brought them to his attention. In any event these letters again demonstrate that Goering was one of the principal conspirators in the Austrian affair.

When the time finally came, on 11th March, 1938, to consummate the Anschluss, Goering was in complete command. Throughout the afternoon and evening of that day he directed by telephone the activities of the defendant Seyss-Inquart and of the other Nazi conspirators in Vienna. The pertinent portions of these telephone conversations, it will be remembered, were read into the record.

It will be recalled that early on the same evening, the 11th March, he dictated to the defendant Seyss-Inquart the telegram which the latter was to send to Berlin, requesting the Nazi Government to send German troops to "prevent bloodshed." Two days later he was able to telephone the defendant Ribbentrop in London and gleefully relate to him his success and that "this story that we had given an ultimatum is just foolish gossip."

If I may interrupt for a moment, that passage I just alluded to was read into the record (Page 260, Part 1).

Similarly, Goering played an important role in the attack on Czechoslovakia. In March, 1938, at the time of the "Anschluss," he had given a solemn assurance to the Czechoslovakian Minister in Berlin that the developments in Austria would in no way have a detrimental influence on the relations between Germany and Czechoslovakia, and he had emphasised the continued earnest attempts on the part of Germany to improve these relations. In this connection he had used the expression: "Ich gebe Ihnen mein Ehrenwort" (I give you my word of honour).

That expression was read previously into the record (Page 123, Part 2).

On the other hand, in his address to German aeroplane manufacturers on the 8th July, 1938, which I have already mentioned, he made his private views on this subject, which were hardly consistent with his solemn official statements, abundantly clear.

On the 14th October, 1938, shortly after the Munich Agreement, at a conference in the Air Ministry, Goering stated that the Sudetenland had to be exploited with all means and that he counted upon a complete industrial assimilation of Czechoslovakia. Meanwhile, as proof before the Tribunal shows, he was deceiving the representatives of the puppet Slovakian government to the same end.

In the following year, with the rape of Czechoslovakia complete, Goering frankly stated what Germany's purpose had been throughout the whole affair. He explained that the incorporation of Bohemia and Moravia into the German economy had taken place, among other reasons, in order to increase the German war potential by exploitation of the industry there.

Goering was also a moving force in the later Crimes against Peace. As the successor designate to Hitler, Chief of the Air Forces and Economic Czar of Greater Germany, he was a party to all the planning for military operations of the Nazi forces in the East and in the West.

In the Polish affair, for example, it was Goering who on the 31st January, 1935, gave assurances to the Polish Government through Count Czembek, as revealed in the Polish White Book, of which I ask the Tribunal to take judicial notice, that "there should be not the slightest fear in Poland that on the German side it" - meaning the German-Polish alliance - "would not be continued in the future." Yet, four years later, Goering helped to formulate plans for the ruthless invasion of Polish territory.

In respect to the attack upon the Soviet Union, the documents already introduced prove that plans for the ruthless exploitation of Soviet territory were made months in advance of the opening of hostilities. Goering was placed in charge of this army of spoliation, whose mission was that of "seizing raw materials and taking over all important concerns."

But these specific instances cited are merely illustrative of Goering's activities in the field of aggressive war. On Pages 20, 21 and 22 of our brief, there appears a list of documents - by no means exhaustive - previously offered by the prosecution, which demonstrate Goering's knowledge of and continued participation in the Nazi war programme.

We turn now to his responsibility for planning and his participation in the procurement of forced labour, the deportation and enslavement of residents of occupied territories, the employment of prisoners of war in war industry, the looting of works of art, and the Germanisation and spoliation of countries overrun by the Nazis.

Evidence previously introduced has detailed the slave labour programme of the Nazi conspirators and has shown its two purposes, both of them criminal. The first was to satisfy the labour requirements of the Nazi war machine by forcing residents of occupied countries to work in Germany. The second purpose was to destroy or weaken the peoples of the occupied territories. It has been shown that millions of foreign workers were taken to Germany, for the most part under pressure and generally by physical force, that these workers were forced to work under conditions of indescribable brutality and degradation, and that often they were used in factories and industries devoted exclusively to the production of munitions of war.

Goering was at all times implicated in the slave labour programme. Recruitment and allocation of man-power and determination of working conditions were included in his jurisdiction as Plenipotentiary for the Four Year Plan, and from its beginning a part of the Four Year Plan Office was devoted to such work. I ask the Tribunal in this connection to take judicial notice of our Document 1862-PS, Ordinance for the Execution of the Four Year Plan, dated 18th October, 1936, which appears in 1936

Reichsgesetzblatt, Part 1, p. 887, and, with the permission of the Tribunal, I shall not read it.

Soon after the fall of Poland Goering began the enslavement of large numbers of Poles. On 25th January, 1940, the defendant Frank, the Governor General of Poland, reported to Goering on his directive for:

"Supply and transportation of at least 1,000,000 male and female agricultural and industrial workers to the Reich- among them at least 750,000 agricultural workers of whom at least 50 per cent. must be women, in order to guarantee agricultural production in the Reich and as a replacement for industrial workers lacking in the Reich ..."

which is taken from our Exhibit USA 172, Document 1375.

That orders for this enormous number of workers originated with the defendant Goering is clear from statements in the defendant Frank's diary for 10th May, 1940, already introduced in evidence.

For the harsh treatment given those workers when they reached Germany the defendant Goering is also responsible. On 8th March, 1940, as Plenipotentiary of the Four Year Plan and as Chairman of the Cabinet Council for the Defence of the Reich, he issued a directive entitled: "Treatment of Male and Female Civilian Workers of Polish Nationality in the Reich." I refer to our Document R-148 as proof of that fact. I shall not introduce it at this time into evidence, with the permission of the Tribunal, as it will be introduced by the Soviet prosecution at a later date.

On 29th January, 1942, the Division for the Employment of Labour in the Four Year Plan Office issued a circular, signed by Dr. Mansfeld, the general delegate for labour employment in the Four Year Plan Office, addressed to various civilian and military authorities in the occupied territories, explaining that, and I quote, "any and all methods must be adopted" to force workers to go to Germany. I shall not read from our exhibit, if the Tribunal please, but I would like to offer in evidence, as Exhibit USA 585, Document 1183-PS. This is a circular letter of the Commissioner for the Four Year Plan, dated the 29th January, 1942.

It has been shown previously that on 21st March, 1942, Hitler promulgated a decree appointing the defendant Sauckel Plenipotentiary General for Manpower, directing him to carry out his tasks within the frame-work of the Four Year Plan, and making him directly responsible to Goering as head of the Four Year Plan.

On 27th March, 1942, Goering issued his important Enabling Decree in pursuance of the decree of the Fuehrer of 21st March, 1942. The Tribunal has already judicially noted this decree, which is our Document 1666-PS.

Since the defendant Sauckel was an authority under the Four Year Plan, the defendant Goering retains full responsibility for the enormous War Crimes committed by Sauckel as Plenipotentiary-General for Man-power. These crimes have been the subject of our presentations on Slave Labour and on the Illegal Use of Prisoners of War.

It was also proven during those presentations that the Nazi conspirators ordered prisoners of war to work under dangerous conditions and in the manufacturing and transportation of arms and munitions of war, in violation of the Laws of War and of Articles 31 and 32 of the Geneva Convention of 27th July, 1929, on Prisoners of War. The defendant Goering had a part in all these crimes.

At a conference on 7th November, 1941, the subject of which was the employment of citizens of the Soviet Union, including prisoners of war, it appears from a memorandum signed by Kurner, who was State Secretary to Goering as Plenipotentiary for the Four Year Plan, that Goering gave certain ruthless directives for the use of Soviet citizens, both prisoners of war and free Soviet workers, as labourers. I refer to our Document 1193-PS which, with the permission of the Tribunal, I shall not offer in evidence at this time and which will be offered by the Soviet prosecution.

In a set of top secret notes of outlines laid down by Goering in what was apparently the same conference of 7th November, 1941, which are already in evidence, the following facts appear:

(1) That, of a total of 5,000,000 prisoners of war, 2,000,000 were employed in war industries;

(2) That it was better to employ P.W.'s than unsuitable foreign workers;

(3) That Poles, Dutchmen, etc., should be seized, if necessary, as P.W.'s and employed as such, if work through free contract cannot be obtained.

These facts, if your Honours please, appear in our Document 1206-PS, which is submitted in evidence as Exhibit USA 215.

In a secret letter from the Reich Minister of Labour to the Presidents of the Regional Labour Exchange Offices, already in evidence, it is furthermore recorded that upon the personal order of the Reich Marshal, the defendant Goering, 100,000 men were to be taken from among the French P.W.'s not yet employed in the armament industry and assigned to the aeroplane armament industry and that gaps in man-power supply resulting therefrom were to be filled by Soviet P.W.'s.

Evidence has also been introduced showing the organised, systematic programme of the Nazi conspirators for the cultural impoverishment of every country in Europe. The continuous connection of the defendant Goering with these activities has been substantiated.

In October, 1939, Goering requested Dr. Muhlmann to undertake immediately the "securing" of all Polish art treasures. In his affidavit, already offered, Dr. Muhlmann states that he was the special deputy of the Governor General of Poland, the defendant Frank, for the safeguarding of art treasures in the Government General from October, 1939, to September, 1943, and that the defendant Goering, in his capacity as chairman of the Reich Defence Council, had commissioned him with this duty.

Muhlmann also confirms that it was the official policy of the defendant Frank to take into custody all important art treasures which belonged to Polish public institutions, private collections and the Church, and that such art treasures were actually confiscated.

It appears also from a report made by Dr. Muhlmann on 16th July, 1943, on his operations, that at one time, 31 valuable sketches by the artist Albrecht Durer were taken from a Polish collection and personally handed to the defendant Goering who took them to the Fuehrer's headquarters.

The part played by Goering in the looting of art by the Einsatzstab Rosenberg has been shown. We refer to Exhibit USA 368, Document 141-PS, which is an order dated 5th November, 1940, already read in evidence, in which Goering directs the Chief of the Military Administration in Paris and the Einsatzstab Rosenberg to dispose of the works of art brought to the Louvre in the following priority:

"(1) Those works of art regarding which the Fuehrer has reserved for himself the decision as to their use.

(2) Those works of art which serve to complete the Reich Marshal's collection.

(3) Those works of art and library stocks, the use of which seems useful to the establishing of higher institutes of learning.

(4) Those works of art that are suited for German museums."

In view of the high priority afforded by the foregoing order to the completion of the defendant's own collection, it is not surprising to find that Goering continued to aid the operations of the Einsatzstab Rosenberg. It has been established that on 1st May, 1941, Goering issued an order under his own signature to all Party, State and Wehrmacht Services requesting them to give all possible support and assistance to the Chief of Staff of Reichsleiter Rosenberg.

By May, 1942, Goering was able to boast of the assistance which he had rendered to the work of the Einsatzstab Rosenberg. In our Document 1051-PS, which has been read in evidence (Page 68, Part 3), he is shown writing to the defendant Rosenberg that he personally supports the work of the Einsatzstab wherever he can do so and that he attributes the seizure of such a large number of art treasures to the assistance he was able to render the Einsatzstab.

Thus the defendant Goering's responsibility for the planning of the looting of art, which was actually accomplished by the Einsatzstab Rosenberg, would seem clear.

Details of the execution of the Germanisation and spoliation policies in both the Western and Eastern countries occupied by the German armies will be presented subsequently by the French and Soviet prosecution. The responsibility of the defendant Goering, in his capacity as Plenipotentiary for the Four Year Plan, as President of the Cabinet Council for the Defence of the Reich and in other capacities, will be further demonstrated by that evidence.

The plans of the Nazi conspirators with respect to Poland have been shown by evidence already offered. The Nazis purported to incorporate the four Western provinces of Poland into the German Reich. In the remaining portions occupied by them they set up the Government General. It has been shown that the Nazis planned to Germanise the so-called incorporated territories ruthlessly, by deporting the Polish intelligentsia, Jews and dissident elements to the Government General for eventual elimination, by confiscating Polish property, by sending those so deprived of their property to Germany as labourers, and by importing German settlers. It was specifically planned to exploit the people and material resources of the territory within the Government General by taking whatever was needed to strengthen the Nazi war machine, thus impoverishing this region and reducing it to a vassal state.

The defendant Goering, together with Hitler and Lammers and with the defendants Frick and Hess, on 8th October, 1939, signed the decree by which certain parts of Polish territory were incorporated into the Reich.

Purporting to act by virtue of the foregoing decree, Goering, as Plenipotentiary of the Four Year Plan, signed an order on 30th October, 1939, concerning the introduction of the Four Year Plan in the Eastern territories.

In his directive dated 19th October, 1939, Goering stated that the task for the economic treatment of the various administrative regions would differ, depending on whether a country was to be incorporated politically into the German Reich or whether the Government General was involved, which, in all probability, would not be made a part of Germany.

He went on to say:

"In the first-mentioned territories the reconstruction and expansion of the economy, the safeguarding of all their production facilities and supplies must be aimed at, as well as a complete incorporation into the Greater German economic system at the earliest possible time. On the other hand, there must be removed from the territories of the Government General all raw materials, scrap materials, machines, etc., which are of use for the German war economy. Enterprises which are not absolutely necessary for the meagre maintenance of the bare existence of the population must be transferred to Germany, unless such transfer would require an unreasonably long period of time and would make it more practical to exploit those enterprises by giving them German orders to be executed at their present location."

From the foregoing documents the complicity of the defendant Goering in the plans for the ruthless exploitation of Poland appears clear. But his fine hand also may be found behind the remainder of the Nazi plans for Poland. As an illustration, it was the defendant Goering who signed, with Hitler and the defendant Keitel, the secret decree of 7th October, 1939, which entrusted Himmler with the task of executing the Germanisation programme. That secret decree was read into evidence (Page 428, Part 2).

Evidence already introduced has shown from the mouths of Himmler, the defendant Frank and others just what this appointment involved in human suffering and degradation.

Similarly, it was the defendant Goering who, by virtue of his powers as Plenipotentiary for the Four Year Plan, issued a decree on 17th September, 1940, concerning confiscation in the incorporated Eastern territories. This decree applied to "property of citizens of the former Polish State within the territory of the Greater German Reich, including the incorporated Eastern territories." I ask the Tribunal to take judicial notice of our Document 1665-PS, which is an "Order concerning Treatment of Property of Nationals of the former Polish State," cited in 1940 Reichsgesetzblatt, Part 1, Page 1270. I shall read from this document:

"Article 1.

(1) Property of nationals of the former Polish State within the area of the Greater German Reich, including annexed Eastern territories, is subject to confiscation, administration by commissioner and sequestration in accordance with the following regulations."

I now pass to Article II.

(1) Confiscation will be applied in case of property belonging to:

    (a) Jews.

    (b) Persons who have fled or who have absented themselves for longer than a temporary period.

(2) Confiscation may be applied:

    (a) If the property is needed for the public good, especially for purposes of national defence or the strengthening of German nationhood.

    (b) If the owners or other persons entitled to it emigrated into the, then, area of the German Reich after 1st October, 1918."

I pass now to Article IX, the first part:

"(1) Sequestered property can be confiscated in favour of the Reich by the competent office, if the public weal, particularly the defence of the Reich or the consolidation of the German nationality, requires it."

Evidence has also been introduced by the United States showing the extent to which the spoliation of Soviet territory and resources and the barbarous treatment inflicted on Soviet citizens were the result of plans long made and carefully drawn up by the Nazis before they launched their aggressive war on the Soviet Union. The Nazis planned to destroy the industrial potential of the Northern regions occupied by their armies and so to administer the production of food in the South and South-East, which normally produced a surplus of food, that the population of the Northern region would inevitably be reduced to starvation because of diversion of such surplus food to the German Reich. It has been shown also that the Nazis planned to incorporate Galicia and all of the Baltic countries into Germany and to convert the Crimea, an area north of the Crimea, the Volga territory and the district around Baku into German colonies.

By 29th April, 1941, almost two months prior to the invasion of the Soviet Union, it appears that Hitler had entrusted the defendant Goering with the overall direction of the economic administration in the area of operations and in the areas under political administration. It further appears that Goering had set up an economic staff and subsidiary authorities to carry out this function.

The form of this organisation created by Goering and the duties of its various sections appear clearer in a set of directives "for the operation of the economy in the newly occupied territories" issued by Goering, as Reich Marshal of the Greater German Reich, in June, 1941. These directives are contained in the important "Green Portfolio" which, curiously enough, was printed by the Wehrmacht. By the terms of these directives it is stated that "The orders of the Reich Marshal cover all economic fields, including nutrition and agriculture. They are to be executed by the subordinate economic offices."

An "Economic Staff East" was charged with the execution of orders transmitted to it from higher authority. One sub-division of this staff, the Agricultural Section, was charged with the following functions: "Nutrition and agriculture, the economy of all agricultural products, provision of supplies for the Army in co-operation with the Army Groups concerned." Excerpts from the "Green Portfolio" have already been admitted as Exhibit USA 315, but I will offer at this time some additional excerpts in support of the facts I have just related. I would like to offer, as Exhibit USA 587, our Document 1743-PS. This is another copy of the "Green Portfolio," and I want to offer this portfolio to show to the Tribunal that these directives were originally published in June, 1941. Document EC-472, which is already in evidence as Exhibit USA 315, was a revised edition published in July, 1941. In other words, the economic plan for the invasion was ready when the Wehrmacht actually marched into the Soviet Union on 22nd June, 1941.

As appears from the foregoing directives, it was a sub-division of the economic organisation set up by the defendant Goering, the Agricultural Section of the "Economic Staff East," which rendered a top secret report on 23rd May, 1941, containing a set of policy directives for the exploitation of Soviet agriculture. It will be recalled that these directives contemplated abandonment of all industry in the food deficit regions, with certain exceptions, and the diversion of food from the food surplus regions to German needs, even though millions of people would inevitably die of starvation as a result. Those directives have already been read into evidence (Page 4, Part 3).

Minutes of a meeting at Hitler's headquarters on 16th July, 1941, kept by the defendant Bormann, have also been read in part in evidence. It was at this meeting that Hitler stated that the Nazis never intended to leave the countries then being occupied by their armies, that although the rest of the world was to be deceived on this point, nevertheless, "this need not prevent us taking all necessary measures - shooting, desettling, etc. - and we shall take them." That quotation, may it please the Tribunal, was taken from Exhibit USA 317, our Document L-221. Then Hitler discussed making the Crimea and other parts of the Soviet Union into German colonies. The defendant Goering was present and participated in this conference.

As a final illustration it appears from a memorandum dated 16th September, 1941, which is our Exhibit 318, that Goering presided over a meeting of German military officials concerned with the better exploitation of the occupied territories for the

German food economy. In discussing this topic, he said:

> "In the occupied territories, on principle, only those people are to be supplied with an adequate amount of food who work for us. Even if one wanted to feed all the other inhabitants, one could not do it in the newly occupied Eastern areas. It is, therefore, wrong to funnel off food supplies for this purpose, if it is done at the expense of the Army and necessitates increased supplies from home."

From the foregoing documents, participation of the defendant Goering in the Nazi plans for committing wholesale War Crimes in occupied territories is, we submit, clear.

I turn, now, to Goering's planning and his participation in inhumane acts committed against civilian populations before and during the war. It has been shown that shortly after becoming Prime Minister of Prussia in 1933, Goering created the Gestapo in Prussia, which became a model for that instrument of terror as it was extended to the rest of Germany. Concentration camps were established in Prussia in the spring of 1933 under his administration, and these camps were then placed under the charge of the Gestapo, of which he was chief.

The extent to which Goering and the other Nazi conspirators employed these institutions as agencies for the commission of their crimes already appears from the evidence. In 1936 Himmler became chief of the German Police. Thereafter Goering was able to devote his attention chiefly to the task of creating the German Air Force and to the task of preparing the nation economically for aggressive war. However, he continued to be concerned with these institutions of his creation. An example of this is shown in our Document 1584-PS-1, already introduced as Exhibit USA 221, which is a teletype sent by Goering to Himmler in which he requested the latter to place at his disposal as great a number of concentration camp inmates as possible, as the situation of air warfare made the subterranean transfer of industry necessary.

In his reply, Himmler advised Goering by teletype that a survey on the employment of prisoners in the aviation industry showed that 36,000 were being employed for the purposes of the Air Forces and that an increase to a total of 90,000 prisoners was being contemplated.

Evidence has been introduced as to medical experiments performed on human beings at the concentration, camp at Dachau, and the part played by Field Marshal Milch, State Secretary and Deputy to Goering as Air Minister, for whose acts the latter must bear full responsibility, is abundantly clear from letters written by Milch to General Wolff on 20th May, 1942, and to Himmler in August, 1942, both of which have been read in evidence (Page 161, Part 3), our Document 343-PS.

Finally, I turn to Goering's participation in the elimination of all members of the Jewish race from the economic life of Germany and in the extermination of all Jews in the continent of Europe.

In 1935 the defendant Goering, as President of the Reichstag, made a speech urging that body to pass the infamous Nuremberg Racial Law. I offer, as Exhibit USA 588, our Document 3458-PS, which is an excerpt from Ruhle's "Das Dritte Reich," Page 257. Goering said:

> "God has created the races. He did not want equality and therefore we energetically reject any attempt to falsify the concept of race purity by making it equivalent with racial equality. We have experienced what it means when a people has to live in accordance with the laws of an equality that is alien to its kind and contrary to nature. For this equality does not exist. We have never acknowledged such an idea and therefore must reject it also, as a matter of

principle, in our laws, and we must acknowledge that purity of race which Nature and Providence have destined."

Again, to show his official attitude, as revealed on 26th March, 1938, in a speech in Vienna, I offer as Exhibit USA 437 our Document 3460-PS, starting with Page 348. Goering said:

"I must address a serious word to the city of Vienna. The city of Vienna can no longer rightfully be called a German city. So many Jews live in this city. Where there are 300,000 Jews, you cannot speak of a German city.

Vienna must once more become a German city, because it must perform important tasks for Germany in Germany's Ostmark. These tasks lie in the sphere of culture as well as in the sphere of economics. In neither of them can we, in the long run, put up with the Jew.

This task, however, should not be attempted by inappropriate interference and stupid measures but must be done systematically and carefully.

As Delegate for the Four Year Plan, I commission the Reichsstatthalter in Austria jointly with the Plenipotentiary of the Reich to consider and take any steps necessary for the redirection of Jewish commerce, i.e., for the Aryanisation of business and economic life, and to execute this process in accordance with our laws, legally but inexorably."

Acting within the framework of economic preparation for aggressive war, the Nazi conspirators then began the complete elimination of Jews from economic life preparatory to their physical annihilation. The defendant Goering, as head of the Four Year Plan, was in active charge of this phase of the persecution.

The first step in his campaign was the Decree of 26th April, 1933, requiring registration of all Jewish property. Both Goering and the defendant Frick signed that law. It is already in evidence.

I beg the Tribunal's pardon. I would like the Tribunal to take judicial notice of that decree, which is our Document 1406-PS and cited as 1938 Reichsgesetzblatt, part 1, Page 414.

Now, armed with the information thus secured, the Nazi conspirators were fully prepared to take the next step. The killing of von Rath, a German Legation Secretary, in Paris on 9th November, 1938, was made the pretext for widespread "spontaneous" riots, which included the looting and burning of many Jewish synagogues, homes and shops, all carefully organised and supervised by the Nazi conspirators. The defendant Goering was fully informed of the measures taken. The teletype orders of 10th November, 1938, given by Heydrich are already in evidence (Page 364, Part 2). A letter which Heydrich wrote to Goering on the following day has also been read. It is our Document 3058-PS, Exhibit USA 508. In it Himmler summarises the so-called "spontaneous" riots that had taken place. He reported the day after the riot that, in so far as the official reports from the district police were concerned, he was able to state that 815 shops were destroyed, 171 dwelling houses set on fire or destroyed, and that all this indicated only a fraction of the actual damage caused, as far as arson is concerned. He also said that:

"Due to the urgency of the reporting, the reports received to date are entirely limited to general statements such as 'numerous' or 'most shops destroyed.'"

Therefore the figures given must have been exceeded considerably.

"191 synagogues were set on fire and another 76 completely destroyed. In addition, 11 parish halls, cemetery chapels and similar buildings were set on fire and 3 more completely destroyed.

20,000 Jews were arrested."

36 deaths were reported, and those seriously injured numbered a further 36. Immediately after these so-called "spontaneous" riots of 9th November, Goering acted as chairman at the Reich Ministry of Air of a meeting devoted to the Jewish question, which meeting was also attended by the defendant Funk and other conspirators. The stenographic report on that meeting is an extraordinary document, and it does not make pretty reading. It is our Document 1816-PS, already offered as Exhibit USA 261. I should like to read certain passages that have not as yet been read into the Record. I read from the top of the first page, the first two paragraphs of Page 1 of the German original; Goering speaks:

"Gentlemen, to-day's meeting is of a decisive nature. I have received a letter written on the Fuehrer's order by the Stabsleiter of the Fuehrer's Deputy Bormann, requesting that the Jewish question be now, once and for all, co-ordinated and solved one way or another. And yesterday once again the Fuehrer requested me by phone to take co-ordinated action in the matter.

Since the problem is mainly an economic one, it is from the economic angle that it will have to be tackled. Naturally a number of legal measures will have to be taken, which fall into the sphere of the Minister of Justice, and into that of the Minister of the Interior; and certain propaganda measures will be taken care of by the office of the Minister of Propaganda. The Minister of Finance and the Minister of Economic Affairs will take care of problems falling into their respective departments."

Specific measures to effect the Aryanisation of Jewish business were then discussed. A representative of German insurance companies was called in to assist in the solving of the difficulties created by the fact that most of the Jewish stores and other property destroyed in the rioting were, in fact, insured, in some cases, ultimately by foreign insurance companies. All present were agreed that it would be unfortunate to pass a law which would have the effect of allowing foreign insurance companies to escape liability. The defendant Goering then suggested a characteristic solution, and I pass to Page 10. In German it is the third full paragraph on Page 311. Goering said:

"No, I do not even dream of refunding the insurance companies the money. The companies are liable. No, the money belongs to the State. That is quite clear. That would indeed be a present for the insurance companies. You make a wonderful petitum there. You will fulfil your obligations; you may count on that."

It is superfluous to quote further from the extensive discussion of all phases of persecution of the Jews that took place at this meeting. It is sufficient to point out that on the same day the defendant Goering, over his own signature, promulgated three decrees, putting into effect the most important matters decided at this meeting. In the first of these decrees a collective fine of one billion Reichsmark was placed on all German Jews. I ask the Tribunal to take judicial notice of that decree, which is our Document 1412-PS and appears in 1938 Reichsgesetzblatt, Part 1, Page 1579.

The second decree, entitled "A Decree on Elimination of Jews from German Economic Life" barred Jews from trades and crafts. I ask the Tribunal to notice judicially that decree, which is our Document 2875-PS, cited in 1939 Reichsgesetzblatt, Part 1, Page 1580.

The third decree, entitled "Decree for the Restoration of the Appearance of the Streets of Jewish Economic Enterprise" took care of the insurance question raised in the morning's meeting by providing that insurance due to the Jews for various losses sustained by them was to be collected by the State.

I ask the Court to notice judicially that decree also. It is our Document 2694-PS and appears in 1938 Reichsgesetzblatt, Part 1, Page 1591.

THE PRESIDENT: Shall we break off for ten minutes there?

(A recess was taken.)

THE PRESIDENT: Mr. Albrecht, the Tribunal thinks that these methods, which are really methods which we have already had under consideration, might be presented in a more summary way than you have given them, and if you can possibly shorten the matters with which you are dealing now by summarising more than you are, it will be more useful to the Tribunal and will save time.

MR. ALBRECHT: My Lord, I think I am practically through with this point with which I am dealing, and I think I shall not have to take more than five or ten minutes.

THE PRESIDENT: Very well, but I may say that the same observation will apply to those who follow.

MR. ALBRECHT: May it please the Tribunal, the material I alluded to before the recess is, we feel, merely illustrative of the energetic manner in which Goering took part in driving the Jews from economic life at this period. Two other documents would seem to be pertinent on this point.

I would like to offer our Document 069-PS as Exhibit USA 589, which is a circular letter dated 17th January, 1939, signed by the defendant Bormann, distributing a directive of the defendant Goering with respect to certain discriminations to be applied in the housing of the Jews. I will be content with the summarisation, if the Court please, and I do not intend to read further from that document.

The second document I desire to offer is 1208-PS, which I offer as Exhibit USA 590. That is an order of the defendant Goering as Commissioner for the Four Year Plan, dated 10th December, 1938, prescribing the manner in which exploitation of Jewish property is to be undertaken and warning that any profit resulting from the elimination of Jews from economic activity is to go to the Reich.

There is no need, I believe, to read excerpts from the document, except that I do wish to call the attention of the Tribunal to the fact that the Goering letter is addressed to all the chief agencies of the Reich, to all the political leaders and leaders of the affiliated organisations of the Party, to all Gauleiter, to all Reichsstatthalter, or Governors, and to the various local heads of the German Lander and subdivisions thereof.

As the German armies moved into other countries, the anti-Jewish laws were extended, often in a more stringent form, to the occupied territories. Many of the decrees were not signed by the defendant Goering himself, but were issued on the basis of decrees signed by him.

Nevertheless, in his capacity as Commissioner for the Four Year Plan or as Chairman of the Ministerial Council for National Defence, Goering did himself sign a number of anti-Jewish decrees for occupied territories, including the decrees enumerated on Pages 47 and 48 of our brief, of which I ask the Tribunal to take judicial notice.

During the later years of the war the programme of the Nazi conspirators for the complete physical annihilation of all Jews in Europe achieved its full fury. While the execution of this anti-Jewish programme was for the most part handled by the S.S. and the Security Police, the defendant Goering remains implicated to the last in the final efforts to achieve a Nazi "solution" of the Jewish problem.

On 31st July, 1941, he wrote a letter to the conspirator Heydrich, which is the final document to which I wish to draw the Tribunal's attention. It is a fitting climax to our presentation on this defendant, your Honour. The reason why it was addressed to the notorious Heydrich, the predecessor of the defendant Kaltenbrunner, need not strain our imagination. This Document, 710-PS, which has already been admitted as Exhibit USA 509, in connection with the case on the Gestapo. While it has already been read into evidence, I would like, with the Court's permission, to close my presentation with the reading of that letter. Goering writes to Heydrich:

"Complementing the task that was assigned to you on 24th January, 1939, which dealt with arriving at a thorough furtherance of emigration and evacuation, a solution of the Jewish problem as advantageous as possible, I hereby charge you with making all necessary preparations in regard to organisational and financial matters for bringing about a complete solution of the Jewish question in the German sphere of influence in Europe. Wherever other governmental agencies are involved, these are to cooperate with you.

I charge you furthermore to send me, before long, an overall plan concerning the organisational, factual and material measures necessary for the accomplishment of the desired solution of the Jewish question."

The presentation made to the Tribunal on the individual responsibility of the defendant Goering has been intended to be merely illustrative of the mass of documentary evidence which reveals the leading part played by this conspirator in every phase of the Nazi conspiracy. Thus, we submit that his responsibility for the crimes with which he has been charged under Count One of the Indictment has been established.

May it please the Tribunal, this completes the presentation of the responsibility of the defendant Goering. We will now proceed with the arrangement made with the British delegation on the presentation showing the individual responsibility of the defendant von Ribbentrop, by Sir David Maxwell Fyfe.

SIR DAVID MAXWELL FYFE: May it please the Tribunal, if the Tribunal would be good enough to look at Appendix A of the Indictment on page 28 of the English Text, they will find the particulars relating to the defendant, this defendant, and they will find that the allegations regarding him fall into three divisions.

After reciting the offices which he held, the appendix of the Indictment goes on to say that the defendant Ribbentrop used the foregoing positions, his personal influence, and his intimate connection with the Fuehrer in such a manner that he promoted the accession to power of the Nazi conspirators as set forth in Count One of the Indictment, and permitted preparation for war as set forth in Count One of the Indictment.

In the second section he participated in the political planning and preparation of the Nazi conspirators for Wars of Aggression and Wars in Violation of International Treaties, Agreements and Assurances as set forth in Count One and Count Two of the Indictment.

In accordance with the Fuehrer's principle, he executed and assumed responsibility for the execution of the foreign policy plans of the Nazi conspirators, as set forth in Count One of the Indictment.

Then the third section: he authorised, directed and participated in War Crimes, as set forth in Count Three of the Indictment, and Crimes against Humanity, set forth in Count Four of the Indictment, including, moreover, the crimes against persons and property in occupied territories. I hope it might be useful to the Tribunal if I follow that order. In regard to these allegations in the Indictment we collected the evidence for each of them in turn, and I therefore proceed to put in first the allegation that this defendant promoted the accession to power of the Nazi conspirators.

The Tribunal notes already that the defendant held various offices and these are listed in his own certified statement, which has already been put in as Exhibit USA 5,

Document 2829-PS. And I think it would be convenient if I very briefly explained the different activities and offices of the defendant which are dealt with in that list. It will be seen that he became a member of the Nazi Party in 1932, but, according to the semi-official statement in the archives, he had begun to work for that Party before that time. That semi- official statement goes on and says that he succeeded in extending his business connections to political circles. Having joined in 1930 the service of the Party, at the time of the final struggle for power in the Reich, Ribbentrop played an important, if not strikingly obvious, part in the bringing about of the decisive meetings between the representatives of the President of the Reich and the heads of the Party, who had prepared the entry of the Nazis into power on 30th January, 1933. Those meetings, as well as those between Hitler and von Papen, took place in Ribbentrop's house in Berlin-Dahlem.

This defendant was therefore present and active at the inception of the Nazi securing of power after that. For a short period he was adviser to the Party on questions of foreign affairs. His title was first "Collaborator to the Fuehrer on matters of Foreign Policy" and he later became representative in matters of foreign policies of the Staff of the Deputy. This was followed by membership in the Nazi Reichstag in November, 1933, and in the Party organisations be became an Oberfuehrer in the S.S. and was subsequently promoted to Gruppenft1hrer and to Obergruppenfuehrer. Thereafter he obtained the official governmental positions.

On the 24th April he was appointed Delegate of the Reich Government on matters of Disarmament. It was after Germany had left the disarmament conference. In this capacity he visited foreign capitals. He was then given a more important, and certainly a more designing, title: the German Minister Plenipotentiary at Large; and it was in that capacity that he negotiated the Anglo-German Naval Agreement of 1935.

In March, 1936, after the Nazi Government had reoccupied the Rhineland, which had been demilitarised in accordance with the terms of the Versailles and Locarno Treaties, and the matter was brought before the Council of the League of Nations, the defendant addressed the Council in defence of the action of Germany. His next position began on 11th August, 1936, when he was appointed Ambassador in London. He occupied that position for a period of some eighteen months, and his activities there, while having their own interest, are not highly relevant to the matters now before the Tribunal. In his capacity as German Minister Plenipotentiary at Large - an office still held by him - he signed the original Anti-Comintern Pact with Japan in November, 1936, and also the additional pact by which Italy joined it in 1937.

Finally, so far as this part of these cases is concerned, in February, 1938, this defendant was appointed Foreign Minister in place of the defendant von Neurath and simultaneously was made a member of the Secret Cabinet Council (Geheimer Kabinettsrat) established by decree of Hitler of that date. That takes us up to the period of his holding the office of Foreign Minister, and his action in that capacity will be dealt with in detail later on.

I refer the Tribunal, without reading further, because I have already summarised it, to the extract from "Das Archiv," Document D-472, which I now put in as Exhibit GB 130; also to the membership extract of the S.S., which consists in the examination of the descent of S.S. leaders - D-636 - and which I insert as Exhibit GB 131. Again I shall not trouble the Tribunal with the details which show his rank, which I have already mentioned. There is no question of any honorary rank. It stated the rank of Gruppenfuehrer, and, of course, it gives his ancestry in detail, in order to deal with the law relating to that subject. It also deals with the adoption of the "von," but the defendant's evidence is now to deal with much more serious matters than barren controversies with the Almanach de Gotha.

But there is one other new document which I shall put before the Tribunal in this part of the case, which is Exhibit GB 129, Document 1337-PS, which shows the establishment, of the Secret Cabinet Council and membership in the Foreign Ministry. These are the activities of this defendant in the earlier part of this career, and in the submission of the prosecution they show quite clearly that he assisted willingly, deliberately, intentionally and keenly in the militarily bringing of the Nazis into power and into the earlier stage of their obtaining control of the German State.

I now come to the second allegation in the Indictment, that this defendant participated in political planning and preparation with the Nazi conspirators for wars of aggression and wars in violation of international Treaties, agreements and assurances; and again it might help the tribunal if I took this up quite shortly, in order of aggressions, and stated briefly the constituent allegations that we make, and the references to matters before the Tribunal, referring the Tribunal only to any new document which I may now present.

The first is the Anschluss with Austria, and there the Tribunal will remember that the defendant Ribbentrop was present at a meeting at Berchtesgaden on 12th February, 1938, at which Hitler and von Papen met the Austrian Chancellor von Schuschnigg and his foreign minister, Guide Schmidt. The Tribunal will find the official account of that interview in Document 2461-PS, which I put in as Exhibit GB 132, and the Tribunal will find, I submit, a truthful account of the interview in Exhibit USA 72, Document 1780- PS, which is the diary of the defendant Jodl; and the relevant entries are those for the 11th and 12th February, 1938. They are extremely short, and I shall ask if the Tribunal will be kind enough to allow me to read from them. They do show quite clearly the case for the prosecution - the pressure that was used in Chancellor Schuschnigg's interview. It is at the foot of the first page in the document book, Document 1780-PS is the number.

And on the 11th of February and the days following the defendant Jodl writes:

"In the evening and on 12th February, General Keitel with General von Reichenau and Sperrle at Obersalzberg. Schuschnigg, together with R. G. Schmidt, are again being put under the heaviest political and military pressure. At 23.00 hours Schuschnigg signs protocol.

13th February: in the afternoon General Keitel asks Admiral Canaris and me to come to his apartment. He tells us that the Fuehrer's order is to the effect that military pressure by shamming military action should be kept up until the 15th. Proposals for these deceptive manoeuvres are drafted and submitted to the Fuehrer by telephone for approval.

At 2.40 o'clock the agreement of the Fuehrer arrived. Canaris went to Munich, to the Counter-Intelligence Office VII and initiated the different measures.

The effect is quick and strong. In Austria the impression is created that Germany is undertaking serious military preparations."

It is rather interesting, after reading the frank statement of the defendant Jodl, to look at the pale words of the official statement which I have also put in. That is the view of the meeting with Schuschnigg, which the prosecution placed before this Court.

Will the Tribunal be good enough to ignore an allegation that appears in the trial brief that this defendant visited Mussolini before the Anschluss, as is stated by a member of his staff. At that time it was disputed by another member. Therefore, I would rather the Tribunal ruled it out.

The next point, on which there is no dispute, is the telephone conversation which took place between the defendant Goering and the defendant Ribbentrop on the 13th March, 1938, when the latter was still in London. The Tribunal will remember that that was dealt with fully by my friend, Mr. Alderman. It was passing on what the prosecution submits was a completely false statement: that there was no ultimatum. The facts of the ultimatum were explained by the earlier telephone conversations with the defendant Goering in Vienna. Defendant Goering then passed that on to the defendant Ribbentrop in London in order that he might propagate the story - of there being no ultimatum - in political circles in London. That appears in the telephone conversation which is Exhibit USA 76, Document 2949-PS, and, I say, it is fully dealt with (Page 260, Part 1).

The third action which this defendant took occurred after his return from London. Although he bad been appointed Foreign Minister in February, he had gone back to London to clear up his business at the Embassy and he was still in London until after the Anschluss had actually occurred, but his name appears as a signatory of the law making Austria a province of the German Reich. That is Document 2307-PS, which I now put in as Exhibit GB 133. And there is a reference in the Reichsgesetzblatt, which is given. These were the actions of the defendant with regard to Austria.

Then we come to Czechoslovakia, and there you have an almost perfect example of aggressive work in its various ways. Again I simply remind the Tribunal of the outstanding points with the greatest brevity. First, there is the question of stirring up trouble inside the country against which aggression is going to be used.

This defendant, as Foreign Minister, was concerned with the setting up of the Sudeten Germany under Henlein, and the contacts between the Foreign Office and Henlein are shown in Exhibits USA 93, 94, 95 and 96. These are Documents 3060-PS, 2789-PS, 2788-PS and 3059-PS. They have all been read by my friend, Mr. Alderman, but I simply mention to the Tribunal their purpose: to stir up the Sudeten-German movement in order to act with the Government of the Reich.

Then, after that, the defendant Ribbentrop was present on the 28th May, 1938, at the Hitler conference, at which the latter gave the necessary instructions to prepare the attack on Czechoslovakia. That was dealt with previously (Page 6, Part 2). And I want to put before the Tribunal Document 2360- PS as Exhibit GB 134, which is a report of a speech of Hitler's in the "Volkischer Beobachter"; and, if the Tribunal would be good enough to look at it, it is a useful date to fix with regard to the aggression against Czechoslovakia, because that was the day on which Hitler, on his own proclamation, had decided that aggression was to take place against that country.

The extract which I have taken is quite short and, if the Tribunal would look at it, the important passage is:

> "On the basis of this unbearable provocation, which was still further emphasised by a truly infamous persecution and terrorising of our Germans there, I have now decided to solve the Sudeten-German question in a final and radical manner."

That was in January, 1939. Then he goes on to say:

> "On 28th May I gave the order for the preparation of military steps against this State, to be concluded by 2nd October."

The important point is that the 28th of May was the date when the "Fall Grun" for Czechoslovakia was the subject of orders, and it was thereafter put into effect to come to fruition at the beginning of October. That is the second stage: "To lay well in advance your plans of aggression. The third stage is to see that the neighbouring

States are not likely to cause you trouble."

So we find that on the 18th July, 1938, this defendant had a conversation with the Italian Ambassador Attolico, at which the attack on Czechoslovakia was discussed. That is Exhibit USA 85, Document 2800-PS. And there were further discussions which are contained in Exhibit USA 86 and 87, which are Documents 2791-PS and 2792-PS.

I think it is sufficient for me to say to the Tribunal that the effect of these documents is that it was made clear to the Italian Government that the German Government was going to move against Czechoslovakia.

The other country which was interested was Hungary, because Hungary had certain territorial ideas with regard to parts of the Czechoslovakian Republic.

So, on the 23rd and 25th of August, this defendant was present at the discussions and had discussions himself with the Hungarian politicians Imredy and Kania, and these are found in Exhibits USA 88 and 89, Documents 2796-PS and 2797- PS.

This defendant attempted to get assurances of Hungarian help, and the Hungarian Government at the time was not too ready to commit itself to action, although it was ready enough with sympathy. These are to be found in the documents which I have mentioned. And, again, unless the Tribunal desires, I shall not read any document that I summarised that way.

Now I have already mentioned that there had been contact with the Sudeten-Germans. That was the long-term grievance that had to be exploited. But the next stage was to have a short-term grievance and to stir up trouble, preferably at the fountain-head. And so, between the 16th and 24th September, we find the German Foreign Office, of which this defendant was the head, stirring up trouble in Prague, and that is shown very clearly in Exhibits USA 97 to 101, which are Documents 2858-PS, 2855- PS, 2854-PS, 2853-PS and 2856-PS. I have read them in order of date. It would be interesting for the Tribunal to look at these. They ought to follow quite shortly the document thay [sic] have just been looking at, beginning with 2858. Here you have the document of the 19th September coming from the Foreign Office to the German Embassy in Prague:

> "Please inform Deputy Kundt at Conrad Henlein's request to get in touch with the Slovaks at once and induce them to start demands."

The others deal with questions of arrest and the action that would be taken against any Czechs in Germany in order to make the position more difficult.

That was the contribution which this defendant made to the pre-Munich crisis. After, as the Tribunal will remember, on the 29th September, 1938, the Munich agreement was signed. That is Exhibit GB 23, Document TC-23, which I have already read to the Tribunal.

And, after that - I just remind the Tribunal of an interesting document which shows the sort of action which the Wehrmacht expected and the advice that the Wehrmacht expected from the Foreign Office.

You have, on the 1st of October, Document C-2, which is Exhibit USA 90 and that is a long document putting forward an almost infinite variety of breaches of International Law, which were likely to arise or might have arisen from the action in regard to Czechoslovakia; and on all these points the opinion of the Foreign Office is sought. That, of course, remained a hypothetical question at that time because no war resulted.

THE PRESIDENT: Can you give us the number of that document?

SIR DAVID MAXWELL FYFE: Yes, C-2, My Lord, Exhibit USA 90.

Then, if the Tribunal please, we come to the second stage in the acquiring of

Czechoslovakia. That is, having obtained the Sudetenland, arranging that there would be a crisis in Czechoslovakia which would be an excuse for taking the rest. The Tribunal will remember the importance of this because it is the first time that the German Government went outside its own statement about not going beyond German blood.

On that point, again, this defendant was active. On the 13th March, as events were moving to a climax, he sent a telegram to the German Minister in Prague, who was under him, telling him to "make a point of not being available if the Czech Government wants to get in touch with you in the next few days." That is Exhibit USA 116, Document 2815-PS.

At the same time this defendant saw a delegation of pro-Nazi Slovaks in Berlin at a conference with Hitler. Tiso, one of the heads of the pro-Nazi Slovaks, was directed to declare an independent Slovak State, in order to assist in the disintegration of Czechoslovakia. That is Exhibit USA 117, Document 2802-PS, and the Tribunal might care to compare it with a previous meeting with another Slovak, Tuca, a month before, which is shown in Document 2790-PS, Exhibit USA 110. So that this defendant was again assisting in the task of proposing internal trouble.

Then, on the 14th March, 1939, the next day, Hacha, the President of Czechoslovakia, was called to Berlin. This defendant was present at the meeting and the Tribunal will remember the usual pressure and threats which resulted in the aged President's permission to hand over the Czechoslovak State to Hitler. The Tribunal will find that subject dealt with on Pages 96-97, Part 2, and the relevant exhibit is Exhibit USA 118, Document 2798-PS, which is the minutes of the meeting between Hitler and Hacha that this defendant attended. You will also find it dealt with in Exhibit USA 126, Document 3061-PS, which is the Czechoslovakian Government Report.

That was the end of the Czech part of Czechoslovakia. The following week this defendant signed a treaty with Slovakia which I now put in. It is Document 1439-PS, and I put it in as Exhibit GB 135, and the important part is Article 11, under which the German Government was given the right to construct military posts and installations and keep them garrisoned within Czechoslovakia. That is 1439-PS, which I put in as GB 135. I am not going to read it at length, but I hope the Tribunal will stop me if there are any of these documents which they would like read instead of summarised. In that way this defendant, by the terms of that treaty, after completely finishing Bohemia and Moravia as an independent state, had got military control in Slovakia.

Before I pass to Poland, there is one interesting little point on the northern Baltic which I put before the Tribunal to show that this defendant could hardly keep his hands out of the internal affairs of other countries, even when it did not seem a very important matter. The Tribunal will remember that on the 3rd April, 1939, as shown in Exhibit GB 4, TC-53- A, Germany had occupied Memelland. It would have appeared, as far as the Baltic States were concerned, that the position was satisfactory; but if the Tribunal will look at Document 2953-PS, which I put in as Exhibit GB 136, and Document 2952-PS, which I put in as Exhibit GB 137, they will find that this defendant acted in close concert with the conspirator Heydrich, who is dead, in stirring up trouble in Lithuania with a group of pro-Nazi people called the "Woldemaras Supporters." Document 2953-PS shows that Heydrich was passing to the defendant Ribbentrop the request for financial support for the ...

THE PRESIDENT: Just one moment, Sir David. Unfortunately, these documents are not in any order.

SIR DAVID MAXWELL FYFE: I am terribly sorry.

THE PRESIDENT: It is very difficult to find them. This follows after 3061 and 1439?

SIR DAVID MAXWELL FYFE: Yes, it follows after 3061. The next one that I referred to, the treaty with Slovakia, 1939, should come after that.

THE PRESIDENT: You are going to read 2953?

SIR DAVID MAXWELL FYFE: Yes, my Lord. That is the one I was going to read. That is a letter from Heydrich to the defendant Ribbentrop and it says:

"Dear Party Comrade v. Ribbentrop,

Enclosed please find a further report about the 'Woldemaras Supporters.' As already mentioned in the previous report the 'Woldemaras Supporters' are still asking for help from the Reich. I therefore ask you to examine the question of financial support brought up again by the 'Woldemaras Supporters' set forth on Page 4, paragraph 2 of the enclosed report and to make a definite decision.

The request of the 'Woldemaras Supporters' for financial support could, in my opinion, be granted. Deliveries of arms should not, however, be made under any circumstances."

Then, 2952, the next document, is a fuller report, and at the end of that there is added, in handwriting, "I support small regular payments, e.g., 2,000 to 3,000 marks quarterly." It is signed "W," who I understand to be the Secretary of State.

I quoted that merely to show the extraordinary interference, even with comparatively unimportant countries.

Then we pass to the aggression against Poland, and again the Tribunal has had that fully dealt with by my friend Colonel Griffith-Jones, but again it might be useful if I just separated the various periods so that the Tribunal will have these in mind. The first was what one might call the Munich period, up to the end of September, 1938, and at that time no language was too good for Poland. The Tribunal will remember the point.

The important exhibits showing that aspect of the case are GB 30, which is Document 2357-PS, Hitler's Reichstag speech on the 20th February, 1938, and then GB 31, Document TC-76, which is the secret Foreign Office memorandum of the 26th August, 1938, and GB 27, Document 73, No. 40...

THE PRESIDENT: What was the number?

SIR DAVID MAXWELL FYFE: I beg your Lordship's pardon. The last one was TC-76.

THE PRESIDENT: Yes, but after that.

SIR DAVID MAXWELL FYFE: The next one was TC-73, No. 40. 73 is the Polish White Book and 40 is the number of the document in the book. It is an extract from the conversation between M. Lipski, the Polish Ambassador, and this defendant.

Finally in this group is Document TC-73, No. 42, Hitler's speech at the Sportpalast on the 26th September, 1938, in which he said that this was the end of his territorial problems in Europe and expressed an almost violent affection for the Poles.

Now the next stage was between Munich and the rape of Prague, and in the following stage-part of the German aggressions in Czechoslovakia having been accomplished and parts still remaining to be done - there is a slight change but still a friendly atmosphere. That begins with a conversation between this defendant and M. Lipski, which is contained in Exhibit GB 27, Document TC-73, No. 44.

There this defendant put forward very peaceful suggestions for the settlement of the Danzig issue. The Polish reply is in Exhibit GB 28, TC-75.

THE PRESIDENT: You did not give the date of those, did you?

SIR DAVID MAXWELL FYFE: The first one is 24th October, 1938; the Polish reply which says that it is unacceptable that Danzig should return to the Reich, but makes suggestions for a bilateral agreement, is the 31st October, 1938. Between these dates, the Tribunal will remember, according to Document C-137, Exhibit GB 33, dated the 21st October, the German Government had made its preparations to occupy Danzig by surprise. But, although these preparations were made, still, some two months later, on the 5th January, 1939, while the rape of Prague had not yet taken place, Hitler was suggesting to M. Beck, the Polish Foreign Minister, a new solution. That is contained in Document TC-73, No. 48, Exhibit GB 34, the interview of Hitler and Beck on the 5th January, 1939.

Then this defendant saw M. Beck on the next day and said there was no violent solution of Danzig, but a further building up of friendly relations. That is contained in Exhibit GB 35, Document TC-73, No. 49. Not content with that, this defendant went to Warsaw on the 25th January, and, according to the report of his speech contained in Document 2530-PS, Exhibit GB 36, talked of the continued progress and consolidation of friendly relations; and that was capped by Hitler's Reichstag speech on the 30th January, 1939, in the same sort of tone, contained in Exhibit GB 37, Document TC-73 No. 57. That was the second stage-the mention of Danzig in honoured words - because, of course, the rape of Prague had not been attained.

Then one has to remember, as one comes to the summer, the meeting at the Reich Chancellery on the 23rd May, 1939, which is reported in Document L-79, Exhibit USA 27. It has been read many times to the Tribunal, and I only remind them of this point; that this is the document where Hitler makes quite clear, and states in his own words, that Danzig has nothing to do with the real Polish question. "I have to deal with Poland because I want Lebensraum. in the East." That is the effect of that portion of the document which has been read so often to the Tribunal-that Danzig was merely an excuse.

It is important to have in mind, if I may respectfully suggest it, that that meeting was on the 23rd May, 1939, because there is an interesting corroboration of the attitude of mind-in showing how clearly this defendant Ribbentrop had adopted the attitude of mind of Hitler - in the introduction to Count Ciano's diary, which was put in as Exhibit USA 166, Document 2987-PS; but I do not think this part of the diary, the introduction, has been read before. It is Document 2987-PS, and it comes after L-79, which is the Little Schmundt File, just after the Obersalzberg Document. It is set forth in the trial brief, if the Tribunal will care to follow it there. Count Ciano says:

> "In the summer of 1939 Germany advanced her claim against Poland, naturally without our knowledge; indeed, Ribbentrop had several times denied to our Ambassador that Germany had any intentions of carrying the controversy to extremes. Despite these denials I remained in doubt; I wanted to make sure for myself, and on 11th August I went to Salzburg. It was in his residence at Fuschl that Ribbentrop informed me, while we were waiting to sit down at the table, of the decision to start the fireworks, just as he might have told me about the most unimportant and common-place administrative matter. 'Well, Ribbentrop,' I asked him, while we were walking in the garden, 'what do you want? The Corridor or Danzig?' 'Not any more,' and he stared at me through those cold Musee Grevin eyes. 'We want war.'"

I remind the Tribunal how closely that corroborates the statement that Hitler had made at his Chancellery conference on the 23rd May - that it was no longer a question of Danzig or the Corridor, it was a question of war to achieve Lebensraum in the East.

Then I remind the Tribunal, without citing, that the "Fall Weiss" for operation against Poland is dated the 3rd and 11th April, 1939, which certainly shows that preparations were already in hand.

And then there is another reference in Count Ciano's diary which also has not been read and which makes this point quite clear. Again, if the Tribunal will take it as set out in the trial brief, I will read it, as it has not been read before:

> "I have collected the conference records of my conversations with Ribbentrop and Hitler. I shall only note some impressions of a general nature. Ribbentrop is evasive every time I ask him for particulars of the forthcoming German action. He has a guilty conscience. He has lied too many times about German intentions towards Poland not to feel embarrassment now over what he must tell me and what he is preparing to do.
>
> The will to fight is unalterable. He rejects any solution which might satisfy Germany and prevent the struggle. I am certain that, even if the Germans were given everything they demanded, they would attack just the same, because they are possessed by the demon of destruction.
>
> Our conversation sometimes takes a dramatic turn. I do not hesitate to speak my mind in the most brutal manner. But this does not shake him in the least. I realise how little weight this view carries in German opinion.
>
> The atmosphere is icy. And the cold feeling between us is reflected in our followers. During dinner we do not exchange a word. We distrust each other. But I at least have a clear conscience. He has not."

Whatever other defects there may have been about Count Ciano, there cannot be an appreciation of the situation which is more heavily corroborated by supporting documents than his diagnosis of the situation in the summer of 1939.

Then we come to the next stage in the German plan, which was sharp pressure on the claim for Danzig shown immediately after Czechoslovakia had been formally dealt with on the 15th of March. It is shown how closely it followed the completion of the rape of Prague. The first sharp raising of the claim was on the 21st March, as shown in Exhibit GB 38, Document TC-73, No. 61. That developed, as the Tribunal has heard from Colonel Griffith-Jones.

Then we come to the last days before the war, and one interesting sidelight is that Herr von Dirksen, the German Ambassador to the Court of St. James, returned from London on the 18th August, 1939; and I put in the extract from the interrogation of the defendant Ribbentrop, which is Document D-490. I put that in as GB 138.

I do not intend to read it to the Tribunal because it can be summarised in this way; that the defendant Ribbentrop has certainly no recollection of ever having seen the German Ambassador to the Court of St. James after his return. He thinks he would have remembered him if he had seen him and he accepts the probability that he did not see him. And there is the point, when it was well known that war with Poland would involve England and France, that either he was not sufficiently interested in opinion in London to take the trouble to see his ambassador or else, as he rather suggests, that he had appointed so weak and ordinary a career diplomat to London that his opinion was not taken into account, either by Ribbentrop himself or by Hitler. In either case, he was completely uninterested in anything which his ambassador might have to tell him as to opinion in London or the possibility of war. And I conceive myself speaking with great moderation in putting it this way, that in the last days before the 1st September, 1939, this defendant did whatever he could to avoid peace with Poland and to avoid anything which might hinder the encouraging of the war which we know he wanted. He did that, well knowing that war with Poland would involve Great Britain and France. These details were given in full by Colonel Griffith-Jones.

I am not going through them again, but I have, for the convenience of the Tribunal, referred to the transcript (Pages 144 to 176, Part 2), and M. Lipski summarised all that took place in his report of the 10th October, 1939, which is Document TC-73, No. 147, Exhibit GB 27.

Now these are the actions of this defendant in the Polish matter. I am glad to inform the Tribunal that with regard to the other countries they are very much shorter than with regard to Poland.

I now come to Norway and Denmark. I remind the Tribunal of the fact, if it cares to take cognisance thereof, that on the 31st May, 1939, the defendant Ribbentrop, on behalf of Germany, signed a non-aggression pact with Denmark, which provided that "The German Reich and the Kingdom of Denmark will under no circumstances go to war or employ force of any other kind against one another." This is Exhibit GB 77, Document TC-24. And just to fix the date, the Tribunal will remember that on the 7th April, 1940, the German armed forces invaded Denmark and at the same time they invaded Norway.

With regard to Norway there are three documents which show that this defendant was fully informed of the earlier preparations for that act of aggression. The Tribunal will remember that my friend, Major Elwyn Jones, did indicate, with some particularity, the relations between Quisling and the defendant Rosenberg. But Rosenberg in this case also required the help of the defendant Ribbentrop and, if the Tribunal would be good enough to turn to Document 957-PS, which I am putting in as Exhibit GB 139, they will see the first of the documents which connect this defendant with the earlier Quisling activities.

The first one, 957-PS, is a letter from defendant Rosenberg to this defendant and it begins:

"Dear Party Comrade von Ribbentrop:

Party Comrade Scheidt has returned and has made a detailed report to Privy Councillor von Grundherr, who will address you on this subject. We agreed the other day that two to three hundred thousand Reichsmark would be made immediately available for the said purpose. Now it turns out that Grundherr states that the second instalment can be made available only after eight days. But as it is necessary for Scheidt to go back immediately, I request you to make it possible that this second instalment be given to him at once. With a longer absence of Party Comrade Reichsamtsleiter Scheidt the connection with your representatives would also be broken up, which just now, under certain circumstances, could be very unfavourable.

Therefore I trust that it is in everybody's interest, if P.M. Scheidt goes back immediately."

That was the 24th February.

Now the next document is a report from Rosenberg to Hitler, and if the Tribunal will be good enough to turn to Page 4 - this is on the Quisling activities - they will find that that passage is sufficient to show how this defendant was connected with it.

This is a report from Rosenberg to Hitler:

"Apart from financial support which was forthcoming from the Reich in currency, Quisling had also been promised a shipment of material for immediate use in Norway, such as coal and sugar. Additional help was promised. These shipments were to be conducted under cover of a new trade company, to be established in Germany, or through especially selected existing firms, while Hagelin was to act as consignee in Norway. Hagelin had already conferred with the respective Minister of the Nygaardsvold Government, as, for instance, the Minister of Supply and Commerce, and had been assured permission for the import of coal. At the same time the coal transports were to serve, possibly, to supply the technical means necessary to launch Quisling's political action in Oslo with German help. It was Quisling's plan to send a number of selected, particularly reliable men to Germany for a brief military training course in a completely isolated camp. They were then to be detailed as area and language specialists to German Special Troops, who were to be taken to Oslo on the coal barges to accomplish a political action. Thus Quisling planned to get hold of his leading opponents in Norway, including the King, and to prevent all military resistance from the very beginning. Immediately following this political action and upon official request of Quisling to the Government of the German Reich, the military occupation of Norway was to take place. All military preparations were to be completed previously. Though this plan contained the great advantage of surprise, it also contained a great number of dangers which could possibly cause its failure. For this reason it received quite dilatory treatment, while at the same time it was not disapproved as far as the Norwegians were concerned.

In February, after a conference with General Field Marshal Goering, Reichsleiter Rosenberg informed the Secretary in the Office of the Four Year Plan, Wohltat, only of the intention to prepare coal shipments to Norway to the named confidant Hagelin. Further details were discussed in a conference between Secretary Wohltat, Staff Director Schickedanz and Hagelin. Since Wohltat received no further instructions from the General Field Marshal, Foreign Minister von Ribbentrop - after a consultation with Reichsleiter Rosenberg - consented to expedite these shipments through his office. Based on a report of Reichsleiter Rosenberg to the Fuehrer it was also arranged to pay Quisling ten thousand English pounds per month for three months, commencing on the 15th March, to support his work."

This was paid through Scheidt, the man who was mentioned before.

Now the other document, D-629, is a letter from defendant Keitel to Ribbentrop, dated the 3rd April, 1940. I need trouble the Tribunal only with the first paragraph. Keitel says:

"Dear Herr von Ribbentrop:

The military occupation of Denmark and Norway has been, by command of the Fuehrer, long in preparation by the High Command of the Wehrmacht. The High Command of the Wehrmacht has therefore had ample time to occupy itself with all the questions connected with the carrying out of this operation. The time at your disposal for the political preparation of this operation is, on the contrary, very much shorter. I believe myself, therefore, to be acting in accordance with your ideas in transmitting to you herewith, not only these wishes of the Wehrmacht which would have to be fulfilled by the Governments in Oslo, Copenhagen and Stockholm for purely military reasons, but also a series of requests which certainly concern the Wehrmacht only indirectly but which are, however, of the greatest importance for the fulfilment of its task."

Then he proceeds to ask the Foreign Office to get in touch with certain commanders. The important point for which I read it to the Tribunal, as far as I know for the first time, is that there we have the defendant Keitel saying quite clearly that the military occupation of Denmark and Norway has been long in preparation. And it is interesting when one looks back to the official life of Ribbentrop, which is contained in the archives and is Document D-472. I am quoting a sentence only because of the interesting contrast.

> "With the occupation of Denmark and Norway on the 9th April, 1940, only a few hours before the landing of British troops in these territories, the battle began against the Western Powers."

Then it goes on to Holland and Belgium.

It is quite clear that, whoever else had knowledge or whoever else was ignorant, this defendant Ribbentrop had been up to his neck in the Quisling plottings, and it is made clear to him, a good week before the invasion started, that the Wehrmacht and the defendant Keitel had long been preparing this particular act of aggression.

I think, my Lord, that is really all the evidence on the aggression against Norway because, again, the story was put forward fully by my friend, Major Elwyn Jones.

THE PRESIDENT: We will adjourn now.

(The Tribunal adjourned until 10.00 hours on the 9th January, 1946.)

Thirtieth Day: Wednesday, January 9th, 1946

SIR DAVID MAXWELL FYFE: If the Tribunal please, when the Tribunal adjourned I had just dealt with the last of the two Norway documents, which I now put in as Exhibits GB 140 and GB 141. Their numbers were 004-PS and D-629.

My Lord, for convenience, the first document to which I shall refer in a few minutes will be Document 1871-PS.

THE PRESIDENT: I have that here.

SIR DAVID MAXWELL FYFE: My Lord, before I come to that, I just want to say one word about the aggression against the Low Countries: Belgium, the Netherlands and Luxembourg.

The facts as to the aggression against these countries, during the period when this defendant was Foreign Minister, were stated in full by my friend Mr. Roberts, and if I give the Tribunal the reference (Pages 198 to 211, Part 2) I do not need to detain the Tribunal on that part of the case.

I only remind the Tribunal that the action of this defendant as Foreign Minister, to which attention may be called, is the making of a statement on the 10th May, 1940, to representatives of the foreign Press with regard to the reasons for the German invasion of the Low Countries, and these reasons were, in my respectful submission, demonstrated to be false by the evidence called by Mr. Roberts, which appears in that part of the transcript.

My Lord, I then proceed to the aggression in South-eastern Europe against Greece and Yugoslavia, and the first moment of time in that regard is the meeting at Salzburg in August, 1939, at which the defendant von Ribbentrop participated, when Hitler announced that the Axis had decided to liquidate certain neutrals. That document is 1871-PS, which I now put in as Exhibit GB 142, and the passage to which I should like to refer the Tribunal is on Page 2 of the English version, two-thirds down the page in the middle of the fifth paragraph, six lines from the top. Your Lordship will find the words "Generally speaking."

THE PRESIDENT: Yes.

SIR DAVID MAXWELL FYFE: I desire to quote from there:

> "Generally speaking, it would be best to liquidate the pseudo-neutrals one after the other. This is fairly easily done, if one Axis partner protects the rear of the other, who is just finishing off one of the uncertain neutrals, and vice versa. Italy may consider Yugoslavia such an uncertain neutral. At the visit of Prince Regent Paul he (the Fuehrer) suggested, particularly in consideration of Italy, that Prince Paul clarify his political attitude towards the Axis by a gesture. He had thought of a closer connection with the Axis, and Yugoslavia's leaving the League of Nations. Prince Paul agreed to the latter. Recently the Prince Regent was in London and sought reassurance from the Western Powers. The same thing was repeated that happened in the case of Gafencu, who was also very reasonable during his visit to Germany and who denied any interest in the aims of the Western democracies. Afterwards it was learned that he had later assumed a contrary standpoint in England. Among the Balkan countries the Axis can completely rely only on Bulgaria, which is, in a sense, a natural ally of Italy and Germany."

Then missing a sentence:

"At the moment when there was a turn to the worse for Germany and Italy, however, Yugoslavia would join the other side openly, hoping thereby to give matters a final turn to the disadvantage of the Axis."

That demonstrates the policy with regard to uncertain neutrals.

Then, as early as September, 1940, this defendant reviewed the war situation with Mussolini. This defendant emphasised the heavy revenge bombing raids on England and the fact that London would soon be in ruins. It was agreed between the parties that only Italian interests were involved in Greece and Yugoslavia, and that Italy could count on German support.

Then von Ribbentrop went on further to explain to Mussolini the Spanish plan for the attack on Gibraltar and Germany's participation therein, and that he was expecting to sign the Protocol with Spain bringing the latter country into the war on his return to Berlin.

This is Document 1842-PS, which is the next document in the book to the one at which the Tribunal has just been looking, and the passage with regard to Greece and Yugoslavia occurs in the middle of the first page, if I might just read a very short extract:

"With regard to Greece and Yugoslavia, the Foreign Minister stressed that it was exclusively a question of Italian interests, the settling of which was a matter for Italy alone, and in which Italy would be certain of Germany's sympathetic assistance."

I do not think I need trouble the Tribunal with the rest.

THE TRIBUNAL (Mr. Biddle): I think you had better read the next paragraph.

SIR DAVID MAXWELL FYFE:

"But it seemed to us to be better not to touch on those problems for the time being, but to concentrate instead on the destruction of England with all our forces. Where Germany was concerned, she was interested in the Northern German districts (Norway, etc.), and this was acknowledged by the Duce."

I am very grateful to you, your Honour.

That I put in as Exhibit GB 143.

A month or two later, in January, 1941, at the meeting between Hitler and Mussolini, in which this defendant participated, the Greek operation was discussed. Hitler bad stated that the "German troops in Roumania were for use in the planned campaign against Greece. That document is C-134, which was put in as Exhibit GB 119, and therefore I do not propose to give it again, but to give the Tribunal the reference to the points which are mentioned at the foot of Page 3 of the English text.

With regard to that meeting there is a cross-reference in Count Ciano's diary, Count Ciano having attended as Italian Foreign Minister, and he recalls his impression of that meeting in the diary for the 20th-21st of January by saying:

"The Duce was, on the whole, pleased with the conversation. I am less pleased. Above all, because Ribbentrop, who had always been so boastful in the past, told us, when I asked him outright how long the war would last, that he saw no possibility of its ending before 1942."

Despite that somewhat pessimistic statement to Count Ciano, a short time later, three weeks later, when it was a question of encouraging the Japanese, this defendant took a more optimistic line.

On the 13th February, 1941, he saw Ambassador Oshima, the Japanese Ambassador, and that is the conversation that appears in Document 1834-PS, which is Exhibit USA 129. That was read previously, and again I simply give the reference on Page 3 of the English version.

The second and last paragraph dealt with the optimistic account of the military position and the position of Bulgaria and Turkey. I do not think I need read it further, because it gives the Tribunal the reference.

Then, after that, in March, this defendant put forth his efforts to get Yugoslavia to join the Axis, and on the 25th March the defendant, in a note to the Prime Minister Ovstkovitch - and this is Document 2450-PS, which is Exhibit GB 123 - gave the assurance:

"The Axis power governments, during this war, will not direct a demand to Yugoslavia to permit the march or transportation of troops through the Yugoslav State or territory."

After that, it is only fair to point out that there was the coup d'etat in Yugoslavia. General Simovics took over the Government, and two days after the assurance which I just read, at the meeting of the 27th March, 1941, at which this defendant was present, Hitler outlined the military campaign against Yugoslavia and promised the destruction of Yugoslavia and the demolition of Belgrade by the German Air Force. That is contained in Document 1746-PS, which is Exhibit GB 120, and that was read by my friend Colonel Phillimore, at an earlier stage, so I don't need to read it again.

The final action of this defendant with regard to Yugoslavia was that after the invasion of Yugoslavia, von Ribbentrop was one of the persons directed by Hitler to draw up the boundaries for the partition and division of Yugoslavia. The preliminary directive for that was Document 1195-PS, which I now put in as Exhibit GB 144.

We now come to the aggression against the Soviet Union, and the first -

THE PRESIDENT: Has that been read, 1195-PS?

SIR DAVID MAXWELL FYFE: No, it has not. I am much obliged, your Lordship. I will now read the relevant sentence with regard to this.

On Page 2, Section 2, your Lordship will see the words "the drawing up of boundaries."

THE PRESIDENT: Yes.

SIR DAVID MAXWELL FYFE: And in paragraph 1 it says:

> "If the drawing up of boundaries has not been laid down in the above Part 1, it will be carried out by the Supreme Command of the Armed Forces in agreement With the Foreign Office" - that is the defendant - "the Plenipotentiary for the Four Year Plan" - the defendant Goering - "and the Reich Minister of the Interior."

THE PRESIDENT: Who is Reich Minister of the Interior?

SIR DAVID MAXWELL FYFE: I think the defendant Frick.

THE PRESIDENT: Yes, I think it was.

SIR DAVID MAXWELL FYFE: My Lord, I am grateful to your Lordship. I had forgotten that had not been read before.

Now then, as I say, we come to the aggression against the Soviet Union, and the first document which has not been put in so far, which I now put in as Exhibit GB 145, is TC-25, the German-Soviet Non-Aggression Pact.

On 23rd August, 1939, this defendant had signed the German- Soviet Non-Aggression Pact. Now, the first point at which this defendant seems to have considered special problems of aggression against the Soviet Union was just after the 20th April, 1941, when the defendant Rosenberg and this defendant met or communicated to consider the problems which were expected to arise in Eastern occupied territory. This defendant appointed his Counsellor, Grosskopf, to be his liaison man with Rosenberg and also assigned a Consul General, called Brautigam, who had many years5 experience in the U.S.S.R. as collaborator with Rosenberg.

That is shown in Document 1039-PS, which is Exhibit USA 146. I did not propose to read it again as it had been read. That passage to which I have referred is the first paragraph on the top of Page 2, beginning "After notification to the Reich Foreign Minister." It is that paragraph which I have just mentioned.

That was in April, 1941. The following month, on 18th May, 1941, the German Foreign Office prepared a declaration setting forth operational zones in the Arctic Ocean, the Baltic and Black Seas, to be used by the German Navy and the Air Force, in the coming invasion of the Soviet Union. That is the next document, C-77, which I now put in as Exhibit GB 146, and it is very short. Therefore, I think I should quote it; it has not been read before:

> "The Foreign Office has prepared for the use in Barbarossa the attached draft of a declaration of operational zones. The Foreign Office has, however, reserved its decision as to the date when the declaration will be issued as well as the discussion of particulars."

These last two documents show quite clearly that this defendant was again implicated in the preparation for this act of aggression. Then, on the 22nd June, 1941, this defendant announced to the world that the German armies were invading the U.S.S.R., as was seen by the Tribunal in the film shown on the 11th December. And how untrue were the reasons given, is shown by the report of his own Ambassador in Moscow who said that everything was being done to avoid a conflict. The Tribunal will find the reference to that in my learned friend, the Attorney General's speech (Page 84, Part 2).

We now come to the aggression which involved Japan and was directed against the United States of America. And there the initial document is 2508-PS, which I now put in as Exhibit GB 147. That shows that on the 25th November, 1936, as a result of negotiations of this defendant as Ambassador at Large, Germany and Japan had signed the Anti-Comintern Pact. I do not think that has been read, but if I may, I will just read the introduction, the recital that gives the purposes of the agreement:

> "The Government of the German Reich and the Imperial Japanese Government, recognising that the aim of the Communist Internationale, known as the Comintern, is to disintegrate and subdue existing States by all the means at its command; convinced that the toleration of interference by the Communist Internationale in the internal affairs of the nations not only endangers their internal peace and social well-being, but is also a menace to the peace of the world; desirous of co-operating in the defence against Communist subversive activities, have agreed as follows."

And then there follow the effective terms of the agreement under which they will act together for five years. It is signed by this defendant.

On the 27th September, 1940, this defendant, as Foreign Minister, signed the Tripartite Pact with Japan and Italy, thereby bring about a full-scale military and economic alliance for the creation of a new order in Europe and East Asia. That is 2643-PS; Exhibit USA 149, and it has been read.

Then, on the 13th February, 1941 - that is, a month or two later - this defendant was urging the Japanese to attack British possessions in the Far East. And that is shown in Document 1834-PS, which is Exhibit USA 129, and which has already been read by my friend, Mr. Alderman. That was in February.

Then, in April, 1941, at a meeting between Hitler and Matsuoka, representing Japan, at which this defendant was present, Hitler promised that Germany would declare war on the United States in the event of war occurring between Japan and the United States as a result of Japanese aggression in the Pacific. That is shown in Document 1831-PS, Exhibit USA 33, which has already been read and which I did not intend to read again.

Then, the next document which reinforces that point is 1882- PS, which is Exhibit USA 153. If I might trouble the Tribunal with just two short paragraphs of that; it is interesting, showing the psychological development of this defendant and his views at that time. It is the first two paragraphs in the document that are quoted, under the heading "Pages 2 and 3 it is on the first page of the document:

> "Matsuoka then spoke of the general high morale in Germany, referring to the happy faces he had seen everywhere among the workers during his recent visit to the Borsig Works. He expressed his regret that developments in Japan had not as yet advanced as far as in Germany and that in his country the intellectuals still exercised considerable influence.
>
> The Reich Foreign Minister replied that at best a nation which had realised its every ambition could afford the luxury of intellectuals, most of whom are parasites, anyway.
>
> A nation, however, which has to fight for a place in the sun must give them up. The intellectuals ruined France; in Germany they had already started their pernicious activities when National Socialism put a stop to these doings; they will surely be the cause of the downfall of Britain, which is to be expected with certainty."

Then, it continues on the usual lines. That was on the 5th April.

Then, the next stage; within a month after the German Armies invaded the Soviet Union, the 22nd June, 1941, Ribbentrop was urging his Ambassador in Tokyo to do his utmost to cause the Japanese Government to attack the Soviet in Siberia, and that is proved by two documents which have already been put in: 2896-PS, which is Exhibit USA 155, a telegram to the German Ambassador in Tokyo, one Ott; and 2897-PS, Exhibit 156, which is the reply from Ambassador Ott. Both of these were read by my friend, Mr. Alderman, and I won't trouble the Tribunal again.

The next document, which is D-656, is a new document which I put in as Exhibit GB 148. That was captured from the Japanese, and it is a message, intercepted, which was sent by the Japanese Ambassador in Berlin just before the attack on the United States. If I might just read one short extract from this defendant's speech - on the 29th November, 1941, that is, roughly, a week before Pearl Harbour, Ribbentrop was saying this. It is in paragraph 1, and I will read it all because it is new:

> "Ribbentrop opened our meeting by again inquiring whether I had received any reports regarding the Japanese-United States negotiations. I replied that I had received no official word.
>
> Ribbentrop: 'It is essential that Japan effect the New Order in East Asia without losing this opportunity. There never has been and probably never will be a time when closer co-operation under the Tripartite Pact is so important. If Japan hesitates at this time and Germany goes ahead and establishes her European New Order, all the military might of Britain and the United States will be concentrated against Japan.
>
> As the Fuehrer said to-day, there are fundamental differences between Germany and Japan, and the United States, as to their very right to exist. We have received advice to the effect that there is practically no hope of the Japanese-United States negotiations being concluded successfully, because of the fact that the United States is putting up a stiff front.
>
> If this is indeed the fact of the case, and if Japan reaches a decision to fight Britain and the United States, I am confident that that will not only be to the interest of Germany and Japan jointly, but would bring about favourable

results for Japan herself.'

Then the Ambassador replied:

'I can make no definite statement, as I am not aware of any concrete intentions of Japan. Is Your Excellency indicating that a state of actual war is to be established between Germany and the United States?'

The defendant Ribbentrop: 'Roosevelt is a fanatic, so it is impossible to tell what he would do.'

Then: 'Concerning this point, in view of the fact that Ribbentrop has said in the past that the United States would undoubtedly try to avoid meeting German troops, and from the tone of Hitler's recent speech, as well as that of Ribbentrop's, I feel that the German attitude toward the United States is being considerably stiffened. There are indications at present that Germany would not refuse to fight the United States if necessary."

Then the next part, Section 2, is an extremely optimistic prognosis of the war against the Soviet Union. I do not think, in view of the date in which we are reading it, that I need trouble the Tribunal with that.

There are then a few remarks about the intended landing operations against England, which I shall not read at this time.

If the Tribunal would go to Part III, there again we get the international attitude of mind of this defendant - at the foot of Page 2, Part III, and I am quoting:

"In any event, Germany has absolutely no intention of entering into any peace with England. We are determined to remove all British influence from Europe. Therefore, at the end of this war, England will have no influence whatsoever in international affairs. The Island Empire of Britain may remain, but all of her other possessions throughout the world will probably be divided three ways by Germany, the United States and Japan. In Africa, Germany will be satisfied with, roughly, those parts which were formerly German colonies. Italy will be given the greater share of the African colonies. Germany desires, above all else, to control European Russia."

And, after hearing this defendant, the Ambassador said, and I quote:

"I am fully aware of the fact that Germany's war campaign is progressing according to schedule, smoothly. However, suppose that Germany is faced with the situation of having not only Great Britain as an actual enemy, but also having all of those areas in which Britain has influence and those countries which have been aiding Britain as actual enemies as well. Under such circumstances, the war area will undergo considerable expansion, of course. What is your opinion of the outcome of the war under such an eventuality?"

The defendant Ribbentrop:

"We would like to end this war during next year" - that is, 1942. "However, under certain circumstances, it is possible that it will have to be continued on the following year. Should Japan become engaged in a war against the United States" -

THE PRESIDENT: You are going a little bit too fast.

SIR DAVID MAXWELL FYFE: If your Lordship pleases. I am sorry. I will go back to the paragraph I have just finished.

The defendant Ribbentrop - and I am still quoting:

"We would like to end this war during next year. However, under certain circumstances it is possible that it will have to be continued into the following year.

Should Japan become engaged in a war against the United States, Germany, of course, would join the war immediately. There is absolutely no possibility of Germany's entering into a separate peace with the United States under such circumstances. The Fuehrer is determined on that point."

That document associates this defendant in the closest possible way with the aggression by Japan against the United States.

Another new document, which is also an intercepted Japanese diplomatic message, is the next one, D-657, which I put in as Exhibit GB 149. If I might read the first two sentences, they show what it is - and I quote:

"The Japanese Ambassador says: 'At 1 p.m. to-day - the 8th December - I called on Foreign Minister Ribbentrop and told him our wish was to have Germany and Italy issue formal declarations of war on America at once. Ribbentrop replied that Hitler was then in the midst of a conference at general headquarters, discussing how the formalities of declaring war could be carried out so as to make a good impression on the German people, and that he would transmit your wish to him at once and do whatever he was able to have it carried out promptly. At that time Ribbentrop told me that on the morning of the 8th' - that is, before the declaration of war - 'Hitler issued orders to the entire German Navy to attack American ships whenever and wherever they might meet them.'

It goes without saying that this is only for your secret information."

Then, as a matter of fact, as the Tribunal are aware, on the 11th December, 1941, the defendant Ribbentrop, in the name of the German Government, announced a state of war between Germany and the United States.

The next stage concerns his attempt to get Japan to attack the Soviet Union.

In Ribbentrop's conversations with Oshima, the Japanese Ambassador, in July, 1942, and in March and April, 1943, he continued to urge Japanese participation and aggression against the Soviet Union. This is shown in Document 2911-PS, which has been put in as Exhibit USA 157 and already read, and Document 2954-PS, which I now put in as Exhibit GB 150. That is a new document, and if I may I will just indicate the effect of it by a very short quotation. This is a discussion between the defendant Ribbentrop and Ambassador Oshima. It begins:

"Ambassador Oshima declared that he has received a telegram from Tokyo, and he is to report, by order of his Government, to the Reich Minister for Foreign Affairs the following:

The suggestion of the German Government to attack Russia was the subject of a common conference between the Japanese Government and the Imperial Headquarters, during which the question was discussed in detail and investigated exactly. The result is the following: The Japanese Government recognises absolutely the danger which threatens from Russia and completely understands the desire of its German ally that Japan on her part will also enter the war against Russia. However, it is not possible for the Japanese Government, considering the present war situation, to enter into the war. It is rather of the conviction that it would be in the common interest not to start the war against Russia now. On the other hand, the Japanese Government would never disregard the Russian question."

And then, in the middle of the next paragraph, this defendant returns to the attack. The third sentence - it begins on the fourth line - says:

"However, it would be more correct that all the powers, allied in the Three Power Pact, should combine their forces to defeat England and America, but also, Russia together. It is not good when one part must fight alone."

Then the pressure on Japan to attack Russia is shown again in the next document, 2929-PS, which was put in as Exhibit USA 159. And, in closing this part of the case, if I may, I will read that. It is very short.

"The Reichsminister for Foreign Affairs then stressed again that without any doubt this year presented the most favourable opportunity for Japan, if she felt strong enough and had sufficient anti-tank weapons at her disposal, to attack Russia, who certainly would never again be as weak as she is at the moment" - the moment being 18th April, 1943.

If the Tribunal please, that concludes my evidence on the second allegation dealing with aggressive war, and I submit that the allegation in the Indictment is more than amply proved.

The third allegation is that the defendant Ribbentrop authorised, directed or participated in War Crimes and Crimes against Humanity.

Of course, I am considering this from the point of view of planning these crimes only. The execution of the crimes will be dealt with by my friends, my Soviet colleagues, but it is relevant to show how this defendant participated in the planning of such crimes.

I deal, first, with the killing of Allied aviators; secondly, with the destruction of peoples in Europe; and thirdly, with the persecution of the Jews.

First, the killing of Allied aviators:

With the increasing air raids on German cities in 1944 by the Allied Air Forces, the German Government proposed to undertake a plan to deter Anglo-American fliers from further raids on the Reich cities. In a report of a meeting at which a definite policy was to be established, there is stated what was the point of view that this defendant Ribbentrop had been urging. That is in Document 735-PS, which I now put in as Exhibit GB 151. That is a discussion of a meeting at the Fuehrer's Headquarters on the 6th June, 1944. If I may, I will read the first paragraph:

"Obergruppenfuehrer Kaltenbrunner informed the Deputy Chief of W.F.S.T. in Klessheim, on the afternoon of the 6th June, that a conference on this question had been held shortly before between the Reich Marshal, the defendant Goering; the Reich Foreign Minister, the defendant von Ribbentrop; and the Reichsfuehrer S.S. Himmler. Contrary to the original suggestion made by the Reich Foreign Minister, who wished to include every type of terror attack on the German civilian population, that is, also bombing attacks on cities, it was agreed in the above conference that only strafing attacks, aimed directly at the civilian population and their property, should be taken as the standard for the evidence of a criminal action in this sense. Lynch law would have to be the rule. There was, however, no question of trial by court martial or handing over to the police."

That is to say, this defendant was pressing that even where there was an attack on a German city, the airmen should be handed over to be lynched by the crowd. The others were saying that such action should be restricted to cases where there were attacks by machine guns, and the like, on the civilian population.

I do not think we need trouble with paragraph (a) of the statement of the Deputy Chief of W.F.S.T. The importance of (a) goes because Kaltenbrunner says that there were no such cases as were mentioned.

If you look at (b):

"Deputy Chief of the W.F.S.T. mentioned that, apart from lynch law, a procedure must be worked out for segregating those enemy aviators who are suspected of criminal action of this kind, until they are received into the reception camp for aviators at Oberursel; if the suspicion were confirmed, they would be handed over to the S.D. for special treatment."

As I understand that, it means that if they were not lynched under the first scheme, by the crowd, then they were to be kept apart from prisoners of war, where they would, of course, be subject to the Protecting Powers' intervention. And if the suspicion were confirmed, they would be handed over to the S.D. to be killed.

Then, in paragraph 3, we have what was decided as justifying the lynch law. Paragraph 3 says:

"At a conference with Colonel von Brauchitsch, representing the C.-in-C., Air Force, on the 6th June, it was settled that the following actions were to be regarded as terror actions justifying lynch law:

Low-level attacks with machine-guns on the civilian population, single persons as well as crowds.

Shooting our own men in the air who had baled out.

Attacks with aircraft armament on passenger trains in the public service.

Attacks with machine-guns on military hospitals, hospitals, and hospital trains, which are clearly marked with the Red Cross."

These were to be the subject of lynching and not, as this defendant had suggested, cases where there was merely the bombing of a city.

Then on the next page, the last page of this document, We have a somewhat curious comment from the defendant Keitel:

"Remarks by the Chief of the O.K.W. on the agenda dated 6th June, 1944."

The number thereon is that of the document at which the Tribunal has just been looking.

"Most secret; Staff Officers only.

If one allows the people to carry out lynch law, it is difficult to enforce rules.

Ministerial direktor Berndt got out and shot the enemy aviator on the road. I am against legal procedure. It does not work out."

That is signed by Keitel.

Then the remarks of the defendant Jodl appear:

"This conference is insufficient. The following points must be decided quite definitely in conjunction with the Foreign Office:

1. What do we consider as murder?

Is R.R. in agreement with point 3 (b)?

2. How should the procedure be carried out?

   (a) By the people?

   (b) By the authorities?

3. How can we guarantee that the procedure be not also carried out against other enemy aviators?

4. Should some legal procedure be arranged or not?

Signed Jodl."

It is important, I respectfully submit, to note that this defendant and the Foreign Office were fully aware of these breaches of the laws and usages of war, and indeed the clarity with which the Foreign Office perceives that there were breaches of laws and usages of war is furthered by the next document-728-PS, which I now put in as Exhibit GB 152. That is a document from the Foreign Office, approved of by the defendant Ribbentrop and transmitted by one of his officials called Ritter; and the fact that it is approved by this defendant is specifically stated in the next document, 740-PS, which I put in as Exhibit GB 153. I do not think this document has been read before, and therefore, again, I would like to read just one or two passages in it. It begins:

"In spite of the obvious objections, based on International Law and foreign politics, the Foreign Office is basically in agreement with the proposed measures.

In the examination of the individual cases, a distinction must be made between the cases of lynching and the cases of special treatment by the Security Service (S.D.).

1. In the cases of lynching, the precise establishment of the circumstances deserving punishment, according to points 1-4 of the communication of 15th June, is not very essential. First, the German authorities are not directly responsible, since death will have occurred before a German official became concerned with the case. Furthermore, the accompanying circumstances will be such that it will not be difficult to depict the case in an appropriate manner upon publication. Hence, in cases of lynching, it will be of primary importance correctly to handle the individual cases upon publication.

2. The suggested procedure for special treatment by the S.D. (Security Service), including subsequent publication, would be tenable only if Germany, on this occasion, would openly at the time repudiate the commitments of International Law, presently in force, and still recognised by Germany. When an enemy aviator is seized by the Army or by the Police, and is delivered to the Air Forces (P.W.) Reception Camp, Oberursel, he has received, by this very fact, the legal status of a prisoner of war.

The Prisoner of War Agreement of 27th July, 1929, establishes definite rules on the prosecution and sentencing of prisoners of war, and the execution of the death penalty, as for example in Article 66: Death sentences may be carried out only three months after the Protective Power has been notified of the sentence; in Article 63: A prisoner of war will be tried only by the same courts and under the same procedure as members of the German armed forces. These rules are so specific that it would be futile to try to cover up any violation of them by clever wording of the publication of an individual incident. On the other hand, the Foreign Office cannot recommend, on this occasion, a formal repudiation of the Prisoner of War Agreement.

An emergency solution would be to prevent suspected fliers from ever attaining a legal prisoner of war status; that is, that immediately upon seizure they be told that they are not considered prisoners of war, but criminals, that they would not be turned over to the agencies having jurisdiction over prisoners of war; that, therefore, they would not go to a prisoner of war camp; but that they would be tried in a summary procedure. If the evidence at the trial should reveal that the special procedure is not applicable to a particular case, the fliers concerned may subsequently be given the status of prisoner of war by transfer to the Air Forces (P.W.) Reception Camp, Oberursel.

Naturally, not even this expedient will prevent the possibility of Germany being accused of the violation of existing treaties or even the adoption of reprisals upon German prisoners of war. At any rate, this solution would enable us clearly to define our attitude, thus relieving us of the necessity of openly having to renounce the present agreements or of the need of having to use excuses, which no one would believe, upon the publication of each individual case."

I do not want to take this in detail, but I ask the Tribunal to look at the first sentence of Section 3:

"It follows from the above that the main weight of the action will have to be placed on lynchings. Should the campaign be carried out to such an extent that the purpose, to wit: 'the deterrence of enemy aviators,' is actually achieved, which goal is favoured by the Foreign Office, then the strafing attacks by enemy fliers upon the civilian populations must be stressed in a completely different propagandist manner."

I do not think I need trouble the Tribunal, but that shows quite clearly the defendant's point of view. If the Tribunal would look at the next document, it is stated at the beginning of the second paragraph:

"Ambassador Ritter has advised us by telephone on 29th June that the Minister for Foreign Affairs has approved this draft."

That is the position as to the treatment of aviators, where there is, in my suggestion, a completely cold-blooded and deliberate adoption of a procedure evading International Law.

The second section is the destruction of the peoples in Europe. With regard to Poland, again I will not go into details, but I remind the Tribunal of the evidence of the witness Lahousen (Pages 275-6, Part 1), and his cross- examination on the 1st December (Pages 318-20, Part 1).

Secondly, Bohemia and Moravia: on the 16th March, 1939, there was promulgated the decree of the Fuehrer and Reichschancellor, signed by Ribbentrop, concerning the Protectorate of Bohemia and Moravia. That is already in as Exhibit GB 8 - Document TC-51. The effect of that was to place the Reich Protector in a remarkable position of supremacy under the Fuehrer. The only part which I would like the Tribunal to have in mind is Article 5, and sub- Article 2:

"It shall be the duty of the Reich Protector, as representative of the Fuehrer and Chancellor of the Reich, and as Commissioner of the Reich Government, to see to the observance of the political principles laid down by the Fuehrer and Chancellor of the Reich.

3. The members of the government of the protectorate shall be confirmed by the Reich Protector. The confirmation may be withdrawn.

4. The Reich Protector is entitled to inform himself of all measures taken by the government of the protectorate and to give advice. He can object to measures calculated to harm the Reich, and, in case of danger, issue ordinances required for the common interest.

5. The promulgation of laws, etc., and the execution of administrative measures and valid sentences are to be suspended if the Reich Protector raises an objection."

As a result of this law, the two Reich Protectors of Bohemia and Moravia, and their various deputies, were appointed, and then there were committed the various crimes, which will be detailed by my Soviet colleague.

Similarly, with regard to the Netherlands, on the 8th May, 1940, a decree of the Fuehrer was signed by Ribbentrop concerning the exercise of governmental authority in the Netherlands; and that is Document D-639, which I put in as Exhibit GB 154, Section 1 says:

"The occupied Netherlands territories will be administered by the 'Reich Commissioner for the Occupied Netherlands Territories' ... the Reich Commissioner is guardian of the interests of the Reich and vested with supreme civil authority.

Dr. Artur Seyss-Inquart is hereby appointed Reich Commissioner for the Occupied Netherlands Territories."

On the basis of this decree, the Reich Commissioner - the defendant Seyss-Inquart - promulgated such orders as that of the 4th July, 1940, dealing with the confiscation of property of those who had, or might have furthered activities hostile to the German Reich, and tentative arrangements were made for the resettlement of the Dutch population. This will be dealt with fully by my French colleague.

I simply, for the moment, put in as a matter of reference the general order of the defendant Seyss-Inquart, which is Exhibit GB 155, the document being 2921-PS. I do not intend to read it. I have summarised the effect of it, and it will be dealt with more fully by my French colleagues.

I want the Tribunal to appreciate, with regard to these two matters of Bohemia and the Netherlands, that the charge against this defendant is laying the basis and procuring the governmental structure under which the War Crimes and Crimes against Humanity were directed.

I also formally put in Exhibit GB 156, the discussion on the question of the Dutch population, which is contained in Document 1520-PS. Again, I have explained it generally and I do not want to occupy time by reading it in full now.

Finally, I come to the persecution of the Jews. In December, 1938, the defendant Ribbentrop, in a conversation with M. Bonnet, who was then Foreign Minister of France, expressed his opinion of the Jews. That was reported by the United States Ambassador, Mr. Kennedy, to the State Department. The report of Mr. Kennedy is Document L-205, which I now put in as Exhibit GB 157. If I might read to the Tribunal the second paragraph which concerns this point:

"During the day we had a telephone call from Berenger's office in Paris. We were told that the matter of refugees had been raised by Bonnet in his conversation with von Ribbentrop. The result was very bad. Ribbentrop, when pressed, had said to Bonnet that the Jews in Germany, without exception, were pickpockets, murderers and thieves. The property they possessed had been acquired illegally. The German Government had therefore decided to treat them as the criminal elements of the population. The property which they had acquired illegally would be taken from them. They would be forced to live in the districts of the criminal classes. They would be under police observation like other criminals. They would be forced to report to the police as other criminals were obliged to do. The German Government could not help it if some of these criminals escaped to other countries which seemed so anxious to have them. It was not, however, willing to let them take along with them the property which they had acquired through illegal operations. There was in fact nothing that it could or would do."

That succinct statement of this defendant's views on Jews is elaborated in a long document which he had sent out by the Foreign Office, which is numbered 3358-PS, which I put in as Exhibit GB 158. I do not want to read the whole of that document because it is excessively dreary. It is also an excessively clear indication of the defendant's views on the treatment of Jews; but if the Tribunal would look at, first of all, Page 3, it is headed, "The Jewish Question as a Factor in German Foreign Policy in the year 1938." After the four divisions the document goes on to say:

"It is certainly no coincidence that the fateful year 1938 has brought nearer the solution of the Jewish question, simultaneously with the realisation of the 'idea of Greater Germany,' since the Jewish policy was both the basis and consequence of the events of the year 1938."

That is elaborated. If the Tribunal will turn over to Page 4 at the beginning of the second paragraph, it will see the first sentence:

> "The final goal of German-Jewish policy is the emigration of an Jews living in Reich territory."

Then that is developed at great length through a large number of pages. If the Tribunal would turn to the foot of Page 7, it goes on to say:

> "These examples from reports from authorities abroad can, if desired, be amplified. They confirm the correctness of the expectation, that criticism of the measures for excluding Jews from German Lebensraum, which were misunderstood in many countries for lack of evidence, would only be temporary and would swing in the other direction the moment the population saw with its own eyes and thus learned, what the Jewish danger was to them. The poorer, and therefore the more burdensome the immigrant Jew becomes to the country absorbing him, the more strongly that country will react, and the more desirable is this effect in the interest of German propaganda. The object of this German action is the future international solution of the Jewish question, dictated not by false compassion for the 'United Religious Jewish minority' but by the full consciousness of all peoples of the danger which it represents to the racial composition of the nations."

The Tribunal will appreciate that this document was circulated by the defendant's ministry, widely circulated to all senior Reich authorities and to numerous people before the war, on the 25th January, 1939, just after the statement to M. Bonnet. Apparently the anti-Semitism of the defendant went from - I was going to say from strength to strength, at any rate from exaggeration to exaggeration, for in June, 1944, the defendant Rosenberg made arrangements for an international anti-Jewish Congress to be held in Cracow on the 11th July, 1944. The honorary members were to be von Ribbentrop, Himmler, Goebbels and Frank - I think the defendant Frank. The Foreign Office was to take over the mission of inviting prominent foreigners from Italy, France, Hungary, Holland, Arabia, Iraq, Norway, etc., in order to give an international aspect to the Congress. However, the military events of June, 1944, prompted Hitler to call off the Congress, which had lost its significance by virtue of the Allied landing in Normandy.

That is contained in Document 1752-PS, Exhibit GB 159. At the foot of Page 1, the Tribunal will see the following has been entered as an honorary member - Reich Foreign Minister Joachim von Ribbentrop. So that there is no doubt that this defendant was behind the programme against the Jews, which resulted in the placing of them in concentration camps with anyone else opposed to the Nazi way of life, and it is submitted that he must, as a minister in special touch with the head of the government, have known what was going on in the country and in the camps. One who preached this doctrine, and was in a position of authority, cannot, I submit to anyone who has had any material experience, suggest that he was ignorant of how the policy was carried out.

That is the evidence on the third allegation and I submit, by the evidence which I have recapitulated to the Tribunal, that the three allegations are proved.

With regard to the second, Hitler's own words were:

> "In the historic year of 1938 the Foreign Minister, von Ribbentrop, was of great help to me, in view of his accurate and audacious judgement and the exceptionally clever treatment of all problems of foreign policy."

During the course of the war, this defendant was in close liaison with the other

Nazi conspirators. He advised them and made available to them, in his foreign embassies and legations abroad, information which was required; and at times participated, as I had shown, in the planning of War Crimes and Crimes against Humanity.

It is submitted that all the allegations which were read from Appendix A of the Indictment are completely proved against this defendant. I only wanted the Tribunal to allow me to add one fact on behalf of the British delegation. In the preparation of these briefs we have received great assistance from certain of our American colleagues, and I should like to thank once, but nevertheless, heartily, on behalf of all of us, Dr. Kempner's staff: Captain John W. Auchineloss, Lieutenants Richard Heller and Frederick Felton, Captain J. Robert Claggett, Captain Norman Stoll, and Mr. Karl Lachmann for the great help they have been to us.

THE PRESIDENT: We will adjourn now for ten minutes.

DR. SEIDL (Counsel for the defendant Frank): May it please the Tribunal, I have a motion to make.

THE PRESIDENT: On behalf of whom is your motion?

DR. SEIDL: I want to make a motion which concerns the indictment of Frank by the prosecution. The Charter of the Tribunal contains, in Part IV, regulations for a fair trial, and Article 16 determines that for the purpose of guarding the right of the defendants the following procedure shall be followed. "The Indictment shall include full particulars specifying in detail the charges against the defendants. A copy of the Indictment and of all the documents lodged with the Indictment, translated into a language which he understands, shall be furnished to the defendant at a reasonable time before the trial."

At the beginning of the trial the defendant Frank was handed a copy of the Indictment. This is the Indictment which was read on the first day. This is, if I may say so, a general Indictment. All actions are listed therein which, according to the opinion of the Signatories of the London Agreement, are regarded as Crimes against Peace, War Crimes and Crimes against Humanity. The Indictment does not contain in particular the criminal actions of each defendant. I am now thinking about positive actions, or concrete actions, or omissions.

This morning I received a document. It has the title "The Individual Responsibility of the defendant Hans Frank for Crimes against the Peace, War Crimes and Crimes against Humanity" - or in German "die personliche Verantwortung des Angcklagten Frank fur Verbrechen gegen den Frieden, fur Kriegsverbrechen und Verbrechen gegen die Humanitat." This document is without any table of contents. It consists of 30 typewritten pages. In addition to this document, or Indictment, as I should like to call it, another document book has been given to me; this book here concerning Hans Frank. The first document, as well as the second document, are not in German but in English. This first document is in reality what I should call the Indictment against Frank, because here in this document of 30 pages, for the first time, are listed those individual activities of Frank which are to be regarded as criminal actions. At least one ought to say that this document is an essential part of the Indictment.

THE PRESIDENT: Interrupting you, the Tribunal has already expressed its desire that a motion such as this should be made in writing. The Tribunal considers that a motion of the sort which you are making, if made orally, is a waste of the Tribunal's time. It therefore desires you to put your motion in writing. It will then be considered.

DR. SEIDL: I regret that I had to make this motion now, but I was not able to make it in writing beforehand, having received this document only two and a half hours ago. My motion asks the prosecution that these two documents be given to the defendant Frank in the German language.

THE PRESIDENT: The Tribunal has not got the documents to which you are referring, but it is quite impossible for us to understand the motion you making unless you make it in writing and attach the documents or in some other way describe or explain to us what the documents are. We have not the documents that you are referring to.

DR. SEIDL: Then I shall make my motion in writing.

THE PRESIDENT: Mr. Roberts, can you explain to me what counsel who just spoke is complaining about?

MR. ROBERTS: I gather he was complaining that the trial brief and the document book which had been served on his client, Frank, were in English and not in German.

THE PRESIDENT: Who is dealing with the case against Frank?

MR. ROBERTS: It is being dealt with by the United States.

THE PRESIDENT: Perhaps I had better ask Colonel Storey, then.

COLONEL STOREY: If the Tribunal please, I think what counsel is referring to is the practice we have made of delivering in advance a copy of the document book and a copy of the trial brief. In this particular instance I happen to know that what counsel refers to is the trial address, which is to be read over the microphone, and as a courtesy to defence counsel, copies have been delivered in advance of the presentation, just like the other document books and briefs against the other individual defendants. That is what it is, as I understand it.

THE PRESIDENT: The documents which will be presented against the defendant Frank will be all translated?

COLONEL STOREY: I am sure they will, yes, Sit. I do not know about the individual case, but the instructions are that, as to the documents there will be photostats, each one in German, plus the English translation, for counsel, and that is what has been delivered, plus the trial address, if your Honour pleases. We handed that material to him in advance, it is what the attorney will read over the microphone.

THE PRESIDENT: Colonel Storey, I thought the Tribunal ordered, after consulting the prosecutors as to the feasibility of the scheme, that sufficient translators should be supplied to the defendant's counsel so that such documents, if in the English language, as trial briefs, might be translated to defendant's counsel. You will remember it was suggested that at least four translators, I think, should be supplied to the defendant's counsel.

COLONEL STOREY: If the Tribunal will recall, I think this is what was finally determined; that document books and briefs could be submitted in English and the photostatic copies submitted to defendant's counsel, and that if they wanted additional copies of the German, then they should request them and they would be furnished. I think that is what the final order was.

THE PRESIDENT: There was, at any rate, a suggestion that translators should be ordered to translate such documents as trial briefs.

COLONEL STOREY: That is correct, yes, Sir, and whenever counsel wanted more copies they would request them, and they would be available for them. The translators, for translation of the photostats, would be available if they requested them. Were there any other questions, your Honour?

THE PRESIDENT: Do you mean that translators have not been supplied to defendant's counsel?

COLONEL STOREY: If your Honour pleases, as I understand it, the defendants' Information Centre is now under the jurisdiction of the Tribunal, and my information is - I would like to check it - that when they want extra copies all they have to do is ask for them and they may obtain them, and sufficient translators are available to provide the extra copies if they want them. That is my information. I have not checked it in the last few days, but sufficient copies in English are furnished for all counsel, and these briefs and document books are furnished to them in advance. In this case I am told that the document book and the briefs were furnished.

THE PRESIDENT: Yes.

DR. FRITZ SAUTER (Counsel for defendants Ribbentrop, Funk and von Schirach):

Your Honour, you may be assured that we defence counsel do not like to take up the time of the Tribunal for discussions such as these, which we ourselves would rather avoid. But the question just raised by a colleague of mine is really very unpleasant for us and makes our work extremely difficult.

You see, it does not help us if after agreements are made or regulations issued, the actual practice is entirely different.

Last night, for example, we received a big volume of documents, all documents being in English. Now, in the evening, in prison, we are supposed to discuss with our clients for hours the result of the proceedings - a difficulty which has now been greatly augmented by the installation of wire screens in the consultation room. In addition, we are also required to talk over, volume by volume, documents written in English; and that is practically impossible. One does not receive these documents until the evening of the day before, and it is not possible, even for one who knows English well, to make the necessary preparation.

The same thing is true of the individual accusations, and I do not know whether these individual accusations, as we receive them for each defendant, have also been submitted to the Tribunal.

THE PRESIDENT: Nearly every document which has been referred to in this branch of the case, which has been presented by Mr. Albrecht and by Sir David Maxwell Fyfe, is a document which has been referred to previously in the trial and which must have been before the defendant's counsel for many days, for weeks, and therefore there can be no lack of familiarity with those documents.

Documents which have been referred to, which are fresh documents, are very few indeed and the passages in them, which are now being put in evidence, are all read over the microphone and, therefore, are heard by defendant's counsel in German, and can be studied by German counsel to-morrow morning in the transcript of the shorthand notes. I do not see, therefore, what hardship is being imposed upon German counsel by the method which is being adopted.

You see, the counsel for the prosecution, out of courtesy to counsel for the defendants, have been giving them their trial briefs in English beforehand. But there is no strict obligation to do that and, in so far as the actual evidence is concerned, all of which is contained in documents, as I have already pointed out to you, the vast majority of these documents have already been put in many days ago and have been in the hands of German counsel ever since, in the German language, and also the documents which are now put in.

DR. SAUTER: No, this is not true, your Honour. This is the complaint which we of the defence counsel, since we dislike to approach the Tribunal with such complaints, have been discussing among ourselves, the complaint that we do not receive the German documents. You may be assured, Mr. President, that if things were as you believe, none of us would complain but would all be very grateful; but in reality it is different.

THE PRESIDENT: Dr. Sauter, surely, when you have a reference to a German document, that German document is available to you in the Information Centre. As these documents have been put in evidence, some of them as long ago as the 20th November or shortly thereafter, surely there must have been adequate time for defendant's counsel to study them.

DR. SAUTER: For instance, this morning I received a volume on Funk. I have no idea when this volume will be presented in court - to-day or to-morrow. It is completely impossible for me to study this volume of English documents upon my return from the prison at nine or ten in the evening. That overtaxes the physical strength of a defence counsel. I could study it if it were in German, but even so it is impossible for me to do so until nine or ten in the evening as I have to make a visit to the prison. It is absolutely impossible for us.

THE PRESIDENT: You see, Dr. Sauter, it is not as though you have to cross-examine witnesses immediately after the evidence is given. The documents are put in and it is not for you to get up and argue upon the interpretation of those documents. You will have, I regret to say, a considerable time before you will have to get up and call your own evidence and ultimately to argue upon the documents which are now being put in. Therefore, it is not a question of hours, it is a question of days and weeks before you will have to deal with these documents which are now being put in. And I really do not see that there is any hardship upon defendant's counsel in the system which is being adopted.

And you will not forget that the rule, which, in a sense, penalises the prosecution, is that every document which is put in evidence and every part of the document which is put in evidence, has got to be read in open Court, in order that it should be translated over the earphones and then shall get into the shorthand notes. I am told that the shorthand notes are not available in German the next morning but are only available some days afterwards. But they are ultimately available in German. And, therefore, every defendant's counsel must have a complete copy of the shorthand notes, at any rate up to the recess, and that contains all the evidence that has been given against the defendants, and it contains it in German.

DR. SAUTER: Yes, Mr. President, that which is most dear to us is what we have already asked for many weeks: that the documents, or at least those parts of the documents read, should be given to us in German translation. It is very difficult for us, even if we know English, to translate the documents in the time which is at our disposal. It is impossible for any of us to do this. That is the reason we regret that our wish to get the documents in German is not being taken into consideration. We are conscious of the difficulties and we are very grateful for any assistance given. Be convinced we are very sorry to have to make such requests, but the actual circumstances are very difficult for us. The last word I wish to say is that the conditions are really very difficult for us.

THE PRESIDENT: Dr. Sauter, I am most anxious and the other members of the Tribunal are most anxious that every reasonable facility should be afforded to the defendants and their counsel. But, as I have pointed out to you, it is not necessary for you, for any of you, at the present moment, to get up and argue upon these documents which are now being put in. By the time that you have to get up and argue upon the documents which are now being put in, you will have had ample time in which to consider them in German.

DR. SAUTER: Thank you, Sir.

DR. BOEHM (Counsel for the S.A.): I have repeatedly asked to receive copies of everything presented in English. After the accusation against the S.A. on the 18th or the 19th December, 1945, had already been presented and a document book had been presented as evidence at this time, I received to-day a few photostats, but I have not received most of the photostats or other pertinent translations. This shows that we do not receive the translations right after the court presentation. It shows further that one can never read the session minutes on the next day or on the day after that. The minutes of the last session ...

THE PRESIDENT: We are not dealing with the S.A. or the organisations at the present moment. If you have any motion to make, you will kindly make it in writing and we will now proceed with the part of the trial with which we are dealing.

DR. BOEHM: Mr. President, will you permit me one more remark? The minutes of 17th and 18th December, 1945, I have received only to-day.

THE PRESIDENT: Do you mean the transcript?

DR. BOEHM: The German transcript for the 18th and 19th December, 1945, I have received only to-day. You see, it is not a fact that we receive the transcript the day after or only a few days after the session. I received it weeks later, after I asked for it repeatedly. I asked the appropriate offices repeatedly to give me a copy of the document book in German, but I have not got it yet.

THE PRESIDENT: We will inquire into that. One moment. Will the last counsel who was speaking stand up?

I am told that is a special case; that the reason for the delay in the case you have mentioned was that there had been an error in the paging and, therefore, the transcripts of those shorthand notes had to be recopied. I understand that the delay ordinarily is not anything like so long as this.

DR. BOEHM: But I hardly believe that, in so far as the translation of the document book is concerned, this delay is due to those reasons. But even if the delay in this particular case should be justified, it would hamper my defence from week to week. I do not know on the day before what is going to be presented and I do not know for weeks afterwards what has been presented. I am therefore not in a position to study the evidence from the standpoint of the defence counsellor. I do not even know what is contained in the document book. According to the procedure of the trial the evidence should be presented in time. This is, apparently, not the case.

THE PRESIDENT: Perhaps you will kindly make your complaint in writing and give the particulars of it. Do you understand that?

DR. BOEHM: Yes.

THE PRESIDENT: Very well.

MR. ROBERTS: May it please the Tribunal:

It is my duty to present the evidence against Keitel and also against the defendant Jodl, and I would ask the Tribunal's permission, if it is thought right, that those two cases should be presented together in the interests of saving time, a matter which I know we all have at heart.

The story with regard to Keitel and Jodl runs on parallel lines. For the years in question they marched down the same road together. Most of the documents affect them both and, in those circumstances, I submit, it might result in a substantial saving of time if I were permitted to present the case against both of them together.

THE PRESIDENT: Yes.

MR. ROBERTS: Then I shall proceed, if I may, on that basis.

My Lords, may I say, that I fully recognise that the activities of both these defendants have been referred to in detail many times, and quite recently by Colonel Telford Taylor, and my earnest desire is to avoid repetition as far as I possibly can. And may I say, I welcome any suggestions, as I travel the road, which the Tribunal have to offer, to make my presentation still shorter.

There is a substantial document book, document book, number 7, which is a joint document book, dealing with both the defendants. Practically all the documents in that book have already been referred to. They nearly all, of course, have a German origin. I propose to read passages from only nine new documents, and those nine documents, I think, are shown in your Lordship's bundle and in the bundles of your colleagues.

May I commence by referring, as shortly as may be, to the part of the Indictment which deals with the two defendants. That will be found on Page 33 of the English translation. It begins with "Keitel" in the middle of the page, and it says:

"The defendant Keitel between 1938 and 1945 was -" the holder of various offices. I only want to point out there, that although the commencing date is 1938, the prosecution rely on certain activities of the defendant Keitel before 1938, and we submit that we are entitled so to do because of the general words appearing on Page 28 of the Indictment, at the head of the Appendix:

> "The statements hereinafter set forth, following the name of each individual defendant, constitute matters upon which the prosecution will rely, *inter alia*, as establishing their responsibility:"

And then the Tribunal will see: "Keitel used the foregoing positions, his personal influence and his intimate connection with the Fuehrer in such a manner that: he promoted the military preparations for war set forth in Count One of the Indictment" - if I may read it shortly - he participated in the planning and preparation for Wars of Aggression and in Violation of Treaties; he executed the plans for Wars of Aggression and Wars in Violation of Treaties and he authorised and participated in War Crimes and Crimes against Humanity.

Then the defendant Jodl between 1932 and 1945 was the holder of various positions. He "used the foregoing positions, his personal influence, and his close connection with the Fuehrer in such a manner" - and this is not to be found in the text relating to Keitel - "that he promoted the accession to power of the Nazi conspirators and the consolidation of their control over Germany - "

May I say, my Lords, here, that I know of no evidence at the moment to support that allegation that he promoted the Nazi rise to power before 1933. There is plenty of evidence that he was a devoted, almost a fanatical admirer of the Fuehrer, but that, I apprehend, would not be enough.

And then it is alleged against Jodl that he promoted the preparations for war; he participated in the planning and preparation of the war; and that he authorised and participated in War Crimes and Crimes against Humanity.

My Lords, with regard to the position of the defendant Keitel, it is well-known that in February of 1938 he became Chief of the O.K.W., Supreme Commander of all the Armed Forces, and that Jodl became Chief of the Operations Staff, and that is copiously proved, in the shorthand notes, on the documents. Perhaps I ought to refer to his position in 1935, at the time when the reoccupation of the Rhineland was first envisaged. Keitel was head of the Wehrmachtsamt in the Reich War Ministry, and that is proved by a document, 3019-PS, which is to be found in "Das Archiv," and I ask the Court to take judicial notice of that. It is not in the bundle.

Jodl's positions have been proved by his own statement, Document 2865-PS, which is also Exhibit USA 16, and in 1935 he held the rank of Lieutenant Colonel, Chief of the Operations Department of the Landesverteidigung.

May I just refer to the pre-1938 period - that is the pre- O.K.W. period - and to two documents, one of which is new. The first document I desire to mention without reading is 177-EC. I do not want to read it. It is Exhibit USA 390. My Lords, those are the minutes, shortly after the Nazi rise to power, of the Working Committee of the Delegates for Reich Defence. The date is the 22nd May, 1933. Keitel presided at that meeting. The minutes have been read. There is a long discussion as to the preliminary steps for putting Germany on a war footing. Keitel regarded the task as most urgent, as so little had been done in previous years, and perhaps the Tribunal will remember the most striking passage where Keitel impressed the need for secrecy, "documents must not be lost, oral statements can be denied at Geneva."

And I will submit, if I may be allowed to make this short comment, that it is interesting to see in those very early days of 1933, that the Heads of the Armed Forces of Germany concentrated upon using lies as a weapon.

My Lord, the next document I desire to refer to is a new one, and it is EC-405, Exhibit GB 160. I desire to refer to this shortly, because in my submission it shows Jodl to have had knowledge of and complicity in the plan to reoccupy the Rhineland country, contrary to the Versailles Treaty. The Tribunal will see that these are the minutes of the Working Committee of the Reich Defence Council, dated the 26th June, 1935.

The Court will see that, a quarter of the way down the page, in subparagraph (F), Lt.-Colonel Jodl gives a dissertation on mobilisation preparation, and it is only the fourth and fifth paragraphs on that same page that I desire to read:

> "The demilitarised zone requires special treatment. In his speech of the 21st May and other utterances, the Fuehrer has stated that the stipulations of the Versailles Treaty and the Locarno Pact regarding the demilitarised zone are being observed. To the Aide Memoire of the French Charge d'affaires on recruiting offices in the demilitarised zone, the Reich Government has replied that neither civilian recruiting authorities nor other offices in the demilitarised zone have been entrusted with mobilisation talks, such as the raising, equipping and arming of any kind of formations for the event of war, or in preparation therefore.
>
> Since political entanglements abroad must be avoided at present" - I stress the "at present" - "under all circumstances, only those preparatory measures that are urgently necessary may be carried out. The existence of such preparations or the intention of them must be kept in strictest secrecy in the zone itself as well as in the rest of the Reich."

My Lord, I need not read more. I submit that this clearly shows Jodl to have had knowledge of the forthcoming breach of Versailles.

My Lord, the day before the Rhineland was reoccupied on the 7th March, 1936, the defendant Keitel issued the directive which has been read before, Document C-194, Exhibit USA 55, ordering an air reconnaissance and certain U-boat movements in case any other nation attempted to interfere with that if reoccupation.

My Lords I pass now to the 4th February, 1938, when the O.K.W. was formed. Shortly after its formation there was issued a handbook which is a new exhibit, from which I want to read short passages. The number of the document is L-211. It is GB 161.

Now, this is dated 19th April, 1938, "Top Secret for Commanders only. Direction of War as a Problem of Organisation." I read only from the appendix which is entitled, "What is the War of the Future?" and if the Court will kindly turn over to the second page, I am going to read 12 lines from the bottom of the page, the line beginning "Surprise."

"Surprise which must be the premise for quick initial success will often require hostilities to begin before mobilisation has been completed or the armies are fully in position.

A declaration of war is no longer necessarily the first step at the start of a war.

The normal rules of war towards neutral nations may be considered to apply only on the basis of whether the operation of these rules will create greater advantages or disadvantages for the warring nation."

It may, of course, be said that those were only theoretical words and they might apply to any other nation who might be minded to make war on Germany. The Court can use its judicial notice of the conditions of things in Europe in 1938 and ask itself whether Germany had any potential aggressor against her.

But, my Lord, I emphasise that passage because I submit it so clearly envisages exactly the way in which Germany did make war in 1939 and in the subsequent years.

My Lord, I now start to tread the road which has been trodden many times already, and which will be trodden so many times again, the road from 1938 and 1941 to the final act of aggression. But I believe that I can treat this period, so far as Keitel and Jodl are concerned, in a very few sentences because I submit that the documents which are already in, which have been read and re-read into the record, demonstrate quite clearly that Keitel, as would only be expected, he being Chief of the Supreme Command of all the Armed Forces, and Jodl, as would only be expected also, he being Chief of the Operations Staff, were vitally and intimately concerned with every single act of aggression which took place successively against the various victims of Nazi aggression.

My Lord, you should have in front of you the document book and the trial brief in which those documents are set out under the heading. If I might take first the aggression against Austria, your Lordship will remember in Jodl's diary on the 12th February, 1938, how Keitel, who was something more than a mere soldier, put heavy pressure upon Schuschnigg - that is Document 1780-PS, Jodl's diary-how on the following day, Keitel wrote to Hitler - Document 1775- PS, Exhibit USA 73 - suggesting the shamming of military action and the spreading of false but quite credible news.

Then, the actual operation orders for Operation Otto, Exhibits USA 74, 75 and 77, all of the 11th March, 1938, are O.K.W. orders for which Keitel is responsible.

THE PRESIDENT: What are the numbers of them?

MR. ROBERTS: My Lord, C-102, C-103 and C-182. One of them is actually signed or initialled by Keitel, and two are initialled by Jodl. Those are the operation orders for the advance into Austria, the injunction, if the Tribunal remembers, to treat Czech soldiers as hostile and to treat the Italians as friends.

My Lord, that is the first milestone on the road, the occupation of Austria. The second is, is it not -

THE PRESIDENT: Well, perhaps if you are going on to another, we had better adjourn now until two o'clock.

(A recess was taken until 14.00 hours.)

MR. ROBERTS: May it please the Tribunal: I had got to the commencement of the aggression against Czechoslovakia, and the Tribunal will remember that the leading exhibit on that matter is the file 388-PS, USA 26, the "Fall Grun" file. My Lords, that file, in my submission, contains copious evidence against both Keitel and

Jodl, showing that they were doing the normal work of the Chief of the Supreme Command of the Armed Forces and the head of the Operations Staff.

May I remind the Tribunal of Item 2 - I do not want to read any of it. I might just refer to the notes of a meeting on the 21st April, 1938. The important thing to notice is that Keitel and the Fuehrer met alone, showing the intimate connection between the two. And it was at that meeting that preliminary plans were discussed, including the possibility of an incident, namely, the murder of the German Ambassador at Prague.

Item 5 in that file, dated the 20th May, 1938, shows the plans for the political and the military campaign against Czechoslovakia, issued by Keitel.

Item 11, dated the 30th May, 1938, is the directive signed by Keitel for the invasion of Czechoslovakia, with the date given as the 1st October, 1938.

There are many items which are initialled by Jodl; Item 14 and Item 17, to mention only two.

Perhaps, for the purposes of the note, I should mention the others, Items 24, 36 and 37.

There is the directive, Items 31 and 32, dated 27th September, 1938, signed by Keitel, enclosing orders for secret mobilisation.

Jodl's diary, 1780-PS, contains many references to the forthcoming aggression, particularly the 13th May and the 8th September, and there is a very revealing entry on the 11th September in Jodl's diary - Document 1780-PS-in which he says:

"In the afternoon, conference with the Secretary of State."

THE PRESIDENT: Will you give us the date?

MR. ROBERTS: I beg your Lordship's pardon; 11th September, 1938.

"In the afternoon, conference with Secretary of State Jahnke, from the Ministry of Public Enlightenment and Propaganda, on the imminent common tasks. The joint preparations for refutation of our own violations of International Law and the exploitation of its violations by the enemy were considered particularly important."

I emphasise those words, "our own violations of International Law."

My Lord, as a result of that conference, the Document C-2, which was referred to by my learned leader, Sir David, was prepared, which the Tribunal win remember has in parallel columns the possible breach of International Law and the excuse which is then going to be given for it. It was referred to so recently that I need not refer to it again.

My Lord, I respectfully submit, on that branch of the matter, that there is an overwhelming case that Keitel and Jodl played an important, indeed, a vital part, in the aggression against Czechoslovakia, which led up to the Pact of Munich.

After the Pact of Munich was signed, as has been pointed out many times, the Nazi conspirators at once set about preparations for annexing the remainder of Czechoslovakia.

My Lord, at this point Jodl disappears from the scene for a time, because he goes to do some regimental soldiering as artillery general in Austria-artillery general of the 44th Division - and so it cannot be said that there is any evidence against him from the Munich Pact until the 23rd August, 1939, when be is recalled on the eve of the Polish invasion to take up his duties once more as Chief of the Operational Staff of O.K.W.

So far as Keitel is concerned, on the 21st October, 1938, less than a month after the Munich Pact, he countersigned Hitler's order to liquidate the rest of Czechoslovakia and to occupy Memel - Document C-136, Exhibit USA 104.

On the 24th November, 1938, Document C-137, Exhibit GB 33,. Keitel issued a memorandum about the surprise occupation of Danzig.

On the 17th December, 1939, Document C-138, Exhibit USA 105, he signed an order to the lower formations, "prepare for the liquidation of Czechoslovakia." These preparations were made.

On the 15th March, 1939, Keitel, who, I again repeat, was more than a mere soldier, was present at the midnight conference between the Fuehrer and Hacha, President of Czechoslovakia, when, under a threat of Prague being bombed, Hacha surrendered the rest of his country to the Germans. I refrain from referring to the contents of the minutes, which have been read many times already.

My Lord, so that milestone is past! And again I submit, in all that aggression, it is clear that Keitel was playing a vital part as Hitler's right-hand man, commanding all the Armed Forces under him.

I now pass to the Polish aggression. Keitel was present at the meeting at the Chancellery on 23rd May, 1939, Document L- 79, Exhibit USA 27, when it was said, quoting just a few words, so familiar: that Danzig was not the subject of the dispute; Poland was to be attacked at the first suitable opportunity; Dutch and Belgian air bases must be occupied; declarations of neutrality were to be ignored.

The directive for "Fall Weiss," the invasion of Poland, is Document C-120A, Exhibit GB 41. The date is the 3rd April, 1939. The Tribunal will remember, the plans were to be submitted to O.K.W. by the 1st May, and the forces were to be ready for invasion by the 1st September. And that directive is signed by Keitel.

Document C-126, Exhibit GB 45, is a follow-up of that previous directive, It is dated the 22nd June, 1939. The need for camouflage is emphasised, and it is stated: "Do not disquiet the population." That is signed by Keitel.

On the 17th August, 1939 - Document 795-PS, Exhibit GB 54 - Keitel had a conference with Admiral Canaris about the supplying of Polish uniforms to Heydrich, and it will be noticed in the last paragraph of the note that Admiral Canaris was against the war, and Keitel argued in favour of it. And Keitel made the prophecy that Great Britain would not enter the war.

I submit that Keitel's vital part, again, in the preparation for the aggression against Poland, is clearly established beyond the possibility of dispute.

Jodl, as I have said to the Tribunal, was recalled on the 23rd August, as seen in his diary entry, 1780-PS, where he says that he is recalled to take charge of the Operations Staff. He says:

"Received order from Armed Forces High Command to proceed to Berlin and take over position of Chief of Armed Forces Executive Office."

And then:

"11.00 hours to 13.30 hours - discussion with Chief of Armed Forces High Command. X-Day has been announced for the 26th August. Y-Time has been announced for 04.30 hours."

And I submit that the Tribunal can infer the importance of Jodl to this conspiracy from the fact that on the eve of the war he is recalled to Berlin to take his place at the head of the Operational Staff of the Supreme Command.

So Poland was invaded, and before I pass to the next aggression may I just point out that, according to the evidence of General Lahousen, if the Tribunal accepts it on this point, Keitel and Jodl were in the field with Hitler on the 10th September, 1939. That is in the shorthand note (Pages 274-275, Part 1). I do not suppose there will be any dispute that the head of the High Command and the Chief of his Operation Staff were in the field.

My Lord, I pass now to Norway and Denmark. So far as both are concerned, we see from Document C-54, Exhibit GB 86, that on the 12th December, 1939, Keitel and Jodl were both present at Hitler's conference with Raeder, when the invasion of Norway was discussed, and Keitel's direct responsibility to those operations is shown, in my submission, by Document C-63, Exhibit GB 87, in which Keitel says that the operations against Norway will be "under my direct and personal guidance." And he sets up a planning staff of O.K.W. for the carrying out of those operations.

Jodl's knowledge and complicity, in my submission, are clearly shown also from the entries in his own diary- Document 1809-PS. That is the second part of his diary. And the Tribunal will remember the entry of the 13th March, 1940, in which he records that the Fuehrer was still looking for an excuse for the "Weser" operations. That is the 13th March, my Lord, 1809-PS.

THE PRESIDENT: Yes. The date I have got is the 3rd.

MR. ROBERTS: Page 5 of that actual exhibit, the 13th March, according to my copy.

THE PRESIDENT: Yes, I see.

MR. ROBERTS: "The Fuehrer does not give the order yet for 'Weser.' He is still looking for an excuse."

And then, on the 14th March, "Fuehrer has not yet decided what reason to give for 'Weser' exercise," - which, in my submission, if I may be allowed to make a short comment, shows up in a lurid light the code of honour of the military leaders of Germany - still looking for an excuse.

My Lord, then, as we know, Norway was attacked unawares, and lying excuses were given.

My Lord, the invasion of the Low Countries and Luxembourg, in my submission, is equally clearly shown by the documents to have been controlled and directed by Keitel with Jodl's assistance. The Tribunal already have a note of the conference in May of the lands to be occupied, Documents L- 79. C-62, Exhibit GB 106 is a directive, signed Hitler, on the 9th October, 1939, and another directive, signed Keitel, on the 15th October. C-62 comprises two documents, the 9th October and 15th October, two directives, one signed Hitler, and one signed Keitel, both giving orders for the occupation of Holland and Belgium.

My Lord, Document C-10, Exhibit GB 108, dated the 8th November, is Keitel's operation orders for the 7th Parachute Division to make an airborne landing in the middle of The Hague.

Document 440-PS, Exhibit GB 107, dated the 20th November, 1939, signed Keitel, is a further directive for the invasion of Holland and Belgium.

Document C-72, Exhibit GB 109, 7th November, 1939, the 10th May, 1940, 18 letters, 11 signed by Keitel, 7 signed by Jodl: The Fuehrer is postponing A-Day because of the weather.

My Lord, Jodl's diary is also eloquent on that subject. That is Document 1809-PS. Several entries, perhaps I need not refer to them again, relating to these forthcoming operations, culminating with the one on the 8th May, which perhaps the Tribunal will remember, when Jodl says: "Alarming information from Holland," and he expresses righteous indignation that the wicked Dutchmen should erect roadblocks and make mobilisation preparations.

So those three neutral countries were invaded, and I submit there is copious and overwhelming evidence that these two men were in charge of the military organisations which made those invasions possible.

I pass now to the planning for the aggression against Greece and Yugoslavia.

Document 1541-PS, Exhibit GB 117, dated 13th December, 1940, Hitler's order for "Marita," the operation against Greece, signed by Hitler, and a copy to Keitel, namely, O.K.W.

Document 448-PS, Exhibit GB 118, 11thJanuary, 1941, Keitel initialled a Hitler order for the Greek operation.

Document C-134, Exhibit GB 119, 20th January, 1941, both Keitel and Jodl are present at the conference with Hitler, Mussolini and others when the operations against Greece and Yugoslavia are discussed.

Document C-59, Exhibit GB 121, 19th February, 1941, the dates of the operations against "Marita" are filled in by Keitel.

Document 1746-PS, Exhibit GB 120, 27th March, 1941, a conference with Hitler, Keitel and Jodl present, the decision to attack and destroy Yugoslavia is announced, and the Fuehrer said: "I am determined to destroy Yugoslavia. I shall use unmerciful harshness to frighten other neutrals"; and these two soldiers were present when that was said.

My Lord, I submit that on that, the complicity of these two men for that aggression is amply proved.

My Lord, I pass to "Barbarossa." Document 446-PS, Exhibit USA 31, dated 18th December, 1940, Hitler's order for the "Barbarossa" operation, initiated by Keitel and Jodl. Hitler says, the Tribunal will remember, that he intends to overthrow Russia in a single rapid campaign.

Document 872-PS, Exhibit USA 134, 3rd February, 1941, a discussion with Hitler, Keitel and Jodl, re: "Barbarossa" and "Sonnenblume," North African suggestions. Hitler said: "When 'Barbarossa' commences, the world will hold its breath and make no comments."

Then, Document 447-PS, Exhibit USA 135, dated 13th March, 1941, that is an operation order signed by Keitel, re: the administration of the areas which are to be occupied, showing again that Keitel was more than a mere soldier; this is civil administration.

Document C-39, Exhibit USA 138, 6th June, 1941, timetable for "Barbarossa," signed by Keitel, and Jodl gets a sixth copy.

Document C-78, Exhibit USA 139, 9th June, 1941, is Hitler's order to Keitel and Jodl to attend the pre-"Barbarossa" conference on the 14th June, 1941, eight days before the operation.

My Lord, on those facts and documents on the position of these two defendants, I again respectfully submit that their participation in this aggression is overwhelmingly proved.

The last aggression is with regard to the provoked persuasion of Japan to commit an aggression against the United States of America. My Lord, there are two key documents, and both Keitel and Jodl are implicated by both of them. The first is C-75, Exhibit USA 151, dated 5th March, 1941. It is an O.K.W. order signed by Keitel, copy to Jodl, "Japan must be drawn actively into the war" is a quotation from it.

Then Document C-152, Exhibit GB 122, 18th March, 1941, the meeting between Hitler, Raeder, Keitel and Jodl - Japan to seize Singapore. That is the relevant extract from that.

My Lord, on those acts of aggression and those preparations for aggression, I submit that the case against these two men is overwhelming. It is clear, in my submission, that there could be no defence open to them except that they were obeying the orders of a superior. That defence is not open to them under this Charter. No doubt all these wicked schemes germinated in the wicked brain of Hitler, but he could not carry them out alone. He wanted men nearly as wicked and nearly as unscrupulous as himself.

My Lord, I now pass very rapidly to the question of War Crimes and Crimes against Humanity. It has already been proved that Keitel signed the "Nacht und Nebel" decrees, committing persons to incarceration in Germany where all trace of them was lost. That is Document L-90, Exhibit USA 503.

There is one fresh document that I desire to put in. Colonel Telford Taylor put in C-50, Keitel's order as to ruthless action in the "Barbarossa" campaign. There is one complementary document to that, C-51, which is GB 162, Keitel's order dated the 27th July, 1941:

> "In accordance with the regulations concerning classified material the following offices will destroy all copies of the Fuehrer's decree of 13th May, 1941" - that is, Document C-50, the "Barbarossa" decree - "issued in the communication mentioned above:
>> (a) All offices upwards to the rank of 'General Commands' inclusive" - My Lord, that means that corps commanders and downwards should destroy copies.
>> "(b) Group commands of the armoured troops" - that again means offices of the armoured corps below the rank of corps commanders should destroy the copies.
>> "(c) Army commands and offices of equal rank, if there is an inevitable danger that they might fall into the hands of unauthorised persons."

That is to say that even higher generals, if the war approaches closely to them, should destroy these documents rather than there should be any chance of them being captured.

> "The validity of the decree is not affected by the destruction of the copies. In accordance with paragraph III it remains the personal responsibility of the commanding officers to see to it that the offices and legal advisers are instructed in time, and that only these sentences are confirmed, which correspond to the political intentions of the High Command."

That was with regard to German soldiers not being tried by court martial for offences against Soviet troops.

> "This order will be destroyed together with the copies of the Fuehrer's decree."

My Lord, I submit that the anxiety on the part of the O.K.W., presided over by Keitel, to destroy that, I suggest illegal, barbarous order is significant.

My Lord, I desire now to put in another document which is almost the last document in the bundle, UK-20. Your Lordship will find it flagged at the end of the bundle. It is from the Fuehrer's headquarters, 26th May, 1943.

It says:

> "Ref.: Treatment of supporters of de Gaulle who fight for the Russians.
> French airmen serving in the Soviet air forces have been shot down on the Eastern Front for the first time. The Fuehrer has ordered that employment of French troops in the Soviet forces is to be counteracted by the strongest means. It is therefore ordered: (1) Supporters of de Gaulle who are taken prisoner on the Eastern Front will be handed over to the French Government for proceedings in accordance with O.K.W. order."

And then I read paragraph (3):

> "Detailed investigations are to be made in appropriate cases against relatives of Frenchmen who fight for the Russians, if these relatives are resident in the

occupied area of France. If the investigation reveals that relatives have given assistance to facilitate escape from France then severe measures are to be taken."

My Lord, I offer that as Exhibit GB 163.

My Lord, there is a document which I feel I should put in, which is the next document in the bundle, and is UK-57, Exhibit GB 164. This is the last document, I think, in the bundle. My Lord, it is from the "Ausland Abwehr" - I believe it is from the Intelligence Foreign Department. It is to the O.K.W. and it is signed the 4th January, 1944. My Lord, the heading is: "Re counteraction to Kharkov show trial." Paragraph 2 is all that I read:

"The documents concerning Commandos have been asked for and thoroughly investigated by the Reich Security Main Office. In five cases members of the British armed forces were arrested as participants. Thereupon they were shot in accordance with the order of the Fuehrer. It would be possible to attribute to them breaches of International Law and to have them posthumously sentenced to death by a tribunal. Up to the present no breaches of International Law could be proved against Commando participants."

My Lord, I read no more, and I submit that that is clearly an admission of murder, not warfare at all.

My Lord, Keitel's comments are to be found in the top left-hand corner of that document: "We want documents on the basis of which we can institute similar proceedings. They are reprisals which have no connection with battle actions. Legal justifications are superfluous."

THE PRESIDENT: Is that not at the top signed by Keitel?

MR. ROBERTS: It is typewritten in the office copy, which is the original.

THE PRESIDENT: There is no actual signature.

MR. ROBERTS: No.

MR. BIDDLE: How does it connect with Keitel then?

MR. ROBERTS: Wehrmacht Chief O.K.W., that is "note of the Chief of O.K.W."

Now, that is the first minute. My Lord, the second minute is on the same subject and it is dated the 6th January, 1944, and there is a large red Keitel "K" initialled on the top of this letter, showing that he got it. My Lord, the first paragraph deals with two officers who were then at Eichstadt Camp in Bavaria. My Lord, there is no importance in that paragraph, because those two officers are still alive.

The second paragraph:

"Attempted attacks on the battleship Tirpitz.

At the end of October, 1942, British Commandos who had come to Norway in a cutter and had orders to carry out an attack on the battleship Tirpitz in Trondheim Fjord by means of a two-man torpedo. The action failed since both torpedoes which were attached to the cutter were lost in the stormy sea. From amongst the crew, consisting of six Englishmen and four Norwegians, a party of three Englishmen and two Norwegians were challenged on the Swedish border. However, only the British seaman Robert Paul Evans, born 14th January, 1922, at London, could be arrested, the others escaped into Sweden.

Evans had a pistol pouch in his possession such as is used to carry weapons under the arm-pit, and also a knuckle-duster. Violence, representing a breach of International Law, could not be proved. He has made extensive statements about the operation. In accordance with the Fuehrer's order he was shot on 19th January, 1943."

Again, I submit, that is murder. Violence representing a breach of International Law could not be proved.

My Lord, then the third paragraph:

"Blowing up of the Glomfjord Power Station.

On 16th September, 1942, ten Englishmen and two Norwegians landed on the Norwegian coast dressed in the uniform of the British Mountain Rifle Regiment, heavily armed and equipped with explosives of every description. After negotiating difficult mountain country they blew up important installations in the power station Glomfjord on 21st September, 1942. The German sentry was shot dead on that occasion. Norwegian workmen were threatened that they would be chloroformed should they resist. For this purpose the Englishmen were equipped with morphia syringes. Several of the participants have been arrested whilst the others escaped into Sweden.

Those arrested are:

Captain Graeme Black, born 9th May, 1911, in Dresden.
Captain Joseph Houghton, born 13th June, 1911, at Bromborough.
Top Sergeant Miller Smith, born 2nd November, 1915, at Middlesbrough.
Corporal William Chudley, born 10th May, 1922, at Exeter.
Rifleman Reginald Makeham, born 28th January, 1914, at Ipswich.
Rifleman Cyril Abram, born 20th August, 1922, in London.
Rifleman Eric Curtis, born 24th October, 1921, in London.

They were shot on 30th October, 1942."

Again there is no suggestion that there was any breach of International Law. They were British seamen and they were in uniform.

Then paragraph 4:

"The sabotage attack against German ships off Bordeaux.

On 12th December, 1942, a number of valuable German ships off Bordeaux were seriously damaged by explosives below water-level. The adhesive mines had been fixed by 5 English sabotage gangs working from canoes. From amongst the 10 participants the following were arrested after a few days."

Then there followed six names, six British names, one an Irishman, a lieutenant; a petty officer; a sergeant and three marines. A seventh soldier named Moffett was found drowned; the remainder apparently escaped into Spain.

The participants proceeded in pairs from a submarine in canoes upstream into the mouth of the River Gironde. They were wearing olive-grey special uniforms. After effecting the explosions they sank the boats and attempted to escape into Spain in civilian clothes, with the assistance of the French civilian population. No special criminal actions during the fight have been discovered. All the arrested, in accordance with orders were shot on 23rd March, 1943. Keitel initialled that document. That document, read by my learned leader Sir David Maxwell Fyfe not so long ago, is 735-PS, quoting Keitel as saying, "I am against legal procedure. It does not work out."

THE PRESIDENT: Would you read the Page 5 which follows that?

MR. ROBERTS: If it will please the Tribunal, that is what I shall do. Page 5: "The Fuehrer's Headquarters, 9th January, 1944. The Chief of O.K.W. has handed the Deputy Chief," - that ought to be W.F.S.T., that is Jodl, - "the enclosed letter with the following account. It is of no importance to establish documentary proof of breaches of International Law. What is important, however, is the collection of material suitable for a propaganda presentation of a show trial. A show trial as such is therefore not meant to take place, but merely a propaganda presentation of cases of breaches of International Law by enemy soldiers, who will be mentioned by name and have already either been punished with death or have to expect the death penalty. The Chief of the O.K.W. asked the Chief of the Foreign Department, Admiral Canaris, to bring with him a corresponding document for his next visit to the Fuehrer's Headquarters," - as the Tribunal heard from my learned friend, Sir David Maxwell Fyfe, when he read Document 735-PS earlier to-day, and Keitel said, "I am against legal procedure. It does not work out."

One can agree with Keitel, after having read that record of what, in my submission, is cold-blooded murder of brave men, brave soldiers and sailors who were fighting for their country; and although this trial has a record of the death of brave men, of the murder of brave men, there are few cases which are more poignant than those shown in the documents to which I have just referred.

I have finished my presentation of the case against Keitel and against Jodl. So far as Jodl's part in the War Crimes and Crimes against Humanity is concerned, he figures much less than Keitel. Of course, he had no power of giving orders or directives, but we see that he at any rate signed and circulated an infamous order of the Fuehrer saying that Commandos ought to be shot and are not to be treated as prisoners of war at all.

In my submission the evidence against these two men is overwhelming and their conviction is demanded by the civilised world.

Your Lordships, Mr. Walter W. Brudno of the American delegation will present the case against Alfred Rosenberg.

MR. WALTER W. BRUDNO: May it please the Tribunal, in connection with the case against the defendant Rosenberg, I wish to offer the document book designated as Exhibit USA EE. This book contains the English translation of all the documents which I will offer into evidence, as well as the English translation of those documents previously offered to which I will refer. The documents are arranged by series in the order of C, L, R, PS and EC, and they are arranged numerically within each series.

Your Honours will note that on the first four pages of the document book there appears a descriptive list of documents. This list is a tabulation of all the documents directly implicating Rosenberg, including those previously offered and those which I will offer into evidence. Those previously offered are keyed to the transcript page of the Record, and to their exhibit numbers. The list is included in the document books

THE PRESIDENT: Will you go a little bit slower.

MR. BRUDNO: Certainly, your Honour. The list is included in the document books made available to the defence. This list will gather together in one place all references to the defendant Rosenberg, which are in the record up to this point. In order to avoid repetition, I will not refer to a great many of the documents previously introduced.

The Indictment at Page 29 charges the defendant Rosenberg under all four Counts of the Indictment. In the presentation which follows, I will show that as charged in Count One, Section IV, subparagraph (D), Rosenberg played a particularly prominent role in developing and promoting the doctrinal techniques of the conspiracy; in developing and promoting beliefs and practices incompatible with Christian teaching, in subverting the influence of the Churches over the German people, in pursuing the programme of relentless persecution of the Jews, and in reshaping the educational system in order to make the German people amenable to the will of the conspirators, and to prepare the people psychologically for waging an aggressive war.

I will also show that Rosenberg played an important role in preparing Germany for the waging of aggressive war through the direction of foreign trade, as charged in Count One, subparagraph (E), Page 6 of the Indictment, and that his activities in the field of foreign policy contributed materially toward the preparation for the aggressions charged in subparagraph (F), Pages 7 to 10 in the Indictment, and the Crimes against Peace, as charged in Count Two.

Finally, I will show that Rosenberg participated in the planning and direction of the War Crimes, and Crimes against Humanity, as specified in paragraph (G), Page 10 of Count One of the Indictment. Particularly, he participated in the planning and directing of the spoliation of art treasures in the Western countries, and in the numerous crimes committed in that part of the Eastern countries formerly occupied by the U.S.S.R.

The political career of the defendant Rosenberg embraced the entire history of National Socialism, and permeated nearly every phase of the conspiracy with which we are concerned. In order to obtain a full conception of his influence upon and participation in the conspiracy, it is necessary to review briefly his political history, and to consider each of his political activities in their relation to the thread of the conspiracy which stretches from the inception of the Party in 1919 to the defeat of Germany in 1945.

It is both interesting and revealing to note that for Rosenberg the 30th November, 1918, marked the "Beginning of political activities with a lecture about the 'Jewish Problem.'" That statement is found at line 2 of the translation of Document 2886-PS, which is an excerpt from a book entitled, "The Work of Alfred Rosenberg," a biography, and I offer this book as Exhibit USA 591.

From the Document 3557-PS, which has excerpts from an official pamphlet entitled, "Dates in the History of the N.S.D.A.P.," and which I offer as Exhibit USA 592, we learn that Rosenberg was a member of the German Labour Party, afterwards the National Socialist German Workers' Party, in January, 1919, and that Hitler joined forces with Rosenberg and his colleagues in October of the same year. Thus Rosenberg was a member of the National Socialist movement even before Hitler himself.

Now I wish to offer Document 3530-PS, which is an extract from "Das Deutsche Fuehrer Lexikon," the year of 1934-35, and I offer it as Exhibit USA 593. In this document we obtain additional biographical data on Rosenberg as follows:

"From 1921 until the present, he was editor of the 'Volkische Beobachter'; editor of the N.S. 'Monatshefte'; in 1930 he became member of the Reichstag and representative of foreign policies for the Party; after April, 1933, he was leader of the foreign political office of the N.S.D.A.P.; was then designated as Reichsleiter; in January, 1934, appointed deputy by the Fuehrer for the spiritual and philosophical education of the N.S.D.A.P., the German labour front and all related organisations."

Document 2886-PS, which I have just referred to, offered as Exhibit USA 591, adds that in July, 1941, Rosenberg was appointed Reichsminister for the Occupied Eastern Territories.

With this general background information in mind, the first phase of proof will deal with Rosenberg as official National Socialist ideologist. The proof, which I will present, will show the nature and scope of the ideological tenets he expounded, and the influence he exerted upon the unification of German thought, a unification which was an essential part of the conspirators' programme for seizure of power and preparation for aggressive war.

Rosenberg wrote extensively on, and actively participated in, virtually every aspect of the National Socialist programme. His first publication was the "Nature, Basic Principles and Aims of the N.S.D.A.P." This publication appeared in 1922. Rosenberg spoke of this book in a speech which we have seen and heard delivered in the motion picture previously introduced as Exhibit USA 167, on Page 2, Part 1, of the transcription of the speech, which is our Document 3054-PS, Rosenberg stated as follows:

"During this time, that is, during the early phase of the Party, a short thesis was written, which nevertheless is significant in the history of the N.S.D.A.P." - this is Rosenberg speaking - "It was always being asked what points of programme the N.S.D.A.P. had, and how they were to be interpreted. Therefore, I wrote the principal programme and aims of the N.S.D.A.P., and this writing made the first permanent connection between Munich and local organisations being organised, and friends within the Reich."

We thus see that the original draftsman of, and spokesman on, the Party programme was the defendant Rosenberg. Without attempting to survey the entire ideological programme advanced by Rosenberg in his various writings and speeches - they are very numerous - I wish to offer into evidence certain of his statements as an indication of the nature and broad scope of the ideological programme which he championed. It will be seen that there was not a single basic tenet of the Nazi philosophy which was not given authoritative expression by Rosenberg. He wrote the "Myth of the Twentieth Century," published in 1930. This book has already been offered as Exhibit USA 352. At Page 479, which your Honour will find on the second page of Document 2553- PS, Rosenberg wrote on the race question as follows:

"The essence of the contemporary world revolution lies in the awakening of the racial type; not in Europe alone but on the whole planet. This awakening is the organic counter movement against the last chaotic remnants of the liberal economic imperialism, whose object of exploitation, out of desperation, has fallen into the snare of Bolshevic Marxism, in order to complete what democracy had begun, the extirpation of the racial and national consciousness."

Rosenberg expounded the "Lebensraum" idea, which was the chief motivation, the dynamic impulse behind Germany's waging of aggressive war. In his journal, the National Socialist "Monatshefte," for May, 1932, which I offer as Exhibit USA 594, our Document 2777-PS, he wrote at Page 199:

"The understanding that the German nation, if it is not to perish in the truest sense of the word, needs ground and soil for itself, and its future generations, and the second sober perception that this soil can no more be conquered in Africa, but in Europe and first of all in the East - these organically determine the German foreign policy for centuries."

Rosenberg expressed his theory as to the place of religion in the National Socialist State in his "Myth of the Twentieth Century," additional excerpts from which are cited in Document 2891-PS; at Page 215 of the "Myth" he wrote as follows:

"We now realise that the central supreme values of the Roman and the Protestant Church as negative Christianity are not suited to our soul, that they hinder the organic powers of the people designated as a Nordic race, that they must give way to them, that they have to be remodelled to conform with Germanic Christianity. Therein lies the meaning of to-day's religious searching."

In the place of traditional Christianity, Rosenberg sought to implant the neo-pagan myth of the blood.

THE PRESIDENT: Do you want to break off here for a recess?

MR. BRUDNO: Yes, your Honour.

(A recess was taken.)

THE PRESIDENT: I have an announcement to make to the defendants' counsel. In view of the applications which were made to the Tribunal this morning, I immediately ordered, on behalf of the Tribunal, that an investigation should be made of the complaints made by defendants' counsel about the delay in the delivery of the transcript of the shorthand notes; and such delay will be remedied at once. The investigation shows that transcripts of the sessions up to and including the 20th December can be completed by this afternoon. The transcripts for the sessions held since the resumption of the trial will be distributed, up to and including the 8th January, by to- morrow evening. Hereafter, the German transcripts will be regularly distributed to the defence counsel within a period of forty-eight hours after the session.

MR. BRUDNO: If your Honour pleases, when the Court rose I had just read it quotation of Rosenberg, in which he expressed his views on Christianity.

In the place of traditional Christianity, Rosenberg sought to implant the neo-pagan myth of the blood. At Page 114 in the "Myth of the Twentieth Century" he stated as follows:

"To-day, a new faith is awakening - the myth of the blood, the belief that the divine being of mankind generally is to be defended with the blood. The faith embodied by the fullest realisation, that the Nordic blood constitutes that mystery which has supplanted and overwhelmed the old sacraments."

Rosenberg's attitudes on religion were accepted as the only philosophy compatible with National Socialism. In 1940, the defendant Bormann wrote to Rosenberg in Document 098-PS, which has been previously introduced as Exhibit USA 350, and I quote:

"The churches cannot be conquered by a compromise between National Socialism and Christian teachings, but only through a new ideology, whose coming you, yourself, have announced in your writings."

Rosenberg actively participated in the programme for elimination of Church influence. The defendant Bormann frequently wrote Rosenberg in this regard, furnishing him information as to proposed action to be instituted against the Churches, and, when necessary, requesting that that action be taken by Rosenberg's department. I refer to documents introduced in connection with the case against the Leadership Corps, such Documents as 070-PS, Exhibit USA 349, which deals with abolition of religious services in the schools; Document 072-PS, Exhibit USA 357, dealing with confiscation of religious property; 064-PS, Exhibit USA 359, which deals with the inadequacy of anti-religious material being circulated to the soldiers; Document 089-PS, Exhibit USA 360, dealing with curtailment of the publication of Protestant periodicals; and Document 122-PS, which is Exhibit USA 362, dealing with the closing of theological faculties.

Rosenberg was particularly avid in his pursuit of what he called the "Jewish Question." On the 28th March, 1941, on the occasion of the opening of the Institute for the Exploration of the Jewish Question, he set the keynote for its activities and indicated the direction which the exploration was to take. I would like to quote from Document 2889-PS, which I offer as Exhibit USA 595. This is an excerpt from the

"Volkischer Beobachter," 29th March, 1941. This is a statement made by Rosenberg on the occasion of the opening of the institute:

> "For Germany the Jewish Question is only then solved when the last Jew has left the Greater German space.
>
> Since Germany with its blood and its nationalism has now broken for ever this Jewish dictatorship for all Europe and has seen to it that Europe as a whole will become free from the Jewish parasitism once more, we may, I believe, also say for all Europeans: for Europe the Jewish Question will be solved only when the last Jew has left the European continent."

It has already been seen that Rosenberg did not overlook any opportunity to put these anti-Semitic beliefs into practice. Your Honour will recall that in Document 001-PS, which was introduced as Exhibit USA 282 in connection with the case on Persecution of the Jews, Rosenberg recommended that instead of executing one hundred Frenchmen as retaliation for attempts on lives of members of the Wehrmacht, there be executed one hundred Jewish bankers, lawyers, etc. The recommendation was made with the avowed purpose of awakening the anti-Jewish sentiment.

Document 752-PS, which was introduced this morning by Sir David Maxwell Fyfe as Exhibit GB 159, discloses that Rosenberg had called an Anti-Semitic Congress in June, 1944, although this Congress was cancelled, due to military events.

In the realm of foreign policy, in addition to demanding Lebensraum, Rosenberg called for elimination of the Versailles Treaty, and cast aside any thought of revision of that Treaty. In his book "The Nature, Principles and Aims of the N.S.D.A.P.," written by him in 1922, he expressed his opinions regarding the Treaty of Versailles. Excerpts from this book are translated in Document 2433-PS, and I offer the book as Exhibit USA 596. He stated as follows:

> "The National Socialists reject the popular phrase 'Revision of the Peace of Versailles' as such a revision might perhaps bring a few numerical reductions in the so- called 'obligations,' but the entire German people would still be, just as before, the slave of other nations."

Then he goes on to expound the second point of the Party:

> "We demand equality for the German people with other nations, the cancellation of the peace treaties of Versailles and St. Germain."

Rosenberg conceived the spread of National Socialism throughout the world, and, as will be subsequently shown, took an active part in promoting the infection of other nations with his creed. In the "Nature, Principles and Aims of the N.S.D.A.P.," he states:

> "But National Socialism still believes that its principles and ideology, though suitable methods of fighting will differ according to individual and racial-national conditions - will be directives far beyond the borders of Germany for the inevitable fights for power in other countries of Europe and in America. There, too, a clear line of thought must be drawn, and the racial- nationalistic fight against the loan-capitalistic and Marxist-internationalism, which is the same in every case, must be taken up. National Socialism believes that, once the great world battle is concluded, after the defeat of the present epoch, there will be a time when the swastika will be woven into the different banners of the Germanic peoples as the Aryan symbol of rejuvenation."

This statement was made in 1922. It is thus seen that the defendant Rosenberg gave authoritative expression to the basic tenets upon which National Socialism was founded, and through the exploitation of which the conspiracy was crystallised in action.

Rosenberg's value to the conspiratorial programme found official recognition through his appointment in 1934 as the Fuehrer's delegate for the entire spiritual and philosophical education and supervision of the N.S.D.A.P. His activities in this capacity were vast and varied.

I now offer in evidence the National Socialist Year Book for the year 1938 as Exhibit USA 597. At Page 180 of this book, which is our Document 3531-PS, the functions of Rosenberg's office as the Fuehrer's delegate are described as follows:

> "The sphere of activity of the Fuehrer's Commissioner for all spiritual and ideological instruction and education of the movement, its organisation, including the 'Strength through Joy,' extends to the detailed execution of all the educational work of the Party and of the affiliated bodies. The office, set up by Reichsleiter Rosenberg, has the task of preparing the ideological education material, of carrying out the teaching programme, and is responsible for the education of those teachers suited to this educational and instructional work." As the Fuehrer's delegate, Rosenberg thus supervised all ideological education and training within the Party.

It was Rosenberg's personal belief that upon the performance of his new functions as ideological delegate depended the future of National Socialism. I offer Document 3532-PS as Exhibit USA 598. This is an excerpt from an article by Rosenberg appearing in the March, 1934, issue of "The Educational Letter." At Page 9 of this publication Rosenberg states:

> "The focus of all our educational work from now on is the service for this ideology, and it depends on the result of these efforts whether National Socialism will die with our fighting generation or whether, as we believe, it really represents the beginning of a new era."

In his capacity as the Fuehrer's delegate for the spiritual and ideological training, Rosenberg assisted in the preparation of the curriculum for the Adolf Hitler schools. These schools, it will be recalled, selected the most suitable candidates from the Hitler Jugend and trained them for leadership within the Party. They were the elite schools of National Socialism. This document, entitled "Documents of German Politics," is already in evidence as Exhibit USA 365. Translations of excerpts from this document are found in Document 3529-PS, Page 389, and read as follows:

> "As stated by Dr. Ley, Reichsorganisationsleiter, on 23rd November, 1937, at Ordensburg Sonthofen, these Adolf Hitler schools, as the first step of the principle of selecting a special elite, form an important branch in the educational system of the National Socialist training of future leaders.
>
> The curriculum has been laid down by Reichsleiter Rosenberg, together with the Reichsorganisationsleiter and the Reich Youth Leader."

Rosenberg exercised further influence in the education of Party members in the establishment of community schools for all organisations of the Party. Document 3528-PS is a translation of Page 297 of the 1934 edition of "Das Dritte Reich," which I offer as Exhibit USA 599. It reads as follows:

> "We support the request of the Fuehrer's Commissioner for the supervision of the whole spiritual and ideological training and instruction of the N.S.D.A.P., Party member Alfred Rosenberg, to organise community schools of all organisations of the N.S.D.A.P. twice a year, in order to show by this common effort the ideological and political unity of the N.S.D.A.P. and the steadfastness of the National Socialist will."

This programme was endorsed by the defendant Schirach as well as by Himmler,

Ley and others.

THE PRESIDENT: Are you not dealing with this rather in a cumulative way? Is it not possible to summarise this evidence against Rosenberg more than you are doing?

MR. BRUDNO: I will try to, your Honour. However, although the Indictment charges, and there is already substantial proof to show that the defendant conspirators used ideological training as an implement in achieving their rise to power and in consolidating their control, there seems to be little evidence as to Rosenberg's position, and I am introducing this evidence in order to show that he played a dominant role in this connection. However, I will try to summarise these documents if I can.

THE PRESIDENT: Well, I have taken down about twenty documents that you have alluded to, all of which deal with Rosenberg's ideological theories.

MR. BRUDNO: Yes, your Honour. I was merely trying to show the scope of his activities.

THE PRESIDENT: Yes.

MR. BRUDNO: Your Honour will recall that it was in his capacity as Fuehrer's delegate that Rosenberg established the Institute for the Exploitation of the Jewish Question in Frankfort. This institute, commonly known as the "Hohe Schule," has been referred to in connection with the exposition of art plunder. Into its library there flowed books, documents and manuscripts which were looted from virtually every country of occupied Europe. Further evidence on this score will be introduced by the Prosecutor of the Republic of France.

Your Honour will also recall, and the record shows (Pages 64 to 73, Part 3) that it was as ideological delegate that Rosenberg conducted the fabulous art looting activities of the Einsatzstab Rosenberg, activities which extended to virtually every country occupied by the Germans. I will not attempt to summarise the extent of the plunder, but merely refer the Tribunal to Document 1015 B-PS, which has already been introduced as Exhibit USA 385 and Document L-188, which has been introduced as Exhibit USA 386. Document 1015 B-PS details the looting of 21,000 artistic treasures, Document L-188, the looting of the contents of over 71,000 Jewish homes in the West. This subject, too, will be further developed by the French Prosecutor.

The importance of Rosenberg's activities as official ideologist of the Nazi Party was not overlooked. In Document 3559-PS, which I wish to introduce as Exhibit USA 600 - this document, incidentally, is the Hart biography of Rosenberg, entitled "The Man and His Work" - it is stated that Rosenberg won the German National Prize in 1937. The creation of this prize, your Honour will recall, was the Nazis' petulant reply to the award of the Nobel Prize to Karl von Ossietzki, an inmate of a German concentration camp. The citation which accompanied the award to Rosenberg read as follows:

> "Alfred Rosenberg has helped with his publications to lay the scientific and intuitive foundation and to strengthen the philosophy of the National Socialist in the most excellent way. The National Socialist movement, and beyond that, the entire German people, will be deeply gratified that the Fuehrer has distinguished Alfred Rosenberg as one of his oldest and most faithful fighting comrades, by awarding him the German National Prize."

The contribution which Rosenberg's book, "The Myth of the Twentieth Century," the foundation of all his ideological propaganda, made to the development of National Socialism was appraised in a publication "Bucher Kunde" in 1942. This publication is our Document 3554-PS, dated November, 1942. I offer it as Exhibit USA 601. The first page sets forth an appraisal of the "Myth of the Twentieth Century."

THE PRESIDENT: Mr. Brudno, you referred us to the "Myth of the Twentieth Century" on several occasions.

MR. BRUDNO: Yes, your Honour.

THE PRESIDENT: We really do not want to hear any more about it.

MR. BRUDNO: I wish to show that this book is regarded as being one of the pillars of the movement and I wish to show also, sir, that it had a circulation of over a million copies.

THE PRESIDENT: Well, I think it is absolutely clear from the evidence which has already been given that Rosenberg was enunciating doctrines of the ideology of the Nazi Party, and I do not think that it is necessary to go any further into details about it.

MR. BRUDNO: Very well. If the Tribunal is satisfied that Rosenberg's ideas formed the foundation for the National Socialist ideological movement, I will pass on.

THE PRESIDENT: Well, you have already brought out the fact that he was appointed the Fuehrer's deputy for that purpose; was he not?

MR. BRUDNO: Yes, your Honour. I shall pass on from that point. I would merely like to make reference, however, to Document 789-PS, which has already been introduced as Exhibit USA 23. This document records a meeting between Hitter and his Supreme Commanders, on which occasion Hitler said: "The building up of our armed forces was only possible in connection with the ideological education of the German people by the Party."

We submit that the contribution which Rosenberg made through formulation and dissemination of National Socialist ideology was fundamental to the conspiracy. As the apostle of neo- paganism, the exponent of the drive for "Lebensraum," and the glorifier of the myth of Nordic superiority, and as one of the oldest and most energetic Nazi proponents of anti-Semitism, he contributed materially to the unification of the German people behind the swastika. He provided the impetus and the inspiration for the National Socialist movement. His doctrines were responsible for the sublimation of morality and the crystallisation of the Nordic dream in the minds of the German people, thereby making them useful tools in the hands of the conspirators and willing collaborators in the prosecution of their criminal plan.

I now pass to the second phase of Rosenberg's criminal activities - his active contribution toward the preparation for aggressive war through the international activities of the A.P.A. - the Foreign Policy Office of the Party.

As previously indicated in my quotation from "Das Deutsche Fuehrer Lexikon" which is Exhibit USA 593, Rosenberg became a Reichsleiter, the highest level of rank in the Leadership Corps, and was made chief of the Foreign Political Office of the Party in April, 1933. The organisation manual of the Party, Document 2319-PS, which I offer as Exhibit USA 602, describes the functions of the A.P.A. as including the influencing of public opinion abroad so as to convince foreign nations that Germany desires peace. The far-flung activities of the A.P.A. are indicated at Page 14 of the translation of this document and are stated as follows:

"1. The A.P.A. is divided into three main offices:

   A. Office for Foreign Areas with its Main Sections-

   (a) England and Far East;

   (b) Near East;

(c) South East;
(d) North;
(e) Old Orient;
(f) Controls, personnel questions, etc.
B. Office of the German Academic Exchange Service.
C. Office of Foreign Commerce.
2. Moreover, there is in the A.P.A. a main office for the Press service and an Educational office."

The Press activities of the A.P.A. were designed to influence world opinion in such a manner as to conceal the conspirators' true purposes and thus facilitate the preparation for waging aggressive war. The activities were carried out on an ambitious scale. I offer into evidence Document 003-PS, which is entitled "A Short Report on the Activities of the A.P.A. of the N.S.D.A.P." It is Exhibit USA 603. The last paragraph on Page 5 of the translation describes the Press activities as follows:

"The Press Division of the A.P.A. is composed of persons who together master all the languages that are in use. Daily they examine approximately 300 newspapers and deliver to the Fuehrer, the deputy Fuehrer and all other interested offices the condensations of the important trends of the entire world Press. The Press Division furthermore conducts exact archives on the attitudes of the most important papers of the world. Many embarrassments during conferences in Germany could have been avoided had one consulted these archives. Further, the Press Division was able to arrange a host of interviews as well as to conduct a great number of friendly foreign journalists to the various official representatives of Germany."

And then:

"Hearst then personally asked me to write often about the position of German foreign policy in his papers. This year five detailed articles have appeared under my name in Hearst papers all over the world. Since these articles, as Hearst personally informed me, presented well-founded arguments, he asked me to write further ones for his paper."

Thus, Rosenberg used his foreign policy office to influence world opinion on behalf of National Socialism.

It is interesting to note in passing that Rosenberg states, at Page 4 of this document, that the Roumanian anti-Semitic leader, Cuza, followed his suggestions as (in Rosenberg's words) "he had recognised in me an unyielding anti-Semite." We will hear more of this affair shortly.

The nature and extent of the activities of the A.P.A. are amply disclosed in a single document. This is the principal document to which I will refer in this phase of the case against Rosenberg. This document bears our number 007-PS and is entitled "Report on the Activities of the Foreign Affairs Bureau of the Party from 1933 to 1943." It is signed by Rosenberg. Portions of Annex 1, attached to the report, have already been read into evidence as Exhibit GB 84. The body of the report and Annex 2 have not been referred to heretofore. As will be seen, the document contains a recital of widespread activities in foreign countries. These activities range from the promotion of economic penetration to fomentation of anti-Semitism; from cultural and political infiltration to the instigation of treason. Activities were carried on throughout the world and extended to such widely separated points as the Middle East and Brazil.

Much of the A.P.A.'s achievements were brought about through the subtle exploitation of personal relationships. Reading from the middle of the first paragraph on Page 2 of the translation, which refers to activities in Hungary, we learn that:

> "The first foreign State visit after the seizure of power took place through the mediation of the Foreign Affairs Bureau. Julius Gombos, who in former years had himself pursued anti-Semitic and racial tendencies, had reached the Hungarian Premier's chair. The Bureau maintained a personal connection with him."

The A.P.A. endeavoured to strengthen the war economy by shifting the source of food imports to the Balkans, as stated in paragraph 3 on Page 2 of the translation:

> "Motivated by reasons of War Economy, the Bureau advocated the transfer of raw material purchases from overseas to the areas accessible by overland traffic routes."

Then he goes on to point out that they had successfully shifted the source of food imports, particularly fruit and vegetable imports, to the Balkans, as a result of the Bureau's activities.

Activities in Belgium, Holland and Luxembourg were confined, according to the report, to "observation of existing conditions" - a phrase which may have broad connotations - and "to the establishment of relations, especially of a commercial nature."

In Iran, the A.P.A. achieved a high degree of economic penetration, in addition to promoting cultural relations. I quote from the middle of the third paragraph on Page 3:

> "The Bureau's initiative in developing, with the help of commercial circles, entirely new methods for the economic penetration of Iran, found expression, in an extraordinarily favourable way, in reciprocal trade relations. Naturally, in Germany, too, this initiative encountered a completely negative attitude and resistance on the part of the competent State authorities, an attitude that at first had to be overcome. In the course of a few years, the volume of trade with Iran was multiplied fivefold, and in 1939, Iran's trade turnover with Germany had attained first place."

In the last sentence on Page 3 -

THE PRESIDENT: Well, now, Mr. Brudno, will you kindly explain to the Tribunal how the paragraph that you just read bears upon the guilt of Rosenberg on this trial?

MR. BRUDNO: If your Honour please, we submit that the conspirators used, as one of the tools of conspiracy, the economic penetration of those countries which they deemed strategically necessary to have within the Axis orbit. The activities of Rosenberg in the field of foreign trade contributed materially, we submit, to the advancement of the conspiracy, as charged in the Indictment.

THE PRESIDENT: Are you suggesting that it is a crime to try and stimulate trade in foreign countries?

MR. BRUDNO: If your Honour pleases, the expression of ideological opinions or the advancement of foreign trade do not, in themselves, constitute a crime, we agree.

THE PRESIDENT: There is nothing here about ideological considerations. It is simply a question of trade.

MR. BRUDNO: Further on, your Honour, he mentions the cultural activities.

THE PRESIDENT: I was confining myself, in order to try to get on, to the particular paragraph that you bad just cited.

MR. BRUDNO: I see, your Honour, we are merely trying to show, Sir, that the Germans used the foreign trade weapon as a material part of the conspiratorial programme.

THE PRESIDENT: As I have said before, it is not possible for me or for any member of this Tribunal to conduct the case of the prosecution for them. We can only tell them when we think they are being irrelevant and cumulative and ask them to try to cut down their presentation. It is for you to cut it down.

MR. BRUDNO: Rosenberg goes on to state, if your Honour pleases, at Page 3 of the translation, that:

> "Afghanistan's neutral position to-day is largely due to the Bureau's activity."

In connection with Arabia, he says:

> "The Arab question, too, became part of the work of the Bureau. In spite of England's tutelage of Iraq, the Bureau established a series of connections to a number of leading personalities of the Arab world, smoothing the way for strong bonds to Germany. In this connection, the growing influence of the Reich in Iran and Afghanistan did not fail to have repercussions in Arabia."

Rosenberg concludes his report with the statement that, with the outbreak of war, he was entitled to consider his task as terminated, and then he says,

> "The exploitation of the many personal connections in many lands can be resumed under a different guise."

I now turn to Annex Two of the report, which is found at Page 9 of the translation. This Annex deals with activities in Roumania. Here the A.P.A.'s intrigue was more insidious, its interference in the internal affairs of a foreign nation more pronounced. After describing the failure of what Rosenberg terms a "basically sound anti-Semitic tendency," due to dynastic squabbles and party fights, Rosenberg describes the A.P.A.'s influence in the unification of conflicting elements. I quote, beginning with the ninth line of the translation:

> "What was lacking was the guiding leadership of a political personality. After manifold groping trials the Bureau believed it had found such a personality - the former Minister and poet, Octavian Goga. It was not difficult to convince this poet, pervaded by instinctive inspiration, that a Greater Roumania, though it had to be created in opposition to Vienna, could be maintained only together with Berlin. Nor was it difficult to create in him the desire to link the fate of Roumania with the future of the National Socialist German Reich in the future. By bringing continuing influence to bear, the Bureau succeeded in inducing Octavian Goga as well as Professor Cuza to amalgamate the parties under their leadership on an anti-Semitic basis. Thus they could carry on with united strength the struggle for Roumania's renaissance internally and her Anschluss with Germany externally. Through the Bureau's initiative both parties, which had heretofore been known by distinct names, were merged as the National Christian Party, under Goga's leadership and with Cuza as Honorary President."

Rosenberg's man, Goga, was supported by two parties, which had not joined the anti-Semitic trend, and Rosenberg states:

> "Through intermediaries, the Bureau maintained constant contact with both tendencies."

Goga, the man supported by Rosenberg, was appointed Prime Minister by the King in December, 1937. The pernicious influence of Rosenberg's ideology had achieved a major triumph, for he states:

> "Thus a second government on racial and anti-Semitic foundations had appeared in Europe, in a country in which such an event had been considered

completely impossible."

I will not deal at any length with the details of the political turmoil that plagued Roumania during the ensuing period.

THE PRESIDENT: Mr. Brudno, I think the Tribunal are satisfied that Rosenberg - I mean satisfied, subject to what Rosenberg himself or his counsel may say that Rosenberg tried to spread his ideology abroad, and we do not require any further detailed proof of that, and we are also satisfied that we have heard enough of the activities of the A.P.A.

MR. BRUDNO: Certainly, your Honour. We feel that if the Tribunal is satisfied, we can pass on.

THE PRESIDENT: Subject, as I said, to anything that Rosenberg may prove.

MR. BRUDNO: Surely. I would merely like to conclude with the statement that the activities of the A.P.A. were, as indicated in this Document 007-PS, primarily responsible for Roumania's joining the Axis. It was a vital link in Germany's chain of military strategy.

I would further like to call to your Honour's attention the evidence which has already been submitted on the activities of the A.P.A. in Norway, activities which led to the treason of Quisling and Hagelin, for which they have been condemned.

I come now to the final phase of the case against the defendant Rosenberg. We have seen how he aided the Nazi rise to power and directed the psychological preparation of the German people for waging aggressive war. I will now offer proof of his responsibility for the planning and execution of War Crimes and Crimes against Humanity committed in the vast areas of the occupied East, which he administered for over three years. These areas included the Baltic States, White Ruthenia, the Ukraine and the Eastern portion of Poland.

I will not attempt, at this stage, to chronicle again the tale of mass murder, spoliation and brutality. We feel that that has already been sufficiently put in evidence, and further evidence on this point will be presented by the prosecution for the U.S.S.R. and for the Republic of France.

We anticipate, however, that Rosenberg will contend that some of these crimes were committed against his wishes, and, indeed, there is some evidence that he protested on occasion - not out of humanitarian reasons but on grounds of political expediency.

We also anticipate that Rosenberg will attempt to place the blame for these crimes on other agencies and on other defendants. The evidence will prove, however, that he himself formulated the harsh policies, in the execution of which the crimes were committed; that the crimes were committed for the most part by persons and agencies within his jurisdiction and control; that any other agencies which participated in the commission of these crimes were invited by Rosenberg to co-operate in the administration of the East, although the brutal methods customarily employed by them were common knowledge; and, finally, that his Ministry lent full co-operation to their activities, despite the criminal methods that were employed.

Rosenberg was actively participating in the affairs of the East as early as 20th April, 1941, two months prior to the German attack upon the Soviet Union. On that date he was designated by Hitler as Commissioner for the Central Control of Questions Connected With the East European Region.

The Hitler Order, by virtue of which he received this appointment, has been read into the record in its entirety as Exhibit USA 143, our Document 865-PS.

The initial preparations undertaken by Rosenberg for fulfilment of his task indicated the extent to which he co- operated in promoting the military plans for aggression. They also show that he understood his task, at the inception, as requiring the assistance of a multitude of Reich agencies and that he invited their co-operation.

Shortly after his appointment by Hitler, Rosenberg conducted a series of conferences with representatives of various Reich agencies, conferences which are summarised in Document 1039-PS, previously offered as Exhibit USA 146. This document indicated the co-operation of the following agencies. It indicated that the co-operation of these agencies was both contemplated and solicited by Rosenberg. The agencies are as follows: O.K.W., O.K.H. and O.K.M., Ministry of Economies, Commissioner for the Four Year Plan, Ministry of the Interior, Reich Youth Leadership, the German Labour Front, Ministry of Labour, the S.S., the S.A. and several others.

These arrangements, it should be noted, were made by Rosenberg in his capacity as Commissioner on Eastern Questions, before the attack on the Soviet Union, before he was appointed as Reich Minister for the Occupied East, in fact, before there was any Occupied East for Germany to administer.

I would like to refer briefly to some of Rosenberg's basic attitudes regarding his new task and the directives which he knew he would be expected to follow. Your Honours will recall that on 29th April, 1941, in Document 1024-PS, previously introduced as Exhibit USA 278, Rosenberg stated that:

"A general treatment is required for the Jewish problem for which a temporary solution will have to be determined (forced labour for the Jews, creation of Ghettos, etcetera)."

On 8th May, 1941, he prepared instructions for all Reich Commissars in the Occupied Eastern Territories. These instructions are found in Document 1030-PS, previously introduced as Exhibit USA 144. The last paragraph, which has not been called to your Honour's attention, reads as follows:

"From the point of view of cultural policy, the German Reich is in a position to promote and direct national culture and science in many fields. It will be necessary that in some territories an uprooting and resettlement of various racial stocks will have to be effected."

In Document 1029-PS, which has been introduced as Exhibit USA 145, Rosenberg directs that the "Ostland" be transformed into a part of the Greater German Reich by Germanising racially possible elements, colonising Germanic races, and banishing undesirable elements.

In a speech which Rosenberg made on 20th June, 1941, your Honour will recall, he stated that the job of feeding Germans was the acme of Germany's claim on the East; that there was no obligation to feed the Russian peoples; that this was a harsh necessity bare of any feelings; that a very extensive evacuation would be necessary; and that the future would hold many hard years in store for the Russians. This speech, your Honour, is in the record as Document 1058-PS, Exhibit USA 147.

On 4th July, 1941, still prior to Rosenberg's appointment as Reich Minister for the Occupied East, a representative of Rosenberg's Bureau attended a conference on the subject of utilisation of labour, and especially of the labour of Soviet prisoners of war. Document 1199-PS is a memorandum of this conference, and I offer it into evidence as Exhibit USA 604. It states that the participants were, among others, representatives of the Commissioner for the Four Year Plan, of the Reich Labour Ministry, of the Reich Food Ministry, and of the Rosenberg Bureau. The first sentence states, and I quote:

"After an introduction by Lieutenant-Colonel Dr. Krull, Lieutenant-Colonel Breyer of the P.W. Department explained that actually there was in effect a prohibition by the Fuehrer against bringing Russian P.W.'s into the Reich for employment, but that one might count on this prohibition being relaxed a little."

The last paragraph records that:

"The chairman summarised the results of the discussion, as indicating that all the interested bureaus unqualifiedly advocated and supported the demand for utilisation of P.W.'s because of manpower needs in the Reich."

On 16th July, 1941, the day before Rosenberg's appointment as Minister of the Occupied East, he attended a conference at the Fuehrer's headquarters, the minutes of which have been introduced as Document L-221, Exhibit USA 317. At that time Hitler stated: "The Crimea has to be evacuated by all foreigners and to be settled by Germans alone."

He further stated that Germany's objectives in the East were threefold, first, to dominate it; second, to administer it; third, to exploit it.

Thus, the character of the administration which was contemplated for the Occupied East was well established before Rosenberg took office as Minister. He knew of these plans and was in accord with them. Persecution of the Jews, forced labour of prisoners of war, Germanisation and exploitation, were all basic points of policy, which Rosenberg knew of at the time he assumed office.

On 17th July, 1941, Rosenberg was appointed Reichminister for the Occupied Eastern Territories. The decree by which he was appointed is in evidence as document 1997-PS, Exhibit USA 319.

I would like now to examine the organisational structure and the chain of responsibility which existed within the Ministry for the Occupied East.

The organisational structure was such as will show that Rosenberg was not merely a straw man. He was the supreme authority with full control.

Document 1056-PS is a mimeographed treatise, entitled "The Organisation of The Administration of the Occupied Eastern Territories." It is undated and unsigned, but we can obtain further information regarding it by reference to EC-347, which is Goering's "Green Folder," already in evidence as Exhibit USA 320.

It is noted that Part II, sub-section A of Document EC-347, is entitled, and I quote:

"Excerpts from the Directives of the Reich Minister for the Occupied Eastern Territories for the Civil Administration," and then in parentheses, "Brown Folder, Part 1, Pages 25 to 30."

The two paragraphs which follow are identical to two paragraphs found at the top of Page 9 of the translation of Document 1056-PS. Thus Document 1056-PS is identified as being a mimeograph of Part I of the Brown Folder which was mentioned in the Green Folder, and was issued by the Reich Minister for the Occupied Eastern Territories.

I now offer Document 1056-PS as Exhibit USA 605. I offer this document for the purpose of proving, from the directives issued by the Rosenberg Ministry itself, the extent of Rosenberg's authority; that he was the supreme civilian authority in the Eastern Territories. The document will show that there was a continuous chain of command from Rosenberg down to the regional administrative officials, a chain of command which extended even to the local prison warden.

The document also will show the relationship which existed between the Rosenberg Ministry and other German agencies, a relationship which varied from full control by Rosenberg to full co-operation with them, made mandatory by his directives and by Hitler's orders.

Finally, the document will show that the various subdivisions of the Ministry were required to submit periodic reports of the situation within their jurisdiction, so that the numerous reports of unspeakable brutality which Rosenberg received, and which are already in the record, were submitted to him pursuant to his orders.

The first paragraph of this significant document states as follows:

"The newly-occupied Eastern Territories are subordinated to the Reich Minister for the Occupied Eastern Territories. By directive of the Fuehrer he established a civil administration there, upon withdrawal of the military administration. He heads and supervises the entire administration of this area and represents the sovereignty of the Reich in the Occupied Eastern Territories."

At the top of Page 2 of the translation is stated, and I quote:

"To the Reich Ministry is assigned a deputy of the Reich Leader S.S. and Chief of the German Police in the Reich Ministry of the Interior."

Part III on Page 2 of the translation defines the responsibility of the Reich Commissars as, and I quote:

"In the Reich Commissariats, Reich Commissars are responsible for the entire civil administration under the supreme authority of the Reich Ministry for the Occupied Eastern Territories. According to the instructions of the Reich Minister for the Occupied Eastern Territories, the Reich Commissar, as a functionary of the Reich, heads and supervises, within his precincts, the entire civil administration. Within the scope of these instructions he acts on his own responsibility."

And then the chain of command is outlined: Subordinate offices, General Commissariats, Main Commissariats, District Commissariats, etc.

In the second last paragraph on Page 3 of the translation it is stated again:

"The Higher S. S. and Police Leader is directly subordinated to the Reich Commissar. However, the Chief of Staff has the general right to secure information from him also.

Great stress is to be placed on close co-operation between him, the Chief of Staff, and the other main department head of the Office of the Reich Commissar, particularly with the one for policies."

To digress from this document a moment, I ask that the Court take judicial notice of the decree signed by Rosenberg, dated 17th July, 1941, and found in the "Verordnungsblatt" of the Reich Minister for the Occupied East, 1942, number 2, Pages 7 and 8.

"This decree provides for the creation of Summary courts for decisions on crimes committed by non-Germans in the East. The courts are to be presided over by a police officer or an S.S. Leader, who have authority to order the death sentence or confiscation of property, and those decisions are not subject to appeal.

The general commissar is given the right to reject a decision."

Thus, the determination of the S.S., of these Summary courts, is made subordinate to the authority of a representative of the Rosenberg Ministry.

At Page 4 of the translation of Document 1056-PS, the position of the General Commissar is defined. It is stated here that:

"The General Commissar forms the administrative office of intermediate appeal."

Three paragraphs down it is stated, and I quote:

"The S.S. and Police Leader assigned to the General Commissar is directly subordinated to him. However, the Chief of Staff has the general right of requiring information from him."

The document goes on to describe the function of the various subdivisions of the Ministry, concluding with Regional Commissars who preside over the local administrative districts. They, too, have police units assigned to them and directly subordinated to them.

THE PRESIDENT: Well, Mr. Brudno, surely that could have been stated in a sentence without referring us to all these passages in this document. I mean, Rosenberg was the Minister for the Eastern Territories. He had under him Reich Commissars and S.S. units, who had the full administration - civil administration - of the Eastern Territories.

If you had stated that, surely that would have been sufficient.

MR. BRUDNO: Very well, your Honour.

I will proceed from that point, then, to merely point out that the economic exploitation of the territory was undertaken in the fullest co-operation with the Commissioner of the Four Year Plan, as shown by paragraph 2 of Page 7 of the translation. It is stated there that the economic inspectorates of the Commissioner of the Four Year Plan will be substantially absorbed in the agencies of the civil administration, after its establishment.

I also wish to call your Honour's attention to the first paragraph on Page 6, which reads as follows:

"The various commissars," it says, "are, aside from the military agencies, the only Reich authorities in the Occupied Eastern Territories. Other Reich authorities may not be established alongside them. They handle all questions of administration of the area which is subordinate to their sovereignty, and all affairs which concern the organisation and activity of the administration, including those of the police, in the supervision of the native agencies and organisation and of the population."

I now turn briefly to the second section of the document which is entitled, "Working Directives for the Civil Administration." The first two paragraphs on Page 9 have been read into the record as part of Document EC-347, Exhibit USA 320. I call particular attention to the statement that the " Hague Rules of Land Warfare, which deal with the administration of a country occupied by a foreign armed power, are not valid."

I continue quoting at, the last paragraph on Page 9:

"The handling of cases of sabotage is a concern of the Senior S.S. and Police Leader, or of the Police Leaders of the lower echelon. In so far as collective measures against the population appear appropriate, the decision about them rests with the competent commissar.

To inflict penalties in cash or kind, as well as to order the seizure of hostages and the shooting of inhabitants of the territory in which the acts of sabotage have taken place, rests only with the General Commissar, unless the Reich Commissar himself intervenes."

I finish with this document by quoting the first sentence at the top of Page 13:

"The District Commissars are responsible for the supervision of all prisons, unless the Reich Commissars intervene."

I will not take the time of the Tribunal, nor burden the record, with a detailed account of the manner in which Rosenberg's plenary authority and power were wielded. There is evidence in the record, and there will be additional evidence presented by the Soviet prosecutor, as to the magnitude of the War Crimes and the

Crimes against Humanity perpetrated against the peoples of the Occupied East.

However, merely to illustrate the manner in which Rosenberg participated in the criminal activities conducted within his jurisdiction, I would like to refer briefly to a few examples.

I call your attention to the document numbered R-135, which was previously introduced as Exhibit USA 289. In this document the prison warden of Minsk reports that 516 German and Russian Jews had been killed, and called attention to the fact that valuable gold had been lost due to the failure to knock out the fillings of the victims' teeth before they were done away with.

These activities took place in the prison at Minsk, a prison which, your Honour will recall from Document 1056, was directly under the supervision of the Ministry for the Occupied East.

For my next illustration I wish to offer Document 018-PS. This has already been introduced as Exhibit USA 186. I would like to read to the Tribunal the first paragraph of Document 018-PS, which has not yet been read into the record. The document reveals that Rosenberg wrote to Sauckel on 21st November, 1942, in the following terms:

> "I thank you very much for your report on the execution of the great task given you, and I am glad to hear that in carrying out your mission you have always found the necessary support, even from the civilian authorities, in the Occupied Eastern Territories. For myself and the officials under my command, this collaboration was and is self-evident, especially since both you and I have, with regard to the solution of the labour problem in the East, represented the same points of view from the beginning."

As late as 11th July, 1944, the Rosenberg Ministry was actively concerned with the continuation of the forced labour programme, in spite of the retreat from the East.

THE TRIBUNAL (Mr. Biddle): After making this generality, Rosenberg goes on to object, at the last here, to the methods used. You have not mentioned that.

MR. BRUDNO: Quite right, your Honour. Those objections are already in the record, Sir, and I was merely referring to this document to show that Rosenberg favoured recruitment from the East, and that his civilian administrators co-operated with the recruitment in spite of the methods used, the methods which were known to Rosenberg, as he reports in the letter himself.

DR. ALFRED THOMA (Counsel for the defendant Rosenberg): High Tribunal. I must, in this connection, protest that the prosecution did not finish reading paragraph I just quoted. For it is declared in the following sentence that an agreement existed between Sauckel and Rosenberg regarding

THE PRESIDENT: I do not think you can have heard, that the United States member of the Tribunal has just made this very point which you are now making to counsel for the United States, and has pointed out to him that he ought to have read there, or drawn attention, at any rate, to the other paragraphs in this document which showed that Rosenberg was objecting to the methods used.

DR. THOMA: High Tribunal. I would like to point to the fact that the prosecution quoted just the first two sentences of a paragraph - the same paragraph continues, however, stating that there was an agreement between him and Sauckel according to which workers were to be treated well in Germany, and for this purpose welfare organisations were to be created. The presentation of the prosecution creates the impression that the defendants Sauckel and Rosenberg had agreed on the use of forced labour without restraint, and on the deportation of the workers from the East.

THE PRESIDENT: As counsel for the United States pointed out, the other passages in the document have already been read. And, naturally, the whole document will be treated as being in evidence.

The Tribunal fully realises the point you are making, that it is not fair to read one passage of a document when there are other passages in the document which show that the passage read is not a full or proper statement of the document.

MR. BRUDNO: If your Honour please, I was not attempting to delude the Tribunal; it was merely in the interest of time that I did not read the balance. The rest is in the record.

THE PRESIDENT: I realise that.

We will adjourn now.

(The Tribunal adjourned until 10th January, 1946, at 1000 hours.)

Thirty-First Day: Thursday, January 10th, 1946

MR. BRUDNO: May it please the Tribunal, when the Tribunal rose yesterday I had finished the submission of proof as to Rosenberg's responsibility and authority in the Occupied Eastern Territories, and was about to conclude my presentation with four brief examples as to the manner in which his authority was exercised. I was in the middle of the third example, which your Honours will recall dealt with Rosenberg's participation in the forced labour programme. I wish to conclude that illustration with reference to Document 199-PS, which we offer as Exhibit USA 606. This document is a letter from Alfred Meyer, Rosenberg's deputy, and is addressed to Sauckel, and dated 11th July, 1944. This time, your Honour will note, it is Rosenberg's Ministry that is urging action. I wish to quote item number I of this letter, which reads as follows:

> "The war employment command formerly stationed in Minsk must continue, under all circumstances, the calling up of young White Ruthenians and Russians for military employment in the Reich. In addition, the Command has the mission to bring boys of 10-14 years of age to the Reich."

My third illustration deals with Rosenberg's exercise of his legislative powers, and I ask the Court to take judicial notice of the decree signed by Lohse, who was Reich Commissar for the Ausland. This decree is published in the Verordnungs Blatt of the Reich Commissar for the Ausland, 1942, No. 38, Pages 158 and 159. It provides for the seizure of the entire property of the Jewish population in the Ausland, including the claims of Jews against third parties. The seizure is made retroactive to the day of occupation of the territory by German troops. This sweeping decree was issued and published by Rosenberg's immediate subordinate, and it must be assumed that Rosenberg knew of it and acquiesced in it.

I now come to my final illustration. This illustration is derived from Document 327-PS, which is already in evidence as Exhibit USA 338.

It is a copy of a secret letter from Rosenberg to Bormann dated 17th October, 1944. It furnishes a graphic account of Rosenberg's activities in the economic exploitation of the Occupied East. I wish to quote from the first paragraph on Page 1, which has not been read into the record. It reads:

> "In order not to delay the liquidation of companies under my supervision, I beg to point out that the companies concerned are not private firms but business enterprises of the Reich, so that actions with regard to them, just as with regard to Government Offices, are reserved to the highest authorities of the Reich. I supervise the following companies."

There follows a list of nine companies - a trading company, an agricultural development company, a supply company, a pharmaceutical company and five banking concerns. On Page 3 of the translation at item I (a), the mission of the trading company is stated to be, and I quote:

> "Collection of all agricultural products as well as commercial marketing, and transportation thereof. (Delivery to Armed Forces and the Reich)."

I now call your attention to item 5 of the same page. It describes the activities of the companies as follows:

"During this period, the Z.O., that is, the Central Trading Corporation, together with its subsidiaries has collected:
Grain — 9,200,000 tons
Meat and meat products — 622,000
Linseed. — 950,000
Butter — 208,000
Sugar — 400,000
Fodder — 2,500,000
Potatoes — 3,200,000
Seeds — 141,000
Other agricultural products — 1,200,000
and — 1,073,000,000 eggs

The following was required for transportation:
1,418,000 freight cars and 472,000 tons shipping space."

In conclusion we submit that the evidence has shown that the defendant Rosenberg played a leading role in the Nazi Party's rise to power by moulding German thought so as to promote the conspirators' ambitions; that he played a leading role in spreading propaganda and intrigue, and in instigating treason in foreign countries, so as to pave the way for the waging of wars of aggression; and that he bears full responsibility for the War Crimes and Crimes against Humanity which were perpetrated in the Occupied Eastern Territories, and which will be further developed by the prosecutor for the U.S.S.R.

This completes the presentation of the case against the defendant Rosenberg. The next presentation will be that of the case against the defendant Frank, which will be presented by Lieutenant-Colonel Baldwin.

LIEUTENANT-COLONEL BALDWIN: May it please the Tribunal, we wish now to deal with the individual responsibility of the defendant Frank. In accordance with the expressed desire of the Tribunal, this presentation has been strictly limited, and, of course, I should welcome any direction from the Tribunal, as to length or method, as I proceed.

First, I must acknowledge my indebtedness to Miss Harriet Zetterberg, of our Legal Staff, and to Doctor Pietrowski, of the Polish Delegation, for their invaluable work, Doctor Pietrowski and the Polish Delegation naturally having a special interest in the defendant Frank.

Aspects of the criminal complicity of the defendant Hans Frank, under Count 1 of the Indictment, have been placed before this Tribunal on several occasions. There remain, however, certain matters for discussion - either novel in presentation or in development - concerning this defendant as an individual, before the United States portions of the prosecution's case against him is completed. Our Soviet colleagues will carry further the heavy complaint against the defendant Frank in their treatment of War Crimes and Crimes against Humanity in the East. We wish here merely to touch upon that evidence which, we believe, irrefutably discloses Frank to have been a tremendously important cog in the machine which conceived, promoted and executed the Nazi Common Plan or Conspiracy. Documents relating to this point have been assembled in a document book bearing the letters "FF." I am informed that these books, as well as explanatory briefs, have been distributed for the use of the members of the Tribunal.

Reference will be made in the course of this argument to the so-called "Frank Diary," portions of which have already been brought to the attention of the Tribunal. It seems appropriate that brief mention should here be made of the contents and source of this diary. It is a set of some 42 volumes detailing the activities of the defendant Frank from 1939 to the end of the war in his capacity as Governor-General of Occupied Poland. It is a record, in short, of each day's business, hour by hour, appointment by appointment, conference by conference, speech by speech, and, in truth we believe, crime by crime. Each volume, excepting the last few, is now handsomely bound, and in those volumes, which deal with the conferences of Frank and his underlings in the Government General, the name of each person attending the meeting is inscribed in his own handwriting on a page preceeding the minutes of the conference itself. It is incredibly shocking to the normal conscience that such a neat history of murder, starvation and extermination should have been maintained by the individual responsible for such deeds, but by now the Tribunal is well aware that the Nazi leaders were sentimentally fond of elaborately documenting their exploits, as witness the Rosenberg volumes displaying the looted art treasures, and the album reporting on the extermination of Jews in the Warsaw Ghetto. The complete set of the "Frank Diary" was found in Bavaria, at Heuhaus, on 18th May, 1945, by the 7th American Army. It was taken to the 7th Army Document Centre at Heidelberg and on or about 20th September, 1945, the collection was sent to the Office of the U.S. Chief of Counsel here at Nuremberg. It is here in Court in its entirety, and now its tones, we submit, are those of accusation, rather than boastful narration.

That the defendant Frank held a position of leadership in the Nazi Party and in the German Government is undeniable, even though, presumably, it would be unfair to him to underestimate his importance in the Nazi Hierarchy and the Third Reich. Like the other defendants in this case, be was a man of far-reaching influence and position, and his office- holding record is already before this Court. It is an affidavit signed by the defendant Frank and identified as Exhibit USA. 7. This document contains a listing of eleven important positions held by Frank in the Party and in the Government, and supports the assertion of influence and position which I have just made, especially since this Tribunal has been fully apprised of the criminal activities of the Nazi organisations and formations.

The machinations of Frank divide themselves logically into two periods. In the one - from 1920 to 1939 - he was, by his own admission, the leading Nazi Jurist, although parenthetically the word "jurist" loses its reputable content when modified by the word "Nazi." In the other period -extending from 10th October, 1939, until the end of the war - he was Governor General of Occupied Poland. While he is most notorious for his persecutions and carrying out of the conspiracy in the latter capacity, it is the opinion of the U.S. prosecution that the defendant Frank's contributions to the Nazi rise to power as the leading "Nazi Jurist" should not pass without mention. It is with this aspect that I shall first deal - the defendant Frank's furtherance of the realisation of the conspirators' programme in the field of law, his knowledge of the criminal purpose of the programme and his active participation therein.

The defendant Frank himself described his role in the Nazi struggle for power in the following words, in the course of his closing remarks at a conference held on 28th August, 1942, at Kressendorf. The remarks appear in the diary and are translated in our document 2233-PS, which, if the Court please, is at Page 54 in the document book.

The numbers of the pages of the document book will be found in the upper right-hand corner in coloured. pencil, either red or blue. The original of this document I now offer in evidence as Exhibit USA 607. In the German text these extracts appear in Part 3 in the 1942 diary volume on Pages 968, 969 and 983. Frank says:

"I have since 1920 continually dedicated my work to the N.S.D.A.P. As a National Socialist I was a participant in the events of November, 1923, for which I received the Blutorden. After the resurrection of the movement in the year 1925, my greater activity in the movement really began, which made me, first gradually, later almost exclusively, the legal adviser of the Fuehrer and of the Reich leadership of the N.S.D.A.P. I was thus the representative of legal interests of the growing Third Reich in a legal-ideological as well as in a practical way."

He goes on to say:

"The culmination of this work I see in the Leipzig Army Trial, in which I succeeded in having the Fuehrer admitted to the famous oath of legality a fact which gave the Movement the legal grounds to expand generously. The Fuehrer indeed recognised this achievement, and in 1926 made me Leader of the National Socialist Lawyers' League; in 1929, Reich Leader of the Reich Legal Office of the N.S.D.A.P.; in 1933, Bavarian Minister of Justice; in 1934, President of the Academy of German Law founded by me; and in December, 1934, Reich Minister without Portfolio. Lastly in 1939, I was appointed to be Governor-General for the Occupied Polish Territories.

So I was, am, and will remain the representative jurist of the struggle period of National Socialism.

I profess myself now, and always, as a National Socialist and a faithful follower of the Fuehrer, Adolf Hitler, whom I have now served since 1919."

It is indeed significant and worth mentioning to the Court -

THE PRESIDENT: Is this an extract from his diary?

LIEUTENANT-COLONEL BALDWIN: Yes, Sir, it is.

THE PRESIDENT: And are the words "Present: Doctor Hans Frank and others" written by him in his diary?

LIEUTENANT-COLONEL BALDWIN: Yes, Sir, they are. Before each of these excerpts, if your Honour pleases, if it was in conference it was indicated which members of the Government generally were present or who made the address.

THE PRESIDENT: Yes.

LIEUTENANT-COLONEL BALDWIN: It is indeed significant and worth mentioning to the Court that the defendant Frank assumes responsibility for the so-called oath of legality at the Leipzig Army Trial. At that trial, in 1930, three army officers are accused of, curiously enough, conspiracy to high treason. The charge was that the defendants in that trial, in their capacity as members of the German Army, tried to form National Socialist cells in the German Army and to influence the German Army to such an extent that in the case of a putsch by the National Socialists the army would not fire at the National Socialists, but would stand at ease instead. All three of the officers were found guilty and sentenced to eighteen months' confinement. At that trial, however, Hitler was a witness, and during the course of the trial testified under oath that the term "revolution," used by him, only meant spiritual revolution in Germany, and that the expression "heads would roll in the sand" meant only that they would do so as a result of legal procedure through State Tribunals, if the National Socialists came to power. This, if the Court please, was the so-called oath of legality, the lie with which the defendant Frank provided his Fuehrer as a facade for the conspiracy and which he, at least in 1942, considered the culmination of his efforts.

As the "Representative Jurist of the struggle period of National Socialism" and in various juridical capacities listed in his affidavit of positions held, defendant Frank was, between 1933 and 1939, the most prominent policy maker in the field of German legal theory. For example, defendant Frank founded the Academy of German Law in 1934 and he was President of this once-potent body until 1942. The statute defining the functions of this Academy conferred upon it wide power to initiate and co-ordinate juridical policies.

This statute appears in the translation at Page 5 in the document book, as our document 1391-PS, and appears in the 1934 Reichsgesetzblatt at Page 605.

We ask the Court to take judicial notice of it. I now quote briefly from the decree:

"It is the task of the Academy for German Law to further the rejuvenation of the Law in Germany. Closely connected with the agencies competent for legislation, it shall further the realisation of the National Socialist programme in the realm of the Law. This task shall be carried out through well-determined scientific methods. The Academy's task shall cover primarily:

1. The composition, initiation, judging and preparing of drafts of law.

2. The collaboration in rejuvenating and unifying the training in jurisprudence and political science.

3. The editing and supporting of scientific publications.

4. The financial assistance for work and research in specific fields of Law and Political Economy."

THE TRIBUNAL (Mr. Biddle): Do you have to read all this? We will take judicial notice of it.

LIEUTENANT-COLONEL BALDWIN: Among the early tasks which defendant Frank set for himself, as policy maker in the field of law, were the unification of the German State, the promotion of racial legislation and the elimination of political organisations other than the Nazi Party. In a radio address given on 20th March, 1934, he announced success in these matters. Our partial English translation of this speech appears as Document 2536-PS, at Page 64 in the document book. The official text of this speech appears in "Dokumente der Deutschen Politik," Volume 11, Pages 294-298. In the German text the extracts which I shall quote appear at Pages 296 and 298, and I win ask the Court to take judicial notice of these passages:

"The first task was that of establishing a unified German State. It was an outstanding historical and juristic-political accomplishment on the part of our Fuehrer that he reached boldly into the historical development and thereby eliminated the sovereignty of the various German States. At last we have now again, after 1,000 years, a unified German State in every respect. It is no longer possible for the world to make calculations to the detriment of the German Government, based on the spirit of resistance inherent in small States, which are set up on an egotistical scale and solely with a view to their individual interest. That is a thing of the past for all times to come."

I pass on now to the second excerpt:

"The second fundamental law of the Hitler Reich is racial legislation. The National Socialists were the first ones in the entire history of human law to elevate the concept of race to the status of a legal term. The German Nation, unified racially and nationally, will in the future be legally protected against any further disintegration of the German race stock."

I pass now to the mention of the sixth:

"The sixth fundamental law was the legal elimination of those political organisations which, within the State, during the period of the reconstruction of the People and the Reich, were once able to place their selfish aims ahead of the common good of the Nation. This elimination has taken place entirely legally. It is not the coming to the fore of despotic tendencies, but the necessary legal consequence of a clear political result of the 14 years' struggle of the N.S.D.A.

In accordance with these unified legal aims," Frank continues, "in all spheres, particular efforts have for months now been made as regards the work of the great reform of the entire field of German Law.

As a leader of the German Jurists, I am convinced that, together with all strata of the German people, we shall be able to construct the legal State of Adolf Hitler in every respect and to such an extent that no one in the world will at any time be able to dare to attack this legal State as regards its laws."

In his speech on the occasion of the Day of the Reich University Professors of the National Socialist Lawyers' League on 3rd November, 1936, the defendant Frank explained to the gathering of professors, the elimination of Jews from the legal field, in accordance with the Nazi plan. Our partial translation of the speech appears as Document 2536- PS, at Page 62 of the document book. The official text appears likewise in "Dokumente der Deutschen Politik," in Volume IV, Pages 225 to 230. I ask the Tribunal to take judicial notice of this. It deals, to summarise -

THE PRESIDENT: I do not think you need it because we have already had documents of the same sort.

LIEUTENANT-COLONEL BALDWIN: As the leading Nazi Jurist, the defendant Frank accepted, condoned and promoted the system of concentration camps and of arrest without warrant. He apparently had no hesitancy in subverting his professional ethics, if he had any, while subverting the legal framework of the German State to Nazi ends. He explains that outrageous departure from civilisation - the concentration camps - in an article on "Legislation and Judiciary in the Third Reich," published in 1936 in the official journal of the Academy of German Law, of which, of course, he was the editor. The partial translation of this article appears as our Document 2533-PS, at Page 61 of the document book. The official German text of the extract appears in "Zeitschrift der Akademie fur Deutsches Recht," 1936, at Page 141, and I will ask the Tribunal to take judicial notice of this. Since the extract is short, I will ask permission to read it. Frank says:

"Before the world we are blamed again and again because of the concentration camps. We are asked, 'Why do you arrest without a warrant of arrest'? I say, put yourselves into the position of our nation. Remember that the very great and still untouched world of Bolshevism cannot forget that here on our German soil we have made final victory for them impossible in Europe."

It can be seen, therefore, that just as other defendants mobilised the military, economic and diplomatic resources for aggressive war, the defendant Frank, in the field of legal policy, geared the German judicial machine for a war of aggression, which war of aggression, as he explained in 1942 to the N.S.D.A.P. political leaders of Galicia at a mass meeting in Lemberg - and I now quote from the "Frank Diary," our Document 2233-PS-S, at Page 50 in the document book, the original of which I offer into evidence as Exhibit USA 607 - bad for its purpose, and I quote:

"To expand the living space for our people in a natural manner."

The distortions and warpings of German law which defendant Frank engineered for the Party gave him, if not the world, vast satisfaction. He reported this to the powerful Academy for German Law in November, 1939, one month after becoming

Governor-General of Occupied Poland. This speech is partially translated in our Document 3445-PS, at Page 73 in the document book. The official text of the speech appears in "Deutsches Recht," 1939, Volume 2, the week of 23rd-30th December, 1939, beginning at Page 2121, and we ask the Court to take judicial notice of this, but would like permission to read the excerpt, as it is very short.

Frank stated:

"To-day we are proud to have formulated our legal principles from the very beginning in such a way that they need not be changed in the case of war. For the rule - right is that which is useful to the nation, and wrong is that which harms it - which stood at the beginning of our legal work, and which established the idea of the people's community as the only standard of the law - this rule also dominates the social order of these times."

If this sentiment has a familiar ring to it, it is because it is a restatement of a Party commandment tailored and furnished by the Party lawyer to fit the Party's concept of law. I allude, of course, to the Party commandment previously commented upon (Page 30, Part 3) in the treatment of the Leadership Corps, which commandment stated, and I quote: "Right is that which serves the movement and thus Germany."

It follows, I think, that the prosecution conceives the defendant Frank to be jointly responsible for all those cruel and discriminatory enabling acts and decrees through which the Nazis crushed minorities in Germany, and consolidated their control over the German State, and prepared it for its early entry upon aggression. It matters not, in our view, that the signature of this lawyer does not appear at the foot of every decree. Enough has been shown, in our submission, to indicate culpability in this regard. There is sufficient, we believe, now in this record - and I refer to decrees cited by Major Walsh in his treatment of the persecution of the Jews and by Colonel Storey in his treatment of the Reich Cabinet - to demonstrate that type of enactment and the consequences thereof, for which we hold the defendant Frank liable. In following this theory, may it please the Tribunal, we are only arriving at conclusions already arrived at for us by the defendant Frank himself.

I now pass to that second and well-known phase of the defendant Frank's official life, wherein he, for five years as chief Party and Government Agent, was bent upon the elimination of a whole people. He was appointed Governor- General of the Occupied Polish Territory by a decree signed by his then Fuehrer, on 12th October, 1939. The decree defined the scope of Frank's executive power and is contained in our Document 2537-PS, at Page 66 in the document book. I shall ask the Tribunal to take judicial notice of this, since it appears in Reichsgesetzblatt, 1939, Part 1, Page 2077.

It merely states that Dr. Frank is appointed as Governor- General of the Occupied Polish Territory; that Dr. Seyss- Inquart is appointed as Deputy Governor-General and that "the Governor-General shall be directly responsible to me," meaning Hitler, he having signed the decree.

While some of the outside world was prone in earlier days to wonder at the apparent efficiency of Nazi administration, we now know that it was often riddled with the petty jealousies of small men in positions of some authority and with jurisdictional fractiousness. No such difficulty existed with the defendant Frank, however, for though he was not without the threat of divided authority, he insisted upon, and was granted, the favour of supreme command within the territorial confines of the General Government. Only two references from his diary, one in 1940 and one in 1942, are necessary to show how all-embracing was his direction and authority.

At a meeting of Department Heads of the Government General on 8th March, 1940, in the Bergakademie, the defendant Frank clarified his status as Governor-General, and these remarks appear in the diary and in our document 2233-PS-N, at Page 42 in the document book, the original of which I offer into evidence as Exhibit USA 173.

In the German text, the extracts appear in the Department Head Meetings, Volume for 1939-40, Pages 6, 7 and 8. Frank says:

> "One thing is certain. The authority of Governor-General as the representative of the Fuehrer and the will of the Reich in this territory is certainly strong, and I have always emphasised that I would not tolerate misuse of this authority. I have allowed this to be known anew at every office in Berlin, especially after Herr Field Marshal Goering on 12th February, 1940, from Karin Hall, had forbidden all Administrative Offices of the Reich, including the Police and even the Wehrmacht, to interfere in administrative matters of the Government General..."

He goes on to say:

> "There is no authority here in the Government General which is higher as to rank, influence and authority than that of the Governor-General Even the Wehrmacht has no governmental or official functions of any kind in this connection; it has only security functions and general military duties - it has no political power whatsoever. The same applies here to the Police and the SS. There is here no State within a State, but we are Representatives of the Fuehrer and of the Reich."

Later, in 1942, at a conference of the District political leaders of the N.S.D.A.P. in Cracow on 18th March, defendant Frank further explained the relationship between the administration and the Reichsfuehrer S.S. Himmler. These remarks appear in the diary and in our Document 2233-PS-R and at Page 48 of the document book, the original of which I offer into evidence, as Exhibit USA 608. In the German text, the extract to be quoted appears at Page 185, of diary volume 1942, Part 1. I quote:

> "As you know" - says Frank - "I am a fanatic as to unity in administration.... It is, therefore, clear that the Higher S.S. and Police Leader is subordinated to me, that the Police is a component of the Government, that the S.S. and Police Leader in the district is subordinated to the Governor, and that the district chief has the authority of command over the Police in his district. This, the Reichsfuehrer S.S. has recognised; in the written agreement all these points are mentioned word for word and signed.
>
> It is also self-evident that we cannot establish a closed set-up here which can be treated in the traditional manner of small States."

THE TRIBUNAL (Mr. Biddle): Do you think all this has to be read?

LIEUTENANT-COLONEL BALDWIN: It is considered important, Sir, by the United States prosecution, in view of the fact that this is the later extract from the diary, and communicates that two years later Frank considered himself to be the Supreme Authority in the Government General. This is a point which we conceive to be of importance, Sir.

May I proceed ?

THE PRESIDENT: Yes.

LIEUTENANT-COLONEL BALDWIN:

> "It would, for instance, be ridiculous if we were to build up here a security police of our own against our Poles in the country, while knowing that the

Poles in West Prussia, in Posen, in Wartheland and in Silesia have one and the same Movement of Resistance. The Reichsfuehrer S.S. and Chief of the German Police thus must be able to carry out, with the aid of his agencies, his police measures concerning the interests of the Reich as a whole. This, however, will be done in such a way that the measures to be adopted will first be submitted to me, and carried out only when I give up consent. In the Government General, the Police are the Armed Forces. As a result of this, the Leader of the Police system will be called by me into the Government of the Government General; he is subordinate to me, or to my deputy, as a State Secretary for the Security System."

At this juncture, it is appropriate to mention that the man who filled the position of State Secretary for Security in the Government General was Frank's Higher S.S. and Police Leader, Kruger.

THE PRESIDENT: Will you read the next page?

LIEUTENANT-COLONEL BALDWIN: May it please the Tribunal, I shall come to that excerpt later.

THE PRESIDENT: In the same document?

LIEUTENANT-COLONEL BALDWIN: Yes, Sir. It seems more appropriate at another point.

The Tribunal may recall that the reports of the extermination of Jews in the Warsaw Ghetto were made in the spring of 1943 by S.S. Leader Stroop - who immediately supervised the operation - to this same Kruger, who was still at that time one of the most influential members of Frank's Cabinet, as State Secretary for Security.

It was inevitable that the grand Common Plan or Conspiracy should have, as its component parts, a host of small plans, each dealing with a particular sphere of activity. These plans, differing from the master plan only in size, are the blueprints for a specific action drawn from the broad policies. Occupied Poland was no exception to this rule. The plan for the administration of Poland was contained in a top secret memorandum of a conference between Hitler and the Chief of the O.K.W., defendant Keitel, entitled, "Regarding Future Relations of Poland to Germany" and dated 20th October, 1939. This report was initialled by General Warlimont. It is our Document 964-PS and may be found at Page 3 of the document book, and I shall offer it into evidence as Exhibit USA 609.

I shall quote, if the Court please, only from paragraphs 1, 3, 4 and 6:

"1. The Armed Forces will welcome it if they can dispose of administrative questions in Poland.

On principle, there cannot be two administrations.

3. It is not the task of the Administration to make Poland into a model province or a model State of the German Order or to put her economically or financially on a sound basis.

The Polish intelligentsia must be prevented from forming a ruling class. The standard of living in the country is to remain low; we want only to draw labour forces from there. Poles are also to be used for the administration of the country. However, the forming of national political groups may not be allowed.

4. The administration has to work on its own responsibility and must not be dependent on Berlin. We do not want to do there what we do in the Reich. The responsibility does not rest with the Berlin Ministries, since there is no German administration unit concerned.

The accomplishment of this task will involve a hard racial struggle which will not allow any legal restrictions. The methods will be incompatible with the principles otherwise adhered to by us.

The Governor General is to give the Polish nation only bare living conditions and is to maintain the basis for military security.

6. Any tendencies towards the consolidation of conditions in Poland are to be suppressed. The 'Polish Muddle' must be allowed to develop. The government of the territory must make it possible for us to purify the Reich territory from Jews and Poles too. Collaboration with new Reich provinces (Posen and West Prussia) only for resettlements (compare Mission Himmler).

Purpose: Shrewdness and severity must be the maxims in this racial struggle, in order to spare us from going to battle on account of this country again."

The defendant Frank was the chosen executor of this programme. He knew its aims, approved of them, and actively carried out the scheme. The Tribunal's attention has already been invited to Exhibit USA 297 wherein (Page 422, Part 2) the defendant Frank expounded the mission which his Fuehrer had assigned to him and according to which he intended to administer in Poland. It contemplated, in brief, ruthless exploitation, deportation of all supplies and workers, reduction of the entire Polish economy to absolute minimum necessary for bare existence of the population, and the closing of all schools. No more callous statement exists than one Frank made in this report, wherein he said, "Poland shall be treated as a colony; the Poles shall be the slaves of the Greater German World Empire."

In December, 1940, Frank submitted to his department heads that the task of administering Poland did truly involve a hard racial struggle which would not allow any legal restrictions. I refer to our Document 2233PS-O, which may be found at Page 45 in the document book. It is taken from the "Frank Diary," and I offer it in evidence as Exhibit USA 173. In the German text the extract to be quoted appears in the volume of the diary entitled "Department Heads Meetings 1939-40," on Pages 12 and 13. I now quote:

"In this country the force of a determined leadership must rule. The Pole must feel here that we are not building him a legal State, but that for him there is only one duty, namely to work and to behave himself. It is clear that this must sometimes lead to difficulties, but you must, in your own interest, see that all measures are ruthlessly carried out in order to become master of the situation. You can rely on me absolutely in this."

As for the Poles and Ukrainians, defendant Frank's attitude was clear. They were to be permitted to slave for the German economy as long as the war emergency continued. Once the war was won, even this cynical interest would cease. I refer to a speech before German political leaders at Cracow on 12th January, 1944. It appears in the "Frank Diary" and as our Document 2233PS-B at Page 60 in the document book. It is the first passage on that page. I offer it in evidence as Exhibit USA 295. In the diary, the German text will be found in the loose-leaf volume covering the period from 1st January to 28th February, 1944, at the entry for 14th January, 1944, at Page 24:

"Once the war is won," Frank tells these leaders - and here we have, may it please the Court, the classic example of the completely brutal statement" Once the War is won, then for all I care, mincemeat can be made of the Poles and the Ukrainians and all the others who run around here-it does not matter what happens."

In accordance with the racial programme of the Nazi conspirators, the defendant

Frank makes it quite clear in his diary that the complete annihilation of Jews was one of his cherished objectives. In Exhibit USA 271, Frank stated in late 1940 in his diary that he could not eliminate all lice and Jews in a year's time. In Exhibit USA 281, he says in his diary in the year 1942 that a programme of starvation rations sentencing, in effect, 1,200,000 Jews to die of hunger, should be noted only marginally. In Exhibit USA 295, he confided to a secret Press conference that in the year 1944 - and this, too, is from the diary - there were still in the Government General perhaps 100,000 Jews.

These facts, if the Tribunal please, are from the diary of the man himself. We do no more here than tabulate the results. The supreme authority within a certain geographic area admits that, in a period of four years' time, up to 3,400,000 persons from that area have been annihilated, pursuant to an official policy and for no crime, but only because of having been born Jews. No words could possibly reveal the inferences of death and suffering which must needs be drawn from these stark facts.

It was a Nazi policy that the population of occupied countries should endure terror, oppression, impoverishment and starvation. The defendant Frank succeeded so well in this regard that he was forced to report to his Fuehrer, in 1943, that, in effect, Poles did not regard the Government General with affection. This report to Hitler was a summary of the first three and one-half years of the defendant Frank's administration. It, better than anything else, can show the conditions as they then existed as a result of the conspiratorial efforts of the defendants.

The report is contained in our document 437-PS, at Page 2 of the document book, and I now offer the original into evidence as Exhibit USA 610. In the German text, the extract to be quoted appears at Pages 10 and 11 of this report by Frank to Hitler dated 19th June, 1943, regarding the situation in Poland. Frank says:

"In the course of time, a series of measures or of consequences of the German rule have lead to a substantial deterioration of the attitude of the entire Polish people to the Government General, These measures have affected either individual professions or the entire population and frequently also - often with crushing severity - the fate of individuals."

He goes on:

"Among these are in particular:

1. The entirely insufficient nourishment of the population, mainly of the working classes in the cities, whose majority is working for German interests.

Until the war of 1939, its food supplies, though not varied, were sufficient and generally secure, due to the agrarian surplus of the former Polish State and in spite of the negligence on the part of their former political leadership.

2. The confiscation of a great part of the Polish estates and the expropriation, without compensation, and resettlement of Polish peasants from manoeuvre areas and from German settlements.

3. Encroachments and confiscations in the industries, in commerce and trade and in the field of private property.

4. Mass arrests and mass shooting by the German Police who applied the system of collective responsibility.

5. The rigorous methods of recruiting workers.

6. The extensive paralysation of cultural life.

7. The closing of high schools, junior colleges, and universities.

8. The limitation, indeed, the complete elimination, of Polish influence from all spheres of State Administration.

9. Curtailment of the influence of the Catholic Church, limiting its extensive influence - an undoubtedly necessary move - and, in addition, until quite recently, the closing and confiscation of monasteries, schools, and charitable institutions."

Indeed, the Nazi plan for Poland succeeded all too well.

THE PRESIDENT: This is only an extract here. Was he saying that these measures were inevitable or that he justified them, or what was he saying in the report?

LIEUTENANT-COLONEL BALDWIN: He was saying, Sir, that the Polish people's attitude to the Government General had substantially deteriorated. The reasons for that deterioration are the listings I gave to the Court. In other words -

THE PRESIDENT: Is that all he said?

LIEUTENANT-COLONEL BALDWIN: No, Sir, that is just taken from Pages 10 and 11 of the report. The report is an extremely long one.

THE PRESIDENT: Well, I suppose you know what the general tenor of the report was.

LIEUTENANT-COLONEL BALDWIN: The general tenor of the report, Sir, was in the nature of a complaint to Hitler, that he, Frank, was having an extremely difficult time in the Government General because of these measures, and because of these happenings in the Government General.

THE PRESIDENT: Very well.

LIEUTENANT-COLONEL BALDWIN: In order to illustrate how completely the defendant Frank is identified with the policies -

DR. SEIDL (Counsel for defendant Frank): After the Tribunal has already asked the prosecutor what purpose should be served by presenting this document, I would like to emphasise here that this is a document of 40 typewritten pages addressed to Hitler, and that Frank criticises these conditions which the prosecution has pointed out, and that in this document he makes large and wide propositions in order to remedy the situation, to which he severely objects.

I shall, when it will be my turn, read the whole document.

THE PRESIDENT: Exactly. You will have full opportunity, when it is your turn, to explain this document, but it is not your turn at the moment.

DR. SEIDL: I only mention that now because the Tribunal itself drew my attention to this point.

THE PRESIDENT: Now, Lieutenant-Colonel Baldwin, I asked you what was the whole contents of the document from which you were reading this paragraph. According to counsel for Frank, the document, which is a very long document, shows that Frank was suggesting remedies for the difficulties which he here sets out. Is that so?

LIEUTENANT-COLONEL BALDWIN: That is so, yes, your Honour.

THE PRESIDENT: Well, I think the -

LIEUTENANT-COLONEL BALDWIN: May it please the Tribunal, I did not cite this portion of that document, as I will later demonstrate, to show that Frank did or did not suggest a remedy for these conditions, but only to explain that these conditions existed at a certain period.

THE PRESIDENT: Well, when you cite a small part of the document, you should make sure that what you cite is not misleading as compared to the rest of the document.

LIEUTENANT-COLONEL BALDWIN: I see, your Honour. I had not considered it to be such in view of the purpose for which I introduced it, which, as I said, was only to suggest a set of conditions which existed at a certain time. I naturally assumed that the defence, as Dr. Seidl has indicated, would carry on with the rest of the document as a defence matter.

THE PRESIDENT: Yes, of course, that is all very well, but the defendant Frank's counsel will speak at some remote date, and it is not a complete answer to say that he will have an opportunity of explaining the document at some future date. It is for counsel for the prosecution to make sure that no extracts which they read can reasonably make a misleading impression upon the mind of the Tribunal.

LIEUTENANT-COLONEL BALDWIN: I shall now state, then, that the extract which was just read was read solely for the purpose of indicating that at a certain period, namely, June, 1943, those conditions existed in Poland, as the result of statements by the Governor-General of Poland.

Would that be satisfactory to the Tribunal?

THE TRIBUNAL (Mr. Biddle): Well, it was not satisfactory to the Tribunal if you did not give us the purport of the document.

LIEUTENANT-COLONEL BALDWIN: Well, Sir, I have not the complete document before me now. Therefore, I cannot read all of it.

THE PRESIDENT: No. What we would like would be, if possible, that when, an extract is made from a document, counsel who are presenting that extract should acquaint themselves with the general purport of the document, so as to make certain that the part that is read is not misleading.

LIEUTENANT-COLONEL BALDWIN: Yes, Sir.

In order to illustrate how completely the defendant Frank is identified with the policies of which the execution is reported in this document, and how thoroughly they were his own policies, and this, if the Tribunal please, regardless of what remedies he may have had in mind in 1943, it is proposed in this last section to take passages from Frank's own diary in proof of his early espousal and execution of these self-same policies.

As to the insufficient nourishment of the Polish population, there was no need for the defendant Frank to have waited until June, 1943, to have reported this fact to Hitler. In September, 1941, defendant Frank's own Chief Medical Officer reported to him the appalling Polish health conditions. This appears in "Frank's Diary" and in our Document 2233-PS-P, at Page 46 in the document book, which I now offer in evidence as Exhibit USA 611. The German text is to be found in the 1941 volume of the diary at Page 830.

I quote:

"Overmedizinalrat Dr. Walbaum expressed his opinion of the health condition of the Polish population. Investigations which were carried out by his department proved that the majority of Poles had only about 600 calories allotted to them, whereas the normal requirement for a human being were 2,200 calories. The Polish population was weakened to such an extent that it would fall an easy prey to spotted fever."

Parenthetically, I think we know that as typhus.

"The number of diseased Poles already amounts to 40 per cent. During the last week alone, 1,000 new spotted fever cases have been officially recorded. That represents so far the maximum number. This health situation represented a serious danger for the Reich and for the soldiers who are coming into the Government General. A spreading of pestilence into the Reich is quite feasible. The increase in tuberculosis, too, is causing anxiety. If the food rations were to be diminished again, an enormous increase of the number of illnesses can be predicted."

While it was crystal-clear from this report that in September, 1941, disease affected 40 per cent. of the Polish population, nevertheless the defendant Frank approved in August, 1942, a new plan which called for a much larger contribution of foodstuffs to Germany at the expense of the non-German population of the Government General. Methods of meeting the new quotas out of the grossly inadequate rations of the Government General and the impact of the new quotas on the economy of the country were discussed at a cabinet meeting of the Government General on 24th August, 1942, in terms which leave no possible doubt that not only was the proposed requisition beyond the resources of the country, but its force was to be distributed on a grossly discriminatory basis. This appears from the "Frank Diary" and in our Document 2233-PS-E, which is at Page 30 in the document book, which I now offer in evidence as Exhibit USA 283. The German text appears in the 1942 conference volume at the conference entry for 24th August, 1942.

I quote the following extract:

> "Before the German people" - Frank says - "are to experience starvation, the Occupied Territories and their people shall be exposed to starvation. In this moment, therefore, we here in the Government General, must also have the iron determination to help the Great German people, our Fatherland.
>
> The Government General, therefore, must do the following: The Government General has taken on the obligation to send 500,000 tons of bread grain to the Fatherland in addition to the foodstuffs already being delivered for the relief of Germany or consumed here by troops of the Armed Forces, Police or S.S. If you compare this with our contributions of last year you can see that this means a six-fold increase over that of last year's contribution of the Government General.
>
> The new demand will be fulfilled exclusively at the expense of the foreign population. It must be done cold- bloodedly and without pity...."

Defendant Frank was not only responsible for reducing the Government General to starvation level, but was proud of the contribution he thereby made to the Reich. I refer to a statement made to the political leaders of the N.S.D.A.P. on 14th December, 1942, at Cracow. It is contained in the "Frank Diary" and is our Document 2233-PS-Z, at Page 57 in the document book, and I now offer it in evidence as Exhibit USA 612. In the German text the extract appears in the 1942 volume of the diary, Part IV, at Page 1331.

Defendant Frank is speaking:

> "I will attempt to get out of the reservoir of this territory everything that is yet to be got out of it ...."

He continues:

> "When you consider that it was possible for me to deliver to the Reich 600,000 tons of bread grain, and, in addition, 180,000 tons to the Armed Forces stationed here; further, an abundance amounting to many thousands of tons of other commodities, such as seed, fats, vegetables, besides the delivery to the Reich of 300 million eggs, etc., you can estimate the significance this territory possesses for the Reich. In order to make clear to you the significance of the consignment from the Government General of 600,000 tons of bread grain, you are referred to the fact that the Government General, by this achievement alone, covers the raising of the bread ration in the Greater German Reich by two- thirds during the present rationing period. This enormous achievement

can rightfully be claimed by us."

Now, as to the resettlement of Polish peasants which defendant Frank mentions secondly in the report to Hitler, although Himmler was given general authority in connection with the conspirators' project to resettle various districts in the conquered Eastern Territories with racial Germans, the projects relating to resettling districts in the Government General were submitted to and approved by the defendant Frank. The plan to resettle Zamosc and Lublin, for example, was reported to him at a meeting to discuss special problems of the district Lublin by his infamous State Secretary for Security, Higher S.S. and Police Leader, Kruger, on 4th August, 1942. It is contained in the "Frank Diary" and in our Document 2233-PS-T, at Page 51 in the document book, which I now offer in evidence as Exhibit USA 607. The German text appears in the 1942 volume of the diary, Part 111, Pages 830, 831 and 832.

I now quote from the report of the conference:

"State Secretary Kruger then continues, saying that the Reichsfuehrer's next urgent plan until the end of the following year would be to settle the following German racial groups in the two districts (Zamosc and Lublin): 1,000 peasant settlements (1 settlement per family of about 6) for Bosnian Germans; 1,200 other kinds of settlements; 1,000 settlements for Bessarabian Germans; 200 for Serbian Germans; 2,000 for Leningrad Germans; 4,000 for Baltic Germans; 500 for Wolhynia Germans, and 200 settlements for Flemish, Danish and Dutch Germans, in all 10,000 settlements for 50,000 to 60,000 persons."

Upon hearing this, the defendant Frank directed that - and I quote:

"... the resettlement plan is to be discussed co-operatively by the competent authorities, and declared his willingness to approve the final plan by the end of September after satisfactory arrangements had been made concerning all the questions appertaining thereto (in particular the guaranteeing of peace and order) so that by the middle of November, as the most favourable time, the resettlement can begin."

THE PRESIDENT: The Tribunal will adjourn now for ten minutes.

(A recess was taken.)

LIEUTENANT-COLONEL BALDWIN: May it please the Tribunal: The way in which the resettlement at Zamosc was carried out was described to defendant Frank by Kruger at a meeting at Warsaw on 25th January, 1943. The report is contained in the "Frank Diary" and is our Document 2233-PS- AA, and appears at Page 58 in the document book. I offer the original of it in evidence as Exhibit USA 613. The German text appears in the Labour Conference Volume for 1943, at Pages 16, 17 and 19. Kruger, in this excerpt, reports that they had settled the first 4,000 in the Kreis Zamosc shortly before Christmas; that, understandably, friends were not made of the Poles in the resettlement programme, and that the Poles had to be chased out. He then stated to Frank, and I quote:

"We are removing those who constitute a burden in this new colonisation territory. Actually, they are the asocial and inferior elements. They are being deported; first brought to a concentration camp, and then sent as labour to the Reich. From a Polish propaganda standpoint, the entire action has an unfavourable effect. For the Poles say:

'After the Jews have been destroyed, then they will employ the same methods to get the Poles out of this territory and liquidate them just like the Jews.'"

Kruger went on to mention that there was a great deal of unrest in the territory as a result, and Frank informed him, that is, Kruger, that each individual case of resettlement would be discussed in the future exactly as that of Zamosc had been.

Although the illegality of this dispossession of Poles to make room for Germans was evident, and although the fact that the Poles who were not only being dispossessed but sent off to concentration camps, became increasingly difficult to handle, the resettlement projects continued in the Government General.

The third item mentioned by Frank-the encroachments and confiscations of industry and private property-was again an early Frank policy. He explained this to his department heads in December, 1939. The report is from his diary and is our Document 2233-PS-K and it appears at Page 40 in the document book. I now offer it in evidence as Exhibit USA 173. The German text appears in the Department Heads Conference Volume for 1939-40 at the entry for 2nd December, 1939, at Pages 2 and 3. Defendant Frank states:

> "Principally it can be said regarding the administration of the Government General: This territory in its entirety is booty of the German Reich, and it thus cannot be permitted that this territory shall be exploited in its individual parts, but that the territory in its entirety shall be economically used and its entire economic worth redound to the benefit of the German people."

Reference is made to Exhibit USA 297, if any further support of an early policy of ruthless exploitation is deemed necessary by the Tribunal. In addition, the decree permitting sequestration in the Government General, heretofore pointed out to the Tribunal (Verordnungsblatt fur das General-Gouvernement No. 6, 27th January, 1940, Page 23), which decree was signed by the defendant Frank, permitted and empowered the Nazi officials to engage in wholesale seizure of property. This was made the easier by the undefined criteria of the decree. The looting of the Government General under this and other decrees has already been presented to the Tribunal on 14th December, 1945, under the subject heading "Germanisation and Spoliation of Occupied Territories," and the Tribunal is respectfully referred to that portion of the record and, in particular, to that segment dealing with the Government General.

The defendant Frank mentioned mass arrests and mass shootings and the application of collective responsibility as the fourth reason for the apparent deterioration of the attitude of the entire Polish people. In this, too, he is to blame, for it was no part of defendant Frank's policy that reprisal should be commensurate with the gravity of the offence. He was, on the contrary, an advocate of the most drastic measures. At a conference of District Political Leaders at Cracow, on 18th March, 1942, Frank stated his policy. This extract is from his diary, and is our Document 2233-PS-R, and will be found at Page 49 in the document book. I offer it in evidence as Exhibit USA 608. The German text may be found in the volume for 1942, of the diary, Part 1, Pages 195 and 196. I quote Frank's statement:

> "Incidentally, the struggle for the achievement of our aims will be pursued cold-bloodedly. You see how the State agencies work. You see that we do not hesitate at anything, and put dozens of people against the wall. This is necessary because here simple consideration says that it cannot be our task at this period, when the best German blood is being sacrificed, to show regard for the blood of another race. For out of that, one of the greatest dangers might arise. One already hears to-day in Germany that prisoners of war, for instance, in Bavaria or Thuringia, are administering large estates entirely independently, while all the men in a village fit for service are at the front. If this state of affairs continues, then a gradual retrogression of Germanism will show itself. One should not underestimate this danger. Therefore, everything

revealing itself as a Polish power of leadership must be destroyed again and again with ruthless energy. This does not have to be shouted abroad; it will happen silently."

And on 15th January, 1944, defendant Frank assured the political leaders of the N.S.D.A.P. that reprisals would be made for German deaths. These remarks are to be found in the "Frank Diary," in our Document 2233-PS-BB, at Page 60 in the document book, the second quotation on that page, the original of which I offer in evidence as Exhibit USA 295. The German text appears in the loose-leaf volume of the diary covering the period from 1st January, 1944, to 28th February, 1944, and appears at Page 13. Frank says quite simply:

"I have not been hesitant in declaring that when a German is shot, up to 100 Poles shall be shot, too."

The whole tragic history of slave labour and recruitment of workers has been placed before this Tribunal in great detail. When the defendant Frank refers to these methods as his fifth reason for disaffection in Poland, in his report to Hitler, he once more cites policies which he executed. Force, violence, and economic duress were all supported by him as means for recruiting labourers for deportation to slavery in Germany. This was an announced policy, and I have already alluded to Exhibit USA 297, which contains verification of this fact.

While, in the very beginning, recruitment of labourers in the Government General may have been voluntary, these methods soon proved inadequate. In the spring of 1940 the question of utilising force came up, and the matter was discussed at an official meeting at which the defendant Seyss-Inquart was also present. I refer to the "Frank Diary" and our Document 2233-PS-N, which the Tribunal will find at Page 43 in the document book. I offer the original in evidence as Exhibit USA 614. The German text appears in the volume of the diary for 1940, Part 11, at Page 333. I quote the conference report:

"The Governor General stated that the fact that all means in the shape of proclamations, etc., did not bring success, leads to the conclusion that the Poles, out of malevolence and guided by the intention of harming Germany by not putting themselves at its disposal, refuse to enlist for working duty. Therefore, he asks Dr. Frauendorfer if there are any other measures not as yet employed to win the Poles on a voluntary basis.

Reichshauptamtsleiter Dr. Frauendorfer answered the question in the negative.

The Governor General emphasised the fact that he will now be asked to take a definite attitude towards this question. Therefore, the question will arise whether any form of coercive measures should now be employed.

The question put by the Governor General to S.S. Lieutenant-General Kruger: Does he see the possibilities of calling Polish workers by coercive means, is answered by Kruger in the affirmative."

In May, 1940, at an official conference - and this record is already before the Tribunal as Exhibit USA 173 - defendant Frank stated that compulsion in recruitment of labour could be exercised, that Poles could be snatched from the streets, and that the best method would be organised raids.

As in the case of persecution of the Jews, the forced labour programme in the Government General is almost beyond belief. I refer to the "Frank Diary" and to our Document 2233-PS-W, which will be found at Page 53 in the document book, the original of which I offer in evidence as Exhibit USA 607. This excerpt is a record, if the Court please, of a discussion between the defendant Sauckel and the defendant Frank at Cracow on 18th August, 1942, and it appears in the 1942 volume of the diary, Part III, at Pages 918 and 920. Frank speaks:

> "I am pleased to report to you officially, Party Comrade Sauckel, that we have up to now supplied 800,000 workers for the Reich."

He continues:

> "Recently you have requested us to supply a further 140,000. I have pleasure in informing you officially that in accordance with our agreement of yesterday, 60 per cent. of the newly requested workers will be supplied to the Reich by the end of October and the balance of 40 per cent. by the end of the year."

Frank continues:

> "Beyond the present figure of 140,000 you can, however, next year reckon upon a higher number of workers from the Government General. For we shall employ the police to conscript them."

How this recruitment was carried out - by wild and ruthless manhunts - is clearly shown in Exhibit USA 178, which is in evidence before the Tribunal. Starvation, violence and death, which characterised the entire slave labour programme of the conspirators, was thus faithfully reflected in the administration of the defendant Frank.

There were, of course, other grounds for uneasiness in Occupied Poland, which the defendant Frank did not mention in his report to Hitler. He does not mention the concentration camps, perhaps because, as a representative jurist of National Socialism, the defendant Frank had himself defended the system in Germany. As Governor General the defendant Frank must be held responsible for all concentration camps within the boundaries of the Government General. These include, among others, the notorious camp at Maidenek and the one at Lublin. As indicated previously, the defendant Frank knew and approved that Poles were to be taken to concentration camps in connection with resettlement projects. He had certain jurisdiction as well in relation to the extermination camp Auschwitz, to which Poles from the Government General were committed by his administration. In February, 1944, Ambassador Counsellor Dr. Schumberg suggested a possible amnesty of Poles who had been taken to Auschwitz for trivial offences and kept there for several months. This, if the Court please, is reported in the "Frank Diary" and is contained in our Document 2233-PS-BB, at Page 60 of the document book. It is the third quotation on that page. I offer the original in evidence as Exhibit USA 295.

THE PRESIDENT: You go too fast. Did you say Page 70?

LIEUTENANT-COLONEL BALDWIN: Page 60, Sir. The German text appears in the loose-leaf volume covering the period 1st January, 1944, to 28th February, 1944, at the conference on 8th February, 1944, on Page 7. I quote:

> "The Governor General will take under consideration an amnesty, probably for 1st May of this year. Nevertheless, one must not lose sight of the fact that the German leadership of the Government General must not now show any sign of weakness."

This, was, and is, the conspirator Hans Frank. The evidence is by no means exhausted, but it is our belief that sufficient proof has been given to this Tribunal to establish his liability under Count I of the Indictment.

As legal adviser of Hitler and the Leadership Corps of the N.S.D.A.P., defendant Frank promoted the conspirators' rise to power. In his various juridical capacities, both in the N.S.D.A.P. and in the German Government, Frank certainly advocated and promoted the political monopoly of the N.S.D.A.P., the racial programme of the conspirators, the terror systems of the concentration camps, and arrests without warrant. His role, early in the Common Plan, was to realise "the National Socialist

Programme in the realm of law," and to give the outward form of legality to this programme of terror, persecution and oppression which had as its ultimate purpose mobilisation for aggressive war.

As a loyal adherent of Hitler and the N.S.D.A.P., defendant Frank was appointed Governor General in 1939 of that area of Poland known as the Government General. Frank had defined justice as that which benefited the German nation. His five years' administration of the Government General illustrates the most extreme extension of that principle.

It has been shown that defendant Frank took the office of Governor General under a programme that constituted in itself a criminal plan or conspiracy, as defendant Frank well knew and approved, to exploit the territory ruthlessly, for the benefit of Nazi Germany, to conscript its nationals for labour in Germany, to close its schools and colleges, to prevent the rise of a Polish intelligentsia, and to administer the territory as a colonial possession of the Third Reich, in total disregard of the duties of an occupying power towards the inhabitants of occupied territory.

Under defendant Frank's administration, this criminal plan was consummated, but the execution went even beyond the plan. Food contributions to Germany increased to the point where the bare subsistence reserved for the Government General under the plan was reduced to a level of mass starvation. The savage programme of exterminating Jews was relentlessly executed. Resettlement projects were carried out with reckless disregard of the rights of the local population, and the terror of the concentration camp followed in the wake of the Nazi invaders.

This statement of evidence has been compiled in large part from statements by the defendant Frank himself, from the admissions found in his diary, official reports, reports of conferences with his colleagues and subordinates, and his speeches. It is, therefore, appropriate that a passage from his diary should be quoted in conclusion. It is our Document 2233-PS-AA. It appears at Page 59 of the document book. I offer the original in evidence as Exhibit USA 613. The German text appears in the 1943 volume of Labour Conference Meetings at the 25th January, 1943, entry on Page 53. In his address, defendant Frank, prophetically enough, told his colleagues in the Government General that their task would grow more difficult. Hitler, he said, could only help them as a kind of "administrative hedge-hog." They must depend on themselves. I quote Frank:

"We are now duty bound to hold together. We must remember that we who are gathered together here figure on Mr. Roosevelt's list of war criminals. I have the honour of being Number One. We have, so to speak, become accomplices in the world historic sense."

This concludes the presentation on the defendant Frank.

May it please the Tribunal, Lieutenant-Colonel Griffith-Jones of the British delegation will now deal with the individual responsibility of the defendant Streicher.

LIEUTENANT-COLONEL GRIFFITH-JONES: If the Tribunal please, it is my duty to present the case against the defendant Julius Streicher.

Appendix A of the Indictment, that paragraph of the Appendix relating to Streicher, sets out the positions which he held and which I shall prove. It then goes on to allege that he used those positions and his personal influence and his close connection with the Fuehrer in such a manner that he promoted the accession to power of the Nazi conspirators and the consolidation of their control over Germany, as set forth in Count 1 of the Indictment; that he authorised, directed and participated in the Crimes against Humanity, set forth in Count 4 of the Indictment, including particularly the incitement of the persecution of the Jews, set forth in

Count 1 and Count 4 of the Indictment.

My Lord, the case against this defendant can be, perhaps, described by the unofficial title that he assumed for himself as "Jew-baiter Number One." It is the prosecution's case that for the course of some twenty-five years, this man educated the whole of the German people in hatred, and that he incited them to the persecution and to the extermination of the Jewish race. He was an accessory to murder, perhaps on a scale never attained before.

With the Tribunal's permission, I propose to prove quite shortly the position and influence that he held, and then to refer the Tribunal to several short extracts from his newspapers and from his speeches, and finally to outline the part that he played in the particular persecutions against the Jews that occurred between the years 1933 and 1945.

My Lord, perhaps, before I start on that, I might say that the document book before the members of the Tribunal is arranged in the order in which I intend to refer to the documents. They are paged, and there is an index at the beginning of the book, and if the Tribunal have got what is called the Trial Brief, it is in effect a note of the evidence to which I shall refer, and again in the order in which I shall refer to it, which may be of some assistance.

My Lord, this defendant was born in 1885. He became a school teacher in Nuremberg and formed a party of his own, which he called the German Socialist Party. The chief policy of that Party, again, was anti-Semitism. In 1922 he handed over his Party to Hitler, and there is a glowing account of his generosity which appears in Hitler's "Mein Kampf," which I do not think it worth occupying the time of the Tribunal in reading. It appears as M-3, and is the first document in the Tribunal's document book. The copy of "Mein Kampf" is already before the Tribunal as Exhibit GB 128.

The appointments that he held in the Party and State were few. From 1921 until 1945, he was a member of the Nazi Party. In 1925 he was appointed Gauleiter of Franconia and he remained as such until about February of 1940, and from the time that the Nazi Government came into power in 1933 until 1945 he was a member of the Reichstag. In addition to that, he held the title of Obergruppenfuehrer in the S.A. All that information appears in Document 2975-PS, which is already in evidence as Exhibit USA 9, and is the affidavit that he made himself.

The propaganda that he carried out throughout those years was chiefly done through the medium of his newspapers. He was the editor and publisher of the journal "Der Sturmer" from 1922 until 1933, and thereafter, the publisher and owner of the paper.

In 1933 he also founded and thereafter, I think, published - certainly was responsible for the daily newspaper called the "Frankische Tageszeitung."

There were, in addition to that, and particularly later, several others, mostly local journals, which he published from Nuremberg.

Those are the positions that he held, and now if I may, I shall quite briefly trace the course of his incitement and propaganda, more or less in chronological order, by referring the Tribunal to the short extracts. I would say this: These extracts are really selected at random. They are selected with a view to showing the Tribunal the various methods that he employed to incite the people against the Jewish race, but his newspapers were crowded with them, week after week, day after day. It is impossible to pick up any copy without finding the same kind of stuff in the headlines and in the articles.

If I might quote from four speeches and articles showing his early activities from 1922 to 1933 - at Page 3 of the Tribunal's document book, M-11 - that is an extract from a speech that he made in 1922 in Nuremberg, and, after abusing the Jews in the first paragraph - I only refer to the last few lines:

"We know that Germany will be free when the Jew has been excluded from the life of the German people."

I pass to the next document, which is M-12, on Page 4. The first document was Exhibit GB 165. That is the book, I understand, that is being given that number, so that the next document, which is taken from the same book, will be the same. Perhaps I might be allowed to read that short extract. It is an extract from a speech:

"I beg you, and particularly those of you who carry the cross throughout the land, to become somewhat more serious when I speak of the enemy of the German people, namely, the Jew. Not out of irresponsibility or for fun do I fight against the Jewish enemy, but because I bear within me the knowledge that the whole misfortune was brought to Germany by the Jews alone.

I ask you once more, what is at stake to-day? The Jew seeks domination not only among the German people but among all peoples. The Communists pave the way for him. Do you not know that the God of the Old Testament ordered the Jews to devour and enslave the peoples of the earth?

The Government allows the Jew to do as he pleases. The people expect action to be taken. You may think about Adolf Hitler as you please, but one thing you must admit. He possessed the courage to attempt to free the German people from the Jew by a national revolution. That was action indeed."

The next short extract appearing on the next page is taken from a speech in April, 1925:

"You must realise that the Jew wants our people to perish. That is why you must join us and leave those who have brought you nothing but war and inflation and discord. For thousands of years the Jew has been destroying the nations."

I ask the Tribunal to note now these last few words: "Let us make a new beginning so that we can annihilate the Jews." My Lord, so far as I have been able to find, that is the earliest expression of annihilation of the Jewish race. Perhaps it gave birth to what was, fourteen years later, to become the official policy of the Nazi Government.

And one further passage from this period. This is April, 1932, M-14, taken from the same book. He starts by saying:

"For 13 years I have fought against Jewry."

I quote the last paragraph only:

"We know that the Jew, whether he is baptised as a Protestant or as a Catholic, remains a Jew. Why can you not realise this, you Protestant clergymen, you Catholic priests, you who have scales before your eyes and serve the God of the Jews, who is not the God of Love but the God of Hate. Why do you not listen to Christ, who said to the Jews: 'You are the children of the Devil'."

That, then, was the kind of performance he was putting up during those early years. When the Nazi Party came to power, they officially started their campaign against the Jews by the boycott of 1st April, 1933. Now, of that boycott the Tribunal have already had evidence, and I would do no more now than to remind the Tribunal in a word of what happened.

The boycott was agreed on and approved of by the whole Government, as was shown in a document which is already before you, 2156-PS, Exhibit USA 262, which was Goebbels' diary.

Streicher was appointed the chairman of the central committee for the organisation of that boycott, which appears in Document 2056-PS, Exhibit USA 263. It was then said that he started his work on Wednesday the 29th.

On that same day the central committee issued a proclamation in which it was said that the boycott would start on Saturday, at 10 a.m. sharp. "Jewry will realise whom it has challenged." That short quotation appears in Document 3387- PS, which is Exhibit USA 566, which is a volume of "Der Sturmer." In actual fact, it is a copy of "Der Sturmer" which is already before the Court.

I would refer the Tribunal to one short passage from an article in the "Nationalsocialistische Partei Korrepondenz," which the defendant wrote on 30th March, 1933, before the boycott was due to start. It is Document 2153-PS, and it appears on Page 12 of the Tribunal's book, which becomes Exhibit GB 166. There he writes, under the title, "Defeat the Enemy of the World! - by Julius Streicher, official leader of the central committee to combat the Jewish atrocity and boycott campaign":

"Jewry wanted this battle. It shall have it until it realises that the Germany of the brown battalions is not a country of cowardice and surrender. Jewry will have to fight until we have won victory.

National Socialists! Defeat the enemy of the world. Even if the world is full of devils, we shall succeed in the end."

As head of the central committee for that boycott, Streicher outlined in detail the organisation of the boycott, in orders which the committee published on the 31st March, 1933, which is the next document in the book, 2154-PS, Exhibit GB 167. I can summarise those.

The committee stressed that no violence was to be employed against the Jews on the occasion of that boycott, but not perhaps for humane reasons; it was because, if there were no violence employed, then Jewish employers would have no grounds for discharging their employees without notice, and no grounds for refusing to pay them any wages.

The Jews were also reported to be apparently transferring businesses to German figureheads in order to alleviate the results of this persecution, and the committee laid it down that any property so transferred was to be considered as Jewish for the purpose of the boycott.

I do not think I need go into that any further. It does show that at that date Streicher was taking a leading part, and a leading part under Government appointment, in the persecution of the Jews.

I would now refer the Court again to a few further extracts to show the form that this propaganda developed as the years went on. At Page 18 of the document book, Document M-20, we have an article in the New Year's issue of a new paper that he had just founded. It was a semi-medical paper called "The People's Health Through Blood and Soil," edited by himself, and it is an example of the really remarkable lengths to which he went in putting over this propaganda against the Jews. I quote:

"It is established for all eternity: alien albumen is the sperm of a man of alien race. The male sperm in cohabitation is partially or completely absorbed by the female, and thus enters her bloodstream. One single cohabitation of a Jew with an Aryan woman is sufficient to poison her blood for ever. Together with the alien albumen she has absorbed the alien soul. Never again will she be able to bear purely Aryan children, even when married to an Aryan. They will all be bastards, with a dual soul and a body of a mixed breed. Their children too will be crossbreeds; that means, ugly people of unsteady character and with a tendency to illnesses. Now we know why the Jew uses every artifice of seduction in order to ravish German girls at as early an age as possible; why the Jewish doctor rapes his female patients while they are under anaesthesia. He wants the German girl and the German woman to absorb the alien sperm of the Jew. She is never again to bear German children. But the blood products of all animals right down to the bacteria, such as the serum, lymph, extracts from internal organs, etc., are also alien albumen. They have a poisonous effect if directly introduced into the bloodstream either by vaccination or by injection. By these products of sick animals the blood is ravished, the Aryan is impregnated with an alien species. The author and abettor of such action is the Jew. He has been aware of the secrets of the race question for centuries, and therefore plans systematically the annihilation of the nations which are superior to him. Science and authorities are his instruments for the enforcing of pseudo-science and the concealment of truth."

That becomes, my Lord, Exhibit GB 168.

The next document, also at the beginning of 1935, an extract from his own paper, "Der Sturmer," entitled "The Chosen People of the Criminals" -

"And all the same, or, let us say, just because of this, the history book of the Jews, which is usually called the Holy Scriptures, impresses us as a horrible criminal romance, which makes the 150 shilling-shockers of the British Jew, Edgar Wallace, grow pale with envy. This 'holy' book abounds in murder, incest, fraud, theft and indecency."

On the 4th of October, 1935 - and the Tribunal will remember that that was the month after the Nuremberg Decrees had been made - he made a speech which is reported in the "Volkischer Beobachter" and is entitled in that newspaper, "Safeguard of German Blood and German Honour." I read the report in that article:

"Gauleiter Streicher speaks at a German Labour Front mass demonstration for the Nuremberg Laws."

Then the first line of the actual article says that he spoke for the second time within a few weeks. I quote only the last two lines of that first large paragraph:

"We have therefore to unmask the Jew, and that is what I have been doing for the past fifteen years."

That remark apparently was met with tempestuous applause. That Document M-34 becomes Exhibit GB 169.

And, my Lord, I think it unnecessary to quote from the next document in the Tribunal's book. It is very much the same type of thing. On Page 22 of the document book, M-6, there is a leading article by Streicher in his "Der Sturmer " of which I would refer only to the last half of the last paragraph, where again he emphasises the part that he himself has taken in this campaign.

"'Der Sturmer's' fifteen years of work of enlightenment has already led an army of those who know - millions strong - to National Socialism. The continued work of 'Der Sturmer' will help to ensure that every German down to the last man will, with heart and hand, join the ranks of those whose aim it is to crush the head of the serpent Pan-Juda beneath their heels. He who helps to bring this about helps to eliminate the devil, and this devil is the Jew."

That document becomes Exhibit GB 170.

The next document - I only include it in the document book again to show the extraordinary length to which he went in his propaganda, and it consists of a photograph of the burning hull of the airship "Hindenburg" when it went on fire in June, 1937, in America. Underneath it the caption includes the comment, "The first radio picture from the United States of America shows quite clearly that a Jew stands behind the explosion of our airship 'Hindenburg.' Nature has depicted quite clearly and quite correctly that devil in human guise."

And although it is not at all clear from that photograph, I think the meaning of that comment is that the cloud of smoke in the air is in the shape of a Jewish face.

On the next page, Document M-4, is a speech he made in September, 1937, at the opening of a bridge in Nuremberg. I would quote only the last paragraph on Page 24. The bridge in question is called the Wilhelm Gustloff bridge, and he says:

> "The man who murdered Wilhelm Gustloff had to come from the Jewish people, because the Jewish text books teach that every Jew has the right to kill a non-Jew, and indeed, that it is pleasing to the Jewish God to kill as many non-Jews as possible.
>
> Look at the road the Jewish people have been following for thousands of years past; everywhere murder, everywhere mass murder. Neither must we forget that behind present-day wars there stands the Jewish financier who pursues his aims and interests. The Jew always lives on the blood of other nations; he needs such murder and such victims. For us who know, the murder of Wilhelm Gustloff is the same as ritual murder."

And then on the next page:

> "We must tell our children that it is the duty of German children at school, and the bigger ones, to learn what this memorial means."

I go to the next paragraph:

> "The Jew no longer shows himself among us openly as he used to. But it would be wrong to say that victory is ours. Full and final victory will have been achieved only when the whole world has been rid of Jews."

That becomes Exhibit GB 171.

Now the next two documents in your document books are simply extracts from the correspondence columns of "Der Sturmer," showing again one of the methods he employed in this propaganda. I do not need to read them. The correspondence columns of all his issues are full of letters coming in from Germans saying that, for instance, some German has been buying her shoes from a Jewish shop and so on, and in that way assisting in the general boycott of the Jews. In other words, they really are a weekly column of libels against the Jews all over Germany.

I pass then to another and particular form of propaganda that he employed, and which he called "Ritual Murder." The Tribunal may well remember that some years ago, I think it started in 1934, this "Der Sturmer" began publishing accounts of Jewish ritual murder which horrified the whole world to such an extent that the Archbishop of Canterbury eventually wrote to "The Times" protesting, as indeed did people from every country in the world, protesting that any Government should allow matter like this to be published in its national newspapers.

He takes his ritual murder, I understand, from a medieval belief that during their Eastertide celebrations the Jews were in the habit of murdering Christian children, and he enlarges upon this and misrepresents this belief, this medieval belief, to show that not only did they do it in the Middle Ages, but that they are still doing it and still want to do it. And if I might just quote one or two passages from his newspapers and show one or two pictures which he published in connection with his campaign of ritual murder, it will illustrate to the Court the type of teaching and propaganda that he was putting up. One Page 29 of the Tribunal's document book, I will quote from the third but last paragraph:

> "This the French front-line soldier should take with him to France: The

German people have taken a new lease of life. They want peace, but if anybody tries to attack them, if anyone tries to torture them again, if anyone tries to push them back into the past, then the world would see another heroic epic; then Heaven will decide where righteousness lies here, or where the Jew has the whip hand and where he instigates massacres, one could almost say the biggest ritual murders of all times. If the German people are to be slaughtered according to the Jewish rites, the whole world will be thus slaughtered at the same time."

And the last paragraph:

"As you have drummed morning and evening prayers into your children's heads, so now drum this into their heads, so that the German people may gain the spiritual power to convince the rest of the world which the Jews desire to lead against us."

That document is M-2, Exhibit GB 172.

And on the following page of the document book there is a reproduction of a photograph taken from the "Der Sturmer" of April, 1937, which illustrates three Jews ritually murdering a girl by cutting her throat, and shows the blood pouring out into a bucket on the ground. The caption underneath that photograph is as follows: "Ritual murder at Polna. Ritual murder of Agnes Hruza by the Jews Hilsner, Erdmann and Wassermann (taken from a contemporary postcard)." That is Exhibit USA 258. It is in a copy of "Der Sturmer," which has already been put in.

There appears in the next page of the document book an extract from that same "Der Sturmer," April, 1937. I will not read it now, because it has been put in and has all been read to the Court. It describes what happens when ritual murder takes place, and the blood is mixed with the bread and drunk by the Jews having their feast. The Tribunal will remember that during the feast the head of the family exclaims, "May all gentiles perish - as the child whose blood is contained in the bread and wine."

That is already Exhibit USA 258, and it has been read in the transcript (Page 381, Part 2).

THE PRESIDENT: Would that be a good time to break off?

LIEUTENANT-COLONEL GRIFFITH-JONES: If your Lordship pleases.

(A recess was taken until 14.00 hours.)

LIEUTENANT-COLONEL GRIFFITH-JONES: May it please the Tribunal, if I might just refer to further copies of "Der Sturmer" on the subject of "ritual murder," the first of which appears on Page 32 of the document book, 2700-PS. It is the copy in Exhibit USA 260. It is an article in "Der Sturmer" of July, 1938:

"Whoever had the occasion to be an eye-witness during the slaughtering of animals, or to see at least a truthful film on the slaughtering, will never forget this horrible experience. It is atrocious, and, unwillingly, he is reminded of the crimes which the Jews have committed for centuries on men. He will be reminded of the ritual murder. History points out hundreds of cases in which non-Jewish children were tortured to death. They also were given the same incision through the throat as is found on slaughtered animals. They also were slowly bled to death while fully conscious."

My Lord, on special occasions, or when he had some particular subject matter to put before the world, he was in the habit of issuing special editions of his newspaper "Der Sturmer." Ritual murder was such a special subject that he issued one of these special editions dealing solely with it. The Tribunal will have a photostatic copy of the complete issue for May, 1939.

Now, I have not attempted to have translated all or indeed any of the articles which appear in that edition. It is perhaps sufficient to look at the pictures, the illustrations, and for me to read the captions which appear underneath the photographs; and I regret that the translations of the captions have not been attached to the Tribunal's copy, but perhaps I may be permitted to refer to the pictures and read the captions for the Tribunal.

The pages are marked in red pencil on the right-hand corner. On Page 1 I see a picture of a child having knives stuck into its side, blood spurting from it, and below the pedestal on which it stands, are five presumably dead children lying on the ground. The caption to that picture is as follows:

"In the year 1476 the Jews in Regensburg murdered six boys. They drew their blood and tortured them to death in an underground vault which belongs to the Jew Josfol. The judges found the bodies of murdered boys. A bloodstained earthen bowl stood on an altar."

On the next page there are two pictures and the captions explain them. The one at the top left-hand corner:

"For the Jewish New Year celebrations in 1913, World Jewry published this picture. On the Jewish New Year and on the Day of Atonement the Jews slaughtered a so-called 'kapores' cock; that is to say, dead cock, whose blood and death is intended to purify the Jews. In 1913 the 'kapores' cock had the head of the Russian Czar Nicholas II. By publishing this postcard the Jews intended to say that Nicholas II would be their next purifying sacrifice. On the 16th of July, 1918, the Czar was murdered by the Jews Jurowsky and Goloschtschekin."

The picture at the bottom of the page, again, shows Jews holding a similar bird, "the 'kapores' cock which has the head of the Fuehrer. The Hebrew script says that one day Jews will kill all Hitlerites. Then they, the Jews, will be delivered from all misfortunes. In due course the Jews will realise that they have reckoned without an Adolf Hitler."

The next page of the newspaper contains reproductions of a lot of previous articles on ritual murder, with a picture of the defendant Julius Streicher at the top.

On the fourth page, a picture at the bottom of the right-hand corner has the caption:

"Jew at the Passover Meal. The wine and Matzeh, unleavened bread, contains non-Jewish blood. The Jew prays before the meal. He prays for death to all non-Jews."

On the fifth page are reproductions from some of the European and American newspaper articles and letters which had been received by those newspapers during the course of the last years, in protest to this propaganda on the subject of ritual murder; and in the centre of it you will see the letter from the Archbishop of Canterbury, written to the editor of "The Times" in protest.

On the next page, Page 6, is another ghastly picture of a man having his throat cut; again the usual spurt of blood falling into a basin on the floor, and the caption to that is as follows:

"The ritual murder of the boy Heinrich, in the year 1345; the Jews in Munich slaughtered a non-Jewish boy. The martyr was declared holy by the Church."

On Page 7 appears a picture representing three ritual murders. On Page 8 there is another photo-picture, "The Holy Gabriel. This boy was crucified and tortured to death by the Jews in the year 1690. The blood was drawn off him."

I think we can pass Pages 9 and 10.

On Page 11 there is shown a piece of sculpture which appears on the wall of the

Wallfahrts Chapel in Wesel and it represents the ritual murder of a boy Werner. It is a somewhat disgusting picture of the boy strung up by his feet and being murdered by two Jews.

Page 12 reproduces another picture taken from the same place. The caption is:

"The embalmed body of 'Simon of Trient' who was tortured to death by the Jews."

Page 13 has another picture; somebody else having a knife stuck into him, more blood coming out into a basin.

On Page 14 are two pictures. The one at the top is said to be the ritual murder of the boy Andreas and the one at the bottom is the picture of a tombstone, the caption of which reads as follows:

"The tombstone of Hilsner."

This is the memorial to a Jewish ritual murderer Leopold Hilsner. He was found guilty of two ritual murders and was condemned to death, by hanging, in two trials. The Emperor was bribed and pardoned him. Masaryk, the friend of the Jews, liberated him from penal servitude in 1918. Even on his tombstone lying Jewry calls this twofold murderer an "innocent victim."

The next page again produces the picture of a woman being murdered by having her throat cut in the same way; and perhaps I might refer to Page 17, which produces a picture of the Archbishop of Canterbury and a picture of an old Jewish man, and the caption says:

"Dr. Lang, the Archbishop of Canterbury, the highest dignitary of the English Church. His ally, a typical example of the Jewish Race."

The last page, Page 18, produces a picture called "Holy Simon who was tortured to death."

My Lord, it is my submission that that document is nothing but an incitement to the people of Germany who read it, an incitement to murder. It is filled with pictures of murder, murder alleged to be against the German people and is an encouragement to all who read it, to revenge themselves, and to revenge themselves in the same way. That document, M-20, becomes Exhibit GB 173.

DR. MARX (Counsel for defendant Streicher): The defendant, Julius Streicher, called my attention this very moment to the fact that he has not been given the opportunity to prove from where these pictures, which have been referred to just now, have been taken. It is, in the opinion of the defence, necessary that the origin of these pictures should be clarified before the Tribunal, otherwise one could think that these pictures had been especially prepared for "Der Sturmer" without any source. Streicher, however, points out that these pictures originate from recognised sources of history. I would therefore like to suggest that the prosecution should submit all its material. I think that the articles of "Der Sturmer" which have been referred to should prove the sources from which Streicher got these pictures.

THE PRESIDENT: Do the articles show the sources? Do the articles themselves indicate the sources?

DR. MARX: Yes. According to Streicher, yes.

LIEUTENANT-COLONEL GRIFFITH-JONES: I should have said so. There was not any intention to misrepresent the matter, that these pictures are taken from original pictures. These were not invented by the newspaper, and in some cases the sources are shown in the caption. This is a collection of medieval pictures and frescoes dealing with this matter. In actual fact the papers show in almost all cases where they come from.

DR. MARX: Thank you.

THE PRESIDENT: You have already given us the dates of them which stated they were medieval.

LIEUTENANT-COLONEL GRIFFITH-JONES: That is so, my Lord. In January, 1938 - and it will be remembered that in 1938 the persecution of the Jews became more and more severe-in January, 1938, for some reason or other, another special issue of "Der Sturmer" was published. If the Tribunal would look at Page 54 of their document book I will quote a short passage from the leading article in that paper, an article written by the defendant.

> "The supreme aim and highest task of the State is therefore to conserve people, blood and race. But if this is the supreme task, any crime against this law must be punished with the supreme penalty. 'Der Sturmer' takes, therefore, the view that there are only two punishments for the crime of polluting the race:
> 1. Penal servitude for life for attempted race pollution.
> 2. Death for committing race pollution."

And again, indeed, if it is now still necessary to show the type of paper this was, if the Tribunal will turn over to the next page it will see the headlines set out for some of the articles that are contained in that edition:

"Jewish race polluters at work."

The next one:

"Fifteen years old non-Jewess ravaged."

The next one:

"A dangerous race polluter. He regards German women as fair game for himself."

The next one:

"The Jewish sanatorium. A Jewish institution for the cultivation of race pollution."

The next one:

"Rape of a feeble-minded girl."

And lastly:

"The Jewish butler. He steals from his Jewish masters and commits race pollution."

The copy of that paper is already in as Exhibit USA 260.

On the next page of the document book - I will quote only the last two lines - is an article appearing in "Der Sturmer," and it is true that it is not an article actually written by the defendant Streicher but by his then editor, Karl Holz:

> "Revenge will break loose one day and will exterminate Jewry from the face of the earth."

And again on Page 37, in September, 1938, "Der Sturmer" has an article in which the last two lines read as follows:

> "A parasite, an enemy, an evil-doer, a disseminator of diseases who must be destroyed in the interest of mankind."

It is my submission to the Tribunal that this is no longer propaganda for the persecution of the Jews, this is propaganda for the extermination of Jews, for the murder not of one man but of millions.

The next document in the document book, on Page 38, has already been put in evidence and read to the Tribunal. It is Exhibit USA 260. It appears in the document book and was read into the transcript (Page 381, Part 2). This is a short article appearing in December, 1938, No. 50 of "Der Sturmer."

I would draw the Tribunal's attention to the next document which is a picture taken from that same copy. It shows the upper part of a girl's body being strangled by the arms of a man with his hands around her neck, and the shadow of the man's face is shown against the background, quite obviously with Jewish features. The caption under that picture is as follows:

"Castration for Race Polluters.

Only heavy penalties will preserve our womenfolk from a tighter grip of the ghastly Jewish claws.

The Jews are our misfortune."

I pass for the moment from "Der Sturmer" to a particular incident that occurred, in which the defendant Streicher took a leading part. It will be remembered that the organised demonstrations against the Jews took place on the 9th and 10th November, 1938. All this propaganda, as I say, was becoming fiercer and more ferocious. In the autumn of that year the defendant Streicher organised the breaking up of the Nuremberg synagogues on the occasion of a meeting of Press representatives in Nuremberg. That incident has in fact been referred to previously in this case and the documents in connection with it are 1724-PS, which were put in as Exhibit USA 266 and were referred to and read in the transcript (Page 384, Part 2).

Gauleiter Julius Streicher was personally to set the crane in motion with which the Jewish symbols were to be torn down from the synagogue. From another document which was also put in, 2711-PS, which became Exhibit USA 267, and was read in the transcript (Page 384, Part 2) also, I quote two lines:

"...the Synagogue is being demolished! Julius Streicher himself inaugurates the work by a speech lasting an hour and a half. By his order then - so to speak as a prelude of the demolition - the tremendous Star of David came off the cupola."

The defendant, of course, took an active part in the November demonstrations of that year. I do not suggest that be was responsible for the idea of them. The evidence against him is confined only to the part that he took in his Gau, in Franconia.

On Page 43 of the document book is an account of the Nuremberg demonstrations as they were reported in the "Frankische Tageszeitung" which, of course, was his paper, on the 11th November. I quote:

"In Nuremberg and Furth it resulted in demonstrations by the crowd against the Jewish murderers. These lasted until the early hours of the morning. Far too long had one watched the activities of the Jews in Germany."

And then I go to the last three lines of that paragraph:

"After midnight the excitement of the populace reached its peak and a large crowd marched to the synagogues in Nuremberg and Furth and burned these two Jewish buildings, where the murder of Germans had been preached.

The fire-brigades, which had been notified immediately, saw to it that the fire was confined to the original outbreak. The windows of the Jewish shopkeepers, who still had not given up hope of selling their junk to the stupid Goims, were smashed. Thanks to the disciplined behaviour of the S.A. men and the police, who rushed to the scene, there was no plundering."

That becomes Exhibit GB 174.

The following document in the document book is the report of Streicher's speech on the 10th November, the day of the demonstration. I will quote from two paragraphs on that page, or rather, starting in the middle of the first paragraph:

"From the cradle, the Jew is not being taught, like we are, such texts as, 'Thou shalt love thy neighbour as thyself,' or 'If you are smitten on the left cheek, offer then your right one.' No, he is told: 'With the non-Jew you can do whatever you like.' He is even taught that the slaughtering of a non-Jew is an act pleasing to God. For 20 years we have been writing about this in 'Der Sturmer,' for 20 years we have been preaching it throughout the world and we have made millions recognise the truth."

I go to the last paragraph:

"The Jew slaughtered in one night 75,000 people; when he emigrated from Egypt he killed all the firstborn, i.e., a whole future generation of Egyptians. What would have happened if the Jew had succeeded in driving the nations into war against us, and if we had lost the war? The Jew, protected by foreign bayonets, would have fallen on us and would have slaughtered and murdered us. Never forget what history has taught us."

My Lord, after the November demonstrations, irregularities occurred in the Gau of Franconia in connection with the organised Aryanisation of Jewish property. Aryanisation of Jewish property was, of course, regulated by the State, and under a decree it had been laid down that the proceeds, or any proceeds that there might be, from taking over Jewish properties and giving them to Aryans, were to go to the State. What apparently happened in Franconia was that a good deal of the proceeds never found their way as far as the State, and as a result Goering set up a commission to investigate what had taken place. We have the report of that commission, and I would refer the Tribunal to certain short passages in it. On Page 45, we see from that report exactly what had been taking place in this defendant Streicher's Gau. I quote from the paragraph where it says "Page 13":

DR. HANS MARX (Counsel for defendant Streicher): The prosecutor intends to refer, as proof of the irregularities which occurred in connection with the Aryanisation of shops in Nuremberg after the 9th November, to a report which the Deputy Gauleiter Holz has given to the examining prosecutor. I would like to protest against the wording of this report. Between Streicher and his Deputy Gauleiter Holz there existed a considerable difference of opinion, if not enmity. His Deputy Gauleiter Holz was the person definitely responsible for the measures taken. It is not at all proven that Streicher had agreed to these measures. It is rather to be assumed that Holz, in order to cover himself, has made statements here which he himself could never stand for if he appeared on the witness stand to-day. Therefore, this report represents the statements of a man who was involved in this matter, of a man who participated in these deeds, of a man who was an enemy of the defendant Streicher. Holz incriminated Streicher on account of the fact that Streicher did not shield him from the Commission and the previous Minister, President Goering. Therefore, I do not think that this report should be used.

THE PRESIDENT: Have you said what you wished to say?

DR. MARX: Yes, Sir.

THE PRESIDENT: The Tribunal considers that this document, being an official document, is admissible under Article XXI, and that the objections which you have made to it are not objections which go to its admissibility as evidence, but go to its weight; and as to that, you will have an opportunity to develop your objections at a later stage when you come to speak. The Tribunal rules that the document is admissible.

LIEUTENANT-COLONEL GRIFFITH-JONES: My Lord, I read from the centre of that Page 45 of the document book:

"Following upon the November demonstrations, the Deputy Gauleiter Holz took up the Jewish questions. His reasons can be given here in detail on the basis of his statement of 25th March, 1939:

The 9th and 10th November, 1938.

In the night of the 9th to the 10th of November and on the 10th November, 1938, events took place throughout Germany which I" - and I emphasise that that is Holz speaking - "considered to be the signal for a completely different treatment of the Jewish question in Germany. Synagogues and Jewish schools were burnt down and Jewish property was smashed both in shops and in private houses. Besides this, a large number of selected Jews were taken to concentration camps by the police. Towards midday we discussed these events in the Gauleiter's house. All of us were of the opinion that we now faced a completely new state of affairs on the Jewish question. By the great action against the Jews, carried out in the night and morning of the 10th November, all guiding principles and all laws on this subject had been made illusory. We were of the opinion (particularly myself) that we should now act on our own initiative in this respect. I proposed to the Gauleiter that, in view of the great existing lack of housing, the best thing would be to put the Jews into a kind of internment camp. Then the houses would become free in a twinkling, and the housing shortage would be relieved, at least in part. Besides that, we would have the Jews under control and supervision. I added 'The same thing happened to our prisoners of war and war internees.' The Gauleiter said that this suggestion was for the time being impossible to carry out. Thereupon I made a new proposal to him. I said that I considered it unthinkable that, after the Jews had had their property smashed, they should continue to be able to own houses and land. I proposed that these houses and this land ought to be taken away from them, and declared myself ready to carry through such an action. I declared that by the Aryanisation of Jewish land and houses a large sum could accrue to the Gau out of the proceeds. I named some millions of marks. I stated that, in my opinion, this Aryanisation could be carried out as legally as the Aryanisation of shops. The Gauleiter's answer was something to this effect: 'If you think you can carry this out, do so. The sum gained will then be used to build a Gau school.'"

I go down now to where it says "Page 18":

"The Aryanisation was accomplished by the alienation of properties, the surrender of claims, especially mortgage claims, and reductions in buying price.

The payment allowed the Jews was basically 10 per cent. of the nominal value or nominal sum of the claim. As a justification for these low prices, Holz claimed, at the Berlin meeting of the 6th February, 1939, that the Jews had mostly bought their property during the inflation period for a tenth of its value. As has been shown by investigating a large number of individual cases selected at random, this claim is not true."

My Lord, I would turn to Page 48 of the document book, which appears in the second part of this report, and that part of the report is really the part containing the findings of the Commission. I quote from the top of the page, Page 48 of the document book.

THE PRESIDENT: Is this still part of the report?

LIEUTENANT-COLONEL GRIFFITH-JONES: This is still part of the report. It is, in fact, the findings of the Commission:

"Gauleiter Streicher likes to beat people with a riding whip but only if he is in the company of several persons assisting him. Usually the beatings are carried out with sadistic brutality.

The best known case is that of Steinruck, whom he beat in the prison cell until the blood came, together with Deputy Gauleiter Holz and S.A. Brigader-General Konig. After returning from this scene to the 'Deutscher Hof' he said: 'Now I am relieved. I needed that again!' Later he also stated several times that he needed another Steinruck case in order to 'relieve' himself.

In August, 1938, he beat Editor Burker at the District House, together with District Office Leader Scholler and his Adjutant, Konig."

To show the authority and power that he held in his Gau, I refer to the last paragraph on that page.

"According to reports of reliable witnesses, Gauleiter Streicher is in the habit of pointing out, on the most varied occasions, that he alone gives orders in the district of Franconia. For instance, at a meeting in the Colosseum in Nuremberg in 1935 he said that nobody could remove him from office. In a meeting at Herkules Hall, where he described how he had beaten Professor Steinruck, he emphasised that he would not let himself be beaten by anybody, not even by an Adolf Hitler.

For, this also must be stated here, in Franconia the Gau acts first and then orders the absolutely powerless authorities to approve."

My Lord, both of those volumes of that, report 1757-PS, will become Exhibit GB 175.

THE PRESIDENT: The Tribunal is not altogether satisfied that that has any bearing on the case against Streicher.

LIEUTENANT-COLONEL GRIFFITH-JONES: My Lord, it is the object of that document to show the kind of treatment and persecution which, the Jews were receiving in the district of Gau over which this defendant ruled; and secondly to show the absolute authority with which this defendant acted in his district. That is the purpose of that document.

As a result, either of that investigation or of some other matter, the defendant was relieved of his position as Gauleiter in February, 1940, but he did not cease from his propaganda or from the control of his newspaper. I would only quote one further short extract from "Der Sturmer," an article written by him on the 4th November, 1943, which appears in the document book on Page 53, is Document 1965- PS, and becomes Exhibit GB 176, and it is an extract of importance:

"It is really the truth that the Jews, so to speak, have disappeared from Europe and that the Jewish reservoir of the East, from which the Jewish plague has for centuries beset the peoples of Europe, has ceased to exist. However, the Fuehrer of the German people at the beginning of the war prophesised what has now come to pass."

My Lord, that article was signed by Streicher, and it is my submission that it shows that he had knowledge of what was going on in the East, of which this Court has had such evidence. That was written November, 1943. In April, 1943, the Tribunal will remember, the Warsaw Ghetto was destroyed. Between April, 1942, and April, 1944, 1,700,000 odd Jews were killed in Auschwitz and Dachau - I quote now from the transcript-and throughout the whole of that period millions of Jews were to die. It is my submission that that article, appearing on the 4th November and signed by him, shows that he knew what was happening, perhaps not the details, but that he knew that the Jews were being exterminated.

I leave "Der Sturmer" and I would draw the attention of the Tribunal quite shortly to a matter which is perhaps as evil as any other aspect of this man's activity, and that is the particular attention that he paid to the instruction, if you can call it that, or the perversion of the children and the youth of Germany. He was not content with inciting the German population. He seized the children as early as he could at their schools, and he started to poison their minds at the earliest possible date. In some of the extracts to which I have already referred, the Tribunal will remember that there are mentions of children and the need for teaching them anti-Semitism. I refer now to Page 54 of the document book, and I would quote four or five lines from the last paragraph, starting in the middle of the last paragraph. It is a report of a speech by Streicher as early as June, 1925, when he says:

> "I repeat, we demand the transformation of the school into a national German institution of education. If we let German children be taught by German teachers, then we shall have laid the foundations for the national German school. This national German school must teach racial doctrine."

I now go to the last line of the first paragraph on the following page:

> "We demand, therefore, the introduction of racial doctrine into the school."

That is in a copy of "Der Sturmer," which has already been put in. It is Exhibit GB 165.

The following Document, M-43, is an extract from the "Frankische Tageszeitung" of the 19th March, 1934, when he addressed the pupils at a girls' school at Preisslerstrasse after they had finished their vocational course. He was continually holding children's meetings and attending children's schools. I quote the third paragraph:

> "Then Julius Streicher spoke about his life, and told them about a girl who at one time went to his school and who fell for a Jew and was finished for the rest of her life."

I need not read the rest. It is all in the same tone. That becomes GB 177.

Every summer they celebrated in Nuremberg what they called their solstice celebration, some pagan rite where the youth of Nuremberg were rallied, organised, or at least encouraged by the defendant Streicher.

On Page 58 of the document book is a report taken from his paper, "Frankische Tageszeitung," of his speech to the Hitler Youth on what they called the "Holy Mountain" near Nuremberg, on the 22nd June, 1935:

> "Boys and girls, look back a little more than ten years ago. A great war - the World War - had whirled over the peoples of the earth and had left in the end a heap of ruins. Only one people remained victorious in this dreadful war, a people of whom Christ said its father is the devil. That people had ruined the German nation in body and soul. Then Adolf Hitler, unknown to anybody, arose from among the people and became the voice which called to a holy war and battle. He cried to the people that everybody should take courage again and rise and give a helping hand to take the devil from the German people, so that the human race might be, free again from these people that have wandered about the world for centuries and millenia, marked with the sign of Cain.
>
> Boys and girls, even if they say that the Jews were once the chosen people, do not believe it, but believe us when we say that the Jews are not a chosen people. Because it cannot be that a chosen people should act among the peoples as the Jews do to-day."

And so on, with similar kind of propaganda. That document will be Exhibit GB 178.

The next Document, M-44, from which I will not read now, becomes GB 179. The Tribunal will see that it was a report of Streicher's address to 2,000 children at Nuremberg at Christmas-time, 1936. Underlined it says: "Do you know who the Devil is?" he asked his breathlessly listening audience. "The Jew, the Jew," resounded from a thousand children's voices.

But he was not content only with writing and talking. He actually issued a book for teachers, a book which he published from his "Der Sturmer" offices, called "The Jewish question and school instruction."

I have not had the whole of that book translated. It is addressed to school teachers. It is intended for their benefit, and it emphasises the necessity of anti-Semitic teaching in schools, and it suggests ways in which the subject can be introduced and handled.

On Page 60 of the document book, M-46, the Tribunal will see a few extracts which have been taken from that book. The preface part of it is as follows:

"The National Socialist State brought fundamental changes into all spheres of life of the German people.

It has also presented the German teacher with some new tasks. The National Socialist State demands that its teachers instruct German children in social questions. As far as the German people is concerned the racial question is a Jewish question. Those who want to teach the child all about the Jew must themselves have a thorough knowledge of the subject."

I will quote from the paragraph opposite Page 5 in the margin. The whole of the rest of the extracts are really suggestions for teachers as to how to introduce the Jewish subject into their teaching, and at Page 5 of the introduction:

"Racial and Jewish questions are the fundamental problems of the National Socialist ideology. The solution of these problems will secure the existence of National Socialism, and with this the existence of our nation for all time. The enormous significance of the racial question is recognised almost without exception to-day by all the German people. In order to attain this recognition, our people had to travel on a long road of suffering."

DR. MARX (Counsel for defendant Streicher): I would like to point out the following: The prosecutor omitted in his presentation to state that the book he referred to was not written by the defendant Streicher, but by the school inspector Fink. If the prosecutor had read the next sentence the Tribunal would have known about this fact. My client has called my attention to this point. I noticed it myself also because the next sentence reads as follows:

"Schulrat Fritz Fink desires to help the German teachers on the road to wisdom with his book: 'The Jewish Question in the Schools.'"

It is perfectly clear that Fink is the author of the book. It is of importance to know that Fink was the author of this book and not Streicher.

THE PRESIDENT: Have you finished what you wish to say?

DR. MARX: Yes, Sir, I have finished what I wanted to say.

THE PRESIDENT: I would point out to you that although the book does appear to have been written by Fritz Fink, which is stated in the paragraph at the top, it has a preface by Streicher, so we may presume that Streicher authorised it; and it was published and printed by "Der Sturmer."

DR. MARX: That is correct. May I add something? I just wanted to call the attention of the Tribunal to the fact that it is not understandable that just that particular sentence was not read. One could be of the opinion that this was an original work of Streicher, in which case the question of whether Streicher agreed with that work would appear of minor importance.

THE PRESIDENT: But you see, Dr. Marx, counsel was reading actually from the preface by Streicher. The last passage that he read, or almost the last, was the preface by Streicher. The last passage I have got marked is the passage on Page 60, which is headed "Preface," and is signed by Julius Streicher, which says in terms that the book was written by School Inspector Fritz Fink.

Let us not take any further time about it.

LIEUTENANT-COLONEL GRIFFITH-JONES: I think I have reached -

THE PRESIDENT: Will you read the last words of that preface on Page 60 there: "Those who take to heart"?

LIEUTENANT-COLONEL GRIFFITH-JONES: If your Lordship pleases, I read towards the end of the paragraph, the first paragraph of the preface:

"Those who take to heart all that has been written with such feeling by Fritz Fink, who for many years has been greatly concerned about the German people, will be grateful to the creator of this outwardly insignificant publication." Then it is signed by Julius Streicher, City of the Reich Party Rallies, Nuremberg, in the year 1937.

I only omitted that last part in the interest of time.

THE PRESIDENT: Yes.

LIEUTENANT-COLONEL GRIFFITH-JONES: That book is Exhibit GB 180. I will just read the last three lines, which I was not able to read before Dr. Marx interposed. The last three lines of the paragraph under "Introduction":

"No one should be allowed to grow up in the midst of our people without this knowledge of the monstrous character and dangerousness of the Jew."

I will not occupy the time of the Tribunal by reading further from that book. The nature of the book I hope is clear. I would only refer to the last three lines on the next page in the document book, taking another extract from it:

"One who has reached this stage of understanding will inevitably remain an enemy of the Jews all his life, and will instil this hatred into his own children."

"Der Sturmer" also published some children's books, although I make it quite clear that I am not alleging that the defendant himself wrote the books. But they were issued from his publishing business, and they are, of course, on the same lines as everything else that was published and issued from that business.

The first of them to which I would call attention was entitled in English or the English translation is as follows: "Do not trust the fox in the green meadow nor the Jew on his oath." It is a picture book for children. There are pictures, all of them offensive, depicting Jews, pictures of which a variety of selections appear in the Tribunal's book. And opposite each picture there is a little story.

On Page 62 of the document book the Tribunal will see the kind of thing which appears opposite each picture. Opposite the picture in the Tribunal's document book appears the following:

"Jesus Christ says: 'The Jew is a murderer through and through.' And when Christ had to die the Lord did not know any other people who would have tortured him to death, so he chose the Jews. That is why the Jews pride themselves on being the chosen people."

The writing opposite the first picture, which depicts a very unpleasant looking Jewish butcher cutting up meat, is as follows:

"The Jewish butcher: He sells half refuse instead of meat. A piece of meat lies on the floor, the cat claws another. This does not worry the Jewish butcher, since the meat increases in weight. Besides, one must not forget, he will not have to eat it himself."

Again, in the interest of time, it is not worth quoting the contents of that book any further. The Tribunal can see the type of book it is, the type of teaching it was instilling into the minds of the children. The pictures speak for themselves.

The second picture is a rather beastly picture of a girl being led away by a Jew. On the next page we see the defendant smiling benignly at a children's party, greeting the little children. The next picture depicts copies of "Der Sturmer" posted on a wall with children looking at them.

The next picture perhaps requires a little explanation. It is a picture of Jewish children being taken away from an Aryan school, led away by an unpleasant-looking father, and all the Aryan children shouting and dancing and enjoying the fun very much.

That book becomes Exhibit GB 181.

THE PRESIDENT: You will not be able, will you, to finish in a short time? Perhaps we had better adjourn now.

LIEUTENANT-COLONEL GRIFFITH-JONES: I have about another 20 minutes.

THE PRESIDENT: We will adjourn now.

(A recess was taken.)

LIEUTENANT-COLONEL GRIFFITH-JONES: My Lord, I had finished describing that one children's book. There is a similar book called "The Poisonous Fungus," which has, in fact, been put in evidence already as Exhibit USA 257. It is a book very much the same in character and appearance. It was put in evidence, but it was not read to the Tribunal, and I would like to read one of the short stories from that book because it shows, perhaps, more strikingly,

I think, than any other extract to which we have referred, the revolting way in which this man poisoned the minds of his listeners and readers.

It is a book of pictures again, with short stories, and Page 69 of the document book shows one of the pictures, a girl sitting in a Jewish doctor's waiting-room.

My Lord, it is not a very pleasant story, but he is not a very pleasant man, and it is only by reading these things that it becomes possible to believe the kind of education that the German children have been receiving during these years, led by this man.

I quote from the story:

"Inge" - that is the girl - "Inge sits in the reception room of the Jew doctor. She has to wait a long time. She looks through the journals which are on the table. But she is much too nervous to read even a few sentences. Again and again she remembers the talk with her mother. Again and again her mind reflects on the warnings of her leader of the League of German Girls. A German must not consult a Jew doctor. And particularly not a German girl. Many a girl that went to a Jew doctor to be cured, found disease and disgrace.

When Inge had entered the waiting-room, she experienced an extraordinary incident. From the doctor's consulting room she could hear the sound of crying. She heard the voice of a young girl: 'Doctor, doctor, leave me alone.'

Then she heard the scornful laughing of a man. And then, all of a sudden it became absolutely silent. Inge had listened breathlessly.

What may be the meaning of all this? she asked herself, and her heart was pounding. And again she thought of the warning of her leader in the League of German Girls.

Inge had already been waiting for an hour. Again she picks up the journals in an endeavour to read. Then the door opens. Inge looks up. The Jew appears.

She screams. In terror she drops the paper. Horrified, she jumps up. Her eyes stare into the face of the Jewish doctor, and this face is the face of the devil. In the middle of this devil's face is a huge crooked nose. Behind the spectacles two criminal eyes. And the thick lips are grinning, a grinning that expresses: 'Now I've got you at last, you little German girl!'

And then the Jew approaches her. His fat fingers snatch at her. But now Inge has composed herself. Before he can grab hold of her, she smacks the fat face of the Jew doctor with her hand. One jump to the door. Breathlessly Inge runs down the stairs. Breathlessly she escapes the Jew house."

Comment is almost unnecessary on a story like that, read by children of the age of those who are going to read the books you have seen.

Another picture which I have included in the book is a picture, of course of the defendant, with his youthful admirers standing around looking at it, and the script opposite that picture, which appears on Page 70 of the document book, included the words, and I quote from the last but one paragraph, "Without a solution of the Jewish question there will be no salvation for mankind."

The page itself contains an account of how some boys attended one of his speeches:

"That is what he shouted to us. All of us could understand him. And when, at the end, he shouted 'Sieg- Heil' for the Fuehrer, we all acclaimed him with tremendous enthusiasm. For two hours Streicher spoke on that occasion. To us it appeared to have been but a few minutes."

One can begin to see the effect that all this was having, from the columns of "Der Sturmer" itself. In April, 1936, there appears only one letter; many others appear in other copies from children of all ages. I quote the third paragraph of this letter, the letter signed by the boys and girls of the National Socialist Youth Hostel at Grossmullen:

"To-day we saw a play on how the devil persuades the Jew to shoot a conscientious National Socialist. In the course of the play the Jew did it, too. We all heard the shot. We would have all liked to jump up and arrest the Jew. But then the policeman came and after a short struggle took the Jew along. You can imagine, 'Der Sturmer,' that we heartily cheered the policeman. In the whole play not one name was mentioned, but we all knew that this play represented the murder by the Jew, Frankfurter. We were very sick when we went to bed that night. None felt like talking to the others. This play made it clear to us how the Jew sets to work."

My Lord, that book is already in evidence, as I have stated. It is GB 170.

To conclude, I would only draw the attention of the Tribunal again to his authority as a Gauleiter. It appears in the Organisation Book of the N.S.D.A.P. for 1938 - which is already in as Exhibit USA 430 - in the description of the duties and authority of Gauleiters: The Gauleiter bears over- all responsibility for the Fuehrer for the sector of sovereignty entrusted to him. The rights, duties and jurisdiction of the Gauleiter result primarily from the mission assigned by the Fuehrer and, apart from that, from detailed direction.

His association with the Fuehrer and with the other defendants - or some of the other defendants-can be seen from the newspapers. On the occasion of his 50th birthday, Hitler paid a visit to Nuremberg to congratulate him. That was on the 13th February, 1935. The account of that meeting is published in the "Volkischer Beobachter" of that date, and I quote as follows:

"Adolf Hitler spoke to his old comrades in battle and to his followers, in words which went straight to their hearts. By way of introduction, he remarked that it was a special pleasure to be present for a short while in Nuremberg, the town of the National-Socialist community which had been steeled in battle, at this day of honour to Julius Streicher, and to be within the circle of the standard bearers of the National-Socialist idea during many years.

Just as they all of them had during the years of oppression unshakeably believed in the victory of the Movement, so his friend and comrade in the battle, Streicher, had stood faithfully at his side at all times. It had been this unshakeable belief that had moved mountains.

For Streicher it would surely be a solemn thought, that this 50th anniversary meant not only the half-way point of a century, but also of a thousand years of German history to him. He had in Streicher a companion of whom he could say that here in Nuremberg was a man who would never waver for a single second, and who would unflinchingly stand behind him in every situation."

That is M-8 and becomes Exhibit GB 182.

The next document is a letter from Himmler published in "Der Sturmer" of April, 1937. That edition is already Exhibit USA 258:

"If in the future years the history of the reawakening of the German people is written, and if already the next generation will be unable to understand that the German people was once friendly to the Jews, it will be stated that Julius Streicher and his weekly paper 'Der Sturmer' have contributed a great deal towards the enlightenment regarding the enemy of humanity.

Signed: For the Reichsfuehrer S.S. Himmler."

That is Exhibit USA 260. A number of these documents are already in evidence in the bound volumes.

Lastly, we have a letter from Baldur von Schirach, the Reich Youth Leader, published in "Der Sturmer" of January, 1938:

"It is the historical merit of 'Der Sturmer' to have enlightened the broad masses of our people in a popular way as to the Jewish world danger. 'Der Sturmer' is right in refusing to fulfil its task in a purely aesthetic manner. Jewry has shown no regard for the German people. We have, therefore, no cause to be considerate and to spare our worst enemy. What we fail to do to-day, our youngsters of to-morrow will have to suffer for bitterly."

My Lord, it may be that this defendant is less directly involved in the physical commission of the crimes against Jews, of which this Tribunal has heard, than some of his co-conspirators. The submission of the prosecution is that his crime is no less the worse for that reason. No Government in the world, before the Nazis came to power, could have embarked upon and put into effect a policy of mass extermination in the way in which they did, without having a people who would back them and support them, and without having a large number of people, men and women, who were prepared to put their hands to their bloody murder. And not even, perhaps, the German people of previous generations would have lent themselves to the crimes about which this Tribunal has heard, the killing of millions and millions of men and women.

It was to the task of educating the people, of producing murderers, educating and poisoning them with hate, that Streicher set himself; and for 25 years he has continued unrelentingly the education - if you can call it so - the perversion of the people and of the youth of Germany. And he has gone on and on as he saw the results of his work bearing fruit.

In the early days he was preaching persecution. As persecutions took place he preached extermination and annihilation; and, as we have seen in the Ghettos of the East, as millions of Jews were being exterminated and annihilated, he cried out for more and more.

That is the crime that he has committed. It is the submission of the prosecution that he made these things possible, made these crimes possible, which could never have happened, had it not been for him and for those like him. He led the propaganda and the education of the German people in those ways. Without him the Kaltenbrunners, the Himmlers, the General Stroops, would have had nobody to carry out their orders. And, as we have seen, he has concentrated upon the youth and the childhood of Germany. In its extent his crime is probably greater and more far-reaching than that of any of the other defendants. The misery that they caused finished with their incarceration. The effects of this man's crimes, of the poison that he has injected into the minds of millions and millions of young boys and girls and young men and women, lives on. He leaves behind him a legacy of almost a whole people poisoned with hate, sadism, and murder, and perverted by him. That German people remain a problem and perhaps a menace to the rest of civilisation for generations to come.

My Lord, I submit that the prosecution's case against this man as set out in the Indictment is proved.

My Lord, Lieutenant Brady Bryson, of the United States delegation, will present to the Court the case against Schacht.

LIEUTENANT BRADY BRYSON: May it please the Tribunal, a document book has been prepared and filed and the appropriate number of copies has been delivered to the defendants.

We ask the Tribunal's permission to file, within the next few days, a trial brief, which now is in the process of preparation.

Our proof against the defendant Schacht is confined to planning and preparation of aggressive war.

THE PRESIDENT: What was it you said about the trial brief?

LIEUTENANT BRYSON: We ask permission to file a trial brief within the next few days, as our brief is not yet ready.

THE PRESIDENT: I see.

LIEUTENANT BRYSON: Our proof against the defendant Schacht is limited to planning and preparation for aggressive war, and to membership in a conspiracy for aggressive war.

The extent of Schacht's criminal responsibility as a matter of law, under the Charter of the Tribunal, will be developed in our brief. Only a few of our 50 odd documents have been previously submitted in evidence. We have taken special pains to avoid repetition and cumulative proof, but for the sake of continuity we would like, in several instances, simply to draw the Tribunal's attention to evidence previously received, with an appropriate reference to the transcript of the record.

Before commencing our proof, we wish to state our understanding that the defendant Schacht's control over the German economy was on the wane after November, 1937, and that by the time of the aggression on Poland his official status had been reduced to that of Minister without Portfolio and personal adviser to Hitler. We know, too, that he is sometimes credited with opposition to certain of the more radical elements of the Nazi Party; and I further understand that at the time of capture by United States forces he was under German detention in a prison camp, having been arrested by the Gestapo in July, 1944.

Be this as it may, our proof will show that at least up until the end of 1937 Schacht was the dominant figure in the rearming of Germany and in the economic planning and preparation for war; that without his work the Nazis would not have been able to wring from their depressed economy the tremendous material requirements of armed aggression; and that Schacht contributed his efforts with full knowledge of the aggressive purposes which he was serving.

The details of this proof will be presented in four parts. First, we will very briefly show that Schacht accepted the Nazi philosophy prior to 1933 and supported Hitler's rise to power.

Second, proof of the contribution of Schacht to German rearmament and preparation for war will be submitted. This evidence will also be brief, since the facts in this respect are well known and have already been touched upon by Mr. Dodd in his preparation of the case on economic preparation for war.

Third, we will show that Schacht assisted the Nazi conspiracy purposely and willingly with knowledge of and sympathy for its illegal ends.

And last, we will prove that Schacht's loss of power in the German Government did not in any sense imply disagreement with the policy of aggressive war.

We turn now to our proof that Schacht helped Hitler to power.

Schacht met Goering for the first time in December, 1930, and Hitler, early in January, 1931, at Goering's house. His impression of Hitler was favourable. I offer in evidence Exhibit USA 615, consisting of an excerpt from a pre-trial interrogation of Schacht, under date of 20th July, 1945, and quote two questions and answers related to this meeting, near the middle of the first page of the interrogation.

THE PRESIDENT: Are you going to give us the exhibit number? You have not given us the other number?

LIEUTENANT BRYSON: This is an interrogation, Sir, and it will not have two.

TIM PRESIDENT: Have you got a number for it?

LIEUTENANT BRYSON: You will find it in your document book in the back, labelled "Schacht Interrogation of 20th July, 1945." I quote from the middle of the first page:

"**Q.** What did he (that is, Hitler) say?

A. Oh, ideas he expressed before, but he was full of will and spirit."

And near the bottom of the page:

Q. What was your impression at the end of that evening?

A. I thought that Hitler was a man with whom one could co-operate."

After this meeting Schacht allied himself with Hitler, and at a crucial political moment in November, 1932, he lent the prestige of his name, which was widely known in banking, financial and business circles throughout the world, to Hitler's cause. I offer in evidence Exhibit USA 616, consisting of excerpts from a pre-trial interrogation of Schacht on 17th October, 1945. I wish to quote beginning at the top of Page 36 of this interrogation. This is the interrogation of 17th October, 1945, at Page 36. I may say that, when I refer to the page numbers, I speak of the page of the document.

"**Q.** Yes, and at that time (referring to January, 1931) you became a supporter, I take it -

A. In the course -

Q. Of Hitler's coming to power.

A. Especially in the course of the years 1931 and 1932."

And I quote further from the lower half of Page 37 of the same interrogation:

"**Q.** But what I mean is - to make it very brief indeed - did you lend the prestige of your name to help Hitler come to power?

A. I have publicly stated that I expected Hitler to come to power, for the first time that I remember, in November, 1932."

I quote further:

"**Q.** And you know, or perhaps you do not, that Goebbels in his diary records with great affection

A. Yes.

Q. The help that you gave him at that time?

A. Yes, I know that.

Q. November, 1932?

A. From the Kaiserhof to the Chancellery and back.

Q. That is right; you have read that?

A. Yes.

Q. And you do not deny that Goebbels was right?

A. I think his impression was, that this was correct at the time."

I now refer the Tribunal to this statement of Goebbels, set forth in Document 2409-A-PS. The entire diary of Goebbels is in evidence as Exhibit USA 262. The entry I wish to read, which appears in 2409-A-PS, was made on 21st November, 1932.

"In a conversation with Dr. Schacht, I assured myself that he absolutely represents our point of view. He is one of the few who accepts the Fuehrer's position entirely."

It is believed that Schacht joined the Party only in the sense that he allied himself with the cause. Dr. Franz Reuter, whose biography of Schacht was officially published in Germany in 1937, has stated that Schacht refrained from formal membership in order to be of greater assistance to the Party. I offer in evidence Document EC-460, Exhibit USA 617, consisting of an excerpt from Reuter's biography, and I quote the last sentence of the excerpt:

"By not doing so - at least until the final assertion and victory of the Party - he was able to assist it (the Party) much better than he would have been able to do had he become an official Party member."

It was Schacht who organised the financial means for the decisive March, 1933, election, at a meeting of Hitler with a group of German industrialists in Berlin. Schacht acted as the sponsor or host of this meeting, and a campaign fund of several million Marks was collected. Without reading therefrom, I offer in evidence Document EC-439, Exhibit USA 618, an affidavit of von Schnitzler under date of 10th November, 1945, which already appears in the record (Pages 130-1, Part 1).

Further evidence on this point is also contained in the excerpt from the interrogation of Schacht on 20th July, 1945, from which I read a part a moment ago. Schacht lent his support to Hitler not only because he was an opportunist, but also because he shared Hitler's ideological principles. Apart from the entry in Goebbel's diary, this may be seen from Schacht's own letter to Hitter, under date of 29th August, 1932, pledging continued support to Hitler after the latter's poor showing in the July 1932 elections. I offer this letter in evidence as Document EC-457, Exhibit USA 619, and quote from the middle of the first paragraph and further from the next to the last paragraph:

"But what you could perhaps do with in these days is a word of most sincere sympathy. Your movement is carried internally by so strong a truth and necessity that victory in one form or another cannot elude you for long."

And further down, and keep in mind that neither Hitler nor Schacht was then in the German Government, Schacht says:

"Wherever my work may take me in the near future, even if you should see me one day within the fortress, you can always count on me as your reliable assistant."

THE PRESIDENT: What do those words mean at the top, "The President of the Reichsbank in retirement"? Are they on the letter?

LIEUTENANT BRYSON: Yes, they are, Sir. Dr. Schacht had previously been a President of the Reichsbank. At this time he was in retirement. You will remember, this is prior to Hitler's accession to power.

THE PRESIDENT: Yes, of course.

LIEUTENANT BRYSON: And then Hitler reinstated Dr. Schacht as President of the Reichsbank after the Nazis had taken over.

THE PRESIDENT: And he put that at the top of his letter, did he?

LIEUTENANT BRYSON: That I cannot say. I will also point out that Schacht signed this letter "With a Vigorous Heil."

We turn now to the second part of our proof, relating to Schacht's contribution to preparation for war.

The detailed chronology of Schacht's official career in the Nazi Government, as set forth in Document 3021-PS, has already been submitted in evidence as Exhibit USA 11. However, it may be helpful at the outset to remind the Tribunal that Schacht was recalled to the Presidency of the Reichsbank by Hitler on 17th March, 1933, which office he continuously held until 20th January, 1939 that he was Acting Minister and then Minister of Economics from August, 1934, until November, 1937; and that he was appointed General Plenipotentiary for War Economy in May, 1935. He resigned as Minister of Economics and General Plenipotentiary for War Economy in November, 1937, when he accepted appointment as Minister without Portfolio, which post he held until January, 1943. His position as virtual economic. dictator of Germany in the four crucial years from early 1933 to the end of 1936 is practically a matter of common knowledge.

Schacht was the guiding genius behind the Nazi expansion of the German credit system for rearmament purposes. From the outset, he recognised that the plan for the German military supremacy required huge quantities of public credit. To that end, a series of measures was adopted which subverted all credit institutions in Germany to the over-all aim of supplying funds for the military machine. I will briefly mention some of these measures.

By Cabinet decree of 27th October, 1933, the statutory reserve of 40 per cent. in gold and foreign exchange required against circulating Reichsbank notes was permanently abandoned. By the Credit Act of 1934, the Government assumed jurisdiction of all credit institutions, and control over the entire banking system was centralised in Schacht as Chairman of the Supervisory Board for the Credit System and President of the Reichsbank. This Act not only enabled Schacht to control the quantity of credit but also its use. On 29th March, 1934, a system of forced corporate lending to the Reich was imposed on German business. And on 19th February, 1935, the Treasury was authorised to borrow funds in any amounts approved by the Reich Chancellor, that is, Hitler.

On these points, I ask the Tribunal to take judicial notice of the Reichsgesetzblatt, 1933, Part 11, Page 827; Reichsgesetzblatt, 1934, Part 1, Page 1203;

Reichsgesetzblatt, 1934, Part 1, Page 295; and Reichsgesetzblatt, 1935, Part 1, Page 198.

THE PRESIDENT: Are they found here in the document book.

LIEUTENANT BRYSON: They are not in the document book, Sir.

I asked only that judicial notice be taken of them as published laws of Germany.

These measures enabled Schacht to embark upon what he himself has termed a "daring credit policy," including the secret financing of a vast amount of armaments through the so-called 'Mefo' Bill (Page 136, Part 1). I offer in evidence Document EC-436, Exhibit USA 620, consisting of a statement, dated 2nd November, 1945, by Emil Puhl, a director of the Reichsbank during Schacht's presidency, and quote the second paragraph thereof as follows:

"In the early part of 1935, the need for financing an accelerated rearmament programme arose. Dr. Schacht, President of the Reichsbank, after considering various techniques of financing, proposed the use of 'Mefo' Bills, to provide a substantial portion of the funds needed for the rearmament programme. This method had as one of its primary advantages the fact that secrecy would be possible during the first years of the rearmament programme, and figures indicating the extent of rearmament, that would have become public through the use of other methods, could be kept secret through the use of 'Mefo' Bills."

The extent of the credit expansion, and the importance of " Mefo " financing, may be seen from Document EC-419, which I now offer as Exhibit USA 621, and which consists of a letter from Finance Minister von Krosigk to Hitler, under date of 1st September, 1938. I quote the following figures from the middle of the first page:

"The development of the Reich debt is as follows: As of 31st December, 1932, Funded Debt: 10.4 billions of Reichsmark. Current Debt: 2.1 billions of Reichsmark. Debt (not subscribed to by public, that is, trade and 'Mefo' Bills of Exchange): 0.

As of 30th June, 1938, Funded Debt: 19 million Reichsmark. Current Debt: 5 million Reichsmark. Debt (not subscribed to by public, that is, trade and 'Mefo' Bills of Exchange): 13.3 billion Reichsmark.

Total, as of 31st December, 1932: 12.5 billion Reichsmark; as of 30th June, 1938: 35.8 billion Reichsmark."

The Reich debt thus tripled -

THE PRESIDENT: Would you read the next section, beginning with the words "Provisions were made to cover."

LIEUTENANT BRYSON:

"Provisions were made to cover the armament expenditures for the year 1938 (the same amount as in 1937) as follows: "Five billions from the budget, that is, taxes; 4 billions from loans; 2 billions from six months treasury notes, which means postponement of payment until 1939; total: 11 billions."

The Reich debt thus tripled under Schacht's management. More than one-third of the total was financed secretly and through the instrumentality of the Reichsbank by "Mefo" and trade bills. It is clear that this amount of financing outside the normal public issues represented armament debt. I read further from Document EC-436, at the beginning of the last long paragraph:

"These 'Mefo' bills were used exclusively for financing rearmament, and when in March, 1938, a new finance programme discontinuing the use of 'Mefo' bills was announced by Dr. Schacht, there was a total volume outstanding of 12 billion Marks of 'Mefo' bills which had been issued to finance rearmament."

The character of Schacht's credit policy and the fact that it was ruthlessly dedicated to the creation of armaments, plainly appear from his own speech delivered on 29th November, 1938.

I offer it in evidence as Document EC-611, Exhibit USA 622, and I quote from Page 6 at the beginning of the last paragraph:

> "It is possible that no bank of issue, in peacetime, carried on such a daring credit policy as the Reichsbank since the seizure of power by National Socialism. With the aid of this credit policy, however, Germany created an armament second to none, and this armament in turn made possible the results of our policy."

Beyond the field of finance Schacht assumed totalitarian control over the German economy generally, in order to marshal it behind the rearmament programme.

He acquired great power over industry as a result of the Nazi reorganisation of German industry along military lines, and in accordance with the so-called "Leadership Principle." On this point I refer the Tribunal to the transcript for 23rd November (Pages 132-4, Part 1) and to Reichsgesetzblatt, 1934, Part 1, Page 1194, of which the Tribunal is asked to take judicial notice.

Schacht also exercised broad powers as a member of the Reich Defence Council, which was secretly established on 4th April, 1933, and the function of which was preparation for war. The Tribunal is referred to the transcript for 23rd November (Page 134, Part 1). I also offer in evidence as Document EC-128, Exhibit U.S.A. 623, a report under date of 30th September, 1934, showing the functions of the Ministry of Economics in this respect. The report reveals concentration upon all the familiar war-time economic problems, including stockpiling, production of scarce goods, removal of industry to secure areas, fuel and power supply for war production, machine tools, control of war-time priorities, rationing, price control, civilian supply, and so on. I wish to read into the record merely an excerpt showing the jurisdiction of the Ministry of Economics, beginning near the top of Page 2 of EC-128:

> "With the establishment of the Reich Defence Council and its permanent committee, the Reich Ministry of Economics has been given the task of making economic preparation for the conduct of the war. There should really be no need to explain the tremendous significance of this task. Everyone remembers how terribly the lack of any economic preparation for war hit us during the world war."

Finally, in 1934, Schacht acquired sweeping powers under legislation which authorised him, as Minister of Economics, to take any measure deemed necessary for the development of the German economy. In this connection reference is made to Reichsgesetzblatt, 1934, Part 1, Page 565, of which the Tribunal is asked to take judicial notice.

The so-called "New Plan," devised by Schacht, was announced in the fall of 1934 shortly after he became Minister of Economics. In this connection the Tribunal is referred to Reichsgesetzblatt, 1934, Part 1, Page 816, and 1935, Part 1, Page 105, with the request that judicial notice be taken thereof. The New Plan was Schacht's basic programme for obtaining the necessary foreign-produced raw materials and foreign exchange required to sustain the rearmament programme.

With respect to the details of the New Plan, I offer in evidence Document EC-437, Exhibit USA 624, consisting of an affidavit of Emil Puhl, dated 7th November, 1945. The entire text is pertinent. Therefore, permission is requested to submit the affidavit without reading therefrom, on condition that French and Russian translations be prepared and filed.

THE PRESIDENT: And German ones supplied, too.

LIEUTENANT BRYSON: We will supply copies. I wish to say that the original is in English, but the affidavit has already been translated into German.

THE PRESIDENT: Yes.

LIEUTENANT BRYSON: This affidavit, by a co-worker of Schacht, describes in detail the many ingenious and often ruthless devices he used, including negotiating "stand- still" agreements, forcing payment in Reichsmark of interest and amortisation on debts incurred in foreign currency, using script and funding bonds for the same purpose; suspending service on foreign-held debt; blocking foreign- held marks; freezing foreign claims in Germany; eliminating unessential foreign expenditures; requisitioning German-held foreign exchange; subsidising exports; issuing restricted marks; bartering under clearing agreements; licensing imports; and controlling all foreign exchange transactions to the favouring of raw materials for armaments.

The Tribunal is also asked to take judicial notice of Reichsgesetzblatt, 1934, Page 997; Reichsgesetzblatt, 1933, Part 1, Page 349, and Reichsgesetzblatt, 1937, Part 1, Page 600, relating to the Clearing Bank, the Conversion Bank, and the maturity of Foreign Loans, all of which decrees are mentioned in the affidavit.

Schacht even went so far as to invest foreign-held Reichsmark on deposit in German banks in rearmament notes, thus, as he put it, financing rearmament with the assets of his political opponents. Without reading therefrom, I refer your Honour to Document 1168-PS, Exhibit USA 37, being a memorandum from Schacht to Hitler, dated 3rd May, 1935, which already appears in the transcript (Pages 187-8, Part 1). Moreover, Schacht even resorted to capital punishment to prevent the loss of foreign exchange when frightened capitalists began to flee from the country. In this connection reference is made to the Law Against Economic Sabotage, found in 1936 Reichsgesetzblatt, Part 1, Page 999, of which the Tribunal is asked to take judicial notice.

Schacht took particular pride in the results which were accomplished under the stringent controls which he instituted under his "New Plan." I refer the Tribunal to Document EC-611, in evidence as Exhibit USA 622, consisting of Schacht's speech in Berlin on 29th November, 1938. I wish to read into the record an excerpt from the top of Page 10:

> "If there is anything remarkable about the New Plan it is again only the fact that German organisation under National Socialist leadership succeeded in conjuring up, in a very short time, the whole apparatus of supervision of imports, direction of exports and promotion of exports. The success of the New Plan can be proved by means of a few figures. Calculated according to quantity, the import of finished products were throttled by 63 per cent. between 1934 and 1937. On the other hand, the import of ores was increased by 132 per cent., of petroleum by 116 per cent., of grain by 102 per cent. and of rubber by 71 per cent."

While President of the Reichsbank and Minister of Economics, Schacht acquired still another key position, that of General Plenipotentiary for War Economy.

He received this appointment from Hitler pursuant to the unpublished Reich Defence Law, secretly enacted on 21st May, 1935. This law is in evidence as 2261-PS, Exhibit USA 24, consisting of a letter from von Blomberg, dated 24th June, 1935, to the Chiefs of the Army, Navy and Air Forces, together with copies of the Reich Defence Law and the Cabinet's memorandum relating thereto Pertinent comments on and excerpts from this document appear in the transcript for 23rd November

(Pages 128 and 134, Part 1). I will simply state, therefore, that by virtue of this appointment, Schacht was put in complete charge of economic planning and preparation for war in peace-time - except for certain direct armament production under control of the War Ministry. Upon the outbreak of war, he was to be the economic Czar of Germany, with complete control over the activities of a number of key Reich industries.

Schacht appointed Wohltat as his deputy and organised a staff to carry out his directives. In this connection I offer in evidence excerpts from a pre-trial interrogation of Schacht under date 17th October, 1945. This document is Exhibit USA 616. I wish to read into the record a question and answer found at the bottom of Page 40 of the document:

"**Q.** Let me ask you a general question, then: Do you take the responsibility as Plenipotentiary for War Economy for the writings that were made and the actions that were done by Wohltat and his assistants?

A. I have to."

I also offer in evidence Document EC-258, Exhibit USA 625, consisting of a status report issued in December, 1937, under the signature of Schacht's deputy Wohltat. The report is entitled "The Preparation of the Economic Mobilisation by the Plenipotentiary for War Economy." Schacht had withdrawn from office immediately prior to the preparation of this report, and it plainly is a recapitulation of his accomplishments while in office. Since the entire text is relevant, we ask permission to submit the document without reading therefrom, on condition that translations into French and Russian be later filed with the Tribunal.

THE PRESIDENT: I do not think this is consistent with the rule laid down by the Tribunal, which was that the translations in the French and Russian language should be submitted at the same time. You are now suggesting that you can submit translations at a later stage.

LIEUTENANT BRYSON: Well, if your Honour pleases, in any event I did not plan to read from the document at this time, and defence counsel have the German original.

THE PRESIDENT: I was not speaking of the defence counsel so much as of the members of the Tribunal.

LIEUTENANT BRYSON: We have the Russian translation in process; it was delayed, and we were unable to get it here by now, but the delay will be very short, and the document is of critical importance to our case.

THE PRESIDENT: How long will it be before it is ready?

LIEUTENANT BRYSON: I would not like to say precisely, Sir, but perhaps within four or five days.

THE PRESIDENT: What did you propose to do now, because it is a very complicated and long document, is it not?

LIEUTENANT BRYSON: It is, and it shows -

THE PRESIDENT: Were you proposing to summarise it?

LIEUTENANT BRYSON: I was proposing to summarise it, Sir, now.

THE PRESIDENT: The Tribunal thinks that if you would summarise it now, and only be permitted to put it in at the stage when you have the translation ready, you may proceed.

LIEUTENANT BRYSON: I will summarise it now, Sir.

This document discloses that before his resignation -

THE PRESIDENT: Will it take long to summarise?

LIEUTENANT BRYSON: Not very long, Sir, no.

THE PRESIDENT: You see, it is 5 o'clock.

LIEUTENANT BRYSON: I think there will be time to summarise it, and then we will stop.

This document discloses that, before his resignation, Schacht had worked out, in amazing detail, his plans and preparations for the management of the economy in the forthcoming war. For example, 180,000 industrial plants in 300 industries had been surveyed with respect to usefulness for war purposes; economic plans for the production of 200 basic materials had been worked out; a system for the letting of war contracts had been devised; allocations of coal, motor fuel and power had been determined; 248 million Reichsmark had been spent on storage facilities alone; evacuation plans for war materials and skilled workers from military zones had been worked out; 80 million war-time ration cards had already been printed and distributed to local areas; and a card-index of some 22 million skilled workers had been prepared.

That concludes the summary, your Honour.

THE PRESIDENT: We will adjourn now.

(The Tribunal adjourned until the 11th January, 1946, at 10.00 hours.)

Thirty-Second Day: Friday, January 11th, 1946

LIEUTENANT BRYSON: If the Tribunal, please, before picking up our line of proof against the defendant Schacht, I would like to supply a point of information.

Yesterday the President of the Tribunal inquired with respect to Document EC-457, Exhibit USA 619. The question raised by the Tribunal was with respect to the words "in retirement" in the letter-head used by Schacht in writing to Hitler in 1932. This is the letter in which Schacht expressed his belief in the truth of the Nazi movement and in which he said that Hitler could always count upon him as a reliable assistant.

The letter-head has printed upon it "The President of the Reichsbank," and after that phrase there is typed the letters "A.D." and I understand that those letters are an abbreviation for a German phrase meaning " in retirement," and that it is customary, or it was customary, in Germany, for retired officials to continue to use their titles with the letters "A.D."

THE PRESIDENT: I see.

LIEUTENANT BRYSON: Yesterday we had just about completed our proof with respect to the contribution of the defendant Schacht to the preparation for war, and I wish to submit one more document on this point. This is Document EC-451, Exhibit USA 626. It consists of a statement by George S. Messersmith, United States Consul- General in Berlin, 1930 to 1934. I will quote therefrom, beginning with the second sentence of the fourth paragraph:

> "It was his" - Schacht's - "financial ability that enabled the Nazi regime in the early days to find the financial basis for the tremendous armament programme and which made it possible to carry it through. If it had not been for his efforts, and this is not a personal observation of mine only, but an opinion which I believe was shared and is shared by every observer at the time, the Nazi regime would have been unable to maintain itself in power and to establish its control over Germany, much less to create the enormous war machine which was necessary for its objectives in Europe and later throughout the world.
>
> The increased industrial activity in Germany incident to rearmament made great imports of raw materials necessary, while at the same time exports were decreasing. Yet Schacht, by his resourcefulness, his complete financial ruthlessness and his absolute cynicism was able to maintain and to establish the situation for the Nazis. Unquestionably, without this complete lending of his capacities to the Nazi Government and all of its ambitions, it would have been impossible for Hitler and the Nazis to develop an armed force sufficient to permit Germany to launch an aggressive war."

We turn now -

THE PRESIDENT: Well, Lieutenant Bryson, I am not sure that that gives a full or quite fair recapitulation of the document. Do you not think perhaps you ought to read the paragraph before?

LIEUTENANT BRYSON:

> "Dr. Schacht always attempted to play on both sides of the fence. He told me,

and I know he told both other American representatives in Berlin and various British representatives, that he disapproved of practically everything the Nazis were doing. I recall on several occasions his saying, after the Nazi Party came into power, that, if the Nazis were not stopped, they were going to ruin Germany and the rest of the world with it. I recall distinctly that he emphasised to me that the, Nazis were inevitably going to plunge Europe into war."

If the Court please, I would like to read also from the last paragraph:

"In my opinion Schacht was in no sense a captive of the Nazis. He was not compelled to devote his time and his capacities to their interest. His situation was such that he would most likely have been able either to work on a much less restrained scale or to abstain from activity entirely. He continued to lend his services to the Nazi Government at every opportunity."

We turn now to the third part of our case against Schacht. The evidence is clear that he willingly contributed his efforts to the Nazi conspiracy, knowing full well its aggressive designs. The Tribunal will recall our proof that Schacht was converted to the Nazi philosophy in 1931 and helped Hitler come to power in 1933. We will now prove, first, that Schacht personally favoured aggression and, second, that in any event he knew Hitler's aggressive intentions.

There is ample evidence to justify the conclusion that Schacht rearmed Germany in order to see fulfilled his strong belief in aggressive expansion as an instrument of German national policy. Schacht had long been a German nationalist and expansionist. He spoke against the Treaty of Versailles at Stuttgart as early as 1927. I offer in evidence Document EC-415, Exhibit USA 627, consisting of a collection of excerpts from speeches by Schacht.

I quote from the top of Page 2:

"The Versailles Dictate cannot be an eternal document, because not only its economic but also its spiritual and moral premises are wrong."

It is common knowledge that he strongly favoured acquisition of colonial territory by Germany. However, he also favoured acquisition of contiguous territory in Europe.

THE PRESIDENT: Are you going to read the passage that follows that at a later stage?

LIEUTENANT BRYSON: At a later stage, if you please, Sir, in connection with another point.

THE PRESIDENT: Very well; go on.

LIEUTENANT BRYSON: On 16th April, 1929, at the Paris Conference in connection with reparations, he said:

"Germany can, in general, pay only if the Corridor and Upper Silesia is handed back to her from Polish possession and if, besides, somewhere on earth colonial territory is made available to her."

THE TRIBUNAL (Mr. Biddle): What are you quoting from?

LIEUTENANT BRYSON: I offer in evidence Exhibit USA 628, consisting of excerpts from a pre-trial interrogation of Schacht on 24th August, 1945.

You will find it in the document book at the back, labelled "Interrogation of 24th August." It is at the top of the first page of the interrogation. This statement was quoted as Schacht's and his reply contains an admission of having made the statement. In his reply he said:

"That Germany could not pay, at the time after I made the statement, has been proved, and that Germany will not be able to pay after this war will be proved in the future."

I wish to point out that this is the very territory which was the subject of armed aggression in September, 1939.

In 1935 Schacht stated flatly that Germany would, if necessary, acquire colonies by force. I offer in evidence Document EC450, designated as Exhibit USA 629. This document consists of an affidavit of S. R. Fuller, Jr., together with a transcript of his conversation with Schacht at the American Embassy in Berlin on 23rd September, 1935. I wish to read from Page 6 of the document where there appears a statement by Schacht in the lower half of the page.

THE PRESIDENT: What is the date of the conversation?

LIEUTENANT BRYSON: The conversation occurred on 23rd September, 1935. The page number of this document is at the bottom, and I quote from Page 6:

"Schacht: Colonies are necessary to Germany. We shall get them through negotiation, if possible, but if not, we shall take them."

In July, 1936, when the rearmament programme was well under way, Schacht again publicly spoke of the Versailles Treaty. This time his language contained an explicit threat of war. I refer the Tribunal again to Document EC-415, which I have previously introduced in evidence as Exhibit USA 627, consisting of a collection of speeches by Schacht. I wish to read from the paragraph beginning in the middle of the first page:

"But the memory of war weighs undiminished upon the disposition of the peoples. That is because, deeper than material wounds, moral wounds are smarting, inflicted by the so-called peace treaties. Material loss can be made up through renewed labour, but the moral wrong which has been inflicted upon the conquered peoples, in the peace dictates, leaves a burning scar on their conscience. The spirit of Versailles has perpetuated the fury of war, and there will not be a true peace, progress or reconstruction until the world desists from this spirit. The German people will not tire of pronouncing this warning."

Later in the same year Schacht publicly advocated the doctrine of "Lebensraum" for the German people. I quote again from Document EC- 415, Exhibit USA 627, being an excerpt from Schacht's speech at Frankfurt on 9th December, 1936, on the second page, the last paragraph:

"Germany has too little living space for her population. She has made every effort, and certainly greater efforts than any other nation, to extract from her own existing small space whatever is necessary for the securing of her livelihood. However, in spite of all these efforts, the space does not suffice."

In January, 1937, Schacht, in a conversation with Ambassador Davies, at least by inference threatened a breach of the peace in demanding a colonial cession. I offer in evidence Document L-111, being Exhibit USA 630, consisting of excerpts from a report under date of 20th January, 1937, by Ambassador Davies to the Secretary of State. I wish to read therefrom, beginning with the second sentence of the second paragraph:

"He" - meaning Schacht - "stated the following: that the present condition of the German people was intolerable, desperate and unendurable; that be had been authorised by his Government to submit proposals to France and England which would -

(1) guarantee European peace;

(2) secure present European international boundaries;

(3) reduce armaments;

(4) establish a new form of a workable League of Nations;

(5) abolish sanctions with new machinery for joint administration; all this based upon a colonial cession that would provide for Germany an outlet for population, a source for foodstuffs, fats and raw materials."

In December, 1937, Ambassador Dodd noted in his diary that Schacht would be willing to risk war for the sake of new territory in Europe. I refer the Tribunal to Document EC-461, consisting of excerpts from Ambassador Dodd's diary.

THE PRESIDENT: The proposal contained in Document 111 was for cession of colonies, was it not?

LIEUTENANT BRYSON: It was, Sir.

I turn now to Document EC-461, consisting of excerpts from Ambassador Dodd's diary. The entire diary has previously been received in evidence as Exhibit USA 58.

I quote some notes on a conversation with Schacht on 21st December, 1937, beginning near the bottom of the second page of EC-461, at the last paragraph:

"Schacht meant what the army chiefs of 1914 meant when they invaded Belgium, expecting to conquer France in six weeks; that is, domination and annexation of neighbouring small countries, especially North and East. Much as he dislikes Hitler's dictatorship he, as most other eminent Germans, wishes annexation without war, if possible; with war, if the United States will keep hands off."

THE PRESIDENT: There is another passage in that book, that diary. I do not know if it is the same date. I am not sure; it probably is not the same date, but it is on the first page of the exhibit, I think, the third paragraph. Is it at a different time?

LIEUTENANT BRYSON: It is a different time, Sir.

THE PRESIDENT: September the 19th of what year?

LIEUTENANT BRYSON: We will check that in the complete volume here, and I think in a minute I will be able to supply the date. In the meantime, would you like me to read, Sir?

THE PRESIDENT: Yes, I think you had better read this.

LIEUTENANT BRYSON:

"He then acknowledged that the Hitler Party is absolutely committed to war and the people, too, are ready and willing. Only a few Government officials are aware of the dangers and are opposed. He concluded: 'But we shall postpone it ten years. Then it may be we can avoid war.'"

THE PRESIDENT: Well, I think you should read the next paragraph, too.

LIEUTENANT BRYSON:

"I remind him of his Bad Eilsen speech some weeks ago and said: 'I agree with you about commercial and financial matters in the main. But why do you not, when you speak before the public, tell the German people they must abandon a war attitude?' He replied: 'I dare not say that. I can only speak on my special subject.'"

THE PRESIDENT: And the next one.

LIEUTENANT BRYSON:

"How then can German people ever learn the real dangers of war, if nobody ever presents that side of the question? He once more emphasised his opposition to war and added that he had used his influence with Hitler - 'a very great man,' he interjected - to prevent war.

The German papers printed what I said at Bremen about commercial relations between our countries, but not a word about the terrible effects and barbarism of war. He acknowledged that and talked very disapprovingly of the Propaganda Ministry which suppresses everything it dislikes. He added, as I was leaving: 'You know a Party comes into office by propaganda and then cannot disavow it or stop it.'"

The date of this conversation was in September, 1934.

THE PRESIDENT: 1934?

LIEUTENANT BRYSON: 1934.

THE PRESIDENT: It is a pity that those years are not stated in the document. It is rather misleading as it is.

LIEUTENANT BRYSON: If the Court please, the exhibit which is in evidence will show the dates.

THE PRESIDENT: Yes, I am not blaming you, but it is misleading, because it looks like September the 19th and December the 21st, and there were three years' interval between. It makes a difference. That is right, is it not?

LIEUTENANT BRYSON: Yes, that is right. I am sorry the excerpt simply shows the page numbers from the exhibit, and not the dates.

Schacht admittedly strained all the resources of Germany to build up a Wehrmacht which would provide Hitler with an instrument for realisation of his desire for Lebensraum. In this connection I offer in evidence Document EC-369, Exhibit USA 631, consisting of a memorandum from the Reichsbank Directorate, signed by Schacht, to Hitler, dated 7th January, 1939. I wish to read the last paragraph of the first page:

> "From the beginning, the Reichsbank has been aware of the fact that a successful foreign policy can be attained only by the reconstruction of the German Armed Forces. It - the Reichsbank - therefore assumed to a very great extent the responsibility of financing the rearmament in spite of the inherent dangers to the currency. The justification thereof was the necessity, which pushed all other considerations into the background, of preparing immediately an armament, out of nothing and furthermore under camouflage, which would make possible a foreign policy which would command respect."

It is clear that the "successful foreign policy" which Schacht thus attributed to rearmament included the Austrian and Czechoslovakian acquisitions. I offer in evidence Document EC- 297A, Exhibit USA 632, being a speech of Schacht's in Vienna after the Anschluss in March, 1938. I quote from the third page and the second full paragraph:

> "Thank God, these things could, after all, not hinder the great German people on their way, for Adolf Hitler has created a communion of German will and German thought. He bolstered it up with the newly strengthened Wehrmacht and he then finally gave the external form to the internal union between Germany and Austria."

With respect to the Sudetenland I refer the Tribunal to Document EC-611, already in evidence as. Exhibit USA 622, being a speech by Schacht on 29th November, 1938, shortly after the Munich settlement. I have earlier read the pertinent remark attributing Hitler's success at that conference to the rearmament made possible by Schacht's financial and economic measures.

This line of proof shows that Schacht entertained an aggressive philosophy with respect to territorial expansion, and justifies the conclusion that he allied himself with Hitler because of their common viewpoint.

We now turn to prove that, whether or not Schacht wanted war, he at least knew

Hitler planned military aggression, for which he was creating the means. He had numerous discussions with Hitler from 1933 to 1937. He knew that Hitler was intent upon expansion to the East, which would mean war, and that Hitler felt he must present the German people with a military victory. I offer in evidence Exhibit USA 633, consisting of an excerpt from a pre-trial interrogation of Schacht on 13th October, 1934, and I read from the second page at the end of the second question:

> "**Q,** What was there in what he" - meaning Hitler - "said that led you to believe he was intending to move towards the East?
> **A.** That is in 'Mein Kampf.' He never spoke to me about that, but it was in 'Mein Kampf.'
> **Q,** In other words, as a man who read it, you understood that Hitler's expansion policy was directed to the East?
> **A.** To the East.
> **Q,** And you thought that it would be better to try to divert Hitler from any such intention and to urge upon him a colonial policy instead?
> **A.** Quite."

I also offer in evidence Document EC-458, Exhibit USA 634, consisting of an affidavit of Major Edmund Tilley under date of 21st November, 1945, with respect to an interview with Schacht on 9th July, 1945. I read the second paragraph:

> "During the course of the discussion Schacht stated to me that he had had numerous talks with Hitler from 1933 to 1937. Schacht stated that from these talks he had formed the impression that, in order to make his hold on the Government secure, the Fuehrer felt that he must present the German people with a military victory."

As early as 1934, Schacht stated his belief that the Nazis would bring war to Europe. I refer the Tribunal to Document EC-451, which I have already submitted in evidence as Exhibit USA 626, consisting of an affidavit under date of 15th November, 1945, by Messersmith, American Consul-General in Berlin, 1930 to 1934. I wish to read from the first page, third paragraph, last sentence.

THE PRESIDENT: You have read it already.

LIEUTENANT BRYSON: If the Court please, there is a little more there which we have not read, which I should like to read.

THE PRESIDENT: You read the whole paragraph. At our invitation you read from the third paragraph down to the bottom of the page.

LIEUTENANT BRYSON: I should like to read the first sentence of the fourth paragraph on Page 1.

THE PRESIDENT: All right.

LIEUTENANT BRYSON:

> "While making these protestations he nevertheless showed by his acts that he was thoroughly an instrument of the whole Nazi programme and ambitions and that he was lending all his extraordinary knowledge and resourcefulness to the accomplishment of that programme."

THE PRESIDENT: Lieutenant Bryson, speaking for myself and for some other members of the Tribunal, we think it is a far better way to deal with a document to deal with it, if possible, once and for all, and not to be coming back to it. It not only wastes time by the fact that the Tribunal have to turn backwards and forwards, backwards and forwards, to the document, but you get a much fairer idea of it if it is dealt with once and for all, although it may cover more, than one subject. I say this, although it may be impossible for you to do it now because of the preparations that you have made. Those who follow you, however, may be able to alter their course. If it is possible, when you get a document with a variety or a number of paragraphs in it which you want to quote, you should quote them all at the same time. Do you follow what I mean?

LIEUTENANT BRYSON: I follow you, your Honour. We have so organised our materials that we have directed our evidence to specific points, and, since the points are separated, we have to separate our quotations.

THE PRESIDENT: I realise that it may be difficult for you.

LIEUTENANT BRYSON: In September of 1934 Ambassador Dodd made a record in his diary of a conversation with Sir Eric Phipps at the British Embassy in Berlin. If the Court please, I will pass over this document, because in response to a question from the Tribunal, I read an excerpt from the document that covers the same point to which I was about to direct myself.

I had just pointed out that Schacht has acknowledged to Ambassador Dodd in September, 1934, his knowledge of the war purposes of the Nazi Party, and we had already shown that in 1935 Schacht had stated that Germany would, if necessary, acquire colonies by force. He must then have known to what length Hitler was prepared to go.

After attending a meeting of the Reich Ministers on 27th May, 1936, in Berlin, Schacht must have known that Hitler was contemplating war. Your Honours may recall, as has been earlier shown, that at this meeting the defendant Goering, who was very close to Hitler, stated that all measures are to be considered from the standpoint of an assured waging of war and that waiting for new methods is no longer appropriate. I refer the Tribunal to Document 1301-FS, from which I will not read, as the quotation is already in evidence as Exhibit USA 123.

On 31st August, 1936, the War Minister, von Blomberg, sent to Schacht a copy of von Blomberg's letter to the defendant Goering. I refer the Tribunal again to Document 1301-PS, previously submitted in evidence as Exhibit USA 123, and read from the middle of Page 19 of the document. The page numbers, if the Court please, on this document, are found in the upper left-hand corner.

> "According to an order of the Fuehrer the setting up of all Air Force units is to be completed by 1st April, 1937. Therefore considerable expenditures have to be made in 1936, which, at the time when the budget for 1936 was made, were planned for later years only."

This intensification of the Air Force programme certainly revealed to Schacht the closeness to war which Hitler must have felt.

I also offer in evidence Document EC-416, Exhibit USA 635, consisting of minutes of the Cabinet meeting of 4th September, 1936, which Schacht attended. I read the statement by Goering found at the top of Page 2 of this document:

> "The Fuehrer and Reich Chancellor has given a memorandum to the General and the Reich War Minister which represents a general instruction. It starts from the basic thought that the showdown with Russia is inevitable."

Schacht thus knew that Hitler expected war with Russia. He also knew of Hitler's ambition towards the East. It must have been plain to him, therefore, that such a war would result from Russian opposition to German military expansion in that direction; that is, Schacht must have known that it would be a war of German aggression.

In January, 1937, the Tribunal will recall, Schacht stated to Ambassador Davies in Berlin that he had "been authorised by his Government" to submit certain proposals to France and England which, in fact, amounted to a bid for colonies under threat of war. If Schacht was acting under instructions from Hitler, he was necessarily familiar with Hitler's aggressive intentions at that time.

In November of 1937 Schacht knew Hitler was determined to acquire Austria, and, at least, autonomy for the Germans of Bohemia, and that Hitler also had designs on the Polish Corridor. I refer the Tribunal to Document L-151, already in evidence as Exhibit USA 70, this being a letter containing a memorandum of a conversation between Schacht and Ambassador Bullitt, dated 23rd November, 1937. I quote the last paragraph on Page 2:

> "Hitler was determined to have Austria eventually attached to Germany and to obtain, at least, autonomy for the Germans of Bohemia. At the present moment he was not vitally concerned about the Polish Corridor, and in his" - Schacht's - "opinion it might be possible to maintain the Corridor, provided Danzig were permitted to join East Prussia, and provided some sort of bridge could be built across the Corridor, uniting Danzig and East Prussia with Germany."

To digress for just a moment, Schacht here was really speaking for himself as well as for Hitler. We have seen from his speech of 29th March, 1938, in Vienna, his enthusiasm for the Anschluss after the event. He was even then working hard for its achievement. In this connection I refer the Tribunal to the transcript (Page 228, Part 1) for evidence of Schacht's having subsidised the Nazis' preliminary agitation in Austria.

In addition to the foregoing direct evidence, the Tribunal is asked to take into consideration the fact that to such a man as Schacht the events of the period certainly bespoke Hitler's intention. Schacht was a close collaborator of Hitler and a member of the Cabinet during the period of the Nazi agitation in Austria, the introduction of conscription, the march into the Rhineland, the overthrow of the Republican Government in Spain, the ultimate conquest of Austria, and the acquisition of the Sudetenland by a show of force. During this period the Reich's debt tripled under the stress of mounting armament. The expenditure rose from three-quarters of a billion Reichsmark in 1932 to eleven billion Reichsmark in 1937, and fourteen billion Reichsmark in 1938. During the entire period 35 billion Reichsmark were spent on armaments. It was a period in which the burning European foreign policy issue was the satisfaction of Germany's repeated demands for additional territory. Hitler, committed to a policy of expansion, was taking great risks in foreign policy and laying the greatest stress upon utmost speed in preparation for war.

Certainly, in this setting, Schacht did not proceed in ignorance of the fact that he was assisting Hitler and Germany along the road toward armed aggression.

We turn now to our last line of proof with respect to Schacht's loss of power in the Hitler regime. In November, 1937, Schacht resigned his offices as Minister of Economics and General Plenipotentiary for the War Economy. At that time he accepted the appointment as Minister without Portfolio and he also continued as President of the Reichsbank.

Our evidence will show that: (a) this change in position was no more than a clash between two power-seeking personalities, Goering and Schacht, which Goering, being closer to Hitler, won, (b) their policy differences were concerned only with the method of rearming, and (c) Schacht's loss of power in no sense implies an unwillingness to assist armed aggression.

There was an issue of policy between Goering and Schacht, but it was concerned only with the method, and not the desirability of war preparations. Schacht emphasised foreign trade as a necessary source of rearmament material during the transitory period until Germany should be ready to strike. Goering was a protagonist of complete self-sufficiency. Hitler supported Goering, and Schacht, his pride wounded and bitterly resenting Goering's intrusion in the economic field, finally stepped out.

I refer the Tribunal to Document 1301-PS, previously submitted in evidence as Exhibit USA 123, containing notes of a conversation between Schacht and Thomas on 2nd September, 1936. These are found on Page 21 of the document, from which I quote:

"President Schacht summoned me to-day at 13.00 hours and requested me to forward the following to the Minister of War: That he, Schacht, had returned from the Fuehrer with the greatest anxiety, since he could not agree to the economic programme planned by the Fuehrer.

The Fuehrer wants to speak at the Party Convention about economic policy and wants to emphasise there that we now want to get free with all our energy from foreign countries, by production in Germany.

Schacht requests urgently that the Reichsminister of War warn the Fuehrer of this step."

And three paragraphs further down:

"If we now shout out abroad our decision to make ourselves economically independent, then we cut our own throats, because we can no longer survive the necessary transitory period."

Nevertheless, Hitler announced the Four Year Plan of self-sufficiency a few days later in Nuremberg, and, against Schacht's wishes, Goering was named Plenipotentiary of the Four Year Plan.

At this point I refer the Tribunal to the interrogation of Schacht on 16th October, 1945, being Exhibit USA 636. I wish to read, beginning near the bottom of Page 9 of the document:

"**Q.** And the Four Year Plan came in when?

A. It was announced in September, 1936, on the Party Day.

Q. Do you say that from the time that the Four Year Plan came in in September, 1936, you were ready to rid yourself of your economic duty?

A. No. At that time I thought that I might maintain my position even against Goering.

Q. Yes. In what sense?

A. That he would not interfere with affairs which I had to manage in my ministry.

Q. As a matter of fact, his appointment was not met with favour by you?

A. I would not have appointed a man like Goering who did not understand a bit about all these things."

Schacht and Goering immediately became embroiled in a conflict of jurisdiction. On 26th November, 1936, Goering issued a directive regarding raw and synthetic material production. I offer in evidence Document EC-243, Exhibit USA 637, consisting of a copy of this directive. It shows that Goering's Office for Raw and Synthetic Materials pre-empted control over large economic areas previously in the hands of Schacht. As an example, I shall quote from paragraph 5 of the directive on Page 4 of the document:

"The planning and determination of objectives, as well as the control over the execution of the tasks which must be accomplished within the framework of the Four Year Plan, are the responsibility of the Office for German Raw and

Synthetic Materials, which supersedes the authorities Which have heretofore been in charge of these tasks."

On 11th December, 1936, Schacht found it necessary to order all supervisory offices in the Ministry of Economics to accept instructions from him alone. I offer in evidence Document EC-376, Exhibit USA 638, consisting of a circular letter from Schacht to all supervisory offices under date of 11th December, 1936, and I quote from the second paragraph:

"The supervisory offices are obliged to accept instructions from me alone. They must answer all official inquiries of the Office for German Raw Materials in order to give any information at any time to the fullest extent."

And a little further down:

" ... I herewith authorise the supervisory offices to take the necessary measures for themselves. In case doubts should arise concerning the requests of the above offices, and these doubts cannot be removed by oral negotiations with the specialised workers of these offices, I should be informed immediately. I will then order in each case the necessary steps to be taken."

The military sided with Schacht, who had rearmed them so well. I offer in evidence Document EC-420, Exhibit USA 639, consisting of a draft of a memorandum by the Military Economic Staff, dated 19th December, 1936. I wish to read from paragraph number 1:

"(1) The control of war economy in the civilian sector in case of war is possible only for that person who in peace-time has made preparations for war at his own responsibility.

Upon recognition of this fact, Reichsbank President Dr. Schacht was appointed Plenipotentiary General for War Economy a year and a half ago, and an Operations Staff was attached to his office."

And then paragraph number 2:

"(2) The Military Economy Staff does not deem it compatible with the principle laid down in number 1, paragraph 1, if the Plenipotentiary General for War Economy is now placed under the Minister President General Goering's command."

In January, 1937, the Military Weekly Gazette published an article warmly praising Schacht's achievements in rearmament. Without reading it, I offer in evidence Document EC-383, Exhibit USA 640, containing this article, a pertinent quotation from which already appears in the transcript for 23rd November (Page 137, Part 1).

Shortly thereafter Schacht attempted to force a showdown with Goering by temporarily refusing to act in his capacity as Plenipotentiary. I offer in evidence Document EC-244, Exhibit USA 641, consisting of a letter from von Blomberg, the Minister of War, to Hitler under date of 23rd February, 1937. I read the second paragraph of this letter as follows:

"The President, Dr. Schacht, has notified me that he is not acting in his capacity as Plenipotentiary for the time being, since in his opinion there exists a conflict between the powers conferred upon him and those of General Goering. Because of this the preparatory mobilisation steps in the economic field are delayed."

Schacht obviously was using his importance to the war preparations as a lever.

THE PRESIDENT: Lieutenant Bryson, does the defendant Schacht admit in his interrogation that the reason for his giving up his office was the difference of opinion between him and the defendant Goering?

LIEUTENANT BRYSON: He does, Sir, and the defendant Goering states so in his interrogation.

THE PRESIDENT: Is it necessary to go into the details of their quarrel?

LIEUTENANT BRYSON: If the Court will be satisfied that this was the cause of Schacht's resignation -

THE PRESIDENT: If they both say so -

LIEUTENANT BRYSON: And that the cause was not his unwillingness to join in with the aggressive intentions of the Nazis at that time, I shall be perfectly satisfied to confine our evidence to the interrogations of Schacht and Goering.

THE PRESIDENT: Does he suggest that in his interrogation - that that might have been the reason?

LIEUTENANT BRYSON: I will find out, Sir, but our case against Schacht is premised upon conspiracy.

THE PRESIDENT: If the defendant Schacht wants to set up such a case as that, you could apply to be heard in rebuttal.

LIEUTENANT BRYSON: Well, we shall be satisfied then to eliminate a number of our items of evidence, including the controversy between Goering and Schacht, and content ourselves with the interrogations.

THE PRESIDENT: Yes.

LIEUTENANT BRYSON: If the Court please, we are almost at the time of the break. Perhaps during the break we can arrange our evidence.

THE PRESIDENT: Yes, we will adjourn now for ten minutes.

(A recess was taken.)

PROFESSOR HERBERT KRAUS (Counsel for defendant Schacht): We agree that the question of the disagreement between the defendant's Goering and Schacht need not be discussed further at this time. But we shall come back to and deal in detail with the question how far these disagreements had any bearing on the plan for an aggressive war.

LIEUTENANT BRYSON: If the Tribunal Please, we have eliminated part of our proof. I would simply like to put in a letter from Goering and an interrogation of Schacht, which will finish up the question of the disagreement.

Under date of 5th August, 1937, Schacht wrote a critical letter to Goering, who replied with a twenty-four page letter on 22nd August, 1937. Goering's letter reviews their many differences in detail. I offer it as Document EC-493, Exhibit USA 642, and I wish to read only one statement, found in the middle of Page 13:

> "In conclusion, I should like to refer to remarks which you made in a paragraph of your letter entitled 'The Four Year Plan' about your general attitude toward my work in regard to the economic policy. I know and I am pleased that at the beginning of the Four Year Plan you promised me your loyal support and co-operation, and that you repeatedly renewed this promise even after the first differences of opinion had occurred and had been removed in exhaustive discussions. I deplore all the more having recently formed the impression which is confirmed by your letter, that you are increasingly antagonistic toward my work in the Four Year Plan. This explains the fact that our collaboration has gradually become less close."

Schacht and Goering were reconciled by written agreement on 7th July, 1937, but subsequently again fell into disagreement, and Hitler finally accepted Schacht's resignation as Minister of Economics on 26th November, 1937, simultaneously appointing him Minister without Portfolio, and, later, Schacht's resignation was extended to his position as Plenipotentiary for War Economy. Without reading it, I offer in evidence Document EC-494, Exhibit USA 643, as proof of this fact.

Now, finally, I wish to refer the Tribunal to the interrogation of Schacht, under date of 16th October, 1945, Exhibit USA 636, and I wish to read from Page 12 of the document near the bottom:

"**A.** It may amuse you if I tell you that the last conversation" - this is Schacht speaking - "I had with Goering on these topics was in November, 1937, when Luther for two months had tried to unite Goering and me, and to induce me to co-operate again with Goering and maintain my position as Minister of Economics. Then I had a last talk with Goering, and at the end of this talk Goering said, 'But I must have the right to give orders to you.' Then I said, 'Not to me, but to my successor.' I never have taken orders from Goering, and I would never have done it, because he was a fool in economics and I knew something about it, at least.

Q. Well, I gather that was a culminating, progressive personal business between you and Goering. That seems perfectly obvious.

A. Certainly."

In all this abundant and consistent evidence there is not the slightest suggestion that Schacht's withdrawal from these two posts represented a break with Hitler in the field of contemplated military aggression. Indeed, Hitler was gratified that Schacht would still be active in the Government as President of the Reichsbank and as Minister without Portfolio. I offer in evidence Document L-104, Exhibit USA 644, consisting of a letter to the United States Secretary of State from Ambassador Dodd, under date of 29th November, 1937, enclosing a translation of Hitler's letter of 26th November, 1937, to Schacht. I quote the last two sentences of Hitler's letter, found on Page 2 of the document:

"If I accede to your wish it is with the expression of deepest gratitude for your so excellent achievements, and in the happy consciousness that, as President of the Reichsbank Directorate, you will make available to the German people and me, for many years more, your outstanding knowledge and ability and your untiring energy. Delighted at the fact that in the future, also, you are willing to be my personal adviser, I appoint you as from to-day a Reich Minister."

Schacht did continue, obviously still in full agreement with Hitler's aggressive purpose. He was still President of the Reichsbank at the time of the taking of Austria in March, 1938. In fact, the Reichsbank took over the Austrian National Bank. On this point I refer the Tribunal to Reichsgesetzblatt 1938, Part 1, Page 254, and ask that judicial notice be taken thereof. Further, Schacht even participated in the planning of the absorption of Austria. In this connection I introduce into evidence Document EC- 421, Exhibit USA 645, consisting of excerpts from minutes of a meeting of the staff of General Thomas on 11th March, 1938, at 15.00 hours. I quote therefrom as follows:

"Lieutenant-Colonel Hunerm reads directive of the Fuehrer of 11th March concerning the 'Action Otto' and informs us that 'The Economy War Service Law' has been put in force. He then reads Directives 1 and 2, and gives special orders to troops for crossing the Austrian borders. According to that, at Schacht's suggestion, no requests should take place, but everything should be put in Reichsmark on an exchange basis of two Schillinge to one Reichsmark."

On the conversion of the Austrian Schilling the Tribunal is asked also to take judicial notice of Reichsgesetzblatt, 1938, Part 1, Page 405.

The Tribunal, of course, is already familiar with the public approval by Schacht of the Anschluss, in his Vienna speech of 21st March, 1938, and your Honours will also recall Schacht's pride in Hitler's use of the rearmed Wehrmacht at Munich, as expressed in his speech of 29th November, 1938. Both speeches were subsequent to his resignation in November, 1937.

We come now to the removal of Schacht from the Presidency of the Reichsbank in January, 1939. The reason for this development is quite clear. Schacht lost confidence in the credit capacity of the Reich and was paralysed with the fear of a financial collapse. He felt that the maximum level of production had been reached, so that an increase in banknote circulation would only cheapen money and bring on inflation. In this attitude he ceased to be useful to Hitler, who was about to strike, and wished to tap every ounce of available Government credit for military purposes.

I refer the Tribunal to Document EC-369, which I have previously submitted in evidence as Exhibit USA 631. This document is a memorandum from the Reichsbank Directorate to Hitler, under date of 7th January, 1939, in which Schacht reviews in detail his fears of inflation. The seriousness of the situation may be seen generally from the entire text. I wish to quote several of the more crucial statements - one from the last paragraph on Page 3, the second sentence:

> "We are, however, faced with the fact that approximately three billion Reichsmark of such drafts cannot now be paid, though they will be due in 1939."

I quote from the upper half of Page 4:

> "Exclusive of the Reichsbank there are approximately six billion Reichsmark 'Mefo' drafts which can be discounted against cash payment at any time at the Reichsbank, which fact represents a continuous danger to the currency."

And I quote finally from the concluding paragraph of the memorandum:

> "We are convinced that the effects on the currency caused by the policy of the last ten months can be mended, and that the danger of inflation again can be eliminated by strict maintenance of a balanced budget. The Fuehrer and Reich Chancellor himself has, again and again, publicly rejected an inflation, as foolish and fruitless.
>
> We therefore ask for the following measures:
>
> (1) The Reich as well as all the other public offices must not incur expenditure or assume guarantees and obligations that cannot be covered by taxes, or by those funds which can be raised through loans without disturbing the long-term investment market.
>
> (2) In order to carry out these measures effectively, full financial control over all public expenditures must be restored to the Reich Minister of Finance.
>
> (3) The price and wage control must be rendered effective. The existing mismanagement must be eliminated.
>
> (4) The use of the money and investment market must be at the sole discretion of the Reichsbank."

It is clear that Schacht's fear was genuine and is a complete explanation of his departure from the scene. He had good reason to be afraid. In fact, the Finance Minister had already recognised the situation in September, 1938. I refer the Tribunal to Document EC-419, Exhibit USA 621, which I have already submitted in evidence, and which consists of a letter under date of 1st September, 1938, from Krosigk to Hitler, in which Krosigk gives a warning of an impending financial crisis. I quote from the bottom of Page 2:

THE PRESIDENT: Is that not really cumulative of what you have already read?

LIEUTENANT BRYSON: We will be glad to omit it, Sir; it is cumulative.

Schacht was not only afraid of a financial crisis, but he was afraid that he personally would be held responsible for it. I offer in evidence an affidavit of Emil Puhl, a director of the Reichsbank and co-worker of Schacht, dated 8th November, 1945, designated as Document EC-438, Exhibit USA 646, and I read therefrom, beginning at the bottom of the second page:

> "When Schacht saw that the risky situation which he had sponsored was becoming insoluble, he was more and more anxious to get out. This desire to get out of a bad situation was for a long time the 'Leitmotiv' of Schacht's conversation with the Directors of the bank."

In the end, Schacht escaped by deliberately stimulating his dismissal from the Presidency of the Reichsbank. I offer in evidence Exhibit USA 647, consisting of excerpts from an interrogation of von Krosigk under date of 24th September, 1945, and I wish to read several statements, beginning at the very bottom of the second page:

> "I asked Schacht to finance for the Reich before the last day of the month the sum of one hundred or two hundred millions. It was this quite usual procedure which we had used for years, and we used to give back this money after a couple of days. Schacht this time refused, and said that he was not willing to finance a penny because he wanted, as he said, that, it should be made clear to Hitler that the Reich was bankrupt. I tried to explain that these were not the proper grounds for discussing the whole question of finance, because the question of financing very small sums for a few days beyond the last days of the month never would bring Hitler to the conviction that the whole financing was impossible. As far as I remember now, it was Funk who told Hitler something about this conversation; then Hitler asked Schacht to call upon him. I do not know what they said, but the result certainly was the dismissal of Schacht."

THE PRESIDENT: Just give me again the reference to that document that you were reading from.

LIEUTENANT BRYSON: This is the interrogation of von Krosigk under date of 24th September, 1945. I wish to read further, continuing on Page 3:

> "**Q.** Now did Schacht ever say anything to you to the effect that he wanted to resign because he was in opposition to the continuance of the rearmament programme?
>
> **A.** No, he never said it in this specific form, but in some conversations he certainly said it several times, in his own way, that he had conflicts with Goering so that, in answer to that, I did not take these things very seriously.
>
> **Q.** Well, let me put it in this way, and please think carefully about this. Did Schacht ever say that he wanted to resign because he realised that the extent of the rearmament programme was such as to lead him to the conclusion that it was in preparation for war rather than for defence?
>
> **A.** No, he never did.
>
> **Q.** Was Schacht ever quoted to you to this effect by any of your colleagues or by anybody else?
>
> **A.** No.
>
> **Q.** Now, after Keitel took over the position of Chief of the Wehrmacht, there were still meetings between Schacht and you with Keitel in place of

Blomberg?

A. Yes.

Q. Did Schacht ever say anything at these meetings to indicate that, except for the technical question of the financing through the Reichsbank directly, he was opposed to a further programme of rearmament, or to the budget of the Wehrmacht?

A. No, I do not think he ever did."

The defendant Goering has also confirmed this testimony. I refer the Tribunal to the interrogation of Goering under date of 17th October, 1945, this being Exhibit USA 648. I read from this interrogation on 17th October, 1945, from the lower half of the third page:

"**Q.** I want to ask you this specifically. Was Schacht dismissed from the Reichsbank by Hitler for refusing to participate any further in the rearmament programme?

A. No, it was because of his utterly impossible attitude in this matter regarding this advance, which had no connection with the rearmament programme."

Hitler dismissed Schacht from the Reichsbank on 20th January, 1939. Without reading, I offer in evidence Document EC-398, Exhibit USA 649, consisting merely of a brief note from Hitler to Schacht announcing his dismissal.

From all of the foregoing it is clear that Schacht's dismissal in no sense reflected a parting of the ways with Hitler on account of proposed aggression. This fact may also be seen from Document EC-397, Exhibit USA 650, consisting of Hitler's letter to Schacht under date of 19th January, 1939, the text of which I wish to read:

"On these occasions of your recall from office as President of the Reichsbank Directorate, I take the opportunity of expressing to you my most sincere and warmest gratitude for the services which you have rendered repeatedly to Germany and to me personally in this capacity, during long and difficult years. Your name, above all, will always be connected with the first epoch of the national rearmament. I am happy to be able to avail myself of your services for the solution of new tasks in your position as Reich Minister."

In fact, Schacht continued as Minister without Portfolio until January, 1943.

I wish to conclude by saying that the evidence shows: first, that Schacht's work was indispensable to Hitler's rise to power and to the rearmament of Germany; second, that Schacht personally was favourably disposed towards Aggression and knew Hitler intended to and would break the peace; and, third, that Schacht retired from the scene for reasons wholly unrelated to the imminence of illegal aggression.

As long as he remained in power, Schacht was working as eagerly for the preparation of aggressive war as any of his colleagues. He was beyond any doubt most effective and valuable in this connection. His assistance in the earlier phase of the conspiracy made their later crimes possible. His withdrawal from the scene reflected no moral feeling against the use of aggressive warfare as an instrument of national policy. He personally struggled to retain his position. By the time he lost it he had already completed his task in the conspiracy, namely, to provide Hitler and his colleagues with the physical means and economic planning necessary to launch and maintain the aggression. We do not consider that, having prepared the Wehrmacht for assault upon the world, he should now be permitted to find refuge in his loss of power before the blow was struck.

This concludes our case against the defendant Schacht, and Lt. Meltzer follows me with the presentation of the American case against the defendant Funk.

LIEUTENANT BERNARD D. MELTZER: May it please the Tribunal, the documents bearing upon defendant Funk's responsibility have been assembled in a document book marked "HH," which has been filed with the Tribunal and has also been made available to defence counsel. The same is true of the brief. The documents have been arranged in the book in the order of their presentation. Moreover, to facilitate reference, the pages of the document book have been numbered consecutively in red. I wish to acknowledge the invaluable collaboration of Mr. Sidney Jacoby, who sits to my right, in the selection and analysis of these documents.

We propose to submit evidence concerning five phases of defendant Funk's participation in the conspiracy:

First, his contribution to the Nazi seizure of power;

Second, his role in the Propaganda Ministry and in the related agencies, and his responsibility for the activities of that Ministry;

Third, his responsibility for the unrelenting elimination of Jews, first from the so-called cultural professions and then from the entire German economy;

Fourth, his collaboration in the paramount Nazi task to which all other tasks were subordinated preparation for aggressive war;

And finally, we propose to mention briefly the evidence concerning his active participation in the waging of aggressive war.

We turn now to the evidence showing that defendant Funk actively promoted the conspirators' accession to power and their consolidation of control over Germany. Soon after he joined the Nazi Party in 1931 defendant Funk began to hold important positions, first within the Party itself and then within the Nazi Government. Funk's positions have, in the main, been listed in Document 3533-PS, which is a statement signed by both defendant Funk and his counsel. This document has been made available in the four working languages of these proceedings, and a copy in the appropriate language should be available in each of your Honours' document books. It is accordingly requested that this document, which is Exhibit USA 651, be received into evidence without the necessity of its being read in its entirety.

Your Honours will observe that there are certain deletions and reservations after some of the items listed in Document 3533-PS. These were inserted by defendant Funk. The words which he wished deleted are enclosed in parentheses. His comments are underscored and followed by asterisks.

We wished to avoid troubling the Tribunal with a detailed discussion of all these contested points. Accordingly, we collected in Document 3563-PS relevant excerpts from certain German publications. This document has also been made available in the four working languages. Moreover, we submit that the Tribunal can properly take judicial notice of the publications referred to in the document. However, in order to facilitate reference, we request that it be received in evidence as Exhibit USA 652.

In connection with item (b) on the top of Page 1 of Document 3533- PS - your Honours will find that on Page 1 of the document - your Honours will observe that defendant Funk has in effect denied that he was Hitler's personal economic adviser in the 1930's. However, the excerpts from the four German publications set forth on Pages 1 and 2 of Document 3563-PS directly contradict this denial.

We submit that it will be clear from the documents just referred to that defendant Funk, soon after he joined the Party, began to operate as one of the Nazi inner circle. Moreover, as a Party economic theorist during its critical days in 1932, he made a significant contribution to its drive for mass support by drafting its economic slogans. In this connection I would refer to Document 3505-PS, which is a biography entitled, in the English translation, "Walter Funk - A Life for Economy." This biography was written by one Oesterreich in German, and published by the Central Publishing House of the Nazi Party. I offer this document in evidence as Exhibit USA 653. I wish to quote now from Page 1 of the translation of this document, the centre of the page. The corresponding page of the German document is Page 81:

> "In 1931 he" - that is, Funk - "became a member of the Reichstag. A document of his activity at the time is the 'Economic Construction Programme of the N.S.D.A.P.' which was formulated by him in the second half of the year 1932. It received the approval of Adolf Hitler and was declared binding on all Gau leaders, speakers on the subject, and Gau advisers on the subject, and others of the Party."

Thus defendant Funk's slogans became the economic gospel for the Party organisers and spellbinders.

Defendant Funk, however, was much more than one of the Nazi Party's economic theorists; he was also involved in the highly practical work of soliciting campaign contributions for the Party. As liaison man between the Party and the large German industrialists he helped to place the industrialists' financial and political support behind Hitler. Defendant Funk, in an interrogation conducted on 4th June, 1945, admitted that he helped to finance the highly critical campaign of 1932. I offer in evidence Document 2828-PS as Exhibit USA 654, and I quote from the bottom of Page 43 ...

THE PRESIDENT: Lt. Meltzer, is not this really all cumulative and detailed evidence to support what the defendant Funk has already agreed with reference to his office? On Page 1 you have the admission that he was a member of the Nazi Party, chief of the division of the Central Nazi Party, and chairman of the committee of the Nazi Party on economic policy, and then it goes on from A to U with views of the various offices which he held and which he admits he held. But surely to go into the details of those positions is unnecessary.

LIEUTENANT MELTZER: If your Honour pleases, the admission of the various positions listed do not, in our judgement, indicate in any way defendant Funk's participation in the fund-raising for the Nazi Party.

THE PRESIDENT: The fund-raising?

LIEUTENANT MELTZER: The fund-raising. Now, it is a possible inference from those positions that he did engage in the solicitation of campaign contributions. However, it did seem to us relevant to mention most briefly direct evidence of that aspect of his activity.

THE PRESIDENT: Very well, if you say there is nothing in these offices which covered the matter you are going to deal with; well and good.

LIEUTENANT MELTZER: Defendant Funk, in an interrogation conducted on 4th June, 1945, admitted, as I said a minute ago, that he helped to finance this highly critical campaign.

THE PRESIDENT: You see, Lieutenant Meltzer, the heading that you have so conveniently given to us is that he contributed to the seizure of power. Well now, nearly every one of the headings A to U on Page 1, which he admits, is evidence that he contributed to seizure of power. Is it your object to propose that he also helped to raise funds? The contribution to the seizure of power is not in itself a crime; it is only a step.

LIEUTENANT MELTZER: Very well, your Honour. There is one aspect, however, of his activity in that regard which I should like to mention; that is, in connection with his fund-raising activities. He was present at a meeting in Berlin early in 1933; and I am referring to the document which records that in the course of that meeting Hitler and Goering submitted an exposition of certain basic elements of the Nazi programme. The reference to this meeting is found in Document 2828-PS, which your Honours will find on Page 28 of the document book. I wish to quote the following question and answer:

> "Q. About 1933, we have been informed, certain industrialists attended a meeting in the home of Goering before the election in March. Do you know anything about this?
>
> A. I was at the meeting. Money was not demanded by Goering but by Schacht. Hitler left the room, and then Schacht made a speech asking for money for the election. I was there as an impartial observer, since I was friendly with the industrialists."

The character and importance of Funk's work with the large industrialists is emphasised in his biography which I referred to earlier, and I will simply invite your Honours' attention to the relevant pages of that book, which are 83 and 84.

THE PRESIDENT: I do not understand why you read that passage. If you wanted to show that he was at the meeting, it would be merely sufficient to say that he was at the meeting. I do not think those two sentences that you read help us in the very least.

LIEUTENANT MELTZER: If the Tribunal please, those two sentences do not refer to the meeting. Those two sentences refer to the biography which sums up the defendant Funk's general contribution to the Nazi accession to power, and I thought it might be of interest to the Tribunal to see the attitude of a German writer to this aspect of the defendant's career.

THE PRESIDENT: It seems to me you referred to the meeting.

LIEUTENANT MELTZER: I was referring your Honour to Pages 32 and 33 of the document book, and to clarify this point may I read briefly from the biography:

> "No less important than Funk's accomplishments in the programmatic field in the years 1931 and 1932 was his activity at that time as the Fuehrer's liaison man to the leading men of the German industry, trade, commerce and finance. On the basis of his past work his personal relations with the German economic leaders were broad and extensive. He was now able to enlist them in the service of Adolf Hitler, and not only to answer their questions authoritatively, but to convince them and win their backing for the Party. At that time this was terribly important work; every success achieved meant a moral, political and economic strengthening of the fighting force of the Party, and contributed toward destroying the prejudice that National Socialism is merely a party of class hatred and class struggle."

THE PRESIDENT: Again, I do not see that that has helped the Tribunal in the least.

LIEUTENANT MELTZER: After Funk had helped, Hitler become Chancellor; as Press Chief of the German Government, he participated in the early Cabinet meetings, in the course of which the conspirators planned the strategy by which they would secure the passage of the Presidential Emergency Decree, which was passed on 24th March, 1933. Funk's presence at these meetings is revealed by Document 2962-PS, which has already been received in evidence and by Document 2963-PS offered as Exhibit USA 656. Your Honours will recall that this decree marked the real seizure of political power in Germany.

Soon after this the defendant Funk assumed an important role in the Ministry of

Propaganda. The record shows that the Ministry became one of the most important and vicious of Nazi institutions, and that propaganda was fundamental to the achievement of the Nazi programme within and outside Germany. We do not propose to review those matters but rather to present evidence showing, as we have said, that the defendant Funk took a significant part in the propaganda operations.

The Ministry was established on 13th March, 1933, with Goebbels as Chief and defendant Funk as Under Secretary, second in command.

As Under Secretary defendant Funk was not only Goebbels' chief aide but was also the organiser of the large and complex propaganda machine, I wish to offer in evidence Document 3501-PS, which will be found on Page 47 of your document book as Exhibit USA 657. This document is an affidavit signed on 19th December, 1945, by Max Amann, who held the position of Reich Leader of the Press and President of the Reich Press Chamber. I should like to read the second sentence of the first paragraph and the entire second paragraph:

"In carrying out my duties and responsibilities I became familiar with the operation and the organisation of the Reich Ministry of Propaganda and Enlightenment, and managed the Ministry. Funk was the soul of the Ministry, and without him Goebbels could not have built it up. Goebbels once stated to me that Funk was his 'most efficient man.' Funk exercised comprehensive control over all of the media of expression in Germany: over the Press, the theatre, radio and music. As Press Chief of the Ministry, Funk held daily meetings with the Fuehrer and a daily Press conference in the course of which he issued the directives governing the materials to be published by the German Press."

In addition to his position as Under Secretary, Funk had many other important jobs in the Propaganda Ministry and in its subordinate agencies. These positions have already been listed in Document 3533-PS. I wish, however, to refer in particular to Funk's position as Vice-President of the Reich Chamber of Culture. This position was, of course, related to his functions in the Propaganda Ministry.

In his dual capacity he directly promoted two vital and related Nazi policies. The first was the regimentation of all creative activities in the interests of Nazi political and military objectives. The second was the complete elimination of Jews and dissidents from the so-called cultural professions. A full discussion of the methods by which these policies were effectuated, has been included in the brief which was submitted as part of Exhibit USA E. Accordingly, we will not go into that matter now unless the Tribunal so wishes.

In view of the defendant Funk's major role in the Propaganda Ministry, it is natural to find Nazi writers stressing his responsibility for the Nazi perversion of culture. In this connection, I will simply invite the Tribunal's attention to Pages 94 and 95 of Oesterreich's biography, which has already been referred to.

After defendant Funk left the Ministry of Propaganda and became Minister of Economics in 1938 he continued to advance the anti- Jewish programme. For example, on 14th June, 1938, he signed a decree providing for the registration of Jewish enterprises. This decree, which became the foundation for the ruthless economic persecution which followed, is found in the Reichsgesetzblatt, 1938, Part 1, Page 627. It is requested that the Tribunal take judicial notice of this and all subsequent references to the Reichsgesetzblatt. May I add that the brief on defendant Funk gives the document numbers of translations of decrees and other German publications of which the Tribunal will be requested to take judicial notice.

THE PRESIDENT: Would that be a convenient time to break off?

LIEUTENANT MELTZER: Yes, your Honour.

THE TRIBUNAL: Before we do so, Sir David Maxwell Fyfe, I see that one of the counsel, Colonel Phillimore, I think, is proposing to call certain witnesses. The Tribunal would like to know who those witnesses are, and what subject their evidence is going to deal with.

SIR DAVID MAXWELL FYFE: Would the Tribunal like to know now? I would like to let them know if it is convenient.

THE TRIBUNAL: If you could, it would be convenient now.

SIR DAVID MAXWELL FYFE: Yes. The first witness is Korvetten Kapitaen Mohle, who was a captain on defendant Donitz's staff, and he will prove the passing on of the Donitz Order of 17th September, 1942. I think that is the main point that he deals with. I think he deals also with the destruction of some rescue ships, but that is the main point.

The second witness is Lieutenant Heisig. He will deal primarily with lectures of the defendant Donitz, in which he advocated the destruction of the crews of merchant ships. That is the general effect of the evidence.

THE PRESIDENT: Thank you.

(A recess was taken until 14.00 hours.)

THE PRESIDENT: Lieutenant Meltzer, are you intending to call any witnesses this afternoon?

LIEUTENANT MELTZER: No, Sir. There is another member of the prosecution, Sir, who I believe is intending to call a witness, Mr. Dodd.

THE PRESIDENT: In connection with the case against Funk?

LIEUTENANT MELTZER: No, your Honour.

THE PRESIDENT: Or in connection with the case against somebody else?

LIEUTENANT MELTZER: Yes, Sir.

THE PRESIDENT: Who is it in connection with, Raeder?

LIEUTENANT MELTZER: I believe Mr. Dodd might offer -

THE PRESIDENT: Raeder, is it?

LIEUTENANT MELTZER: No, Sir. Mr. Dodd might offer a better explanation than I on the purpose of calling the witness.

THE PRESIDENT: Mr. Dodd?

MR. DODD: Yes, Sir. Your Honour, the witness is offered in connection with the defendants Rosenberg, Funk, Frick, Sauckel, and Kaltenbrunner.

THE PRESIDENT: I see. The evidence relates to concentration camps, does it?

MR. DODD: It does, your Honour.

THE PRESIDENT: I see.

MR. DODD: This witness would have been called at the time that we presented the other proof, but for the fact that he was before the Military Court at Dachau at that time and was not available.

THE PRESIDENT: I see; thank you.

LIEUTENANT MELTZER: May it please the Tribunal, before we adjourned we were dealing with defendant Funk's role in the economic persecution of the Jews. As your Honours will recall, in November of 1938 the death of von Rath in Paris was exploited by the Nazis as a pretext for intensifying the persecution of the Jews. The new policy was directed at the complete elimination of the Jews from the economic life of Germany. The evidence we will offer will show that defendant Funk took a significant part in both the formulation and execution of that policy. In this connection I would refer the Tribunal to Document 1816-PS which is already in the record. This document is a report of the meeting on the Jewish question. It will be found, your Honour, on Page 52 of the document book. This meeting was held under Goering's chairmanship on 12th November, 1938. In opening the meeting defendant Goering stated, and I quote now from Page 1 paragraph 1, of the translation - the corresponding page of the German document is also Page 1:

"To-day's meeting is of a decisive nature. I have received a letter written on the Fuehrer's orders, requesting that the Jewish question be now, once and for all, co-ordinated and solved one way or another."

Defendant Funk came to this meeting well prepared. He had a law already drafted which he submitted with the following explanation - I quote again from Document 1816-PS, Page 15:

"I have prepared a law elaborating that, effective 1st January, 1939, Jews shall be forbidden to operate retail stores and wholesale establishments as well as independent artisan shops. They shall be further prohibited from keeping employees or offering any ready products on the market. Wherever a Jewish shop is operated, the police shall shut it down. From 1st January, 1939, a Jew can no longer be employed as an enterpriser as stipulated in the law for the Organisation of National Labour of 20th January, 1934."

I believe we may omit the rest. It is all in the same tenor.

THE PRESIDENT: Yes.

LIEUTENANT MELTZER: The substance of defendant Funk's draft law promptly found its way into the Reichsgesetzblatt. On 12th November, 1938, defendant Goering signed a decree entitled, and I quote, "For the Elimination of Jews from the German Economic Life," and in section 4 he authorised defendant Funk to implement the provisions of the decree by issuing the necessary rules and regulations. An examination of the provisions of this decree, which is set forth in the Reichsgesetzblatt, 1938, Part 1, Page 1580, will reveal how well it deserved its title "For the Elimination of the Jews from the German Economic life."

Soon after the passage of the decree of 12th November defendant Funk delivered a speech on the Jewish question. He made it clear that the programme of economic persecution was part of the larger programme of extermination, and he boasted of the fact that the new programme ensured the complete elimination of Jews from the Germany economy. I offer in evidence Document No. 3545-PS as Exhibit USA 659. This document, which is found on Page 76 of the document book, is a certified photostatic copy of Page 2 of the "Frankfurter Zeitung" of 17th November, 1938. I quote a brief portion of that speech:

"The State and the economy constitute a unit. They must be directed according to the same principles. The best proof thereof has been rendered by the most recent development of the Jewish problem in Germany. One cannot exclude the Jews from the political life and yet let them live and work in the economic sphere."

I shall omit the rest, with the request that the Tribunal take judicial notice of this reprint from the German newspaper, the "Frankfurter Zeitung."

I wish, however, to refer to just one more decree signed by defendant Funk himself. On the 3rd of December, 1938, he signed a decree which imposed additional and drastic economic disabilities upon the Jews, and subjected their property to confiscation and forced liquidation. This decree is set forth in the Reichsgesetzblatt, 1938, Part 1, Page 1709. Defendant Funk himself has admitted and deplored his responsibility for the economic persecution of the Jews. I offer in evidence Document

3544-PS as Exhibit USA 660. This document, which is the last document in connection with this phase of the case, is an interrogation of defendant Funk dated 22nd October, 1945. Your Honours will find it on Pages 102 and 103 of the document book. I wish to quote from Pages 26 to 27 of the interrogation. The corresponding page of the German translation is Page 21. Although I propose to quote enough to place defendant Funk's statements in their proper context, I do not, of course, intend to give any credence to his attempts at self-justification:

"**Q.** All the decrees excluding the Jews from industry were yours, were they not?"

Now, omitting the first nine lines of the reply:

"**A.** So far as my participation in this Jewish affair is concerned, that was my responsibility, and I regretted later on that I ever did participate. The Party had always brought pressure to bear on me to make me agree to the confiscation of Jewish property, and I had refused repeatedly. But, later on, when the anti-Jewish measures and the force against Jews came into effect, something legal had to be done to prevent the looting and confiscation of all Jewish property.

Q. You knew that the looting and all that was done at the instigation of the Party, did not you?"

Here defendant Funk wept, and answered:

"Yes, most certainly. That is when I should have left, in 1938. Of that I am guilty; I am guilty; I admit that I am a guilty party here."

In the Propaganda Ministry defendant Funk, as we have seen, helped solidify the German people in favour of war. When he moved on to his position as Minister of Economics, and to other positions which will appear, he used his talents even more directly for the conspirators' main task: preparation for war. Immediately before defendant Funk took over the Ministry of Economics from defendant Schacht in 1938 there was a major reorganisation of that Ministry's functions which integrated it with the Four Year Plan as the supreme command of the German military economy. This reorganisation was effected by a decree, dated 4th February, 1938, signed by Goering as Commissioner of the Four Year Plan. This decree is set forth in an official monthly bulletin issued by Goering and entitled, in the English translation, "The Four Year Plan," Volume 11, Page 105. It is requested that the Tribunal take judicial notice of this publication.

At this point I would simply note that that decree makes it clear that defendant Funk assumed a critical role in the task of economic mobilisation during a decisive period. Indeed, in 1938 he was directly charged with the task of preparing the German economy for war. By a secret decree he was made Chief Plenipotentiary for Economics and assumed the duties which once had been discharged by defendant Schacht. In this connection I refer to Document 2194-PS, which has already been placed in evidence. This document, which is found on Page 111 of your Honours' document books, consists of a letter dated 6th September, 1939, and that letter transmitted a copy of the Reich Defence Law of 4th September, 1938. It is this enclosure that we wish to deal with now. I wish to quote from Page 4 of the translation paragraphs 2 to 4:

"It is the task of the G.B.W." - that is the Chief Plenipotentiary for Economics - "to put all economic forces into the service of the Reich defence and to safeguard economically the life of the German nation. To him are subordinate:

the Reich Minister of Economics;
the Reich Minister of Nutrition and Agriculture;
the Reich Minister of Labour," and so on.

"He is furthermore responsible for directing the financing of the Reich defence within the realm of the Reich Finance Ministry and the Reichsbank."

To quote one more paragraph: "The G.B.W. must carry out the demands of the O.K.W., which are of considerable importance for the Armed Forces; and he must insure the economic conditions for the production of the armament industry directed immediately by O.K.W. according to its demands." This law, in essence, re-enacted the provisions previously passed in the Reich Defence Law of 1935, and I will not trouble the Tribunal with further reading. I do wish to note, however, that the law was, at the specific direction of Hitler, kept secret, and that it was signed by defendant Funk, among others, as Chief Plenipotentiary for Economics. Your Honours will find defendant Funk's signature on the next to the last page of the document, and I invite your attention to the names of his co-signatories.

Defendant Funk, in a speech which he delivered on 14th October, 1939, explained how, as Chief Plenipotentiary for Economics, he had for a year and a half prior to the launching of the aggression against Poland advanced Germany's economic preparations for war. I offer in evidence Document 3324-PS as Exhibit USA 661. This document is a German book by Berndt and von Wedel entitled, in the English translation, "Germany in the Fight." That book reprints the defendant's speech. I quote now from Page 2 of the translation of Document 3324-PS, which is found on Page 116 of the document book. The translation of this speech is somewhat awkward, and with the Tribunal's permission I would rephrase it somewhat, without changing its substance in the slightest:

"Although all economic and financial departments were harnessed to the task of the Four Year Plan under the leadership of General Field Marshal Goering, Germany's economic preparation for war was also secretly advanced in another sector for well over a year, namely, through the formation of a national guiding apparatus for special war economy tasks which would have to be accomplished the moment that war became a fact. For this work all economic departments were combined into one administrative authority, the General Plenipotentiary for Economy, to which position the Fuehrer appointed me one and a half years ago."

THE PRESIDENT: What was the date of that?

LIEUTENANT MELTZER: The date of that speech, Sir, is October.

THE PRESIDENT: The 14th of October?

LIEUTENANT MELTZER: The 14th October, 1939.

In his dual capacity as Chief Plenipotentiary for Economics and Minister of Economics, defendant Funk was naturally advised of the requirements which the conspirators' programme of aggression imposed on the German economy. In this connection I would invite the Tribunal's attention to Document 1301-PS, which is already in evidence. As your Honours will recall, this document is a top secret report of the conference held in defendant Goering's office on 14th October, 1938. Your Honours will find it on Page 142 of the document book. I shall simply summarise the relevant portions of this document.

During the conference Goering referred to the world situation and to Hitler's directive to organise a gigantic armament programme. He thereupon directed the Ministry of Economics to increase exports in order to obtain the foreign exchange necessary for stepping up armament. He added, as your Honours will recall, that the

Luftwaffe must be increased fivefold, that the Navy should arm more quickly, and that the Army should accelerate the production of weapons for attack. Defendant Goering's words, directed at Funk, among others, were the words of a man already at war, and his emphasis on quintupling the Luftwaffe and on the production of weapons for attack was that of a man waging aggressive war.

After Schacht's departure Funk was a key figure in the preparation of plans to finance the war. This was natural, since he, after 1939, occupied three positions crucial to war finance, Two we have already named: Minister of Economics and Chief Plenipotentiary for Economics. In addition, he was President of the Reichsbank.

Funk's role in war financing is illustrated by Document 3562-PS, which I now offer in evidence as Exhibit USA 662. This document was found in the captured files of the Reich Ministry of Economics. It consists in part of a letter from the Chief Plenipotentiary for Economics, signed on his behalf by Dr. Posse. The letter is dated 1st June, 1939, and encloses the minutes of a conference concerning the financing of the war which was held under the chairmanship of Funk's Undersecretary in the Ministry of Economics, Dr. Landfried. A copy of the document which I have offered into evidence bears a marginal note on Page 1 in the bottom left-hand corner, dated 5th June, stating, and I quote: "To be shown to the Minister" - that is, Funk - "for his information."

During the course of the meeting, which was attended by twelve officials, five of whom were directly responsible to defendant Funk in his various capacities, the conferees discussed a memorandum regarding war finance which had been prepared by the Chief Plenipotentiary for Economics on 9th May, 1939. I wish to quote briefly from Page 2 of the English translation, which is found on Page 153 of your Honours' document book:

> "Then a report was made of the contents of the notes on the question of internal financing of war of 9th May of this year, in which the figures given to me by the Reich Minister of Finance are also discussed. It was pointed out that the General Plenipotentiary for Economy is primarily interested in introducing into the legislation for war finance, the idea of financing war expenditures by anticipating future revenues to be expected after the war."

If I may quote another brief excerpt from this important memorandum, which is found on Page 2 of the English translation, Page 153 of your document books:

> "State Secretary Neumann first submitted for discussion the question of whether the production would be able to meet, to the assumed extent, the demands of the army, especially if the demands of the army, as stated in the above report, should increase to approximately 14 billions in the first three months of war. He stated that, if the production potential of the present Reich territory is taken as a basis, he doubts the possibility of such an increase."

It is plain then that defendant Funk exercised comprehensive authority over large areas of the German economy, whose proper organisation and direction were critical to effective war preparation. The once powerful military machine, which rested on the foundation of thorough economic preparation, was a tribute to the contribution which defendant Funk had made to Nazi aggression.

Funk made this contribution with full knowledge of the plans for military aggression. A compelling inference of such knowledge would arise from the combination of several factors: from Funk's long and intimate association with the Nazi inner circle, from the very nature of his official functions, from the war-dominated setting of Nazi Germany, and from the fact that force and the threat of force had become the primary and the open instruments of German foreign policy. And the final element in weighing the question of defendant Funk's knowledge is, of course, the fact that, at the same time that defendant Funk was making economic preparation, specific plans for aggression were being formulated, plans which were later carried out and plans which could be effectively carried out only if they were synchronised with the complementary economic measures.

The conclusion concerning defendant Funk's knowledge is reinforced beyond any question by considering, in the light of the factors described above, the more specific and direct evidence which has already been placed into the record. We have seen from Document 1760-PS that defendant Funk had told Mr. Messersmith that the absorption of Austria by Germany was a political and economic necessity, and that it would be achieved by whatever means were necessary.

We have already referred to Document 1301-PS, in which defendant Goering laid down directives which could be understood only as directives to prepare the economic basis for aggression. And Document 3562-PS has revealed that defendant Funk was making detailed plans for financing the war, that is, of course, a particular war, the war against Poland. In this connection I wish to refer to another vital piece of evidence which has already been introduced in the record. It is the letter dated 25th August, 1939, which defendant Funk wrote to Hitler. In that letter, as your Honours will recall, defendant Funk expressed his gratitude at being able to experience those world-shaking times, and to contribute to those tremendous events. And he thanked Hitler for approving his proposals, designed to prepare the German economy for the war.

Moreover, the record contains evidence showing that defendant Funk, both personally and through his representatives, participated in the economic planning which preceded the military aggression against the Soviet Union. I would refer the Tribunal to Document 1039-PS, which revealed that in April of 1941 defendant Rosenberg, who had been appointed deputy for the centralised treatment of problems related to the occupation of the Eastern Territories, that is, the Soviet Union, discussed with defendant Funk the economic problems which would arise when the plans for aggression in the East matured. And Document 1039-PS also reveals that defendant Funk appointed one Dr. Schlotterer as his deputy, to collaborate with Rosenberg in connection with the exploitation of the Eastern Territories and that Schlotterer met with defendant Rosenberg almost daily.

It is clear, then, that Funk participated in every phase of the conspirators' programme, from their seizure of power to their final defeat. Throughout he worked effectively, if sometimes more quietly than others, on behalf of the Nazi programme, a programme which, from the very beginning, he knew contemplated the use of ruthless terror and force within Germany and, if necessary, outside of Germany. He bears, we submit, a special, a direct and a heavy responsibility for the commission of Crimes against Humanity, Crimes against Peace and War Crimes. The record makes it clear, if we may summarise the evidence, that by virtue of his activities in the Ministry of Propaganda and in the Ministry of Economics, he is responsible for stimulating and engaging in the unrelenting persecution of the Jews and other minorities, for psychologically mobilising the German people for aggressive war, and for weakening the willingness and capacity of the conspirators' intended victims to resist aggression. It is also clear, we submit, that defendant Funk, with full knowledge of the conspirators' purposes, in his capacity as Minister of Economics, President of the Reichsbank and Chief Plenipotentiary for Economics, actively participated in the mobilisation of the German economy for aggression. In these capacities, and as a member of the Ministerial Council for Defence and the Central Planning Board he also participated in the waging of aggressive war. Moreover, by virtue of his membership in the Central Planning Board which, as your Honours will recall from Mr. Dodd's presentation, formulated and directed the programme for the enslavement, the exploitation and degradation of millions of foreign workers; defendant Funk also shares special responsibility for the Nazi Slave Labour programme.

The French prosecution, I am informed, will deal with this matter in greater detail. Moreover, the French and Soviet prosecutions will submit evidence showing that defendant Funk actively participated in the programme for the criminal looting of the resources of occupied territories.

MR. THOMAS DODD: May it please the Tribunal, we would like to call at this time the witness Dr. Franz Blaha.

THE PRESIDENT (To the witness): Is your name Franz Blaha?

THE WITNESS (In Czech): Dr. Franz Blaha.

THE PRESIDENT: Will you repeat this oath: I swear by God the Almighty and Omniscient that I will speak the truth, the clear truth, and will withhold and add nothing.

(The witness repeated the oath.)

THE PRESIDENT: You can sit down if you wish.

DIRECT EXAMINATION QUESTIONS BY MR. DODD:

Q. You are Dr. Franz Blaha, a native and a citizen of Czechoslovakia; are you not?

A. *(In Czech)* Yes.

Q. I understand that you are able to speak German, and for technical reasons I suggest that we conduct this examination in German, although I know your native tongue is Czech; is that right?

A. *(In Czech)* In the interest of the case I am willing to testify in German for the following reasons:

1. For the past seven years, which are the subject of my testimony, I have lived exclusively in German surroundings.

2. A large number of special and technical expressions relating to life in and about the concentration camps are purely German inventions, and no appropriate equivalent for them in any other language can be found.

Q. Dr. Blaha, by education and training and profession you are a Doctor of Medicine?

A. *(In German)* Yes.

Q. And in 1939 you were the head of a hospital in Czechoslovakia?

A. Yes.

Q. You were arrested, were you not, by the Germans in 1939, after they occupied Czechoslovakia?

A. Yes.

Q. And were you confined in various prisons between 1939 and 1941?

A. Yes.

Q. From 1941 to April of 1945 you were confined at Dachau Concentration Camp?

A. Yes, until the end.

Q. When that camp was liberated by the Allied Forces?

A. Yes.

Q. You executed an affidavit in Nuremberg on the 9th day of January of this year, did you not?

A. Yes.

MR. DODD: This affidavit, if it please the Tribunal, bears the Document number 3249-PS, and I wish to offer it at this time. It is Exhibit USA 663. I feel that we can reduce the extent of this interrogation by approximately three-fourths through the submission of this affidavit and I should like to read it. It will take much less time to read this affidavit than it would to go through it in question and answer form, and it covers a large part of what we expect to elicit from this witness.

THE PRESIDENT: Very well.

MR. DODD: I would not have read it if we had had time to have a Russian and French translation, but unfortunately that was not possible in the few days we had.

"I, Franz Blaha, being duly sworn, depose and state as follows:

I studied medicine in Prague, Vienna, Strassburg and Paris and received my diploma in 1920. From 1920 to 1926 I was a clinical assistant. In 1926 I became chief physician of the Iglau Hospital in Moravia, Czechoslovakia. I held this position until 1939, when the Germans entered Czechoslovakia, and I was seized as a hostage and held a prisoner for co-operating with the Czech Government. I was sent as a prisoner to the Dachau Concentration Camp in April, 1941, and remained there until the liberation of the camp in April, 1945. Until July, 1941, I worked in a Punishment Company. After that I was sent to the hospital and subjected to the experiments in typhoid being conducted by Dr. Murmelstadt. After that I was to be made the subject of an experimental operation, and only succeeded in avoiding this by admitting that I was a physician. If this had been known before I would have suffered, because intellectuals were treated very harshly in the Punishment Company. In October, 1941, I was sent to work in the herb plantation, and later in the laboratory for processing herbs. In June, 1942, I was taken into the hospital as a surgeon. Shortly afterwards I was directed to conduct a stomach operation on 20 healthy prisoners. Because I would not do this I was put in the autopsy room, where I stayed until April, 1945. While there I performed approximately 7,000 autopsies. In all, 12,000 autopsies were performed under my direction.

From mid-1941 to the end of 1942 some 500 operations on healthy prisoners were performed. These were for the instruction of the S.S. medical students and doctors and included operations on the stomach, gall bladder, spleen and throat. These were performed by students and doctors of only two years' training, although they were very dangerous and difficult. Ordinarily they would not have been done except by surgeons with at least four years' surgical practice. Many prisoners died on the operating table and many others from later complications. I performed autopsies on all of these bodies. The doctors who supervised these operations were Lang, Murmelstadt, Wolter, Ramsauer and Kahr. Standartenfuehrer Dr. Lolling frequently witnessed these operations.

During my time at Dachau I was familiar with many kinds of medical experiments carried on there with human victims. These persons were never volunteers but were forced to submit to such acts. Malaria experiments on about 1,200 people were conducted by Dr. Klaus Schilling between 1941 and 1945. Schilling was personally asked by Himmler to conduct these experiments. The victims were either bitten by mosquitoes or given injections of malaria sporozoites taken from mosquitoes. Different kinds of treatment were applied, including quinine, pyrifer, neosalvarsan, antipyrin, pyramidon and a drug called 2516 Behring. I performed autopsies on bodies of people who died from these malaria experiments. 30 to 40 died from the malaria itself. 300 to 400 died later from diseases which proved fatal because of the physical condition resulting from the malaria attacks. In addition there were deaths resulting from poisoning due to overdoses of neosalvarsan and pyramidon. Dr. Schilling was present at the time of my autopsies on the bodies of his patients.

In 1942 and 1943 experiments on human beings were conducted by Dr. Sigismund Rascher to determine the effects of changing air pressure. As many as 25 persons were put at one time into a specially constructed van in which pressure could be increased or decreased as required. The purpose was to find out the effects of high altitude and of rapid parachute descents on human beings. Through a window in the van I have seen the people lying on the floor of the van. Most of the prisoners who were made use of, died as a result of these experiments, from internal hemorrhages of the lungs or brain. The rest coughed blood when taken out. It was my job to take the bodies out and to send the internal organs to Munich for study as soon as they were found to be dead. About 400 to 500 prisoners were experimented on. Those not dead were sent to invalid blocks and liquidated shortly afterwards. Only a few escaped.

Rascher also conducted experiments on the effect of cold water on human beings. This was done to find a way for reviving aviators who had fallen into the ocean. The subject was placed in ice cold water and kept there until he was unconscious. Blood was taken from his neck and tested each time his body temperature dropped one degree. This drop was determined by a rectal thermometer. Urine was also periodically tested. Some men lasted as long as 24 to 36 hours. The lowest body temperature reached was 19 degrees C., but most men died at 25 degrees C., or 26 degrees C. When the men were removed from the ice water attempts were made to revive them by artificial warmth from the sun, from hot water, from electro-therapy or by animal warmth. For this last experiment prostitutes were used and the body of the unconscious man was placed between the bodies of two women. Himmler was present at one such experiment. I could see him from one of the windows in the street between the blocks. I have personally been present at some of these cold water experiments when Rascher was absent, and I have seen notes and diagrams on them in Rascher's laboratory. About 300 persons were used in these experiments. The majority died. Of those who lived many became mentally deranged. Those not killed were sent to invalid blocks and were killed, just as were the victims of the air pressure experiments. I only know two who survived - a Yugoslav and a Pole, both of whom have become mental cases.

Liver puncture experiments were performed by Dr. Brachtl on healthy people, and on people who had diseases of the stomach and gall bladder. For this purpose a needle was jabbed into the liver of a person and a small piece of the liver was extracted. No anaesthetic was used. The experiment is very painful and often had serious results, as the stomach or large blood vessels were often punctured, and haemorrhage resulted. Many persons died of these tests, for which Polish, Russian, Czech and German prisoners were employed. Altogether these experiments were conducted on about 175 people.

Phlegmone experiments were conducted by Dr. Schutz, Dr. Babor, Dr.

Kieselwetter and Professor Lauer. Forty healthy men were used at a time, of whom 20 were given intra-muscular, and 20 intravenous injections of pus from diseased persons. All treatment was forbidden for three days, by which time serious inflammation and in many cases general blood poisoning had occurred. Then each group was divided again into groups of 10. Half were given chemical treatment with liquid and special pills every 10 minutes for 24 hours. The rest were treated with sulfanamide and surgery. In some cases all of the limbs were amputated. My autopsy also showed that the chemical treatment had been harmful and had even caused perforations of the stomach wall. For these experiments Polish, Czech and Dutch priests were ordinarily used. Pain was intense in such experiments. Most of the 600 to 800 persons who were used finally died. Most of the others became permanent invalids and were later killed.

In the autumn of 1944 there were 60 to 80 persons who were subjected to salt water experiments. They were locked in a room and for five days were given nothing to swallow but salt water. During this time their urine, blood and excrement were tested. None of these prisoners died, possibly because they received smuggled food from other prisoners. Hungarians and Gipsies were used for these experiments.

It was common practice to remove the skin from dead prisoners. I was commanded to do this on many occasions. Dr. Rascher and Dr. Wolter in particular asked for this human skin from human backs and chests. It was chemically treated and placed in the sun to dry. After that it was cut into various sizes for use as saddles, riding breeches, gloves, house slippers and ladies' handbags. Tattooed skin was especially valued by S.S. men. Russians, Poles and other inmates were used in this way, but it was forbidden to cut out the skin of a German. This skin had to be from healthy prisoners and free from defects. Sometimes we did not have enough bodies with good skin and Rascher would say, 'All right, you will get the bodies.' The next day we would receive 20 or 30 bodies of young people. They would have been shot in the neck or struck on the head so that the skin would be uninjured. Also we frequently got requests for the skulls or skeletons of prisoners. In those cases we boiled the skull or the body. Then the soft parts were removed and the bones were bleached and dried and reassembled. In the case of skulls it was important to have a good set of teeth. When we got an order for skulls from Oranienburg the S.S. men would say, 'We will try to get you some with good teeth.' So it was dangerous to have a good skin or good teeth.

Transports arrived frequently in Dachau from Studthof, Belsen, Auschwitz, Mauthausen and other camps. Many of these were 10 to 14 days on the way without water or food. On one transport which arrived in November, 1942, I found evidence of cannibalism. The living persons had eaten the flesh from the dead bodies. Another transport arrived from Compiegne in France. Professor Limousin of Clermont-Ferrand, who was later my assistant, told me that there had been 2,000 persons on this transport when it started. There was food available but no water. Eight hundred died on the way and were thrown out. When it arrived after twelve days more than 500 persons were dead on the train. Of the remainder, most died shortly after arrival. I investigated this transport because the International Red Cross complained, and the S.S. men wanted a report that the deaths had been caused by fighting and rioting on the way. I dissected a number of bodies and found that they had died from suffocation and lack of water; it was mid-summer and 120 people had been packed into each car.

In 1941 and 1942 we had in the camp what we called invalid transports. These were made up of people who were sick or for some reason incapable of working. We called them Himmelfahrt Commandos. About 100 or 120 were ordered each week to go to the shower baths. There, four people gave injections of phenol evipan, or benzine, which soon caused death. After 1943 these invalids were sent to other camps for liquidation. I know that they were killed because I saw the records, and they were marked with a cross and the date that they left, which was the way that deaths were ordinarily recorded. This was shown both on the card index of the Camp Dachau and the records in the town of Dachau. One thousand to two thousand went away every three months, so there were about five thousand sent to death in 1943, and the same in 1944. In April, 1945, a Jewish transport was loaded at Dachau and was left standing on the railroad siding. The station was destroyed by bombing, and they could not leave. So they were just left there to die of starvation. They were not allowed to get off. When the camp was liberated they were all dead.

Many executions by gas or shooting or injections took place in the camp itself. The gas chamber was completed in 1944, and I was called by Dr. Rascher to examine the first victims. Of the eight or nine persons in the chamber there were three still alive, and the remainder appeared to be dead. Their eyes were red and their faces were swollen. Many prisoners were later killed in this way. Afterwards they were removed to the crematorium, where I had to examine their teeth for gold. Teeth containing gold were extracted. Many prisoners who were sick were killed by injections while in hospital. Some prisoners killed in the hospital came through to the autopsy room with no name or number on the tag which was usually tied to their big toe. Instead the tag said: 'Do not dissect.'

I performed autopsies on some of these and found that they were perfectly healthy, but had died from injections. Sometimes prisoners were killed only because they had dysentery or vomited, and gave the nurses too much trouble. Mental patients were liquidated by being led to the gas chamber and injected there or shot. Shooting was a common method of execution. Prisoners would be shot just outside the crematorium and carried in. I have seen people pushed into the ovens while they were still breathing and making sounds, although if they were too much alive they were usually hit on the head first.

The principal executions about which I know from having examined the victims, or supervised such examinations, are as follows: In 1942 there were five thousand to six thousand Russians held in a separate camp inside Dachau. They were taken on foot to the Military Rifle Range near the camp in groups of five hundred or six hundred and shot. These groups left the camp about three times a week. At night we used to go out to bring the bodies back in carts and then examine them. In February, 1944, about 40 Russian students arrived from Moosburg. I knew a few of the boys in the hospital. I examined them after they were shot outside the crematorium. In September, 1944, a group of 94 high-ranking Russians were shot, including two military doctors who had been working with me in the hospital. I examined their bodies. In April, 1945, a number of prominent people who had been kept in the bunker were shot. They included two French generals, whose names I cannot remember, but I recognised them from their uniform. I examined them, after they were shot. In

1944 and 1945 a number of women were killed by hanging, shooting and injections. I examined them and found that in many cases they were pregnant. In 1945, just before the camp was liberated, all 'Nacht und Nebel' prisoners were executed. These were prisoners who were forbidden to have any contact with the outside world. They were kept in a special enclosure and were not allowed to send or receive any mail. There were 30 or 40, many of whom were sick. These were carried to the crematorium on stretchers. I examined them and found they had all been shot in the neck.

From 1941 on the camp became more and more overcrowded. In 1943 the hospital for prisoners was already overcrowded. In 1944 and in 1945 it was impossible to maintain any sort of sanitary condition. Rooms, which held three hundred or four hundred persons in 1942, were filled with one thousand in 1943, and in the first quarter of 1945 with two thousand or more. The rooms could not be cleaned because they were too crowded, and there was no cleaning material. Baths were available only once a month. Latrine facilities were completely inadequate. Medicine was almost non-existent. But I found, after the camp was liberated, that there was plenty of medicine in the S.S. hospital for all the camps, if it had been given to us for use.

New arrivals at the camp were lined up out of doors for hours at a time. Sometimes they stood there from morning until night. It did not matter whether this was in the winter or in the summer. This occurred all through 1943, 1944 and the first quarter of 1945. I could see these formations from the window of the autopsy room. Many of the people who had to stand in the cold in this way became ill from pneumonia and died. I had several acquaintances who were killed in this manner during 1944 and 1945. In October, 1944."

THE PRESIDENT: Too fast.

MR. DODD:

"In October, 1944, a transport of Hungarians brought spotted fever into the camp, and an epidemic began. I examined many of the corpses from this transport and reported the situation to Dr. Hintermayer, but was forbidden, on penalty of being shot, to mention that there was an epidemic in the camp. He said that it was sabotage, and that I was trying to have the camp quarantined so that the prisoners would not have to work in the armaments industry. No preventive measures were taken at all. New healthy arrivals were put into blocks were an epidemic was already present. Infected persons were also put into these blocks. So the thirteenth block, for instance, died out completely, three times. Only at Christmas, when the epidemic spread into the S.S. camp, was a quarantine established. Nevertheless, transports continued to arrive.

We had 200 to 300 new typhus cases and 100 deaths caused by typhus each day. In all, we had 28,000 cases and 15,000 deaths, In addition to those that died from the disease my autopsies showed that many deaths were caused solely by malnutrition. Such deaths occurred in all the years from 1941 to 1945. They were mostly Italians, Russians and Frenchmen. These people were just starved to death. At the time of death they weighed 50 to 60 pounds. Autopsies showed their internal organs had often shrunk to one-third of their actual size.

The facts stated above are true: This declaration is made by me voluntarily and without compulsion. After reading over the statement I have signed and executed it at Nuremberg, Germany, this 9th day of January, 1946.

(Signed) Dr. Franz Blaha.

Subscribed and sworn to before Second-Lieutenant Daniel F. Margolies."

DIRECT EXAMINATION

(Resumed.)

MR. DODD:

Q. Dr. Blaha, will you state whether or not visitors came to the camp of Dachau while you were there?

A. Many visitors came to our camp, so that it many times seemed to us that we were not confined in a camp but in an exhibition or a zoo. At times almost every day there was a visit or an excursion of military men, of political men from schools, from different medical and other institutions, and also many members of the Police, S.S. and the Armed Forces; also -

THE PRESIDENT: Will you pause so as to give the interpreter's words time to come through; do you understand?

THE WITNESS: Yes. Also some State officials came to the camp. Regular inspections were made month by month by Obergruppenfuehrer Pohl; also by Prof. Gradel, Inspector of Experimental Stations, Standartenfuehrer Dr. S.S. Reichsfuehrer, Lolling and others.

MR. DODD: The presiding Justice has suggested that you pause, and it would be helpful if you paused in the making of your answers so that the interpreters can complete their interpretation.

THE WITNESS: Yes.

Q. Are you able to state how long these visits lasted on an average?

A. That depended on the sort of visits being made. Some lasted for half an hour to an hour, some for three or four hours.

Q. Were there prominent Government people who visited the camp at any time while you were there?

A. While I was there many prominent people came to our camp: Reichsfuehrer Himmler came to Dachau several times and also was present at the experiments. I was present myself on three occasions. Others also were there. I myself have seen three Ministers of State, and of several others I have heard that they were in camp - through the political prisoners, Germans - who knew these people. I also twice saw high-ranking Italian officers and once a Japanese officer.

Q. Do you remember the names of any of these prominent Government people, do you remember more particularly who any of them were?

A. Besides Himmler there was Bormann, also Gauleiter Wagner, Gauleiter Giesler; Ministers of State Frick, Rosenberg, Funk, Sauckel; also the General of Police Daluege, and others.

Q. Did these people whom you have just named take tours around the camp while you were there?

A. In general the tour through the camp was so arranged that the visitors were first taken to the kitchen, then to the laundry, then to the hospital, i.e., usually to the surgical station, then to the malaria station of Prof. Schilling and the experimental station of Dr. Rascher. Then they proceeded to a few "blocks," particularly those of the German prisoners, and often they also visited the chapel which, however, had been furnished inside for German priests only. Often, also, different personalities were presented and introduced to the visitors. It was so arranged that always, first of all, a "green" (professional criminal) was selected who was introduced as a murderer; then the Mayor of Vienna, Dr. Schmitz, was usually presented as the second one, then a high-ranking Czech officer, then a homosexual, a gipsy, a Catholic Bishop or other high Polish churchman, then a university professor; in this order so that the visitors could amuse themselves.

Q. Now did I understand you to name Kaltenbrunner as one of those visitors there, or not?

A. Yes, Kaltenbrunner also came there. He was there, together with General Daluege. That was, I believe, in the year 1943. I was also interested in General Daluege who then, after Heydrich's death, had become Protector of Bohemia and Moravia, and I wanted him to be pointed out to me.

Q. Did you see Kaltenbrunner there yourself?

A. Yes. He was pointed out to me. I had not seen him previously.

Q. Did I understand you to mention Frick as one of those whom you saw there?

A. Yes, it was in the year of 1944, the first half of 1944.

Q. Where did you see him? Where in the camp did you see him?

A. I saw him from the hospital window as he was entering the hospital with his staff, and several other people.

Q. Do you see the man whom you saw there that day, by the name of Frick, in this Court-room now?

A. Yes. The fourth man in the first row from the right.

Q. I understand you also named the name Rosenberg as one of those whom you saw there?

A. I can recall that it was shortly after my arrival in the concentration camp at Dachau that there was a visit, and it was then that my German comrades pointed Rosenberg out to me.

Q. Do you see that man in this Court-room now?

A. Yes. He is two further to the left in the first row.

Q. I also understood you to name Sauckel as one of those who were present in the camp?

A. Yes, but I did not see him personally; I merely heard that he had visited certain factories and armament plants, and that was in 1943, 1, believe.

Q. Was it general knowledge in the camp at that time that a man named Sauckel visited the camp, and particularly the munition plant?

A. Yes, that was general knowledge in the camp.

Q. I also understood you to name one of those who visited this camp as Funk?

A. Yes. He was also present at a visit, and II can remember that it was on the occasion of a State conference of the Axis Powers in Salzburg or Reichenhall. It was the custom on such occasions, when there was a Party convention or a celebration in Munich, Berchtesgaden, or Salzburg, that several personalities would come from the celebrations to Dachau for a visit. That was also the case with Funk.

Q. Did you personally see Funk there?

A. No, I did not see Funk personally; I merely heard that he was there.

Q. Was that general knowledge in the camp at that time?

A. Yes. We knew beforehand that he was to come.

Q. Were there any visits after the end of the year 1944, or in the months of 1945?

A. There were some visits still, but very few, because there was a typhus epidemic in the camp at that time, and quarantine was imposed.

Q. Doctor, you are now a director of a hospital in Prague, are you not?

A. Yes.

MR. DODD: I have no further questions to ask of the witness.

THE PRESIDENT: Do any other counsel for the prosecution wish to ask any questions?

(Colonel Pokrovsky indicated assent.) We will adjourn for a ten minute recess.

(A recess was taken.)

COLONEL POKROVSKY: I would like permission to ask this witness several questions.

BY COLONEL POKROVSKY:

Q. Tell us, witness, do you know what were the particular functions of the concentration camp at Dachau; was it really, so to speak, a concentration camp of extermination?

A. Until the year 1943 it was really an extermination camp. After the year 1943 a good many factories and munition plants were also established, inside the camp, and particularly after the bombardments got underway, and then it became more a work camp. But as far as the results are concerned there was no difference, because the prisoners had to work so hard while going hungry that they died from hunger and exhaustion instead of from beatings.

Q. Must I understand you this way, that, in fact, even up to and since 1943 Dachau was a camp of extermination and that there were different ways of extermination?

A. That is so.

Q. How many, according to your own observations, went through this camp of extermination, Dachau; how many internees came originally from the U.S.S.R.; how many passed through the camp?

A. I cannot state that exactly, only approximately. First, after November, 1941, there were exclusively Russian prisoners of war in uniform. They had separate camps, and were liquidated within a few months. In the summer of 1942, those who remained out of, I believe, 12,000 prisoners of war, were transported to Mauthausen, and, as I learned from the people who came from Mauthausen to Dachau, they were liquidated in gas chambers.

Then, after the Russian prisoners of war, the Russian children were brought to Dachau. There were, I believe, 2,000 boys, 6 to 17 years old. They were kept in one or two special blocks. They had to suffer extremely from the "greens," who beat them constantly. These boys also ...

THE PRESIDENT: You are going too fast.

BY COLONEL POKROVSKY:

Q. What do you mean when you refer to the "greens"?

A. Those were the so-called professional criminals. They beat these young boys and gave them the hardest work. They worked particularly in the plantations where they were used instead of horses and engines, to pull ploughs, machines, and steam rollers. Also in all transport commandos Russian children were used exclusively. At least 70 per cent. of them died of tuberculosis, and those who remained were then sent to a special camp in the Tyrol in 1943 or the beginning of 1944.

Then after the children, several thousand so-called Eastern workers were brought in. These were civilians who were removed by force from the Eastern territories to Germany, and then, because of so-called work-sabotage, were put into concentration camps. In addition there were many Russian officers and intellectuals.

Q. I would like to ask you to be more exact in your answers in regard to those people whom you call "greens." Did I correctly understand you when you said that those criminals had the task of supervising those internees arriving at the camp?

A. Yes.

Q. And that these professional criminals were given complete charge of the children so that they, those children of Soviet citizens, and arrivals at the camp could be beaten, ill-treated and sent to such unbearable work that they became tubercular?

A. Yes.

Q. What do you know in regard to executions of the citizens of the U.S.S.R. which were being carried on in this camp?

A. I believe that I am not far from the truth in saying that of all those executed, at least 75 per cent. were Russians, and they were men as well as women, who were brought to Dachau from outside to be executed.

Q. Can you give us more details in regard to the execution of 94 high field and staff officers of the Red Army, which you have already spoken about in reply to the question of my colleague? Who and of what rank were these officers? What were the reasons for their execution? Do you know anything at all about it?

A.In the summer or later spring of 1944 high-ranking Russian officers, generals, colonels, and majors were sent to Dachau. During the next few weeks they were investigated by the Political Department. That is to say, after each interrogation they were completely beaten up and brought to the camp hospital, so that I saw some of them and knew them well. For weeks they simply had to lie on their bellies; we had to remove the paralysed parts of their skin and muscles by operation. Many succumbed to these methods of investigation. The others, 94 people in number, were then, on orders from the R.S.H.A. in Berlin, brought to the crematorium in the beginning of September, 1944, and there, while on their knees, shot through the neck.In addition, later on in the winter and in the spring of 1945, several Russian officers were brought from solitary confinement to the crematorium and there either hanged or shot.

Q. The same kind of question I would like to ask you about the execution of the 40 Russian students. Is it possible for you to give us a few details about the execution?

A. Yes, these Russian students and intellectuals in general - I can recall that a doctor was also among them-were brought from the Moosburg camp to Dachau, and after one month they were all executed. That was in March of 1944.

Q. Do you happen to know what the reason was for their execution? A. The order for it came from Berlin. We did not get to know the reason, because I saw the bodies only after the execution, and the reason had been read aloud before the execution took place.

Q. This execution produced the impression of being one of the stages of the general plan for extermination of the people who entered Dachau?

A. Yes. That was the plan in all executions, and in all transports of invalids, etc., as well as in the case of the epidemics. It was easy to see that this was all part of the general plan for extermination, and particularly - and this I must emphasise - the Russian prisoners were always treated the worst of all.

Q. Would you be so kind as to say what is known to you in regard to those internees who were in the category "Nacht und Nebel," night and fog? Were there many of these internees? Do you know the reason why they were sent to the concentration camp?

A. Many prisoners, so-called "Nacht und Nebel" (night and fog), came to the concentration camp; the people so designated were mostly from the Western countries of Europe, particularly Frenchmen, Belgians and Dutchmen. The Russian people-and this was also the case with the Czechs and also in my own case - frequently had the designation "return undesirable." This actually meant the same.

Shortly before the liberation many of these people were executed on the order of the camp commander, that is, shot in front of the crematorium. Among these people, particularly French and Russians, many had serious cases of typhus and were carried on stretchers to the rifle range with a temperature of 40 degrees.

Q. I believe you mentioned something about a considerable number of prisoners who died of starvation. Could you tell me how large that number was, the number of people who died of starvation?

A. I believe that two-thirds of the entire population of the camp suffered from severe malnutrition, and that at least 25 per cent. of the dead had literally died of starvation. It was called in German "Hungertyphus." Besides, tuberculosis was the most widely spread disease in the camp and spread also because of malnutrition and found most of its victims among the Russians.

Q. I think you said, answering the question of my colleague, that the majority of those who died of starvation and exhaustion were French, Russians and Italians. How do you account for the fact that just those categories of internees died more than other people?

A. Yes.

Q. How do you explain that Russians, French and Italians made up the largest number of those people who died from starvation? Was there any difference in the feeding of internees of different nationalities, or was there some other kind of reason?

A. It was like this: the others, the Germans, Poles, Czechs, who had already been in the camp for some time, had had time - so to speak - to adjust themselves to camp conditions, physically I mean. The Russians deteriorated rapidly. The same was true of the French and the Italians. Moreover, these nationals for the most part arrived suffering from malnutrition from other camps, so that they then soon fell easy prey to the other epidemics and diseases. Also, the Germans, Poles, and many others who worked in the armaments industry had had, since the year 1943, the opportunity to get parcels from home. That, of course, was not the case with citizens of Soviet Russia, France or Italy.

Q. Can you answer the question about what Rosenberg, Kaltenbrunner, Sauckel or Funk saw when they were in the Dachau concentration camp; do you know what they saw and what was shown them?

A. I had no opportunity to follow the course of these visits. Such occasions were afforded only very seldom, when one could see these visitors from the window and could observe where they went. I seldom had the opportunity to be present, as I was in the case of Himmler's visits and those of Obergruppenfuehrer Pohl, and once at the occasion of Gauleiter Giesler's visit, when they were shown the experiments on the patients in the hospital. Of the others I do not know what they individually saw and did in the camp.

Q. Perhaps you had an opportunity to observe the length of the visit of those people in the camp, whether the visit was short, just for a few moments, or whether they stayed there for a long time. I have in mind Rosenberg, Kaltenbrunner, Sauckel and Funk.

A. That depended. Many visitors were there for half an hour, many, as I said before, spent as many as three hours there. We were always able to observe that quite well, because at those times no work could be done, nor was food distributed. We did not carry on our work in the hospital, and had to wait until the signal was given to us that the visitors had left the camp. Otherwise I had no means of finding out in the individual cases how long these visits in the camp lasted.

Q. Can you recall the visits of Kaltenbrunner, Rosenberg, Funk and Sauckel? We want to classify them the same way as you mentioned just now, whether they were brief visits or whether those people stayed there for several hours. Did you understand my question or not?

A. Unfortunately, I cannot make a statement on that because, as I said, the visits took place so frequently that I have difficulty after these years in recalling whether they lasted for a shorter or longer time. Many visits, for instance, from schools, from military personnel, and police schools lasted a whole day.

COLONEL POKROVSKY: Thank you. I have no further questions of this witness at this stage of the sitting.

BY M. DUBOST:

Q. You have alluded to a convoy of deported French people who came from Compiegne, of whom only 1,200 survivors arrived. Were there any other convoys?

A. Yes. There were transports, particularly from Bordeaux, Lyon, and Compiegne, all in the first half of the year 1944.

Q. Were all the transports carried out under the same conditions?

A. The conditions under which these transports were made were, if not the same, at any rate very similar.

Q. Each time upon their arrival you were able to see that there were numerous victims?

A. Yes.

Q. What were the causes of death?

A. The causes of death were that too many people had been packed closely into the cars, which were then locked, and that they did not get anything to eat or drink for several days. Usually they starved or suffocated. Of those who survived many were brought to the camp hospital, and of these again a large number died from various complications and diseases.

Q. Did you make autopsies of the people who died while en route?

A. Yes, my services were demanded particularly for the transport from Compiegne because the rumour was spread that the French, namely the Maquis and the Fascists, had attacked and killed each other in the cars. I had to inspect these corpses, but in no case did I find any signs of violence. Moreover, I took ten corpses as samples, dissected them thoroughly, and sent special reports on them to Berlin. All these people had died of suffocation. I could also note during the autopsy that these were prominent French people. I could tell from their identity papers and uniforms that they were high-ranking French officers, priests, deputies, and well-fed people who had been taken directly from civilian life to the cars to be sent to Dachau.

Q. After you sent your reports to Berlin did the conditions under which the transports were made remain the same?

A. Nothing happened, as usual. Always long reports were written, but ,conditions did not improve at all.

Q. You indicated that some French generals had been put to death shortly before the liberation of the camp. Do you know the names of these generals?

A. Unfortunately I have forgotten these names. I can remember only and I was told so by the prisoners who were kept in the "Bunkers" with them that they were prominent people from Germany and other countries: Pastor Niemoeller, also the Prussian Prince, Schuschnigg, members of the French Government, and many others. I was told that one of the generals who had been shot was a close relative of General de Gaulle. Unfortunately I have forgotten his name.

Q. If I understood you rightly, these generals were prisoners of war who had been transported to this concentration camp?

A. These two generals never were in the concentration camp. They were kept, along with the other prominent people, in the so-called "Kommandantur-Arrest," i.e., in the "Bunker" separated from the camp. On various occasions when they needed medical attention I came into contact with them, but that was very infrequently. Otherwise they did not come into contact with other prisoners at all.

Q. Did they belong to the category of deported people whose return was undesirable, or were they of the category of "Nacht und Nebel"?

A. I do not know. Two days previously all the others who were kept in the "Bunker" were sent by special transport to the Tyrol. That was, I believe, a week or eight days before the liberation.

Q. You indicated that numerous visitors, German military men, students, political men, had toured the camp repeatedly. Can you say if any common people like workers or farmers knew what was going on in this camp?

A. In my opinion, the people who lived in the neighbourhood of Munich must have known of all these things because the prisoners went every day to various factories in Munich and the neighbourhood, and while at work frequently came into contact with the civilian workers. Moreover, the plantations and the factories of the German armament plants were often entered by people making deliveries and also customers, who must have seen what was done to the prisoners, and what they looked like.

Q. Can you say in what way the French were treated?

A. Well, if I said that the Russians were treated worst of all, the French were the second in order. Of course, there were differences in the treatment of the different people. The "Nacht und Nebel" prisoners were treated quite differently, likewise the prominent political personalities and the intellectuals. That was true of all nations. And the workers and peasants were treated in a different way.

Q. If I understood correctly, the treatment reserved for the French intellectuals was particularly rigorous. Do you remember the treatment inflicted on some French intellectuals, and can you tell us their names?

A. As I can recall I had many comrades among the physicians and university professors who worked with me in the hospital. Unfortunately, a large number of them died of typhus. Most of the French, in fact, died of typhus. I can remember best of all Professor Limousin. He arrived in very poor condition with the transport from Compiegne. I took him into my department as assistant pathologist. Then I also knew the Bishop of Clermont- Ferrand. There were also other physicians and university professors whom I knew. I remember Professor Roche, Dr. Lemartin, and there were many others, but I have forgotten their names.

Q. In the course of the conversations which you had with Dr. Rascher were you informed of the purpose he pursued by these experiments?

A. I did not understand the question.

Q. Were you informed of the purpose of the medical and biological experiments made by Dr. Rascher in the camp?

A. Well, Dr. Rascher made exclusively so-called Air Force experiments in the camp. He was a major in the Air Force and was assigned to investigate the conditions to which parachutists were subjected and, further, the conditions of those people who had to make an emergency landing on the sea or had fallen into the sea. According to scientific rules, in so far as I can judge, there was no purpose at all. Just as in the case of all these experiments, it was simply useless murder, and it is particularly amazing that learned university professors and physicians were capable of carrying out these experiments according to plan. These experiments were much worse than all the liquidations and executions, because all the victims of these experiments simply had their suffering prolonged, as various medicines, such as vitamins, hormones, tonics and injections, which were not available for common patients, were provided for these patients, so that the experiments might last longer, and give those people more time to observe their victims.

Q. I am speaking now of the experiments of Dr. Rascher only; had he received the order to make these experiments, or did he make them on his own initiative?

A. These experiments were made on Himmler's direct orders; also, Dr. Rascher had close relations with Himmler, and was like a relative of his. Himmler visited Dr. Rascher very often, and Dr. Rascher repeatedly visited Himmler.

Q. Have you any information regarding the qualifications of the physicians who were making these experiments? Were they always S.S. men, or were they members of medical faculties of academies who did not belong to the S.S.?

A. That depended. For example, the malaria station was headed by Professor Klaus Schilling of the Koch Institute in Berlin. The phlegmine station also had several university professors. The surgical station was manned solely by S.S. doctors. In the Air Force station there were exclusively S.S. and military doctors. It was not always the same. Dr. Bleibeck from Vienna conducted the experiments with sea-water.

Q. Were the studies for the Luftwaffe made on the order of Himmler only?

A. Yes.

Q. Do you know - this is the last question - how many Frenchmen passed through this camp?

A. I believe at least eight or ten thousand people arrived at the camp. I know, furthermore, very well that, particularly during the last period, several thousand French prisoners marched on foot from the Western camps, especially from Natzweiler, Studthof, etc., and that only very small remnants of these ever reached Dachau.

M. DUBOST: Thank you.

BY THE PRESIDENT:

Q. Can you tell us to what branches of the German service those who were employed at the camp belonged?

A. If I understood you correctly, the highest authority on everything going on in the camp was the so-called R.S.H.A. in Berlin. All orders came from Berlin; also in the experimental stations a certain definite number of subjects for the experiments was assigned from Berlin, and if the experimenting doctors needed a larger number, new requests had to be sent to Berlin.

Q. Yes, but what I want to know is, to what branch of the service the men belonged who were employed in the camp.

A. They were all S.S. men, and most of them from the S.D. During the last days, at the very end, a few members of the Armed Forces were there as guards, but the men in charge were exclusively S.S. men.

Q. Were there any of the Gestapo there?

A. Yes, that was the so-called Political Department, which was directed by the Chief of the Munich Gestapo. It had control of all the interrogations, regulations, proposed executions, transports, and transports of invalids. Also, all the people who were provided for the experiments had to be approved by the Political Department.

THE PRESIDENT: Do any of the defendants' counsel want to cross-examine the witness?

CROSS-EXAMINATION
BY DR. SAUTER (Counsel for defendant Funk):

Q. Witness, you told us that at one time the defendant Funk also was at Dachau, and you informed us, if I understood you correctly, that this happened on the occasion of some celebration or State conference between the Axis Powers. I ask you to exert your memory a bit and tell us when that was approximately. Perhaps you could tell us the year, maybe also the season, and perhaps you could also state which political celebration was in question.

A. As far as Funk is concerned, I can remember that it was, I believe, a conference of finance ministers. It had been reported in the papers that this was to take place at that time, and we were informed ahead of time that some of the ministers would come to Dachau. Such a visit was actually made in the next few days, and Minister Funk was said to have been among the visitors. It was, I believe, during the first half of the year 1944. I cannot say that with absolute certainty.

Q. You mean to say during the first half of 1944, on the occasion of a conference of finance ministers?

A. Yes.

Q. Where did that conference take place?

A. If I remember correctly - I did not write that down, of course - it was either in Salzburg or Reichenhall or Berchtesgaden, somewhere in the neighbourhood of Munich, I believe.

Q. From who did you learn at that time that within the next few days, or the day after, the next high-ranking visitors would arrive?

A. We always received an order to prepare for such a visit. Elaborate preparations were always made; everything was cleaned up, everything had to be in order, as you will understand; and those people whose presence might be undesirable or might even, in a certain sense, be dangerous, had to disappear. Thus, in the case of all such high-ranking visitors, we received an order from the Camp Commandant one or two days ahead of time. And these visitors were also always accompanied by the Camp Commander.

Q. By the Camp Commander. Now, if you know that the defendant Funk was there and people talked about it, then, I think, they would have mentioned also what other persons were present at this visit made by the defendant Funk.

A. I cannot remember. There were always many different prominent people.

Q. Other visitors interest me. I am interested only whether or not at that particular visit, which was said to have been made by Funk, word was passed around the camp that such and such persons were with him?

A. I cannot remember that now.

Q. You cannot remember. Can you remember whether afterwards, perhaps on the next day or the day after, something was said about that, perhaps by people who had seen the visitors?

A. Yes, we always discussed that; but now I can no longer remember who were named on these occasions.

Q. Witness, I am not interested in any other visit, but in this specific visit, as long as I do not say anything to the contrary. In this case I should like to know whether or not anything was said later on about the persons who were there with Funk.

A. That I do not know: there were so many visits. For instance, after one visit, the very next day there would be another visit announced.

Q. Now, you do also remember the visit that Funk made, do you not?
A. Yes.

Q. Well, if other finance ministers were there, one would think that you would recall them too.
A. No, I cannot remember that. It may be that the people with whom I talked did not know these other persons.

Q. Do you know why - or to put it differently - which departments of the camp the visitor Funk was said to have visited? At any rate he did not come to you?
A. No; he did not come to the Department of Pathology.

Q. He did not. But you were also prepared?
A. Yes. All departments had always to be prepared, even if the visitors did not come. It also happened at times that a visit was announced, and then, for one reason or another, nothing came of it.

Q. Witness, as regards these observations of yours that you have related to us to-day, have you been interrogated in regard to them many times already?
A. I was interrogated on these matters for the first time before the Military Court at Dachau.

Q. Did you also at that time say that Funk had been there? I repeat, did you before the Military Court at Dachau say anything to the effect that Funk had been present?
A. Yes, I said the same thing before the Court at Dachau.

Q. About Funk?
A. Also about Funk.

Q. But is it true, witness? I ask again whether it is really true, because you are here as a witness under oath.
A. Yes.

Q. You were interrogated also the day before yesterday?
A. Yes.

Q. Did you, at that time, also make these statements about Funk?
A. I said the same thing at the interrogation conducted by the prosecution.

Q. Is that also in the affidavit which I believe you signed?
A. I signed no affidavit.

Q. You signed no affidavit?
A. No; I simply signed what has just been read by the prosecution.

Q. Well, that is an affidavit.
A. Yes, but in that affidavit there is no mention of these visits.

Q. Why then did not you mention these visits the day before yesterday?
A. I was asked about it orally, and the prosecutor told me that these matters would be taken up orally in the Courtroom.

Q. Were you then also told where the defendants sit in the Courtroom?
A. No. Before the Military Court I was shown all the pictures and I was asked to identify to the Court the various people. I identified the three whom I said to-day that I had seen in person. Funk and others I did not name.

Q. You did not name Funk?
A. I did not say that I had personally seen him or that I could identify him.

Q. But when the pictures were shown to you did you see these defendants in the pictures?

A. Yes.

Q. Now, if I understand you correctly, you knew to-day where, for instance, Funk or Frick or anyone else was sitting?

A. Funk I do not know personally, because I never saw him at that time.

Q. Were you not told when the pictures were shown to you at Dachau, "This is Funk; look at him; do you know him"?

A. No; it was done quite differently.

Q. How?

A. All the pictures were shown to me and I was to say whom of these individuals I had seen at the Dachau camp. Of these people I named these three. In regard to the other pictures there was no further discussion whatsoever.

Q. Well, Dr. Blaha, when your hearing started and you were asked by the President or by the Prosecutor, you made a statement, I believe, in the Czech language.

A. No.

Q. What then?

A. In the German language.

Q. No, everyone heard that that was not German, but it was obviously Czech.

A. The first sentences only.

Q. The first sentences only; I therefore, ask that it also be included in the Court transcript for practical purposes. I ask you to state and to repeat quite literally, giving the true sense, that which you said then, because we are interested in that from the point of view of the defence.

A. I believe that it was included in the transcript because an English translation was added to my statement, and the Czech sentences were also translated.

Q. I do not believe that Czech is being translated. But please repeat what you said then; we did not hear it.

A. I said that I was ready, since it is technically impossible to use my native tongue in the hearing, to give my testimony in German, because I have lived through all these events which occurred during the last seven years and which are now the subject of this trial in German surroundings, and also the special and new expressions referring to life in the camp can be found only in German, and in no other dictionary can you find such suitable and expressive terms as in the German language.

DR. SAUTER: Then I have no further questions; thank you.

DR. THOMA (Counsel for defendant Rosenberg):

Q. Witness, were the inmates of the concentration camp Dachau bound to secrecy?

A. No. Of course, if someone was discharged from the camp by the Gestapo - those were very few cases-particularly in the case of the Germans who were then drafted, one had to sign . . .

THE PRESIDENT (interposing): More slowly, please.

A. ... one had to sign a so-called statement of secrecy.

BY DR. THOMA:

Q. Could the inmates of the camp, those inside the camp, who worked on farms, etc. talk to the other workers about the conditions in the camp?

A. Yes, there were opportunities, because the people worked in the same rooms and factories with various other workers, civilian workers. That was so in the German armament industry, on the plantations, and in all factories, in Munich and surrounding districts.

Q. If I understood you correctly, you said previously that visitors, people who delivered things, and customers also, had an opportunity to observe these conditions in the camp without difficulty.

A. Yes. Many of these people went through all the plantation as well as the branches of the various factories and observed the life in these places.

Q. And what did they see there in the way of atrocities and ill-treatment?

A. No, I believe they saw how the people worked, what they looked like and what was produced there. For instance, I can remember one example quite well. At that time I was working on the plantations. We were pulling a heavy steam roller, 16 men and a party of girls passed. When they passed, their leader said very loudly, so that we all could hear it, "Look, those people there are so lazy that it looks as if they'd rather have a team of horses pull it." That was supposed to be funny.

Q. Witness, when did you first have occasion, after your liberation from the concentration camp, to tell other people about those horrible atrocities which you related to us to-day?

A. I did not understand that; please repeat.

Q. When did you first have an opportunity, after your discharge or liberation from the concentration camp, to tell an outsider about these horrible atrocities?

A. Immediately after the liberation. I was at that time, as chief physician of the concentration camp, interrogated by the American Investigating Corps, and it was to this corps that I told this story for the first time, and I also gave them various proofs, diagrams, and the case histories, which I had saved from being burnt.

Q. That prosecutor believed the information you gave without further ado?

A. Yes.

Q. Witness, you said that the defendant Rosenberg was shown to you in the concentration camp Dachau shortly after you arrived there? When was that?

A. In the year 1941; first half of 1941.

Q. First half?

A. I believe so, yes.

Q. Can you perhaps remember the month?

A. I cannot remember. I arrived in April; that is why I assume it was perhaps from April to July, or so.

Q. To July, from April to July, 1941?

A. I believe so.

Q. Was Rosenberg at that time in uniform?

A. He was in uniform.

Q. In what uniform?

A. I believe it was an S.S. uniform.

Q. S.S. uniform?

A. It was a - I cannot say that very precisely - but he was in uniform.

Q. All right, you remember prima facie that it was an S.S. uniform, that is a black uniform?

A. No, at that time the S.S. did not any longer wear the black uniform, because after the beginning of the war they wore field uniforms and other similar uniforms.

Q. Then, you assume it was a grey uniform?

A. Something like that; whether it was grey or yellow or brown I do not remember any more.

Q. That is just the point: whether it was grey, brown, or yellow. Was it a field uniform?

A. I do not remember any longer, because from 1939 I was in the concentration camp, and anyway I am not familiar with the various German uniforms, ranks and branches of the Army, and so forth.

Q. But you just said that during the war they changed the uniform.

A. Yes, the people in the Gestapo also changed it. When I was taken prisoner in 1939, all Gestapo personnel wore this black uniform. After the beginning of the war most of them were either green or grey uniforms.

Q. May I ask you again: Now did Rosenberg wear a war uniform or a peacetime uniform?

A. I believe it was a war uniform.

Q. War uniform? The defendant Rosenberg was pointed out to you by another comrade, was he not?

A. Yes.

Q. At what distance?

A. Well, he was just going down the camp street. That was perhaps 30 or 40 degrees.

Q. Thirty or 40 metres you mean?

A. Well, 30 metres; 30 paces I wanted to say, 30 to 40 paces.

Q. And had you previously seen photographs of Rosenberg? Did you connect any idea with the name Rosenberg?

A. Yes.

Q. And when this comrade showed you Rosenberg, was it then necessary for him to say: "This is Rosenberg"? Did you not recognise him already from having seen him in the pictures which you had previously

A. I cannot remember that. But when he showed him to me I did remember that I knew him already from the various pictures in the newspapers.

Q. May I ask you to describe the precise sequence of events, how it happened; where you were standing, where Rosenberg came from, and who was in his company.

A. Who was in his company? I knew only the Camp Commander.

Q. Who was it at that time?

A. Camp Commander was Pierkowski, Sturmbannfuehrer Pierkowski.

Q. Do you know whether he is still alive?

A. No, I do not.

Q. The Camp Commander?

A. Pierkowski.

Q. Yes?

A. Then the Lagerfuehrer Ziel and Hoffmann. I knew them.

Q. You knew them. Now were you in your room and looking out of the window?

A. No, we were in one of the so-called block streets. This led into another through which the visitors passed.

Q. And what was said to you?

A. "Look, there goes Rosenberg."

Q. Was Rosenberg alone?

A. No, he was with these other persons.

Q. That is to say, only with the Camp Commander?

A. No, there were many other people with him.

Q. That is to say, he had an escort, a staff?

A. I do not know whether that was Rosenberg's staff, but there were a number of persons.

Q. A number of persons? Witness, the defendant Rosenberg assures me most definitely that he has never been to the concentration camp at Dachau. Is no error possible here?

A. I believe I am not mistaken. Besides the German in question knew Rosenberg very well, I believe.

Q. How do you know that?

A. Because he told me so definitely. Otherwise, I have no way of knowing it.

THE PRESIDENT: Dr. Thoma.

DR. THOMA: Yes.

THE PRESIDENT: You will forgive me if I point out to you that this is intended to be an expeditious trial and that it is not right to take up too much time upon small points like this.

DR. THOMA: I ask your permission to remark that the question whether or not Rosenberg was in the concentration camp is a very important question of decisive significance. I thank you.

BY DR. PANNENBECKER (Counsel for defendant Frick):

The defendant Frick states that he has never been in Dachau Camp. I should like, therefore, in order to clarify the facts, to ask the following questions:

Q. Witness, at what distance do you believe you saw Frick?

A. I saw him from the window as he passed with a number of people.

Q. Did you know Frick before?

A. Yes, from pictures.

Q. From pictures? Did you recognise him yourself, or did some friend tell you that it was Frick?

A. A number of us saw him and I looked at him particularly because at that time he was already Protector of Bohemia and Moravia. For that reason I had a personal interest in recognising him.

Q. Did Frick wear a uniform?

A. I do not believe so.

Q. Did you recognise anybody who was with him, anyone from his staff or from the camp command?

A. From the camp command? I did not know his staff. Of the camp command there was Camp Commander Weiter, and his adjutant, Otto.

Q. Could you name anyone of your comrades who also recognised him?

A. There were many comrades of mine who at that time were standing at the window. Unfortunately, I cannot say who they were, because, as you will understand, so many things happened during life in the concentration camp, as on an assembly line, that one cannot record these things accurately in one's memory. One remembers only the more important events.

Q. Did you recognise him at once of your own accord when he passed by, or had it been talked over previously that Frick was expected?

A. No, it was not discussed then. It was simply said that a high-ranking visitor was to come, and we were waiting for this high-ranking visitor. We were not told beforehand who was to come.

Q. Did you recognise Frick immediately now in the Courtroom, or did you know beforehand that he was sitting in the fourth seat here?

A. No, I recognised him quite well, because I have already seen him repeatedly in various pictures.

Q. How did that happen?

A. Because he is a well-known person in Bohemia and Moravia.

Q. You then believe that any error is completely out of question?

A. I believe so.

DR. PANNENDECKER: May I then ask the Court whether Frick himself may take the stand to testify that he has never seen the camp Dachau? I want to make this motion now so that, if necessary, the witness might be confronted with Frick.

THE PRESIDENT: Counsel for the defendants will understand that they will have the opportunity, when it comes to their time to present their cases, to call all the defendants, but they will not have an opportunity of calling them now. They will have to wait until the case for the prosecution is over, and they will then have an opportunity, each of them, to call the defendant for whom they appear, if they wish to.

DR. PANNENBECKER: I simply thought, that since the witness is available now

(Dr. Kubuschok approached the lectern.)

THE PRESIDENT: It is now 5 o'clock, and unless you are going to be very short - are you going to be very short?

BY DR. KUBUSCHOK (Counsel for the Reich Cabinet): Yes, Sir.

Q. Witness, you said that when prominent visitors came to the camp, for instance, Reich Ministers, extensive preparations were made beforehand. You also said that undesirable persons were removed. Maybe you could supplement that statement. I am interested to know the purpose of these preparations.

A. My meaning is that everything had to be in order. In our infirmary all the patients had to lie in bed quietly, everything was washed and prepared and the instruments were polished, as was usually the case when high-ranking visitors came. We were not allowed to do anything, there were no operations no bandages; and no food was given out before the visit had terminated.

Q. Could you perhaps tell me which undesirable persons were to be removed, as you said before?

A. Well, the Russians in particular were always kept strictly in their blocks. It was said that there was a fear of possible demonstrations, assassinations, etc.

Q. Were prisoners kept out of sight because they showed outward signs of any ill-treatment?

A. It goes without saying that before visits nobody was struck, beaten, hanged or executed.

Q. Summing up, the purposes of these preparations were not to give the guests a view of the real concentration camp?

A. Not of the cruelties.

Q. Thank you.

THE PRESIDENT: The Court will not sit in open session to-morrow, Saturday, and will only sit in the morning on Monday because there is work to be done in the closed session to-morrow and on Monday afternoon. I thought it would be convenient for counsel to know that.

The Court will now adjourn.

(The Tribunal adjourned until 10.00 hours, on 14th January, 1946.)

Thirty-Third Day: Monday, January 14th, 1946

THE PRESIDENT: Would you have the witness brought in? I think one of the defendants' counsel was about to cross-examine him.

DR. BABEL (Counsel for the S.S. and S.D.): I would like to put the following question to the witness. I am asking these questions in order to understand better the previous statements of the witness and for my own information.

The witness was from 1941 to 1945 in the concentration camp and should be well informed on conditions as they were. His memory seems to be excellent.

CROSS-EXAMINATION OF DR. FRANZ BLAHA
(resumed):
BY DR. BABEL:

Q. Do you know how the relations of the inmates changed during the various periods of time; I mean the relations between the political and criminal inmates? What was the number of the political and criminal inmates?

A. In Dachau it was not always the same. There were political and actual criminals and the so-called "asocial" elements. Naturally, I am just speaking about the German prisoners, the members of the other nations were only political prisoners. The German inmates alone were divided into red, green and black prisoners.

Q. Can you indicate their approximate relations? About half, three-quarters, one-fourth?

A. I am sorry, I did not hear you.

Q. Can you give me figures? About how many of these - half, three-quarters, or how many? Can you give me an approximate number?

A. I would say about 5,000 German prisoners. Out of that number, 3,000 were political prisoners; about 2,000 were considered green and black.

Q. Was it like that during the whole four or five-year period?

A. It changed periodically because many died; some Germans left; many were drafted; and there were many new arrivals. In the last year there were always more and more political prisoners, for many of the green were taken to the front.

Q. What approximately was their total number in 1941, 1943, and 1945?

A. We had 8 to 9,000 in 1941; in 1943 from 15 to 20,000; and toward the end of 1944 until the beginning of 1945 we had more than 70 to 80,000.

Q. One more question: You mentioned you had first worked on the plantations. What do you mean by that?

A. Plantations, that refers to a large estate of the S.S. where many spices, medical herbs and things of that sort were raised.

Q. Was this plantation inside the camp?

A. No, it was in the near vicinity of the camp, not a part of it.

Q. You mentioned armament works; and I gathered from your testimony that these armament factories were partially within the camp and partially without. Is that true?

A. At first they were only outside the camp. Then, as a result of the bombings, certain sections were moved into the interior of the concentration camp.

Q. Now, regarding the guards: What was the number of the guards in 1941?

A. The actual guard duty was done by about three S.S. companies; but at Dachau there were in addition a large garrison of S.S. and a Kommandantur. Guards were taken from other S.S. formations from time to time, when it was necessary. The number varied, and depended on how many guards were needed. For regular duty there were about three companies.

Q. Did they serve guard in the armament plants during working hours?

A. Yes. Every labour detachment had a commander and, in addition, these so-called guards, who went with the detachment to their place of work and brought the prisoners back again to the camp.

Q. While you were at the camp, did you notice any mistreatment of the prisoners by these guards in the course of their daily activities.

A. Yes; many.

Q. Often?

A. Yes.

Q. For what reasons?

A. The reasons varied, depending upon the nature of the guards or the commandant.

Q. You said you were busy and active?

A. Quite busy.

Q. How did you have the opportunity to observe such mistreatment?

A. I performed many autopsies of people either shot at work or beaten to death. I dissected these bodies and reported on these autopsies.

Q. You said they were shot. Did you see these shootings yourself?

A. No.

Q. How do you know that they were shot?

A. I received the bodies from their place of work, and my duty was to ascertain the cause of death: whether the man has been beaten to death, whether the skull or ribs were fractured, or whether there were internal haemorrhages. Had he been shot, a record had to be made - an official report - sometimes; sometimes, but rarely, when an investigation was made, I was called in as witness.

DR. BABEL: Thank you.

THE PRESIDENT: Mr. Dodd, do you wish to re-examine the witness.

MR. DODD: I have no further questions to ask the witness at this time.

THE PRESIDENT: Does any other member of the prosecuting staff want to re-examine? Colonel Pokrovsky?

COLONEL POKROVSKY: At this stage of the trial I have no more questions to ask the witness.

THE PRESIDENT: Then the witness can go.

MR. DODD: I should like to ask the Tribunal at this time to take judicial notice of the findings and the sentences imposed by the Military Court at Dachau, Germany on the 13th day of December, 1945. The findings were dated the 12th and the sentences on the 13th. I have here a certified copy of the findings and the sentences, Document 3590-PS, which I should like to offer as Exhibit USA 664.

THE PRESIDENT: Have copies of this been given to the defendants?

MR. DODD: Yes. They have been sent to the defendant's counsel Information Room.

THE PRESIDENT: Very well.

MR. DODD: I have one other matter that I should like to take up very briefly before the Tribunal this morning. It is concerned with a matter that arose after I had left the Courtroom to return to the United States.

On the 13th December we offered in evidence Document 3421- PS, and Exhibits USA 252 and 254. They were, respectively, the Court will recall, sections of human skin taken from human corpses and preserved; and a human head, the head of a human being, which had been preserved. On the 14th day of December, according to the record, counsel for the defendant Kaltenbrunner addressed the Tribunal and complained that the affidavit, which was offered, of one Pfaffenberger, failed to state that the camp commandant at Buchenwald, Koch, along with his wife, was condemned to death for having committed precisely these atrocities, this business of tanning the skin and preserving the head. And in the course of the discussion before the Tribunal the record reveals that Counsel for the defendant Bormann, in addressing the Tribunal, stated that it was highly probable that the prosecution knew that the German authorities had objected to this camp commandant Koch and, in fact, knew that he had been tried and sentenced for doing precisely these things. And there was some intimation, we feel, that the prosecution, having this knowledge, withheld it from the Tribunal. Now, I wish to say that we had no knowledge at all about this man Koch at the time that we offered the proof; we did not know anything about him except that he had been the Commandant, according to the affidavit. But, subsequent to this objection we had an investigation made, and we have found that he was indeed tried in 1944 by an S.S. court, but not for having tanned human skin nor for having preserved a human head, but for having embezzled money, for what, as the judge who tried him tells us - was a charge of general corruption, and for having murdered someone with whom he had some personal difficulties. Indeed, the judge, a Dr. Morgen, tells us that he saw the tattooed human skin and he saw a human head in Commandant Koch's office, and that he saw a lampshade there made out of human skin. But there were no charges at the time that he was tried for having done these things.

I would also point out to the Tribunal, that, we say, the testimony of Dr. Blaha sheds further light on whether or not these exhibits, USA 252 and 254, were isolated instances of that atrocious kind of conduct. We have not been able to locate the affiant. We have made an effort to do so, but we have not been able to locate him thus far.

THE PRESIDENT: Locate whom?

MR. DODD: The affiant Pfaffenberger, the one whose affidavit was offered.

THE PRESIDENT: Very well, Mr. Dodd.

DR. KAUFMANN (Counsel for defendant Kaltenbrunner): The statement just made is undoubtedly significant, but it would be of importance if we had the proof and the documents which served to convict the Commandant and his wife, for Kaltenbrunner told me that it was known in the whole S.S. that the Commandant Koch and his wife had also - I am emphasising "also" - been convicted because of these things. It had been made known that the size, the magnitude of the penalty had been determined by their inhuman behaviour.

THE PRESIDENT: Wait a minute. As you were the counsel who made the allegation that the Commandant Koch had been put to death for his inhuman treatment, it would seem that you are the party to produce the judgement.

DR. KAUFMANN: I never had the sentence in my hand. I depended on the information which Kaltenbrunner gave me personally and orally.

THE PRESIDENT: It was you who made the assertion. I do not care where you got it from. You made the assertion; therefore it is for you to produce the document.

DR. KAUFMANN: Yes, Sir.

COLONEL PHILLIMORE: May it please the Tribunal: briefs and document books have been handed in. The documents in the document book are in the order in which I shall refer to them, and the references to them in the briefs are also in that order. On the first page of the brief is set out the extract from Appendix A of the Indictment, which deals with the criminality of this defendant.

THE PRESIDENT: Are you dealing first of all with Raeder or with Donitz?

COLONEL PHILLIMORE: With Donitz. My learned friend, Major Elwyn Jones, will deal with Raeder immediately after.

THE PRESIDENT: The Tribunal will adjourn for ten minutes.

(A recess was taken.)

COLONEL PHILLIMORE: My Lord, may I proceed?

THE PRESIDENT: Very well.

COLONEL PHILLIMORE: Briefs and documents books have been handed in. The documents are in the document book in the order in which I shall refer to them, and the references in the brief to the documents are in that same order. On the first page of the brief is set out the extract from the Indictment as Appendix A, which deals with the allegations against this defendant. It sets out the positions he held, and charges him, first, with promoting the preparations for war, set forth in Count 1; second, with participating in the military planning and preparation for wars of aggression and wars in violation of international treaties, agreements, and assurances, set forth in Count 1 and 2 of the Indictment; and, thirdly, with authorising, directing, and participating in the war crimes, set forth in Count 3 of the Indictment, including particularly the crimes against persons and property on the high seas.

Now, if at any place I appear to trespass on Count 3, it is with the consent and courtesy of the Chief Prosecutor for the French Republic.

My Lord, on the second page of the brief are set out first the positions held by the defendant Donitz, and the document in question is the first document in the document book, 2887- PS, which has already been put in as Exhibit USA 12. The members of the Tribunal will see that after his appointment in 1935 as Commanding Officer of the Weddigen U-boat Flotilla - that was, in fact, the flotilla to be formed after the end of the World War in 1918 - the defendant, who was in effect then Commander of U-boats, rose steadily in rank, as the U-boat arm expanded, until he became an Admiral. And then, on the 30th of January, 1943, he was appointed Gross Admiral and succeeded the defendant Raeder as Commander-in-Chief of the German Navy, retaining his command of the U-boat arm. Then on the 1st of May, 1945, he succeeded Hitler as leader of Germany.

My Lord, as appears from a number of documents which I shall put in evidence, the defendant was awarded the following decorations: On the 18th of September, 1939, the Iron Cross, first class, for the U-boat successes in the Baltic during the Polish campaign; this award was followed on the 21st of April, 1940, by the high award of the Knight's Cross to the Iron Cross, while on the 7th of April, 1943, he received personally from Hitler the Oak Leaf to the Knight's Cross of the Iron Cross, as the two hundred and twenty-third recipient, for his outstanding services in building up the German Navy and, in particular, the offensive U-boat arm for the coming war. And now I put in the next document in the document book, D-436, which becomes Exhibit GB 183. That is an extract from the official publication Das Archiv on the defendant's promotion to Vice-Admiral. It is dated the 27th of September, 1940, and I read the last two sentences:

"In four years of untiring and, in the fullest sense of the word, uninterrupted work of training, he succeeds in developing the young U-boat armed personnel and material till it is a weapon of a striking power, unexpected even by the experts. More than three million gross tons of enemy shipping sunk in only one year, achieved with only a few boats, speak better than words of the service of this man."

The next document in the document book, 1463-PS, which I put in as Exhibit GB 184, is an extract from the diary of the German Navy, 1944 edition, and it serves to emphasise the contents of that last document. My Lord, I will not read from it. The relevant passage is on Page 2, and, if I might summarise that, it describes in detail the defendant's work in building up the U-boat arm, his ceaseless work in training night and day to close the gap of seventeen years during which no training had taken place, his responsibility for new improvements, and for devising the "pack" tactics which were later to become so famous. And then his position is summarised further at the top of Page 3. If I might read the last two sentences of the first paragraph on that page:

"In spite of the fact that his duties took on immeasurable proportions since the beginning of the huge U-boat construction programme, the chief was what he always was and always will be: the leader and inspiration to all the forces under him."

And then the last sentence of that paragraph:

"In spite of all his duties he never lost touch with his men, and he showed a masterly understanding in adjusting himself to the changing fortunes of war."

It was not, however, only his ability as a naval officer which won the defendant these high honours: his promotion to succeed the defendant Raeder as Commander-in-Chief of the Navy, the personal position he acquired as one of Hitler's principal advisers, and finally - earlier candidates such as Goering, having betrayed Hitler's trust or finding the position less attractive than they had anticipated - the doubtful honour of becoming Hitler's successor. These honours he owed to his fanatical adherence to Hitler and to the Party, to his belief in the Nazi ideology with which he sought to indoctrinate the Navy and the German people, and to his masterly understanding in adjusting himself to the changing fortunes of war, referred to in the diary, and which the Tribunal may think, when I have referred them to the document, may be regarded as synonymous with the capacity for utter ruthlessness. His attitude to the Nazi Party and its creed is shown by his public utterances.

I turn to the next document in the document book, D-443, which I put in to become Exhibit GB 185. It is an extract from a speech made by the defendant at a meeting of commanders of the Navy in Weimar on the 17th December, 1943. It was subsequently circulated by the defendant as a top-secret document for senior officers only, and by the hand of officers only. My Lord, if I might read:

"I am a firm adherent of the idea of ideological education. For what is it in the main? Doing his duty is a matter of course for the soldier. But the full value, the whole weight of duty done, is only complete if the heart and spiritual conviction lend themselves to the idea. The result of duty done is then quite different from what it would be if I only carried out my task literally, obediently and faithfully. It is therefore necessary for the soldier to support the execution of his duty with all his mental, all his spiritual energy; and for this his conviction, his ideology are indispensable. It is therefore, necessary for us to train the soldier uniformly, comprehensively, that he may be adjusted ideologically to our Germany. Every dualism, every dissension in this connection, or every divergence or unpreparedness imply a weakness in all circumstances. He in whom this grows and thrives in unison is superior to the other. Then, indeed, the whole importance, the whole weight of his conviction comes into play. It, is also nonsense to say that the soldier or the officer must have no politics. The soldier embodies the State in which he lives, he is the representative, the articulate exponent of his State. He must, therefore, stand with his whole weight behind this State.

We must travel this road from our deepest conviction. The Russian travels along it. We can only maintain ourselves in this war if we take part in it, with holy zeal, with all our fanaticism.

Not I alone can do this; it can only be done with the aid of the man who holds the production of Europe in his hand, with Minister Speer. My ambition is to have as many warships for the Navy as possible so as, to be able to fight and to strike. It does not matter to me who builds them."

My Lord, that last sentence is of importance in connection with a later document. The Tribunal will see, when I come to this, that the defendant was not above employing concentration camp labour for this purpose.

I put in the next document in the document book, D.-640, which becomes Exhibit GB 186. It is an extract from a speech on the same subject by the defendant, as Commander-in-Chief of the Navy, to the Commanders-in-Chief on the 15th February, 1944. My Lord, it is cumulative except that I think the last two sentences add something if I might read them:

"From the very start the whole of the officer corps must be so indoctrinated that it feels itself co-responsible for the National Socialist State in its entirety. The officer is the exponent of the State, the idle chatter that the officer is non-political is sheer nonsense."

Now, the next document is 2879-PS, which I put in to become Exhibit GB 187. It consists of three extracts from speeches. The first is from a speech made by the defendant to the German Navy and the German people on Heroes' Day, the 12th March, 1944.

"German men and women!

... What would have become of our country to-day, if the Fuehrer had not united us under National Socialism! Split into parties, beset with the spreading poison of Jewry and vulnerable to it, and lacking, as a defence, our present uncompromising world outlook, we would long since have succumbed to the burdens of this war and been subject to the merciless destruction of our adversaries...."

My Lord, the next extract is from a speech to the Navy on the 21st July, 1944. It again shows the defendant's fanaticism. It is perhaps worth reading the first sentence:

"Men of the Navy! Holy wrath and unlimited anger fill our hearts because of the criminal attempt which was to have cost the life of our beloved Fuehrer. Providence wished it otherwise, watched over and protected our Fuehrer, and did not abandon our German Fatherland in the fight for its destiny."

And then he goes on to deal with the fate which should be meted out to these traitors.

The third extract deals with the introduction of the German salute into the Armed Forces. I do not think I need read it, but as the members of the Tribunal will see, it was the defendant Keitel, and this defendant, who were responsible for the alteration of the salute in the German Forces and the adoption of the Nazi salute - together with Goering - Pardon me, I should have said, the defendants Goering, Keitel and Donitz.

The next document is a monitored report of the speech made on the German wireless by this defendant, announcing the death of Hitler and his own succession. It is D-444. I put it in to become Exhibit GB 188, and I read a portion of it. The time is 22.26 hours marked on the document. I read therefrom:

> "It has been reported from the Fuehrer's headquarters that our Fuehrer, Adolf Hitler, has died this afternoon in his battle headquarters at the: Reich Chancellery, fallen for Germany, fighting to the last breath against Bolshevism. On the 30th April the Fuehrer nominated Grand Admiral Donitz to be his successor. The Grand Admiral and Fuehrer's successor will speak to the German nation."

And then, the first paragraph of the speech:

> "German men and women, soldiers of the German Armed Forces. Our Fuehrer, Adolf Hitler, is dead. The German people bow in deepest sorrow and respect. Early he had recognised the terrible danger of Bolshevism and had dedicated his life to the fight against it. His fight having ended, he died a hero's death in the capital of the German Reich, after having led an unmistakably straight and steady life."

Then, that document also contains an order of the day issued by the defendant, which is very much to the same effect.

Apart from his services in building up the U-boat arm, there is ample evidence that the defendant as Commander-in-Chief of U-boats, took part in the planning and execution of aggressive war against Poland, Norway and Denmark. The next document in the document book, C-126/C, has already been put in as Exhibit GB 45. It is a memorandum by the defendant Raeder, dated the 16th May, 1939, and I will call the attention of the Tribunal to the distribution. The sixth copy went to the Fuehrer der Unterseeboote, that is to say, to the defendant Donitz. It is a directive for the invasion of Poland, "Fall Weiss," and I will not read it. It has already been read.

The next document, C-126/E, on the second page of that same document, has also been put in as Exhibit GB 45. It again is a memorandum from the defendant Raeder's headquarters, dated the 2nd August, 1939. It is addressed to the Fleet, and then Flag Officer U-boats - that is, of course, the defendant - and it is merely a covering letter for operational directions for the employment of U-boats which are to be sent into the Atlantic as a precaution in case the intention of carrying out "Fall Weiss" should remain unchanged. The second sentence is important:

> "Flag Officer U-boats is handing in his operational orders to SKL" - that is, the Seekriegsleitung, the German Admiralty - "by 12th August. A decision on the sailings of U-boats for the Atlantic will probably be made in the middle of August."

The next document, C-172, I put in as Exhibit GB 189. It consists of the defendant's own operational instructions to his U-boats for the operation "Fall Weiss." It is signed by him. It is not dated, but it is clear from the subject-matter that its date must be before the 16th July, 1939. I do not think the substance of the document adds anything. It is purely an operational instruction, giving effect to the document already put in, C-126/6, the directive by Raeder.

My Lord, the next document, C-122, has already been put in as Exhibit GB 82. It is an extract from the War Diary of the Naval War Staff of the German Admiralty, dated the 3rd October, 1939, and records the fact that the Chief of the Naval War Staff has called for views on the possibility of taking operational bases in Norway. It has already been read, and I would merely call the Tribunal's attention to the passage in brackets, in the paragraph marked (d).

"Flag Officer U-boats already considers such harbours extremely useful as equipment and supply bases for Atlantic U-boats to call at temporarily."

The next document, C-5, has already been put in as Exhibit GB 83. This in from the defendant, as Flag Officer U-boats, addressed to the Supreme Command of the Navy, the Naval War Staff. It is dated the 9th October, 1939, and it sets out the defendant's view on the advantages of Trondheim and Narvik as bases. The document proposes the establishment of a base at Trondheim with Narvik as an alternative.

Now the next document, C-151, has already been put in as Exhibit GB 91. It is the defendant's operation order to his U-boats for the occupation of Denmark and Norway, and the operation order, which is top secret, dated the 30th March, is termed "Hartmut." The members of the Tribunal will remember that the document, in the last paragraph, said:

"The naval force will, as they enter the harbour, fly the British flag until the troops have landed, except presumably at Narvik."

The preparations for war against England are perhaps best shown by the disposition of the U-boats under his command on the 3rd September, 1939, when war broke out between Germany and the Western Allies. The locations, of the sinkings in the following week, including that of the Athenia which will be dealt with by my learned friend, Major Elwyn Jones, provide corroboration. On that, I would put in two charts; I put them in as D-652, and they become Exhibit GB 190.

My Lord, I have copies here for the members of the Tribunal. They have been prepared by the Admiralty. There are two charts. The first sets out the disposition of the submarines on the 3rd September, 1939. There is a certification attached to the chart, in the top left-hand corner, which I should read:

"This chart has been constructed from a study of the orders issued by Donitz between 21st August, 1939, and 3rd September, 1939, and subsequently captured. The chart shows the approximate disposition of submarines ordered for 3rd September, 1939, and cannot be guaranteed accurate in every detail, as the file of captured orders are clearly not complete, and some of the submarines shown apparently had received orders at sea on or about 3rd September to move to new operational areas. The documents from which this chart was constructed are held by the British Admiralty in London."

My Lord, there are two points I would make on that first chart. First, it will be apparent to members of the Tribunal that U-boats which were in those positions on the 3rd September, 1939, had left Kiel some considerable time before. The other point which I would make is important in connection with my learned friend Major Elwyn Jones' case against the defendant Raeder, and that is the location of the U-boat U-30. The members of the Tribunal may care to bear it in mind while looking at the charts now.

The second chart sets out the sinkings during the first week of the war, and the location of the sinking of the Athenia will be noted. There is a short certification in the left- hand corner of the Tribunal's copies:

"This chart has been constructed from the official records of the British Admiralty in London. It shows the position and sinkings of the British merchant vessels lost by enemy in the seven days subsequent to 3rd September, 1939."

My Lord, I turn to the defendant's participation in War Crimes and Crimes, against Humanity.

The course of the war waged against neutral and Allied merchant shipping by the U-boats followed, under the defendant's directions, a course of consistently increasing ruthlessness. The defendant displayed his masterly understanding in adjusting himself to the changing fortunes of war. From the very early days, merchant ships, both Allied and neutral, were sunk without warning; and when operational danger zones had been announced by the German Admiralty, these sinkings continued to take place both within and without those zones. With some exceptions in the early days of the war, no regard was taken for the safety of the crews or passengers of sunk merchant ships, and the announcement claiming a total blockade of the British Isles merely served to confirm the established situation, under which U-boat warfare was being conducted without regard to the established rules of international warfare or the requirements of humanity.

The course of the war at sea during the first eighteen months is summarised, by two official British reports made at a time when those who compiled them were ignorant of some of the actual orders issued, orders which have since come to hand.

My Lord, I turn to the next document in the document book. It is D-641 (a), which I put in to become Exhibit GB 191. It is an extract from an official report of the British Foreign Office concerning German attacks on merchant shipping during the period 3rd September, 1939, to September, 1940, that is to say, the first year of the war, and it was made shortly after September, 1940.

My Lord, if I might quote from the second paragraph on the first page:

"During the first twelve months of the war, 2,081,062 tons of Allied shipping comprising 508 ships have been lost by enemy action. In addition, 769,213 tons of neutral shipping, comprising 253 ships, have also been lost. Nearly all these merchant ships have been sunk by submarine, mine, aircraft or surface craft, and the great majority of them were sunk while engaged on their lawful trading voyages. 2,836 Allied merchant seamen have lost their lives in these ships.

In the last war the practice of the Central Powers was so remote from the recognised procedure that it was thought necessary to set forth once again the Rules of Warfare, in particular as applied to submarines. This was done in the Treaty of London, 1930, and in 1936 Germany acceded to the rules. The rules laid down:

(1) In action with regard to merchant ships, submarines must conform to the rules of International Law to which surface vessels are subjected.

(2) In particular, except in the case of persistent refusal to stop on being summoned, or of active resistance to visit and search, a war ship, whether surface vessel or submarine, may not sink or render incapable of navigation a merchant vessel without having first placed passengers, crew and ships' papers in a place of safety. For this purpose, the ship's boats are not regarded as a place of safety unless the safety of the passengers and crew is assured in the existing sea and weather conditions, by the proximity of land, or the presence of another vessel which is in a position to take them on board."

Then, the next paragraph:

"At the beginning of the present war, Germany issued a Prize Ordinance for the regulation of sea warfare and the guidance of her naval officers. Article 74 of this ordinance embodies the submarine rules of the London Treaty. Article 72, however, provides that captured enemy vessels may be destroyed if it seems inexpedient or unsafe to bring them into port, and Article 73/(1) and (2) makes the same provision with regard to neutral vessels which are captured for sailing under enemy convoy, for forcible resistance, or for giving assistance to the enemy. These provisions are certainly not in accordance with the traditional British view, but the important point is that, even in these cases, the Prize Ordinance envisages the capture of the merchantman before its destruction. In other words, if the Germans adhered to the rules set out in their own Prize Ordinance, we might have argued the rather fine legal point with them, but we should have no quarrel with them, either on the broader legal issue or on the humanitarian one. In the event, however, it is only too clear that almost from the beginning of the war the Germans abandoned their own principle, and waged war with steady disregard for International Law, and for what is, after all, the ultimate sanction of all law, the protection of human life and property from arbitrary and ruthless attacks."

I pass to the third paragraph on the next page which sets out two instances:

"On the 30th September, 1939, came the first sinking of a neutral ship by a submarine without warning and with loss of Life. This was the Danish ship Vendia bound for the Clyde in ballast. The submarine fired two shots and shortly after torpedoed the ship. The torpedo was fired when the master had already signalled that he would submit to the submarine orders, and before there had been an opportunity to abandon ship. By November, submarines were beginning to sink neutral vessels without warning as a regular thing. On the 12th November the Norwegian Arne Kjode was torpedoed in the North Sea without any warning at all. This was a tanker bound from one neutral port to another. The master and four of the crew lost their lives and the remainder were picked up after many hours in open boats. Henceforward, in addition to the failure to establish the nature of the cargo, another element is noticeable, namely an increasing recklessness as to the fate of the crew."

And then dealing with attacks on Allied merchant vessels, certain figures are given.

Ships sunk — 241

Recorded attacks — 221

Illegal attacks — 112

At least 79 of these 112 ships were torpedoed without warning.

THE TRIBUNAL (Mr. Biddle): Then they were not illegally sunk, however?

COLONEL PHILLIMORE: Yes, Sir.

THE TRIBUNAL (Mr. Biddle): According to this document, the Germans have been given the benefit of the doubt.

COLONEL PHILLIMORE: Oh, yes, I should have read that sentence; I am obliged to your Honour.

I pass to the second report, D641/b. It is part of the same document and is put in as Exhibit GB 191. It is a report covering the next six months from 1st September, 1940 -

THE PRESIDENT: Are you not reading Page 3?

COLONEL PHILLIMORE: If your Lordship pleases, I have read a great deal of the report and there, are passages that I had not considered important.

THE PRESIDENT: I have not myself read it, but I think -

COLONEL PHILLIMORE: If I might read the first two paragraphs on Page 3:

"By the middle of October, submarines were sinking merchant vessels without any regard to the safety of the crews. Yet four months later the Germans were still officially claiming that they were acting in accordance with their Prize Ordinance. Their own semi-official commentators, how-ever, had made the position clear. As regards neutrals, Berlin officials had early in February stated that any neutral ship that is either voluntarily or under compulsion bound for an enemy port - including contraband control harbours - thereby loses its neutrality and must be considered hostile. At the end of February the cat was let out of the bag by a statement that a neutral ship which obtained a navicert from a British Consul, in order to avoid putting into a British contraband control base, was liable to be sunk by German submarines, even if it was bound from one neutral port to another. As regards Allied ships, in the middle of November, 1939, a Berlin warning was issued against the arming of British vessels. By that date a score of British merchantmen had been illegally attacked by gunfire or torpedo from submarines, and after that date some fifteen more unarmed Allied vessels were torpedoed without warning. It is clear therefore, that not only was the arming fully justified as a defensive measure, but also that neither before nor after this German threat did the German submarines discriminate between armed and unarmed vessels."

The last paragraph is merely a summing up; it does not add anything. Turning to 641/b, which is a similar report covering the next six months, if I might read the first five paragraphs of Page 1:

"On the 30th January, 1941, Hitler proclaimed: 'Every ship, with or without convoy, which appears before our torpedo tubes is going to be torpedoed.'"

On the face of it, this announcement appears to be uncompromising; and the only qualification provided by the context is that the threats immediately preceding it are specifically addressed to the peoples of the American Continent. German commentators, however, subsequently tried to water it down by contending that Hitler was referring only to ships which attempted to enter the area where the German "total blockade" was alleged to be in force.

"From one point of view it probably matters little what exactly was Hitler's meaning, since the only conclusion that can be reached, after a study of the facts of enemy warfare on merchant shipping, is that enemy action in this field is never limited by the principles which are proclaimed by enemy spokesmen, but solely by the opportunities or lack of them which exist at any given time."

THE PRESIDENT: Colonel Phillimore, is not this document you are now reading really legal argument?

COLONEL PHILLIMORE: My Lord, some of it is. The difficulty is to leave those parts and take in the facts.

THE PRESIDENT: Very well.

COLONEL PHILLIMORE: The third paragraph, if I might leave the rest of the second, is as follows:

"The effect of the German total blockade is to prohibit neutral ships from entering an enormous stretch of sea round Britain (the area extends to about 500 miles west of Ireland, and from the latitude of Bordeaux to that of the Faroe Islands), upon pain of having their ships sunk without warning and their crews killed. As a matter of fact, at least thirty-two neutral ships, exclusive of those sailing in British convoys, have been sunk by enemy action since the declaration of the 'total blockade.'"

Then the last sentence in the following paragraph deals with the sinking of merchant ships without warning:

"Yet, though information is lacking in many cases, details are available to prove that, during the period under review, at least thirty-eight Allied merchant ships exclusive of those in convoys have been torpedoed without warning in or near the 'total blockade' area.

That the Germans themselves have no exaggerated regard for the area is proved by the fact that of the thirty- eight ships referred to at least sixteen were torpedoed outside the limits of the war-zone."

My Lord, the next page deals with a specific case illustrating the matter set out above. It is in the first paragraph of that page, the third sentence:

"The sinking of the City of Benares on the 17th September, 1940, is a good example of this. The City of Benares was an 11,000-ton liner with 191 passengers on board, including nearly 100 children. She was torpedoed without warning just outside the 'war zone,' with the loss of 258 lives, including 77 children. It was blowing a gale, with hail and rain squalls and a very rough sea when the torpedo struck her at about 10 p.m. In the darkness, and owing to the prevailing weather conditions, at least four of the twelve boats lowered were capsized. Others were swamped and many people were washed right off. In one boat alone 16 people, including 11 children, died from exposure; in another 22 died, including 15 children: In a third 21 died. The point to be emphasised is not the unusual brutality of this attack, but rather that such results are inevitable when a belligerent disregards the rules of sea warfare as the Germans have done and are doing."

I think the rest of that paragraph is not important.

I turn to the next document, D-641/C, which is part of Exhibit GB 191.

THE PRESIDENT: It is clear, I suppose, from that statement of facts that there was no warning whatever given?

COLONEL PHILLIMORE: No, my Lord.

THE PRESIDENT: We think that you should read the next paragraph too.

COLONEL PHILLIMORE: If your Lordship pleases.

"There are hundreds of similar stories, stories of voyages for days in open boats in Atlantic gales, of men in the water clinging for hours to a raft and gradually dropping off one by one, of crews being machine-gunned as they tried to lower their boats or as they drifted away in them, of seamen being blown to pieces by shells and torpedoes and bombs. The enemy must know that such things are the inevitable result of the type of warfare he has chosen to employ."

My Lord, the rest is very much to the same general effect.

The next document, D-641/C, is merely a certificate giving the total sinkings by U-boats during the War (1939 to 1945) as 2,775 British, Allied and neutral ships totalling 14,572,435 gross registered tons.

My Lord, it is perhaps worth considering one example not quoted in the above reports of the ruthless nature of the actions conducted by the defendants' U-boat commanders, particularly as both British and German versions of the sinkings are available. I turn to the next document, "The sinking of S.S. Sheaf Mead." That is D-644, which I put in as Exhibit GB 192. If I might read the opening paragraph:

"The British S.S. Sheaf Mead was torpedoed without warning on 27th May, 1940 - "

THE PRESIDENT: This is the German account, is it not?

COLONEL PHILLIMORE: This is actually in the form of a British report. It includes the German account in the shape of a complete extract from the log.

THE PRESIDENT: It bears the words, Top Secret?

COLONEL PHILLIMORE: Yes, my Lord, this was at the time a top secret document. That was some while ago.

"The British S.S. Sheaf Mead was torpedoed without warning on 27th May, 1940, with the loss of 31 of the crew. The commander of the U-boat responsible is reported to have behaved in an exceptionally callous manner towards the men clinging to upturned boats and pieces of wood. It was thought that this man was Kapitanleutnant Ohrn of U-37: The following extract from his log for 27th May, 1940, leaves no doubt on the matter and speaks for itself as to his behaviour."

Again, turning to the relevant extract from the log, on the second page, the time is marked on the document as 15.54.

"Surface. Stern is under water" - referring to the ship which has been torpedoed - "Stern is under water. Bows rise higher. The boats are now on the water. Lucky for them. A picture of complete order. They lie at some distance. The bows rear up quite high. Two men appear from somewhere in the forward part of the ship. They leap and rush with great bounds along the deck down the stern. The stem disappears. A boat capsizes. Then a boiler explosion. Two men fly through the air, limbs outstretched. Bursting and crashing. Then all is over. A large heap of wreckage floats up. We approach it to identify the name. The crew have saved themselves on wreckage and capsized boats. We fish out a buoy. No name on it. I ask a man on the raft. He says, hardly turning his head -'Nix Name.' A young boy in the water calls 'Help, help, please!' The others are very composed. They look damp and somewhat tired. An expression of cold hatred is on their faces. On to the old course. After washing the paint off the buoy, the name comes to light: Gretastone, Glasgow, 5,006 gross registered tons."

"On to the old course" means merely that the U-boat makes off.

Then the next page of that document contains an extract from the report of the Chief Engineer of the Sheaf Mead. The relevant paragraphs are the first and the last:

"When I came to the surface I found myself on the port side, that is, nearest to the submarine, which was only about five yards away. The submarine captain asked the steward the name of the ship, which he told him, and the enemy picked up one of our life-buoys, but this had the name Gretastone on it, as this was the name of our ship before it was changed to Sheaf Mead last January."

In the last paragraph:

"She had cut-away bows, but I did notice a net-cutter. Two men stood at the side with boat-hooks to keep us off.

They cruised around for half an hour, taking photographs of us in the water. Otherwise they just watched us, but said nothing. Then she submerged and went off, without offering us any assistance whatever."

THE PRESIDENT: Is. there any suggestion in the German report that any warning was given?

COLONEL PHILLIMORE: No, my Lord. It is quite clear, indeed, that it was not.

Under the time, 14.14, there is a description of the sighting of the ship and the difficulty in identifying; and then at the top of the page:

"The distance apart is narrowing. The, steamship draws in quickly, but the position is still 40-50. I cannot see the stern yet. Tube ready. Shall I or not? The gunnery crews are also prepared. On the ship's side a yellow cross in a small, square, dark blue ground. Swedish? Presumably not. I raise the periscope a little. Hurrah, a gun at the stern, an ack-ack gun or something similar. Fire! It cannot miss..."

and then the sinking.

Now that it is possible to examine some of the actual documents by which the defendant and his fellow conspirators issued their orders in disregard of International Law, you may think the compilers of the above reports understated the case. These orders cover not only the period referred to in the reports, but also the subsequent course of the war. It is interesting to note in them the steps by which the defendants progressed. At first they were content with breaching the rules of International Law to the extent of sinking merchant ships, including neutral ships, without warning, where there was a reasonable prospect of being able to do so without discovery. The facts already quoted show that the question of whether ships were defensively armed or outside the declared operational areas was, in practice, immaterial.

I go to the next document in the document book, C-191, which I put in as Exhibit GB 193. That is a memorandum by the German Naval War Staff, dated 22nd September, 1939. It sets out:

"Flag Officer U-boats intends to give permission to U- boats to sink without warning any vessels sailing without lights."

Reading from the third sentence:

"In practice there is no opportunity for attacking at night, as the U-boats cannot identify a target which is a shadow, in a way that entirely obviates mistakes being made. If the political situation is such that even possible mistakes must be ruled out, U-boats must be forbidden to make any attacks at night in waters where French and English naval forces or merchant ships may be situated. On the other hand, in sea areas where only English units are to be expected, the measures desired by Flag Officer U-boats can be carried out; permission to take this step is not to be given in writing, but need merely be based on the unspoken approval of the Naval War Staff.

U-boat commanders should be informed by word of mouth, and the sinking of a merchant ship must be justified in the War Diary as due to possible confusion with a warship or an auxiliary cruiser. In the meanwhile, U-boats in the English Channel have received instructions to attack all vessels sailing without lights."

Now I go to the next document, C-21, which I put in as Exhibit GB 194. My Lord, this document consists of a series of extracts from the War Diary of the German Naval War Staff of the German Admiralty. The second extract, on Page 5, relates a conference with the head of the Naval War Staff, "Report on the 2nd January, 1940," and then reading:

"(1) Report by Ia." - That is the Staff Officer Operations on the Naval War Staff.

THE PRESIDENT: Should not you read above that, paragraph 1 (b)?

COLONEL PHILLIMORE: Yes, if your Lordship pleases. It is important. The others are much to the same effect. If I might read it:

"Report by Ia," - This is one report by Ia on Directive of Armed Forces High Command of 30th December.

"According to this, the Fuehrer, on report of Commander- in-Chief in Navy, has decided:

(a) Greek merchant vessels are to be treated as enemy vessels in the zone blockaded by U.S.A. and Britain.

(b) In the British Channel all ships may be attacked without warning. For external consumption these attacks should be given out as hits by mines.

Both measures may be taken with immediate effect."

The next extract, report by Ia, that is, the Staff Officer Operations on the Naval

War Staff on Directive of Armed Forces High Command, dated 30th December:

"Referring to intensified measures in naval and air warfare in connection with 'Fall Gelb.' In consequence of this directive, the Navy shall authorise, simultaneously with the general intensification of the war, the sinking by U-boats, without any warning, of all ships in those waters near the enemy coasts in which mines can be employed. In this case, for external consumption, pretence should be made that mines are being used. The behaviour of, and use of weapons by, U-boats should be adapted to this purpose."

And then the third extract, dated 6th January, 1940:

" ... the Fuehrer has in principle agreed (see minutes of report of C.-in-C. Navy of 30th December) to authorise firing without warning whilst maintaining the pretence of mine hits, in certain parts of the American blockade zone."

Well, then the order is given to Flag Officer U-boats carrying out that decision.

The next extract, dated 18th January, 1940, adds to some extent and, if I may read it:

"The High Command of the Armed Forces has issued the following Directive dated 17th January, cancelling the previous order concerning intensified measures of warfare against merchantmen.

The Navy will authorise, with immediate effect, the sinking without warning by U-boats of all ships in those waters near the enemy coasts in which the use of mines is possible."

My Lord, that is an extension of the area.

"U-boats must adapt their behaviour and employment of weapons to the pretence, which is to be maintained in these cases, that the hits were caused by mines. Ships of the United States, Italy, Japan and Russia are exempted from these attacks."

Well, then there is a note emphasising the point about maintaining the pretence of mine hits, and the last extract is, I think, purely cumulative.

The next document, C- 118, I put in as Exhibit GB 195. This is an extract from the B.D.U. War Diary, that is to say, the defendant's War Diary. It is dated 18th July, 1941, and it consists of a further extension of that order by the cutting down of the protected categories.

"Supplementary to the order forbidding, for the time being, attacks on U.S. warships and merchant vessels in the operational area of the North Atlantic, the Fuehrer has ordered the following:

(1) Attacks on U.S. merchant vessels sailing in British or U.S. convoys, or independently, is authorised in the original operational area which corresponds in its dimensions to the U.S. blockade zone, and which does not include the sea-route U.S. to Iceland."

As the members of the Tribunal will have seen from these orders, at one date the ships of a particular neutral under certain conditions could be sunk while those of another could not. It would be easy to put before the Tribunal a mass of orders and instances to show that the attitude to be adopted toward ships of particular neutrals changed at various times. The point is that the defendant conducted the U-boat war against neutrals with complete cynicism and opportunism. It all depended on the political relationship of Germany toward a particular country at a particular time, whether her ships were sunk or not.

My Lord, I turn to the next document in the document book, D- 642, which I put in as Exhibit GB 196. My Lord, this is a series of orders; the first I should say of a series of orders leading up to the issue of an order which enjoined the U-boat commanders not merely to abstain from rescuing crews, which is the purpose of this order, not merely to give them no assistance, but deliberately to annihilate them.

My Lord, in the course of my proof of this matter, I shall call two witnesses. The first witness will give the Court an account of a speech made by the defendant at the time that he issued the order, describing the policy, or his policy toward the rescue of Allied troops - that it must be stopped at all costs.

The second witness is the officer who actually briefed crews on the order.

My Lord, this document is an extract from the standing orders of the U-boat Command, an extract from Standing Order No. 154, and it is signed by the defendant.

> "Paragraph (e). Do not pick up survivors or take them with you. Do not worry about the merchant ship's boats. Weather conditions and distance from land play no part. Have a care only for your own ship and strive only to attain your next success as soon as possible. We must be harsh in this war. The enemy began the war in order to destroy us, so nothing else matters."

THE PRESIDENT: What is the date of that?

COLONEL PHILLIMORE: My Lord, that order, the copy we have, is not dated, but a later order, No. 173, which was issued concurrently with an operational order, is dated the 2nd May, 1940. The Tribunal may take it, it is earlier than the 2nd May, 1940. My Lord, that is a secret order.

THE PRESIDENT: Earlier than May, 1940?

COLONEL PHILLIMORE: Earlier than May, 1940.

It was, however, in 1942, when the United States entered the war with its enormous ship-building capacity, that the change thus brought about necessitated a further adjustment in the methods adopted by the U-boats and the defendant; and the defendant was guilty of an order, which intended not merely the sinking of merchant ships, not merely the abstention from rescue of the crews, but their deliberate extermination.

My Lord, the next document in the document book shows the course of events. It is D-423, and I put it in as Exhibit GB 197. It is a record of a conversation between Hitler and the Japanese Ambassador Oshima, in the presence of the defendant Ribbentrop, on the 3rd January, 1942.

> "The Fuehrer, using a map, explains to the Japanese Ambassador the present position of marine warfare in the Atlantic, emphasising that what he considers his most important task is to get the U- boat warfare going in full swing. The U-boats are being reorganised. Firstly, he had recalled all U-boats operating in the Atlantic. As mentioned before, they would now be posted outside United States ports. Later, they would be off Freetown and the larger boats even as far down as Capetown."

And then, after further details:

> "After having given further explanations on the map, the Fuehrer pointed out, that, however many ships the United States built, one of their main problems would be the lack of personnel. For that reason, even merchant ships would be sunk without warning with the intention of killing as many of the crew as possible. Once it gets around that most of the seamen are lost in the sinkings, the Americans would soon have difficulties in enlisting new people. The training of sea-going personnel takes a very long time. We are fighting for our existence and our attitude cannot be ruled by any humane feelings. For this reason he must give the order that, in case foreign seamen could not be taken

prisoner, which is not always possible on the sea, U-boats were to surface after torpedoing and shoot up the lifeboats.

Ambassador Oshima heartily agreed with the Fuehrer's comments, and said that the Japanese, too, were forced to follow these methods."

My Lord, the next document, D-446, I put in as Exhibit GB 198. I do not propose to read it. It is an extract from B.D.U. War Diary of 16th September, 1942, and it is part of the story in the sense that it was on the following day that the order I complain of was issued, and the defence will, no doubt, wish to rely on it. It records an attack on a U-boat which was rescuing survivors, chiefly the Italian survivors of the Allied liner Laconia when it was attacked b~ an Allied aircraft.

My Lord, the next document, D-630, I put in as Exhibit GB 199. It contains four documents. The first is a top secret order, sent to all commanding officers of U-boats from the defendant's headquarters, dated 17th September, 1942.

"1. No attempt of any kind must be made at rescuing members of ships sunk, and this includes picking up persons in the water and putting them in lifeboats, righting capsized lifeboats and handing over food and water. Rescue runs counter to the rudimentary demands of warfare for the destruction of enemy ships and crews.

2. Orders for bringing in captains and chief engineers still apply.

3. Rescue the shipwrecked only if their statements will be of importance to your boat.

4. Be harsh, having in mind that the enemy takes no regard of women and children in his bombing attacks on German cities."

Now, my Lord, that is of course a very carefully worded order. Its intentions are made very clear by the next document on that same page, which is an extract from the defendant's War Diary; and I should say here, as appears from the copy handed into the Court, that the War Diary is personally signed by the defendant Donitz. It is the War Diary entry for 17th September, 1942.

"The attention of all commanding officers is again drawn" - and I would draw the Tribunal's attention to the word "again" - "to the fact that all efforts to rescue members of the crews of ships which have been sunk, contradict the most primitive demands for the conduct of warfare by annihilating enemy ships and their crews. Orders concerning the bringing in of the captains and chief engineers still stand."

The last two documents on that page consist of a telegram from the commander of the U-boat Schacht to the defendant's headquarters and the reply. Schacht had been taking part in the rescue of survivors from the Laconia. The telegram from Schacht dated the 18th September, 1942, reads:

"163 Italians handed over to Annamite. Navigating officer of Laconia and another English officer on board." - And then it goes on setting out the position of English and Polish survivors in boats.

The reply sent on the 20th: "Action as in wireless telegram message of 17th September was wrong. Boat was detailed to rescue Italian allies and not for the rescue of English and Poles."

It is a small point, but, of course, "detailed" means before the bombing incident had ever occurred.

And then as for the next document, D-663, that was issued later and may not yet have been inserted in the Tribunal's document book; D-663 I put in as Exhibit GB 200.

My Lord, this is an extract from an operation order, "Operation Order Atlantic No.

56," dated 7th October, 1943, and the copy put in is part of sailing orders to a U-boat. As I shall prove through the second witness, although the date of this order is 7th October, 1943, in fact it is only a reproduction of an order issued very much earlier, in the autumn of 1942.

> "Rescue ships: A so-called rescue ship is generally attached to every convoy, a special ship of up to 3,000 gross registered tons, which is intended for the picking up of survivors after U-boat attacks. These ships are, for the most part, equipped with a ship-borne aircraft and large motorboats, are strongly armed with depth charge throwers, and are very manoeuvrable, so that they are often called 'U-boat traps' by the commander."

And then, the last sentence:

> "In view of the desired destruction of ship's crews, their sinking is of great value."

If I might just sum up those documents, it would appear from the War Diary entry of 17th September, that orders on the lines discussed between Hitler and Oshima were, in fact, issued, but we have not captured them. It may be that they were issued orally and that the defendant awaited a suitable opportunity before confirming them. The incident of the bombing of the U-boats detailed to rescue the Italian survivors from the Laconia afforded the opportunity, and the order to all commanders was issued. Its intent is very clear when you consider it in the light of the War Diary entry. The wording is, of course, extremely careful, but to any officer of experience its intention was obvious, and he would know that deliberate action to annihilate survivors would be approved under that order.

You will be told that this order, although perhaps unfortunately phrased, was merely intended to stop a commander from jeopardising his ship by attempting a rescue, which had become increasingly dangerous, as a result of the extended coverage of the ocean by Allied aircraft; and that the notorious action of the U-boat Commander Eck in sinking the Greek steamer Peleus and then machine-gunning the crew on their rafts in the water, was an exception; and that, although it may be true that a copy of the order was on board, this action was taken solely, as he himself swore, on his own initiative.

I would make the point to the Tribunal that if the intention of this order was to stop the rescue attempts in the interests of the preservation of the U-boat, first of all it would have been done by calling attention to Standing Order 154.

Second, this very fact would have been prominently stated in the order. Drastic orders of this nature are not drafted by experienced staff officers without the greatest care and an eye to their possible capture by the enemy.

Third, if it was necessary to avoid the risks attendant on standing by or surfacing, not only would this have been stated but there would have been no question of taking any prisoners at all, except possibly in circumstances where virtually no risk in surfacing was to be apprehended.

Fourth, the final sentence of the first paragraph would have read very differently.

Fifth, if, in fact, and the prosecution do not for one moment accept it, the defendant did not mean to enjoin murder, his order was so worded that he cannot escape the responsibility which attaches to such a document.

My Lord, I would call my first witness, Peter Heisig.

(Peter Josef Heisig took the stand.)

BY THE PRESIDENT:

Q. What is your name?

A. My name is Peter Josef Heisig.

THE PRESIDENT: say this: "I swear by God the Almighty and Omniscient that I will speak the pure truth and will withhold nothing and add nothing."
(The witness repeated the oath in German.)
DIRECT EXAMINATION BY COLONEL PHILLIMORE:
Q. Peter Josef Heisig, are you an Oberleutnant zur See in Germany?

A. I am an Oberleutnant zur See in the German Navy.

Q. Were you captured on the 27th December, 1944, and now held as a prisoner of war?

A. Yes.

Q. Did you swear an affidavit on 27th November, 1945?

A. Yes.

Q. And is that your signature? *(A document, D-566 was submitted to the witness.)*

COLONEL PHILLIMORE: My Lord, that is the Document D-566.

A. That is the document I signed.

COLONEL PHILLIMORE: I put that in as Exhibit GB 201.

Q. Will you take your mind back to the autumn of 1942? What rank did you hold at that time?

A. I was a midshipman at the Second U-boat Training Division.

Q. Were you attending a course there?

A. I took part at the training course for U-boat officers of the watch.

Q. Do you remember the last day of the course?

A. On the last day of the course, Grand Admiral Donitz, who was then Commander-in-Chief of the U-boats, reviewed the Second Training Division.

Q. And what happened at the end of this tour?

A. At the end of his visit - not at the end of his visit, but rather during his visit, Gross Admiral Donitz made a speech to the officers of the Second U-boat Division.

Q. Can you fix the date of his visit?

A. I remember the approximate date; it must have been at the end of September or the beginning of October, 1942.

Q. Now, will you give the Tribunal - speaking slowly - an account of what Admiral Donitz said in his speech?

A. Grand Admiral Donitz said in his speech: The successes of the U-boats have diminished. Strong enemy air controls. account for that. New ack-ack guns have been developed, which will make it possible for the U-boats to fight off enemy aircraft in the future. Hitler had personally given him the assurance that U-boats, first of all branches, would be equipped with these ack-ack guns. It could be expected that the old successes would be reached again within a few months. Then Grand Admiral Donitz referred to his good relations with Hitler, and spoke about the German armament programme.

He answered an interpolated question regarding a newspaper article, according to which the United Nations were building more than a million tons of merchant shipping every month. He doubted, at first, the credibility of this estimate and said a figure given by President Roosevelt was the basis for it. Grand Admiral Donitz spoke shortly about Roosevelt as a person, about the American production programme, and the armament potential. He further mentioned that the Allies met with great difficulty in manning their ships. Seamen considered the route across the Atlantic very dangerous because German U- boats were sinking Allied ships in great numbers. Many of the Allied seamen had been torpedoed more than once. News like that is spreading and frightens seamen from going to sea again. Some of then even were trying to escape before a crossing of the Atlantic so that the Allied authorities were compelled, if necessary, to retain them aboard by force. Such observations would be favourable to the Germans. First, the fact that the Allies are manufacturing much commercial shipping; and, second, that the Allies have many difficulties in manning these newly built ships.

Grand Admiral Donitz concluded that the problem of the personnel represents a very serious matter for the Allies. The losses in personnel mean a special setback to the Allies, as, first, they have few reserves and second -

Q. I do not want to interrupt you, but did he say anything about rescues at all? You have told us about the Allied losses and how serious they were.

A. Yes, he mentioned rescues, but I would like to speak about that later.

Grand Admiral Donitz said that the losses of the Allies were heavy, first of all because they had no reserves and, second, because the training of new seamen requires a very long time. It is difficult for him to understand how submarines -

THE PRESIDENT: Colonel Phillimore, just a moment. I do not think we want to hear the whole of Admiral Donitz' speech. We want to hear the material part of it.

COLONEL PHILLIMORE:

Q. Now, you have dealt with the question of losses. Will you come to the crucial part of the speech, at the end, and deal with that? What did the Grand Admiral go on to say?

DR. THOMA (Counsel for defendant Rosenberg): The testimony of the witness does not concern me directly, but I have certain problems. According to German law, German criminal law, the witness has to tell everything that he knows on the matter. When asked about a speech made by Grand Admiral Donitz, he should not, at least according to German law, report only those things to the Tribunal which, in the opinion of the prosecution, are unfavourable to the defendant. I believe this principle should apply in these proceedings also whenever a witness is questioned.

THE PRESIDENT: The Tribunal is not bound by German law. I have already said that the Tribunal does not desire to hear from this witness all of Admiral Donitz' speech.

It will be open to any of the counsel for the defendants to cross-examine this witness. Your intervention is therefore entirely unnecessary.

COLONEL PHILLIMORE:

Q. Now, will you deal with the crucial parts of the Grand Admiral's speech?

A. Grand Admiral Donitz continued his speech as follows: Under the given situation he could not understand how German U-boats, contrary to their own safety, could let the crews be saved; it would be absolutely working for the enemy, and these rescued crews would sail again on new ships.

Now total war at sea was to be instituted. The men - the seamen - as well as the ships - were to be a target for the U-boats, and through this it was to be made impossible for the Allies to use this personnel again on a new ship. On the other hand, it was to be expected that in America and the other Allied countries a strike was likely, for already a part of the seamen did not want to go back to sea.

Now if, according to our tactics, the sea war were to be harsher, it would have heavy repercussions along those lines. If this is considered harsh, we should also remember that our wives and our families at home are being bombed.

That was the speech of Grand Admiral Donitz in respect to its main points.

Q. Now, about how many officers were present and heard that speech?

A. I have nothing practical to give you about the number of men, I can only give you an estimate. I would say, roughly, 120 officers.

COLONEL PHILLIMORE: My Lord, the witness is available for cross-examination.

THE PRESIDENT: Does the United States prosecutor wish to ask any question?

(No response.)

The Soviet prosecutor?

(No response.)

The French prosecutor?

(No response.)

Now, any of the defendants' counsel may cross-examine the witness.

DR. KRANZBUEHLER (Counsel for defendant Donitz): I represent Grand Admiral Donitz.

THE PRESIDENT: Counsel will understand that what I said to Dr. Thoma was not intended to interfere with your cross-examination; it was only intended to save time. The Tribunal did not desire to hear unimportant passages in the defendant Donitz' speech. Therefore, they did not want to hear them from this witness. However, you are at liberty to ask any questions that you please.

CROSS-EXAMINATION BY DR. KRANZBUEHLER:

Q. Oberleutnant Heisig, you yourself took part in an action against the enemy?

A. Yes.

Q. On which boat were you, and who was your commander?

A. I was on U-877 and Finkeisen was the Kapitanleutnant.

Q. Please repeat your answer.

A. I was on U-877, and the commander was Kapitanleutnant Finkeisen.

Q. Were you successful?

A. Our boat was sunk when cruising in the zone of combat.

Q. Before you had ever sunk an enemy ship?

A. Yes.

Q. The boat was sunk by which enemy weapon?

A. Depth charges sank us. Two Canadian frigates had sighted our U-boat and destroyed it through depth bombs.

Q. Your testimony to-day differs slightly from the statement that you made on the 27th November, and in an essential point. How did you come to make this statement of the 27th November?

A. I made the statement in order to help my comrades who were put before a court martial in Hamburg and sentenced to death for the murder of ship-wrecked sailors.

Q. Your declaration, your affidavit, starts by stating that you had received reports that German sailors were accused of murder, and you felt yourself duty-bound to give the following affidavit.

Which report had you received, and when?

A. At the beginning of the Hamburg proceedings against Kapitanleutnant Eck and his officers I was a prisoner of war in England. I understood from the radio and from the newspapers that these officers were to be sentenced. Knowing one of these accused officers very well, a Lieutenant Hoffmann, having conversed with him on this subject, repeatedly, two or three times, I felt it my duty to come to his assistance and to help him by my testimony.

Q. In your hearing on the 27th November were you not told that the death sentence against Eck and Hoffmann had already been pronounced?

A. I do not know whether it was on the 27th November. I know only that I was told here of the fact that the death sentence had been carried out. The date I cannot remember; I was in several hearings.

Q. Can you, having knowledge of these connections, still maintain that the speech given by Grand Admiral Donitz made some remark concerning the shooting of shipwrecked sailors?

A. No; we gathered that from his words, that total war was to be carried on against ships and men, from his reference to the bombings. We assumed that, and I talked about it to my comrades on the way back. We were convinced that Admiral Donitz meant that. He did not express it clearly.

Q. Did you speak to any of your superiors at the school about this point?

A. On the same day I left school. But I can remember that one of my superiors, whose name I do not recall - and I do not recall in which connection I had this conversation - did speak about the same topic. We were advised that officers were to be at the bridge ready to annihilate shipwrecked sailors, should this possibility arise, and should it be necessary.

Q. One of your superiors told you that?

A. Yes, but I cannot remember in which connection and where. I received plenty of advice from my superiors, and on many things.

Q. Was it at school?

A. No; I left school the same day.

Q. At school were you advised on the permanent orders of war?

A. Yes, we were.

Q. Was there one word in these standing orders that shipwrecked sailors were to be shot or their rescue apparatus destroyed?

A. Nothing was said with regard to that in the regulations, but from an innuendo of Captain Rollmann, then the chief of our officers' company, I felt entitled to assume that a short time prior to that some order had arrived by telegram that rescue measures were prohibited and that, on the other hand, sea warfare should be fought with radical means. That is, it was to be carried on in a harsher manner.

Q. Do you see in the prohibition of rescue measures the same thing as in the shooting of shipwrecked sailors?

A. We came to this -

Q. Please answer my question. Does it mean the same to you?

A. No.

Q. Thank you.

DR. KRANZBUEHLER: I have no further questions.

THE PRESIDENT: Dr. Thoma, I am afraid the Tribunal will have to adjourn now, and I have an announcement to make. You may cross-examine to-morrow.

DR. THOMA: Thank you.

THE PRESIDENT: As I have already said, the Tribunal will not sit in open session this afternoon.

The announcement that I have to make is in connection with the organisations which are alleged to be criminal under Article 9 of the Charter, and this is the announcement:

The Tribunal has been giving careful consideration to the duty imposed upon it by Article 9 of the Charter.

It is difficult to determine the manner in which the representatives of the named organisations shall be permitted to appear in accordance with Article 9, without considering the exact nature of the case presented for the prosecution.

For this reason, the Tribunal has come to the conclusion that, at this stage of the trial, with many thousands of applications being made, the case for the prosecution should be defined with more precision than appears in the Indictment.

In these circumstances, therefore, it is the intention of the Tribunal to invite argument from the counsel for the prosecution and for the defence, at the conclusion of the case by all prosecutors, in regard to the questions hereinafter set forth.

The questions which need further consideration are as follows: 1. The Charter does not define a criminal organisation, and it is therefore necessary to examine the test of criminality which must be applied, and to decide the nature of the evidence to be admitted.

Many of the applicants who have made requests to be heard assert that they were conscripted into the organisation, or that, they were ignorant of the criminal purposes of the organisation, or that they were innocent of any unlawful acts.

It will be necessary to decide whether such evidence ought to be received to rebut the charge of the criminal character of the organisation, or whether such evidence ought more properly to be received at the subsequent trials under Article 10 of the Charter, when the organisations have been declared criminal, if the Tribunal so decides.

2. The question of the precise time within which the named organisation is said to have been criminal is vital to the decision of the Tribunal.

The Tribunal desires to know from the prosecution at this stage whether it is intended to adhere to the limits of time set out in the Indictment.

3. The Tribunal desires to know whether, in the light of the evidence, any class of persons included within the named organisations should be excluded from the scope of the declaration, and which, if any.

In the indictment of the Leadership Corps of the Nazi Party, the prosecution have reserved the right to request that political leaders of subordinate grades or ranks, or of other types or classes, be exempted from further proceedings without prejudice to other proceedings or actions against them.

Is it the intention of the prosecution to make any such request? If so, it should be done now.

4. The Tribunal would be glad if the prosecution would also:

(a) summarise in respect of each named organisation the elements which in their opinion justify the charge of being a criminal organisation;

(b) indicate what acts on the part of individual defendants, indicted in this trial - in the sense used in Article 9 of the Charter - justify declaring the groups or organisations, of which they are members, to be criminal organisations;

(c) submit in writing a summary of proposed findings of fact as to each organisation, with respect to which a finding of criminality is asked.

The Tribunal hopes it is not necessary to say to the prosecution that it is not seeking to interfere with the undoubted right of the prosecution to present its case in its own way, in the light of the full knowledge of all the documents and facts which it possesses, but the duty of the Tribunal under Article 9 of the Charter makes it essential at this time to have the case clearly and precisely defined.

This announcement will be communicated to the Chief Prosecutors and to Defence Counsel in writing.

(The Tribunal adjourned until 15th January, 1946, at 10.00 hours.)

Thirty-Fourth Day: Tuesday, January 15th, 1946

THE PRESIDENT: Do any of the other counsel for the defence wish to cross-examine this witness (referring to Peter Joseph Heisig, interrogated the previous day)?
(There was no response.)
Then, Colonel Phillimore, do you wish to re-examine?
COLONEL PHILLIMORE: No, my Lord, I have no further questions.
THE PRESIDENT: Then the witness can go.
COLONEL PHILLIMORE: Before I call my second witness, Karl-Heinz Moehle, an affidavit by him is the next document in the document book.
(Karl-Heinz Moehle took the stand.)
THE PRESIDENT:
Q. What is your name?
A. Karl-Heinz Moehle.
Q. Will you repeat this oath: "I swear by God the Almighty and Omniscient that I will speak the pure truth and will withhold and add nothing."
(The witness repeated the oath in German.)
THE PRESIDENT: You can sit down if you wish.
DIRECT EXAMINATION BY COLONEL PHILLIMORE:
Q. Karl-Heinz Moehle, you held the rank of Corvette Captain in the German Navy?
A. Yes, Sir.
Q. Did you serve in the German Navy since 1930?
A. Yes, Sir.
Q. Will you tell the Tribunal what decorations you hold?
A. I hold the General Service Cross, the Iron Cross Second Class, the Iron Cross First Class, the Knights Cross, and the German Cross in Silver.
Q. Did you swear to an affidavit covering a statement you have made on 21st July, 1945?
A. Yes, Sir.
Q. I show you that document and ask you to say whether that is your affidavit.
(Document 382-PS was submitted to this witness.)
A. *(Looking at paper)* Yes, this is my affidavit which I swore to.
COLONEL PHILLIMORE: I put that document in, which is 382-PS, and it becomes Exhibit GB 202.
Q. In the autumn of 1942 were you head of the Fifth U-Boat Flotilla?
A. Yes, I was.
Q. Were you stationed at Kiel?
A. Yes, Sir.
Q. How long did you hold that appointment altogether?
A. For four years.
Q. Was that from June, 1941, until the capitulation?

A. That is correct.

Q. What were your duties as commander of that flotilla?

A. My main duties as chief, covered the fitting out of U- boats which were to be sent to the front, and giving them the orders as well as necessary equipment.

Q. Had you any special responsibility to U-boat commanders in respect of the orders?

A. Yes, Sir, I was responsible for outgoing U-boat commanders knowing all new orders of the U-Boat Command.

Q. Had you any responsibility in explaining the orders?

A. The orders of the U-Boat Command were always very clear and unambiguous. If there were any ambiguities I used to clarify them at the Command itself.

Q. Did you personally see commanders before they went out on patrol?

A. Yes, each commander, before leaving for the front, was briefed.

Q. I will go back if I may, for two or three questions. Did you personally see commanders before they went out on patrol?

A. Yes, Sir, each commander before sailing on patrol was briefed in a session at my office.

Q. And what did that briefing session consist of? Were there any questions on the orders?

A. Yes, Sir, all experiences of previous patrols and any questions of equipment, fitting out, were discussed with the commander at that session. Also, the commanders had an opportunity at the briefing to clarify any ambiguities which might have existed in their minds.

Q. Apart from your briefing sessions, did commanders also go to Admiral Donitz' headquarters for briefing?

A. As far as it was possible, that was done, especially after the Commander-in-Chief of the U-boat arm had transferred his office from Paris to Berlin.

Q. Do you remember an order in the autumn of 1942 dealing with lifeboats?

A. Yes, Sir; in September, 1942, 1 received a wireless message addressed to all commanders at sea, and it dealt with that question.

Q. I show you this document - my Lord, that is the exhibit I have already put in as GB 199.

THE PRESIDENT: What other number has it?

COLONEL PHILLIMORE: It is D-630.

Q. Is that the order you are referring to?

A. Yes, that is the order.

Q. From the time when you were captured until last Friday had you seen that order?

A. No, Sir.

Q. It follows, I think, that the account of the order in your statement was given from recollection?

A. Yes, Sir, only from recollection.

Q. Now, after you got that order did you go to Admiral Donitz' headquarters?

A. Yes, at my next visit to headquarters, where, on receipt of the order, I discussed it with Captain Kuppisch, who was a specialist on the staff of the U-Boat Command.

Q. Will you tell the Tribunal what was said at that meeting?

A. At that meeting I asked Corvette Captain Kuppisch how the ambiguity contained in that order - or I might say, lack of clarity - should be cleared up and defined. He explained the order by two illustrations.

The first example was that of a U-boat in the Outer Bay of Biscay. It was sailing on patrol when it sighted a rubber dinghy carrying survivors of a British plane. Sailing on patrol, i.e., being fully equipped, the U-boat could not take the crew of the plane on board, although, especially at that time, it appeared very desirable to bring back home specialists from shot-down aeroplane crews for useful interrogations. So the commander of the U-boat made a wide circle and continued his patrol. When he returned from his patrol he reported this case to the staff of the Commander-in-Chief of the U-boat arm.

The staff officers upbraided him, saying that, were he unable to bring these specialists home, the right thing to do would have been to attack them, for it could be expected that, in twenty-four hours at the latest, the dinghy would be rescued by British reconnaissance forces, and they -

Q. I do not quite get what you said would have been the correct action to take. You were saying the correct thing to do would have been -

A. The right thing to do would have been to fight these specialists since it was not possible to rescue them, as it could be expected that this aeroplane crew would be found and rescued within a short time by British reconnaissance forces. In the meantime the crew could already have been on another patrol and might have destroyed one or two German boats. The second example -

Q. Did he give you any second example?

A. Yes, Sir. The second example I am going to recount now:

During the first month of the U-boat warfare against the United States a great quantity of tonnage - I do not recollect the exact figure - had been sunk in the shallow waters off the American coast. In these sinkings the crews, for the greater part, were rescued, because of the proximity of land. That was exceedingly regrettable, as the merchant marine not only required tonnage but also crews, and in the meantime these crews were able to man newly built ships.

Q. You have told us about the ambiguity of the order. Are you familiar with the way Admiral Donitz worded his orders?

A. I do not quite understand the question.

Q. Are you familiar with the way Admiral Donitz normally worded his orders?

A. Yes. In my opinion, the order should have read like this: It is pointed out again that, in order to secure the safety of the submarines, rescue measures should not be taken. This is how the order would have been worded - if only rescue measures were to have been forbidden. Therefore -

Q. Are you saying that if it had been intended only to prohibit rescue measures it would have been sufficient to refer to the previous order?

A. Yes, Sir, that would have been enough.

Q. Was that previous order also marked "top secret"?

A. I do not remember that exactly.

Q. What was the propaganda at the time with regard to crews?

A. The propaganda at that time said that the enemy had great difficulties in finding sufficient crews for the mercantile navy and -

THE PRESIDENT: The question as to the propaganda at that time is too general a question for him to answer.

COLONEL PHILLIMORE: If your Honour pleases, I will not press it.

Q. From your knowledge of the way orders were worded, can you tell the Tribunal what you understood this order to mean?

A. It meant, in my own opinion, that rescue measures remained prohibited, that on the other hand it would be desirable that in the case of sinkings of merchantmen there should be no survivors.

Q. And was it because you understood this to be the meaning that you went to Admiral Donitz's headquarters?

A. I did not go to the headquarters of the U-boat Command on account of this order alone; these visits took place rather frequently in order to discuss other questions also, and in order to have the opportunity of being constantly informed on the ideas and opinions of the U-boat Command which I had to transmit to the commanders.

Q. How did you brief commanders on this order?

A. At these briefing sessions I read the wording of the radio message to the commanders without making any commentary. In a few instances commanders have asked me later about the meaning of the message. Then I let them know the two examples as they had been told to me at headquarters.

However, I added that "The Flag Officer U-boats cannot give you such an order officially; everybody has to act according to his own conscience."

Q. Do you remember an order about rescue ships?

A. Yes, Sir.

Q. Can you say what the date of that order was?

A. I do not remember the exact date. However, I think the order was given at the same time as the order of 17th September, 1942.

COLONEL PHILLIMORE: May the witness see the Document D-663 which I put in yesterday?

THE PRESIDENT: Yes.

COLONEL PHILLIMORE: It is the German copy of the document that I am showing him; the original is being held.

(Document D-663 was submitted to the witness.)

THE WITNESS: Yes, Sir, I recognise that order.

Q. You will note that the date on that document is 7th October, 1943.

A. Yes, this order is laid down there in the general Operational Order "Atlantic" No. 56. According to my recollection, this order was already contained in the previous Operational Order 54. It covers the general radius of instructions.

THE PRESIDENT: Colonel Phillimore, is that order in the index here?

COLONEL PHILLIMORE: Yes, my Lord, that is Document D-663, which I put in yesterday as Exhibit GB 200. If it is omitted from the index, it is because, as your Lordship will remember, it is the document we have just received, as I explained yesterday.

Your Lordship will remember the order; it deals with rescue ships attached to convoys, and it was the last sentence to which I referred.

THE PRESIDENT: Yes, I only wanted to get the words of it.

COLONEL PHILLIMORE: Yes, Sir, I have the original here now, and if it is thought necessary the witness may see it, but he has seen a copy.

Q. Do you remember an order about entries in logs?

A. Yes, Sir. At the time - the exact date I do not remember - it had been ordered that sinkings and other acts which were in contradiction to international conventions should not be entered in the log, but should be reported orally after return to the home port.

Q. Would you care to tell us why it is that you are giving evidence in this case?

A. Yes, Sir; because when I was taken prisoner it was claimed that I was the author of these orders, and I do not want to have this charge connected with my name.

COLONEL PHILLIMORE: My Lord, the witness is available for examination by my colleagues and for cross-examination.

THE PRESIDENT: Does any counsel for any defendant wish to ask the witness any questions ?

CROSS-EXAMINATION BY DR. KRANZBUEHLER (Counsel for defendant Donitz):

Q. Corvette Captain Moehle, since when have you been in the U-boat arm?
A. Since the end of 1936.
Q. Do you know Grand Admiral Donitz personally?
A. Yes.
Q. Since when?
A. Since October, 1937.
Q. Do you see him here in this room?
A. Yes.
Q. Where?
A. To the left at the back.
Q. Do you know Grand Admiral Donitz as an Admiral to whom none of his subordinates could speak?
A. No.
Q. Or was it the opposite way?
A. He could be reached by everybody at any time.
Q. Have you been yourself on patrol as commander of a U-boat?
A. Yes, on nine occasions.
Q. From when to when?
A. From the beginning of the war until April, 1941.
Q. How many ships did you sink?
A. I sank twenty ships.
Q. After sinking ships, have you destroyed the rescue possibilities or have you fired at the survivors?
A. No.
Q. Did you have an order to do that?
A. No.
Q. Was it dangerous to the U-boat? Had the danger passed for a U-boat after the attack on a merchantman?
A. No, the danger to the U-boat is not passed when the attack is over.
Q. Why not?
A. Because in most instances when a ship is sunk, the ship is able to send radio messages with its position, and therefore in the last minute it is able to get other ships to the spot.
Q. Is there any principle in the U-boat arm to the effect that fighting comes before rescuing?
A. I never heard of that principle so formulated.
Q. Prior to the order of September, 1942, did you know of any other orders in which rescuing was prohibited when connected with danger to the U-boat?
A. Yes, but I do not know when and in which documents this order was laid down.

It had been ordered that, as a matter of principle, the safety of their own boat was the main concern.

Q. Was this ordered only once, or on several instances?

A. That I cannot say.

Q. Do you know that the order of September, 1942, was given in consequence of an incident in which German U-boats, contrary to orders, had undertaken rescue measures?

A. Yes, Sir.

Q. And the U-boats were then attacked by Allied aircraft?

A. Yes, Sir.

Q. A minute ago you classified the order of September, 1942, as ambiguous, did you not?

A. Yes, Sir.

Q. You interpreted it to the commanders in the sense that the order should comprise the destruction of rescue facilities and of its crews?

A. No, not quite, since I gave the two examples to the commanders only if they made an inquiry, and they themselves could draw that conclusion from these two examples.

Q. In which sentence of the order do you see a hidden request to kill survivors or to destroy rescue facilities? Just a second, I shall read to you a sentence of the order. I read from the Document D-630:

> "(1) No attempt of any kind must be made at rescuing crews of ships sunk, and this includes picking up persons in the water and putting them in lifeboats, righting capsized lifeboats, and handing over food and water. These are absolutely forbidden."

Do you see it in this sentence?

A. No.

Q. "All rescue measures contradict the most primitive demands of warfare that ships and crews should be destroyed."

Do you see that in this sentence?

A. Yes.

Q. Does that sentence contain anything as to the destruction of shipwrecked sailors?

A. No, of crews.

Q. At the end of the order is the phrase "Be harsh." Have you heard that phrase here for the first time?

A. No.

Q. Was this phrase used by the Flag Officer of the U-boats in order to harden commanders and their crews against themselves?

A. Yes.

Q. You have discussed the order with Corvette Captain Kuppisch?

A. Yes.

Q. Do you remember that, exactly?

A. As far as I can rely upon my recollection after such a long time.

Q. Where did that conference take place?

A. At the staff of the U-Boat Command, probably in Paris.

Q. What position did Kuppisch occupy at the time?

A. As far as I can remember, he was the man in charge of enemy convoys, but I could not say that with any certainty.

Q. The superior officer of Kuppisch was Hessler?

A. Superior officer? I would not say so. Hessler was on the same level as Kuppisch, a specialist.

Q. Was Kuppisch's superior Admiral Godt?

A. Yes, in his capacity as Chief of Staff.

Q. Have you spoken to Captain Hessler or Admiral Godt or with the Grand Admiral himself with regard to the interpretation to be given to the order of September?

A. Whether I did with Hessler, I do not remember; but certainly not with Godt or the Grand Admiral himself.

Q. You said Capt. Kuppisch had told you of the opinion which was prevalent at the staff of the U-Boat Command with regard to the attitude taken towards aviators in the Bay of Biscay?

A. Yes.

Q. Did he tell you that it was the opinion of the Grand Admiral himself?

A. I do not remember that. It is too far back. To us, the chiefs of the flotillas, it was a matter of course, that the opinion expressed by a responsible member of the staff, in connection with interpretations, was the official opinion of the U-Boat Command. Admiral Godt was only approached personally in such cases where the Staff Specialists refused to commit themselves, and assume the responsibility for an answer.

Q. Did you not know that the incident with these airmen in the Bay of Biscay had really been just the opposite of what you described?

A. I do not understand.

Q. I continue: that the commander had been reproached because he did not bring home these airmen even if thus forced to end his patrol.

A. No, I do not know that.

Q. Did Corvette Captain Kuppisch tell you in that second example you mentioned, that the shipwrecked sailors should have been killed and rescue facilities near the American coast destroyed?

A. No, he only said it was regrettable that the crews had been rescued.

Q. And you concluded from that that it was desirable to kill the shipwrecked?

A. I did not draw any conclusions, since I passed on these examples without any commentary.

Q. Do you know the standing orders of the U-Boat Command? Do they contain the general principles of U-boat warfare?

A. Yes.

Q. Are there any orders in the standing orders directing or advising the killing of shipwrecked sailors or the destruction of rescue facilities?

A. As far as I know, no.

Q. What kind of secrecy was attached to these standing orders?

A. As far as I remember, "Geheime Kommandosache" - Top Secret.

Q. Do you remember that in Standing Order 511, the following was ordered:

DR. KRANZBUEHLER: Mr. President, I read from an order which I shall submit in evidence later on. I cannot do it now because I have not as yet the original with me.

"Standing Order of Flag Officer U-boats No. 511, 20th May, 1943.

Taking on board officers of sunken ships.

(1) As far as accommodation facilities on board permit, Captains and Chief Engineers of sunken ships are to be brought in. The enemy tries to thwart this intention and has issued the following order: '(a) Masters are not allowed to identify themselves when questioned, but should if possible use sailors selected especially for this purpose. (b) Crew has to state that Masters and Chief Engineers remained on board.' If in spite of energetic questioning it is not possible to find the Masters or the Chief Engineers, then the other ship's officers should be taken aboard.

(2) Masters and officers of neutral ships, which, according to Standing Order No. 101, can be sunk (for instance, Swedish ships outside Goteborg Traffic), are not to be brought in because internment of these officers would violate International Law.

(3) In case the ship's officers cannot be taken prisoner, members of the crew should be taken along, as far as accommodation facilities and further operations permit, for the purpose of interrogation for military and propagandist purposes.

(4) In case of the sinking of a single cruising destroyer, corvette, or trawler, try at all events to take prisoners, if that can be done without endangering the boat. Interrogation of the prisoners at interrogation camps can produce valuable hints as to anti-submarine tactics, devices and weapons used by the enemy; the same applies to air crews of shot down planes."

BY DR. KRANZBUEHLER:

Q. Do you know that order?

A. The order is familiar to me.

Q. Do you know the order 513?

"Standing Order of U-Boat Command, 1st June, 1944, Bringing in of Prisoners.

(1) Statements of prisoners are the safest and best source of information regarding enemy tactics, weapons, location sets and methods, and questioning of prisoners from planes and destroyers may be of the greatest importance to us; therefore, as far as possible and without endangering the boat, the utmost is to be done to take such prisoners.

(2) As prisoners are extremely willing to talk when captured, interrogate them at once on board. It is of special interest to know the manner of locating U-boats by aircraft, whether by radar or by passive location; for instance, by ascertaining, through electricity or heat, the location of the boat. Immediately report prisoners taken, in order to hand them over to returning boats."

Do you know that order?

Have you noticed and tried to clarify a contradiction between those orders concerning the rescue of air crews in each instance, and the story you told about the destruction of air crews?

A. No, because the order of September, 1942, retains the order with regard to bringing in as prisoners the masters and the chief engineers.

Q. Did you hear of any instance in which a U-boat has brought in masters and chief engineers but has killed the rest of the crew?

A. No.

Q. Do you consider it at all possible that such an order can be given-that is, that part of the crew should be rescued and the rest of the crew should be killed?

A. No, Sir. Such an order cannot be given.

Q. Did you hear that a U-boat commander, on the basis of your briefings, had destroyed rescue facilities or had killed shipwrecked sailors?
A. No.
Q. Was it permitted to attack neutral vessels outside the fixed blockaded areas?
A. Only in case they were not marked as neutrals according to specifications.
Q. Was the Flag Officer U-Boat Command very severe in enforcing this order concerning neutral ships?
A. Since such cases are not known to me, I cannot say anything on that subject.
Q. Do you know that the commanders were threatened with court martial if they did not obey the orders given for the protection of neutrals?
A. Yes; I remember one case which happened in the Caribbean Sea.
Q. Do you remember an order of 1944 directing that neutral ships were to be stopped and searched?
A. Yes, it was ordered - I do not remember the date - that, in particular, Spanish and Portugese ships in the North Atlantic should be stopped and searched.
Q. Did you pass on that order to the commanders?
A. As far as I recollect, this order was given in writing and is contained in one of the official sets of orders. I have passed on orders to commanders only in instances where they were not contained in a set of orders.
Q. In passing that order on, did you make an addition as to whether that order should be executed or not?
A. Yes, I remember that I said - when that order came by radio and the commanders did not know of it yet - that they should be exceedingly careful, as far as the stopping of neutrals was concerned, since there existed always the danger that a neutral ship might report the position of the U-boat by radio. Owing to the air superiority of the enemy in the North Atlantic, it would always be safer or better not to be compelled to carry out these stoppings.
Q. Had you orders to make such additional remarks?
A. No. As far as I remember, one of the members of the staff - I think it was Captain Hessler - told me that he emphasised that any stopping of ships, including neutrals, involved increased danger to the U-boat.
Q. Because of the air superiority?
A. Yes.
Q. Has your attention been called to the order concerning the "so-called rescue ships"? Do you remember that?
A. Yes.
Q. Were these rescue ships recognised under International Law as hospital ships, with special markings?
A. As far as I know, no.
Q. What orders existed concerning hospital ships?
A. Where these orders were laid down and whether in writing or not - I do not remember-I only remember that frequently the Flag Officer U-Boats reminded the commanders of the absolute inviolability of hospital ships.
Q. Do you know of any case in which a hospital ship was attacked by U-boats?
A. No; I do not know of such a case.
Q. If the B.D.U. had been interested in destroying helpless human beings, in violation of International Law, the destruction of hospital ships would have been an excellent measure, do you not think so?

A. Without any doubt.

DR. KRANZBUEHLER: No further questions.

THE PRESIDENT: Does any other defence counsel wish to cross-examine this witness?

(No response.)

BY THE TRIBUNAL (Mr. Biddle):

Q. Did you ever save any of the survivors of the vessels that you torpedoed?

A. No, Sir. I have not been in a position to do that, due to the military situation.

Q. You mean to say it was dangerous to your boat to do it?

A. Not only that. A great part of the sinkings which I did took place in a convoy or in a high, rough sea, so that it was impossible to undertake any rescue measures.

THE TRIBUNAL (Mr. Biddle): That is all.

THE PRESIDENT: Colonel Phillimore, do you wish to re-examine?

COLONEL PHILLIMORE: My Lord, I have about three questions.

THE PRESIDENT: Very well.

RE-EXAMINATION BY COLONEL PHILLIMORE:

Q. When you were a U-boat commander yourself, what were the orders with regard to rescue?

A. At the beginning of the War we had been told that the safety of your own boat was the decisive thing, and that the boat should not be endangered by rescue measures. Whether these orders had been laid down in writing at the outbreak of the War I do not remember.

Q. When you got this order of 17th September, 1942, did you take it merely as prohibiting rescue or as going further?

A. When I received that order, I noticed that it was not unambiguous, as orders of the B.D.U. normally were, that in this order there was a definite ambiguity.

Q. You have not answered my question. Did you take the order to mean that a U-boat commander should merely abstain from rescue measures, or as something further?

A. I interpreted that order to go further in some way, although not as an actual order; but that it was considered desirable.

Q. The instance you were given about the Bay of Biscay, had you any knowledge of the facts of that incident?

A. No, the surrounding circumstances of that case were not known to me.

Q. What were the actual words in which you passed that order on to commanders?

A. I told the commanders, literally the following: "We approach now a very delicate and difficult chapter; it is the question of the treatment of life-boats. The Flag Officer U-Boats has issued the following radio message in September, 1942." Thereupon I read the radio message of September, 1942, in full.

In most instances the chapter was then closed; no commander had any question to ask. In some few instances the commanders asked, "How should that order be interpreted?" In that case I gave the two examples as a means of interpretation. And then I added that officially such a thing cannot be ordered, that everybody has to reconcile that with his own conscience.

Q. Do you remember any comment being made by commanding officers after they had read the order?

A. Yes, Sir. Several commanders, following the reading of the order without any commentary being given, uttered the opinion, "That is very clear, but damned hard."

COLONEL PHILLIMORE: My Lord, I have no further questions.

THE PRESIDENT: The Tribunal will adjourn for 10 minutes.

(A recess was taken.)

COLONEL PHILLIMORE: My Lord, I would not put before the Tribunal two cases where that order of the 17th September, 1942, was apparently put into effect. The first case is set out at the next document in the document book, which is D- 645. My Lord, I put that document in and it becomes Exhibit GB 203.

It is a report of the sinking of a steam trawler, a fishing trawler, the Noreen Mary, which was sunk by U-247 on 5th July, 1944. The first page of the document contains an extract from the log of the U-boat. The time reference 19-43 on the document is followed by an account of the firing of two torpedoes which missed, and then, at 20.55, the log reads:

"Surfaced.

Fishing vessels: (Bearings given of 3 ships).

Engaged the nearest. She stops after three minutes."

Then there is an account of a shot fired as the trawler lay stopped, and then, the final entry:

"Sunk by flak, with shots into her side. Sank by the stern."

The tribunal will notice there is no mention in the log of any action against the torpedoed or the shipwrecked seamen.

THE PRESIDENT: Why is it entered as 5.7.1943?

COLONEL PHILLIMORE: My Lord, that is an error.

THE PRESIDENT: An error?

COLONEL PHILLIMORE: It is a typing error. I should have pointed it out.

My Lord, the next page of the document is a comment on the action by the U-boat command, and the last line reads:

"Recognised success: Fishing vessel Noreen Mary sunk by flak."

Then there is an affidavit by James MacAlister, who was a deckhand on board the Noreen Mary at the time of the sinking. My Lord, reading the last paragraph on the first page of the affidavit. He has dealt earlier with having seen the torpedo tracks which missed the trawler. The last paragraph reads:

"At 21.10 hours, while we were still trawling, the submarine surfaced on our starboard beam, about 50 yards to the North-east of us, and without any warning immediately opened fire on the ship with a machine gun. We were 18 miles West from Cape Wrath, on a North- westerly course making 3 knots. The weather was fine and clear, sunny, with good visibility. The sea was smooth, with light airs."

My Lord, then there is an account of the firing in the next paragraph, and then, if I might read from the second paragraph on Page 2.

THE PRESIDENT: Why not read the first?

COLONEL PHILLIMORE: If your Lordship please:

"When the submarine surfaced I saw men climbing out of the conning tower. The skipper thought at first the submarine was British, but when she opened fire he immediately slackened the brake to take the weight off gear (that is, the trawler), and increased to full speed, which was about 10 knots. The submarine chased us, firing her machine gun, and with the first rounds killed two or three men, including the skipper, who were on deck and had not had time to take cover. The submarine then started using a heavier gun from her conning tower, the first shot from which burst the boiler, enveloping everything in steam and stopping the ship.

By now the crew had taken cover, but in spite of this all but four were killed. The submarine then commenced to circle round ahead of the vessel, and passed down her port side with both guns firing continuously. We were listing slowly to port all the time but did not catch fire.

The mate and I attempted to release the lifeboat, which was aft, but the mate was killed whilst doing so, so I abandoned the attempt. I then went below into the pantry, which was below the waterline, for shelter. The ship was listing more and more to port, until finally at 22.10 she rolled right over and sank, and the only four men left alive on board were thrown into the sea. I do not know where the other three men had taken cover during this time, as I did not hear or see them until they were in the water.

I swam around until I came across the broken bow of our lifeboat, which, was upside down and managed to scramble on top of it. Even now the submarine did not submerge, but deliberately steamed in my direction and when only 60 to 70 yards away fired directly at me with a short burst from the machine gun. As their intention was quite obvious, I fell into the water and remained there until the submarine ceased firing and submerged, after which I climbed back onto the bottom of the boat. The submarine had been firing her guns for a full hour."

My Lord, then the affidavit goes on to describe the Second Engineer and others attempting to rescue themselves and to help each other, and then they were picked up by another trawler.

The last paragraph on that page:

"Whilst on board the Lady Madeleine the Second Engineer and I had our wounds dressed. I learned later that the Second Engineer had 48 shrapnel wounds, also a piece of steel wire 21 inches long embedded in his body."

And there is a sentence on which I do not rely, and the last sentence:

"I had 14 shrapnel wounds."

My Lord, and then the last two paragraphs of the affidavit:

"This is my fourth war-time experience, having served in the whalers Sylvester (mined) and New Seville (torpedoed), and the trawler Ocean Tide, which ran ashore.

As a result of this attack by U-boats, the casualties were six killed, two missing, two injured."

My Lord, the next document, D-647, I put in as Exhibit GB 204. My Lord, this is an extract from a statement given by the Second Officer of the ship Antonico, torpedoed, set afire, and sunk, on the 28th September, 1942, on the coast of French Guiana. The Tribunal will observe that the date of the incident is some eleven days after the issue of the order. My Lord, I would read from the words "that the witness saw the dead," slightly more than halfway down on the first page. An account has been given of the attack on the ship, which by then was on fire:

"That the witness saw the dead on the deck of the Antonico as he and his crew tried to swing out their lifeboat; that the attack was sudden, lasting almost 20 minutes; and that the witness already in the lifeboat tried to get away from the side of the Antonico in order to avoid being dragged down by the said Antonico and also because she was the aggressor's target; that the night was dark, and it was thus difficult to see the submarine, but that the fire aboard the Antonico lit up the locality in which she was submerging, helping the enemy to see the two lifeboats trying to get away; that the enemy ruthlessly machine-gunned the defenceless sailors in No. 2 lifeboat, in which the witness found himself, and killed the Second Pilot Amoldo de Andrade de Lima, and wounded three of the crew; that the witness gave orders to his company to throw themselves overboard to save themselves from the bullets; in so doing, they were protected and out of sight behind the lifeboat, which was already filled with water; even so the lifeboat continued to be attacked, At that time the witness and his companions were about 20 metres in distance from the submarine."

My Lord, I have not got the U-boat's log in that case, but you may think that, in view of the order with regard to entries in logs, namely, that anything compromising should not be put in, it would be no more helpful than in the case of the previous incident.

My Lord, the next document, D-646/A, I put in as Exhibit GB 205. It is a monitored account of a talk by a German Naval War Reporter on the long wave propaganda service from Friesland. The broadcast was in English, and the date is 11th March, 1943. It is, if I may quote:

"Santa Lucia, in the West Indies, was an ideal setting for romance, but nowadays it was dangerous to sail in these waters - dangerous for the British and Americans and for all the coloured people who were at their beck and call. Recently a U-boat operating in these waters sighted an enemy windjammer. Streams of tracer bullets were poured into the sails and most of the Negro crew leaped overboard, Knowing that this might be a decoy ship, the submarine steamed cautiously to within 20 yards, when hand grenades were hurled into the rigging. The remainder of the Negroes then leaped into the sea. The windjammer sank. There remained only wreckage. Lifeboats packed with men, and sailors swimming. The sharks in the distance licked their teeth in expectation. Such was the fate of those who sailed for Britain and America."

My Lord, the next page of the document I do not propose to read. It is an extract from the log of the U-boat believed to have sunk this ship. It was in fact the U-105.

My Lord, I read that because, in my submission, it shows that it was the policy of the enemy at the start to seek to terrorise crews, and it fits in with the order with regard to rescue ships and the killing of seamen.

If I might say so, in view of the cross-examination, the prosecution do not complain of rescue ships being attacked. They are not entitled to protection. The point of the order was that they were to be given priority in attack, and the order, therefore, is closely allied with the order of the 17th September, 1942. In view of the Allied building programme, it had become imperative to prevent the ships being manned.

My Lord, I pass to the period after the defendant had succeeded the defendant Raeder. My Lord, the next document is 2098-PS. It has been referred to but not, I think, put in. I put it in formally as Exhibit GB 206. My Lord, I will not read it. It merely sets out that the defendant Raeder should have the equivalent rank of a Minister of the Reich, and I ask the Tribunal to infer that on succeeding Raeder the defendant Donitz would presumably have succeeded to that right.

THE PRESIDENT: This is from 1938 onward?

COLONEL PHILLIMORE: From 1938 onward.

The next document, D-648, I put in as Exhibit GB 207. It is an affidavit by an official, or rather it is an official report certified by an official of the British Admiralty.

The certificate is on the last page, and it sets out the number of meetings the dates of the meetings and those present, on the occasion of meetings between the defendant Donitz or his representative with Hitler, from the time that he succeeded Raeder until the end. The certificate states:

"I have compiled from them" - that is, from captured documents - "the attached list of occasions on which Admiral Donitz attended conferences at Hitler's headquarters. The list of other senior officials who attended the same conferences is added when this information was contained in the captured documents concerned. I certify that the list is a true extract from the collective documents which I have examined, and which are in the possession of the British Admiralty, London."

My Lord, I will not go through the list. I would merely call the Tribunal's attention to the fact that either Admiral Donitz or his deputy, Konteradmiral Voss, was present at each of these meetings; and that amongst those who were also constantly there were the defendants Speer, Keitel and Jodl, Ribbentrop and Goering, and also Himmler or his Lieutenants Fegelein or Kaltenbrunner.

My Lord, the inference which I ask the Tribunal to draw from the document is that from the time that he succeeded Raeder, this defendant was one of the rulers of the Reich, and was undoubtedly aware of all decisions, major decisions of policy.

My Lord, I pass to the next document, C-178, that has already been put in as Exhibit USA 544. It is an internal memorandum of the Naval War Staff, written by the division dealing with International Law to another division, and the subject is the order with regard to the shooting of Commandos of 18th October, 1942, with which the Tribunal, I think, are familiar.

The point of the document is that some doubt appeared to have arisen in some quarters with regard to the understanding of the order, and in the last sentence of the memorandum it is suggested, "As far as the Navy is concerned, it remains to be seen whether or not this case should be used to make sure, after a conference with the Commander-in-Chief of the Navy, that all departments concerned have an entirely clear conception regarding the treatment of members of Commando units."

My Lord, whether that conference took place or not I do not know. The document is dated some 11 days after this defendant had taken over from the defendant Raeder.

But the next document in the book, D-649, which I put in as Exhibit GB 208, is an instance of the Navy in July of that year, July, 1943, handing over to the S.D. for shooting, Norwegian and British naval personnel, whom the Navy decided came under the terms of the order. My Lord, it is an affidavit by a British barrister-at-law who served as judge advocate at the trial of the members of the S.D. who executed the order.

Paragraph I sets out that the deponent was judge advocate at the trial of 10 members of the S.D. by a military court held at the Law Courts, Oslo, Norway, which sat on Thursday, 29th November, 1945, and concluded its sitting on Tuesday, 4th December, 1945.

My Lord, the next paragraph sets out who convened the court, and the names of the prosecuting and defending counsel, and the third paragraph states:

"The accused were charged with committing a war crime, in that they at Ulven, Norway, in or about the month of July, 1943, in violation of the laws and usages of war, were concerned in the killing" - and then there follows the names of six personnel of the Norwegian Navy, including one officer, and one leading telegraphist of the Royal Navy, prisoners of war.

I might read from paragraph 4:

"There was evidence before the Court, which was not challenged by the defence, that Motor Torpedo Boat No. 345 set out from Lerwick in the Shetlands on a naval operation for the purpose of making torpedo attacks on German shipping off the Norwegian coast, and for the purpose of laying mines in the same area. The persons mentioned in the charge were all the crew of the torpedo boat."

Paragraph 5: "The defence did not challenge that each member of the crew was wearing uniform at the time of capture, and there was abundant evidence from many persons, several of whom were German, that they were wearing uniform at all times after their capture."

Paragraph 6: "On 27th July, 1943, the torpedo boat reached the island of Aspo off the Norwegian coast, north of Bergen. On the following day the whole of the crew were captured and were taken on board a German naval vessel which was under the command of Admiral von Schrader, the Admiral of the West coast. The crew were taken to Bergenhus where they had arrived by 11 p.m. on 28th July. The crew were there interrogated by Lieut. H. P. W. Fanger, a Naval Lieutenant of the Reserve, on the orders of Korvettenkdaitan Egon Drascher, both of the German Naval Intelligence Service. This interrogation was carried out upon the orders of the staff of the Admiral of the West coast. Lieut. Fanger reported to the Officer in Charge of the Intelligence Branch at Bergen that in his opinion all the members of the crew were entitled to be treated as prisoners of war, and that officer in turn reported both orally and in writing to the Sea Commander, Bergen, and in writing to the Admiral of the West coast.

Paragraph 7: The interrogation by the Naval Intelligence Branch was concluded in the early hours of 29th July, and almost immediately all the members of the crew were handed over on the immediate orders of the Sea Commander, Bergen, to Obersturmbannfuehrer of the S.D., Hans Wilhelm Blomberg, who was at that time Kommandeur of the Sicherheitspolizei at Bergen. This followed a meeting between Blomberg and Admiral von Schrader, at which a copy of the Fuehrer order of the 18th October, 1942, was shown to Blomberg. This order dealt with the classes of persons who were to be excluded from the protection of the Geneva Convention and were not to be treated as prisoners of war, but when captured were to be handed over to the S.D. Admiral von Schrader told Blomberg that the crew of this torpedo boat were to be handed over, in accordance with the Fuehrer order, to the S.D.

Paragraph 9: The S.D. then conducted their own interrogation -

THE PRESIDENT: You can summarise the rest, cannot you?

COLONEL PHILLIMORE: If your Lordship pleases.

My Lord, paragraph 9 described the interrogation by officials of the S.D., and that these officials took the same view as the Naval Intelligence officers, that the crew were entitled to be treated as prisoners of war; that despite this they were taken out and shot by an execution squad composed of members of the S.D.

Then there is a description of the disposal of the bodies.

My Lord, the last paragraph is perhaps important in connection with the case against the defendant Keitel.

THE PRESIDENT: Yes, read it.

COLONEL PHILLIMORE:

"(11) It appeared from the evidence that in March or April, 1945, an order from the Fuehrer Headquarters, signed by Keitel, was transmitted to the

German authorities in Norway. The substance of the order was that members of the crews of Commando raids who fell into German captivity were from that date to be treated as ordinary prisoners of war. This order referred specifically to the Fuehrer order referred to above."

The members of the Tribunal will of course have noted the date; it was time to put their affairs in order.

My Lord, the next document, C-158, I put in as Exhibit GB 209. It consists of two extracts from minutes of conference, on the 19th and 20tb February,

1945, conferences between the defendant Donitz and Hitler. If I might read the first and last sentence of the first extract:

"The Fuehrer is considering whether or not Germany should renounce the Geneva Convention."

That is, of course, the 1929 prisoners of war convention. And the last sentence:
"The Fuehrer orders the Commander-in-Chief of the Navy to consider the pros and cons of this step and to state his opinion as soon as possible."

Then the second extract; the defendant Donitz states his opinion in the presence of the defendant Jodl and the representative of the defendant Ribbentrop. It is the last two sentences on which I rely:

"On the contrary, the disadvantages" - that is, the disadvantages of renouncing the convention - "outweigh the advantages. Even from a general standpoint it appears to the Commander-in-Chief that this measure would bring no advantage. It would be better to carry out the measures considered necessary without warning, and at all costs to save face with the outer world."

My Lord, it is no small matter, that document, when one reflects that it was to that convention that we owe the fact that upwards of 165,000 British and 65,000 to 70,000 American prisoners of war were duly recovered at the end of the war. And to advocate breaching that convention, preferably without saying so, is not a matter to be treated lightly.

My Lord, the next document, C-171, I put in as Exhibit GB 210. It is another extract from the minutes of a meeting between the defendant Donitz and Hitler, the 1st July, 1944. The extract is signed by the defendant:

"Regarding the General Strike in Copenhagen, the Fuehrer says that the only weapon to deal with terror is terror. Court-martial proceedings create martyrs. History shows that the names of such men are on everybody's lips, whereas there is silence with regard to the many thousands who have lost their lives in similar circumstances without court-martial proceedings."

My Lord, the next document, C-195, I put in as Exhibit GB 211. It is a memorandum signed by the defendant, dated late in 1944. There is no specific date on the document, but it is late in 1944, in December, I think, of 1944. The distribution on the third page includes Hitler, Keitel, Jodl, Speer and the Supreme Command of the Air Force.

My Lord, if I might read the second paragraph. He is dealing with the review of German shipping losses.

"Furthermore, I propose reinforcing the shipyard working parties by prisoners from the concentration camps, and as a special measure for relieving the present shortage of coppersmiths, especially in U-boat construction, I propose to divert coppersmiths from the construction of locomotives to ship-building."

Then he goes on to deal with sabotage, and the last two paragraphs on that page are:

"Since, elsewhere, measures for exacting atonement taken against whole working parties amongst whom sabotage occurred, have proved successful, and, for example, the shipyard sabotage in France was completely suppressed, possibly similar measures for the Scandinavian countries will come under consideration."

THE PRESIDENT: Do you need to read any more than that?

COLONEL PHILLIMORE: My Lord, no. The last sentence of the document in the next page is:

"Item 2 of the summing-up reads: '12,000 concentration camp prisoners will be employed in the shipyards as additional labour (security service agrees to this).'" That is the S.D.

My Lord, this man was one of the rulers of Germany, and, in my submission, that document alone is sufficient to condemn him. It was not for nothing that at these meetings Himmler and his Lieutenants, Fegelein and Kaltenbrunner, were present.

My Lord, they were not there to discuss U-boats or the use of battleships. It is clear, in my submission, from this document that this defendant knew all about concentration camps and concentration camp labour, and as one of the rulers of Germany he must bear his full share of that responsibility.

My Lord, I pass to the last document, D-650, which I put in as Exhibit GB 212.

My Lord, this contains the orders issued by the defendant in April. The document, in my submission, shows the defendant's fanatical adherence to the Nazi creed, and his preparedness, even at that stage, to continue a hopeless war at the expense of human life and with the certainty of increased destruction and misery to the men, women and children of this country. I read the last paragraph on the second page:

"I therefore demand of the commanding officers of the Navy: That they clearly and unambiguously follow the path of military duty, whatever may happen. I demand of them that they stamp out ruthlessly all signs and tendencies among the men which endanger the following of this path."

Then he refers to an order:

"I demand from Senior Commanders that they should take just as ruthless action against any commander who does not do his military duty. If a commander does not think he has the moral strength to hold his position as a leader in this sense, he must report this immediately. He will then be used as a soldier in this fateful struggle, in some position in which he is not burdened with any tasks as a leader."

And then the last paragraph on that page, from the secret Baltic Order of the Day of 19th April, he gives an example of the type of under-officer who should be promoted:

"An example: In a prison camp of the auxiliary cruiser Cormorau, in Australia, a petty officer acting as camp senior officer, had all Communists, who made themselves noticeable among the inmates of the camp systematically done away with, in such a way that the guards did not notice it. This petty officer is sure of my full recognition for his decision and his execution. After his return, I shall certainly promote him, as he has shown that he is fitted to be a leader."

My Lord, of course the point is not whether the facts were true or not, but the type of order that he was issuing. My Lord, if I might just sum up, the defendant was no plain sailor, playing the part of a service officer, loyally obedient to the orders of the Government of the day; he was an extreme Nazi who did his utmost to indoctrinate the Navy and the German people with the Nazi creed. It is no coincidence that it was he who was chosen to succeed Hitler; not Goering, not Ribbentrop, not Goebbels, not Himmler. He played a big part in fashioning the U-boat, fleet, one of the most deadly weapons of aggressive war. He helped to plan and execute aggressive war, and we cannot doubt that he knew well that these wars were in deliberate violation of treaties. He was ready to stoop to any ruse where he thought he would not be found out, such as breaches of the Geneva Convention or of neutrality, where they might hope to maintain that sinking was due to a mine. He was ready to order, and did order, the murder of helpless survivors of sunken ships, an action only paralleled, by that of his Japanese ally.

My Lord, there can be few countries where widows or parents do not mourn for men of the merchant navies whose death was due to the callous brutality with which, at the orders of this man, the German U-boats did their work.

My Lord, my learned friend, Major Elwyn Jones, will now deal with the defendant Raeder.

MAJOR ELWYN JONES: May it please the Tribunal, it is my duty to present to the Tribunal the evidence against the creator of the Nazi Navy, the defendant Raeder. The allegations against him are set out in Appendix A of the Indictment at Pages 33 and 34, and the Tribunal will see that the defendant Raeder is charged with promoting and participating in the planning of the Nazi wars of aggression; with executing those plans; and with authorising, directing and participating in Nazi War Crimes, particularly war crimes arising out of sea warfare.

At the outset the Tribunal may find it convenient to look at Document 2888-PS, which is already before the Tribunal as Exhibit USA 13, which the Tribunal will find at Page 96 of the document book. That is a document which sets out the offices and positions held by the defendant Raeder. The Tribunal will see that he was born in 1876 and joined the German Navy in 1896. By 1915 he had become commander of the Cruiser Koln. In 1928 he became an admiral, chief of naval command, and head of the German Navy. In 1935 he became Commander-in-Chief of the Navy. In 1936, on Hitler's 47th birthday, he became General Admiral, a creation of Hitler's. In 1937 he received the high Nazi honour of golden badge of honour of the Nazi Party. In 1938 he became a member of the secret cabinet council. And in 1939 he reached the empyrean of Grand Admiral, a rank created by Hitler, who presented Raeder with a marshal's baton. In 1943 he became Admiral Inspector of the German Navy, which, as the Tribunal will shortly see, was a kind of retirement into oblivion, because from January, 1943 on, as the Tribunal has heard, Donitz was the effective commander of the German Navy.

In these eventful years of Raeder's command of the German Navy from 1928 to 1943 he played a vital role. I would like, in the first instance, to draw the Tribunal's attention to Raeder's part in building up the German Navy as an instrument of war to implement the Nazis' general plan of aggression.

The Tribunal is by now familiar with the steps by which the small navy permitted to Germany under the Treaty of Versailles was enormously expanded under the guidance of Raeder. I will do no more than to remind the Tribunal of some of the milestones upon Raeder's road to Nazi mastery of the seas, which mercifully he was unable to attain.

With regard to the story of Germany's secret rearmament in violation of the Treaty of Versailles, I would refer the Court to the Document C-156, which is already before the Court as Exhibit USA 41, and which the Tribunal will find at Page 26 of the document book. That document, as the Tribunal will remember, was "A history of the fight of the German Navy against Versailles, 1919 to 1935," which was published secretly by the German Admiralty in 1937. The Tribunal will remember that that history shows that before the Nazis came to power the German Admiralty was deceiving not only the governments of other countries, but its own legislature and, at one stage, its own government. Its secret measures of rearmament ranged from experimental U-boat and E-boat building to the creation of secret intelligence and finance organisations. I only propose to trouble the Tribunal with a reference to the last paragraph at Page 33 of the document book, which refers to the role of Raeder in this development. It is an extract from Page 75 of this Document C- 156, and it reads:

"The commander-in-chief of the Navy, Admiral Raeder, had received hereby a far-reaching independence in the building and development of the Navy. This was only hampered insofar as the previous concealment of rearmament had to be continued in consideration of the Versailles Treaty."

As an illustration of Raeder's concealment of rearmament, I would remind the Tribunal of the Document C-141, Exhibit USA 47, which is at Page 22 of the document book. In that document Raeder states that:

"In view of Germany's treaty obligations and the disarmament conference, steps must be taken to prevent the first E-Boat-Half-Flotilla from appearing openly as a formation of torpedo-carrying boats, as it was not intended to count these E-boats against the number of torpedo-carrying boats allowed us."

The next document, C-135, which will be Exhibit GB 213, and which is at Page 20 of the document book, is of unusual interest because it suggests that even in 1930 the intention ultimately to attack Poland was already current in German military circles. This document is an extract from the history of war organisation and of the scheme for mobilisation. The German text of this document is headed "850/38," which suggests that it was written in the year 1938. The extracts read:

"Since under the Treaty of Versailles all preparations for mobilisation were forbidden, these were at first confined to a very small body of collaborators and only of a theoretical nature. Nevertheless, there existed at that time an 'Establishment Order,' and Instructions for Establishment, the forerunners of the present-day scheme for Mobilisation.

An Establishment Organisation and adaptable instructions for establishment were drawn up for each A-year, cover name for mobilisation year.

As stated, the 'Establishment Organisations' of that time were to be judged purely theoretically, for they had no positive basis in the form of men and material. They provided, nevertheless, a valuable foundation for the establishment of a War Organisation as our ultimate aim."

Paragraph two:

"The crises between Germany and Poland, which were becoming increasingly acute, compelled us, instead of making theoretical preparation for war, to prepare in a practical manner for a purely German-Polish conflict.

The strategic idea of a rapid forcing of the Polish base of Gdynia was made a basis, and the fleet on active service was to be reinforced by the auxiliary forces which would be indispensable to attain this strategic end, and the essential coastal and flak batteries, especially those in Pillau and Swinemunde were to be taken over. Thus in 1930 the Reinforcement Plan was evolved."

If the Tribunal turns over the page to paragraph 3, to the second sub-paragraph:

"Hitler had made a clear political request to build up for him in five years, that is to say, by the 1st April, 1938, armed forces which he could place in the balance as an instrument of political power."

Now that entry points to the fact that the Nazi seizure of power in 1933 was a signal to Raeder to go full speed ahead on rearmament. The detailed story of this development has already been told by my American colleague, Mr. Alderman, and I would simply refer the Court in the first place to Document C-189, Exhibit USA 44, which is at Page 66 of the document book. In that document Raeder tells Hitler in June, 1934, that the German fleet must be developed to oppose England, and that therefore from 1936 on the big ships must be armed with big guns to match the British King George class of battle-ship. It further, in the last paragraph, refers to Hitler's demand that the construction of U-boats should be kept completely secret, especially in view of the Saar plebiscite. In November, 1934, Raeder had a further talk with Hitler on the financing of naval rearmament, and on that occasion Hitler told him that in case of need he would get Doctor Ley to put 120 to 150,000,000 marks from the Labour Front at the disposal of the Navy. The reference to that is the Document C-190, Exhibit USA 45, at Page 67 of the document book. The Tribunal may think that that proposed fraud upon the German working people was a characteristic Nazi manifestation.

THE PRESIDENT: Would that be a convenient time to break off?

MAJOR. ELWYN JONES: If your Lordship pleases.

(A recess was taken until 14.00 hours.)

MAJOR ELWYN JONES: May it please the Tribunal, the next document I desire to draw to the Tribunal's attention is Document C-23, Exhibit USA 49, at Page 3 of the document book, which states that the true displacement of certain German battleships exceeded by 20 per cent. the displacement reported to the British. That, I submit, is typical of Raeder's use of deceit.

The next document, to which I refer briefly, is C-166, Exhibit USA 48, Page 36 of the document book. It is another such deceitful document, which orders that auxiliary cruisers, which were being secretly constructed, should be referred to as "transport ships."

Then there is Document C-29, Exhibit USA 46, at Page 8 of the document book, which is signed by Raeder and deals with the support given by the German Navy to the German armament industry, and, I submit, is an illustration of Raeder's concern with the broader aspects of Nazi policy, and of the close link between Nazi politicians, German service chiefs and German armament manufacturers.

THE PRESIDENT: Has that been put in before?

MAJOR ELWYN JONES: It has been put in before, my Lord, as Exhibit USA 46.

A final commentary on post-1939 naval rearmament is Document C-155, at Page 24 of the document book, which is a new document and will be Exhibit GB 214, and is a letter from Raeder to the German Navy, dated 11th June, 1940. The original, which is now submitted to the Tribunal, shows the very wide distribution of this letter. There is provision in the distribution list for 467 copies. This letter of Raeder's is a letter both of self-justification and of apology. The extracts read:

"The most outstanding of the numerous subjects of discussion in the Officers' Corps are the torpedo positions, and the problem, whether the naval building programme, up to autumn 1939, envisaged the possibility of the outbreak of war as early as 1939, or whether the emphasis ought not to have been laid, from the first, on the construction of U-boats.

If the opinion is voiced in the Officers' Corps, that the entire naval building programme has been wrongly directed, and if, from the first, the emphasis should have been on the U-boat weapon and after its consolidation on the large ships, I must emphasise the following matters:

The building up of the Fleet was directed according to political demands, which were decided by the Fuehrer. The Fuehrer hoped, until the last moment, to be able to put off the threatening conflict with England until 1944-45. At that time the Navy would have had available a fleet with a powerful U-boat superiority and a much more favourable ratio as regards strength in all other types of ships, particularly those designed for warfare on the high seas.

The development of events forced the Navy, contrary to the expectation even of the Fuehrer, into a war which it had to accept while still in the initial stage of its rearmament. The result is that those who represent the opinion that the emphasis should have been laid, from the start, on the building of the U-boat arm, appear to be right. I leave undiscussed, how far this development, quite apart from difficulties of personnel, training and dockyards, could have been appreciably improved in any way in view of the political limits of the Anglo-German Naval Treaty. I leave also undiscussed, how the early and necessary creation of an effective air force slowed down the desirable development of the other branches of the forces. I indicate, however, with pride, the admirable and, in spite of the political restraints in the years of the Weimar Republic, far-reaching preparation for U-boat construction, which made the immensely rapid development of the U-boat arm, both as regards equipment and personnel, possible immediately after the assumption of power."

There the Tribunal sees no trace of reluctance in co-operating with the Nazi programme. On the contrary, the evidence points to the fact that Raeder welcomed and became one of the pillars of Nazi power. Now it will be my purpose to develop the relationship between Raeder, the Navy and the Nazi Party. The prosecution's submission is that Raeder, more than anyone else, was responsible for securing the unquestioned allegiance of the German Navy to the Nazi movement, an allegiance which Donitz was to make even more firm and fanatical.

Raeder's approval of Hitler was shown particularly clearly on 2nd August, 1934, the day of Hindenburg's death, when he and all the men under him swore a new oath of loyalty with considerable ceremony, this time to Adolf Hitler and no longer to the Fatherland. The oath is found in Document D-481, at Page 101 of the document book. That will be Exhibit GB 215, and it may be of interest to the Court to see what the new oath was.

The last paragraph reads:

"The oath of allegiance taken by members of the Armed Forces reads as follows:

I swear this holy oath by God: that I will implicitly obey the Leader of the German Reich and People, Adolf Hitler, the Supreme Commander of the Armed Forces and that, as a brave soldier, I will be willing to stake my life at any time for this oath."

The Tribunal will see that for his Fatherland, Raeder substituted the Fuehrer.

I am not proposing to take the Tribunal's time by reiterating the steps by which the German Navy was progressively drawn into the closest alliance with the Nazi Party. I would remind the Court of facts of history, like the incorporation of the swastika into the ensign under which the German Fleet sailed, and the wearing of the swastika on the uniform of naval officers and men, which are facts which speak for themselves.

The Nazis, for their part, were not ungrateful for Raeder's obeisance and collaboration. His services in rebuilding the German Navy were widely recognised by Nazi propagandists and by the Nazi Press. On his 66th birthday, the chief Party organ, the "Volkischer Beobachter," published a special article about him, to which I desire to draw the Tribunal's attention. It is at Page 100 of the document book; it is Document D-448, Exhibit GB 216. It is a valuable summing up of Raeder's contribution to Nazi development:

> "It was to Raeder's credit - writes the 'Volkischer Beobachter' - to have already built up by that time a powerful striking force from the numerically small fleet, despite the fetters of Versailles.
>
> With the assumption of power through National Socialism, began the most fruitful period, also, in the reconstruction of the German Fleet.
>
> The Fuehrer openly expressed his recognition of Raeder's faithful services and unstinted co-operation, by appointing him General-Admiral on 20th April, 1936."

THE PRESIDENT: Do you think it necessary to read the entire document?

MAJOR ELWYN JONES: I was going to turn to the last paragraph but one, my Lord, which I think is helpful.

> "As a soldier and a seaman, the General-Admiral has proved himself to be the Fuehrer's first and foremost naval collaborator."

This, in my submission, is a summing up of his status and position in Nazi Germany.

I now propose to deal with Raeder's personal part in the Nazi conspiracy. The evidence indicates that Raeder, from the time of the Nazi seizure of power, became increasingly involved in responsibility for the general policies of the Nazi State.

Long before he was promoted to General-Admiral in 1936 he had become a member of the very secret Reich Defence Council, joining it when it was founded on 4th April, 1933. And thus, at an early date, he was involved, both militarily and politically, in the Nazi conspiracy. The relevant document upon that is Document EC-177, Exhibit USA 390, at Page 68 of the document book, which I would remind the Tribunal contains the classic Nazi directive:

> "Matters communicated orally cannot be proved; they can be denied by us in Geneva."

On the 4th February, 1938, Raeder was appointed to be a member of a newly formed Secret Advisory Council for Foreign Affairs, and the authority for that statement is Document 203 1 -PS, at Page 88 of the document book, which will be Exhibit GB 217.

Three weeks after this, a decree of Hitler's stated that, as well as being equal in rank with a Cabinet Minister, Raeder was also to take part in the sessions of the Cabinet. That has already been established in Document 2098-PS, which was submitted as Exhibit GB 206.

In my submission, therefore, it is thus clear that Raeder's responsibility for the political decisions of the Nazi State was steadily developed from 1933 to 1938 and that, in the course of time, he had become a member of all the main political advisory bodies. He was, indeed, very much a member of the inner councils of the conspirators, and, I submit, must carry, with them, the responsibility for the acts that led to the German invasion of Poland in 1939 and the outbreak of the war.

As an illustration, I would remind the Tribunal that Raeder was present at two of the key meetings at which Hitler openly declared his intention of attacking neighbouring countries. I refer the Tribunal to Document 386-PS, which is Exhibit

USA 25 and is found at Page 81 of the document book, which the Tribunal will remember is the record of Hitler's conference at the Reich Chancellery on 5th November, 1937, about matters which were said to be too important to discuss in the larger circle of the Reich Cabinet. This document, which Mr. Alderman submitted, establishes conclusively that the Nazis premeditated their crimes against peace.

Then there was the other conference of Hitler's on the 23rd May, 1939, the minutes of which are found in Document L-79, Exhibit USA 27, at Page 74 of the document book. That, the Tribunal will remember, was the conference at which Hitler confirmed his intention to make a deliberate attack upon, Poland at the first opportunity, well knowing that this must cause widespread war in Europe.

Now, those two were key conferences. At many, many others Raeder was also present to place his knowledge and professional skill at the service of the Nazi war machine.

His active promotion of the military planning and preparation for the Polish campaign is by now well-known to the Tribunal, and I am not proposing to, reiterate that evidence again. Once the war did start, however, the defendant Raeder showed himself to be a master of the most typical of the conspirator's techniques, namely, that of deceit on a grand scale. There are few better examples of this allegation than that of his handling of the case of the Athenia.

The Athenia, as the Tribunal will be aware, was a passenger liner which was sunk on the evening of 3rd September, 1939, when she was outward bound to America, about one hundred lives being lost.

On 23rd October, 1939, the Nazi Party paper, the "Volkischer Beobachter, published, in screaming headlines, the story, "Churchill sank the Athenia." I would refer the Court to Document 3260-PS, at Page 97 of the document book, which will be Exhibit GB 218, and I would also like the Tribunal to, look for a moment at the copy of the "Volkischer Beobachter" here, and see the scale on which this deliberate lie was perpetrated. I have a photostat of the relevant page of the "Volkischer Beobachter" for that day. The Tribunal will see that on this front page, with the big red underlining, there are the words: "Churchill found guilty this time."

The extract from the "Volkischer Beobachter," which is at Page 97 of the document book, reads as follows:

"Churchill sank the Athenia.

The above picture" - and the Tribunal will see it is a fine picture of this fine ship - "shows the proud Athenia, the ocean giant, which was sunk by Churchill's crime. One can clearly see the big radio equipment on board the ship. But nowhere was an SOS heard from the ship. Why was the Athenia silent? Because her captain was not allowed to tell the world anything. He very prudently refrained from telling the world that Winston Churchill attempted to sink the ship, through the explosion of an infernal machine. He knew it well, but he had to keep silent. Nearly fifteen hundred people would have lost their lives if Churchill's original plan had resulted as the criminal wanted. Yes, he longingly hoped that the one hundred Americans on board the ship would find death in the waves so that the anger of the American people, who were deceived by him, should be directed against Germany, as the presumed author of the deed. It was fortunate that the majority escaped the fate intended for them by Churchill. Our picture on the right shows two wounded passengers. They were rescued by the freighter City of Flint; and as can be seen here, turned over to the American coastguard boat Gibb for further medical treatment. They are an unspoken accusation against the criminal Churchill.

Both they and the shades of those who lost their lives call him before the Tribunal of the world and ask the British people, 'How long will his office, one of the richest in tradition known to Great Britain's history, be held by a murderer?"

Now, in view of the maliciousness of this "Volkischer Beobachter" announcement, and in fairness to the men of the British Merchant Navy, I think it is proper that I should say, that contrary to the allegation in this Nazi sheet, the Athenia of course made repeated wireless distress signals which were in fact intercepted and answered by His Majesty's ship Electra, in escort, as well as by the Norwegian steamer Knut Nelson and the yacht Southern Cross.

I shall submit evidence to the Tribunal to establish that, in fact, the Athenia was sunk by the German U-boat U-30. So unjustifiable was the torpedoing of the Athenia, however, that the German Navy embarked upon a course of falsification of their records and on other dishonest measures, in the hope of hiding their guilty secret. And for their part, as the Tribunal has seen, the Nazi propagandists indulged in their favourite falsehood of seeking to shift the responsibility to the British.

The Captain of the U-boat 30, Oberleutnant Lemp, was later killed in action, but some of the original crew of the U-30 have survived to tell the tale, and they are now prisoners of war. And so that the truth of this episode may be placed beyond a peradventure, I submit to the Tribunal an affidavit by a member of the crew of the U-30; as to the sinking of the Athenia and as to one aspect of the attempt to conceal the true facts.

I refer to document C-654, Exhibit GB 219, at Page 106 of the document book. The affidavit reads:

"I, Adolf Schmidt, Official Number N 1043-33T, do solemnly declare that:

I am now confined to Camp No. 133, Lethbridge, Alberta.

On the first day of war, 3rd September, 1939, a ship of approximately 10,000 tons was torpedoed in the late hours of the evening by the U-30.

After the ship was torpedoed and we surfaced again, approximately half an hour after the explosion, the Commandant called me to the tower in order to show me the torpedoed ship.

I saw the ship with my very eyes, but I do not think that the ship could see our U-boat at that time on account of the position of the moon.

Only a few members of the crew had an opportunity to go to the tower in order to see the torpedoed ship.

Apart from myself, Oberleutnant Hinsch was in the tower when I saw the steamer after the attack.

I observed that the ship was listing.

No warning shot was fired before the torpedo was launched.

I myself observed much commotion on board the torpedoed ship.

I believe that the ship had only one smoke stack.

In the attack on this steamer one or two torpedoes were fired which did not explode, but I myself heard the explosion of the torpedo which hit the steamer.

Oberleutnant Lemp waited until darkness before surfacing.

I was severely wounded by aircraft 14th September, 1939.

Oberleutnant Lemp shortly before my disembarkation in Reykjavik, 19th September, 1939, visited me in the forenoon in the petty officers' quarters where I was lying severely wounded.

Oberleutnant Lemp then had the petty officers' quarters cleared in order to be alone with me.

Oberleutnant Lemp then showed me a declaration under oath according to which I had to bind myself to mention nothing concerning the incidents of 3rd September, 1939, on board the U-30.

This declaration under oath had approximately the following wording: I, the undersigned, swear hereby that I shall keep secret all happenings of 3rd September, 1939, on board the U-30, from either foe or friend, and that I shall erase from my memory all happenings of this day.'

I signed this declaration under oath, which was drawn up by the Commandant in his own handwriting, very illegibly with my left hand.

Later on in Iceland when I heard about the sinking of the Athenia, the idea came into my mind that the U-30 on the 3rd September, 1939, might have sunk the Athenia, especially since the Captain caused me to sign the above-mentioned declaration.

Up to to-day I have never spoken to anyone concerning these events.

Due to the termination of the war I consider myself freed from my oath."

Donitz's part in the Athenia episode is described in an affidavit which he has sworn, which is D-638, Exhibit GB 220, at Page 102 of the document book. The affidavit was sworn in English, and I invite the Tribunal to look at it and observe the addition, in Donitz's handwriting, of four words at the end of the affidavit, the significance of which will be seen in a moment.

The defendant Donitz states:

"U-30 returned to harbour about mid-September. I met the captain, Oberleutnant Lemp, on the lockside at Wilhelmshaven, as the boat was entering harbour, and he asked permission to speak to me in private. I noticed immediately that he was looking very unhappy, and he told me at once that he thought he was responsible for the sinking of the Athenia in the North Channel area. In accordance with my previous instructions he had been keeping a sharp lookout for possible armed merchant cruisers in the approaches to the British Isles, and had torpedoed a ship which he afterwards identified as the Athenia from wireless broadcasts, under the impression that she was an armed merchant cruiser on patrol. I had never specified in my instructions any particular type of ship as armed merchant cruiser, nor mentioned any names of ships. I despatched Lemp at once by air to report to the S.K.L. at Berlin; in the meantime, I ordered complete secrecy as a provisional measure. Later on the same day or early on the following day, I received a verbal order from Kapitan zur See Fricke" - who was head of the Operations Division of the Naval War Staff - "that:

(1) The affair was to be kept a total secret.

(2) The O.K.M. considered that a court-martial was not necessary as they were satisfied that the captain had acted in good faith.

(3) Political explanations would be handled- by the O.K.M.

I had had no part whatsoever in the political events in which the Fuehrer claimed that no U-boat had sunk the Athenia.

After Lemp returned to Wilhelmshaven from Berlin, I interrogated him thoroughly on the sinking and formed the impression that, although he had taken reasonable care, he had still not taken sufficient precautions to establish fully the identity of the ship before attacking. Prior to the occurrence of this incident I had given very strict orders that all merchant vessels and neutrals were to be treated according to prize law. I accordingly placed him under cabin arrest, as I felt certain that he would be acquitted by a court-martial which would, however, entail unnecessary publicity" - and then Donitz has added the words "and too much time."

It is right, I think, that I should add that Donitz's suggestion that the captain of the U-30 sank the Athenia in mistake for a merchant cruiser must be considered in the light of a document which Colonel Phillimore submitted - Document C-191, Exhibit GB 193, dated; 22nd September, 1939 - which contained Donitz's order that "the sinking of a merchant ship must be justified in the War Diary as due to possible confusion with a warship or an auxiliary cruiser."

Now, the U-30 returned to Wilhelmshaven on 27th September, 1939. I submit another fraudulent naval document, Document D- 659, Page 110 of the document book, which will be Exhibit GB 221, which is an extract from the War Diary of the Chief of U-boats, and it is an extract for 27th September, 1939. The Tribunal will see that it reads:

"U-30 comes in.
She had sunk:
S.S. Blairlogies,
S.S. Fanad Head."

There is no reference at all, of course, to the sinking of the Athenia.

But perhaps the most elaborate forgery in connection with this episode was the forgery of the log book of the U-30, which was responsible for sinking the Athenia. I now submit that original log book to the Tribunal as Document D-662, which will be Exhibit GB 222, and an extract from the first and relevant page of it is found at Page 111 of the document book. I would like the Tribunal to examine the original, if you will be good enough to do so, because the prosecution's submission is that the first page of that log book is a forgery, but a forgery which shows a curiously un-German carelessness about detail. The Tribunal will see that the first page of the text is a clear substitute for pages that have been removed. The dates in the first column of that page are in Arabic numerals. On the second and more authentic looking page, and throughout the other pages of the log book, they are in Roman numerals.

The Tribunal will also see that all reference to the action of the sinking of the Athenia on 3rd September is omitted. The entries are translated in Page 111 of the document book for the Court's assistance.

The log book shows that the position at 14.00 hours, of the U-30 on 3rd September, is given as A.L. 0278, which the Tribunal will notice is one of the very few positions quoted at all upon that page, and which was, in fact, some 200 miles west of the position where the Athenia was sunk. The course due South, which is recorded in the log book, and the speed of 10 knots -those entries are obviously designed to suggest that the U-30 was well clear of the Athenia's position on the 3rd September.

Finally, and most curiously, the Tribunal will observe that Lemp's own signature upon the page dealing with the 3rd September differs from the other signatures in the text. Page 1 shows Lemp's signature with a Roman "p" as the final letter of his name. On the other signatures, there is a script "p", and the inference I submit is that either the signature is a forgery or it was made up by Lemp at some other, and probably considerably later date.

Now, in my submission, the whole of this Athenia story establishes that the German Navy under Raeder embarked upon deliberate fraud. Even before receiving Lemp's reports, the German Admiralty had repeatedly denied the possibility that a German U-boat could be in the area concerned. The charts which showed the disposition of U-boats and the position of sinking of the Athenia, which Colonel Phillimore introduced, have shown the utter dishonesty of these announcements, and my submission upon this matter is this: Raeder, as head of the German Navy, knew all the facts. Censorship and information control in Nazi Germany were so complete that Raeder, as head of the Navy, must have been party to the falsification published in the "Volkischer Beobachter," which was a wholly dishonourable attempt by the Nazi conspirators to save their faces with their own people, and to uphold the myth of an infallible Fuehrer backed by an impeccable war machine.

The Tribunal has seen that truth mattered little in Nazi propaganda, and it would appear that Raeder's camouflage was not confined to painting his ships or sailing them under the British flag, as he did in attacking Norway and Denmark. With regard to that last matter, the invasion of Norway and Denmark, I think it is hardly necessary that I should remind the Tribunal of Raeder's leading part in that perfidious Nazi assault, the evidence as to which has already been presented. I think I need only add Raeder's proud comment upon those brutal invasions, which is contained in his letter in Document C-155 at Page 25 of the document book, which is already before the Tribunal as Exhibit GB 214. That document, which is a letter of Raeder's to the Navy, part of which I have already read, states:

"The operations of the Navy in the occupation of Norway will for all time remain the great contribution of the Navy to this war."

Now, with the occupation of Norway and much of Western Europe safely completed, the Tribunal has seen that Hitler turned his eyes towards Russia. Now, in fairness to Raeder, it is right that I should say that Raeder himself was against the attack on Russia and tried his best to dissuade Hitler from embarking upon it. The documents show, however, that Raeder approached the problem with complete cynicism. He did not object to the aggressive war on Russia because of its illegality, its immorality, its inhumanity. His only objection to it was its untimeliness. He wanted to finish England first before going further afield.

The story of Raeder's part in the deliberations upon the war against Russia is told in Document C-170, at Page 37 of the document book, which has already been submitted as Exhibit USA 136. That document consists of extracts from a German compilation of official naval notes by the German Naval War Staff.

The first entry, at Page 47 of the document book, which bore the date of 26th September, 1940, which is at Page 11 of Document C-170, showed that Raeder was advocating to Hitler an aggressive Mediterranean policy in which; of course, the Navy would play a paramount role, as opposed to a continental land policy. The entry reads:

"Naval Supreme Commander with the Fuehrer: Naval Supreme Commander presents his opinion about the situation: the Suez Canal must be captured with German assistance. From Suez, advance through Palestine and Syria; then Turkey will be in our power. The Russian problem will then assume a different appearance. Russia is fundamentally frightened of Germany. It is questionable whether action against Russia from the North will then be still necessary."

The next entry is at Page 48 of the document book for 14th November:

"Naval Supreme Commander with the Fuehrer: Fuehrer is still inclined to instigate the conflict with Russia. Naval Supreme Commander recommends putting it off until the time after victory over England, since there is heavy strain on German forces and the end of war is not in sight."

Then there is the entry on Page 50 for 27.12.40:

"Naval Supreme Commander emphasises again that strict concentration of our entire war effort against England as our main enemy is the most urgent need of the hour. On the one side England has gained strength by the unfortunate Italian conduct of the war in the Eastern Mediterranean, and by the increasing American support. On the other hand, however, she can be hit mortally by a strangulation of her ocean traffic, which is already taking effect. What is being done for submarine and naval force construction is much too little. Our entire war potential must work for the conduct of the war against England; thus for the Navy and Air Force, every dispersion of strength prolongs the war and endangers the final success. Naval Supreme Commander voices serious objections against Russia campaign before the defeat of England."

At Page 52 of the document book, on 18th February, 1941, there is the entry:

"Chief, Naval Operations (S.K.L.) insists on the occupation of Malta even before 'Barbarossa'."

On the next page, for 23rd February, there is this interesting entry:

"Instruction from Supreme Command, Armed Forces (O.K.W.) that seizure of Malta is contemplated for the fall of 1941 after the execution of 'Barbarossa.'" - which the Tribunal may think is a sublime example of wishful thinking.

The next entry, for 19th March, 1941, which is at Page 54 of the document book, shows that by March of 1941 Raeder had begun to consider what prospects of naval action the Russian aggression had to offer. There is the entry:

"In case of 'Barbarossa,' Supreme Naval Commander describes the occupation of Murmansk as an absolute necessity for the Navy, Chief of the Supreme Command Armed Forces considers compliance very difficult."

In the meantime, the entries in this document show that Mussolini, the flunkey of Nazism, was crying out for a more active Nazi Mediterranean policy. I refer the Court to Page 57 of the document book, the entry for 30th May:

"Duce demands urgently decisive offensive Egypt-Suez for autumn 1941; 12 divisions are needed for that; 'That stroke would be more deadly to the British Empire than the capture of London'; Chief, Naval Operations agrees completely."

And then, finally, the entry for 6th June, indicating strategic views of Raeder and the German Navy at this stage, reads as follows. It is at Page 58 of the document book:

"Naval Supreme Commander with the Fuehrer: Memorandum of the Chief, Naval Operations. Observation on the strategic situation in the Eastern Mediterranean after the Balkan campaign, and the occupation of Crete, and further conduct of the War."

A few sentences below:

"The memorandum points with impressive clarity to the decisive aims of the war in the Near East, which have been made tangible by the successes in the Aegean area. The memorandum emphasises that the offensive utilisation of the present favourable situation must take place with the greatest acceleration and energy, before England has again strengthened her position in the Near East with help from the United States of America. The memorandum, however, realises the unalterable fact that the campaign against Russia would be opened very shortly, demands that the undertaking 'Barbarossa" which, because of the magnitude of its aims, naturally stands in the foreground of the operational plans of the Armed Forces leadership, must under no circumstances lead to an abandonment, diminishing or delay of the conduct of the War in the Eastern Mediterranean."

Thus Raeder was, throughout, seeking an active role for his Navy in the Nazi war plans.

Now, once Hitler had decided to attack Russia, Raeder sought a role for the Navy in the campaign against Russia, and the first naval operational plan against Russia was a particularly perfidious one. I refer the Tribunal to Document C-170 from which I have just been reading, at Page 59 of the document book. There the Tribunal will see an entry for 15th June, 1941:

"On the proposal of Chief Naval Operations, use of arms against Russian submarines, South of the Northern boundary of the Oland danger zone (declared area) is permitted immediately; ruthless destruction is to be aimed at."

The defendant Keitel provided a characteristically dishonest pretext for this action in his letter, Document C-38, which is at Page 11 of the document book and which will be Exhibit GB 223. The Tribunal sees that Keitel's letter is dated 15th June, 1941:

"Subject: Offensive action against enemy submarines in the Baltic Sea.

To: High Command of the Navy-O.K.M. (S.K.L.).

Offensive action against submarines South of the line Memel-Southern tip of Oland is authorised if the boats cannot be definitely identified as Swedish during the approach by German naval forces.

The reason to be given up to B-day is that our naval forces are believed to be dealing with penetrating British submarines."

Now, that was on 15th June, 1941, and the Tribunal will remember that the Nazi attack on Russia did not take place until the 22nd of June of 1941. In the meantime, Raeder was urging Hitler, as early as 18th March, 1941, to enlarge the scope of the world war by inducing Japan to seize Singapore. The relevant document is C-152, Exhibit GB 122, at Page 23 of the document book. There is just one paragraph which I would like to be permitted to read. The document describes the audience of Raeder with Hitler on 18th March and the entries in it, in fact, represent Raeder's own views:

"Japan must take steps to seize Singapore as soon as possible, since the opportunity will never again be as favourable (whole English Fleet contained; unpreparedness of U.S.A. for war against Japan; inferiority of U.S. Fleet vis-a-vis the Japanese). Japan is indeed making preparations for this action, but according to all declarations made by Japanese officers she will only carry it out if Germany proceeds to land in England. Germany must therefore concentrate all her efforts on spurring Japan to act immediately. If Japan has Singapore, all other East Asiatic questions regarding the U.S.A. and England are thereby solved (Guam, Philippines, Borneo, Dutch East Indies).

Japan wishes if possible to avoid war against U.S.A. She can do so if she determinedly takes Singapore as soon as possible."

The Japanese, of course, as events proved, had different ideas from that.

By 20th April, 1941, the evidence is that Hitler had agreed with this proposition of Raeder's of inducing the Japanese to take offensive action against Singapore. I refer the Tribunal again to Document C-170 and to an entry at Page 56 of the document book, for 20th April, 1941. A few sentences from that read:

"Naval Supreme Commander with the Fuehrer: Naval Supreme Commander asks about result of Matsuoka's visit, and evaluation of Japanese-Russian pact. Fuehrer has informed Matsuoka, 'that Russia will not be touched if she behaves in a friendly manner according to the treaty. Otherwise, he reserves action for himself.' Japan-Russia pact has been concluded in agreement with Germany, and is to prevent Japan from advancing against Vladivostok, and to cause her to attack Singapore."

Now an interesting commentary upon this document is found in Document C-66, at Page 13 of the document book. At that time the Fuehrer was firmly resolved on a surprise attack on Russia, regardless of what was the Russian attitude to Germany. This, according to reports coming in, was frequently changing, and there follows this interesting sentence:

"The communication to Matsuoka was designed entirely as a camouflage measure and to ensure surprise."

The Axis partners were not even honest with each other, and this, I submit, is typical of the kind of jungle diplomacy with which Raeder associated himself.

I now, with the Tribunal's permission, turn from the field of diplomacy to the final aspect of the case against Raeder, namely, to crimes at sea.

The prosecution's summary is that Raeder throughout his career showed a complete disregard for any international rule or usage of war which conflicted in the slightest with his intention of carrying through the Nazi programme of conquest. I propose to submit to the Tribunal only a few examples of Raeder's flouting of the laws and customs of civilised States.

Raeder has himself summarised his attitude in the most admirable fashion in Document U.K. 65, which the Tribunal will find at Page 98 of the document book, and which will be Exhibit GB 224. Now that document, UK 65, is a very long memorandum compiled by Raeder and the German Naval War Staff on 15th October, 1939: that is to say, only a few weeks after the war started. It is a memorandum on the subject of the intensification of the war at sea, and I desire to draw the Tribunal's attention to the bottom paragraph at Page 98 of the document book. It is headed: "Possibilities of future naval warfare."

"1. Military requirements for the decisive struggle against Great Britain.

Our naval strategy will have to employ all the military means at our disposal as expeditiously as possible. Military success can be most confidently expected if we attack British sea communications wherever they are accessible to us with the greatest ruthlessness; the final aim of such attacks is to cut off all imports into and exports from Britain. We should try to consider the interests of neutrals in so far as it is possible without detriment to military requirements. It is desirable to base all military measures which may be taken on existing International Law; however, measures which are considered necessary from a military point of view, provided a decisive success can be expected from them, will have to be carried out, even if they are not covered by existing International Law. In principle, therefore, any means of warfare which is effective in breaking enemy resistance should be used on some legal conception," - the nature of which is not specified - "even if that entails the creation of a new code of naval warfare.

The Supreme War Council will have to decide what measures of military and legal nature are to be taken. Once it has been decided to conduct economic warfare in its most ruthless form, in fulfilment of military requirements, this decision is to be adhered to under all circumstances, and under no circumstances may such a decision for the most ruthless form of economic warfare, once it has been made, be dropped or released under political pressure from neutral powers; that is what happened in the World War to our own detriment. Every protest by neutral powers must be turned down. Even threats of further countries, including the U.S. coming into the war, which can be expected with certainty should the war last a long time, must not lead to a relaxation in the form of economic warfare once embarked upon. The more ruthlessly economic warfare is waged, the earlier will it show results and the sooner will the war come to an end. The economic effect of such military measures on our own war economy must be fully recognised and compensated through immediate re-orientation of German war economy, and the redrafting of the respective agreements with neutral States; for these are the final words: for this, strong political and economic pressure must be employed if necessary."

I submit that those comments are most revealing, and the general submission of the prosecution is that, as an active member of the inner council of the Nazi State up to 1943, Raeder, promoting such ideas as these, must share responsibility for the many War Crimes committed by his confederates and underlings in the course of the war.

But quite apart from this over-all responsibility of Raeder, there are certain crimes which the prosecution submits were essentially initiated and passed down the naval chain of command by Raeder himself.

I refer to Document C-27, at Page 7 of the document book, which will be Exhibit GB 225. These are minutes of a meeting between Hitler and Raeder on 30th December, 1939. 1 will read, with the Court's approval, the second paragraph beginning:

"The Chief of the Naval War Staff requests that full power be given to the Naval War Staff in making any intensification suited to the situation and to the means of war. The Fuehrer fundamentally agrees to the sinking without warning of Greek ships in the American prohibited area, and of neutral ships in those sections of the prohibited American area in which the fiction of mine danger can be upheld, e.g., the Bristol Channel."

At this time, of course, as the Tribunal knows, Greek ships were neutral. I submit that this is yet another demonstration of the fact that Raeder was a man without principle.

This incitement to crime was, in my submission, a typical group effort, because in Document C-12, which is at Page 1 of the document book, the Tribunal will see that a directive to the effect of those naval views was issued on 30th December, 1939, by the O.K.W., being signed by the defendant Jodl. And that Document C-12 will be Exhibit GB 226. It is an interesting document. It is dated 30th December, 1939, and it reads:

"On 30th December, 1939, according to a report of the Oberbefehlshaberder Marine, the Fuehrer and Supreme Commander of the Armed Forces decided that:

(1) Greek merchant ships in the area around England declared by U.S.A. to be a barred zone are to be treated as enemy vessels.

(2) In the Bristol Channel, all shipping may be attacked without warning where the impression of a mining incident can be created.

Both measures are authorised to come into effect immediately."

Another example of the callous attitude of the German Navy when it was under Raeder's command, towards neutral shipping, is found in an entry in Jodl's diary -

THE PRESIDENT: I think perhaps you should read the pencil note, should you not?

MAJOR ELWYN JONES: The pencil note on Document C-12 reads:

"And to (1) Attack must be carried out without being seen. The denial of the sinking of these steamships in case the expected protests are made must be possible."

As I was saying, my Lord, another example of the callous attitude of Raeder's Navy towards neutral shipping is found in an entry in Jodl's diary for 16th June, 1942, at Page 112 of the document book, which is Document 1807-PS, and will be Exhibit GB 227. This extract from Jodl's diary is dated 16th June, 1942, and it reads:

"The operational staff of the Navy (S.K.L.), applied on 29th May for permission to attack the Brazilian sea and air forces. The S.K.L. considers that a sudden blow against the Brazilian warships and merchant ships is expedient at this juncture (a) because defence measures are still incomplete; (b) because there is the possibility of achieving surprise; and (c) because Brazil is to all intents and purposes fighting Germany at sea."

This, the Tribunal will see, was a plan for a kind of Brazilian "Pearl Harbour" because the Tribunal will recollect that war did not in effect break out between Germany and Brazil until 22nd August, 1942.

Raeder himself also caused the Navy to participate in War Crimes ordered by other conspirators, and I shall give one example only of that. On 28th October, 1942, as Document C-179, Exhibit USA 543, at Page 63 of the document book shows, the head of the operations division of the Naval War Staff promulgated to naval commands Hitler's notorious order of 18th October, 1942, with regard to the shooting of Commandos, which, in my submission, amounted to denying the protection of the Geneva Convention to captured Commandos.

The Tribunal will remember the document is dated 28th October, 1942, and it reads:

"Enclosed please find a Fuehrer order regarding annihilation of terror and sabotage units.

This order must not be distributed in writing by Flotilla leaders, Section Commanders or Officers of this rank.

After verbal notification to subordinate sections the above officers must hand this order over to the next higher section which is responsible for its withdrawal and destruction."

What clearer indication could there be than the nature of these instructions as to the naval command's appreciation of the wrongfulness of the murders Hitler ordered?

THE PRESIDENT: Shall we adjourn now for ten minutes?

MAJOR ELWYN JONES: I have drawn the Tribunal's attention to the circulation of Hitler's order to shoot Commandos. I now draw the Tribunal's attention to an example of the execution of that order by the German Navy during the period when Raeder was its Commander.

My learned friend, Mr. Roberts, has already given the Tribunal an account of a Commando operation of December, 1942, which had as its objective an attack on shipping in Bordeaux harbour. The Tribunal will recollect that the Wehrmacht account he quoted, U.K. 57, Exhibit GB 164, stated that six of the ten participants in that Commando raid were arrested and that all were shot on 23rd March, 1943. In connection with that episode the prosecution has a further document throwing more light on this Bordeaux incident, and showing how much more expeditiously the Navy under Raeder had implemented Hitler's order on this particular occasion. I draw the Court's attention to Document C-176, at Page 61 of the document book, Exhibit GB 228.

That document consists of extracts from the war diary of Admiral Bachmann, who was the German Flag Officer in charge of Western France. The first entry, at Page 61, is dated 10th December, 1942, and reads:

"About 10.15. Telephone call from personal representative of the Officer-in-Charge of the Security Service in Paris, S.S. Obersturmfuehrer Dr. Schmidt, to Flag Lieutenant, requesting postponement of the shooting, as interrogation had not been concluded.

After consultation with the Chief of Operations Staff the Security Service had been directed to get approval direct from Headquarters.

18.20. Security Service, Bordeaux, requested Security Service authorities at Fuehrer's headquarters to postpone the shooting for three days. Interrogations continued for the time being."

The next day, 11th December, 1942:

"Shooting of two prisoners was carried out by a unit belonging to the naval officer in charge, Bordeaux, in the presence of an officer of the Security Service, Bordeaux, on order of the Fuehrer."

Then there is a note in green pencil in the margin opposite the entry which reads:

"Security Service should have done this. Phone Flag Officer in Charge in future cases."

The Tribunal will therefore see from this Document, C-176, that the first two gallant men to be shot as a result of the Bordeaux operation were actually put to death by a naval firing party on 11th December, 1942. They were Sergeant Wallace and Marine Ewart, who had the misfortune to be captured on 8th December in the preliminary stages of the operation.

Of interest is the comment of the Naval War Staff upon this shooting, which is found in Document D-658.

THE PRESIDENT: What do the last two lines in Document C-176 about the operation being "particularly favoured" mean?

MAJOR ELWYN JONES: "The operation was particularly favoured by the weather conditions and the dark night" - that presumably, my Lord, is a reference to the operation of the Marine Commandos in successfully blowing up a number of German ships in Bordeaux harbour. Alternatively, I am advised by the naval officer who is assisting me, that it probably is a reference to the conditions prevailing at the time of the shooting of the two men.

THE PRESIDENT: I should have thought so.

MAJOR ELWYN JONES: I stand corrected by the representative of the British Navy upon my interpretation of the matter.

THE PRESIDENT: Does not it indicate that naval men had done it?

MAJOR ELWYN JONES: The shooting was in fact, as the entry of 11th December shows, carried out by a naval party-by units belonging to the naval officer in charge of Bordeaux.

THE PRESIDENT: Yes.

MAJOR ELWYN JONES: I was seeking to draw the Tribunal's attention to the comment of the Naval War Staff upon that shooting, which is in Document D-658, at Page 109, Exhibit GB 229. It reads:

"The Naval Commander, West France, reports that during the course of the day, explosives with attachable magnets, mapping material dealing with the mouth of the Gironde, aerial photographs of the port installations at Bordeaux, camouflage material and food and water for several days were found. Attempts to salvage the canoe were unsuccessful. The Naval Commander, West France, has ordered that both soldiers be shot immediately for attempted sabotage, if their interrogation, which has begun, confirms what has so far been discovered; their execution has, however, been postponed in order to obtain more information.

According to a Wehrmacht report, both soldiers have meanwhile been shot. The measure would be in accordance with the Fuehrer's special order, but is nevertheless something new in International Law, since the soldiers were in uniform."

I submit that that last sentence shows very clearly that the Naval High Command, under. Raeder, accepted allegiance to the Nazi conspiracy as of greater importance than any question of moral principle or of professional honour and integrity. This operation of the shooting of those two Commandos was, as I submit, not an act of war, but a murder of two gallant men, and it is upon this sombre note that it is my duty to summarise this part of the prosecution's case against the defendant Raeder.

The prosecution's submission is that he was not just a military puppet carrying out political orders. The Tribunal has seen that, before the Nazis came, he had worked actively to rebuild the German Navy behind the back of the Reichstag. When the Nazis seized power, he unreservedly joined forces with them. He was the prime mover in transferring the loyalty of the German Navy to the Nazi Party. He was as much a member of the inner councils of the Nazis as possibly any other defendant. And he was a member of their main political advisory bodies.

He was well aware of their aggressive designs, and I submit he assisted in their realisation not only as a military technician, but also as a mendacious politician, and he furthered, as I have submitted, their brutal methods of warfare. Yet of all these conspirators, Raeder was one of the first to fall from his high position. It is in fact true that the extension of war beyond the boundaries of Poland came as a disappointment to him. His vision of a Nazi Armada mastering the Atlantic reckoned without Ribbentrop's diplomacy and Hitler's ideas of strategy.

I would draw the Tribunal's attention to Document C-161, at Page 35 of the document book, which is an extract, GB 230, from a memorandum of Raeder, dated 10th January, 1943, just before his retirement, entitled, "The Importance of German Surface Forces for Conducting the War by the Powers Signatory to the Three-Power-Pact." The material entry reads:

"It was planned by the leaders of the National Socialist Reich to give the German Navy by 1944-45 such a strength that it would be possible to strike at the British vital arteries in the Atlantic with sufficient ships, fighting power and range.

The war having begun five years earlier, in 1939, the construction of these forces was still in its initial stages."

The Tribunal will see from that document how completely Raeder was cheated in his ambitious plans, by miscalculation as to when his high seas fleet would be required. The Tribunal has seen that Raeder made a great effort to recover some of his lost glory, with his attack on an inoffensive Norway. He made many efforts to liven up the war at sea, both at the expense of neutrals and also of the customs and laws of the sea. But his further schemes were disregarded by his fellow conspirators, and in

January, 1943, Raeder retired, and thereafter he was a leader in name only.

I invite the Court's attention to Document D-655, at Page 108 of the document book, Exhibit GB 231, which is a record in Raeder's handwriting of his interview with Hitler on 6th January, 1943, which led to Raeder's retirement. I am proposing to read only the fifth paragraph, in which Raeder records:

"If the Fuehrer was anxious to demonstrate that the parting was of the friendliest character and wished that the name Raeder should continue to be associated with the Navy, particularly abroad, it would perhaps be possible to make an appointment to General Inspector, giving appropriate publicity in the Press, etc. But a new C.-in- C. Navy with full responsibility for this office must be appointed. The position of Inspector General, or whatever it was decided to call it, must be purely nominal. Hitler," the record reads, "accepted this suggestion with alacrity. The Inspector General could perhaps carry out special tasks for him, make tours of inspection, etc. The name of Raeder was still to be associated with the Navy. After C.-in-C. Navy had repeated his request, the Fuehrer definitely agreed to 30th January as his release date. He would like to think over the details."

This was Raeder's twilight, and indeed a very different occasion from the period of his ascendancy in 1939, when on 12th March Raeder spoke on the occasion of the German Heroes' Day. I now refer the Court to the final document on Raeder, an account of that speech in March, 1939, which is at Page 103 of the document book, in Document D-653, Exhibit GB 232. The first paragraph reads:

"Throughout Germany celebrations took place on the occasion of Hero Commemoration Day. On 12th March, 1939, these celebrations were combined for the first time with the celebration of the freedom to rearm. The day's chief event was the ceremony held in the Berlin State Opera House in Unter den Linden. In the presence of Hitler and representatives of the Party and Armed Forces, General Admiral Raeder made a speech, extracts from which are given below."

I turn to Page 2 of the record, Page 104 of the document book, to about the fifteenth line.

"National Socialism," says Raeder, "which originates from the spirit of the German fighting soldier, has been chosen by the German people as its ideology. The German people follow the symbols of its regeneration with the same great love and fanatical passion. The German people has had practical experience of National Socialism and it has not been imposed, as so many critics believe. The Fuehrer has shown his people that in the National Socialist racial community lies the greatest and invincible source of strength, whose dynamic power ensures not only peace at home, but also enables us to make use of all the Nation's creative powers."

There follow eulogies of Hitler, and, a few sentences below:

"This is the reason for the clear and unsparing summons to fight Bolshevism and international Jewry, whose race- destroying activities we have sufficiently experienced on our own people. Therefore, the alliance with all like- minded nations who, like Germany, are not willing to allow their strength, dedicated to construction and peaceful work at home, to be disrupted by alien ideologies as by parasites of a foreign race"

Then a few sentences on:

"If later on we instruct in the technical handling of weapons, this task demands that the young soldier should also be taught National Socialist ideology and the problems of life. This part of the task, which becomes for us both a duty of honour and a demand which cannot be refused, can and will be carried out if we stand shoulder to shoulder and in sincere comradeship to the Party and its organisations."

The next sentence:

"The Armed Forces and the Party thus became more and more united in attitude and spirit."

And then just two sentences on the next page:

"Germany is the protector of all Germans within and beyond our frontiers. The shots fired at Almeria are proof of that."

That refers, of course, to the bombardment of the Spanish town of Almeria, carried out by a German naval squadron on 31st May, 1937, during the course of the Spanish Civil War.

There are further references to the Fuehrer and his leadership, and then a final sentence of the first paragraph of Page 3:

"They all planted into a younger generation the great tradition of death for a holy cause, knowing that with their blood they will lead the way towards the freedom of their dreams."

My submission is that that speech of Raeder's is the final proof of his deep personal involvement in the Nazi conspiracy. There is the mixture of heroics and fatalism that led millions of Germans to slaughter. There are boasts of violence used on the people of Almeria. There is the lip service to peace by a man who planned conquest. "Armed Force and Party have become more and more united in altitude and spirit" - there is the authentic Nazi voice. There is the assertion of racialism. Finally, there is the anti-Semitic gesture, Raeder's contribution to the outlook that produced Belsen. Imbued with these ideas he became an active participant on both the political and military level in the Nazi conspiracy to wage wars of aggression and to wage them ruthlessly.

MR. ALBRECHT: May it please the Tribunal, the United States will continue with the presentation, showing the individual responsibility of the defendant von Schirach. It will be made by Captain Sprecher.

CAPTAIN SPRECHER: May it please the Tribunal, it is my responsibility to present the individual responsibility of the defendant Schirach for Crimes against the Peace, War Crimes and Crimes against Humanity as they concern directly the Common Plan or Conspiracy.

The prosecution contends that the defendant Schirach is guilty of having exercised a leading part in the Nazi conspiracy from 1925 until the Nazi downfall.

The conspiratorial acts and the criminality of the defendant Schirach may be grouped for purposes of convenience into three principal phases: (1) his early support of the conspirators over the period 1925-29; (2) his leadership and direction of German youth over the period 1929-45; (3) his leadership of the Reichgau Vienna as chief representative of the Nazi Party and the Nazi State in Vienna for the period July, 1940 to 1945. The presentation will take up each of these principal phases after a brief listing of all the principal positions which Schirach held.

In presenting first a listing of the positions held by Schirach, it is not intended immediately to describe the functions of each of these positions. In so far as a description of the functions of any particular position is still felt necessary at this stage of the trial, it will be given later during the discussion of Schirach's conspiratorial acts as Nazi Youth Leader and as Nazi official in Vienna.

For the consideration of the Tribunal, we have submitted a brief on this subject.

The document book contains English translations of 29 documents. Although we feel that we have reduced the number of documents to the minimum, the document book is still large. But Schirach's subversion of German youth is a large subject, even apart from any of his other acts. Most of these documents are from German publications, of which the Tribunal can take judicial notice. Therefore, in most cases, it is intended only to paraphrase these documents, unless the Tribunal in particular instances will indicate that they would like fuller treatment.

Before passing to the proof, I want to express my appreciation, particularly to Major Hartley Murray, Lt. Fred Nisbergall at my right, and Mr. Norbert Hailpern, for their assistance in research, analysis, translation, and organisation of these materials.

Schirach agrees he held the following positions: They are found in two affidavits, an affidavit of certificate and one affidavit of report dated December, 1945, which is Document 3302-PS, document book, Page 110.

I want to offer that affidavit as Exhibit USA 665. The certificate, which I will only rely on for one point, is Document 2973-PS. It is already in evidence as Exhibit USA 14.

Turning first to Document 3302-PS: This affidavit shows that Schirach was a member of the Party from 1925 to 1945; that he was a Leader of the National Socialist Student League from 1929 to 1931; that he was Leader of the Hitler Youth Organisation from 1931 to 1940. In 1931 and 1932 Schirach was Reich Youth Leader on the staff of the S.A. Supreme Command, where at that time all Nazi youth organisations were centralised. Also, Schirach was Reich Youth Leader of the N.S.D.A.P. from 1931 to 1940.

In 1932 Schirach became an independent Reich Leader (Reichsleiter) in the Party. Upon acquiring this relatively independent position, he no longer remained on the staff of the S.A. Supreme Command, since Nazi youth affairs thereafter, with the creation of the Reich Youth Leadership, were directly subordinate to Hitler, with Schirach at the helm. We had that kind of condition existing in the Party where, under the leadership principle, at the pinnacle you had one man, Schirach, and you no longer had the youth affairs under the S.A. However, within the S.A., Schirach retained the rank and the title of a Gruppenfuehrer throughout the period from 1931 to 1941, and in that year, 1941, he was elevated to the rank of an S.A. Obergruppenfuehrer, a rank which Schirach continued to hold in the S.A. until the collapse.

Schirach was Reich Leader of Youth Education in the N.S.D.A.P. from 1932 until the collapse. In other words, from before the Nazis came to State power until the final downfall, this defendant held the high position of a Reichsleiter, a Reich Leader, inside the Party.

Now, in addition to these positions in the Party, Schirach held the following positions in the Nazi State:

Reich Youth Leader, 1933 to 1940; Reich Governor (Reichsstatthalter) of the Reichsgau Vienna, 1940 to 1945; Reich Defence Commissioner of Vienna, 1940 to 1945.

Now, although Schirach gave up some of his positions with respect to the leadership of German youth in 1940, when he accepted these positions in Vienna, he still continued to hold after that time the Party position of Reich Leader for Youth Education in the N.S.D.A.P. Moreover, he was given a very special position: Deputy to the Fuehrer for the Inspection of the Hitler Youth, the organisation which he, of course, had led until 1940. He continued in these last two positions until the downfall.

The certificate, Document 2973, the only thing I rely on there, in this particular presentation, is to show that Schirach was a member of the Reichstag from 1932 to 1945.

We next take up acts showing that Schirach actively promoted the N.S.D.A.P. and its affiliated youth organisations before the Nazis seized power. Schirach was an intimate and servile follower of Hitler from the year 1925. In that year, when he was only 18 years old, Schirach joined the Nazi conspirators by becoming a member of the Party. Upon special request of Hitler, he went to Munich to study Party affairs. He became active in converting students to National Socialism. I am paraphrasing there, your Honours, from paragraph 2 of Schirach's own affidavit, Document 3302-PS, found at Page 110 of the document book.

Now, this was the start of conspiratorial activities which Schirach thereafter continued for two decades in a spirit of unbending loyalty to Hitler and to the principles of National Socialism. Hitler's early personal attentions to this defendant bore fruit for the conspirators, and we find Schirach's stature in the Party circles rapidly growing through those early years.

In 1929 Schirach was made national leader of the entire National Socialist German Students' League. He retained this position for two years, until 1931. Document 3464-PS, document book, Page 121, is an extract from the 1936 Edition of the Party Manual, USA Exhibit 666, which I would like to offer in evidence. This makes it clear that the purpose of the Nazi Students' League was the ideological and political conversion of students, in universities and technical schools, to National Socialism.

After 1931 Schirach devoted his full time to Party work. Schirach was elected a Nazi member of the Reichstag in 1932, and therefore he played his part in the unparliamentary conduct of the Nazi Reichstag members during the last months of the existence of the Reichstag as an independent instrument of government.

Some of the best evidence concerning Schirach's support of the conspiracy in its early stages comes from Schirach's own words in his book "The Hitler Youth." Excerpts from this book are found in Document 1458-PS, document book, Page 1. It is offered in evidence as Exhibit USA 667, Now, since this book, your Honours, covers many years and many topics, I shall have to refer to it occasionally later on.

An example of Schirach's servile loyalty to Hitler during the early years is, found at Page 17 of this book, Page 12 of your document book. There he writes of his early years of Party activity as follows:

"We were not yet able to account for our conception in detail. We, simply believed. And when Hitler's book, 'Mein Kampf,' was published, it was our bible, which we almost learned by heart in order to answer the questions of the doubters and superior critics. Almost everyone who, to-day is leading youth in a responsible position, joined us in those years."

Before 1933 Schirach moved throughout Germany, leading demonstrations, summoning German youth to membership in the Hitler Youth. When the Hitler Youth and the wearing of its uniform were forbidden by law, Schirach continued his activities by illegal means. Of this period he himself writes, at Page 26 of his book on "The Hitler Youth," Pages 16 and 17 of your document book, as follows:

"At this time the H.J. (the Hitler Jugend) gained its best human material. Whoever came to us during this illegal time, boy or girl, risked everything. With pistols in our pockets we drove through the Ruhr district while stones came flying after us. We jumped every time we heard a bell ring, because we lived in constant fear of arrests and expected our houses to be searched."

At Page 27 of the same book, Page 18 of your Honours' document book, Schirach indicates that, in the early intra- Party fight between Hitler and Strasser, Schirach clung steadfastly to the Hitler clique, and then, in discussing Strasser, he exchanged confidences only with Hitler and the defendant Streicher. It is hardly necessary to argue, that such an intimate of the Fuehrer himself was advised, from the beginning, of the general purposes, plans, and methods of the conspiracy.

As an interesting sidelight, I believe a number of those conferences, you will note, took place in Schirach's apartment in Munich, and that Hitler used to come there occasionally.

Schirach was the leading Nazi conspirator in destroying all independent youth organisations; and in building the Nazi youth movement. In connection with this point, the attention of the Tribunal is invited to the brief of the United States Chief of Counsel entitled "The Reshaping of Education, Training of Youth," which was written for the United States Chief of Counsel by Major Hartley Murray, and to the documents cited therein under the section headed "b". "The Nazi conspirators supplemented the School System by Training Youth through the Hitler Jugend." These documents were offered in evidence in document book "c" in the earlier phase of this trial. The attention of the Tribunal is also called to the motion picture "The Nazi Plan," which was shown before the Tribunal on 11th December, insofar as that film involved the defendant Schirach and his Hitler youth organisation. Occasions when Schirach's activities are shown in this film are noted in Document 3054-PS, the index and the guide to this film, which is already in evidence as Exhibit USA 167.

It was the task of Schirach to perpetuate the Nazi regime through generations, by poisoning the minds of youth with Nazi ideology and preparing youth for aggressive war. This poisoning will long outlive the defendant. Indeed, one of the principal purposes of this exposure must be to bring to those German youths who survived the Nazi-created catastrophe a true picture of this man whom Nazi propaganda presented as a great youth hero; a man against whom the living breath of free criticism and the truth itself could make no answer before German youth or before the German people, for more than ten years.

Again, from Schirach's own hand in his book, "The Hitler Youth," we have crystal-clear evidence concerning the methods and the tactics employed by this defendant in his destruction of independent youth organisations, and their incorporation into the Hitler Youth. At Page 32, Pages 19 and 20 of your Honours' document book, Schirach states that in 1933 the new Cabinet ministers were too over-burdened to solve the youth question by their own initiative; that therefore he, Schirach, then leader of the Hitler Youth, commissioned one of his confederates to lead fifty members of the Berlin Hitler Youth in a surprise raid on the Reich Committee of German Youth Organisations. This raid resulted in the destruction of the Reich Committee, and in its absorption within the Hitler Youth, and was closely followed by a second surprise raid of like success upon the Youth Hostels Organisation, Page 33, "The Hitler Youth," found at Pages 20 and 21 of the document book.

Now, after these successful showings of force and terror, Schirach's star climbed higher. He was appointed youth leader of the German Reich in June, 1933, in a solemn ceremony before Hitler. Concerning his next steps, Schirach writes at Pages 35 and 36 of his book, Page 22 of the document book, as follows:

> "The first thing I did was to dissolve the Greater German League. Since I headed all German youth organisations and I had the right to decide on their leadership, I did not hesitate for a moment to take this step, which was, for the Hitler Youth, the elimination of an unbearable state of affairs."

Schirach accomplished the dissolution and destruction of most youth organisations by orders which he issued and signed as youth leader of the German Reich. This is shown by the order contained in Document 2229-PS, your document book, Page 65, which is offered in evidence as Exhibit USA 668.

By this one order of Schirach nine youth organisations were dissolved, including the Boy Scout movement.

The Protestant and Catholic youth organisations were the last to be destroyed and absorbed by the Hitler Youth. Schirach accomplished the absorption of the Protestant youth organisation by agreement with the Hitler-appointed Reich Bishop Ludwig Muller, Page 38 of "The Hitler Youth," Page 24 of the document book. Schirach's objective in forcing all German youth into the Hitler Youth was finally accomplished in December, 1936, by the basic law on the Hitler Youth. Document 1392-PS is a decree, 1936, Reichsgesetzblatt, Part 1, Page 993, of which, of course, the Tribunal may take judicial notice. This law declared in part, and your Honours, I read from this because it shows so clearly the nature of what was to happen and what was already happening to German youth under Schirach.

THE PRESIDENT: Is it set out in the document book?

CAPTAIN SPRECHER: Yes, Sir.

THE PRESIDENT: What page?

CAPTAIN SPRECHER: It is Document 1392-PS. It is at Page 6 of your document book.

"The future of the German nation depends on its youth, and German youth shall have to be prepared for its future duties. All of the German youth in the Reich is organised within the Hitler Youth. The German youth, besides being reared within the family and school, shall be educated physically, intellectually, and morally in the spirit of National Socialism, to serve the people and the community through the Hitler Youth. The task of educating the German youth through the Hitler Youth is being entrusted to the Reich Leader of German Youth in the N.S.D.A.P."

The first executive order on this basic law concerning the Hitler Youth was issued on 25th March, 1939. If you refer to Page 40 of your document book, this decree, 1939, Reichsgesetzblatt, Part 1, Page 709, among other points, confirms the exclusive nature of Schirach's responsibility concerning German youth. I will quote only one sentence:

"The Youth Leader of the German Reich is solely competent for all missions of the physical, ideological, and moral education of the entire German youth outside home and school."

THE PRESIDENT: Captain Sprecher, I think you have told us enough now to satisfy us that von Schirach was in charge of the ideological education of German youth, and completely in charge of it.

CAPTAIN SPRECHER: Yes, Sir.

THE PRESIDENT: And we do not desire to hear any more of it.

CAPTAIN SPRECHER: I understand.

In exercising his far-reaching control over German youth, Schirach naturally relied on the common techniques of the Nazi conspirators, including the leadership principle, the nature of which has already been established before this Tribunal. The Tribunal will find a galling glorification and explanation of the leadership principle as it was applied to German youth in Schirach's book, "The Hitler Youth," at Page 68, translated at Page 32 of the document book. I will not read from that.

In his affidavit, Document 3302-PS, paragraph 5, Schirach states:

"It was my task to educate the youth in the aims, ideology, and directives of the N.S.D.A.P., and beyond this to direct and to shape them."

Naturally, Schirach established and directed an elaborate propaganda apparatus to accomplish a thorough-going poisoning of the minds of German youth. Document 3349-PS, your document book, Page 114, is offered in evidence as Exhibit USA 666.

This is an excerpt from Pages 452 and 453 of the 1936 edition of the Party Manual This document will show that the Reich Youth Leadership, "Reichsjugendfuehrung," of the N.S.D.A.P., prepared and published numerous periodicals, ranging from a daily Press service to monthly magazines. This document also shows that the propaganda office of the Hitler Youth maintained, through liaison agents, a political and ideological connection with the propaganda office of the N.S.D.A.P. and with the Propaganda Ministry, both of which of course were headed by the conspirator Goebbels.

Schirach shares with the conspirator Dr. Robert Ley, Reich Organizationsleiter of the N.S.D.A.P., the responsibility for the establishment and general administration of the Adolf Hitler Schools. This is shown by a joint statement of Ley and Schirach in the year 1937, which is found in the document book at Page 100. It is our Document 2653-PS, offered in evidence as Exhibit USA 669. This document shows that these Adolf Hitler Schools were open free of charge to outstanding and proved members of the Young Folk, the junior section of the Hitler Youth organisation. It further shows that the object of these, schools was the building of youthful leadership for the Nazi Party and the Nazi State apparatus.

Schirach extended his education of German youth into the field of law and the legal profession, even though these fields were principally under the control of the defendant Frank. Proof is found in Document 3459-PS, Page 120 of the document book. This is a one-page extract from an account of the Congress of German Law in 1939. It is offered as Exhibit USA 670. This document shows that beyond purely technical education in law it was considered by the conspirators to be the task of the Party to exercise influence upon the ideological conceptions of the, Young Law Guardians League. This league was a junior organisation of the National Socialist Law Guardians League, a Nazi-controlled organisation of lawyers.

Now, at this Congress to which the document refers, an official of the Youth Law Guardians declared that ignorance of the simplest legal principles could best be fought within the Hitler Youth and that, therefore, the legal education programme of the Hitler Youth was to receive the broadest support.

Obergebietsfuehrer Arthur Axmann, then the subordinate of Schirach, and who in 1940 was to succeed him as leader of the Hitler Youth, was at that time - namely, May, 1939 - appointed the chairman of a Youth Legal Committee for the establishment of the Youth Law. He was appointed by the defendant Frank.

THE PRESIDENT: Captain Sprecher, I do not think I made it quite clear that the Tribunal is not really interested in these details by which the defendant von Schirach acquired his power over the German youth. You have told us sufficient to establish in our minds, so far at any rate, that he managed to get absolute command over the German youth. The only thing that seems to me to be material, at the present stage, is whether or not you can show us any direct evidence that the defendant Schirach was a party to the aggressive aims of the Reich leaders, or to any War Crimes or to any Crimes against Humanity. Unless you can show us that, your address to us is really not useful to us at this stage.

CAPTAIN SPRECHER: I plan to take up directly, your Honour, the question of the militarisation of youth. I did want to make one reference at this point to the relation of the Hitler Youth to the League for Germandom Abroad, if that is satisfactory to your Honour.

THE PRESIDENT: The League for Germandom Abroad?

CAPTAIN SPRECHER: Yes, Sir.

THE PRESIDENT: Well, that may bear on the aggressive aims of the Reich Leaders.

CAPTAIN SPRECHER: Schirach extended the influence of the Hitler Youth beyond the borders of Germany, by means of co-operation between the Hitler Youth and the League of Germandom Abroad, the V.D.A. This is proved by an agreement made in 1933 between Schirach and leaders of the V.D.A. which is contained in Document L-360-H, document book Page 3. This is offered in evidence as Exhibit USA 671.

Now, Schirach discusses in his book, "The Hitler Youth," under the chapter heading "Work Abroad" (that is Chapter 4 of the book, Pages 34 to 38 of the document book) some of the connections of the Hitler Youth with such Nazi ideas as Lebensraum - colonial policy - as an ideological weapon.

I will not read from that, since it also covers to a certain extent

THE PRESIDENT: Did it talk about "Lebensraum"?

CAPTAIN SPRECHER: It actually used the word, "Lebensraum." At Page 36 of the document book there is reference made to the "Ostraum," space in the East -

THE PRESIDENT: I thought the document you were dealing with was L-360 on Page 3.

I **CAPTAIN SPRECHER:** I am sorry. I had gone on from there to speak about Schirach's book.

Document 1458-PS, and I had mentioned that at Pages 34 to 38 of that book there were references concerning the Nazi ideas of colonial policy and "Lebensraum," and that this book by Schirach indicated that the Hitler Youth was charged with spreading those ideas.

He uses the word "Ostraum" in speaking of space in the East, and he discusses German Youth organisations abroad and the German schools in these countries. And then I wish particularly to point out on Page 37 the following sentence:

> "It will be taken into consideration concerning this schooling that the guiding line of German population policy which aims at the utilisation of the space in the East will not be violated."

Now, in concluding the question of the ideological significance of the Hitler Youth, I would like to ask your indulgence while I make a short quotation from that master Nazi ideologist, the defendant Alfred Rosenberg. This is Document 130-PS, your document book, Page 122, which is offered as Exhibit USA 672. Rosenberg was making an answer to some inquiries of the defendant Bormann about the expediency of initiating some legal proceedings against the Churches in 1939. Rosenberg replied, apparently, by enclosing an article which he had written the year before, and it is from this article that I wish to quote:

> "We have made quite good progress in carrying the N.S. ideology to German Youth. What there is still left of Catholic Youth are only small groups, which will be absorbed as time goes on. The Hitler Youth is the absorbing sponge which nobody can resist. Furthermore, our programme for education in all categories of our schools has been built up already, with such an anti-Christian and anti-Jewish tendency, that the generation growing up now will be safe from the black 'swindle'."

I use that extract, your Honour, in connection with the expectancy of these conspirators themselves with respect to the Hitler Youth and what it was to do to the mind of young Germans.

Now, the conspirators devoted a great deal of energy to the perpetuation of their scheme of things by selecting and training successors for Nazi leadership, selecting and training and acquiring active Nazis for the rank and file of the N.S.D.A.P. and its affiliated organisations, including the S.A. and the S.S. which are alleged here to be criminal organisations.

A number of orders issued by the Party Chancellery under the heading, "Successor Problems," show the dominant part assumed by Schirach and his Hitler Youth in this field. Our Document 3348-PS, "Selections from Volume I of the Decrees, Regulations and Announcements of the Party Chancellery," already marked in evidence as Exhibit USA 410, contains some of these orders, which I will not take the time to read. But, they are all contained on one page - 113 - of your document book.

Only Hitler Youth members who distinguished themselves were to be admitted to the Party. Nazi leaders were directed to absorb full-time Hitler Youth Leaders into their staffs, so as to offer them practical experience and thus secure necessary successors for the Leadership Corps, which is also alleged as a criminal organisation. This pivotal and central function of the Hitler Youth in the domination of German life by the Party is also shown at Pages 80 and 81 of the 1938 Party Manual, Exhibit USA 430, found at Page 74 of the document book.

THE PRESIDENT: That last page, Page 113, does that refer to any of the matters to which I drew your attention? It is simply the organisation of the youth; it has nothing to do with any criminal aims.

CAPTAIN SPRECHER: Your Honour, it certainly is the contention of the prosecution that any man who took an active part in furnishing, for these criminal organisations, young members, committed a crime.

THE PRESIDENT: I quite understand that, and that is why I told you that we were satisfied that so far you had shown that he had acquired absolute control over and was the leader of the German youth. The only thing we want to hear about at this stage is whether he was a party to the schemes for aggressive war, to War Crimes, or to Crimes against Humanity. That is what we want to hear, and we do not want to hear anything else.

CAPTAIN SPRECHER: Your Honours, may I pass, then, to the connection of Hitler Youth to the S,S. Document 2396-PS, which is found at Page 69 of the document book and which is offered as Exhibit USA 673, has a quotation in it concerning the "Streifendienst" of the Hitler Youth, the "Streifendienst" being the patrol Service, a type of self- police organisation of the Hitler Youth. The quotation which I intend to read will indicate how this organisation became the principal supplier of the S.S.

Are your Honours interested in hearing that quotation concerning the Hitler Youth as the main source of the S.S.?

THE PRESIDENT: Yes, perhaps; I have not read it.

CAPTAIN SPRECHER: This document is an agreement between Schirach and Himmler. It was concluded in October, 1938. It bears, I think, partial quoting:

"Organisation of the 'Streifendienst.'

1. Since the 'Streifendienst' in the Hitler Youth has to perform tasks similar to those of the S.S. for the whole movement, it is organised as a special unit for the purpose of securing recruits for the General S.S. However, as much as possible, recruits for the S.S. Special Troops, for the S.S. Death Head Units,

and for the officer candidate schools, should also be taken from these formations."

I am passing down now to 4-a, the second part, which is underlined in red in your book:

"The selection of 'Streifendienst' members is made according to the principles of racial selection of the Schutzstaffel. The competent officials of the S.S., primarily unit leaders, race authorities, and S.S. physicians, will be consulted for the admission tests."

Passing to 5:

"To ensure from the beginning a good understanding between Reich Youth Leadership and Reich S.S. Leadership, a liaison office will be arranged from the Reich Youth Leadership to the S.S. Main Office starting 1st October, 1938. The appointment of other leaders to the S.S. sections is a subject for a future agreement."

Then, going down to what I think is the most striking quotation, your Honour, 6:

"After the organisation is completed, the S.S. takes its replacement primarily from these Streifendienst members. Admission of youths of German blood, who are not members of the Hitler Youth, is then possible only after information and advice of the competent Bann Leaders."

Now, the Bann leader referred to there was the local leader of the Hitler Jugend, and without his consent no one could go into the S.S. after that agreement was made, which was in October, 1938.

Now, the second agreement which Schirach made with Himmler was made in December, 1938. It is Document 2567-PS, Page 98 of the document book. It is offered in evidence as Exhibit USA 674. It states that the Farm Service of the Hitler Youth

"is, according to education and aim, particularly well suited as a recruiting agency for the S.S., General S.S. and the armed section of the S.S., S.S. Special Troops, and S.S. Death Head battalions."

The agreement concludes by stating that Farm Service members of the Hitler Youth who pass the S.S. admission tests will be taken over by the S.S. immediately after leaving the Hitler Youth Farm Service.

I might point out to your Honours that this meant that, after that time, any Hitler Youth member who was in the Farm Service was obliged to go into the S.S.

And now, to come directly to the point you have been inquiring about, your Honour:

Throughout the six years of Nazi political control over Germany before the launching of aggressive war, Schirach was actively engaged in militarising German youth. From the beginning, the Hitler Youth was set up along military lines with uniforms, ranks, and titles. It was regimented and led in military fashion under the leadership principle.

If your Honours will take any edition whatsoever of the Organisation Book, the Party Manual, and turn to the table, beginning with Tables 54 and 90, through the book, you will see the very striking insignia of the Hitler Youth, and how much it resembles the normal military insignia. You will further notice that one of the most prominent insignia is an "S" of the same type that the Nazis used with respect to the S.S. You will notice that part of the uniform was a long knife.

THE PRESIDENT: Is not that all a part of what they are pleased to call the Nazi ideology? I mean, the Fuehrership principle, military training?

CAPTAIN SPRECHER: There is a relation between all of these things, perhaps, and the leadership principle, because the leadership principle dominated absolutely every aspect of German life. However, your Honour, I suggest that showing to you, in this graphic way, the similarity between the uniform of the Hitler Youth and military uniforms, has some bearing upon the preparation for aggressive wars, about which I am further to speak in just a moment.

Now, Document 2654-PS, found at Page 102 of your document book is a whole book given over to just this question of the organisation and the insignia of the Hitler Youth.

The Tribunal will see how the Hitler Youth was divided into branches or divisions which were very similar to military divisions.

That document is offered as Exhibit USA 675. I will refer no further to it.

Now, in a speech in February, 1938, when the conspirators had already dropped some of the camouflage which surrounded their earlier military preparations for the wars, which we have recently suffered, Hitler discussed the military training of the Hitler Youth in the "Volkischer Beobachter" of 21st February, 1938. This is our Document 2454-PS, found at Page 97 of the document book. It is offered as Exhibit USA 676.

Hitler there said that thousands of German boys had received specialised training through the Hitler Youth in naval, aviation, and motorised groups, and that over 7,000 instructors had trained more than one million Hitler Youth members in rifle shooting. That was February, 1938, shortly before the Anschluss. Note the progress of military training within the Hitler Youth between then and August, 1939, just one month before the invasion of Poland.

At that time the defendant Schirach and the defendant Keitel, as Chief of the High Command, entered into another one of those informative agreements, which many of these defendants liked to make among themselves. It is Document 2398-PS, your document book Page 72. It is offered as Exhibit U.S.A. 677. It is taken from "Das Archiv" which, in introducing the actual agreement, declared that this agreement was "the result of close co-operation" between Schirach and Keitel. The agreement itself states, in part:

> "While it is exclusively the task of the Hitler Youth to attend to the training of their units in this direction, it is suitable, in the sense of a uniformed training corresponding to the demands of the Wehrmacht, to support the leadership of the Hitler Youth for their responsible task as trainers and educators in all fields of training for defence by special courses."

And then, passing down towards the end, you will note this quotation within the agreement: "A great number of courses are in progress."

Your Honour, if I may take about five minutes, I can finish this one section on the aggressive war phase.

THE PRESIDENT: Very well.

CAPTAIN SPRECHER: Whereas Hitler, in February, 1938, mentioned that 7,000 Hitler Youth leaders were engaged in training German youngsters in rifle shooting, Schirach and Keitel, in their agreement of August, 1939, note the following:

> "Thirty thousand Hitler Youth leaders are already being trained annually in field service. The agreement with the Wehrmacht gives the possibility of roughly doubling that number. The billeting and messing of the Hitler Youth leaders is done, according to the regulations for execution already published, in the barracks, drill grounds, etc., of the Wehrmacht, at a daily cost of 25 pfennigs."

Just as Schirach dealt with the head of the S.S. in obtaining zealous recruits for organised banditry and the commission of atrocities, so also he dealt with the head of the Wehrmacht in furnishing young men as human grist for the mill of aggressive war.

The training of German youths runs through the Nazi conspiracy as an important central thread. It is one of the manifestations of Nazism which has shocked the entire civilised world. The principal responsibility for the planning and execution of the Nazi youth policy falls upon this defendant.

I wish to take merely one' sentence from his own affidavit, paragraph. 5, Document 3302-PS, so that there can be no doubt before this Tribunal or before the world, indeed, as to this defendant's own feeling of responsibility:

"I feel myself responsible for the policy of the Youth Movement in the Party and later within the Reich." I underline the phrase "I feel myself responsible."

Your Honour, that is a convenient breaking point before coming to a discussion of Schirach's connection to War Crimes and Crimes against Humanity.

THE PRESIDENT: Very well.

(The Tribunal adjourned until 10.00 hours on 16th January, 1946.)

Thirty-Fifth Day: Wednesday, January 16th, 1946

CAPTAIN SPRECHER: May it please the Tribunal, I now pass to activities which involve Schirach in the commission of Crimes against Humanity as they bear directly on Count 1. The presentation of all specific acts will deal with the Reichsgau Vienna, but first allow me to refer back to two important points in the previous proof, which will show that Schirach bears, responsibility for War Crimes and Crimes against Humanity which bring in the whole of Europe. Through his agreements with Himmler he provided, through the Hitler Youth, many if not most of the S.S. men who administered, in the main, the concentration camps, and whose War Crimes and Crimes against Humanity throughout Europe generally are notorious.

Nor should we pass to further specific acts of Schirach without mentioning one more thing, that he cannot escape responsibility for implanting in youth the Nazi ideology generally, with its tenets of a master race, "sub-human" peoples, and "Lebensraum" and world domination. For such notions were the psychological prerequisites for the instigation and for the tolerance of the atrocities which zealous Nazis committed throughout Germany and the occupied countries.

To present Schirach's responsibilities for crimes committed within the Reichsgau Vienna, where Schirach was Gau Leader and Reich Governor from July, 1940, until the downfall, the general basic functions of these two offices must be held in mind.

The first document I refer to is 1893-PS. This is an extract from the Party Manual of 1943 and therefore catches Schirach in midstream in his activities in the Reichsgau Vienna. That is Page 42 of the document book, and Pages 70, 71, 75, 98, 136 and 140b of the Party Manual, extracts from each of those pages appearing in your document book.

The following highlights concerning the Gau Leader's functions will appear, and I propose only to paraphrase. Since your Honour may take judicial notice of the Party Manual, you may check at your leisure unless you wish me to read from any one of these specific orders. These orders make it appear that the Gau Leader was the highest representative of Hitler in his Gau, that he was the bearer of sovereignty, the top "Hoheitstrager," and that he had sovereign political rights. Beyond that he was responsible for the entire political situation in his Gau. He could call - and we believe this is important - he could call upon S.A. and S.S. leaders as "needed in the execution of a political mission." Beyond that he was obliged to meet at least once a month with the leaders of the affiliated Party organisations within his Gau, and this course included the S.S.

Now, the position of the Reich Governor in Vienna is somewhat special. After the Anschluss the State of Austria was abolished and Austria was divided into 7 Reich Gaue. The most important of these Gaue was the Reichsgau Vienna, of which Schirach was Governor. Reference to any statistical manual of the Reich at this time will establish that at that time Vienna had a population of over two million people. Therefore it was certainly one of the principal cities of the Reich., The Tribunal is asked to take judicial notice of the decree, 1939 Reichsgesetzblatt, Part I, Page 777, our Document 3301-PS, found at Page 107 of the document book. This is the basic law on the administrative reorganisation of Austria. It was enacted in April, 1939, a little more than a year before Schirach became Governor. This law shows that

Schirach, as Governor, was the lieutenant of the head of the German State, Hitler; that he could issue decrees and orders within the limitations set by the Supreme Reich Authorities; that he was especially under the administrative supervision of the defendant Frick, Reich Minister of the Interior; and that he was also the first mayor of the city of Vienna. For the same period that Schirach was Gau Leader, and Reich Governor of Vienna, he was also Reich Defence Commissioner of Vienna, and after 1940, of course, the Reich was engaged in war.

Because of his far-reaching responsibilities and authority in these positions, the prosecution contends that Schirach must be held guilty, specifically, of all the crimes of the Nazi conspirators in the Reichsgau. Vienna, on the ground that he either initiated, approved, executed or abetted these crimes. Specific examples follow which, in fact, demonstrate that Schirach was actively and personally engaged in Nazi crimes and that, when he became boastful, a characteristic never lacking in most of these defendants, he himself admitted his own involvement in acts which are crimes within the competence of this Tribunal.

I come first to slave labour.

The slave labour programme naturally played its part in staffing the industries of as large and important a city as Vienna. The general nature of this programme and the crimes flowing therefrom have, in part, been set before you by Mr. Dodd. The Soviet prosecutors will present further acts later on. Our Document 3352-PS, found at Page 116 of your document book, which I would like to offer as Exhibit USA 206, gives extracts from a number of orders of the Party Chancellery. Each of these orders, from which the extracts have been taken, bear on the Gau Leader's responsibility for the placing and use of manpower. They prove quite simply, and in unmistakable language, that the Gau Leaders, under the direction of the experienced old Gau Leader Sauckel, who was Plenipotentiary for Manpower, became the supreme integrating and co-ordinating agents of the Nazi conspirators in the entire manpower programme. At Page 116 of your document book (Page 508 of the original volume of orders) which I may say is also indicated at each place there in the quotation notation, the defendant Goering is shown to have agreed, as leader of the Four Year Plan, to Sauckel's suggestion that the Gau Leaders be utilised to assure the highest efficiency in manpower. At Page 117 of your document book (Page 511 of the order of the Party Chancellery), Sauckel in July, 1942, makes the Gau Leaders his special plenipotentiaries for manpower within their Gaue, with the duty of establishing a harmonious co-operation of all interests concerned. In effect the Gau Leader became the supreme arbitrator for all the conflicting interests that exist during wartime with respect to claims upon manpower. Under this same order, the Provisional Labour Offices and their staffs were "directed to be at the disposal of the Gau Leaders for information and advice and to fulfil the suggestions and demands of the Gau Leader for the purpose of improvements in manpower." At Pages 118 and 119 of your document book (Page 567 of the Party Chancellery Order) the defendant Sauckel ordered that his special plenipotentiaries, the Gau Leaders, familiarise themselves with the general regulations on Eastern workers. He stated that his immediate objective was "to avoid that politically inept factory heads - "

THE PRESIDENT: Where is this?

CAPTAIN SPRECHER: That is at Pages 118 and 119, towards the end of the entire document:

He stated that his immediate objective was "to avoid that politically inept factory heads give too much consideration to the care of Eastern workers and thereby cause justified annoyance among the German workers."

We submit to the Tribunal that if Schirach, as Gau Leader, was required to interest himself in such manpower details as are concerned with the alleged annoyance of German workers for the consideration given to Eastern workers, it is unnecessary to press further into the detailed workings of the manpower programme to establish Schirach's connection with, and responsibility for, the Slave Labour Programme in the Reichsgau Vienna.

I now pass to the persecution of the Churches.

The elimination of the religious youth organisations while Schirach was Chief Nazi Youth Leader has already been noted. In March, 1941, two letters, one from the defendant Bormann, the other from the conspirator Hans Lammers -

THE PRESIDENT: Captain Sprecher, have you any other evidence which connects von Schirach with the problem of manpower?

CAPTAIN SPRECHER: I had planned on presenting nothing further, your Honour. I felt that; in view of the fact that our Soviet colleagues are going further with the details of the manpower programme, particularly in the East, the main objective under Count 1 should merely be to show the general responsibility of the defendant Schirach for the Slave Labour Programme, and the question of specific acts will have to be taken from the other proof in the record, which will come into the record later.

THE PRESIDENT: Very well.

CAPTAIN SPRECHER: There is just one further point: When I come to the treatment of the Jews, in a few minutes, there will be one or two specific examples.

THE PRESIDENT: You are now going to deal with the persecution of Churches, is that right?

CAPTAIN SPRECHER: Yes, Sir.

Now, the Tribunal is referred to Document R-146, at Page 5 of the document book. This is offered as Exhibit USA 678.

I am a little in doubt, your Honours, as to whether I should read all this document, in view of our common anxiety to pass rapidly on; but perhaps I may paraphrase it, and if you are not satisfied I will read it.

These documents establish clearly that, during a visit by Hitler to Vienna, Schirach and two other officials brought a request to the Fuehrer, that the confiscations of church property in Austria, made on various pretexts, should be made in favour of the Gaue rather than of the Reich. Later the Fuehrer decided the issue in favour of the position which had been taken by Schirach, namely, in favour of the Gaue. I use this merely to connect Schirach with the persecution of the Churches, concerning which there has been a great deal of evidence before this time.

THE TRIBUNAL (Mr. Biddle): None of it is in evidence yet. You have not put anything in evidence. We cannot take judicial notice of something unless you ask us to.

CAPTAIN SPRECHER: Your ruling is that this would not be in evidence unless I read it?

THE TRIBUNAL (Mr. Biddle): I am not making any ruling; I was merely pointing out to you that we have nothing in evidence on the last document.

CAPTAIN SPRECHER: I think, under the circumstances, I had better read this document.

"Munich, 20th March, 1941, Brown House.

Circular Letter No. 5g.

To all Gau Leaders.

Subject Matter: Sequestration of Church Properties.

Valuable church properties have lately had to be sequestered to a large extent, especially in Austria; according to reports of the Gauleiter to the Fuehrer, these sequestrations were frequently caused by offences against ordinances relating to war economy (e.g. hoarding of food-stuffs of various kinds, textiles, leather-goods, etc.). In other cases they were caused by offences against the law relating to malicious attacks against the State, and in some cases because of prohibited possession of firearms. Obviously no compensation is to be paid to the Churches for sequestrations made because of the above-mentioned reasons.

With regard to further sequestrations, several Austrian Gau Leaders have attempted to clarify the question, on the occasion of the Fuehrer's last visit to Vienna, who should acquire such sequestered properties. Please take note of the Fuehrer's decision, as contained in the letter written by Reich Minister Dr. Lammers to the Reich Minister of the Interior, dated 14th March, 1941. I enclose copy of extracts thereof.

(Signed) M. Bormann."

I had offered that document as Exhibit USA 678. Do you still wish me to read the enclosure that went with it?

THE TRIBUNAL (Mr. Biddle): I do not wish you to read anything; I was simply pointing out that, as you had not read it, it was not in evidence.

CAPTAIN SPRECHER: In that event I will continue, your Honour. The copy reads as follows:

"Berlin, 14th March, 1941.

The Reich Minister and Chief of the Reich Chancellery.

To the Reich Minister of the Interior.

Subject: Draft of an ordinance supplementing the provisions on confiscation of property inimical to People and State.

The Reich Governors and Gauleiter von Schirach, Dr. Jury and Eigruber complained recently to the Fuehrer that the Reich Minister of Finance still maintains the point of view that confiscation of property inimical to the People and State should be made in favour of the Reich, and not in favour of the Reich Gaue. As a consequence the Fuehrer has informed me that he desires the confiscation of such properties to be effected in favour of the respective Reich Gau in whose area the confiscated property is situated, and not in favour of the Reich."

THE PRESIDENT: You need not read any more of it.

CAPTAIN SPRECHER: I pass over now to the Jewish persecution.

The prosecution submits, finally, that Schirach authorised, directed, and participated in anti-Semitic measures. Of course, the whole ideology and teaching of the Hitler Youth was predicated upon the Nazi racial myth. Before the war, Schirach addressed a meeting of the National Socialist German Students' League, the organisation he headed from 1929 to 1931.

Document 2441-PS is offered as Exhibit USA 679, an affidavit by Gregor Ziemer. I wish to read merely from the bottom of Page 95 of the document book to the end of the first paragraph at the top of Page 96.

The deponent Ziemer is referring to a meeting at Heidelberg, Germany, which he personally attended, some time before the war, at which Baldur von Schirach addressed the Students' League, which he himself had at one time led.

THE PRESIDENT: What is this document?

CAPTAIN SPRECHER: It is an affidavit of Gregor Ziemer.

"He" - meaning Schirach - "declared that the most important phase of German university life in the Third Reich was the programme of the N.S.D.S.T.B. He extolled various activities of the Bund. He reminded the boys of the service they had rendered during the Jewish purge. Dramatically, he pointed across the river to the old university town of Heidelberg where several burnt-out synagogues were mute witnesses of the efficiency of Heidelberg students. These skeleton buildings would remain there for centuries as inspiration for future students, as warning to enemies of the State."

To attempt to visualise the true extent of the fiendish treatment of Jews under Schirach, we must look to his activities in the Reichsgau, Vienna, and to the activities of his assistants, the S.S. and the Gestapo, in Vienna.

Document 1948, Page 63 of your document book, is offered as Exhibit USA 680. You will note it is on the stationery of the last Governor of Vienna.

THE PRESIDENT: Captain Sprecher, I have been reading on in this Document 2441-PS, on Page 96 of the document book. It seems to me you ought to read the next three paragraphs on Page 96, from the place where you left off.

CAPTAIN SPRECHER: Yes, Sir.

THE PRESIDENT: The second, third, and fourth paragraphs.

CAPTAIN SPRECHER:

"Even as old Heidelberg Castle was evidence that Old Germany had been too weak to resist the invading Frenchmen who destroyed it, so the black remains of the synagogues would be a perpetual monument reminding the coming generations of the strength of New Germany.

He reminded the students that there were still countries which squandered their time and energy with books and wasteful discussions about abstract topics of philosophy and metaphysics. Those days were over. New Germany was a land of action. The other countries were sound asleep.

But he was in favour of letting them sleep. The more soundly they slumbered, the better opportunity for the men of the Third Reich to prepare for more action. The day would come when German students of Heidelberg would take their places side by side with legions of other students to conquer the world for the ideology of Nazism."

I was about to refer, your Honours, to Document 1948-PS, which is found at Page 63 of your document book, and which I offer as Exhibit USA 680. This, you will note, is on the stationery of the Reich Governor of Vienna, The Reichsstatthalter in Vienna.

"7th November, 1940. Subject: Compulsory labour of able- bodied Jews. (1) Notice.

On 5th November, 1940, telephone conversation with Colonel (Standartenfuehrer) Huber of the Gestapo. The Gestapo has received directions from the Reich Security Main Office (R.S.H.A.) as to how able-bodied Jews should be drafted for compulsory labour service. Investigations are being made at present by the Gestapo to find out how many able-bodied Jews are still available, in order to make plans for the contemplated mass projects. It is assumed that there are not many more Jews available. If some should still be available, however, the Gestapo has no scruples in using the Jews even for the removal of the destroyed synagogues.

S.S. Colonel Huber will report personally to the 'Regierungsprasident' in this matter.

I have reported to the Regierungsprasident accordingly. The matter should be kept further in mind."

The signature is by Fr. Fischer.

I want to call the Court's attention to the significance of the title "Regierungsprasident." The S.S. Colonel, you will note, was to report to the Regierungsprasident. If you will refer back again to the decree which set up the Reichsgau Vienna, 1939 Reichsgesetzblatt, Part 1, page 777, you will find that the Regierungsprasident was Schirach's personal representative within the governmental administration of Vienna.

Now, it seems to us that this Document 1948-PS which was signed by Fischer, concerning compulsory labour of able- bodied Jews, answers the argument that persons of the rank of Gauleiter were ignorant of the atrocities of the Gestapo and the S.S. in their own locality. It shows further that even the assistants of the Gau Leaders were informed of the details of the persecution projects which were afoot at the time.

Schirach also had concern for, and knowledge of, the housing shortage in Vienna, which was alleviated for some members of the alleged "Master Race" who succeeded to the houses of the luckless Jews who were moved into oblivion in Poland.

On 3rd December, 1940, the conspirator Lammers wrote a letter to Schirach. It is our Document 1950-PS, Page 64 of your document book, and it is offered in evidence as Exhibit USA 681. The letter is very short:

"Berlin, 3rd December, 1940."

It is on the stationery of the Reich Minister and Chief of the Reich Chancellery, and it is marked "secret." To the Reich Governor in Vienna, Gauleiter von Schirach:

"As Reichsleiter Bormann informs me, the Fuehrer has decided, after receipt of one of the reports made by you, that the 60,000 Jews still residing in the Reichsgau Vienna shall be deported as rapidly as possible - that is, while the war is still going on - to the Government General, because of the housing shortage prevalent in Vienna.

I have informed the Governor General in Cracow, as well as the Reichsfuehrer S.S., about this decision of the Fuehrer, and I request you also to take cognisance of it."

Signed " Lammers."

As a last piece of illustrative evidence against this youngest member of the defendants in the dock, I take something from his own lips, which was published for all Vienna, and indeed, for all Germany and the world to know, even at that time. It appears in the Vienna edition of the "Volkischer Beobachter," on 15th September, 1942, Document 3048-PS, your document book, Page 106. It is already in evidence as Exhibit USA 274.

I would like to point out that these words were uttered before the so-called European Youth League in Vienna in 1942.

The Tribunal will recall that Schirach was still Reich Leader for Youth Education in the N.S.D.A.P. at that time:

"Every Jew who exerts influence in Europe is a danger to European culture. If anyone reproaches me with having driven from this city, which was once the European metropolis of Jewry, tens of thousands upon tens of thousands of Jews into the ghetto of the East, I feel myself compelled to reply, 'I see in this an action contributing to European culture'."

Although Schirach's principal assistance to the conspiracy was made in his commitment of the German Youth to the conspirators' objectives, he also stands guilty of heinous Crimes against Humanity, as a Party and governmental administrator of high standing after the conspiracy had reached its inevitable involvement in wars of aggression.

This completes, your Honours, the presentation on the individual responsibility of the defendant Schirach.

The prosecution will next take up the responsibility of the defendant Martin Bormann, and the presentation will be made by Lieutenant Lambert.

DR. FRITZ SAUTER (Counsel for defendant von Schirach): Mr. President, as to the various errors made in the case against Schirach, I shall state my position when the defence has its turn. But I should like to take the opportunity now of pointing out an error in translation in one of the documents. It is in Document 3352-PS.

It is an order of the Reich Chancellery to the subordinate offices, and this order mentions that the work departments had to be at the disposal of the Gauleiter under certain circumstances. In the German original of this order it reads as follows: "Anregungen und Wunsche."

THE PRESIDENT: Which page of the document is it?

DR. SAUTER: I think, Page 512 of Document 3352-PS, on Page 117 of the document book.

This German expression "Anregungen und Wunsche" has been translated "suggestions" (for "Anregungen") and "demands" (for "Wunsche").

The first translation, the translation for "Anregungen," we consider to be correct; but the second translation, namely, "demands" for "Wunsche," we consider false, because, so far as we know, this word is "Befehle" or "Forderungen" in German. We should consider, it correct if for the English translation "demands" could be substituted by another word, "wishes," which is an exact translation of the word "Wunsche." I do not know whether I have pronounced the word correctly in English. That is all I have to say for the time being. Thank you very much.

THE PRESIDENT: Do you wish to say anything about that?

CAPTAIN SPRECHER: I think that Dr. Sauter has made a very good point. I have checked with the translator beside me, your Honour, and the German word "Wunsche" has been translated too strongly.

THE PRESIDENT: Very well.

LIEUTENANT THOMAS F. LAMBERT, JR.: May it please the Tribunal, the prosecution comes now to deal with the defendant Bormann, and to present the proofs establishing his responsibility for the crimes set forth in the Indictment. And if the Tribunal will allow, we should like to observe on the threshold that, because of the absence of the defendant Bormann from the dock, we believe that we should make an extra effort to make a solid record in the case against him, out of fairness to defence counsel and for the convenience of the Tribunal.

I offer the document book supporting this trial address as Exhibit USA JJ, together with the trial brief against the defendant Bormann.

The defendant Bormann bears a major responsibility for promoting the accession to power of the Nazi conspirators, the consolidation of their total power over Germany and the preparation for aggressive war set forth in Count 1 of the Indictment.

Upon the record of this trial the Nazi Party and its Leadership Corps were the main vehicles and the fountain-head of the conspiracy.

Now, following the flight of the defendant Hess to Scotland, in May, 1941, Bormann became Executive Chief of the Nazi Party. His official title was Chief of the Party Chancery. Before that date Bormann was Chief of Staff to the defendant Hess, the Deputy of the Fuehrer.

By virtue of these two powerful positions - Chief of the Party Chancery and Chief of Staff to the Deputy of the Fuehrer - Bormann stands revealed as a principal architect of the conspiracy. Subject only, and we stress, subject only to the supreme authority of Hitler, Bormann engineered and employed the vast powers of the Party, its agencies and formations, in furtherance of the Nazi conspiracy, he employed the Party to impose the will of the conspirators upon the German people, and he then directed the powers of the Party in the drive to dominate Europe.

Accordingly, the defendant Bormann is blameworthy for the multiple crimes of the conspiracy, and for the multiple crimes committed by the Party, its agencies and the German people, in furthering the conspiracy.

It might be helpful to give a very brief sketch of the career in conspiracy of the defendant Bormann.

Bormann began his conspiratorial activities more than 20 years ago. In 1922, When only 22 years of age, he joined the Organisation Rossbach, one of the illegal groups which continued the militaristic traditions of the German Army, and employed terror against the small struggling pacifist minority in Germany. While he was District Leader for this organisation in Mecklenburg, he was arrested and tried for his part in a political assassination which, we suggest, indicates his disposition to use illegal methods to carry out purposes satisfactory to himself. On 15th May, 1924, he was found guilty by the State Tribunal for the Protection of the Republic, and sentenced to one year in prison.

Upon his release from prison in 1925, Bormann resumed his subversive activities. He joined the militarist organisation, "Frontbann," and in the same year he joined the Nazi Party and began his ascent to a prominent position in the conspiracy. In 1927 he became Press-Chief for the Party Gau of Thuringia. In other words, referring back to the case against the Leadership Corps, he became an important staff officer of a Gauleiter. On 1st April, 1928, he was made District Leader, Bezirksleiter, in Thuringia, and business manager for the entire Gau.

We come now to a particularly important point involving Bormann's link with the S.A. From 15th November, 1928, to August, 1930, he was on the staff of the Supreme Command of the S.A. Now, the Tribunal has heard the demonstration of the criminality of the S.A., and knows full well that this was a semi-military organisation of young men, whose main mission was to get control of the streets, and to impose terror on oppositional elements of the conspiracy.

Our submission at this stage is that, by virtue of Bormann's position on the staff of the Supreme Command of the S.A., he shares responsibility for the illegal activities of the S.A. in furtherance of the conspiracy.

In August, 1930, Bormann organised the Aid Fund, "Hilfskasse," of the Nazi Party, of which he became head. Through this fund he collected large sums for the alleged purpose of aiding the families of Party members who had been killed or injured while fighting for the Party.

As the Tribunal knows, on 30th January, 1933, the conspirators and their Party took over the Government of Germany. Shortly thereafter, in July, 1933, Bormann was given the number three position in the Party, that of Chief of Staff to the defendant Hess, the Deputy of the Fuehrer. At the same time, he was made a Reichsleiter and, as the Tribunal knows, that makes him a member of the top level of the alleged illegal organisation, the Leadership Corps of the Nazi Party.

In November, 1933, he was made a member of the Reichstag.

I request the Tribunal to take judicial notice of the authoritative German publication "The Greater German Reichstag" edition of 1943. The facts which I have recited in the foregoing sketch of defendant Bormann's career are set forth on Page 167 of that publication, the English translation of which appears in Document 2981-PS of the document book now before the Tribunal.

With respect to Bormann's conviction for political murder, I offer in evidence Document 3355-PS, Exhibit USA 682, which is the affidavit of Dr. Robert M. W. Kempner, and I quote therefrom briefly as follows:

"I, Robert M. W. Kempner, an expert consultant of the War Department, appeared before the undersigned attesting officer and, having been duly sworn, stated as follows:

In my capacity as Superior Government Counsellor and Chief Legal Advisor of the pre-Hitler Prussian Police Administration, I became officially acquainted with the criminal record of Martin Bormann, identical with the defendant Martin Bormann now under indictment before the International Military Tribunal in Nuremberg, Germany.

The official criminal record of Martin Bormann contained the following entry:

Bormann, Martin, sentenced on 15th May, 1924, by the State Tribunal for the Protection of the Republic, in Leipzig, Germany, to one year in prison, for having been an accomplice in the commission of a political murder. Signed: Robert M. W. Kempner." End of quotation.

THE PRESIDENT: Lt. Lambert, I do not think it is necessary for you, when dealing with a document of that sort, to read the formal parts. If you state the nature of the document and read the material part, you need not deal with the formal parts; for instance, "I, Robert Kempner, an expert consultant," and all that. Do you understand me?

LIEUTENANT LAMBERT: Thank you very much, Sir, for a very helpful suggestion.

As defendant Hess' Chief of Staff, Bormann was responsible for receiving and passing on to the defendant Hess the, demands of the Party in all fields of State action. These demands were then guaranteed by the defendant Hess by virtue of his participation in the legislative process, his power with respect to the appointment and promotion of government officials, and his position in the Reich Cabinet.

I come now, to what seems to be an important point, which ties up the defendant Bormann with the S.D. and the Gestapo. As Chief of Staff of the defendant Hess, Bormann took measures to reinforce the grip of the Gestapo and the S.D. over the German civil population. I request the Tribunal to notice judicially a Bormann order of 14th, February, 1935, set forth in the official publication, "Decrees of the Deputy of the Fuehrer," Edition 1937, Page 257.

I quote merely the pertinent portions of that decree, The English version of which is set forth in our Document 3237- PS, which reads as follows.

THE PRESIDENT: If it is a document of which we can take judicial notice, it is sufficient for you to summarise it without reading it.

LIEUTENANT LAMBERT: I appreciate that, Sir. This quotation is so succinct and so brief that we perhaps could avoid summarisation.

THE PRESIDENT: Very well, go on.

LIEUTENANT LAMBERT:

"The Deputy of the Fuehrer expects that Party Offices will now abandon all distrust of the S.D. and will support it wholeheartedly in solving the difficult tasks with which it has been entrusted in order to protect the Movement and our people.

Because the Work of the Party is primarily benefited by the work of the S.D., it is inadmissible that its expansion be upset by prejudiced attacks when individuals fail. On the contrary, it must be wholeheartedly assisted. Signed, Bormann Chief of Staff to the Deputy of the Fuehrer."

That is with respect to Bormann's support of the S.D.

I deal now with Bormann's effort to support the work of the Gestapo.

THE PRESIDENT: Lt. Lambert, would not it be sufficient to say that that document indicates the support Bormann promised to the S.D.?

LIEUTENANT LAMBERT: I was anxious merely on one point, Sir, that a document was not in evidence unless it had been quoted.

THE PRESIDENT: Well, you began by asking us to take judicial notice of it. If we can take judicial notice of it - it need not be quoted.

LIEUTENANT LAMBERT: Then with respect to Bormann's efforts to reinforce the grip of the Gestapo, I request the Tribunal to notice judicially a Bormann order of 3rd September, 1935, calling on Party agencies to report to the Gestapo all persons who criticise Nazi institutions or the Nazi Party. This decree appears in the official Party publication "Decrees of the Deputy of the Fuehrer," 1937, at Page 190. The English translation is set forth in our Document 3239- PS. I shall summarise the effect of this document shortly. In its first paragraph it refers to a law of 20th December, 1934. As the Tribunal will recall, this law gave the same protection to Party institution and Party uniforms as enjoyed by the State; and in the first and second paragraphs of this decree it is indicated that: whenever a case came up involving malicious or slanderous attack on Party members or the Nazi Party or its institutions, the Reich Minister of Justice would consult with the Deputy of the Fuehrer in order to take joint action against the offenders. Then, in, the third paragraph, Bormann gives his orders to all Party agencies with respect to reporting to the Gestapo, individuals who criticised the Nazi Party or its institutions. I quote merely the last paragraph.

THE PRESIDENT: Well, I took down what you said in your first sentence, which was that the document showed that he was ordering that a report should be made to the Gestapo on anyone criticising the Party. Well, that is sufficient, it seems to me, and all that you said after that is cumulative.

LIEUTENANT LAMBERT: There is, however, one brief point, if I may be permitted, which I should like to emphasise, about the last paragraph, because I think it is helpful to the prosecution's case against the Leadership Corps of the Nazi Party.

The Tribunal will recall that it asked certain very material questions with respect to whether the prosecution's evidence involved the rank and file of the Leadership Corps. In the last paragraph of this decree Bormann instructs the Ortsgruppenleiter - now that is way down in the Leadership Corps hierarchy under Kreisleiter and Gauleiter - to report to the Gestapo, persons who criticise Nazi Party institutions. Now, an important point with respect to the link between Bormann and the S.S. The Tribunal has already received the evidence establishing the criminality of the S.S. In this connection, I respectfully request the Tribunal to notice judicially the July, 1940, issue of "Das Archiv," our Document 3234-PS. On Page 399 of that publication, under date 21st July, 1940, it is stated that the Fuehrer promoted defendant Bormann from Major-General to Lieutenant-General in the S.S. Accordingly, we respectfully submit that Bormann is chargeable and jointly responsible for the criminal activities of the S.S.

After the flight of the defendant Hess to Scotland, in May, 1941, the defendant Bormann succeeded him as Head of the Nazi Party under Hitler, with the title Chief of the Party Chancery. I request the Tribunal to take judicial notice of a decree of

24th January, 1942, 1942 Reichsgesetzblatt, Part 1, Page 35. In our conception this is an extremely important decree, because by virtue of it the participation of the Party in all legislation and in government appointments and promotions had to be undertaken exclusively by Bormann. He was to take part in the preparation - and we emphasise that - as well as the enactment and promulgation of all Reich laws and enactments; and further, he had to give his assent to all enactments of the Reich Laender, that is, the States, as well as all decrees of the Reich Governors. All communications between State and Party officials had to pass through his hands. And, as a result of this law, we respectfully submit, Bormann is chargeable for every enactment, issued in Germany after 24th January, 1942, which facilitates and furthers the conspiracy.

It will be helpful, I believe, to point out and to request the Court to take judicial notice of a decree of 29th May, 1941, 1941 Reichsgesetzblatt, Part 1, Page 295. In this decree Hitler ordered that Bormann should take over all powers and all offices formerly held by the defendant Hess. I request the Tribunal to take judicial notice of another very important decree, that of the Ministerial Council for the Defence of the Reich, 16th November 1942.

THE PRESIDENT: Are these documents set out in the document book?

LIEUTENANT LAMBERT: Yes, Sir.

THE PRESIDENT: You have not given us the reference.

LIEUTENANT LAMBERT: That is true, Sir. I recall from memory, although I have not got it in my manuscript, that document, that important decree of 24th January, 1942, is, I believe, our Document 2001-PS.

I now request the Tribunal to take judicial notice of the important decree of the Ministerial Council for the Defence of the Reich, dated 16th November, 1942, 1942 Reichsgesetzblatt, Part, 1, Page 649. Under this decree, all Gauleiter who were under Bormann by virtue of his position as Chief of the Party Chancery, were appointed Reich Defence Commissars and charged with the co-ordination, supervision, and management of the aggressive Nazi war effort.

From then on the Party, under Bormann, became the decisive force in planning and conducting the aggressive Nazi war economy.

On 12th April, 1943, as is shown in the publication "The Greater German Reichstag," 1943 Edition, Page 167, our Document 2981-PS, Bormann was appointed Secretary of the Fuehrer, and we submit that this fact testifies to the intimacy and influence of the defendant Bormann with the Fuehrer and enlarges his role in, and responsibility for, the conspiracy.

We now come to the important point of Bormann's executive responsibility for the acts of the "Volkssturm." I request the Tribunal to notice judicially a Fuehrer Order of 18th October, 1944, which was published in the official " Volkischer Beobachter," 20th October, 1944 edition, in which Hitler appointed Bormann political and organisational leader of the "Volkssturm." This is set forth in our Document 3018-PS. In this decree Himmler is made the military Leader of the "Volkssturm," but the organisational and political leadership is entrusted to Bormann. The Tribunal will know that the "Volkssturm " was an organisation consisting of all German males between 16 and 60. By virtue of his leadership of the "Volkssturm" Bormann was instrumental in needlessly prolonging the war, with a consequential destruction of the German and the European economy, and a loss of life and destruction of property.

We come now to deal with the responsibility of the defendant Bormann with respect to the persecution of the Church. The defendant Bormann authorised, directed and participated in measures involving the persecution of the Christian

Church. The Tribunal, of course, has heard much in this proceeding concerning the acts of the conspiracy involving the persecution of the Church. We have no desire now to rehash that evidence. We are interested in one thing alone, and that is nailing on the defendant Bormann his responsibility, his personal, individual responsibility, for that persecution.

I shall now present the proofs showing the responsibility of Bormann with respect to such persecution of the Christian Churches.

Bormann was among the most relentless enemies of the Christian Church and Christian Clergy in Germany and in German-occupied Europe. I refer the Tribunal, without quoting therefrom, to Document D-75, previously introduced in evidence as Exhibit USA 348, which contains a copy of the secret Bormann decree of 6th June, 1941, entitled "The Relationship of National Socialism to Christianity." In this decree, as the Tribunal will well recall, Bormann bluntly declared that National Socialism and Christianity were incompatible, and he indicated that the ultimate aim of the conspirators was to assure the elimination of Christianity itself.

I next refer the Tribunal, without quotation, to Document 098-PS, previously put in as Exhibit USA 350. This is a letter from the defendant Bormann to the defendant Rosenberg, dated 22nd February, 1940, in which Bormann reaffirms the incompatibility of Christianity and National Socialism.

Now, in furtherance of the conspirators' aim to undermine the Christian Churches, Bormann took measures to eliminate the influence of the Christian Church from within the Nazi Party and its formations. I now offer in evidence Document 113-PS, as Exhibit USA 683. This is an order of the defendant Bormann, dated 27th July, 1938, issued as Chief of Staff to the Deputy of the Fuehrer, Hess, which prohibits clergymen, from holding Party offices. I shall not take the time of the Tribunal to put this quotation upon the, record. The point of it is, as indicated, that Bormann issued an order-forbidding the appointment of clergymen to Party positions.

THE PRESIDENT: Perhaps this would be a good time to break off for ten minutes.

(A recess was taken.)

LIEUTENANT LAMBERT: May it please the Tribunal, we are dealing with the efforts of the defendant Bormann to expel and eliminate from the Party all Church and religious influence.

I offer in evidence Document 838-PS, as Exhibit USA 684. I shall not burden the record with extensive quotation from this exhibit, but merely point out that this is a copy of a Bormann decree dated 3rd June, 1939, which laid it down that followers of Christian Science should be excluded from the Party.

The attention of the Tribunal is next invited to Document 840-PS, previously introduced in evidence as Exhibit USA 355. The Tribunal will recall that this, was a Bormann decree of 14th July, 1939, referring with approval to an earlier Bormann decree of 9th February, 1937, in which he had ruled, that in the future all Party members who entered the clergy or who undertook the study of theology were to be expelled from the Party.

I next offer in evidence Document 107-PS, Exhibit USA 3M. This is a circular directive of the defendant Bormann dated 17th June, 1938, addressed to all Reichsleiters and Gauleiters, top leaders of the Leadership Corps of the Nazi Party, transmitting a copy of directions relating. to the non-participation of the Reich Labour Service in religious celebrations. The Reich Labour Service, the Tribunal will recall, compulsorily incorporated all Germans within its organisation.

DR. BERGOLD (Counsel for defendant Bormann): The member of the prosecution has just submitted a number of documents, in which he proves that, on the suggestion of Bormann, members of the Christian religion were to be excluded from the Party, or from certain organisations. I beg the High Tribunal to allow the member of the prosecution to explain to me how and why Bormann's activity, that is, the exclusion of Christians from the Party, can be a War Crime. I cannot gather this evidence from the trial brief. The Party is described as a criminal conspiracy. Is it a crime to exclude certain people from membership in a criminal conspiracy? Is that considered a crime? How and why is the exclusion of certain members from the Party a crime?

THE PRESIDENT: Counsel will answer you.

LIEUTENANT LAMBERT: If the Tribunal will willingly accommodate argument at this stage, we find that the question -

THE PRESIDENT: Only short argument.

LIEUTENANT LAMBERT: Yes, Sir - admits of a short, and, as it seems to us, easy answer.

The point we are now trying to prove - and evidence is abounding on it - is that Bormann had a hatred and an enmity and took oppositional measures towards the Christian Church. The Party was the repository of political power in Germany. To have power one had to be in the Party or subject to its favour. By his efforts, concerted, continuing and consistent, to exclude clergymen, theological students or any persons sympathetic to the Christian, religion, Bormann could not have chosen a clearer method of showing and demonstrating his, hatred and his distrust of the Christian religion and those who supported it.

THE PRESIDENT: Counsel for Bormann can present his argument upon this subject at a later stage. The documents appear to the Tribunal to be relevant.

LIEUTENANT LAMBERT: With the Tribunal's permission, I had just put in Document 107-PS and pointed out that it transmitted directions relating to the non-participation of the Reich Labour Service in religious celebrations. I quote merely the fourth and fifth paragraphs of Page 1 of the English translation of Document 107-PS, which reads as follows:

> "Every religious discussion is forbidden in the Reich Labour Service because it disturbs the comrade-like harmony of all working men and women.
>
> For this reason also, every participation of the Reich Labour Service in Church, i.e., religious, arrangements and celebrations is not possible."

The attention of the Tribunal is next invited to Document 070-PS, previously put in as Exhibit USA 349. The Tribunal will recall that this was a letter from Bormann's office to the defendant Rosenberg, dated 25th April, 1941, in which Bormann declared that he had achieved progressive success in reducing and abolishing religious services in schools, and in replacing Christian prayers with National Socialist mottoes and rituals. In this letter, Bormann also proposed a Nazified morning service in the schools, in place of the existing confession and morning service.

In his concerted efforts to undermine and subvert the Christian churches, Bormann authorised, directed and participated in measures leading to the closing, reduction and suppression of theological schools, faculties and institutions. The attention of the Tribunal is invited to Document 116-PS, Exhibit USA 685, which I offer in evidence. This is a letter from the defendant Bormann to the defendant Rosenberg, dated 24th January, 1939, enclosing, for Rosenberg's cognisance, a copy of Bormann's letter to the Reich Minister for Science, Training and Public Education. In the enclosed letter, Bormann informs the Minister as to the Party's position in favour of restricting and suppressing theological faculties. Bormann states that, owing to war conditions, it had become necessary to reorganise the German high schools, and in view of this situation, he requested the Minister to restrict and suppress certain theological faculties.

I now quote from the first paragraph on Page 3 of the English translation of Document 116-PS, which reads as follows:

"I, therefore, would like to see you put the theological faculties under appreciable limitations in so far as, according to the above statements, they cannot be entirely eliminated. This will concern not only the theological faculties at universities, but also the various State institutions which, as seminaries having no affiliation with any university, still exist in many places. I request you not to give any express explanations to churches or other institutions and to avoid public announcement of these measures. Complaints and the like, if they are to be answered at all, must be countered with this explanation, that these measures are carried out in the course of planned economy, and that the same is being done to other, faculties. I would be glad, if the professorial chairs thus made vacant could then be turned over to the fields of research newly created in recent years, such as racial research and archaeology.

"Martin Bormann."

In our submission, what this document comes to is a request from Bormann to this effect: "Please close down the religious faculties and substitute in their place Nazi faculties and university chairs, with the mission of investigating racialism, cultism, Nazi archaeology." This sort of thing was done in the Hohe Schule, as was so clearly demonstrated in the prosecution's case against the plundering activities of the Einsatzstab Rosenberg.

The attention of the Tribunal is next invited to Document 122-PS, previously put in as Exhibit USA 362. The Tribunal will recall that 122-PS is a letter from the defendant Bormann to the defendant Rosenberg, dated 17th April, 1939, transmitting to Rosenberg a photostatic copy of the plan of the Reich Minister of Science, Training and Public Education for the combining and dissolving of certain specified theological faculties. In his letter of transmittal, Bormann requested Rosenberg "to take cognizance and prompt action" with respect to the proposed suppression of religious institutions.

I next offer in evidence Document 123-PS, Exhibit USA 686. This is a confidential letter from the defendant Bormann to the Minister of Education, dated 23rd June, 1939, in which Bormann sets forth the Party's decision to order the suppression of numerous theological faculties and religious institutions. The Tribunal will note that the letter lists 19 separate religious institutions with respect to which Bormann ordered dissolution or restriction.

After directing the action to be taken by the Minister in connection with the various theological faculties, Bormann stated as follows, and I quote from the next to last paragraph of Page 3 of the English translation of Document 123-PS:

"In the above I have informed you of the Party's wishes, after thorough, investigation of the matter with all Party offices. I would be grateful if you would initiate the necessary measures as quickly as possible. With regard to the great political significance which every single case of such a combination will have for the Gau concerned, I ask you to take these measures, and particularly to fix dates for them always in agreement with me."

I next offer in evidence, without quotation, Document 131- PS, as Exhibit USA 687. In summary, without quotation therefrom, this is a letter from the defendant

Bormann to the defendant Rosenberg, dated 12th December, 1939, relating to the suppression of seven professorships in the near-by University of Munich.

Now, I deal briefly with the responsibility of Bormann for the confiscation of religious property and cultural property. Bormann used his paramount power and position to cause the confiscation of religious property and to subject the Christian churches and clergy to a discriminatory legal regime.

I offer in evidence Document 099-PS, Exhibit USA 688. This is a copy of a letter from Bormann to the Reich Minister for Finance, dated 19th January, 1940, in which Bormann demanded a great increase in the special war tax imposed on the churches. I quote from the first two paragraphs of Page 2 of the English translation of this document, which reads as follows:

> "As it has been reported to me, the war contribution of the churches has been specified from 1st November, 1939 on, at first, for a period of three months, at R.M. 1,800,000 per month, of which R.M. 1,000,000 are to be paid by the Protestant church, and R.M. 800,000 by the Catholic church per month. The establishment of such a low amount has surprised me. I see from numerous reports that the political communities have to raise such a large war contribution, that the execution of their tasks, partially very important - for example, in the field of public welfare - is, endangered. In consideration of that, a larger quota from the churches appears to be absolutely appropriate."

The question may arise: Of what criminal effect is it to demand larger taxes from church institutions? As to this demand of Bormann's taken by itself, the prosecution would not suggest that it had a criminal effect, but when viewed within the larger frame of Bormann's demonstrated hostility to the Christian Church, and his efforts, not merely to circumscribe but to eliminate it, we suggest that this document has probative value in showing Bormann's hostility and his concrete measures to effectuate that hostility against the Christian churches and clergy.

I next refer the Tribunal to Document 089-PS, previously put in as Exhibit USA 360. The Tribunal will recall that this was a letter from Bormann to Reichsleiter Amann, dated 8th March, 1940, in which Bormann instructed

Amann, Reichsleiter of the Press, to make a sharper restriction in paper distribution against religious writings, in favour of publications, more acceptable to the Nazi ideology.

I next offer in evidence Document 066-PS, as Exhibit USA 689. This is a letter from the defendant Bormann to the defendant Rosenberg, dated 24th June, 1940, transmitting a draft of a proposed discriminatory Church Law for Danzig and West Prussia. This decree is a direct abridgement of religious freedom, for in paragraph 1 - I do not quote, but briefly and rapidly summarise - the approval of the Reich Deputy, for Danzig and West Prussia is required as a condition for the legal competence of all religious organisations.

Paragraph 3 of the decree suspended all claims of religious organisations and congregations to State or municipal subsidies, and prohibited religious organisations from exercising their right of collecting dues without the approval of the Reich Deputy.

In paragraph 5 of the decree, the acquisition of property by religious organisations was made subject to the approval of the Reich Deputy. All credit rights acquired by religious organisations prior to 1st January, 1940, were required to be ratified by the Reich Deputy in order to become actionable.

I now offer in evidence Document 1600-PS, Exhibit USA 690. This comprises correspondence of Bormann during 1940 and 1941, relating to the confiscation of religious art treasures. I quote the text of the second letter set forth on Page 1 of the English translation of Document 1600-PS, which is a letter from the defendant Bormann to Dr. Posse of the State Picture Gallery in Dresden, dated 16th January, 1941, which reads as follows, and I quote:

"Dear Dr. Posse:

Enclosed herewith I am sending you the picture of the altar from the convent in Hohenfurt, near Kruman. The convent and its entire property will be confiscated in the immediate future because of the attitude, hostile to the State, of its inhabitants. It will be up to you to decide whether the pictures shall remain in the convent at Hohenfurt or be transferred to the museum at Linz after its completion.

I shall await your decision in the matter.

Bormann."

The Tribunal may know that, in what is described as Hitler's last will and testament, he makes a bequest of all the art treasures he had in the museum at Linz, and from a legal point of view he uses the euphemism "art treasures which I have bought."

This document, on its face, suggests how at least certain of the properties, the art treasures in the museum at Linz, were acquired.

Finally, as the war drew increasing numbers of German youth into the Armed Forces, the defendant Bormann took measures to exclude and eliminate all religious influence from the troops. The attention of the Tribunal is invited to Document 101-PS, previously put in as Exhibit USA 361. The Tribunal will recall that this is a letter from the defendant Bormann dated 17th January, 1940, in which Bormann pronounced the Party's opposition to the circulation of religious literature to the members of the German Armed Forces. In this letter Bormann stated that if the influence of the Church upon the troops was to be effectively fought, this could only be done by producing, in the shortest possible time, a large amount of Nazi pamphlets and publications.

I now offer in evidence Document 100-PS, as Exhibit USA 691. This is a letter from the defendant Bormann to Rosenberg, dated 18th January, 1940, in which Bormann declares, that the publication of Nazi literature for army recruits as a counter measure to the circulation of religious writings was the "most essential demand of the hour."

I forbear from quoting from that document. Its substance is indicated.

I now request the Tribunal to notice judicially the authoritative Nazi publication entitled "Decrees of the Deputy of the Fuehrer," edition of 1937, and I quote from Page 235 of this volume, the pertinent and important decree issued by the defendant Bormann to the Commissioner of the Party Directorate, dated 7th January, 1936, the English version of which is set forth in the English, translation of our Document 3246-PS. In this one sentence Bormann aims and directs the terror of the Gestapo against dissident church members, who crossed the conspirators, and I quote:

"If parish priests or other subordinate Roman Catholic leaders adopt an attitude of hostility towards the State or Party, it shall be reported to the Secret State Police (Gestapo) through official channels.

(Signed) Bormann."

By leave of the Tribunal, I come now to deal with the responsibility of the defendant Bormann for the persecution of the Jews.

Again, the prosecution seeks not to rehash the copious evidence in the record on the persecution of the Jews, but rather to limit itself to evidence fastening on the defendant Bormann his individual responsibility for that persecution. Bormann shares the deep guilt of the Nazi conspirators for their odious programme in the persecution of the Jews. It was the defendant Bormann, we would note, who was charged by Hitler with the transmission and implementation of the Fuehrer's orders for the liquidation of the so-called Jewish problem.

Following the Party-planned and Party-directed programme of 8th and 9th November, 1938, in the course of which a large number of Jews were killed and harmed, Jewish shops pillaged and wrecked, and synagogues set ablaze all over the Reich, the defendant Bormann, on orders from Hitler, instructed the defendant Goering to proceed to the "final settlement of the Jewish question" in Germany.

The attention of the Tribunal is invited to Document 1816- PS, previously put in as Exhibit USA 261. The Tribunal is well acquainted with this document. It has frequently been referred to. The Tribunal knows that it is the minutes of a conference on the Jewish question, held under the direction of Goering on the 12th November, 1938. I quote only the first sentence of that document which fastens the responsibility upon Bormann and which reads as follows:

> "Goering (speaking): Gentlemen, to-day's meeting is of a decisive nature. I have received a letter written on the Fuehrer's orders by the Chief of Staff of the Fuehrer's Deputy, Bormann, requesting that the Jewish question be now, once and for all, co-ordinated and solved in one way or another."

The Tribunal is well aware of the proposals, the discussions and the actions taken in this conference that constituted the so-called "settlement of the Jewish question."

As a result of this conference, a series of anti-Jewish decrees and measures were issued and adopted by the Nazi conspirators. I offer in evidence Document 069-PS, Exhibit USA 589. This is a decree of Bormann, dated 17th January, 1939, in which Bormann demands compliance with the new anti- Jewish regulations, rising and flowing from the Goering conference just referred to, under which Jews were denied access to housing, travel and other facilities of ordinary life. I quote the Bormann order, which appears at Page 1 of the English translation of Document 069-PS, which reads as follows:

> "According to a report of General Field Marshal Goering, the Fuehrer has made some basic decisions regarding the Jewish question. The decisions are brought to your attention on the enclosure. Strict compliance with these directives is requested.
>
> (Signed) Bormann."

In the interests of expediting the proceedings, I shall resist the temptation to quote extensively from the enclosed order in Bormann's letter of transmittal. In effect, the crux of it is that Jews are denied sleeping compartments in trains, the right to give their trade to certain hotels in Berlin, Munich, Nuremberg, Augsburg and the like. They are banned and excluded from swimming pools, certain public squares, resort towns, mineral baths and the like. The stigma, the degradation and the inconvenience in the ordinary affairs of life promoted by this decree are plain.

I next request the Tribunal to notice judicially the decree of 12th November, 1938, 1938 Reichsgesetzblatt, Part 1, Page 1709, quite familiar to this Tribunal, for it was the decree which excluded Jews from economic life. This decree forbade Jews to operate retail shops and it was a decree which went far to eliminate Jews from economic life.

Now, Bormann also acted through other State agencies to wipe out the economic existence of large sections of the Jewish population. In that respect I request the Tribunal to notice judicially the authoritative Nazi publication entitled "Decrees of the Deputy of the Fuehrer," edition of 1937, our Document 3240-PS. At Page 383 of this publication there appears a decree of the defendant Bormann, dated 8th January, 1937, reproducing an order of the defendant Frick, issued at Bormann's instigation, denying financial assistance to government employees who employed the services of Jewish doctors, lawyers, pharmacists, morticians and other professional classes. I shall forbear from quoting the text of that decree. Its substance is as given. I If it please the Tribunal, for the benefit of the translators I shall continue reading from Page 25 of the manuscript.

After the outbreak of war, the anti-Jewish measures increased in intensity and brutality. Thus, the defendant Bormann participated in the arrangements for the deportation to Poland of 60,000 Jewish inhabitants of Vienna - in co-operation with the S.S. and the Gestapo. I have no doubt that the Tribunal received this document in connection with the case against von Schirach, it is our Document 1950-PS, and on its face it points out - "Lammers says - Bormann has informed von Schirach of your proposal to bring about the deportations." I limit myself to pointing out that single, solitary fact.

When Bormann succeeded the defendant Hess as Chief of the Party Chancery, he used his vast powers in such a way that he was a prime mover in the programme of starvation, degradation, spoliation and extermination of the Jews, and we use those terms advisedly, subject to the Draconian rule of the conspirators.

I request the Tribunal to notice judicially the decree of 31st May, 1941, 1941 Reichsgesetzblatt, Part 1, Page. 297, which was signed by the defendant Bormann and which extends the discriminatory Nuremberg laws to the annexed Eastern Territories. I request the Tribunal to notice judicially the Eleventh Ordinance under the Reich Citizenship Law of 25th November, 1941, 1941 Reichsgesetzblatt, Part 1, Page 722, signed by defendant Bormann, which ordered the confiscation of the property of all Jews who had left Germany or who had been deported.

I request the Tribunal to notice judicially an order of Bormann's dated 3rd October, 1941.

THE PRESIDENT: You have not given us the PS numbers of either the decree of 31st May, 1941, or the one after that.

LIEUTENANT LAMBERT: I confess dereliction of duty there. These decrees, in translated form, are all in the document book. I have not, in my manuscript, their PS citation. However, in the brief now filed with or soon to be delivered to the Tribunal, these decrees are given with their PS numbers opposite.

THE PRESIDENT: 3354-PS and 3241-PS.

LIEUTENANT LAMBERT: That is very good of you, Sir, thank you.

I request the Tribunal to notice judicially an order of the defendant Bormann, dated 3rd October, 1941, Volume 11 of the publication "Decrees, Orders and Announcements," Page 147. This is our Document 3243-PS, which announces a Ministry of Food's decree, issued at Bormann's instigation, which deprived Jews of many essential food items, all special sickness and pregnancy rations for expectant mothers, and ordered confiscation of food parcels sent to the beleaguered Jews from the sympathetic outside world.

I now request the Tribunal to notice judicially the Thirteenth Ordinance under the Reich Citizenship Law of 1st July, 1943, 1943 Reichsgesetzblatt, Part 1, Page 372, signed by the defendant Bormann, under which all Jews were completely withdrawn from the protection of the ordinary courts and handed over to the exclusive jurisdiction of Himmler's police. This is our Document 1422-PS.

With leave of the Tribunal, I respectfully request the opportunity to underline the significance of that decree. In a society which desires to live under the rule of law, men are judged only after appearance before and adjudication by a Court of Law. The effect of this decree was to remove all alleged Jewish offenders from the jurisdiction of the Courts of Law and to turn them over to the police. The police were to have jurisdiction over alleged Jewish offenders, not the Courts of Law.

The result of this law was soon forthcoming, a result for which the defendant Bormann shares the responsibility. On 3rd July, 1943, Himmler issued a decree, out Document 3085- PS, 1943 Ministry of Interior Gazette, Page 1085. I respectfully request the Tribunal to take judicial notice of this decree, which charged the Himmler police and Gestapo with the execution of the foregoing ordinance, closing the courts to the Jews and entrusting them to Himmler's police.

Finally, with respect to Bormann's responsibility for the persecution of the Jews, I request the Tribunal to notice judicially a decree of Bormann's dated 9th October, 1942, Volume 11, Decrees, Regulations and Announcements, Pages 131- 2. It declared that the problem of eliminating for ever, millions of Jews from Greater German territory, could no longer be solved by emigration merely, but only by the application of ruthless force in special camps in the East.

THE TRIBUNAL (Mr. Biddle): To what are you referring there?

LIEUTENANT LAMBERT: That, Sir, is Document 3244-PS.

We had desired at the outset, Sir, to quote this decree in full, as an irrefutable answer to a question put by defence counsel some days ago in cross-examination, as to whether or not the anti-Semitic policies of the conspirators were the policies merely of certain demented members of the conspiracy, and not the concerted, settled policy of the conspiracy itself. Time does not permit the full quotation of this decree, but with the indulgence of the Tribunal, I will offer the essence of this decree in a brief sentence or two.

Bormann starts out by saying: "Recently, rumours have been spread throughout the Reich as to violent things we are doing with respect to the Jews. These rumours are being brought back to the Reich by our returning soldiers, after what they saw in the East. If we are to combat their effect, then our attitude, as I now outline it to you officially, must be communicated to the German civil population." Bormann then reviews what he terms the two-thousand-year-old struggle against Judaism, and he divides the Party's programme into two spheres: the first, the effort of the Party and the conspirators to expel the Jews from the economic and social life of Germany. Then he adds: "When we started rolling with our war, this measure by itself was not enough; we had to resort to forced emigration and set up our camps in the East." He then goes on to say, "as our armies have advanced in the East, we have overrun the lands to which we have sent the Jews and now these emigration measures, our second proposal, are no longer sufficient."

Then he comes to the proposal, the considered proposal of himself and the Party Chancery - "We must transport these Jews Eastward and farther Eastward and place them in special camps for forced labour" - and I quote now merely the last sentence of Bormann's decree:

> "It lies in the very nature of the matter that these problems, which in part are very difficult, can be solved only with ruthless severity in the interest of the final security of our people. Bormann."

With leave of the Tribunal, I come now to deal -

THE PRESIDENT: Is it signed by Bormann? It does not appear to be. I thought you said, "Bormann."

LIEUTENANT LAMBERT: That is what I said, true, Sir.

If the Tribunal will refer to Document 3244-PS, it will be clear that this is a Bormann decree, issued from the Office of the Deputy of the Fuehrer. It is true, in this translation of the decree, Sir, Bormann's name is not affixed, but in the original volume it is very clear that this is a decree of Bormann's, issued from the Party Chancery. The prosecution so assures the Tribunal and accepts responsibility for that submission.

With leave of the Tribunal, I now come to deal with the responsibility of the defendant Bormann for overt acts, for the commission and planning of a wide variety of crimes in furtherance of the conspiracy. The Tribunal knows the vast powers that Bormann possessed; that has already been put in evidence. Our point is that he used these powers, buttressed by his position as Secretary to the Fuehrer, attending all the conferences at the Fuehrer's Headquarters - that he used these vast powers in the planning, the authorisation and the participation in overt acts, denominated War Crimes and Crimes against Humanity.

The attention of the Tribunal is invited to Document L-221, previously put in as Exhibit USA 317. The Tribunal knows that this document is a comprehensive report, dated 16th July, 1941, made by the defendant Bormann just three weeks after the invasion of the territory of the Soviet Union by Germany. It is a report of a twenty-hour conference at Hitler's Field Headquarters with the defendants Goering, Rosenberg, Keitel, and with Reich Minister Lammers. This conference resulted in the adoption of detailed plans and directives for the enslavement, depopulation, Germanisation and annexation of extensive territories in the Soviet Union and other countries of Eastern Europe.

In his report on this conference, set forth in Document L-221, Bormann included numerous proposals of his own for the execution of these plans.

Later the defendant Bormann took a prominent part in implementing the conspiratorial programme. The attention of the Tribunal is invited to Document 072-PS, previously put in as Exhibit USA 357. The Tribunal will recall that this is a letter from the defendant Bormann to the defendant Rosenberg, dated 19th April, 1941, dealing with the confiscation of cultural property in the East. I quote merely the last two paragraphs of the English translation of Document 072-PS, which reads as follows:

> "The Fuehrer emphasised that in the Balkans the use of your experts" - I parenthetically insert that that is the experts of the Einsatzstab Rosenberg organisation, the plundering organisation - "the use of your experts would not be necessary, since there were no objets-d'art to be confiscated. In Belgrade, only the collection of Prince Paul existed, which would be returned to him completely. The remaining material of the lodges, etc., would be seized by the men of S.S. Gruppenfuehrer Heydrich.
>
> The libraries and objets d'art of the monasteries, confiscated in the Reich, were to remain for the time being in these monasteries, in so far as the Gauleiters had not determined otherwise. After the war, a careful examination of the stock could be undertaken. Under no circumstances, however, should a centralisation of all the libraries be undertaken. Signed Bormann."

I now offer in evidence Document 061-PS, Exhibit USA 692. This is a secret letter from Bormann, dated 11th January, 1944, in which Bormann discloses - and we stress this, very important as it seems to us, - the existence of large-scale operations to drain off commodities from German-occupied Europe for delivery to the bombed-out population in Germany. The Tribunal knows that the Hague Regulations and the laws of war permit the requisitioning of goods and services only for the use of the

Army of Occupation and for the needs of the administration of the area. This proposal and this action represents the requisitioning of materials in occupied areas for the use of the folk at home, of the Home Front.

I now quote the first two paragraphs of the English translation of Bormann's letter of 11th January, 1944, set forth in the English translation of our Document 061-PS, which reads as follows:

> "Since the supply of textiles and household goods for the bombed populations is becoming increasingly difficult, the proposition was repeatedly made to effect purchases in the occupied territories in greater proportions. Various district leaders (Gauleiter) proposed to let these purchases be handled by suitable private merchants who know these districts and have corresponding connections.
>
> I have brought these proposals to the attention of the Reich Minister of Economics, and am quoting his reply of 16th December, 1943, on account of its fundamental importance: 'I consider it a specially important task to make use of the economic power of the occupied territories for the Reich. You are aware of the fact that, since the occupation of the Western territories, purchases in these countries have been affected in very large proportions. Raw materials, semi-finished products and stocks in finished goods have been rolling into Germany for months; valuable machines were sent to our armaments industry. Everything was done at that time to increase our armament potentialities. Later on the shipments of these important economic goods were replaced by the so-called distribution of orders from industry to industry."

I shall end the quotation there. The rest is not material to the matter.

In the course of the war - and this is of utmost importance, in the view of the prosecution -

THE PRESIDENT: Is it clear that that was confiscation?

LIEUTENANT LAMBERT: It was not suggested, Sir, that it was confiscation. Our point was that The Hague Regulations allow requisitions in return for payment only for the needs of the Army of Occupation and for the needs of administration of the occupied area. This represents, as it seems to us, a requisitioning programme for the needs of the Home Front. It is on that point that we offer it.

We come now to what the prosecution considers a most important point against the defendant Bormann. In the course of the war Bormann issued a series of orders establishing Party jurisdiction over the treatment of prisoners of war, especially when employed as forced labour.

The Tribunal knows that, under the Geneva Convention of 1929 relating to prisoners of war, prisoners of war are the captives, not of the troops who take them, or even of the army which captures them, but of the capturing power; and it is the capturing power which has jurisdiction over and responsibility for them.

By the series of decrees now to be put in, Bormann asserts and establishes Nazi Party jurisdiction over Allied prisoners of war. In the exercise of that Party jurisdiction he called for excessively harsh and brutal treatment of such prisoners.

I now offer in evidence Document 232-PS as Exhibit USA, 643, This is a decree of the defendant Bormann, dated 13th September, 1944, addressed, will the Tribunal please note, to all Reichsleiter, Gauleiter, and Kreisleiter, and leaders of, the Nazi affiliated organisations-numerous levels, that is, of the Leadership Corps of the Nazi Party-a decree establishing Nazi Party jurisdiction over the use of prisoners of war for forced labour.

I quote the first three paragraphs of Bormann's order set forth on Page 1 of the English translation of Document 232-PS, which reads as follows:

"The regulations, valid until now, on the treatment of prisoners of war, and the tasks of the guard units, are no longer justified in view of the demands of the total war effort."

The prosecution would intrude to ask the question: Since when do the exigencies of the war effort repeal or modify the provisions of International Law?

"Therefore, the Supreme Command (O.K.W.) of the Armed Forces, on my suggestion, issued the regulation, a copy of which is enclosed. The following observations are made on its contents:

(1) The understanding exists between the Chief of the Supreme Command of the Armed Forces (O.K.W.) and myself, that the co-operation of the Party in the commitment of prisoners of war is inevitable. Therefore, the officers assigned to the prisoner of war system have been instructed to co-operate most closely with the bearers of sovereignty (Hoheitstrager). The commandants of the prisoner-of-war camps have to detail, immediately, liaison officers to the Kreisleiter.

Thus the opportunity will be afforded the Hoheitstrager to alleviate existing difficulties locally, to exercise influence on the behaviour of guards units - and this is the point we underline - and to better assimilate the commitment of prisoners of war to the political and economic demands."

Will the Tribunal permit me to observe that on the face of this order, addressed to Reichsleiter, Gauleiter and Kreisleiter, and to the officials of the Leadership Corps, in the terms of the order itself, Hoheitstrager are referred to as co-operating media in this scheme.

The Tribunal has graciously given me an opportunity to observe that this decree is addressed to Reichsleiter, Gauleiter, Kreisleiter, and to the leaders of the affiliated and controlled Nazi organisations. As the Tribunal knows, within the Leadership Corps of the Nazi Party, the Kreisleiter is a pretty low level. He is a county leader. On the face of the decree itself the co-operation of the Hoheitstrager is directed, and the Tribunal knows, under the evidence presented against the Leadership Corps, that Hoheitstrager range all the way from the Reichsleiter on the top, down to and including the 500,000 or so Blockleiter implicated.

I next offer in evidence Document D-163-PS, as Exhibit USA 694. This is a letter of the defendant Bormann, dated 5th November, 1941, and addressed, the Tribunal will please note, to all Reichsleiter, Gauleiter and Kreisleiter (the last just mere county leaders), transmitting to these officials of the Leadership Corps of the Nazi Party the instructions of the Reich Minister of the Interior, prohibiting decent burials with religious ceremonies for Russian prisoners of war. I quote the pertinent portions of these instructions, beginning with the next to the last sentence of Page 1 of the English translation of D-163, which reads as follows:

"To save costs, Service Departments of the Army will generally be contacted regarding transport of corpses (furnishing of vehicles) whenever possible. No coffins will be indented for the transfer and burial. The body will be completely enveloped with strong paper (if possible, oil, tar, asphalt paper) or other suitable material. Transfer and burial is to be carried out unobtrusively. If a number of corpses have to be disposed of, the burial will be carried out in a communal grave. In this case, the bodies will be buried side by side (but not on top of each other) and in accordance with the local custom regarding depth of graves. Where a graveyard is the place of burial a distant part will be chosen. No" - we repeat - "No burial ceremony or decoration of graves will be allowed."

I now offer in evidence Document 228-PS, Exhibit USA 695. This is a Bormann circular, dated 25th November, 1943, issued from the Headquarters of the Fuehrer demanding harsher treatment of prisoners of war and the increased exploitation of their manpower. I now quote the Bormann circular which is set forth on Page 1 of the English translation of Document 228-PS, which reads as follows:

> "Individual Gau-administrations often refer in reports to a too indulgent treatment of P.W.'s on the part of the guard personnel. In many places, according to these reports, the guarding authorities have even developed into protectors and caretakers of the P.W.'s.
>
> I informed the Supreme Command of the Armed Forces of these reports, with the comment that the productive German working population absolutely cannot understand it, if, in a time in which the German people is fighting for existence or non-existence, P.W.'s - hence our enemies - are leading a better life than the German working man, and that it is an urgent duty of every German who has to do with P.W.'s, to bring about a complete utilisation of their manpower.
>
> The Chief of P.W. affairs in the Supreme Command of the Armed Forces has now given the unequivocal order, attached hereto in copy form, to the commanders of P.W.'s in the military districts. I request that this order be brought orally to the attention of all party office holders in the appropriate manner.
>
> In case complaints about unsuitable treatment of P.W.'s still come to light, they are to be immediately communicated to the commanders of the P.W.'s with a reference to the attached order."

The Tribunal will note, of course, that, on the face of the decree, Bormann instructs that these orders be communicated orally to all Party officials, and that surely must include the members of the Leadership Corps of the Nazi Party.

THE PRESIDENT: Speaking for myself, I do not see anything particularly wrong in that communication.

LIEUTENANT LAMBERT: On that point, Sir, we submit that if you take a document which says: "We wish to utilise all the possible labour power of P.W.'s under our control, and to get this result by suitable means" probably it tends to appear unexceptional. But viewing this document in relation to the other evidence already in and to be presented, which show a concerted and settled policy by Bormann and his co- conspirators to -

THE PRESIDENT: Well, it is not necessary to argue it.

LIEUTENANT LAMBERT: Yes, Sir. Thank you, Sir.

The attention of the Tribunal is invited to Document 656-PS, previously put in as Exhibit USA 339. The Tribunal will recall that this is a secret Bormann circular transmitting instructions of the Nazi High Command of 29th January, 1943, providing for the enforcement of labour demands on Allied prisoners of war through the use of weapons and corporal punishment. I quote a brief excerpt from these instructions, beginning with the third sentence of the third numbered paragraph of Page 2 of the English translation of Document 656-PS, which reads as follows, and I quote:

> "Should the prisoner of war not fulfil his order, then he" - that is the guard unit, the guard personnel - "then he has, in the case of the most pressing need and danger, the right to force obedience with arms if he has no other means.

He can use arms as much as is necessary to attain his goal. If the assistant guard is not armed, then he is authorised to force obedience by other applicable means."

The Tribunal knows that under the Geneva Prisoners of War Convention of 1929, when prisoners of war prove derelict and refuse to carry out proper orders of the captive power or its forces, such prisoners of war are subject to court martial and military proceedings as if they were serving under their own forces. Here is a decree which, on its face, authorises or attempts to authorise guard personnel to use the rifle or other suitable means of violence, and, of course, your Lordship will understand it was this type of document we had in mind when we suggested that the decree of Bormann should be considered in the light of his other orders relating to the treatment of prisoners of war.

THE PRESIDENT: The Tribunal will adjourn now.

(A recess was taken.)

LIEUTENANT LAMBERT: The Tribunal will recall that at the close of the morning session I had been putting in a series of decrees of the defendant Bormann in which he called for increasingly harsh and severe treatment of Allied prisoners of war. These instructions issued by the defendant Bormann culminated in his decree of 30th September, 1944. The attention of the Tribunal is invited to Document 058-PS, previously put in as Exhibit USA 456. The Tribunal will recall that this decree of the defendant Bormann removed jurisdiction over all prisoners of war from the Nazi High Command and transferred it to Himmler. The decree also provided that all P.W. camp commanders should be under the orders of the local S.S. commanders. By virtue of this order, Hitler was enabled to proceed, with his programme of inhuman treatment and even extermination of Allied prisoners of war.

We now proceed to put in what the prosecution conceive to be extremely important and extremely, incriminating evidence against Bormann and the co-conspirators, that is, the responsibility of the defendant Bormann for the organised lynching of Allied airmen. I offer in evidence Document 062- PS, Exhibit USA 696, and I very respectfully request the Tribunal to turn to this document. On its face it is an order dated 13th March, 1940, by the defendant Hess addressed to Reichsleiters, Gauleiters and other Nazi officials and organisations. In this order these Party officials are instructed by the defendant Hess to direct the German civil population to arrest or liquidate all baled-out Allied fliers. I call the attention of the Tribunal to the third paragraph on the first page of the English translation of Document 062-PS. In the third paragraph Hess directs that these instructions, which I shall soon read, are to be passed out only orally to all - will the Tribunal please mark that - to all District Leaders or Kreisleiters, Ortsgruppenleiters, Zellenleiters and even the Block Leaders; that is to say, this order must be passed out by all the officials of the Leadership Corps to the Hoheitstrager, ranging from Reichsleiter down to and including the Blockleiter.

Now turn to Document 062-PS, and the Tribunal will find the instructions which Hess demanded be disseminated by the Leadership Corps orally: the lynching of Allied fliers. These directions are headed: "About behaviour in case of landings of enemy planes or parachutists." The first three instructions I omit, as not material to the basic point now being made. Instruction 4 reads, and I quote:

"Likewise enemy parachutists are immediately to be arrested or liquidated."

It speaks for itself and requires no further comment from the prosecution.

Now in order to ensure the success of this scheme ordered by the defendant Hess, Bormann issued a secret letter, dated 30th May, 1944, to the officials - if the Tribunal will please mark - of the Leadership Corps of the Nazi Party, prohibiting any police measures or criminal proceedings against German civilians who had lynched or murdered Allied airmen. This document, our 057-PS, has been previously put in and received by the Tribunal in connection with the prosecution's case against the alleged criminal organisation, the Leadership Corps of the Nazi Party.

Now, may it please the Tribunal, that such lynchings, organised, authorised and consented to by defendant Bormann, actually took place, has since been fully and indisputably demonstrated by, trials by American Military Commissions, which have resulted in the conviction of German civilians for the murder of Allied fliers. I request the Tribunal to take judicial notice of Military Commission Order No. 2, Headquarters 15th U.S. Army, dated 23rd June, 1945. This order is our Document 2559-PS. This order imposed the sentence of death upon a German civilian for violation of the laws and usages of war in murdering an American airman who had baled out and landed without any means of defence.

The Tribunal will note, from that order of the American Military Commission, the 15th August, 1944, as the date of the crime; Bormann's order was dated May, 1944.

I request the Tribunal to notice judicially Military Commission Order No. 5, Headquarters 3rd U.S. Army and Eastern Military District, dated 18th October, 1945. This order is set forth in Document 2560-PS. This order imposed a sentence of death upon a German national for violating the laws and usages of war by murdering, on or about 12th December, 1944, an American airman who landed in German territory.

We could cite further orders of American and other Allied Military Commissions sentencing German civilians to death for the lynching and murdering of Allied airmen who had baled out and landed without means of defence on German territory, We think our point is made by taking the time of the Tribunal to cite those two orders.

As previously mentioned in the trial address, on 20th October 1944, when Nazi defeat in the war had become certain, Bormann assumed political and organisational command of the newly-formed Volkssturm, the People's Army. By virtue of ordering the continued resistance by the Volkssturm, Bormann bears some responsibility for the resistance which prolonged the aggressive war for months.

I come now, if it please the Tribunal, to present the proofs showing that Bormann authorised, directed and participated in a wide variety of Crimes against Humanity in aid of the conspiracy. Bormann played an important role in the administration of the Forced Labour Programme. I offer in evidence Document D-226, Exhibit USA 697. This is a Speer circular, a circular of the defendant Speer, of 10th November, 1944, transmitting Himmler's instructions that the Party and the Gestapo should co-operate in securing a larger productivity from the millions of impressed foreign workers in Germany. I quote the second numbered paragraph of Page 2 of the English translation of Document D-226, which reads as follows:

> "All men and women of the N.S.D.A.P., its subsidiaries and affiliated bodies in the works" - meaning of course factories - "will, in accordance with instructions from their Kreisleiters, be warned by their Local Group Leaders" - we intrude to say that means Ortsgruppenleiters - "and be put under obligation to play their part in keeping foreigners under the most careful observation. They will report the least suspicion to the works foreman, which he will pass on to the Defence Deputy or, where such a Deputy has not been appointed, to the Police Department concerned, whilst at the same time reporting to the works manager and the Local Group Leader (the Ortsgruppenleiter) to exert untiringly and continuously their influence on

foreigners, both in word and deed, in regard to the certainty of German victory and the German will to resist, thus producing a further increase of output in the works. Party members, both men and women, and members of Party organisations and affiliated bodies must be expected, more than ever before, to conduct themselves in an exemplary manner."

Now, in a word, the significance of that decree: It is true, it is a circular of Speer's, reciting an arrangement between himself and Himmler, but the effect of the arrangement is to impose the onus, and the continuous task of supplying foreign workers, on Party members, a Party which, as the Tribunal knows, Bormann headed as executive chief.

Under the decree of 24th January, 1942, no such directive could have been issued without the participation of Bormann, both in its preparation and its enactment.

I now offer in evidence Document 025-PS as Exhibit USA 698. This is a conference report dated 4th September, 1942, which states that the recruitment, importation, mobilisation, and grading of 500,000 female domestic workers. from the East would be handled exclusively by the defendant Sauckel, Himmler, and the defendant Bormann. I quote the first two sentences of the third paragraph of the English translation of Document 025-PS, which reads as follows:

"The Fuehrer has ordered the immediate importation of 400,000 to 500,000 female domestic Eastern workers from the Ukraine between the ages of 15 and 35, and has charged the General Deputy for Labour Mobilisation with the execution of this action, which is to end in about three months. In connection with this - this is also approved by Reichsleiter Bormann - the illegal bringing of female housekeepers into the Reich by members of the Armed Forces or various other agencies, is to be allowed subsequently and, furthermore, irrespective of the official recruiting, is not to be prevented."

I now quote from the first sentence of the last paragraph on Page 4 of the English translation of Document 025-PS, and this is the part that brings in the defendant Bormann with the scheme:

"Generally one gathered from this conference that the questions concerning the recruitment and mobilisation, as well as the treatment of female domestic workers from the East, are being handled by the General Deputy for Labour Mobilisation, the Reichsfuehrer S.S., and the Chief, of the German Police and the Party Chancery, and that the Reich Ministry for the Occupied Territories of the East is in these questions considered as having no or only limited competence."

The Party Chancery is here mentioned in terms, and Bormann was the leader of the Party Chancery, as the Tribunal knows.

Now the defendant imposed his will on the administration of the German-occupied areas, and insisted on the ruthless exploitation of the inhabitants of the occupied East. The attention of the Tribunal is respectfully invited to Document R-36, previously put in as Exhibit USA 344. The Tribunal is well acquainted with this document, for it has been referred to several times in these proceedings, and knows that this is an official memorandum of the Ministry for Eastern Territories, dated 19th August, 1942, which states that the repressive views of the defendant Bormann, with respect to the inhabitants of the Eastern areas, actually determined German occupational policies in the East. The Tribunal recalls the now almost notorious quotation from this Document R-36, which purports to paraphrase and constitute the essence of Bormann's views with respect to German occupational policy in the East. So often has it been quoted that I shall resist the temptation to repeat it, but in essence it comes to this. Bormann in effect says:

"The Slavs are to work for us. In so far as we do not need them, they may die. They should not receive the benefits of the German public health system. We do not care about their fertility. They may practise abortion and use contraceptives; the more the better. We do not want them educated; it is enough if they can count up to one hundred. Such stooges will be the more useful to us. Religion we leave to them as a diversion. As to food, they will not get any more than is absolutely necessary. We are the masters; we come first."

We respectfully submit this as an accurate paraphrase and summary of the text of that document, Document R-36.

The attention of the Tribunal is next respectfully invited to Document 654-PS, previously put in as Exhibit USA 218. The Tribunal will recall that this is a conference report, dated 18th November, 1942, embodying an agreement between the Minister of Justice and Himmler, entered into by Bormann's suggestions, under which all inhabitants of the Eastern occupied areas are subjected to a brutal police regime in the place of an ordinary, judicial system. This agreement refers all disputes between the Party, Reich Minister for Justice and Himmler to Bormann for settlement.

Now, because Bormann issued these and related orders, we submit that he bears a large share of the responsibility for the discriminatory treatment and the extermination of great numbers of persons in German-occupied areas of the East.

With the indulgence of the Tribunal, I put the substance of what I have been privileged to present in a few words. We have shown that Bormann, only 45 years old at the time of Germany's defeat, contributed his entire adult life to the furtherance of the conspiracy. His crucial contribution to the conspiracy lay in his direction of the vast powers of the Nazi Party in advancing the multiple objectives of the conspiracy. First as Chief of Staff to the defendant Hess and then as leader, in his own name, of the Party Chancery, subject only to Hitler's supreme authority, he applied and directed the total power of the Party and its agencies to carry into execution the plans of the conspirators. He used his great powers to persecute the Christian Church and clergy, and was an unrepentant foe of the fundamentals of the Christianity with which he warred.

He actively authorised and participated in measures designed to persecute the Jews, and his was a strong hand in pressing down the crown of thorns of misery on the brow of the Jewish people, both in Germany and in German-occupied Europe.

As Chief of the Party Chancery and Secretary to the Fuehrer, Bormann authorised, directed and participated in a wide variety of War Crimes and Crimes against Humanity, including, without limitation, the lynching of Allied airmen, the enslavement and inhuman treatment of the inhabitants of German-occupied Europe, the cruelty of impressed labour, the breaking up of homes contrary to the clear provisions of the Hague regulations, and the planned persecution and extermination of the civil population of Eastern Europe.

May it please this Tribunal, every schoolboy knows that Hitler was an evil man. The point we respectfully emphasise is that, without chieftains like Bormann, Hitler would never have been able to seize and consolidate total power in Germany, but would have been left to walk the wilderness alone.

Bormann was, in truth, an evil archangel to the Lucifer of Hitler, and, although he may remain a fugitive from the justice of this Tribunal, with an empty chair in the dock, he cannot escape responsibility for his illegal conduct.

And we close with what seems to us an extremely important point. Bormann may not be here, but under the last sentence of Article 6 of the Charter, every defendant in this dock shown in our evidence to have been a leader, an organiser, an inciter and an accomplice of this conspiracy is responsible for the acts of all persons in furtherance of the general scope of the conspiracy. Resting squarely on this proposition we submit, even though Bormann is not here, that every man in the dock shares responsibility for his criminal acts. And with this we close. The name of Bormann is not "written in water," but will be remembered as long as the record of your Honours' Tribunal is preserved.

I now have the privilege of introducing Lieutenant Henry Atherton, who will present the case for the prosecution against the individual defendant Seyss-Inquart.

LIEUTENANT HENRY ATHERTON: May it please the Tribunal, the prosecution has prepared a trial brief for the convenience of the Tribunal showing the individual responsibility of the defendant Seyss-Inquart. Copies of this brief are now being handed to the Tribunal. At the same time the document books which bear the letters "KK" and which contain translations of the evidence referred to in the brief, or to be introduced in evidence at this time, are also being handed to the Tribunal. At the outset I wish to make clear my intention to deal at this time only with the individual responsibility of Seyss-Inquart for the crimes charged in Counts 1 and 2 of the Indictment. Evidence to show his guilt as charged under Counts 3 and 4 of the Indictment, that is, evidence specifically directed thereunto, is to be introduced later by the Prosecutors of the French Republic and the Soviet Union.

Seyss-Inquart has agreed that he held the following positions in State and Party, and I am referring now to Document 2910-PS, which is Exhibit USA 17. He was State Councillor of Austria from May, 1937, to 12th February, 1938. He was Minister of Interior and Security of Austria from 16th February, 1938, to 11th March, 1938; Chancellor of Austria from 11th March to 15th March, 1938; Reich Governor of Austria from 15th March, 1938, to 1st May, 1939; Reich Minister without Portfolio from 1st May, 1939, until September of that year; Member of the Reich Cabinet from 1st May, 1939, until the end of the war; Chief of the Civil Administration of South Poland from the early part of September, 1939, until 12th October, 1939; Deputy Governor- General of Poland under the defendant Frank from 12th October, 1939, until May, 1940; and, finally, Reich Commissioner of the Occupied Territories of the Netherlands from 29th May, 1940, until the end of the war. He has also agreed that he became a member of the National Socialist Party on 13th March, 1938, and that he was appointed a General in the S.S. two days later.

Now this list of positions which Seyss-Inquart has agreed that he held, if the Tribunal please, shows the place which he held in the Nazi Common Plan or Conspiracy. It shows his steady rise to greater influence and power, and especially it emphasises his particular talent, his skill in effecting the enslavement of the smaller nations surrounding Germany, for the benefit of what he called the Greater German Reich.

Now the defendant Seyss-Inquart first became a member of the Nazi conspiracy in connection with the Nazi assault on Austria. Mr. Alderman has shown how the Nazis implemented their diplomatic and military preparations for this event by intensive political preparations within Austria.

The ultimate purpose of these preparations was to secure the appointment of Nazis, or persons known to be sympathetic to them, to key positions in the Austrian Government, particularly that of Minister of the Interior and Security, which controlled the police, thus permitting quick suppression of all opposition to the Nazis when the time came.

For this purpose Seyss-Inquart was a most effective tool, the first of the so-called Quislings or traitors used by the Nazis to further their aggressions and to fasten their hold on their victims. Seyss-Inquart has admitted his membership in the Party only from 13th March, 1938, but I want to show that he was closely affiliated with them at a much earlier time. For this purpose I now offer in evidence Document 3271-PS as Exhibit USA 700.

Reading from Page 9 of the translation, he says in this letter, which is a letter to Himmler, dated 19th August, 1939:

"As far as my membership in the Party is concerned, I state that I was never asked to join the Party but had asked Dr. Kier in December, 1931, to clarify my relationship with the Party, since I regarded the Party as the basis for the solution of the Austrian problem.... I paid my membership fees, as I believe, directly to the 'Gau' Vienna. These contributions also took place after the period of suppression. Later on I had direct contact with the Ortsgruppe in Dornbach. My wife paid these fees, but the 'Blockwart'"- and I believe that is another word for 'Blockleiter" - was never in doubt, considering that this amount, forty shillings per month, was a difficult accomplishment for my wife and myself, and I was in every respect treated as a Party member."

Seyss-Inquart, in the last sentence of the paragraph says:

"In every way, therefore, I felt as a Party member, considered myself a Party member, as stated, as far back as December, 1931."

Now, if the Tribunal please, and before I leave this letter, I want just to refer to one or two sentences which the Tribunal will find in the third paragraph on Page 7 of the translation. Referring to a meeting which he had had with Hitler, Seyss-Inquart says:

"I left this discussion a very upright man with the unspeakably happy feeling of being permitted to be a tool of the Fuehrer."

The truth of the matter is that Seyss-Inquart was an active supporter of the Nazis at all times after 1931. But after the Nazi Party in Austria was declared illegal in July, 1934, he avoided too notorious a connection with the Nazi organisation, in order to safeguard what the Nazis called his good legal position. By this device he was better able to use his connections with Catholics and others in his work of infiltration for his Nazi superiors.

The Tribunal will remember, as Document 2219-PS, Exhibit USA 62, a letter from Seyss-Inquart to Goering of 14th July, 1939, in which Seyss-Inquart makes this clear. It was in this letter also that he said:

"Yet I know that I cling with unconquerable tenacity to the goal in which I believe; that is Greater Germany and the Fuehrer."

The evidence which Mr. Alderman introduced told in detail the manner in which the Nazi conspirators carried out their assault on Austria. I do not intend to attempt to review any part of this evidence. I merely wish to refer the Tribunal to two documents, which are particularly important in showing the part played by this defendant. I refer to the Rainer report to, Gauleiter Burckel, dated 6th July, 1939, which relates the part played by the Austrian Nazi Party, the defendant Seyss-Inquart, and others, between July, 1934, and March, 1938, and the astonishing record of telephone calls between the defendant Goering, or his agents in Berlin, and Seyss-Inquart and others in Vienna on 11th March, 1938. The Rainer report is Document 812-PS, Exhibit USA 61, and was read into the record beginning at Page 502 of the English version and continuing for a number of pages thereafter. The transcript of the telephone calls is Document 2949-PS, Exhibit USA 76, and was introduced first at Page 566 of the English record.

Now, in order to supplement this and further to show that part played by Seyss-Inquart, I wish now to introduce in evidence the voluntary statement which Seyss-Inquart signed with advice of his counsel on 10th December, 1945. This is Document 3425-PS, and I offer it as Exhibit USA 701.

In this statement, Seyss-Inquart explains, from his point of view, his part in bringing about the Anschluss. I want to read first just a few -sentences from the second paragraph on the first page. It states - and I quote:

"In 1918 I became interested in the Anschluss of Austria with Germany. From that year on I worked, planned and collaborated with others of a like mind to bring about a union of Austria with Germany. It was my desire to effect this union of the two countries in an evolutionary manner, and by legal means."

Omitting just a sentence or two:

"I supported also the National Socialist Party as long as it was legal, because it declared itself with particular determination in favour of the Anschluss. From 1932 onwards I made financial contributions to this party, but I discontinued financial support when it was declared illegal in 1934."

Then passing down another couple of sentences:

"From July, 1936, onwards I tried to help the National Socialists to regain their legal status and, finally, to participate in the Austrian Government. During this time, particularly after the Party was forbidden in July, 1934, I knew that the radical element of the Party was engaged in terroristic activities, such as attacks on railroads, bridges, telephone communications, etc. I knew that the governments of both Chancellors, Dollfuss and Schuschnigg, although they held in principle the same total German viewpoint, were opposed to the Anschluss then, because of the National Socialist regime in the Reich. I was sympathetic towards the efforts of the Austrian Nazi Party to gain political power and corresponding influence, because they were in favour of the Anschluss."

Now, briefly summarising, the Tribunal will note that the defendant tells how his appointment as State Councillor in May, 1937, was the result of an agreement between Austria and Germany in July, 1936, which Rainer agreed Seyss-Inquart had helped to bring about; and that his appointment as Minister of the Interior and Security was one of the results of the agreement between Schuschnigg and Hitler at Berchtesgaden, 12th February, 1938. He admits too that, after the appointment and the agreement, the Austrian National Socialists engaged in more and more widespread demonstrations. He tells how, immediately after this appointment as Minister of the Interior and Security, he went directly to Berlin and talked with Himmler and Hitler; and then, finally, he describes the events of that day, of 11th March, 1938, when with the full support of German military power he became Chancellor.

I do not want to quote at length from that description, because the Tribunal knows already what happened. Reading from the middle of Page 3, he says:

"At 10 o'clock in the morning, Glaise-Horstenau and I went to the Bund Chancellery, and conferred for about two hours with Dr. Schuschnigg. We told him all that we knew, particularly about the possibility of disturbances and preparations by the Reich.

The Chancellor said that he would give his decision by 14.00 hours. While I was with Glaise-Horstenau and Dr. Schuschnigg, I was repeatedly called to the telephone to speak to Goering."

THE PRESIDENT: Has this been read already?

LIEUTENANT ATHERTON: No, Sir, this document has not been in before.

THE PRESIDENT: Very well.

LIEUTENANT ATHERTON:

"He informed me that the agreement of 12th February had been cancelled and demanded Dr. Schuschnigg's resignation and my appointment as Chancellor."

The Tribunal has heard the other side of that story, the, actual telephone conversations. And then, finally, the next two paragraphs; he tells how Keppler repeatedly urged him to send a telegram calling on Germany to send troops, and that at first he refused but finally acquiesced, and I now read from the next to the last paragraph:

"As I am able to gather from the records available, I was requested about 10 p.m. to give my sanction to another somewhat altered telegram about which I informed President Miklas and Dr. Schuschnigg. Finally President Miklas appointed me Chancellor, and a little while later he approved my list of proposed ministers."

If the Tribunal will recall, the telegram in question called on Hitler, on behalf of the Provisional Austrian Government, to send German troops as soon as possible in order to support it in its task and help it to prevent bloodshed. The text of the telegram, as printed in Vol. 6 of the "Dokumente der Deutschen Politik," appears as Document 2463-PS of the document book. It is interesting to note that the text of this telegram is substantially identical with that dictated by Goering over the 'phone to Keppler, on the evening of 11th March, which appears on Page 575 of the record.

Now, on the next morning, again referring to the statement of the defendant, he admits that he telephoned Hitler -

THE TRIBUNAL (Mr. Biddle): Are you reading?

LIEUTENANT ATHERTON: No, Sir, I am summarising.

MR. BIDDLE: If you do not read it, it is not in evidence.

LIEUTENANT ATHERTON: In that event I will read a little further. I read now the last paragraph on Page 3:

"During the morning of 12th March I had a telephone conversation with Hitler, in which I suggested that, while German troops were entering Austria, Austrian troops, as assembled, should march on the Reich. Hitler agreed to this suggestion, and he agreed to meet in Linz in Upper Austria later on, on the same day. He then flew to Linz with Himmler, who had arrived in Vienna from Berlin. I greeted Hitler on the balcony of the City Hall and said that Article 88 of the Treaty of St. Germain was now inoperative."

I have referred to the slavish manner in which, as the evidence has shown, Seyss-Inquart carried out orders conveyed to him by telephone from Goering on 11th March, 1938, in his negotiations with Chancellor Schuschnigg and President Miklas. This relationship had in fact existed for some time. Early in January, 1938, Seyss-Inquart, although he then held an important position in the Austrian Government, had already considered himself as holding a mandate from the Nazi conspirators in Berlin in his negotiations with his own Government. As evidence of the way in which this happened, I offer Document 3473-PS as Exhibit USA 581. This is a letter from Keppler to Goering, dated 6th January, 1938, in which he states, and I quote:

"Dear General:

Councillor of State, Dr. Seyss-Inquart, has sent a courier to me with the report that his negotiations with the Federal Chancellor, Dr. Schuschnigg, have fallen to the ground, so that he feels compelled to return the mandate entrusted to him."

Dr. Seyss-Inquart desires to have a discussion with me regarding this before he acts accordingly. May I ask your advice, whether at this moment such a step, entailing automatically also the resignation of the Federal Minister von Glaise-Horstenau, appears indicated, or whether I should put forth efforts to postpone such an action?"

The letter is signed by Keppler. On top of the original is a brief note apparently attached by the secretary of the defendant Goering and dated Karinhall, 6th January, 1938, reading as follows:

"Keppler should be told by telephone:

(1) He should do everything to avoid the resignation of Councillor of State Dr. Seyss-Inquart and State Minister von Glaise-Horstenau. If some difficulties should arise, Seyss-Inquart should come to him first of all."

Now, as a result of this directive, apparently telephoned to Keppler, the latter, on 8th January, 1938, wrote a letter to Seyss-Inquart. I now offer this letter, which is Document 3397-PS in evidence, as Exhibit USA 702. Keppler writes, and the Tribunal will remember that Keppler was, at that time, Secretary of State in charge of Austrian Affairs of the German Government:

"Dear State Councillor:

To-day I had a visit from Mr. Pl. who gave us a report of the state of affairs, and informed us that you are seriously considering the question of whether or not you are forced to hand back the mandate entrusted to you.

I informed General Goering of the situation in writing, and G. just informed me that I should try my utmost to prevent you, or anyone else, from taking this step. This is also in the same vein as G.'s conversation with Dr. J. before Christmas; at any rate, G. requests you to undertake nothing of this nature under any circumstances before he himself has the opportunity of speaking with you once more.

I can also inform you that G. is, furthermore, making an effort to speak to Ll., in order that certain improper conditions be eliminated by him."

Then the letter is signed by Keppler.

The two letters together, if the Tribunal please, show clearly enough the extent to which this defendant was a tool, the extent to which he was being used at that time by the conspirators in their planning for their assault on Austria. Now, once German troops were in Austria and Seyss- Inquart had become Chancellor, he lost no time carrying out the plans of his Nazi fellow-conspirators.

I next offer in evidence Document 3254-PS, which is a memorandum written by the defendant Seyss-Inquart entitled "The Austrian Question." It is Exhibit USA 704. I offer it only because of the description which he gives of the manner in which he secured the passage of an Austrian Act in annexing Austria to Germany. He said that on 13th March German officials brought him a proposal for inviting Austria into Germany. They reported that -

THE PRESIDENT: Are you quoting?

LIEUTENANT ATHERTON: I now quote from the middle of Page 20 of the English text:

"I called a meeting of the Council of Ministers, after having been told by Wolff that the Bund President would make no difficulties in regard to that realisation; he would return to his home in the meantime and would await me there. On my proposal the Council of Ministers, assembled in the meantime, adopted the draft bill to which my law section had made some formal modifications. The vote on the 26th April had been planned already in the first draft. According to the provisions of the Constitution of 1st May, 1934, any fundamental modification of the Constitution could be decided by the Council of Ministers, with the approbation of the Bund President. A vote or a confirmation by the nation was in no way provided for. In the event that the Bund President should, for any reason, either resign his functions or be for some time unable to fulfil them, his prerogatives were to go over to the Bund Chancellor. I went to the Bund President with Dr. Wolff. The President told me that he did not know whether this development would be of benefit to the Austrian Nation, but that he did not wish to interfere, and preferred to resign his functions, so that all rights would come into my hands according to the Constitution."

And then, omitting two or three sentences to the top of Page 21:

"Thereafter I returned to Linz, where I arrived about midnight and reported to the Fuehrer the accomplishment of the Anschluss law."

The same day Germany formally incorporated Austria into the Reich by a decree, and declared it to be a province of the German Reich, in violation of Article 80 of the Treaty of Versailles. I ask the Court to take judicial notice of, Document 2307-PS, which is the decree to this effect, published in 1938 Reichsgesetzblatt, Part 1, Page 237.

If the defendant Seyss-Inquart seems unduly modest as to the part which he played in undermining the Government to which he owed allegiance, his fellow conspirators were quick to recognise the importance of his contributions. In a speech on the 26th March, 1938, the defendant Goering said - and I am reading now from Document 3270-PS, Exhibit USA 703, which is an extract from the "Dokumente der Deutschen Politik," Volume 6, Page 183:

"A complete unanimity between the Fuehrer and the N.S. Confidants inside of Austria existed.... If the N.S. rising succeeded so quickly and thoroughly and without bloodshed, it is first of all due to the intelligent and decisive firmness of the present Reichsstatthalter Seyss- Inquart and his confidants."

I want, before leaving the matter of the Anschluss, to stress this once more, because this was a time of great importance, and it was Seyss-Inquart who held the key position in this first open attack on another country. Had it not been for his part - as has been shown - things might have gone very differently; and if there were no other place where he was connected with the conspirators' plans for aggression, this would be sufficient to rank him with the foremost of the conspirators.

Now, passing on, Mr. Alderman has shown the way in which Seyss-Inquart co-operated with the conspirators in integrating Austria as fully as possible into the Reich, making its resources available to the Reich - its resources of wealth and its resources of manpower.

In furtherance of the conspirators' plan Reichsstatthalter Seyss-Inquart, for the first time, demonstrated his talent for the persecution of Jewish citizens. In an address in Vienna on 26th March, 1938, which will be found at Page 2326 of the record, he recalls that Goering expressly commissioned this defendant, as Reichsstatthalter, to institute anti-Semitic measures.

And the Tribunal will remember from previous evidence the kind of wholesale larceny which this involved. So successfully did Seyss-Inquart perform his task that at the meeting of the Air Ministry, under the chairmanship of the defendant Goering on the 12th November, 1938, Fischbock, a member of Seyss-Inquart's official family, was able to relate the efficiency with which the Civil Administration in Austria dealt with the so-called "Jewish Question." I refer to Document 1816-PS, Exhibit USA 261 - and I am reading first from Page 14 of the English translation. The Tribunal will note that this is the third full paragraph from the bottom of Page 14:

"Your Excellency:

In this matter we have already a very complete plan for Austria. There are 12,000 Jewish artisans and 5,000 Jewish retail shops in Vienna. Before the National Revolution we had already a definite plan for tradesmen, regarding this total of 17,000 stores. Of the shops of the 12,000 artisans about 10,000 were to be closed definitely and 2,000 were to be kept open. 4,000 of the 5,000 retail stores should be closed and 1,000 should be kept open, that is, were to be Aryanised. According to this plan, between 3,000 and 3,500 of the total of 17,000 stores would be kept open, all others closed. This was decided following investigations in every single branch, and according to local needs, in agreement with all competent authorities, and is ready for publication as soon as we receive the law which we requested in September; this law shall empower us to withdraw licences from artisans, quite independent of the Jewish Question." Goering said, "I shall have this decree issued to-day."

Then, if the Tribunal please, I just wish to read one more sentence from the middle of the next page, in which Fischbock says:

"Out of 17,000 stores 12,000 or 14,000 would be shut down and the remainder Aryanised or handed over to the Bureau of Trustees which is operated by the State."

And Goering replies:

"I have to say that this proposal is grand. This way the whole affair would be wound up in Vienna, one of the, Jewish capitals, so to speak, by Christmas or by the end of the year."

The defendant Funk then says, "We can do the same thing over here."

In other words, Seyss-Inquart's so-called solution was so highly regarded that it was considered a model for the rest of the Reich.

The task of integrating Austria into the Reich being substantially complete, the Nazi conspirators were able to use Seyss-Inquart's expert services for the subjugation of other peoples. As an illustration I refer the Tribunal to Document D-571, Exhibit USA 112, which has already been read in evidence. The Tribunal will recall that from this document it appeared that on the 21st March, 1939, an official of the British Government reported from Prague to Viscount Halifax that a little earlier, on the 11th of March, 1939, Seyss-Inquart, Burckel and five German generals attended a meeting of the Cabinet of the Slovak Government, and told them that they should proclaim the independence of Slovakia, that Hitler had decided to settle the question of Czechoslovakia definitely (this has been read in Court to- day) and that, unless they did as they were told, Hitler would disinterest himself in their fate. It just gives an indication of the manner in which this man continued to be busy in the aggressive plans of these Nazi conspirators.

Now, early in September, 1939, after the opening of the attack against Poland, Seyss-Inquart became Chief of the Civil Administration of South Poland. A few weeks later, on 12th October, 1939, Hitler promulgated a decree providing that territories occupied by German troops, except those incorporated within the German Reich, should be subject to the authority of the Governor-General of the Occupied Polish Territories, and he appointed the defendant Frank as Governor-General and the defendant Seyss-Inquart as Deputy Governor-General. This decree will be found in the 1939 Reichsgesetzblatt, Part I, Page 2077, and I ask the Tribunal to take judicial notice of it. Shortly thereafter, on 26th October, 1939, Frank promulgated a decree establishing the administration of the Occupied Polish Territories, of which he was Governor. This decree is published in the "Dokumente der Deutschen Politik" and appears in the document book as 3468-PS. I am informed that this book, Volume 7, will be Exhibit USA 705, and I offer it as such.

Article III of the decree provided that the Chief of the Office of the Governor-General and the Senior S.S. and Police Leaders should be directly subordinate to the Governor-General and his Deputy. The Deputy, of course, was the defendant Seyss-Inquart.

The significance of that provision is obvious in the light of the evidence which the Tribunal has heard and will hear. I ask the Tribunal to take judicial notice of it.

As Deputy Governor-General of the Polish Occupied Territories, Seyss-Inquart seems to have had the job of setting up a German Administration throughout this territory; that is, he worked under the defendant Frank, but did much of the work of interviewing the various local leaders, telling them what they should do. As an illustration I offer in evidence a report of a trip which Seyss-Inquart and his consultants took between the 17th and 22nd of February, 1939. This is our Document 2278-PS, and I offer it as Exhibit USA 706. If the Tribunal please, I have misstated that date or period. It was 17th to the 22nd November, 1939 - in other words, shortly after the administration was set up. On the first page of the English translation - and I now quote from the second full paragraph- the following appears:

> "At 3 p.m. Reich Minister Dr. Seyss-Inquart addressed the department heads of the District Chief and stated, among other things, that the chief guiding rule for carrying out German administration in the Government General must be solely the interests of the German Reich. A stern and inflexible administration must make the7 area of use to German economy, and, so that excessive clemency may be guarded against, the results of the intrusion of the Polish race into German territory must be brought, to mind."

This report is too long, if the Tribunal please, to quote from at too great length, but if the Tribunal will turn over to Page 7, I would like to read in some extracts of what occurred while the defendant was in Lublin. From the report it appears that the defendant Seyss-Inquart, after meeting the various local German administrative officers, "then expounded the principles" - and I am now quoting from the top of Page 7 - "in accordance with which the administration in the 'Government' must be conducted."

Then, omitting a sentence:

> "The resources and inhabitants of this country would have to be made of service to the Reich, and only within these limits could they prosper. Independent political thought should no longer be allowed to develop. The Vistula area might perhaps be still more important to German destiny than the Rhine. The Minister than gave as a guiding theme to the District Leaders: 'We will further everything which is of service to the Reich and will put an end to everything which may harm the Reich.' Dr. Seyss-Inquart then added that the Governor-General wished that those men who were fulfilling a task for the Reich here should receive a post with material benefits in keeping with their responsibility and achievements."

Then, if the Tribunal will turn over two more pages, the reporter is describing a sightseeing tour which was made to the village of Wlodawa, Cycow - and I quote:

> "Cycow is a German village ..." - passing down a couple of sentences - Reich

Minister Dr. Seyss-Inquart made a speech in which he pointed out that the fidelity of these Germans to their nationality now found its justification and reward through the strength of Adolf Hitler."

And then the next sentence, apparently thrown in by the reporter:

"This district with its very marshy character could, according to District Chief Schmidt's deliberations, serve as a reservation for the Jews, a measure which might possibly lead to heavy mortality among the Jews."

THE PRESIDENT: We might break off here for ten minutes.

(A recess was taken.)

LIEUTENANT ATHERTON: If the Tribunal please, at the time the Tribunal rose, I was in the process of considering the functions of the defendant Seyss-Inquart, his place as Deputy Governor-General of Poland, between 1939 and 1940.

Now the Tribunal has already heard evidence of the atrocities which were perpetrated by the administration which Seyss-Inquart thus helped to create. The Prosecutors for the Soviet Union will present to the Tribunal more evidence of such atrocities. For our present purposes, to show the importance of the work which this man did to further the Nazi plan for the Government General of Poland, it is enough to quote a few words from the diary of the defendant Frank.

On the occasion of what was apparently a farewell lunch to Seyss-Inquart, when he became Reich Commissar of the Netherlands, Frank said - and I now quote from Document 3465- PS, Pages 5 10 and 511 of Volume 2, the 1940 volume of the diary, which is Exhibit USA 614:

"I am extremely glad, Mr. Reich Commissar and Reich Minister, to assure you, in this hour of your departure, that the months of our collaboration with you belong to the most precious memories of my life, and that your work in the Government General will be remembered forever in the building of the coming World Empire of the German nation."

Passing down a little, if the Tribunal please, Frank went on to say:

"In the construction of the Government General your name will forever take a place of honour as an originator of this organisation and this State system. I express our thanks, Mr. Reich Minister, for your collaboration and for your creative energy."

Then reading the last two or three sentences:

"During the hard times common work united us here in the East, but it is at the same time the starting point for a gigantic power development of the German Reich. Its perfection will show the development of the greatest energy unit which has ever been in the history of the world. In this work you were placed by the Fuehrer very effectively, in the most important position."

And to these remarks the defendant Seyss-Inquart replied - and I now quote from the second page of the translation:

"I learned here a lot, many things which I did not understand before at all, and mainly on account of the initiative and firm leadership as I found them in my friend Dr. Frank."

Then, omitting a sentence:

"I will now go to the West, and I want to be quite open with you. With my whole heart I am present, because my whole attitude is one directed toward the East. In the East we have a National-Socialist mission; over there, in the West, we have a function; that may be the difference."

I submit, if the Tribunal please, that the sentences which I have just read show clearly enough the conscious participation of the defendant Seyss-Inquart in the Polish phase of the conspiracy.

Thus equipped with experience gained in Poland and under the defendant Frank, Seyss-Inquart was ready to undertake his last and most ambitious task, the enslavement of the Netherlands. The ruthless manner in which he performed it marks his position in the Nazi Common Plan or Conspiracy.

I ask the Tribunal first to take judicial notice of a decree of Hitler of 18th May, 1940, which is found in 1940 Reichsgesetzblatt, Part 1, Page 778. The translation will be found in the book as Document 1376-PS. By Section I of this decree it is provided that:

"The Reich Commissar is protector of the interests of the Reich and will represent the supreme power of the Government within the civil sphere. He will be directly subordinated to me and will receive directives and orders from me."

Section 3 provides that:

"The Reich Commissar may use German Police forces to carry out his orders. The German Police forces are at the disposal of the German military commander in so far as military necessities require this and if the missions of the Reich Commissar permit it."

Then by Paragraph or Section 5 of the law it is provided that the Reich Commissar may promulgate laws by decree, such orders to be published in the "Verordnungsblatt" for the Occupied Territory of the Netherlands, a publication which I shall hereafter refer to merely as the "Verordnungsblatt."

On 29th May, 1940, acting within these powers, the defendant promulgated an order covering the exercise of governmental authority in the Netherlands, and this appears as 3588-PS in the document book. I ask the Tribunal to take judicial notice of its contents.

That will contain two decrees. I am now referring to the first one.

By Section 1 of this decree the defendant modestly purports to assume, to the extent required for the fulfilment of his duties, "all powers, privileges and rights heretofore vested in the king and the Government, in accordance with the Constitution and the laws of the Netherlands." That is a direct quotation.

And then Section 5 of the order entrusts the maintenance of public peace, safety and order to the Netherlands Police Force, unless the Reich Commissar calls on German S.S. or Police Forces for the enforcement of his orders. It further provides that the investigation and combating of all activities hostile to the Reich and Germanism shall be the concern of the German Police Force.

On 3rd June, 1940, a further decree was promulgated, concerning the organisation and establishment of the Office of the Reich Commissar. This decree is found in the "Verordnungsblatt" for 1940, Number 1, at Page 11, and is the second decree under Document 3588-PS. This decree provided for general commissioners on the staff of the Reich Commissar to head four enumerated sections, one of which, the Superior S.S. and Police Chief, was to head the section for Public Safety. It was provided by Section 5 of this decree that this official should command the units of the military S.S. and German Police Forces transferred to the occupied Netherlands territories, supervise the Netherlands central and municipal Police Forces, and issue to them necessary orders.

Section 11 provided that the Reich Commissar alone -

THE PRESIDENT: Lieutenant Atherton, do not you think that we can assume that the defendant Seyss-Inquart, who had been appointed to administer the occupied territory of the Netherlands, had all these powers and that you can turn your attention to what he did under those powers?

LIEUTENANT ATHERTON: Yes, Sir, I will do that, but I wanted to make plain to the Tribunal, because of the peculiar set- up of this German Police Force, the fact that he was granted the power to give orders to them, and not only that, but that he customarily did. If that point is made clear, as I believe it is, in these two decrees, I will pass on to the next matter.

THE PRESIDENT: I think the Tribunal has no doubt that an officer under the Reich who had got the powers of the administrator of an occupied territory could make use of the Police Forces.

LIEUTENANT ATHERTON: Yes, Sir.

THE PRESIDENT: It is really a matter that we should be prepared to assume until it is proved to the contrary.

LIEUTENANT ATHERTON: I agree, Sir.

THE PRESIDENT: We would wish you to turn your attention to show what he did, under those powers, which constitute crimes.

LIEUTENANT ATHERTON: Yes, Sir. It is not our intention at this time to go into the crimes against persons and property, which the defendant Seyss-Inquart is responsible for in the Netherlands, in any detail, because evidence of Nazi barbarity in this country is to be presented by our associates, the Prosecutors for the French Republic. It is our purpose only to show a few illustrations, and to give some idea of the scope of this defendant's activities and his responsibilities, as evidence of his part in the execution of the Nazi's Common Plan or Conspiracy, which it is our part to prove.

Now, in the first place, there will be much evidence to show that the defendant was responsible for widespread spoliation of property. Merely as an illustration of the way in which he was implicated in the smallest parts of this, I offer in evidence Document 176-PS, as Exhibit USA 707.

This document is a report on the activities of the "Work- Group Netherlands," a part of the Einsatzstab-Rosenberg, on which the Tribunal has already heard, evidence. Quoting from the first page of this report, the first sentence:

"The Work-Group Netherlands of the Einsatzstab Reichsleiter Rosenberg began its work in agreement with the competent representative of the Reich Commissar, during the first days of September, 1940."

The report then proceeds to detail the property taken from Masonic Lodges and similar institutions. Reading from page - I believe it is Page 3 - of this report, the very bottom:

"An extremely precious library, containing invaluable works on Sanscrit, was confiscated and packed into 96 cases, when the 'Theosophische' Society in Amsterdam was dissolved. A number of smaller libraries belonging to the Spiritists, the Esperanto movement, the Bellamy movement, the International Bible Students and various other minor international organisations, were packed into seven cases; texts belonging to various minor Jewish organisations were packed into four cases; and a library of the 'Anthroposophic Society' in Amsterdam into three.

It is safe to say that the stocks of books confiscated, packed and so far sent to Germany by the Work-Group, are of extraordinary scientific value, and will contribute an integral part of the library of the 'Hohe Schule.'"

The money value of these libraries can only be estimated, but must surely amount to from 30,000,000 to 40,000,000 Reichsmark. Then, quoting from the very end of the report:

"The Work-Group, in executing the aforementioned tasks is bound strictly to the pace set by the Reich Commissar for the handling of the Jewish questions and those of the international organisations."

As Reich Commissar, it was one of the functions of the defendant Seyss-Inquart to supervise the execution of the conspirators' programme for deportation of Dutch citizens to Germany for slave labour. The Tribunal will recall that Mr. Dodd read into evidence at Page 1372 a portion of a transcript of an interrogation of the defendant Sauckel, on 5th October, 1945, in which it appeared that the quotas for the workers for Holland were agreed upon, and then the numbers given to the Reich Commissar Seyss-Inquart to fulfil; and after the quota was given to Seyss-Inquart, it was his mission to fulfil it with the aid of Sauckel's representative. And then the Tribunal will recall that Mr. Dodd, having shown the defendant Seyss-Inquart's part in recruitment for slave labour in this fashion, and his responsibility for it, read into the record (Page 307, Part 2) some portions from Document 1726-PS, Exhibit USA 195, which showed the numbers of Netherlands citizens deported to the Reich at various times. Since that is all a matter of record, I will not go into it again.

In the Netherlands, as in Austria and elsewhere, Seyss- Inquart was relentless in his treatment of Jewish Netherlanders. To illustrate his attitude, I offer in evidence Document 3430-PS, which consists of extracts from the defendant's book, "Four Years in the Netherlands. Collected Speeches." It becomes Exhibit USA 708. In a speech in Amsterdam on 13th March, 1941 - and I am now quoting from Page 57 of the original book, the last extract on the translation - Seyss-Inquart said:

"The Jews, for us, are not Dutch. They are those enemies with whom we can come to neither an armistice nor to peace. This applies here, if you wish, for the duration of the occupation. Do not expect an order from me which stipulates this, except regulations concerning police matters. We will beat the Jews wherever we meet them, and those who join them must bear the consequences. The Fuehrer declared that the Jews have played their final, act in Europe, and therefore they have played their final act."

Now, as promised, the defendant Seyss-Inquart proceeded to promulgate the long series of decrees which first threatened to deprive the Jewish people in the Netherlands of their property, of their rights, and degraded them to something lower than the lowest, and which eventually resulted in their deportation to Poland. These decrees, all signed by Seyss-Inquart, are collected in our brief, Page 65. I ask the Court to take judicial notice of them, By way of illustration, the first to which I wish to refer appears in the document book as 3333-PS, and it is a decree of 26th October, 1940, requiring the registration of businesses belonging to Jews as defined in the decree, including partnerships or corporations in which Jews owned a substantial interest. You have seen that this type of law was the inevitable prelude to mass confiscation of the property of Jews under the Nazi administration. In a law found in "Verordnungsblatt," Volume 6, Page 99, 14th February, 1941, 3325-PS, Dutch universities and colleges were limited in the registration of Jewish students. This of itself does not seem important, but it is a part of the programme to take away from these people their rights and degrade them. Document 3328-PS is a decree published in "Verordnungsblatt, " No. 44, at Page 841, of 23rd October, 1941. This prevented Jews from exercising any profession or trade without authorisation from administrative authorities, and permitted such authorities to order the termination of any employment contract concerning Jews.

As a final illustration I refer in passing to Document 3336- PS, a decree published in the "Verordnungsblatt," No. 13, Page 289, and dated 23rd May, 1942. This decree required all Jews to make written declaration of claims of any kind, under which they might be beneficiaries, at a banking firm known as Lippmann-Rosenthal and Company, which was actually an agency of the Reich at Amsterdam. The decree gave the bank - this named bank - all rights to dispose of the claim, and provided that payment to the bank should be released in full. This type of Nazi decree was, of course, a forerunner of ultimate deportation to the East, and allowed the Nazis to snatch the insurance.

Evidence of the success of this defendant's efforts to annihilate all Jews in the Netherlands has already been read into the record. The Court will find that Major Walsh - again reading from the report of the Netherlands Government, Exhibit USA 195, at Page 1497 - showed that out of 140,000 Jewish Netherlanders, 117,000 were deported, over 115,000 of them to Poland - over 80 per cent. The evidence has shown what was the probable fate of most of these people, and I shall not dwell on it further.

Finally, I want to say a few words about the responsibility of this defendant for the systematic terror practised against the inhabitants of the occupied territory by the Nazis throughout the occupation. Referring again to the collected speeches in Document 3430-PS, on 29th January, 1943, the defendant left little doubt of his point of view. He said, and I quote:

> "It is also clear, now more than ever, that every resistance which is directed against this fight for existence must be suppressed. Some time ago the representatives of the Churches had written to the Wehrmacht Commander and to me, and they presented their ideas in regard to the execution of death sentences which the Wehrmacht Commander announced in the meantime. To this I can say only the following: At the moment in which our men, fathers and sons with iron determination, look towards their fate in the East, and unflinchingly and steadfastly perform their highest pledge, it is unbearable to tolerate conspiracies whose goal is to weaken the rear of this Eastern front. Whoever dares this must be annihilated. We must be severe and become even more severe against our opponents. This is the command of a relentless sequence of events and for us, perhaps, unhumanly hard but our holy duty. We remain human because we do not torture our opponents. We must remain hard in annihilating them."

I do not offer any evidence of the commission of these crimes, because that is to be done by Prosecutors of the French Republic. But the position of the defendant Seyss-Inquart as Reich Commissar, the control which he exercised, which has been shown, particularly over the S.S. and Police, and the attitude of the man himself will make clear his authorisation and participation in the crimes to be proved and are a further indication of his part in the Common Plan.

Seyss-Inquart supported the Nazi Party as early as 1931. He was a traitor to the government to which he owed allegiance and in which he held high office. With full knowledge of the ultimate purposes of the conspirators he bent every effort to integrate Austria into the Reich and to make its resources and manpower, as well as its strategic position, available for the Nazi war machine. He performed these tasks with such ruthless efficiency that he was chosen thereafter for key positions in the enslavement of Poland and the Netherlands - the positions which he filled with such satisfaction to his superiors, that ultimately he came to be one of the foremost and most detested leaders in this Common Plan. As such, under Article 6 of the Charter, he is responsible for all acts performed by any persons in the execution of that plan. As such he is guilty of the crimes charged to him under Counts 1 and 2 of the

Indictment.

I wish to introduce to the Tribunal at this time Dr. Robert M. W. Kempner, who will represent the prosecution in the next phase of the case dealing with the defendant Frick.

DR. KEMPNER: May it please the Tribunal: There have been distributed to the Tribunal and to all defence counsel trial briefs and documents relating to the defendant Frick. The trial brief prepared by my colleague Karl Lachmann sets forth in great detail evidence, in the form of both documents and decrees, against the defendant Wilhelm Frick, English translations of the evidentiary material referred to in the trial brief are included in the document book prepared by my colleague, Lt. Felton. This book has been marked "LL."

Defendant Frick's great contribution to the Nazi conspiracy was in the field of governmental administration. He was the administrative brain which devised the machinery of State for Nazism, who geared that machinery for aggressive war.

In the course of his active participation in the Nazi conspiracy, from 1923 to 1945, the defendant Frick occupied a number of important positions. Document 2978-PS, which has previously been introduced as Exhibit USA 8, lists the positions in detail. The original was signed by the defendant Frick on 14th October, 1945. I do not repeat these positions; they are known to the Court. Frick's past activity on behalf of the Nazi conspirators was his participation in promoting their rise to power. Frick betrayed, in his capacity as law enforcement official of the Bavarian Government, his own Bavarian Government, by participating in the Munich Beer Hall Putsch of 8th November,, 1923. Frick was tried and sentenced, together with Hitler, on a charge of complicity in treason. His position in the Putsch is described in a record of the proceeding called "The Hitler Trial before the Peoples' Court in Munich," published in Munich in 1924.

I will ask this Tribunal to take judicial notice of this record of these proceedings. Hitler's appreciation of Frick's assistance is evidenced by the fact that he honoured Frick by mentioning his name in "Mein Kampf." Only two other defendants in this proceeding share this honour; namely, Hess and Streicher. I ask the Tribunal to take judicial notice of the favourable mentioning of defendant Frick in "Mein Kampf," German edition, 1933, Page 403.

During the period after the Putsch, Frick made further contributions to the Nazi conspiracy. I should like to refer briefly to Document 2513-PS, an excerpt on Pages 36 and 38 from a Report entitled "The National Socialist Workers Party as an Association Hostile to the State and to the Republican Form of Government and Guilty of Treasonable Activity." This Report has been previously introduced as Document 2513-PS, Exhibit USA 235. It is an official report of the criminal activities of Hitler, Frick and other Nazis prepared by the Prussian Ministry of the Interior in 1930. It states that Frick, next to Hitler, can be regarded as the most influential representative of the Nazi Party at that time. This document reported that at the 1927 Party Congress in Nuremberg, Frick said that the Reichstag would first be misused by the Nazi Party, would then be, abolished, and that its abolition would, open, the way for racial dictatorship. The document also reported that Frick stated in a speech in 1929 at Pyritz that "this fateful struggle will first be taken up with the ballot, but this cannot continue indefinitely, for history has taught, us that in battle blood must be shed and iron broken."

Back in 1927 Frick's prominent role in helping to bring the Nazis to power was recognised when, on 23rd January, 1930, he was appointed Minister of the Interior and Education in the State of Thuringia.

THE PRESIDENT: Are you passing from that document now? I thought you were reading from 2513.

DR. KEMPNER: No, this is an introduction of the next document.

THE PRESIDENT: I see, Dr. Kempner.

DR. KEMPNER: I just started to refer to the fact that Adolf Hitler at this time, when Frick was Minister of the Interior in the State of Thuringia, was an undesirable alien, not a German citizen. In his capacity as Minister of Thuringia the defendant Frick began his manipulations to provide Adolf Hitler, the undesirable alien, with German citizenship, an essential step towards the realisation of the Nazi conspiracy.

This lack of German citizenship was highly detrimental to the cause of the Nazi Party because, as an alien, Hitler could not become a candidate for the Reich Presidency in Germany.

It was the defendant Frick who solved this problem by an administrative manoeuvre. We now introduce in evidence Document 3564-PS, Exhibit USA 709. This document is an affidavit by Otto Meissner of 27th December, 1945. Meissner was former State secretary and chief of Hitler's Presidential Chancellery. The last two sentences of this affidavit read as follows:

> "Frick also, in collaboration with Klagges, Minister of Brunswick, succeeded in naturalising Hitler as a German citizen in 1932, by having him appointed a Brunswick government official (Ministerialrat). This was done in order to make it possible for Hitler to run as a candidate for the office of President in the Reich."

When Hitler came to power on 30th January, 1933, Frick was duly awarded a prominent post in the new regime as Reich Minister of the Interior. In this capacity he became responsible for the establishment of totalitarian control over Germany, an indispensable prerequisite for the preparation of aggressive warfare. Frick assumed responsibility for the realisation of a large part of the Nazi conspirators' programme, through both administration and legislation.

I must explain very briefly the significance of the Ministry of the Interior in the Nazi State to show the contribution made by Frick to the conspiracy. I offer, as evidence of Frick's extensive jurisdiction as Minister of the Interior, Document 3475-PS, Exhibit USA 710, which is part of the official German manual for administrative officials, dated 1943. I ask the Tribunal to take judicial notice of Frick's jurisdiction mentioned in this document. The names of the men who, according to this document, worked under Frick's supervision, and I stress this point "worked under Frick's supervision" are symbolic. They are listed on Page 1 of the English translation. Here we find among the subordinates of Frick "Reich Health Leader Dr. Conti," "Reichsfuehrer S.S. and Chief of the German Police Heinrich Himmler" and "Reich Labour Service Leader Hierl." This document shows Frick as supreme commander of three important pillars of the Nazi State: the Nazi Health Service, the Nazi Police System and the Nazi Labour Service.

The wide variety of Frick's activities as Reich- Minister of the Interior can be judged from the following catalogue of his functions, enumerated in the following pages of the manual. He had final authority over constitutional questions, drafted legislation, had jurisdiction over governmental administration and civil defence and was final arbiter in all questions concerning race and citizenship. The manual also lists sections of the ministry concerned with administrative problems for the occupied territories and annexed territories, the New Order in the Southeast, the Protectorate of Bohemia and Moravia and the New Order in the East. He also had full jurisdiction in the field of civil service, including such matters as appointment, tenure, promotion and dismissal.

The defendant Frick used his wide powers as Reichsminister of the Interior to advance the cause of the Nazi conspiracy. To accomplish this purpose, he drafted and signed the laws and decrees which abolished the autonomous State governments, the autonomous local governments, and the political, parties in Germany other than the Nazi Party.

In 1933 and 1934, the first two years of the Nazi regime, Frick signed about 235 laws or decrees, all of which are published in the "Reichsgesetzblatt." I should like to refer briefly to a few of the more important laws and decrees, such as the law of 14th July, 1933, outlawing all political parties other than the Nazi Party, Reichsgesetzblatt, 1933, Part 1, Page 479 (Document 1388A-PS); then the law of 1st December, 1933, securing the unity of party and State, Reichsgesetzblatt, 1933, Part 1, Page 1016 (Document 1395-PS); the law of 30th January, 1934, transferring the sovereignty of the German States to the Reich, Reichsgesetzblatt, 1934, Part 1, Page 75 (Document 3068-PS); the German Municipality Act of 30th January, 1935, which gave Frick's Ministry of the Interior final authority to appoint and dismiss all mayors of municipalities throughout Germany, Reichsgesetzblatt, 1935, Part 1, Page 49 (Document 2008-PS); and, finally, the Nazi Civil Service Act of 7th April, 1933, which provided that all civil servants must be trustworthy as defined by Nazi standards and also must meet the Nazi racial requirements, published in Reichsgesetzblatt, 1933, Part 1, Page 175 (Document 1397-PS).

One category of Frick's activities, however, deserves special notice; that is, the crushing of opposition by legally camouflaged police terror. This is shown by the book, "Dr. Wilhelm Frick and His Ministry," our Document 3119-PS, which is in evidence as Exhibit USA 711, written by Frick's under-secretary and co-conspirator, Hans Pfundtner, apparently written to establish Frick's eternal contribution to the creation of the Nazi's Thousand Year Reich. It states, and I quote briefly from Page 4, paragraph 4, of the English translation:

> "While Marxism in Prussia was crushed by the hard fist of the Prussian Prime Minister, Hermann Goering, and a gigantic wave of propaganda was initiated for the Reichstag elections of 5th March, 1933, Dr. Frick prepared the complete seizure of power in all States of the Reich. All at once the political opposition disappeared. All at once the Main (River) line was eliminated - from this time on only one will and one leadership reigned in the German Reich."

How was this done? On 28th February, 1933, the day after the Reichstag fire, civil rights in Germany were abolished. This decree was published in the Reichsgesetzblatt, 1933, Page 83, and an English translation of it appears in the document book as 1390-PS. I refer to this decree at this time because it carries the signature of the Reich Minister of the Interior Frick. And, now something important. It is stated at the beginning of the decree, which was published on the morning after the Reichstag fire, that the suspension of civil rights is decreed as a defence measure against Communist acts of violence endangering the State. At the time of publication of this decree, the Nazi Government announced that a thorough investigation had proven that the Communists had set fire to the Reichstag building. I do not intend to go into the controversial issue of who set fire to the Reichstag, but I should like to offer proof that the official Nazi statement, that the Communists were responsible for the fire, was issued without any investigation, and that the preamble of the decree which had Frick's signature was a mere subterfuge.

I offer in evidence a very short excerpt of an interrogation of defendant Goering, dated 13th October, 1945, our Document 3593-PS, Exhibit USA 712, and I should like to read the following brief portion, beginning on Page 4:

My question to Goering: "How could you tell your Press agent, one hour after the Reichstag caught fire, that the Communists did it, without investigation?"

Goering's answer: "Did the Public Relations Officer say that at that time?"

My answer: "Yes. He said you said it."

Goering: "Is it possible when I came to the Reichstag, the Fuehrer and his gentlemen were there. I was doubtful at that time, but it was their opinion that the Communists had started the fire."

My question: "But you were the highest law enforcement official in a certain sense. Daluege was your subordinate. Looking back at it now, and not in the excitement that existed there at the time, was it not too early to say without any investigation that the Communists had started the fire?"

Goering: "Yes, that is possible, but the Fuehrer wanted it this way."

Question: "Why did the Fuehrer want to issue at once a statement that the Communists had started the fire?"

Answer: "He was convinced of it."

Question: "Is it right when I say he was convinced without having any evidence or any proof of that at this moment?"

Goering: "That is right, but you must take into account that at that time the Communist activity was extremely strong, that our new government as such was not very secure."

THE PRESIDENT: Dr. Kempner, what has that got to do with Frick?

DR. KEMPNER: He signed the decree, as I said before, abolishing civil liberties, on the morning after, pointing out that there was a Communist danger. On the other side, this Communist danger was a mere subterfuge and was one of the things which finally led to the second World War.

The defendant Frick not only abolished civil liberties within Germany, but he also became the organiser of the huge police network of the Nazi Reich.

Parenthetically, I may state that before this time there was no unified Reich police system; the individual German States had police forces of their own.

I ask the Tribunal to take judicial notice of the decree of 17th June, 1936, signed by Frick and published in the Reichsgesetzblatt, 1936, Page 487. An English translation of this decree is in the document book as Document 2073-PS. Section 1 of this Frick decree reads as follows:

"For the unification of police duties in the Reich, a Chief of German Police is instituted in the German Ministry of the Interior, to whom is assigned the direction and conduct of all police affairs."

And from Section 2 we learn that it was the defendant Frick and Hitler, the signers of the decree, who appointed Himmler as Chief of the German Police.

Paragraph 2 of Section 2 of the decree states that Himmler was, and I quote, "subordinated individually and directly to the Reich and Prussian Minister of the Interior." And, of course, that is Frick.

The official chart of the German police system, Document 1852-PS, which has already been introduced into evidence as Exhibit USA 449, clearly shows the position of the Reich Minister of the Interior, Frick, as the supreme commander of the entire German police system, including the notorious R.S.H.A., of which the defendant Kaltenbrunner became chief, under Frick, in January, 1943.

The defendant Frick used his authority over the newly centralised police system for the promotion of the Nazi conspiracy. The Tribunal may take judicial notice of

Frick's decree of 20th September, 1936, published in the "Ministerial Gazette of the Reich" ("Ministerialblatt des Reichs- und Preussischen Ministeriums des Innern"), 1936, Page 1343, Document 2245-PS.

In this decree Frick reserved for himself the authority to appoint inspectors of the Security Police, subordinated them to his district governors, the Oberprasidenten, and ordered them to have a close co-operation with the Party and the Armed Forces.

Another example of the use of his activities in the police sphere is in his ordinance of 18th March, 1938, concerning the Austrian Anschluss, in which Frick authorised the Reichsfuehrer of the S.S. and Police, Himmler, to take security measures in Austria without regard to previous legal limitations. This decree is published in the Reichsgesetzblatt, 1938, Page 262, and appears in the document book as 1437-PS.

I shall not here repeat the evidence concerning the criminal activities of the German police, over which the defendant Frick had supreme authority. I should simply like to refer the Tribunal to the presentations already made on the subject of concentration camps and the Gestapo, two of the police institutions under Frick's jurisdiction. But I should like to show that not only Himmler's subordinate machine but also Frick's Ministry itself was familiar with these institutions. Therefore, I now offer into evidence Document 1643-PS, as Exhibit USA 713.

This document is a synopsis of correspondence between the Reich Ministry of the Interior and its field offices from November, 1942, through August, 1943, on the subject of the legal aspects of the confiscation of property by the S.S. for the enlargement of the concentration camp at Auschwitz. At the bottom of Page 1 and the top of Page 2 of the English translation there appears a synopsis of the minutes of a meeting held on 17th and 18th December, 1942, concerning the confiscation of this property. These minutes indicate that a further discussion was to be held on the subject on 21st December, 1942, between the representatives of the Reich Minister of the Interior and the Reichsfuehrer S.S. On Page 2 there appears also a summary of a teletype letter dated 22nd January, 1943, from Dr. Hoffmann, representing the Reich Minister of the Interior, to the District Governor in Kattowitz.

The summary begins as follows, and I quote:

"The territory of the Auschwitz Concentration Camp will be changed into an independent estate" - which means an administrative territory of itself.

The fact that the defendant Frick demonstrated personal interest in a concentration camp became known through the testimony of Dr. Blaha, to which I should like to refer the Tribunal, in which he testified that Frick visited the Dachau Camp in 1943.

The next aspect of the participation of the defendant Frick in the Nazi conspiracy concerns his promotion of racial persecution and racialism, involving the wiping out of the Jews.

In addition to the many other responsibilities of Frick, this vast administrative empire covered the entire area of the enactment and administration of racial legislation.

I refer again to Document 3475-PS, "The Manual for German Administrative Officials," previously introduced, and I refer to Pages 2 and 4, showing that Frick was administrative and legislative guardian and protector of the German race.

In order to avoid any repetition, I shall not quote the various acts drafted by Frick's Ministry against the Jews. The presentation concerning persecution of the Jews made by Major Walsh before the Christmas recess listed a number of decrees signed by Frick, including the infamous Nuremberg laws and the laws depriving Jews of their property and their rights of citizenship, and stigmatising them with the Yellow Star.

But the activities of Frick's Ministry were not restricted to the commission of such crimes, camouflaged in the form of legislation. The police field offices, subordinate to Frick, participated in the organisation of such terroristic activities as the pogrom of 9th November, 1938.

I refer to a series of Heydrich's orders and reports concerning the organisation of these pogroms - or, as they were termed-by Heydrich, "spontaneous riots" - Documents 3051-PS and 3058-PS, Which are already in evidence as Exhibits USA 240 and 508.

Three days after this pogrom of 9th November, 1938, Frick, his Under-Secretary Stuckart and his subordinates, Heydrich and Deluege, participated in a conference on the Jewish question under the chairmanship of the defendant Goering. At this meeting the various measures were discussed which the individual governmental departments should initiate against the Jews. A stenographic record of this meeting, Document 1816-PS, is already in evidence as Exhibit USA 261. May I briefly refer to the bottom of Page 23 of the English translation, where we find Goering's concluding remarks:

"Also the Ministry of the Interior and the police will have to think over what measures have to be taken."

This remark shows that Goering regarded it as Frick's duty to follow up by administrative devices the pogrom, organised by Frick's own subordinates.

In the foregoing presentation we have shown that the defendant Frick, as a member of the conspiracy, devised the machinery of the State for Nazism. In the following presentation we will show that Frick actively supported the preparation of the Nazi State for war.

May we begin this portion by showing that Frick was in sympathy with the flagrant violations by Germany of her treaties of non-aggression. This is clearly shown by the affidavit of Ambassador Messersmith, Document 2385-PS, previously introduced as Exhibit USA 68. I shall quote only one sentence from this affidavit, Page 4, line 10. It reads as follows:

"High-ranking Nazis with whom I had to maintain official contact, particularly men such as Goering, Goebbels, Ley, Frick, Frank, Darre and others, repeatedly scoffed at my attitude to the binding character of treaties and openly stated to me that Germany would observe her international undertakings only so long as it suited Germany's interests to do so."

In May, 1935, by his appointment as General Plenipotentiary for the Administration of the Reich, Frick became one of the big three in charge of preparing Germany for war. The other two members of the triumvirate were the Chief of the O.K.W. and the General Plenipotentiary for Economy, at that time the defendant Schacht. Frick has admitted that he held the position of General Plenipotentiary since 21st May, 1935, the date of the original secret Reich Defence Law. I refer to his statement of positions, Document 2978-PS, Exhibit USA 8.

His functions as General Plenipotentiary are outlined in the Reich Defence Law of 4th September, 1938, which was classified top military secret and appears in our document book as 2494-PS, Exhibit USA 36. Under this law of 1938, paragraph 3, tremendous power was concentrated in the hands of Frick as General Plenipotentiary for Administration. In addition to the offices under his supervision as Minister of the Interior, the law made the following offices subordinate to Frick for the purpose of carrying out the directives of the law: Reich Minister of Justice, Reich Minister of Education, Reich Minister for Religious Matters and the Reich Office for Planning.

Frick admitted the significant part he played in the preparations for war as a member of the triumvirate, in a speech made on 7th March, 1940, at the University of Freiburg. Excerpts appear in the document book as 2608-PS, which I offer in evidence as Exhibit USA 714. I think it would be helpful if the Tribunal would allow me to read two short paragraphs, beginning at the top of Page 1 of the English translation:

"The organisation of the non-military national defence fits organically into the entire structure of the National Socialist government and administration. This state of affairs is not exceptional, but a necessary and planned part of the National Socialist order. Thus, the conversion of our administration and economy to wartime conditions has been accomplished very quickly and without any friction-avoiding the otherwise very dangerous change of the entire structure of the State.

The planned preparation of the administration for the possibility of a war has already been carried out during peacetime. For this purpose the Fuehrer appointed a Plenipotentiary General for the Reich Administration and a Plenipotentiary General for Economy."

Many of Frick's contributions to the preparation of the German State for war are outlined in detail in the book "Dr. Wilhelm Frick and His Ministry," which is already in evidence as Document 3119-PS. May I quote two short sentences from the top of Page 3 of the English translation:

"Besides, the leading co-operation of the Reich Minister of the Interior in the important field of 'military legislation,' and thus in the establishment of our Armed Forces, has to be particularly emphasised. After all, the Reich Minister of the Interior is the civilian minister of the defence of the country, who in this capacity, together with the Reich War Minister, not only signed the military law of 12th May, 1935, but in his capacity as Supreme Chief of the General and Inner Administration, as well as of the police, has also received from the Fuehrer and Reich Chancellor important powers in the fields of the recruitment system and of military supervision."

I have previously mentioned that, as Minister of the Interior, Frick was responsible for the administrative policy in occupied and annexed territories. It was his Ministry which introduced the new German order throughout the vast territory of Europe occupied by the German Armed Forces, and the defendant Frick exercised these powers. I request that the Tribunal take judicial notice of three decrees signed by Frick, introducing German law into Austria, the Sudetenland and the Government General of Poland respectively: Decree of 13th March, 1938, Reichsgesetzblatt, 1938, Part 1, Page 237, Article 8 (Document 2307-PS); Decree of 1st October, 1938, Reichsgesetzblatt,1938, Part 1, Page 1331, paragraph 8 (Document 3073-PS); Decree of 12th October, 1939, Reichsgesetzblatt, 1939, Part 1, Page 2077, paragraph 8 (1) (Document 3079-PS).

Frick's Ministry also arranged the selection and assignment of hundreds of occupation officials for the Soviet territory even before the invasion. This fact appears in a report by the defendant Rosenberg of April, 1941, on preparations for the administration of occupied territory in the East. May I refer to Page 2, paragraph 2, of Document 109-PS, which has previously been introduced as Exhibit USA 146.

One category of Frick's contribution to the planning of and preparation for aggressive war deserves special notice. This is the systematic killing of persons regarded as useless to the German war machine, such as the insane, the crippled and aged, and foreign labourers who were no longer able to work. These killings were carried out in nursing homes, hospitals and asylums. The Tribunal will recall that the defendant Frick, in his capacity as Reich Minister of the Interior, had jurisdiction over public health and all institutions. May I refer again briefly to the "Manual for German Administrative Officials," Document 3475-PS, this time to Pages 3, 4 and 7 of the English partial translation. There the following are mentioned as Frick's jurisdictional areas: "Health Administration," "Social Hygiene," "Racial Improvement and Eugenics," "Reich Plenipotentiary for Sanatoria and Nursing Homes."

As proof that Frick's jurisdiction covered the death cases in these institutions, I now offer in evidence Document 621- PS, Exhibit USA 715. This is a letter of 2nd October, 1940, from the Chief of the Reich Chancellery, Dr. Lammers, to the Reichsminister of Justice, informing the latter that material concerning the death of inmates of nursing homes had been transmitted to the Reichsminister of the Interior for further action. In fact, the defendant Frick not only had jurisdiction of these establishments, but he was one of the originators of a secret law organising the murdering.

I now offer Document 1556-PS, Exhibit USA 716. This is an official report dated December, 1941, of the Czechoslovak War Crimes Commission entitled "Detailed Statement of the Murdering of Ill and Aged People in Germany." I should like to quote very brief excerpts from this report. Paragraphs 1, 2 and 3 read as follows:

"(1) The murdering can be traced back to a secret law which was issued some time in the summer of 1940.

(2) Besides the Chief Physician of the Reich, Dr. L. Conti, the Reichsfuehrer S.S. Himmler, and the Reichsminister of the Interior Dr. Frick, as well as other men, the following participated in the introduction of this secret law ..." (other names listed).

"(3) As I have already stated, there were-after careful calculation at least 200,000 mainly mentally deficient, imbeciles, besides neurological cases and medically unfit people - these were not only incurable cases - and at least 75,000 aged people."

The most striking example of the continued killings in these institutions, which were under Frick's jurisdiction and operated under the order of which Frick was a co-author, is the famous Hadamar case.

Your Honour, may I ask you whether I can have ten more minutes to end this presentation, because the Chief Prosecutors agreed, as I understood, to start tomorrow morning the case of the French, and I have just ten more minutes.

THE PRESIDENT: Yes, very well.

DR. KEMPNER: Thank you, your Lordship.

I refer to the Hadamar case. I now offer in evidence Document 615-PS, Exhibit USA 717.

THE TRIBUNAL (Mr. Biddle): What is this last report that you spoke about. Whose is it?

DR. KEMPNER: The Czechoslovak War Crimes Commission report. After I have shown the general scheme, of which Frick was a co-author, I would like to show that Frick's ministry was acquainted with the things that were going on under his organisational authorship, and therefore I am quoting now a letter showing that he was acquainted with these killings, and that these killings had even become public knowledge. For this reason I offer in evidence Document 615-PS, Exhibit USA 717. This document is a letter from the Bishop of Limburg, of 13th August, 1941, to the Reichsminister of Justice. Copies were sent to the Reichsminister of the Interior - this means Frick - and to the Reichsminister for Church Affairs. I quote:

"About 8 kilometres from Limburg, in the little town of Hadamar, on a hill overlooking the town, there is an institution which had formerly served various purposes and of late had been used as a nursing home this institution was renovated and furnished as a place in which, by consensus of opinion, the above-mentioned euthanasia has been systematically practised for months - approximately since February, 1941. The fact has become known beyond the administrative district of Wiesbaden, because death certificates from a Registry Hadamar-Monchberg are sent to the home communities."

And I quote further:

"Several times a week buses arrive in Hadamar with a considerable number of such victims. School children of the vicinity know this vehicle and say: 'There comes the murder-box again.' After the arrival of the vehicle, the citizens of Hadamar watch the smoke rise out of the chimney and are tortured with the ever-present thought of the miserable victims, especially when repulsive odours annoy them, depending on the direction of the wind.

The effect of the principles at work here are: Children call each other names and say, 'You're crazy; you'll be sent to the baking oven in Hadamar.' Those who do not want to marry or find no opportunity say, 'Marry, never! Bring children into the world so they can be put into the bottling machine!" You hear old folks say, 'Do not send me to a State hospital! After the feeble-minded have been finished off, the next useless eaters whose turn will come are the old people.'

... The population cannot grasp that systematic actions are carried out which, in accordance with paragraph 211 of the German criminal code, are punishable with death....

Officials of the Secret State Police, it is said, are trying to suppress discussion of the Hadamar occurrences by means of severe threats. In the interest of public peace this may be well intended. But the knowledge and the conviction and the indignation of the population cannot be changed by it; the conviction will be increased with the bitter realisation that discussion is prohibited with threats, but that the actions themselves are not prosecuted under penal law."

I quote the last paragraph of the letter, the postscript:

"I am submitting copies of this letter to the Reich Minister of the Interior and the Reich Minister for Church Affairs." - Initialled by above.

Nevertheless, the killings carried out in these institutions under the secret law created by defendant Frick, Himmler and others continued year after year.

THE PRESIDENT: Was any answer made to that letter?

DR. KEMPNER: No answer has been found. I have other letters which I am not able to quote here to-day which bear the words: "Please do not answer."

THE PRESIDENT: "Please do not answer?"

DR. KEMPNER: So that it should be unanswered.

Nevertheless, the killings carried out in these institutions under the secret law created by defendant Frick, Himmler and others continued year after year. I offer in evidence Document 3592-PS, Exhibit USA 718, which is a certified copy of the charge, specifications, findings and sentence of the U.S. Military Commission at Wiesbaden, against the individuals who operated the Hadamar Sanatorium, where many Russians and Poles were murdered. In this particular proceeding seven defendants were charged with the murder in 1944 of 400 persons of Polish and Russian nationality, and three of the defendants were sentenced to be hanged; the other four were sentenced to confinement with hard labour.

Now I come to the last page of my presentation, the final case of Frick's responsibility, which arises under his position as Reich Protector of Bohemia and Moravia for the period from 20th August, 1943, until the end of the war. I think it is not necessary to say anything about the functions of the Protector of Bohemia and Moravia; these broad powers are known to the Court.

THE PRESIDENT: Before you pass from 3592-PS, is it clear that that trial related to the killing of Polish and Russian nationals in nursing homes or institutions of that sort?

DR. KEMPNER: It is absolutely clear in this document, the sentence of the Military Commission of Hadamar for Wiesbaden.

THE PRESIDENT: Will you show me where that is?

DR. KEMPNER: Document 3592-PS. I quote:

> "Specification: In that Alfons Klein, Adolf Wahlmann, Heinrich Ruoff, Karl Willig, Adolf Merkle, Irmgard Huber, and Phillip Blum, acting jointly and in pursuance of a common intent and acting for and on behalf of the then German Reich, did, from or about 1st July, 1944 until about 1st April, 1945, at Hadamar, Germany, wilfully, deliberately, and wrongfully aid, abet and participate in the killing of human beings of Polish and Russian nationality; their exact names and number being unknown, but totalling over 400, and who were then and there confined by the German Reich as an exercise of belligerent control."

THE PRESIDENT: It does not show that it came within the jurisdiction of the Ministry of the Interior.

DR. KEMPNER: Sometime ago I referred to the Manual of the German Administrative Officials. This manual points out very clearly that nursing homes, sanitaria, and similar establishments are under the supervision of the Ministry of the Interior.

THE PRESIDENT: I follow that; but this document does not refer to nursing homes. That is what I was asking you.

DR. KEMPNER: Yes, it says only Hadamar. It is, in fact, the Hadamar nursing home. This portion was not given by the Judge Advocate General, but I am willing to give later a more extended document showing that Hadamar is a common name for the so-called Hadamar killing mill, which is a nursing home.

Now I come to the last paragraph of my presentation.

THE PRESIDENT: Wait a moment, Dr. Kempner. Counsel for the defence wishes to speak. There is the gentlemen standing by your side.

DR. PANNENBECKER (Counsel for defendant Frick): From Document 3592-PS, which was just read, I cannot find that the defendant Frick is connected with the document in any way.

THE PRESIDENT: Surely it is not necessary for you to get up and repeat what I have just said.

DR. PANNENBECKER: I would like to add something else.

THE PRESIDENT: I beg your pardon.

DR. PANNENBECKER: I would like to add that the defendant Frick since August, 1943, was not Minister of the Interior, and for that reason this document cannot be used against him.

THE PRESIDENT: And it does not give the date of the death of these people. At any rate, until Dr. Kempner produces something to show that this was a nursing home and in a time during which the defendant Frick was Minister of the Interior, the Tribunal will not treat it as being evidence which implicates Frick.

DR. KEMPNER: I quoted this killing in Hadamar for two reasons: First, because the Ministry of the Interior has become acquainted, as I said before, with the letter of the Bishop of Limburg, in 1941, when Frick was Minister of the Interior and knew about these facts; and I quoted the military decision for this reasons that these killings were still going on in 1944 and 1945 under a law of which the defendant Frick was the co-author.

The final phase of Frick's responsibility arises under his position as Reich Protector of Bohemia and Moravia for the period from 20th August, 1943, until the end of the war. I have not to prove his function but I shall mention one example, and I offer in evidence Document 3589-PS, Exhibit USA 720, which is a supplement to an official Czechoslovak report on German crimes against Czechoslovakia. I would like to quote only the following brief passage from this report:

> "During the tenure of office of defendant Wilhelm Frick as Reich Protector of Bohemia and Moravia, from August, 1943, until the liberation of Czechoslovakia in 1945, many thousands of Czechoslovak Jews were transported from the Terezin ghetto in Czechoslovakia to the concentration camp at Oswieczim (Auschwitz) in Poland and were there killed in the gas chambers."

Brought from the territory over which Frick was Protector to the gas chamber.

Thus, we submit, it has been shown that the defendant Frick was a key conspirator from 1923 until the Allied armies crushed the resistance of the Nazi Armed Forces. Frick's guilt rests on his own record, and on the record of his co-defendants, with whom he is co-responsible under our Charter.

I would like to express my appreciation for the assistance rendered in connection with the preparation of this case by my colleagues, Mr. Karl Lachmann, Lt. Frederick Felton, and Captain Seymour Krieger.

(The Tribunal adjourned until 10.00 hours on 17th January, 1946.)

Thirty-Sixth Day: Thursday, January 17th, 1946

THE PRESIDENT: I call upon the counsel for France.

M. FRANCOIS DE MENTHON: The conscience of the peoples, who only yesterday were enslaved and tortured both in soul and body, calls upon you to judge and to condemn the most monstrous attempt at domination and barbarism of all times, both in the persons of some of those who bear the chief responsibility and in the collective groups and organisations which were the essential instruments of their crimes.

France, twice in thirty years invaded, in the course of wars both of which were launched by German imperialism, bore almost alone, in May and June, 1940, the weight of armaments accumulated by Nazi Germany over a period of years in a spirit of aggression. Although temporarily crushed by superiority in numbers, material and preparation, my country never gave up the battle for freedom and was at no time absent from the field. The engagements undertaken and the will for national independence would have sufficed to assure France's support of General de Gaulle in the camp of the democratic nations, but if our fight for freedom slowly took the shape of a popular uprising, at the call of the men of the Resistance belonging to all social classes, to all creeds and to all political parties, it was not only because, while our soil and our souls were crushed by the Nazi invader, our people refused to submit to wretchedness and slavery, but even more because they refused to accept the Hitlerian dogmas which were in absolute contradiction to their traditions, their aspirations and their human calling.

France, which was systematically plundered and ruined; France, so many of whose sons were tortured and murdered in the jails of the Gestapo or in concentration camps; France, which was subjected to the still more horrible grip of demoralisation and return to barbarism diabolically imposed by Nazi Germany, asks of you, above all in the name of the heroic martyrs of the Resistance who are among the greatest heroes of our national legend, that justice be done.

France, so often in history the spokesman and the champion of human liberty, of human values, of human progress, through my voice to-day becomes also the interpreter of the martyred peoples of Western Europe, Norway, Denmark, the Netherlands, Belgium, Luxembourg, peoples more than all others devoted to peace, peoples who are among the noblest of humanity by reason of their aspirations and their worship of the values of civilisation, peoples who have shared our sufferings and have refused, like us, to give up liberty and sacrifice their souls before the assault of Nazi barbarism. France here becomes their interpreter to demand that justice be done.

THE PRESIDENT: One moment, M. de Menthon, the Russian translation is not coming through.... It is all right now.

M. DE MENTHON: The tortured peoples' craving for justice is the basic foundation of France's appearance before your High Tribunal. It is not the only one, nor perhaps the most important one. More than toward the past, our eyes are turned toward the future.

We believe that there can be no lasting peace and no certain progress for humanity, which still to-day is torn asunder, suffering and anguished, except through the co-operation of all peoples and through the progressive establishment of a real international society.

Technical procedure and diplomatic arrangements will not suffice. There can be no well-balanced and enduring nation without a common consent in the essential rules of social living, without a general standard of behaviour before the claims of conscience, without the adherence of all citizens to identical concepts of good and evil; there is no domestic law which in defining and punishing criminal violations is not founded on criteria of a moral order which are accepted by all - in a word, without a common morality. There can be no society of nations to-morrow without an international morality, without a certain community of spiritual civilisation, without an identical hierarchy of values; International Law will be called upon to recognise and guarantee the punishment of the gravest violations of the universally accepted moral laws. This morality and this International Criminal Law, indispensable for the final establishment of peaceful co-operation and of progress on lasting foundations, are inconceivable to us to-day after the experience of past centuries and more especially of these last years, after the incredible and awesome sacrifices and the sufferings of men of all races and of all nationalities unless they are built on the respect of the human person, of every human person whosoever he may be, as well as on the limitation of the sovereignty of States.

But in order that we may have the hope of founding progressively an international society, through the free co- operation of all peoples, on this morality and on this International Law, it is necessary that, after having premeditated, prepared and launched a war of aggression which has caused the death of millions of men and the ruin of a great number of nations, after having thereupon piled up the most odious crimes in the course of the war years: Nazi Germany shall be declared guilty and her rulers and those chiefly responsible punished as such. Without this sentence and without this punishment the nations would no longer have any faith in justice. When you have declared that crime is always crime, whether committed by a national entity against other nations or by one individual against another, you will thereby have affirmed that there is only one standard of morality which applies to international relations as well as to individual relationships, and that on this morality are built prescriptions of law recognised by the international community; you will then have truly begun to establish an international justice.

This work of justice is equally indispensable for the future of the German people. These people have been for many years intoxicated by Nazism; certain of their eternal and deep- seated aspirations, under this regime, have found a monstrous expression; their entire responsibility is involved, not only by their general acceptance but by the effective participation of a great number of them in the crimes committed. Their re-education is indispensable. This represents a difficult enterprise and one of long duration. The efforts which the free people will have to make in order to reintegrate Germany in an international community cannot succeed in the end if this re-education is not carried out effectively. The initial condemnation of Nazi Germany by your High Tribunal will be a first lesson for these people and will constitute the best starting-point for the work of the revision of values and of re-education which must be its great concern during the coming years.

This is why France sees fit to ask the Tribunal to qualify juridicially as crimes, both the war of aggression itself and those acts in violation of the morality and of the laws of all civilised countries which have been committed by Germany in the conduct of the war, to impose the supreme penalty on those who are chiefly responsible, and to declare criminal the members of the various groups and organisations which were the principal perpetrators of the crimes of Nazi Germany.

Your High Tribunal, established by the four nations signatory to the agreement of 8th August, 1945, acting in the interests of all the United Nations, is qualified to mete out to Nazi Germany the justice of the free peoples, the justice of liberated humanity.

The establishment by our four Governments of a Tribunal competent to judge the crimes committed by those principally responsible in Nazi Germany is based solidly on the principles and usage of International Law. As an eminent British jurist has recently reminded us, the practice and the doctrine of International Law have always given to belligerent States the right to punish enemy war criminals who fall into their power. It is an incontestable rule of International Law which no author has ever contested. It is not, anew doctrine. It was born with the birth of International Law. Francisco de Vittoria and Grotius laid its foundations. The German authors of the seventeenth and eighteenth centuries developed the doctrine.

Thus Johann Jacob Moser, a positivist writer of the eighteenth century, said: "Enemy soldiers who act in violation of International Law, should they fall into the hands of their adversaries, are not to be treated as prisoners of war. They can suffer the same fate as thieves or murderers." The prosecutions which the United States, Great Britain, the Union of Soviet Socialist Republics and France are to-day carrying out against the men and the organisations appearing before your High Tribunal under the Indictment read in Berlin on 18th October, 1945, therefore have an unimpeachable juridical foundation: the right, universally recognised by international doctrine, of bringing war criminals before a punitive jurisdiction.

This right is strengthened by legal considerations that are perhaps even more irrefutable.

The principle of the territorial application of penal laws gives to every State the right to punish crimes committed on its territory. The application of the territorial principles covers the violations of. International Law in territory subject to military occupation; these violations are the chief source of war crimes. But the crimes committed by the defendants were not directed against any given State, in any given occupied territory. The National Socialist conspirators, against whom we ask that justice be done, directed the policy of the Third Reich. All the States which were occupied and temporarily enslaved by their Armed Forces have been equally victims both of the illicit war which they launched and of the methods used by them in the conduct of this war.

There is therefore no single State which could legitimately claim the privilege of trying these criminals. Only an International Tribunal, emanating from the combined United Nations, which were yesterday at war with Germany, can rightly claim this privilege. That is why the declaration as to enemy atrocities made at the end of the Moscow Conference in October, 1943, had provided that the leaders of Nazi Germany would, after the joint victory of the Allies, be brought before an International Jurisdiction. There is, therefore, nothing new from a juridical point of view in the principle of justice which you are called upon to render. Far from being merely an affirmation of power on the part of the victors, your competence is founded on the recognition by International Law of the territorial jurisdiction of sovereign States.

The transfer by these States of their juridical power to an International Court constitutes a notable progress in the setting up of an inter-State punitive procedure. It does not constitute any innovation in the legal foundation of the justice which you are called upon to render.

The penal qualification of the facts may seem more open to juridical objections. This horrible accumulation and maze of Crimes against, Humanity both includes and goes beyond the two more precise juridical notions of Crimes against Peace and

War Crimes. But I think - and I will revert later separately to Crimes against Peace and War Crimes - that this body of Crimes against

Humanity constitutes, in the last analysis, nothing less than the perpetration, for political ends and in a systematic manner, of Common Law crimes such as theft, looting, ill-treatment, enslavement, murders and assassinations, crimes that are provided for and punishable under the penal laws of all civilised States.

No general objection of a juridical nature, therefore, appears to hamper your task of justice.

Moreover, the Nazi accused would have no ground to argue on alleged lack of written texts to justify the penal qualification that you will apply to their crimes.

The juridical doctrine of National Socialism admitted that in domestic criminal law even the judge can and must supplement the law. The written law no longer constituted the Magna Carta of the delinquent. The judge could punish when, in the absence of a provision for punishment, the National Socialist sense of justice was gravely offended.

How could a judge under the Nazi regime supplement the law?

In his search for a semi-legal solution he acted in the manner of a legislator. Proceeding from the firm basis of the National Socialist programme, he sought the rule which he would have proclaimed had he been a legislator. The defendant Frank, in his speech at the Juristentag in 1936, declared:

> "Say to yourself at each decision you have to make, how would the Fuehrer decide in my place? At each decision which you must make, ask yourself: Is this decision in accordance with the National Socialist conscience of the German people? Thus you will have a firm basis of conscience which will also bear for all time, in your own sphere of decisions, the authority of the Third Reich, based on the popular National Socialist unity and on the recognition of the will of the Fuehrer Adolf Hitler."

To those who to-morrow will render justice in the name of human conscience the defendant Frank and his accomplices would be ill advised to protest against a lack of written texts with appropriate sanctions, especially as, in addition to various international conventions, these texts, though they be not codified in an inter-State penal code, exist in the penal code of every civilised country.

Mr. Justice Jackson has given you the details of the various phases and aspects of the National Socialist plot, its planning and its development, from the first days of the conspiracy of Hitler and his companions to rise to power, up to the unleashing of innumerable crimes in a Europe almost entirely at their mercy.

Sir Hartley Shawcross has enumerated the various breaches of treaties, of agreements, of promises which were the prelude to the many wars of aggression of which Germany was guilty.

I propose to-day to prove to you that all this organised and vast criminality springs from what I may be allowed to call a crime against the spirit, I mean a doctrine which, denying all spiritual, rational and moral values by which the nations have tried, for thousands of years, to improve human conditions, aims to plunge humanity back into barbarism, no longer the natural and spontaneous barbarism of primitive nations, but a diabolical barbarism, conscious of itself and utilising for its ends all material means put at the disposal of mankind by contemporary science. This sin against the spirit is the original sin of National Socialism from which all crimes spring.

This monstrous doctrine is that of racialism: the German race, composed in theory of Aryans, would be a fundamental and natural concept. Germans as individuals do not exist and cannot justify their existence, except in so far as they belong to the race or Volkssturm, to the popular mass which represents and amalgamates all Germans. Race is the matrix of the German people; proceeding therefrom this people lives and develops as an organism. The German may consider himself only as a healthy and vigorous member of this body, fulfilling within the collectivity a definite technical function; his activity and his usefulness are the exact gauge and justification of his liberty. This national body must be "moulded" to prepare it for a permanent struggle.

The ideas and the bodily symbols of racialism are an integral part of its political system; this is what is called authoritative or dictatorial biology.

The expression "blood" which appears so often in the writings of the Nazi theorists denotes this stream of real life, of red sap which flows through the circulatory system of every race and of all genuine culture as it flows through the human body. To be Aryan is to feel this current passing through oneself, this current which galvanises and vivifies the whole nation. Blood is this region of spontaneous and unconscious life which reveals to each individual the tendencies of the race. The intellectual life must never, in extolling itself, separate us from this elemental basis of the sacred community. Let the individual go into himself and he will receive by direct revelation "the commandments of the blood." Dreams, rites and myths can lead to this revelation. In other words, the modern German can and must bear in himself the call of the old Germany and find again its purity and its youthful primitiveness.

The body and soul unity (Leibdeele, Einheit) of the individual must not be disputed. One reads in the "Nationalsozialistische Monatshefte" of September, 1938:

"It is said that the body belongs to the State and the soul to the Church and to God. It is no longer so. The whole of the individual, body and soul, belongs to the Germanic nation and to the Germanic State."

National Socialism affirms, indeed, that the moral conscience is the result of orthogenetic evolution, the consequence of the most simple physiological functions which characterise the individuality of the body. Therefore, the moral conscience is also subject to heredity and, consequently, subject to the postulate and to the demands of the race.

True, this pseudo-religion does not repudiate the means of reason and of technical activity, but subordinates them rigorously, brings them infallibly to the racial myth.

The individual has no value in himself and is important only as an element of the race. This affirmation is logical if one admits that not only physical and psychological characteristics, but also opinions and tendencies are bound, not to the individual but to the nation. Anyone whose opinions differ from the official doctrine is asocial or unhealthy. He is unhealthy because in the Nazi doctrine the nation is equivalent to the race. Now, the characteristics of the race are fixed. An exception in the formation from the spiritual or moral point of view constitutes a malformation in the same way as does a club-foot or a hare- lip.

That is the totalitarian doctrine which reduces the individual to non-existence save by the race and for the race, without freedom of action or any definite aim; a totalitarian doctrine which excludes every other concept, every other aspiration or requirement save those connected with the race, a totalitarian doctrine which eliminates from the individual every other thought save that of the interest of the race.

National Socialism ends in the absorption of the personality of the citizen into that of the State and in the denial of any intrinsic value of the human person.

We are brought back to the most primitive ideas of the savage tribe. All the values of civilisation accumulated in the course of centuries are rejected, all traditional ideas of morality, justice and law give way to the primacy of race, its instincts, its needs and interests. The individual, his liberty, his rights and aspirations, no longer have any real existence of their own.

In this conception of race it is easy to realise the gulf that separates members of the German community from other men. The diversity of the races becomes irreducible, and irreducible, too, the hierarchy which sets apart the superior and the inferior races. The Hitler regime has created a veritable chasm between the German nation, the sole keeper of the racial treasure, and other nations.

Between the Germanic community and the degenerate population of an inferior variety of man there is no longer any common measure. Human brotherhood is rejected, even more than all the other traditional moral values.

How can one explain in what way Germany, fertilised through the centuries by classic antiquity and Christianity, by the ideals of liberty, equality and special justice, by the common heritage of Western humanism to which she had brought such noble and precious contributions, could have come to this astonishing return to primitive barbarism?

In order to understand it and to try to eradicate for ever from the Germany of tomorrow the evil by which our entire civilisation came so near to perishing, it must be recalled that National Socialism has deep and remote origins.

The mysticism of racial community was born of the spiritual and moral crises which Germany underwent in the nineteenth century, and which abruptly broke out again in its economic and social structure through a particularly rapid industrialisation. National Socialism is, in reality, one of the peaks of the moral and spiritual crisis of modern humanity, convulsed by industrialisation and technical progress. Germany experienced this metamorphosis of economic and social life not only with an extraordinary brutality, but at a time when she did not yet possess the political equilibrium and the cultural unity which the other countries of Western Europe had achieved.

While the inner and spiritual life was weakening, a cruel uncertainty dominated the spirit, an uncertainty admirably defined by the term "Ratlosigkeit" which cannot be translated into French but which corresponds to our popular expression: "One no longer knows in what Saint to believe." This is the spiritual cruelty of the nineteenth century which so many Germans have described with a tragic evocative power. A gaping void opens before the human soul, disoriented by the search for new values.

The natural sciences and the sciences of the mind give birth to absolute relativism; to a deep scepticism regarding the lasting quality of values on which Western humanism has been nurtured for centuries. A vulgar Darwinism prevails, which bewilders and befuddles the brain. The Germans cease to see in human groups and races anything but isolated nuclei in perpetual struggle with one another.

It is in the name of decadence that the German spirit condemns humanism; it sees in the value of humanism and in the elements that derive from it only "maladies," which it attributes to an excess of intellectualism and abstraction of everything that restrains men's passions by subjecting them to common norms. From this point onwards classic antiquity is no longer considered in its aspects of ordered reason or of radiant beauty. In it one sees only civilisations violently enamoured of struggles and rivalries, linked especially to Germany through their so- called Germanic origin.

Sacerdotal Judaism and Christianity in all its forms are condemned as religions of honour and brotherhood, calculated to kill the virtues of brutal force in man.

A cry is raised against the democratic idealism of the modern era, and then against all the internationals.

Over a people in this state of spiritual crisis and of negations of traditional values the culminating philosophy of Nietzsche was to exercise a dominant influence. In taking the will to power as a point of departure, Nietzsche preached not inhumanity but superhumanity. If there is no final cause in the universe, man - whose body is matter which is at once feeling and thinking - may mould the world to his desire, choosing as his guide a militant biology. If the supreme end of humanity is a feeling of victorious fullness which is both material and spiritual, all that remains is to ensure the selection of physical specimens who will become the new aristocracy of masters.

For Nietzsche the industrial evolution necessarily entails the rule over the masses, the automatism and the shaping of the working multitudes. The State endures only by virtue of an elite of vigorous personalities who, by the methods so admirably defined by Machiavelli, which alone are in accord with the laws of life, will lead men by force and by ruse simultaneously, for men are and remain wicked and perverse.

We see the modern barbarian arise. Superior by his intelligence and his wilful energy, freed of all conventional ethics, he can enforce upon the masses obedience and loyalty, by making them believe in the dignity and beauty of labour and by providing them with that mediocre well-being with which they are so easily content. An identical force will, therefore, be manifest in the leaders, by the harmony between their elementary passions and the lucidity of their organising reason, and in the masses, whose dark or violent instincts will be balanced by a reasoned activity imposed with implacable discipline.

Without doubt, the late philosophy of Nietzsche cannot be identified with the brutal simplicity of National Socialism. Nevertheless, National Socialism was wont to glorify Nietzsche as one of its ancestors, and justly so, for he was the first to formulate in a coherent manner criticism of the traditional values of humanism and also, because his conception of the government of the masses by masters knowing no restraint is a preview of the Nazi regime. Besides, Nietzsche believed in the sovereign race and attributed primacy to Germany, whom he considered endowed with a youthful soul and unquenchable resources.

The myth of community which had arisen from the depths of the German soul, unbalanced by the moral and spiritual crises endured by modern humanity, allied itself with the traditional theses of Pan-Germanism.

Fichte's "Speeches to the German Nation" had already, by exalting Germanity, clearly revealed one of the main ideas of Pan-Germanism, namely, that Germany visualises and organises the world as it should be visualised and organised.

The apology for war is equally ancient. It dates back to Fichte and Hegel, who had affirmed that war, through its classifying of peoples, alone establishes justice among nations. In his "Grundlinien der Philosophie des Rechtes," Hegel writes,

> "The moral health of nations is maintained thanks to war, just as the passing breeze saves the sea from stagnation."

The living-space theory appears right at the beginning of the nineteenth century. It is a well-known geographical and historical demonstration which such people as Ratzel, Arthur Dix and Lamprecht took up later on, comparing conflicts between peoples to a savage fight between conceptions and realisations of space, and declaring that all history is moving towards German hegemony.

State totalitarianism also has deep roots in Germany. The absorption of individuals by the State was hoped for by Hegel, who wrote, "Individuals disappear in the presence of the universal substance (that is the People or State idea) and this substance itself shapes the individuals in accordance with its own ends."

Therefore, National Socialism appears in present-day Germany neither as a spontaneous formation which might be due to the consequence of the defeat in 1918, nor as a mere invention of a group of men determined upon seizing power. National Socialism is the ultimate result of a long evolution of doctrines; the exploitation by a group of men of one of the most profound and most tragic aspects of the German soul. But the crime committed by Hitler and his companions will be precisely that of unleashing and exploiting to its extreme limit the latent force of barbarity, which existed before him in the German people.

The dictatorial regime instituted by Hitler and his companions carries with it for all Germans the "soldier- life," that is to say, a kind and a system of life entirely different from that of the bourgeois West and the proletarian East. It amounted to a permanent and complete mobilisation of individual and collective energies. This integral militarisation presupposed complete uniformity of thoughts and actions. It is a militarisation which conforms to the Prussian tradition of discipline.

Propaganda instils into the masses faith, drive and a thirst for the greatness of the community. Those consenting masses find an artificial derivative for their moral anguish and their material cares in theories of race and in a mystical exaltation held in common. Souls which yesterday were wounded and rent asunder once more find themselves united in a common mould.

The Nazi educational system moulds new generations to show no trace of traditional moral teachings, those being replaced by the cult of race and of strength.

The race-myth tends to become a real national religion. Many writers dream of substituting for the duality of religious confessions a world-wide dogma of German conception, which would amount to being the religion of the German race as a race.

In the midst of the twentieth century Germany goes back, of her own free will, beyond Christianity and civilisation to the primitive barbarity of ancient Germany. She makes a deliberate break with all universal conceptions of modern nations. The National Socialist doctrine, which raised inhumanity to the level of a principle, constitutes, in fact, a doctrine of disintegration of modern society.

This doctrine necessarily brought Germany to a war of aggression and to the systematic use of criminality in the waging of war.

The absolute primacy of the German race, the negation of any International Law whatsoever, the cult of strength, the exacerbation of community mysticism made Germany consider recourse to war, in the interests of the German race, logical and justified.

This race would have the incontestable right to grow at the expense of nations considered decadent. Germany is about to resume in the midst of the twentieth century the great invasions of the barbarians. Moreover, most naturally and logically, she will wage her war in barbarous fashion, not only because National Socialist ethics are indifferent to the choice of means, but also because war must be total in its means and in its ends.

Whether we consider a Crime against Peace or War Crimes, we are therefore not faced by an accidental or an occasional criminality which events could explain without justifying it. We are, in fact, faced by systematic criminality, which derives directly and of necessity from a monstrous doctrine put into practice with deliberate intent by the masters of Nazi Germany.

From National Socialist doctrines there arises directly the immediate preparation of Crimes against Peace. As early as February, 1920, in the first programme of the National Socialist Party, Adolf Hitler had already outlined the future basis of German foreign policy. But it was in 1924, in his Landsberg prison, while writing "Mein Kampf," that he more fully developed his views.

According to "Mein Kampf," the foreign policy of the Reich must have as its first objective the return to Germany of her "independence and her effective sovereignty" which is clearly an allusion to the articles of the Treaty of Versailles, referring to disarmament and the demilitarisation of the Rhineland. It would then attempt to reconquer the territories "lost" in 1919, and fifteen years before the outbreak of the Second World War the question of Alsace and Lorraine is clearly raised. It would also have to seek to extend German territories in Europe, the frontiers of 1914 being "insufficient" and it would be indispensable to extend them by including "all Germans" in the Reich, beginning with the Germans of Austria.

After having reconstituted Greater Germany, National Socialism will do everything necessary to "ensure the means of existence" on this planet to the race forming the State, by means of establishing a "healthy relation" between the size of the population and the extent of the territory. By "healthy relation" is meant a situation such that the subsistence of the people will be assured by the resources of its own territory. "A sufficient living space on this earth will alone insure to a people its liberty of existence."

But so far that is but a stage. "When a people sees its subsistence guaranteed by the extent of its territory, it is nevertheless necessary to think of ensuring the security of that territory," because the power of a State "arises directly out of the military value of its geographical situation."

Those ends, Hitler adds, cannot be reached without war. It will be impossible to obtain the re-establishment of the frontiers of 1914 "without bloodshed." How much more would it be impossible to acquire living space if one did not prepare for a "clash of arms."

"It is in Eastern Europe, at the expense of Russia and the neighbouring countries, that Germany must seek new territories. We arrest the eternal march of the Germans towards the South and the West of Europe and cast our eyes towards the East."

But before anything, declares Hitler, it is necessary to crush France's tendency towards hegemony and to have a "final settlement" with this "mortal enemy." "The annihilation of France will enable Germany to acquire afterwards territories in the East." The "settlement of accounts" in the West is but a prelude. "It can be explained only as the securing of our rear defences in order to extend our living-space in Europe."

Henceforth, also, Germany will have to prevent the existence near her territory of a "military power" which might become her rival, and to oppose "by all means" the formation of a State which possibly might acquire sufficient strength to do so, and if that State exists already, to "destroy" it is, for Germans, not only a right but a duty. "Never permit," recommends Hitler to his compatriots, in a passage which he calls his political testament, "the formation in Europe of two Continental powers. In every attempt to set up a second military power on Germany's borders - even if it were in the shape of a State which might possibly acquire that power - you must see an attack on Germany."

War to reconquer those territories lost in 1919, war to annihilate the power of France, war to acquire living-space in Eastern Europe, war, finally, against any State which would be or which might become a counter-weight to the hegemony of the Reich, that is the plan of "Mein Kampf."

In this way, from the inception of National Socialism, he does not recoil from any of the certainties of war entailed by the application of his doctrines.

In fact, from the moment of his accession to power, Hitler and his companions devoted themselves to the military and diplomatic preparation of the wars of aggression which they had resolved to wage.

It is true that even before the accession to power of the National Socialists, Germany had already shown her determination to reconstruct her Armed Forces, notably in 1932 when, on the occasion of the Disarmament Conference, she demanded "equality of rights" as regards armament; and she had already violated in secret the articles of the Treaty of Versailles regarding disarmament. But after the arrival of Hitler to power, German rearmament was to be carried out at a vastly different rate.

On 14th October, 1933, the Reich left the Disarmament Conference and made known, five days later, its decision to withdraw from the League of Nations, under the pretext that it was not granted equality of rights in the matter of armament. France had, however, expressed her readiness to accept equality of rights if Germany would first consent to an international control which would enable the level of existing armaments to be determined. Germany very obviously did not wish to agree to this condition, for an international control would have revealed the extent of the rearmament already carried out in secret by the Reich in violation of the treaties. As a matter of fact, at a Cabinet meeting which took place on 13th October, 1933, the minutes of which have been found, Hitler had declared that he wished to "torpedo" the Disarmament Conference. Under these conditions it is not surprising that the attempts made to resume negotiations with Germany after her withdrawal ended in failure.

When, 18 months later, Hitler's Government decided to re-establish conscription, and to create immediately an Army which would, on a peace establishment, comprise 36 divisions, as well as to create a military air force, it was breaking engagements which Germany had undertaken by the Treaty of Versailles. However, on 3rd February, 1935, France and Great Britain had suggested to the Reich that it resume its place in the League of Nations and prepare a general disarmament convention which would have been substituted for the military articles of the Treaty. At the moment when Hitler was on the point of obtaining, by means of free negotiation, the abolition of the "unilateral burden" which, as he said, the Treaty of Versailles laid on Germany, he preferred to escape any voluntary limitation and any control of armaments by a deliberate violation of a treaty.

When it decided on 7th March, 1936, to denounce the Treaty of Locarno and to reoccupy at once the demilitarised Rhineland area, thereby violating Articles 42 and 43 of the Treaty of Versailles, the German Government alleged that in so doing it was replying to the pact concluded and signed on 2nd May, 1935, between France and the U.S.S.R., and ratified on 27th February, 1936, by the French Chamber of Deputies. It alleged that this pact was contrary to the Treaty of Locarno. This was a mere pretext which was taken seriously by nobody. The Nazi leaders wanted to start building the Siegfried Line as soon as possible in the demilitarised Rhineland area, in order to thwart a military intervention which France might attempt so as to assist her Eastern allies. The decision of 7th March, 1936, was the prelude to the aggressions directed against Austria, Czechoslovakia and Poland.

Internally, rearmament was achieved; thanks to a plan of economic and financial measures which affected every aspect of national life. The entire economic system was directed towards the preparation for war. The members of the Government proclaimed priority of armaments manufacture over all other branches of production. Policy took precedence before economics. The Fuehrer declared: "The people must be resigned for some time to having its butter, fats and meat rationed, in order that rearmament may proceed at the desired rate." The German people did not protest against this order. The State intervened to increase the production of substitute goods which would help to relieve the insufficiency of raw materials and would enable the Reich, in the event of war, to maintain the level of production necessary for the Army and Air Force, even if imports were to become difficult or impossible. The defendant Goering, in September, 1936, inspired the drawing up and directed the application of the Four Year Plan which put Germany's economic system on a war footing. The expenses entailed by this rearmament were assured, thanks to the new system of work treaties. The defendant Schacht, during the three and a half years he was at the head of the Reich Ministry of Economics, brought into being this financial machinery, and thereby played an outstanding role in military preparations, as he himself recalled, after he left the Ministry, in a speech that he made in November, 1938, at the Economic Council of the German Academy.

Germany thus succeeded in three years' time in re-creating a great Army and in forming on the technical plane an organisation entirely devoted to future war. On the 5th November, 1937, when expounding his plan for home policy to his collaborators, Hitler was able to state that rearmament was almost completed.

(A recess was taken.)

M. FRANÇOIS DE MENTHON: While Hitler's Government was giving to the Reich the economic and financial means for a war of aggression he was carrying on simultaneously the diplomatic preparation of that war by attempting to reassure the threatened nations during the period which was indispensable to him for rearmament, and by trying also to keep his eventual adversaries apart from one another.

In a speech on 17th May, 1933, Hitler, while asking for a revision of the Treaty of Versailles, declared that he had no intention of obtaining it by force. He stated that he admitted "the legitimate exigencies of all peoples" and he asserted that he did not want to "Germanise those who are not Germans." He wished to "respect the rights of other nationalities."

The German-Polish Non-Aggression Pact, concluded on 26th January, 1934, which was to reassure for a time the Warsaw Government and to lull it into a state of false security, was principally intended to bar French policy from any action. In a work published in 1939 entitled "Deutschlands Aussenpolitik 1933-39," an official writer, Professor Von Freytag-Loringhoven, wrote that the essential purpose of this pact was to paralyse the action of the Franco-Polish alliance and to "overthrow the entire French system."

On 26th May, 1935, ten days after denouncing the military clauses of the Treaty of Versailles, Germany started negotiations with Great Britain which were to result in the Naval Agreement of 18th June, 1935, negotiations which were intended to reassure British public opinion by showing, it that, while the Reich was desirous of becoming once more a great military Power, it was not thinking of reconstituting a powerful fleet.

Immediately following the plebiscite of 13th January, 1935, which decided the return of the Saar territory to the Reich, Hitler formally declared "that he would make no further territorial demands whatsoever on France."

He was to use the same tactics towards France until the end of 1938. On 6th December, 1938, Ribbentrop came to Paris to sign the Franco-German Declaration which agreed "the frontiers as definite" between the two countries and which stated that the two Governments were resolved, "under reservation of their particular relations with third Powers, to engage in mutual consultation in the event of questions of common interests which might show a risk of leading to international difficulties"; he was then still hoping, to quote the French Ambassador in Berlin, to "stabilise peace in the West in order to have a free hand in the East."

Did not Hitler make the same promises to Austria and Czechoslovakia? He signed on 11th July, 1936, an agreement with the Viennese Government, recognising the independence of Austria, an independence which he was to destroy 20 months later. By means of the Munich Agreement on 29th September, 1938, he promised subsequently to guarantee the integrity of the Czech territory - which territory he invaded less than six months later!

Nevertheless, as early as 5th November, 1937, in a secret conference held at the Reich Chancellery, Hitler had made known to his collaborators that the hour had struck for resolving by force the problem of the living-space required by Germany. The diplomatic situation was favourable to Germany. She had acquired a superiority of armaments which ran the risk of being only a temporary one. Action should be taken without further delay.

Thereupon started the series of aggressions which have already been detailed before this Court. It has also been shown to you that these various aggressions have been made in violation of international treaties and of the principles of International Law. As a matter of fact, German propaganda did not challenge this at the time. It merely stated that those treaties and those principles "had lost any reality whatever with the passage of time." In other words, it simply denied the value of the word once pledged, and asserted that the principles which formed the basis of International Law had become obsolete. This is a reasoning which is in line with the National Socialist doctrines which, as we have seen, do not recognise any International Law, and state that any means is justifiable if it is of a nature to serve the interests of the German race.

However, it is worth while examining the various arguments which German propaganda made use of to justify the long- planned aggression.

Germany set forth, first of all, her vital interests. Could she not be excused for neglecting the rules of the rights of people when she was engaged in a struggle for the existence of her people? She needed economic expansion. She had the right and the duty to protect the German minorities abroad. She was obliged to ward off the encirclement which the Western Powers were directing against the Reich.

Economic expansion was one of the reasons which Hitler put forward, even to his direct associates, in the secret conferences he held in 1937 and 1939 in the Reich Chancellery. "Economic needs," he said, "are the basis of the policy of expansion of Italy and of Japan. They also guide Germany."

But would not Hitler's Germany have been able to seek satisfaction of these needs by peaceful means,? Did she think of obtaining new possibilities for her foreign commerce through commercial negotiations? Hitler did not stop at such solutions. To solve the German economic problems, he saw only one way - the acquisition of agricultural territories - undoubtedly because he was incapable of conceiving these problems under any other form than that of "war economy." If he affirmed the necessity of obtaining this "agricultural space" - to use his own phrase - it was because he saw therein the means of obtaining for the German population the food resources which would protect it against the consequences of a blockade.

The duty of protecting "the German minorities abroad" was the favourite theme which Germany's diplomacy made use of from 1937 to 1939. Obviously it could not serve as an excuse for the destruction of the Czechoslovakian State or for the establishment of the "German Protectorate of Bohemia- Moravia." The fate of the "Sudeten Germans," that of the "Danzig Germans" was the Leitmotiv of the German Press, of the Fuehrer's speeches and of the publications of Ribbentrop's propaganda. Now, is it necessary to recall that in the secret conference of 5th November, 1937, in which Hitler draws up for his associates the plan of action to be carried out against the Czechoslovakian State, he does not say one word about the "Sudeten Germans," and to recall that in the conference of 23rd May, 1939, he declares that Danzig is not the "principal point" of the German-Polish controversy? The "right of nationalities" was, therefore, in his mind only a propaganda method intended to mask the real design, which was the conquest of "living space."

The encirclement directed by the Western Powers against the Reich is the argument which Hitler used when, on 28th April, 1939, he denounced the Naval Agreement which he had concluded in 1935 with Great Britain. This thesis of encirclement occupied a great deal of space in the German White Book of 1939, relative to the origins of the war; but is it possible to speak of encirclement when Germany had, in May, 1939, obtained the alliance with Italy and when, on 23rd August, 1939, she concluded the German-Russian Pact, and can we forget that the diplomatic efforts of France and of Great Britain in respect to Greece, Roumania, Turkey, and Poland are subsequent both to the destruction of the Czechoslovakian State and to the, beginning of the German-Polish diplomatic conflict? Had not the British Prime Minister declared on 23rd March, 1939, before the House of Commons that British policy had only two aims: to prevent Germany from dominating Europe and "to oppose a method which, by the threat of force, obliged the weak States to renounce their independence"? What Hitler Germany called "encirclement" was simply a fence, belatedly built in an attempt to check measureless ambitions.

But German propaganda did not limit itself to this. Did we not see one of its spokesmen point to the contrast between the passivity of France and Great Britain in September, 1938, and the resistance which they showed in 1939 to the Hitler policy, wherefrom it was concluded that the peace would have been maintained if the Western Powers had exercised pressure on Poland to bring it to accept the German demands, as they had exercised pressure the previous year on Czechoslovakia? A strange argument, which is equivalent to saying that Germany would have been willing not to make war if all the Powers had yielded to her will. Is it an excuse for the perpetrators of these violations that France and Great Britain had, for a long time, opposed the violations of the rights of peoples by Germany merely by platonic protests?

Public opinion in France and Great Britain, deceived by Hitler's declarations, may have believed that the designs of National Socialism contemplated only the settlement of the fate of German minorities; it may have hoped that there was a limit to German ambitions; for, ignorant as they were of the secret plans of which we have proof to-day, France and Great Britain allowed Germany to rearm and reoccupy the Rhineland at the very moment when, according to the testimony of Ribbentrop, a military reaction on their part would, in March, 1936, have placed the Reich in a critical situation. They permitted the aggression of March and September, 1938, and it required the destruction of the Czechoslovakian State to make the scope of the German plans clear to the Allies. How can one be astonished that their attitude then changed, and they decided to resist the German plans? How could one still claim that the peace could have been "bought" in August, 1939, by concessions, since the German secret documents prove that Hitler was determined to attack Poland as early as May, 1939, and that he would have been "deeply disappointed" if she had yielded, and that he wished a general war?

In reality the war was implied by the coming to power of the National Socialists. Their doctrine inevitably led to it.

As Sir Hartley Shawcross forcefully brought out before your High Tribunal, a war of aggression is self-evidently a violation of International Law and, more particularly, a violation of the General Treaty for the Renouncement of War of 27th August, 1928, under the name of the Paris Pact, or the Briand-Kellogg Pact, of which Germany is one of the signatories. This Pact continues to constitute a part of International Law.

May I reread Article I of this Treaty?

> "The High Contracting Parties solemnly declare, in the name of their respective peoples, that they condemn recourse to war for the solution of international controversies and renounce it as an instrument of national policy in their reciprocal relations."

Wars of aggression thus ceased, in 1928, to be lawful.

Sir Hartley Shawcross told you, with eloquence, that the Paris Pact, a new law of civilised nations, was the foundation of a better European order. The Paris Pact, which remains the fundamental charter of the law of war, indeed marks an essential step in the evolution of the relations between States. The Hague Convention had regulated the "law of the conduct of war." It had instituted the obligation of recourse to arbitration as a preliminary to any conflict. It had, essentially, established a distinction between acts, of war to which International Law and custom allow recourse and those which it prohibits. The Hague Convention did not even touch upon the principle of war which remained outside the legal sphere. This is, in fact, what is brought into being by the Paris Pact, which regulates "the right of declaration of war."

Since 1928 International Law of war has emerged from its framework of regulations. It has gone beyond the empiricism of The Hague Convention to qualify the legal foundation or recourse to force. Every war of aggression is illegal, and the men who bear the responsibility for bringing it about place themselves by their own will beyond the law.

What does this mean, if not that all acts, committed as a consequence of this aggression, for the carrying on of the struggle thus undertaken, will cease to have the juridical character of acts of war?

May I quote this well-known passage from Pascal?

> "Why do you kill me? Do you not live on the other side of the water? My friend, if you lived on this side, I would be an assassin, and it would be unjust to kill you as I am doing, but since you live on the other side, I am an honourable man, and this is just."

Acts committed in the execution of a war are assaults on persons and goods which are themselves prohibited, but are sanctioned in all legislations. The state of war could make them legitimate only if the war itself was legitimate. Inasmuch as this is no longer the case, since the Briand-Kellogg Pact, these acts become purely and simply common law crimes. As Mr. Justice Jackson has already argued before you with irrefutable logic, any recourse to war is a recourse to means which are in themselves criminal.

This is the whole spirit of the Briand-Kellogg Pact. It was intended to deprive the States which accepted it of the right of having recourse, in their national interests, to a series of acts directed against the physical persons or against the properties of nationals of a foreign Power. Given this formal commitment, those who have ignored it have given the order to commit acts prohibited by the common law of civilised States, and here is involved no special rule of International Law like that which existed previously and which left the said acts of war untouched by any criminal qualifications.

A war perpetuated in violation of International Law no longer really possesses the juridical character of a war. It is truly an act of gangsterism, a systematically criminal undertaking.

This war, or this would-be war, is in itself not only a violation of International Law, but, indeed, a crime, since it signifies the outbreak of this systematically criminal enterprise.

Inasmuch as they could not legally have recourse to force, those who dictated it, and who were the very organs of the State bound by treaties, must be considered as the very source of the numerous assaults upon life and property that are severely punished by all penal law.

One cannot, of course, deduce, from the preceding, the individual responsibility of all the perpetrators of acts of violence. It is obvious that, in an organised modern State, responsibility is limited to those who act directly for the State, they alone being in a position to estimate the lawfulness of the orders given. They alone can be prosecuted and they must be prosecuted. International Law is so powerful that the prestige of the sovereignty of States cannot reduce it to impotence. It is not possible to maintain that crimes against International Law must escape repressive action because, on the one hand, the State is an entity to which one cannot impute criminal intention and upon which one cannot inflict punishment and, on the other, no individual can be held responsible for the acts of the State.

On the other hand, it cannot be objected that, despite the illegality of the principle of recourse to force by Germany, other States have admitted that war existed, and speak of the application of International Law in time of war. It must, in fact, be noted that, even in the case of civil war, the parties have often invoked these rules which, to a certain extent, canalise the use of force. This in no wise implies acquiescence in the principle of its use. Moreover, when Great Britain and France communicated to the League of Nations the fact that a state of war existed between them and Germany as on 3rd September, 1939, they also declared that, in committing an act of aggression against Poland, Germany had violated its obligations, assumed not only with regard to Poland but also with regard to the other signatories of the Paris Pact. From that moment on, Great Britain and France took cognisance, in some way, of the launching of an illegal war by Germany.

Recourse to war implies preparation and decision; it would be futile to prohibit it, if one intended to inflict no chastisement upon those who knowingly took recourse to it, though they had the power of choosing a different path. They must, indeed, be considered the direct instigators of the acts qualified as crimes.

It seems to us that it is evident from all this that the statute of 8th August only established a jurisdiction to judge what was already an international crime, not only before the conscience of humanity but also according to International Law, even before the Tribunal was established.

If it is not contested that a crime has really been committed, is it possible to contest the competence of the International Tribunal to judge it?

There can, indeed, be no doubt that the States bound by the treaty of 1928 had assumed international responsibilities towards the co-signatories, should they act in a way contrary to the agreements undertaken.

International responsibility normally involves the collective State as such, without in principle exposing the individuals who have been the perpetrators of an illegal act. It is within the framework of the State, with which an international responsibility rests, that as a general rule the conduct of the men who are responsible for this violation of International Law may be appraised. They are subject, as the case may be, to political responsibility or to penal responsibility before the assemblies or the competent jurisdictions.

The reason for this is that normally the framework of the State comprises the nationals: the order of the State assumes the exercise of justice over a given territory and with regard to the individuals whom it includes, and the failure of the State in the exercise of this essential mission is followed by the reaction and the protests of third Powers, notably when their own nationals are involved.

But in the present situation there is no German State.

Since the surrender declaration of 5th June, 1945, and until the day when a Government shall have been established by the agreement of the Four Occupying Powers, there will be no organ representing the German State. Under these conditions, it cannot be considered that there exists a German State juridical order, capable of bringing the consequences, arising from a recognition of the responsibility of the Reich for the violation of the Briand-Kellogg Pact, to bear upon those individuals who are, in fact, the perpetrators of this violation in their capacity as organs of the Reich.

To-day supreme authority is being exercised over the whole German territory, in regard to the entire German population, by the Four Powers acting jointly. It must, therefore, be allowed that the States which exercise supreme authority over the territory and population of Germany can submit this guilt to a Court's jurisdiction. Otherwise, the proclamation that Germany has violated the solemn convenant, which it has undertaken, becomes meaningless.

There is involved a penal responsibility incurred for a series of acts, qualified as crimes which were committed against subjects of the United Nations. These acts, which are not juridicially acts of war but which have been committed as such upon the instigation of those who bear the responsibility for the launching of the so-called war, who have committed aggression upon the lives and the property of subjects of the United Nations, may, by virtue of the territorial principle, as we have shown above, be brought before a jurisdiction constituted to this effect by the United Nations, even as war crimes, properly speaking, are now being brought before the tribunals of each country whose nationals have been victims thereof.

Crimes committed by the Nazis in the course of the war, like the war of aggression itself, will be, as Mr. Justice Jackson has demonstrated to you, the manifestation of a concerted and methodically executed plan.

These crimes flow directly, like the war itself, from the National Socialist doctrine. This doctrine is indifferent to the moral choice of means to attain a final success, and for this doctrine the aim of war is pillage, destruction and extermination.

To-day war, totalitarian war in its methods and its aims, is dictated by the primacy of the German race and the negation of any other value. The Nazi conception maintains selection as a natural principle. The man who does not belong to the superior race counts for nothing. Human life and liberty, personality, the dignity of man, have no importance when an adversary of the German community is involved. It is truly "the return to barbarism" with all its consequences. Logically consistent, National Socialism goes to the length of assuming the right, either to exterminate totally races judged hostile or decadent, or to subjugate or put to use individuals and groups capable of resistance in these races. Does not the idea of totalitarian war imply the annihilation of any eventual resistance? All those who in any way may be capable of opposing the New Order and the German hegemony will be liquidated. It thus becomes possible to assure an absolute domination over a neighbouring people that has been reduced to impotence and to utilise, for the benefit of the Reich, the resources and the human material of these people reduced to slavery.

All the moral conceptions which tended to make war more humane are obviously outdated, and still more so all international conventions which bad undertaken to bring some extenuation of the evils of war.

The conquered peoples must concur willingly or by force in the German victory, by their material resources, as well as by their labour potential. Means will be found to subject them.

The treatment to which the occupied countries will be subjected is likewise related to this war aim. As one could read in "Deutsche Volkskraft" of 13th June, 1935:

> "The totalitarian war will end in a totalitarian victory. 'Totalitarian' signifies the entire destruction of the conquered nation and its complete and final disappearance from the historic scene."

Among the conquered peoples distinctions can be made according to whether or not the National Socialists consider them as belonging to the Master Race. For the former, an effort is made to integrate them into the German Reich against their will. For the latter, there is applied a policy of weakening them and bringing about their extinction by every means, from that of appropriation of their property to extermination of their persons. In regard to both groups, the Nazi rulers assault not only property and physical persons, but also the spirits and souls. They seek to align the populations according to the Nazi dogma and behaviour, when they wish to integrate them in the German community; they apply themselves at least to rooting out whatever conceptions are irreconcilable with the Nazi universe; they aim to reduce to the mentality and status of slaves, those men whose nationality they wish to eradicate for the benefit of the German race.

Inspired by these general conceptions as to the conduct to be observed in occupied countries, the defendants gave special orders or general directives, or deliberately identified themselves with such. Their responsibility is that of perpetrators, co-perpetrators or accomplices in the War Crimes systematically committed between 1st September, 1939, and 8th May, 1945, by Germany at war. They deliberately willed, premeditated and ordered these crimes, or knowingly associated themselves with this policy of organised criminality.

We shall expose the various aspects of this policy of criminality as it was pursued in the occupied countries of Western Europe, by dealing successively with Forced Labour, Economic Looting, Crimes against Persons, and Crimes against Mankind.

The conception of total war, which gave rise to all the crimes which were to be perpetrated by the Nazi Germans in the occupied countries, was the basis for the Forced Labour Service. Through this institution, Germany proposed to utilise to the maximum the labour potential of the enslaved populations, in order to maintain the German war production at the necessary level. Moreover, there can be no doubt that this institution was linked with the German plan of "extermination through labour" of the populations adjoining Germany which she regarded as dangerous or inferior.

> A document of the Supreme Command of the Armed Forces of Germany, dated 1st October, 1938, provided for the forced employment of prisoners and civilians for war labour. Hitler in his speech of 9th November, 1941, "did not doubt for a moment that, in the occupied territories which we control at present, we shall make the last man work for us."

From 1942 on, it is under the admitted responsibility of the defendant Sauckel, acting together with the defendant Speer, under the control of the defendant Goering, General Plenipotentiary of the Four Year Plan, that compulsory foreign labour, for the benefit of the war conducted by Germany, was developed to the full.

The most various methods of constraint were utilised simultaneously or successively:

First: Requisition of services under conditions incompatible with Article 52 of

The Hague Convention.

Second: So-called voluntary labour, which consisted of bringing a worker under pressure to sign a contract to work in Germany.

Third: Conscription for compulsory labour.

Fourth: The forcing of war prisoners to work for the German war production and their transformation in certain cases into so-called free workers.

Fifth: The enrolling of certain foreign workers, notably French (Alsatian, people of Lorraine) and Luxembourgers in the German Labour Front.

All these procedures constitute crimes contrary to International Law and in violation of Article 52 of The Hague Convention.

These services requisitions were made under threat of death. Voluntary labour recruiting was accompanied by individual measures of constraint, obliging the workers of occupied territories to sign contracts. The duration of these pseudo-contracts was subsequently prolonged unilaterally and illegally by the German authorities.

The failure of these measures of requisition or the voluntary recruitment of labour led the German authorities everywhere to have recourse to conscription. Hitler declared on 19th August, 1942, in a conference on the Four Year Plan, which was reported by the defendant Speer, that Germany "had to proceed to forced recruiting if sufficient labour were not obtained on a voluntary basis." On 7th November, 1943, the defendant Jodl declared in the course of a speech given in Munich before the Gauleiters:

"In my opinion the time has come to take vigorous, resolute, and unscrupulous measures in Denmark, in Holland, in France and in Belgium in order to force thousands of idle men to carry out this most important work of fortification."

Having accepted the principle of force, the Germans made use of two complementary methods: legal constraint, consisting of promulgating laws regulating obligatory labour; and restraint in fact, consisting of taking necessary measures to oblige workers under penalty of grave sanctions to conform to the issued legislation.

The basis of the legislation on forced labour is the decree of 22nd August, 1942, of the defendant Sauckel, who formulated the charter of forced recruiting in all the occupied countries.

In France, Sauckel got the so-called Government of Vichy to publish the law of 4th September, 1942. This law effected the freezing of all manpower in industries and anticipated the possibility of a requisition of all Frenchmen who might be employed in any work useful to the enemy. All Frenchmen from 18 to 50 years of age, who did not have a job which occupied them more than thirty hours a week, had to prove that they were usefully employed to meet the needs of the country. A decree of 19th September, 1942, and an enabling directive of 24th September regulated the various provisions of this announcement. The law of 4th September, 1942, had been published by the so-called Government of Vichy, following strong pressure exercised by the occupation authorities. Specifically, Dr. Michel, Chief of the Administrative Staff of the German Military Command in France, wrote on 26th August, 1942, a threatening letter to the Delegate General for Franco-German Economic Relations, requesting him that the law be published.

In 1943, Sauckel obtained from the defacto authority a directive under date of 2nd February, stipulating a census of all male Frenchmen born between 1st January, 1912, and 31st December, 1921. He also obtained the passing of the law of 16th February, establishing the Bureau of Compulsory Labour for all young men from 20 to 22 years of age. On 9th April, 1943, Gauleiter Sauckel requested the deportation of 120,000 workers for the month of May and another 100,000 for the month of June. To accomplish this, the so-called Government of Vichy proceeded to mobilise the entire military conscription class of 1942. On 15th January, 1944, Sauckel requested the defacto French authorities to deliver one million men for the first six months of the year, and he caused the adoption of the regulation designated as the law of 1st February, 1944, which extended the possibility of impressing all men from 16 to 60 years of age and women from the age of 18 to 45 for forced labour.

Similar measures were taken in all occupied countries.

In Norway, the German authorities imposed on the so-called Government of Quisling the publication of a law dated 3rd February, 1943, which established the compulsory registration of Norwegian citizens and prescribed their forced enrolment. In Belgium and in Holland, the Bureau of Compulsory Labour was organised directly by ordinances of the occupying Power. In Belgium the ordinances were promulgated by the military command, and in Holland by the defendant Seyss-Inquart, who was Reich Commissar for the occupied Netherland territories. In both of these countries the development of a compulsory labour policy followed the same pattern. Compulsory labour was at first required only within the occupied territories. It was soon extended in order to permit the deportation of workers to Germany. This was achieved, in the case of Holland, by the ordinance of 28th February, 1941, and in Belgium by the ordinance of 6th March, 1942, which established the principle of forced labour. The principle of deportation was formulated in Belgium by means of the ordinance of 6th October, 1942, and in Holland by the ordinance of 23rd March, 1942.

In order to ensure the efficiency of these legal provisions, brutal compulsion was exercised in all countries, numerous round-ups in all large cities. For example, 50,000 persons were arrested in Rotterdam on 10th and 11th November, 1944.

Even more serious than the forced labour of civilian population was the incorporation of labourers from occupied countries in the service of the Reich. This incorporation was not merely the conscription of labourers but meant, in fact, the application of German legislation to the nationals of occupied countries.

In the face of the patriotic resistance of the workers of the different occupied countries, the important results which the German Labour Office had anticipated were far from being fulfilled. However, a large number of workers from the occupied countries were forced to work for the German war effort.

With regard to the Todt Organisation, the labourers who were employed in the West in the construction of the Atlantic Wall totalled 248,000 at the end of March, 1943. In the year 1942, 3,300,000 workers from occupied countries worked for Germany in their own country. 300,000 of these were in Norway, 249,000 in Holland, 650,000 in France. The number of workers deported to Germany and coming from the occupied territories in the West increased in 1942 to the figure of 131,000 Belgians, 135,000 Frenchmen, 154,000 Dutchmen. On 30th April, 1943, 1,293,000 workmen, of whom 269,000 were women from the occupied territories in the West were working for the German War Economy. On 7th July, 1944, Sauckel stated that the number of workers deported to Germany during these first six months of 1944 reached a total of 537,000, of which 33,000 were Frenchmen. On 1st March, 1944, he acknowledged during a conference, held by the Central Office of the Four Year Plan, that there were in Germany, 5,000,000 foreign workers, of whom 200,000 were actually volunteers.

The report of the French Ministry for prisoners of war, deportees and refugees, gives the figure of 715,000 for the total number of men and women who had been deported.

It should be added that, contrary to International Law, the workers who were transported to Germany had to work under labour conditions and living conditions that were incompatible with the most rudimentary regard for human dignity. The defendant Sauckel has himself stated that foreign workers, who could achieve substantial production should be fed so that they could be exploited as completely as possible with the minimum of expense, adding that they should receive less food the moment their production began to decrease, and that no concern should be given to the fate of those whose production capacity no longer presented any interest. Special reprisal camps were organised for those who sought to avoid the compulsion imposed on them. An order of 21st December, 1942, stipulated, that unwilling workers should be sent, without trial, to such camps. In 1943, Sauckel, during an inter-ministerial conference, stated that the co-operation of the S.S. was essential to him in order to fulfil the task with which he had been entrusted. Thus, the crime of forced labour and of deportation gave rise to a whole series of additional crimes, against persons.

The work required of war prisoners did not remain within the legal limits authorised by International Law any more than did that of the civilian labourers. National Socialist Germany obliged prisoners of war to work for the German war production, in violation of Articles 31 and 32 of the Geneva Convention.

National Socialist Germany while exploiting to the fullest extent for the war effort prisoners of war as well as workers for occupied territories, against all international conventions, was at the same time seizing, by every possible means, the wealth of these countries. German authorities applied systematic pillage in these countries. By economic pillage we mean both the taking away of goods of every type and the exploitation on the spot of the national resources for the benefit of Germany's war.

This pillage was methodically organised.

The Germans began by making sure that they had in their possession, in all countries, the necessary means for payment. Thus, they ensured that they could seize, with the appearance of legality, the wealth which they coveted. After freezing the existing purchasing power, they required enormous payments under the pretext of indemnity for the maintenance of occupation troops.

It should be recalled that according to the terms of The Hague Convention, occupied countries may be obliged to assume the burden of the expenses caused by the maintenance of an army of occupation. But the amounts that were exacted under this by the Germans were only remotely related to the actual costs of occupation.

Moreover, they forced the occupied countries to accept a clearing system which operated almost entirely to the exclusive profit of Germany. Imports from Germany were almost non-existent; the goods exported to Germany by the occupied countries, were subject to no regulation.

In order to maintain for the purchasing balance thus created a considerable purchasing power, the Germans attempted everywhere to achieve the stabilisation of prices and imposed a severe rationing system. This rationing system, which left the population with a quality of inferior goods, which was less than the minimum indispensable for their existence, afforded the additional advantage of preserving for the benefit of the Germans the greatest possible portion of the production.

Thus, the Germans seized a considerable part of the stocks and of the production, as a result of operations which had the appearance of legality (requisitions, purchases made with German priority coupons, individual purchase). These transactions were completed by other operations of a clandestine character, which were carried out in violation of the official regulations imposed frequently by the Germans themselves. Thus, the Germans had created a whole organisation for black market purchases. For example, one may read in a report of the German Foreign Ministry of 4th

September, 1942 that the defendant Goering had ordered that purchases on the black market should henceforth extend to goods which until then had not been included, such as household goods, and he prescribed further that all goods which could be useful to Germany should be collected, even if as a result certain signs of inflation appeared in the occupied countries.

While they were transporting to Germany the maximum quantity of goods, of every description, after requisitioning without payment, or by paying with bills which they had irregularly obtained by a simple entry in the clearing account, the Nazi leaders were at the same time trying to impose the resumption of activity in industry for the benefit of Germany's war.

German industrialists had received instructions ordering them to divide amongst themselves the enterprises in the occupied areas which had engaged in a production similar to their own. While having to carry out these orders, these industrialists were required to place such industries in occupied countries firmly under their control by means of different types of financial combinations.

The appearance of monetary legality or contractual legality could in no way hide the fact that economic looting was systematically organised contrary to the stipulations of the International Convention of The Hague. If, according to the stipulations of this Convention, Germany had the right to seize whatever was indispensable for the maintenance of the troops necessary for the occupation, all seizures in excess of these requirements undoubtedly constitute a War Crime, which brought about the economic, ruin of the occupied countries, a long-range weakening of their economic potential and of their means of subsistence, as well as the general undernourishment of the populations. Exact estimates of German transactions in the economic field cannot be formulated at this time. It would be necessary for this purpose to study in detail the activities of several countries over a period of more than four years.

Nevertheless, it has been possible to bring out precisely certain facts, and to give minimum estimates of German spoliations with respect to the different occupied countries.

In Denmark, which was the first country in Western Europe to be invaded, the value of German seizures was nearly 9,000,000,000 crowns. In Norway, German spoliations exceed a total value of 20,000,000,000 crowns.

In the Netherlands, German pillage was effected to such an extent that although Holland is one of the richest countries in the world in relation to its population, it is to-day almost completely ruined, and the financial charges imposed by the occupant exceed 20,000,000,000 florins.

In Belgium, through various schemes, notably the system of occupation indemnity and clearing, the Germans seized far more than 130,000,000,000 Belgian francs of payment balances. The Grand Duchy of Luxembourg also suffered important losses as a result of the action of the occupying power.

Finally, in France, the levying of taxes on means of payments reached a total of 745,000,000,000 francs. In this sum we have not included the 74,000,000,000 francs, which represents the maximum figure which Germany could legally demand for the maintenance of her army of occupation. (Moreover, the seizure of 9,500,000,000 in gold was calculated according to the rate of 1939.)

In addition to the goods settled for in the occupied countries by means of payment extorted from these countries, enormous quantities of goods of every character were purely and simply requisitioned without any indemnity, seized without any explanation, or else stolen. The occupying authorities took not only all raw materials and manufactured goods which could be useful to their war efforts, but they extended their seizures to everything that might help to procure them a credit balance in neutral countries, such as movables, jewels, luxury goods and objects of all kinds. Finally, the art treasures of the countries of Western Europe were likewise looted in the most shameful manner.

The considerable sums which Germany was able to obtain by abusing her power contrary to all the principles of International Law, without providing any compensation, enabled her to carry out, with the appearance of legality, the economic looting of France and of the other countries of Western Europe. The consequence for these countries, from the economic viewpoint, is a loss of their strength which will take long to repair.

But the most serious consequences of these practices affected the population itself. For more than four years, the people of the occupied countries were exposed to a regime of slow starvation, which resulted in an increase in the death rate, a breaking down of the physical stamina of the population and, above all, an alarming deficiency in the growth of children and adolescents.

Such practices, perpetrated and consummated systematically by the German leaders, contrary to International Law and specifically contrary to The Hague Convention, as well as contrary to the general principles of criminal law in force in all civilised nations, constitute War Crimes for which they must answer before your High Tribunal.

(A recess was taken.)

M. FRANCOIS DE MENTHON: Crimes against the physical person: arbitrary imprisonment, ill-treatment, deportations, murder committed by the Germans in the occupied countries, reached proportions beyond what could be imagined, even in the course of a world conflict which took the most odious forms.

These crimes spring directly from the Nazi doctrine and testify to the Reich leaders' absolute disregard for the human individual, to the abolition of any sense of justice or even of pity, to a total subordination of any and all human consideration on the part of the German community.

All these crimes are linked to a policy of terrorism. Such a policy permits the subjugation of occupied countries, without involving a large deployment of troops, and their submission to anything that might be demanded of them. Many of these crimes are moreover tied up with the will to exterminate.

We shall examine in succession executions of hostages, police crimes, deportations, crimes involving prisoners of war, terroristic activities against the Resistance and the massacre of the civilian population.

The execution of hostages constitutes in all countries the first act of terrorism on the part of German occupation troops. From 1940 on, the German Command, notably in France, carried out numerous executions as reprisals for any crime against the German Army.

These practices, contrary to Article 50 of The Hague Convention, which forbids collective sanctions, awaken everywhere a feeling of horror and frequently produce a result contrary to the one sought, by arousing the populations against the occupant.

The occupying authorities then attempted to legalise such criminal practices, thus seeking to have them recognised by the populations as "the right of the occupying power." Veritable "codes for hostages" were promulgated by the German military authorities.

Following the general order issued by the defendant Keitel on 16th September, 1941, Stulpnagel published in France his ordinance of 30th September, 1941. According to the terms of this ordinance, all Frenchmen held by German authorities for any reason whatsoever will be considered as hostages, as well as all Frenchmen who are in the custody of the French authorities on behalf of German organisations. The ordinance of Stulpnagel specifies:

"At the time of the burial of the bodies, burial in a common grave of a rather large number of persons in a particular cemetery must be avoided, since this would create a shrine for pilgrims, which now or later might become a centre for the stimulation of anti-German propaganda."

In the execution of this ordinance the most infamous executions of hostages were carried out.

Following the murder of two German officers, one in Nantes on 2nd October, 1941, and the other at Bordeaux a few days thereafter, the German authorities had 27 hostages shot at Chateaubriant and 21 at Nantes.

On 15th August, 1942, 96 hostages were shot at Mont-Valerien.

In September, 1942, following an assault committed against German soldiers in the Rex moving picture house in Paris, 116 hostages were shot, 46 hostages being taken from the hostage depot of the Fortress at Romainville and 70 from Bordeaux.

In reprisal for the murder of a German official of the labour front, 50 hostages were shot in Paris at the end of September, 1943.

Threats of reprisals on the families of the patriots of the Resistance are related to the same odious policy of hostages. The Kommandatur (garrison de Q) published the following notice in the "Pariser-Zeitung" of 16th July, 1942:

"Near male relatives, brothers-in-law and cousins of the agitators above the age of 18 years will be shot.

All female family members of the same degree of relationship shall be condemned to forced labour.

Children less than 18 years of age, of all above-mentioned persons, shall be sent to a house of correction."

The execution of hostages continued everywhere until the liberation, but in the last period they were no more than one additional feature in the methods of German terrorism, then grown more sweeping.

Among the crimes against persons of which the civilian populations of the occupied countries of the West were victims, those committed by the Nazi police organisations are of the most revolting.

The intervention of the German police who, in spite of certain appearances, did not belong to the armies of occupation, is in itself contrary to International Law.

Their crimes, particularly hateful in the complete disregard for human dignity that they imply, were multiplied during four years throughout all the territories of the West occupied by the German forces.

True, no definite order, no detailed directive emanating directly from one of the defendants or from one of their immediate subordinates and valid for all the German police or for the police of the occupied territories of the West, has been found. But these crimes were committed by a police that was a direct expression of the National Socialist ideology and the undeniable instrument of National Socialist policy for which all the defendants carry the full and entire responsibility.

Before the considerable mass of acts, their similarity, their simultaneousness, their generalisation in time and place, no one would be able to deny that these acts are not only the individual responsibility of those who committed them here or there, but constitute as well the execution of orders from above.

The arrests took place without any of the elementary guarantees recognised in all civilised countries. On a simple, unverified denunciation, without previous investigation, and often on charges brought by persons not qualified to bring them, masses of arbitrary arrests took place in every occupied country.

During the first period of the occupation, the Germans simulated a scrupulous respect for "legality" in the matter of arrests. This legality was that introduced by Nazism in the interior of Germany and did not respect any of the traditional guarantees to which the individuals in civilised countries are entitled. But, rapidly, even this pseudo- legality was abandoned and the arrests became absolutely arbitrary.

The worst treatments were applied to arrested persons even before the guilt of the accused had been examined. The use of torture in the interrogations was almost a general rule. The tortures usually applied were beating, whipping, chaining for several days without a moment of rest for nourishment or hygienic care, immersion in ice water, drowning in a bathtub, charging the bathwater with electricity, electrification of the most sensitive parts of the body, burns at certain places on the body and the pulling out of fingernails. But, moreover, those who carried out these measures had every latitude for unleashing their instinct of cruelty and of sadism against their victims. All those facts, which were of public knowledge in the occupied countries, never led to any punishment whatsoever of their authors on the part of the responsible authorities. It even seems that the torture was more severe when an officer was present.

It is undeniable that the actions of the German police towards the prisoners were part and parcel of a long premeditated system of criminality, ordered by the chiefs of the regime and executed by the most faithful members of the National Socialist organisations.

Aside from the general use of torture on prisoners, the German police perpetrated a considerable number of murders. It is impossible to know the conditions under which many of these murders were carried out. Nevertheless, we have enough information to permit us to discover in them a new expression of the general policy of the National Socialists in the occupied countries. Often the deaths were only the result of the tortures inflicted on the prisoners, but often the murder was deliberately desired and carried out.

The crime which will undoubtedly be remembered as the most horrible among those committed by the Germans against the civilian populations of the occupied countries was that of deportation and internment in the concentration camps of Germany.

These deportations had a double aim: to secure additional labour for the benefit of the German war machine, and to eliminate from the occupied countries and progressively exterminate the elements most opposed to Germanism. They served likewise to empty prisons overcrowded with patriots and to remove the latter for good.

The deportations and the methods employed in the concentration camps were a stupefying revelation for the civilised world. Nevertheless, they also are only a natural consequence of the National Socialist doctrine, according to which man, of himself, has no value except when he is of service to the German race.

It is not possible, yet, to give exact figures. It is probable that one would be making an understatement when speaking of 250,000 for France; 6,000 for Luxembourg; 5,200 for Denmark; 5,400 for Norway; 120,000 for Holland; and 37,000 for Belgium.

The arrests were founded, now under a pretext of a political nature, now on a pretext of a racial nature. In the beginning they were individual; subsequently they took on a collective character, particularly in France from the end of 1941. Sometimes the deportation did not come until after long months of prison, but more often the arrest was made with a direct view to deportation under the system of "protective custody." Everywhere imprisonment in the country of origin was accompanied by brutality, often by tortures. Before being sent to Germany, the deportees were, in general, concentrated in an assembly camp. The formation of a convoy was often the first stage of extermination. The deportees travelled in cattle cars, 80 to 120 per car, no matter what the season. There were few convoys where no deaths occurred. In certain transports the proportion of deaths was more than 25 per cent.

The deportees were sent to Germany, almost always to concentration camps, but sometimes also to prisons.

Admitted to the prisons were those deportees who had been condemned or were awaiting trial. The prisoners there were crowded together under inhuman conditions.

Nevertheless, the prison regime was generally less severe than conditions in the camps. The work there was less out of proportion to the strength of the prisoners, and the prison wardens were less hard than the S.S. in the concentration camps.

It appears to have been the plan followed by the Nazis in the concentration camps, gradually to do away with the prisoners, but only after their working strength had been used to the advantage of the German war effort.

The Tribunal has been told of the almost inconceivable treatment inflicted by the S.S. on the prisoners. We shall take the liberty of going into still further detail, during the course of the statement of the French Prosecution, for it must be fully known to what extent of horrors the Germans, inspired by National Socialist doctrine, could stoop.

The most terrible aspect was perhaps the desire to create moral degradation and debasement in the prisoner until he lost, if possible, all semblance of a human individual.

The usual living conditions imposed on the deportees in the camps were sufficient to ensure slow extermination through inadequate feeding, bad sanitation, cruelty of the guards, severity of discipline, strain of work out of proportion to the strength of the prisoner, and haphazard medical service. Moreover, you already know that many did not die a natural death, but were put to death by injections, gas chambers or inoculations of fatal diseases.

But more speedy extermination was often the case; it was often brought about by ill treatment: communal ice-cold showers in winter in the open air, prisoners left naked in the snow, cudgelling, attacks by dogs, hanging by the wrists.

Some figures will illustrate the result of these various methods of extermination. At Buchenwald, during the first quarter of 1945 there were 13,000 deaths out of 40,000 internees. At Dachau, 13,000 to 15,000 died in the three months preceding the liberation. At Auschwitz, a camp for systematic extermination, the number of murdered persons came to several millions.

As to the total number of those deported from France, the official figure is as follows:

of 250,000 deported only 35,000 returned.

The deportees served as guinea pigs for numerous medical, surgical or other experiments which generally led to their death. At Auschwitz, at Struthoff, in the prison at Cologne, at Ravensbruck, at Neuengamme, numerous men, women and children were sterilised. At Auschwitz, the most beautiful women were set apart, artificially fertilised and then gassed. At Struthoff, a special barracks, isolated from the others by barbed wire, was used to inoculate men, in groups of 40, with fatal illnesses. In the same camp women were gassed whilst German doctors observed their reactions through a peephole arranged for this purpose.

Extermination was often directly effected by means of individual or collective executions. These were carried out by shooting, by hanging, by injections, by gas lorry or gas chamber.

I should not wish to stress further the facts, already so numerous, submitted to your High Tribunal during the preceding days by the American Prosecution, but the representative of France, so many of his people having died in these' camps after horrible sufferings, could not pass in silence over this tragic example of complete inhumanity. This would have been inconceivable in the twentieth century, had not a doctrine of return to barbarism been established in the very heart of Europe.

Crimes committed against prisoners of war, although less known, bear ample testimony to the degree of inhumanity which Nazi Germany had attained.

To begin with, the violations of international conventions committed against prisoners of war are numerous. Many were forced to travel on foot, almost without food, for very long distances. Many camps had no respect for even the most elementary rules of hygiene. Food was very often insufficient; thus a report from the O.K.W. of the N.F.S.P., dated 11th April, 1945, and annotated by the defendant Keitel, shows that 82,000 prisoners of war interned in Norway received the food strictly indispensable to the maintenance of life on the assumption that they were not working, whereas 30,000 of them were really employed on heavy work.

In agreement with the defendant Keitel, acting at the request of the defendant Goering, camps for prisoners belonging to the British and American Air Forces were established in towns which were exposed to air raids.

In violation of the text of the Geneva Convention, it was decided, at a conference held at the Fuehrers headquarters on the 27th January, 1945, in the presence of the defendant Goering, to punish by death all attempts to escape made by prisoners of war when in convoy.

Besides all these violations of the Geneva Convention, numerous crimes, were committed by the German authorities against prisoners of war: execution of captured Allied airmen, murder of Commando troops, collective extermination of certain prisoners of war for no reason whatsoever, for example the matter of 120 American soldiers at Malmedy on 27th January, 1945. Parallel with "Nacht und Nebel," an expression for the inhuman treatment inflicted on civilians, can be put down the "Sonderbehandlung," a "special treatment" of prisoners of war, in which these disappeared in great numbers.

The same barbarism is found in the terroristic activity carried out by the German Army and police against the Resistance.

The order of the defendant Keitel of 16th September, 1941, which may be considered as a basic document, certainly has as a purpose the fight against the Communist movements, but it anticipates that resistance to the Army of Occupation can come from other than Communist sources and decides that every case of resistance is to be interpreted as having a Communist origin. As a matter of fact, in carrying out this general order to annihilate the Resistance by every possible means, the Germans arrested, tortured and massacred men of all ranks and all classes.

To be sure, the members of the Resistance rarely complied with the conditions laid down by The Hague Conventions, which would qualify them to be considered as regular combat forces; they could be sentenced to death as francs-tireurs and executed. But they were assassinated without trial in most cases, often after having been terribly tortured.

After the Liberation, numerous charnel-houses were discovered and the bodies examined by doctors: they bore obvious traces of extreme brutal treatment, cranial tissue had been pulled out, the spinal column had been dislocated, the ribs had been so badly fractured that the chest had been entirely crushed and the lungs perforated, hair and nails had been pulled out.

It is impossible to determine the total number of the victims of German atrocities in the fight against the Resistance. It is certainly very high. In the department of the Rhone alone, for example, the bodies of 713 victims were discovered after the Liberation.

An order of 3rd February, 1944, of the Commander-in-Chief of the Forces in the West, signed "By order, General Sperrle," laid down for the fight against the terrorists immediate reply by firearms and the immediate burning down of all houses from which shots had come. "It is of little importance," the text adds, "if innocent people should suffer. It will be the fault of the terrorists. All commanders of troops who show weakness in repressing the terrorists will be severely punished. On the other hand, those who go beyond the orders received and are too severe will incur no penalty."

The war diary of von Brodowski, commanding the Liaison Headquarters, No. 588, at Clermont-Ferrand, gives irrefutable examples of the barbarous forms which the Germans gave to the struggle against the Resistance. Those caught resisting were almost all shot on the spot. Others were turned over to the S.D. or the Gestapo to be subjected first to torture. The diary of Brodowski mentions "the cleaning up of a hospital" or "liquidation of an infirmary."

The struggle against the Resistance had the same atrocious character in all the occupied territories of the West.

The last months of the German occupation were characterised in France by a strengthening of the policy of terrorism which multiplied the crimes against the civilian population. The crimes which we are going to consider were not isolated acts committed from time to time in this or that locality, but were acts perpetrated in the course of extensive operations, the high number of which can only be explained by general orders.

The perpetrators of these crimes were frequently members of the S.S., but the Military Command shares responsibility for them. In a directive entitled "Fight Against the Partisan Bands," dated 6th May, 1944, the defendant Jodl states that "the collective measures to be taken against the inhabitants of entire villages (including the burning down of these villages) are to be ordered exclusively by the division commanders or the heads of the S.S. troops and of the police."

The war diary of von Brodowski mentions the following:

"It is understood that the leadership of the Sipo and of the S.D. shall be subordinate to me."

These operations are supposedly measures of reprisal which were caused by the action of the Resistance. But the necessities of war have never justified the plundering and heedless burning down of towns and villages, nor the blind massacres of innocent people. The Germans killed, plundered, and burned ,down, very often without any reason whatsoever, whether in the regions and departments of the Ain, in Savoy, Lot, Tarn-and-Garonne, in Vercors, Correze or Dordogne. Entire villages were burned down at a time when the nearest armed groups of the Resistance were tens of kilometres away and the population of these villages had not made a single hostile gesture towards the German troops.

The two most typical examples are those of Maille (in Indre- et-Loire), where on 25th August, 1944, 52 buildings out of 60 were destroyed and 124 people were killed; and that of Oradour-sur-Glane (in the Haute-Vienne). The war diary of von Brodowski makes mention of the latter act in the following manner:

"All the male population of Oradour was shot. The women and children took refuge in the church. The church caught fire from explosives which were stored in the church. (This assertion has been shown to be false.) All the women and all the children perished."

In the scale of criminal undertakings, perpetrated in the course of the war by the leaders of National Socialist Germany, we finally meet a category which we have called: Crimes against Human Status (la condition humaine).

First of all it is important that I should clearly define for the Tribunal the meaning of this term: this classical French expression belongs both to the technical vocabulary of law and to the language of philosophy. It signifies all those faculties, the exercising and developing of which rightly constitute the meaning of human life. Each of these faculties finds its corresponding expression in the order of man's existence in society. His belonging to at least two social groups - the nearest and the most extensive - is translated by the right to family life and to nationality. His relations with the powers constitute a system of obligations and guarantees. His material life as producer and consumer of goods is expressed by the right to work in the widest meaning of this term. Its spiritual aspect implies a combination of possibilities to give out and to receive the expressions of thought, whether in assemblies or associations, in religious practice, in teachings given or received, by the many means which progress has put at his disposal for the dissemination of work of intellectual value: books, Press, radio, cinema. This is the right of spiritual liberty.

Against this human status, against the status of public and civil rights of the human beings in occupied territories, the German Nazis directed a systematic policy of corruption and demoralisation. We shall treat this question last because it is this undertaking which presents a character of the utmost gravity and which has assumed the most widespread prevalence. Man is more attached to his physical integrity and to life than to his property. But in all high conceptions of life, man is even less attached to life than to that which makes for his dignity and quality, according to the great Latin maxim: " Et propter vitam vitandi perdere causas. " On the other hand, if, in the territories occupied by them, the Germans did not, in spite of the importance and extent of their crimes, plunder all the property and goods, and if they did not kill all the people, there remains not a single man whose essential rights they did not change or abolish, and whose condition as a human being they did not violate in some way.

We can even say that in the entire world and as regards all people, even those to whom they reserved the privileges belonging to the superior race and even as, regards themselves, their agents and accomplices, the Nazi leaders committed a major offence against the conscience which mankind has to-day evolved from his status as a human being.

The execution of the enterprise was preceded by its plan: this is manifest in the entire Nazi doctrine and we shall content ourselves by recalling a few of its dominant features. The human status expresses itself, we say, in major statutes, every one of which comprises a complex apparatus of very different provisions. But these statutes are inspired in the laws of civilised countries by a conception essential to the nature of man. This conception is defined in two complementary ideas: The dignity of the human being considered in each and every person individually, on the one hand; and on the other hand, the permanence of the human being considered within the whole of humanity.

Every juridical organisation of the human being in a state of civilisation proceeds from this essential, twofold conception of the individual, in each and in all, the individual and the universal.

Without doubt, to Occidentals this conception usually appears connected with the Christian doctrine, but, if it is exact that Christianity is bound up with its affirmation and diffusion, it would be a mistake to see in it only the teachings of one or even of certain religions. It is a general conception which imposes itself quite naturally on the spirit: it was professed since ancient pre-Christian times, and, in more recent times, the great German philosopher Kant expressed it in one of his most forceful formulas, "A human being should always be considered as an end and never as a means."

The role, as we have already exposed, of the zealots of the Hitlerian myth was to protest against the spontaneous affirmation of the genius of mankind and to pretend to break at this point the continuous progress of moral intelligence. The Tribunal is already acquainted with the abundant literature of this sect. Without a doubt, nobody expressed himself more clearly than the defendant Rosenberg when he declared in the "Myth of the Twentieth Century," Page 539:

"Peoples whose health is dependent on their blood do not know individualism as a criterion of values any more than they recognise universalism. Individualism and universalism, in the absolute sense and historically speaking, are the metaphysics of decadence."

Nazism professes, moreover, that:

"The distance between the lowest human being still worthy of this name, and our higher races, is greater than that between the lowest type of mankind and the best educated monkey."

Thus it is not only a question of abolishing the truly divine conception which religion sets forth as regards man, but even of setting aside all purely human conceptions and substituting for it an animalistic conception.

As a consequence of such a doctrine, the upsetting of the human status appears to be not only a means to which one has recourse in the presence of temporary opportunities, such as those arising from war, but also an aim both necessary and desirable. The Nazis propose to classify mankind in three main categories: that of their adversaries, or persons whom they consider inadaptable to their peculiar constructions - this category can be bullied in all sorts of ways and even destroyed; that of higher man, which they claim is distinguishable by his blood or by some arbitrary means; that of inferior man, which does not deserve destruction and whose vital power should be used in a regime of slavery for the well-being of the "overlords," the masters.

The Nazi leaders proposed to apply this conception wherever they could, in territories more and more extended, to populations ever more numerous, and, in addition, they demonstrated a frightful ambition to succeed in imposing it on intelligent people, to convince their victims and to demand from them, in addition to so many sacrifices, an act of faith. The Nazi war is a war of fanatic religion in which one can exterminate infidels and equally as well impose conversion upon them. It should further be noted that the Nazis aggravated the excesses of those horrible times, for in a religious war converted adversaries were received like brothers, whereas the Nazis never gave their pitiable victims the chance of saving themselves, even by the most complete recantation.

It is by virtue of these conceptions that the Germans undertook the Germanisation of occupied territories, and had, without doubt, the intention of undertaking to Germanise the whole world. This Germanisation can be distinguished from the ancient theories of Pan-Germanism in so far as it is both a Nazification and an actual return to barbarism.

Racialism classifies occupied nations into two main categories; Germanisation means for some a National Socialist assimilation, and for others disappearance or slavery. For human beings of the so-called "higher race," the most favoured condition assigned to them comprises the falling-in with the new concepts of the Germanic community. For human beings of the so-called "inferior race" it was proposed either to abolish all rights while waiting or preparing their physical destruction, or to assign them to servitude. For both, racialism means acceptance of the Nazi myths.

This twofold programme of absolute Germanisation was not carried out in its entirety nor in all the occupied countries. The Germans had conceived it as a lengthy piece of work which they intended to carry out gradually, by a series of successive measures. This progressive approach is always characteristic of the Nazi method. It fits in apparently, both with the variety of obstacles encountered, with the hypocritical desire of sparing public opinion, and with a horrid lust for experimenting and scientific ostentation.

When the countries were liberated, the state of the Germanisation varied a great deal according to the different countries, and in each country according to such and such category of the population. At times the method was driven on to its extreme consequences; elsewhere, one only discovers signs of preparatory arrangements. But it is easy to note everywhere the trend of the same evil, interrupted at different moments in its development, but everywhere directed by the same inexorable movement.

As regards national status, the Germans proceeded to an annexation pure and simple in Luxembourg, in the Belgian cantons of Eupen and of Malmedy, and in the French departments of Alsace and of Lorraine. Here the criminal undertaking consisted both in the abolition of the sovereignty of the State, natural protector of its nationals, and in the abolition for those nationals of the status they had as citizens of this State, a status recognised by domestic and International Law.

The inhabitants of these territories thereby lost their original nationality, ceasing to be Luxembourgers, Belgians or French. They did not acquire, however, full German nationality; they were admitted only gradually to this singular favour, on the further condition that they furnish certain justifications therefor.

The Germans sought to efface in them even the memory of their former country. In Alsace and in Moselle the French language was banned; names of places and of people were Germanised.

New citizens or mere subjects were equally subjected to the obligations, relating to the Nazi regime: to forced labour, as a matter of course, and soon to military conscription. In case of resistance to these unjust and abominable orders - since it was a matter of arming the French against their allies and in reality against their own country - sanctions were brought to bear, not only against the parties concerned, but even against the members of their families, following the theses of Nazi law, which brushes aside the fundamental principles of law against repression.

Persons who appeared recalcitrant to Nazification, or even those who seemed of little use to Nazi enterprises, became victims of large-scale expulsions, driven from their homes in a few short hours with the scantiest of baggage, and despoiled of their property.

Yet this inhuman evacuation of entire populations, which will remain one of the horrors of our century, appears as favourable treatment when compared to the deportations which were to fill the concentration camps, in particular the Stuthoff camp in Alsace.

At the same time that they oppressed the population by force and in contravention of all law, the Nazis undertook, according to their method, to convince the people of the excellence of their regime. The young people especially were to be educated in the spirit of National Socialism.

The Germans did not proceed to the annexation, properly speaking, of other areas than those we have named; it is beyond doubt, however, and confirmed by numerous indications, that they proposed to annex territories much more important by applying to them the same regime, if the war had ended in a German victory. But everywhere they prepared for the abolition or the weakening of the national status by debarring or damaging the sovereignty of the State involved, and by forcing the destruction of patriotic feelings.

In all the occupied countries, whether or not there existed an apparent governmental authority, the Germans systematically disregarded the laws of occupation. They legislated, regulated, administered. Besides the territories annexed outright, the other occupied territories also were in a state that might be defined as a state of pre- annexation.

This leads to a second aspect, which is the attack on spiritual security. Everywhere, although with variation in time and space, the Germans applied themselves to abolishing the public freedoms, notably the freedom of association, the freedom of the Press; and they endeavoured to trammel the essential freedoms of the spirit.

The German authorities subordinated the Press to the strictest censorship, even in matters devoid of military character, a Press, many of whose representatives, moreover, were inspired by them. Manifold restrictions were imposed on industry and on the moving picture business. Numerous works altogether without political character were banned, even textbooks: Religious authorities, themselves, saw their clerical realm invaded, and words of truth could not be heard.

After having curtailed freedom of expression even beyond the degree that a state of war and occupation have justified, the Germans developed their National Socialist propaganda systematically through the Press, radio, film, meetings, books and posters.

All these efforts achieved so little result that one might attempt to-day to minimise their importance. Nevertheless, the propaganda conducted by means most contrary to the respect due to human intelligence, and on behalf of a criminal doctrine, must go down in history as one of the disgraces of the National Socialist regime.

No less did the Germanisation programme compromise human rights in the other broad aspects that we have defined: right of the family, right of professional and economic activity, juridical guarantees. These rights were attacked, these guarantees were curtailed.

The forced labour and the deportations infringed the rights of the family, as well as the rights of labour. The arbitrary arrests suppressed the most elementary legal guarantees. In addition, the Germans tried to impose their own methods on the administrative authorities of the occupied countries and sometimes, unfortunately, succeeded in their attempts.

It is also known that racial discriminations were provoked against citizens of the occupied countries who were catalogued as Jews, measures particularly hateful, damaging to their personal rights and to their human dignity.

All these criminal acts were committed in violation of the rules of international Law and, in particular, of The Hague Convention, which limits the rights of armies occupying a territory.

The fight of the Nazis against the human status completes the tragic and monstrous totality of war criminality of Nazi Germany, by placing her under the banner of the abasement of man, deliberately brought about by the National Socialist doctrine. This gives it its true character of a systematic undertaking of a return to barbarism.

Such are the crimes which National Socialist Germany committed while waging the war of aggression that she launched. The martyred peoples appeal to the justice of civilised nations and request your High Tribunal to condemn the National Socialist Reich in the person of its surviving chiefs.

Let the defendants not be astonished at the charges brought against them, and let them not dispute at all this principle of retroactivity, the permanence of which was guaranteed, against their wishes, by democratic legislation. War crimes are defined by International Law and by the national law of all modern civilisations. The defendants knew that acts of violence against the persons and property and human status of enemy nationals were crimes for which they would have to answer before international justice.

The Governments of the United Nations have addressed many a warning to them since the beginning of the hostilities.

On 25th October, 1941, Franklin Roosevelt, President of the United States of America, and Winston Churchill, Prime Minister of Great Britain, announced that the war criminals would not escape just punishment:

"The massacres of France," said Churchill, "are an example of what Hitler's Nazis are doing in many other countries under their yoke. The atrocities committed in Poland, Yugoslavia, Norway, Holland, Belgium, and particularly behind the German front in Russia, exceed anything that has been known since the darkest and most bestial ages of humanity. The punishment of these crimes should now be counted among the major goals of the war."

During the autumn of 1941, the representatives of the governments of the occupied countries met in London upon the initiative of the Polish and Czech Governments. They worked out an Inter-Allied declaration which was signed on 13th January, 1942. May I remind the Tribunal of its terms:

"The undersigned, representing the Governments of Belgium, of Czechoslovakia, the National Committee of Free France, the Governments of Greece, of Luxembourg, of the Netherlands, of Poland and of Yugoslavia;

Whereas Germany, from the beginning of the present conflict, which was provoked by her policy of aggression, set up in the occupied countries a regime of terror characterised, among other things, by imprisonment, mass expulsions, massacres, and execution of hostages;

Whereas these acts of violence are committed equally by the allies and associates of the Reich, and in certain countries by citizens collaborating with the occupying power;

Whereas international solidarity is necessary in order to prevent these deeds of violence from giving rise to acts of individual or collective violence, and finally in order to satisfy the spirit of justice in the civilised world;

Recalling to mind that International Law and, in particular, The Hague Convention signed in 1907, concerning the laws and customs of land warfare, do not permit belligerents to commit acts of violence against civilians in occupied countries, or to violate laws which are in force or to overthrow national institutions;

Affirming that acts of violence thus committed against civilian populations have nothing in common with the conceptions of an act of war or a political crime as this is understood by civilised nations;

Taking note of the declarations made in this respect on 25th October, 1941, by the President of the United States of America and the British Prime Minister;

Placing among their chief war aims, the punishment by means of organised justice of those guilty of, or responsible for, these crimes, whether they ordered, perpetrated, or shared in them; Having decided to see to it in a spirit of international solidarity that:

(a) those guilty or responsible, whatever their responsibility, shall be sought out, brought to justice, and be judged;

(b) that the sentences pronounced shall be executed;

In faith of which, the undersigned, being duly authorised, to this effect have signed this declaration."

The leaders of National Socialist Germany received other warnings. I refer to the speech of General de Gaulle of 13th January, 1942; that of Churchill on 8th September, 1942; the note of M. Molotov, Commissar of the People for Foreign Affairs of the Soviet Union, of 14th October, 1942; and the second Inter-Allied declaration of 17th December, 1942. The latter was made simultaneously in London, Moscow and Washington after receipt of information according to which the German authorities were engaged in exterminating the Jewish minorities in Europe. In this declaration, the Governments of Belgium, Czechoslovakia, Greece, Luxembourg, the Netherlands, Norway, Poland, the United States of America, the United Kingdom, the Soviet Union, Yugoslavia, and the French National Committee, which represented the continuation of France, solemnly reaffirmed their will to punish the war criminals who are responsible for this extermination.

(A recess was taken.)

M. DE MENTHON: The premises for a just punishment are thus fulfilled. The defendants, at the time when they committed their crimes, knew the will of the United Nations to bring about their punishment. The warnings which were given to them contain a definition which precedes the punishment.

The defendants, moreover, could not be ignorant of the criminal nature of their activities. The warnings of these Allied Governments in effect translated in a political form the fundamental principles of International Law and of national law which permit the punishment of war criminals to be established on positive precedents and positive rules.

The creators of International Law had a presentiment of the concept of war crime, particularly Grotius who elucidated the criminal character of needless acts of war. The Hague Conventions, after the lapse of several centuries, established the first generally binding standards for laws of war. They regulated the conduct of hostilities and occupation procedures; they formulated positive rules in order to limit recourse to force and to bring the necessities of war into agreement with the requirements of human conscience. War Crimes thus received the first definition under which they may be considered; they became a violation of laws and customs of war as codified by The Hague Convention.

Then came the war of 1914. Imperial Germany waged the first World War with a brutality perhaps less systematic and frenzied than that of the National Socialist Reich, but just as deliberate. The deportation of workers, looting of public and private property, the taking and killing of hostages, the demoralisation of the occupied territories constituted, in 1914 as in 1939, the political methods of German warfare.

The Treaty of Versailles was based on The Hague Convention in order to establish the suppression of War Crimes. Under the title "Sanctions," Charter VII, of the Treaty of Versailles discusses criminal responsibility incurred in the launching and waging of the conflict, which was then the Great War. Article 227 accused William of Hohenzollern, previously Emperor of Germany, of a supreme offence against international morality and against the sacred character of treaties. Article 228 acknowledged the right of the Allied and Associated Powers to bring persons guilty of acts contrary to the laws and customs of war before military tribunals.

Article 229 provided that criminals whose acts were not of precise geographical location were to be referred to the inter-allied jurisdiction. The provisions of the Treaty of Versailles were repeated in the conventions which were signed in 1919 and 1920 with the powers allied with Germany, in particular in the Treaty of Saint-Germain and in that of Neuilly. That is how the idea of War Crime was affirmed in International Law. The peace treaties of 1919 not only defined the concept of infringement; they formulated the terms of its suppression. The defendants were aware of this, just as they were aware of the warnings of the Governments of the United Nations. They no doubt hoped that the repetition of the factual circumstances which hampered the punishment of the criminals in 1914 would permit them to escape their just punishment. Their presence before this Tribunal is the symbol of the constant progress which International Law is making in spite of all obstacles.

International Law had given a still more precise definition of the term "War Crime." This definition was formulated by the Commission which the preliminary peace conference appointed on 25th January, 1919, to disentangle the various responsibilities incurred in the course of the war. The report of the Commission of Fifteen of 29th March, 1919, constitutes the historical basis of Article 227 and following of the Treaty of Versailles. The Commission of Fifteen based its investigation of criminal responsibilities on an analysis of the crimes liable to involve them.

A material element enters into the juridical settlement of any infraction. Its definition is, therefore, the more precise as it includes an enumeration of the facts which it encompasses. That is why the Commission of Fifteen set up a list of War Crimes. This list includes 32 infractions. These are particularly:

Murders, massacres, systematic terrorism.
Killing of hostages.
Torture of civilians.
Burying of civilians in inhuman conditions.
Forced labour of civilians in connection with military operations of the enemy.
Usurpation of sovereignty during the occupation of occupied territories.
Forced conscription of soldiers among the inhabitants of the occupied territories.
Attempts to denationalise the inhabitants of occupied territories.
Looting.
Confiscation of property.
Imposition of collective fines.
Wilful devastation and destruction of property.
Violation of other rules concerning the Red Cross.
Ill-treatment of wounded and prisoners of war.
Use of prisoners of war for unauthorised work.

This list, which already includes the grievances against the defendants enumerated in the Indictment and from which we have just quoted a few facts, is significant because the War Crimes which it encompasses all present a composite character. They are crimes against both International Law and national law. Some of these crimes constitute attacks on the fundamental liberties and constitutional rights of peoples and of individuals; they consist in the violation of public guarantees which are recognised by the constitutional Charter of the Nations whose territories were occupied; violation of the principles of liberty, equality and fraternity which France proclaimed in 1789 and which the civilised States guarantee in perpetuity. These War

Crimes are violations of public national law, since they represent a systematic refusal of acknowledgement of all respective rights of both occupying and occupied Power; but they also may be analysed as violations of public national law, since they mean forcibly transforming the constitutional institutions of the occupied territories and the juridical statute of their inhabitants.

More numerous are crimes which constitute attacks on the integrity of the physical person and of property.

They are allied with war law regulations and include violations of International Law and customs.

But the international conventions, it should be remarked, determine the elements constituting an infraction more than they actually establish that infraction itself. The latter existed before in all national legislatures; it was to some extent a part of the juridical inheritance common to all nations; Governments agreed to affirm its international character and to define its contents. International Penal - Law is thus superimposed on national law, which preserves its repressive basis because the War Crime remains, after all, a crime of Common Law. National penal law gives the definition of this. All the acts referred to in Article 6 of the Charter of 8th August, 1945, all the facts encompassed by the Third Count of the Indictment of 18th October, 1945, correspond to the infractions of Common Law provided for and punished by national penal legislation. The killing of prisoners of war, of hostages, and of inhabitants of occupied territories falls, in French law, under Article 295 and following of the Penal Code, which define murder and assassination. The mistreatment to which the Indictment refers would come under the heading of bodily injuries caused intentionally or through negligence, which are defined by Article 309 and following. Deportation is analysed, independently of the murders which accompany it, as arbitrary restraint, which is defined by Articles 341 and 344. Pillage of public and private property and imposition of collective fines are penalised by Article 221 and the following of Military Code of Justice. Article 434 of the Penal Code punishes voluntary destruction, and the deportation of civilian workers may be compared with the forced conscription provided for by Article 92. The oath of allegiance is equivalent to the exaction of a false oath in Article 366, and the Germanisation of occupied territories may be applied to a number of crimes, the most obvious of which is forced incorporation in the Wehrmacht in violation of Article 92. The same equivalents can be found in all modem legislative systems and particularly in German law.

The crimes against persons and property, of which the defendants are guilty, are provided for by all national laws. They present an international character because they were committed in several different countries; from this there arises a problem of jurisdiction of competency which the Charter of 8th August, 1945, has solved as we have previously explained; but this leaves intact the rule of definition.

A crime of Common Law, the War Crime, is, nevertheless, not an ordinary infraction; it has a character peculiarly intrinsic - it is a crime committed on the occasion or under the pretext of war. It must be punished because, even in time of war, attacks on the integrity of the physical person and of property are crimes if they are not justified by the laws and customs of war. The soldier who on the battlefield kills an enemy combatant commits a crime, but this crime is justified by the law of war. International Law, therefore, intervenes in the definition of a War Crime, not in order to give it its essential qualification but in order to fix its outer limits. In other words, every infraction committed on the occasion or under the pretext of hostilities is criminal unless justified by the laws and customs of war. International Law applies the national theory of legitimate defence which is common to all codes of criminal law. The combatant is engaged in legitimate defence on the battlefield; his homicidal action is therefore covered by a justifying fact. But if this justifying fact is taken away the infraction, whether ordinary crime or War Crime remains such in its entirety. To establish the justifying fact, the criminal action must be necessary and proportional to the threat to which it responds. The defendants, against whom justice is demanded of you, can plead no such justification.

Nor can they escape their responsibility by arguing that they were not the physical authors of the crimes. The War Crime involves two responsibilities, distinct and complementary, that of the physical author and that of the instigator. There is nothing heterodox in this conception. It is the faithful representation of the criminal theory of complicity through instructions. The responsibility of the accomplice, whether independent or complementary to that of the principal author, is incontestable. The defendants bear the entire responsibility for the crimes which were committed upon their instructions or under their control.

Finally, they cannot be justified by the pretext that an order from above was given by Hitler to the defendants. The theory of the justifying fact of an order from above has, in national law, definite fixed limits; it does not cover the execution of orders whose illegality is manifest. German law, moreover, assigns only a limited rule to the concept of justification by orders from above. Article 47 of the German Military Code of Justice of 1940, although maintaining in principle that a criminal order from a superior removes the responsibility of the agent, punishes the latter as an accomplice when be exceeded the orders received or when he acted with knowledge of the criminal character of the act which had been ordered. Goebbels once made this juridical concept the theme of his propaganda. On 28th May, 1944, he wrote in an article in the "Volkischer Beobachter" which was submitted to you by the American Prosecution, an article intended to justify the murder of Allied pilots by German mobs:

"The pilots cannot validly claim that as soldiers they obeyed orders. No law of war provides that a soldier will remain unpunished for a hateful crime by referring to the orders of his superior, if their orders are in striking opposition to all human ethics, to all international customs in the conduct of war."

Orders from a superior do not exonerate the agent of a manifest crime from responsibility. Any other solution would, moreover, be unacceptable, for it would testify to the impotence of all repressive policy.

All the more reason why orders from above cannot be the justifying fact for the crimes of the defendants. Sir Hartley Shawcross told you with eloquence that the accused cannot claim that the Crime against Peace was the doing of Hitler alone and that they limited themselves to transmitting the general directives. War Crimes may be compared to the will for aggression; they are the common work of the defendants; the defendants bear a joint responsibility for the criminal policy which resulted from the National Socialist doctrine.

The responsibility for German war criminality, because it constituted a systematic policy, planned and prepared before the opening of hostilities, and perpetrated without interruption from 1940 to 1945, rests with all the defendants, political or military leaders, high officials of National Socialist Germany, and leaders of the Nazi Party.

Nevertheless, some among them appear more directly responsible for the acts taken as a whole, particularly those facts connected with the French charges, that is to say, crimes committed in the Western occupied territories or against the nationals of those countries. We shall cite:

The defendant Goering as Director of the Four Year Plan and President of the Cabinet of Ministers for Reich Defence, the defendant Ribbentrop in his capacity as Minister of Foreign Affairs in charge of the administration of occupied countries, the defendant Frick in his capacity as Director of the Central Office for occupied territories, the defendant Funk in his capacity as Minister of Reich Economy, the defendant Keitel, inasmuch as he had command over the occupation armies, the defendant Jodl, associated in all the responsibilities of the preceding defendant, the defendant Seyss-Inquart in his capacity as Reich Commissar for the occupied Dutch territory from 13th May, 1940, to the end of the hostilities.

We will examine more particularly among these defendants, or among others, those responsible for each category of acts, it being understood that this enumeration is in no wise restrictive.

The defendant Sauckel bears the chief responsibility for compulsory labour in its various forms. As Plenipotentiary for Labour, he carried out the intensive recruiting of workers by every possible means. He is in particular the signer of the decree of 22nd August, 1942, which constitutes the charter for compulsory labour in all occupied countries. He worked in liaison with the defendant Speer, Chief of the Todt Organisation, as General Plenipotentiary for Armament in the office of the Four Year Plan, as well as with the defendant Funk, Minister of Reich Economy, and with the defendant Goering, Chief of the Four Year Plan.

The defendant Goering participated directly in economic looting in the same capacity. He appears to have often sought and derived a personal profit from it. The defendant Ribbentrop in his capacity as Minister of Foreign Affairs was no stranger to these acts. The defendant Rosenberg, organiser and Chief of the "Einsatzstab Rosenberg," is particularly guilty of the looting of works of art in the occupied countries.

The chief responsibility for the murders of hostages lies with the defendant Keitel, the drafter notably of the general order of 16th September, 1941, with his assistant the defendant Jodl, and with the defendant Goering who agreed to the order in question.

The defendant Kaltenbrunner, Himmler's direct associate and chief of all the foreign police and security offices, is directly responsible for the monstrous devices to which the Gestapo had recourse in all occupied countries, devices which are only the continuation of the methods originated in the Gestapo by its founder in Prussia, the defendant Goering.

The defendant Kaltenbrunner is likewise directly responsible for the crimes committed in deportation. Moreover, he visited these camps of deportation, as will be proved by the French delegation in the case of the Mauthausen Camp. The defendant Goering knew of and gave his approval to the medical experiments made on prisoners. The defendant Sauckel forced prisoners by every possible means to work under conditions which were often inhuman, for the German war production.

The defendant Keitel and his assistant the defendant Jodl are responsible for treatment contrary to the laws of war inflicted upon war prisoners, for murders and killings to which they were subjected, as well as for handing over great numbers of them to the Gestapo. The defendant Goering shares their responsibility for the execution of Allied aviators and soldiers belonging to the Commando groups. The defendant Sauckel directed the work of war prisoners for the German war production in violation of International Law.

The defendant Keitel and the defendant Kaltenbrunner share the chief responsibility for the terrorist actions carried out jointly by the German Army and the police forces in the various occupied countries and notably in France against the

Resistance, as well as for the devastations and massacres carried out against the civilian population of several French Departments. The defendant Jodl shares in this responsibility, most particularly through his initial order, "Fight Against Partisan Bands," dated 6th May, 1945, which provides for "collective measures against the inhabitants of entire villages." These blows against mankind are the result of racialist theories of which the defendant Hess,mthe defendant Rosenberg, and the defendant Streicher are among the instigators or propagandists. The defendant Hess participated notably in the elaboration of this subject, which is found in "Mein Kampf."

The defendant Rosenberg, one of the principal theorists of racial doctrine, exercised the function of special delegate for the spiritual and ideological training of the Nazi Party. The defendant Streicher showed himself to be one of the most violent anti-Semitic agitators. In the execution of the policy of Germanisation and Nazification responsibility is shared between the Ministry of Foreign Affairs, that is to say, the defendant Ribbentrop, the General Staff, i.e., the defendants Keitel and Jodl, and the Central Office for all the occupied territories, i.e., the defendant Frick.

The major National Socialist culprits had their orders carried out in the divers Nazi organisations, which we ask you to declare criminal in order that each of their members may be then apprehended and punished.

The Reich Cabinet, the Leadership Corps of the Nazi Party, the General Staff, and the High Command of the German Armed Forces represent only a small number of persons whose guilt and punishment must ultimately result from the evidence, since they participated personally and directly in the decisions, or ensured their execution through some eminent person in the political or military hierarchy, and without being able to ignore their. criminal nature.

The leaders of the Nazi Party are unquestionably in the forefront of those who participated in the criminal enterprise, and around the defendants Keitel and Jodl the military High Command directed the Army to execution of hostages, to pillage, to wanton destruction and to massacres.

But perhaps it will seem to you that the punishment of hundreds of thousands of men who belonged to the S.S., to the S.D., to the Gestapo and to the S.A. will give rise to some objection. I should like to try, should this be the case, to do away with that objection by showing you the dreadful responsibilities of these men. Without the existence of these organisations, without the spirit which animated them, one could not understand how so many atrocities could have been perpetrated. The systematic War Crimes could not have been carried out by Nazi Germany without these organisations, without the men who composed them. It is they who not only executed but willed this body of crimes on behalf of Germany.

It may have seemed impossible to you that the monstrous barbarity of the National Socialist doctrine could have been imposed upon the German people, the heir, as are our people, of the highest values of civilisation. The education by the Nazi Party of the young men who formed the S.S., the S.D., and the Gestapo explains the hold that Nazism exercised over all Germany. They incarnated National Socialism, and permitted it to accomplish, thanks to the guilty passiveness of the whole German population, a part of its purpose. This youth, those who carried out the tenets of the regime, were trained in a veritable doctrine of unmorality, which results from the ideology that inspired the regime. The myth of the race removed from war in the eyes of these disciples of Nazism its criminal character.

If it is proved that a superior race is to annihilate races and peoples that are considered inferior and decadent, incapable of living a life as it should be lived, before what means of extermination will they recoil? These are the ethics of immorality, the result of the most authentic Nietzscheism, which considers that the destruction of all conventional ethics is the supreme duty of man. The crime against race is punished without pity. The crime on behalf of race is exalted without limit. The regime truly creates a logic of crime which obeys its own laws, which has no connection whatsoever with what we consider ethical. With such a point of view, all horrors could have been justified and authorised. So many acts which appear incomprehensible to us, so greatly do they clash with our customary notions, were explained, were formulated in advance in the name of the racial community.

Add that these atrocities and these cruelties were perpetrated within the rigid framework created by the esprit de corps, by the soldierly solidarity which bound individuals and ensured the legitimacy of the crime an unlimited field of action. The individuals who committed them would not only be covered by the regime itself, but spurred on by the discipline and the "camaraderie" of these corps, imbued with Nazi criminality.

The Nazi Youth was invited to go through an extraordinary adventure. Having unlimited power at its disposal thanks to the Party and its massive grip, it was first of all called upon to implement the grandiose dreams of National Socialist Pan-Germanism.

The Party exercised a rigid selection of its youth, and neglected no incentive. It solicited from its youth the desire to distinguish itself, to accomplish exploits beyond the common order and beyond nature. The young Nazis in the Gestapo and the S.S. knew that their acts, no matter how cruel or how inhumane they might be, would always be judged legitimate by the regime, in the name of the racial community, of its needs and of its triumphs. The Nazi Party, thanks to the young men of the S.S., of the S.D., and of the Gestapo, had thus become capable of accomplishing in the field of criminality what no other person or nation could have committed.

The members of these organisations became voluntarily the authors of these innumerable crimes of all kinds, often executed with disconcerting cynicism and with artful sadism in the concentration camps of Germany as well as in the various occupied countries, and especially in those of Western Europe.

The crimes are monstrous. The crimes and the responsibility for them have definitely been established. There is no possible doubt.

But nevertheless, throughout these tranquil sessions of this trial, extraordinary in the history of the world, in view of the exceptional nature of the justice which your High Tribunal is called upon to render before the United Nations and the German people and before all mankind, a few objections may arise in our minds.

It is our duty to discuss this exhaustively, even if it is still only in our subconscious, for soon a pseudo-patriotic propaganda may take hold of Germany, and even may echo in some of our countries.

"Who can say: 'I have a clean conscience, I am without fault'? To use different weights and measures is abhorred by God." This text from the Holy Scriptures has already been mentioned here and there; it will serve to-morrow as a theme of propaganda, but above all, it is profoundly written in our souls. Rising in the name of our martyred people as accusers of Nazi Germany, we have never for a moment suppressed it as an unwonted appeal.

Yes, no nation is without reproach in its history, just as no individual is faultless in his life. Yes, every war in itself brings forth iniquitous evils and entails almost necessarily individual and collective crimes, because it easily unleashes in man the evil passions which always slumber there.

But we can examine our conscience fearlessly in the face of the Nazi culprits; we find no common measure between them and ourselves.

If this criminality had been accidental, if Germany had been forced into war, if crimes had been committed only in the excitement of combat, we might question ourselves in the light of the Scriptures. But the war was prepared and deliberated upon long in advance, and up to the very last day it would have been easy to avoid it without sacrificing any of the legitimate interests of the German people. And the atrocities were perpetrated during the war, not under the influence of a mad passion or of a warlike anger or of an avenging resentment, but as a result of cold calculation, of perfectly conscious methods, of a pre-existing doctrine.

The truly diabolical enterprise of Hitler, and of his companions, was to assemble, in a body of dogmas formed around the concept of race, all the instincts of barbarism, repressed by centuries of civilisation, but always present in men's innermost nature, all the negations of the traditional values of humanity, without which nations, as well as individuals, question their conscience in the troubled hours of their development and of their life; to construct and to propagate a doctrine which organises, regulates and aspires to command crime.

The diabolical enterprise of Hitler, and of his companions, was also to appeal to the forces of evil in order to establish his domination over the German people, and subsequently the domination of Germany over Europe and perhaps over the world. It planned to incorporate organised criminality into a system of government, into a system of international relations and into a system of warfare, by unleashing within a whole nation the most savage passions.

Nationalism and serving their people and their country will perhaps be their explanation; far from constituting an excuse, if any excuse were possible in view of the enormity of their crime, these explanations would make them still more serious. They have profaned the sacred idea of the Fatherland by linking it to a willed return to barbarism.

In its name they obtained, half by force, half by persuasion, the adherence of a whole country, formerly among the greatest in the order of spiritual values, and have sunk it to the lowest level. The moral confusion, the economic difficulties, the obsession with the defeat of 1918, and with the loss of might and the Pan-Germanic tradition, are the basis of the empire of Hitler and of his companions over a people thrown off its balance; to abandon oneself to force, to renounce moral concern, to satisfy a love of collectivity, to revel in lack of restraint, are the natural temptations strongly implanted in the German, which the Nazi leaders exploited with cynicism. The intoxication of success and the madness of greatness completed the picture, and put practically all Germans, some without doubt unconsciously, in the service of the National Socialist doctrine, by associating them with the diabolical enterprise of their Fuehrer and his companions.

Opposing this enterprise arose men of various countries and different classes, all of them animated by the common bond of their human lot. France and Great Britain entered the war only to remain faithful to their given word. The peoples of the occupied countries, tortured in body and soul, never renounced their liberty, nor their cultural values, and it was a magnificent epic of clandestine opposition and of resistance which, through a splendid heroism, testifies to the spontaneous refusal of the populations to accept the Nazi myths. Millions and millions of men of the Soviet Union fell to defend, not only the soil and independence of their country, but also their humanitarian universalism. The millions of British and American soldiers who landed on our unhappy continent carried in their hearts the ideal of freeing from Nazi oppression both the occupied countries and the peoples who, willingly or by force, had become the satellites of the Axis and the German people itself.

They were all of them together, whether in uniform or not, fighters for the great hope which throughout the centuries has been nourished by the suffering of the peoples, the great hope for a better future for mankind.

Sometimes this great hope expresses itself with difficulty, or loses its way, or deceives itself, or knows the dread return to barbarism, but it persists always and finally constitutes the powerful lever which brings about the progress of humanity despite everything. These aspirations always reborn, these concerns constantly awakened, this anguish unceasingly present, this perpetual combat against evil, form in a definitive manner the sublime grandeur of man. National Socialism only yesterday imperilled all of this.

After that gigantic struggle where two ideologists, two conceptions of life were at grips, in the name of the people whom we represent here, and in the name of the great human hope for which they have so greatly suffered, so greatly fought, we can without fear and with a clean conscience rise as accusers of the leaders of Nazi Germany.

As Mr. Justice Jackson said so eloquently at the opening of this trial: "Civilisation would not survive if these crimes were to be committed again," and he added: "The true plaintiff in this Court is civilisation."

Civilisation requires from you, after this unleashing of barbarism, a verdict which will also be a sort of supreme warning at the hour when humanity appears still, at times, to enter the path of the organisation of peace only with apprehension and hesitation.

If it is our wish that on the morrow of the cataclysm of war the sufferings of martyred countries, the sacrifices of victorious nations, and also the expiation of guilty people will engender a better humanity, justice must strike those guilty of the enterprise of barbarism from which we have just escaped. The reign of justice is the most exact expression of the great human hope. Your decision can make a decisive stage in its difficult pursuit.

Undoubtedly, even to-day, this justice and this punishment have become possible only because, as a first condition, free peoples emerged victorious from the conflict. This is actually the link between the force of the victors and the guilt of the vanquished leaders who appear before your High Tribunal.

But this link signifies nothing else but the revelation of the wisdom of nations that justice, in order to impose itself effectively and constantly upon individuals and upon nations, must have force at its disposal. The common will to put force in the service of justice inspires our nations and commands our whole civilisation.

This resolution is brilliantly confirmed to-day in a judicial case where the facts are examined scrupulously in all their aspects, the penal nature of the offence rigorously established, the competency of the Tribunal incontestable, the rights of the defence intact, and total publicity ensured.

Your verdict, pronounced under these conditions, can serve as a foundation for the moral uplift of the German people, a first stage in its integration into the community of free countries. Without your verdict, history might incur the risk of repeating itself, crime would become epic, and the National Socialist enterprise a last Wagnerian tragedy; and new Pan-Germanists would soon say to the Germans: "Hitler and his companions were wrong because they finally failed, but we must begin again some day on other foundations the extraordinary adventure of Germanism."

After your verdict, if only we know how to enlighten this people and watch over their first steps on the road to liberty, National Socialism will be inscribed permanently in their history as the crime of crimes which could lead it only to material and moral perdition, as the doctrine which they should for ever avoid with horror and scorn, in order to remain faithful, or rather become once more faithful, to the great norms of common civilisation.

The eminent international jurist and noble European, Politis, in his posthumous book entitled "International Ethics," reminds us that, like all ethical rules, those which should rule international relations will never be definitely established unless all peoples succeed in convincing themselves that there is definitely a greater profit to be gained by observing them than by transgressing them. That is why your judgement can contribute to the enlightenment of the German people and of all peoples.

Your decision must be inscribed as a decisive act in the history of International Law in order to prepare the establishment of a true international society excluding recourse to war and enlisting force permanently in the service of the justice of nations; it will be one of the foundations of this peaceful order to which nations aspire on the morrow of this frightful torment. The need for justice of the martyred peoples will be satisfied, and their sufferings will not have been useless to the progress of mankind.

THE PRESIDENT: M. de Menthon, would you prefer to continue the case on behalf of France this afternoon, or would you prefer to adjourn?

M. DE MENTHON: We are at the disposal of the Court.

THE PRESIDENT: Well then, if that is so, I think we had better go on until 5 o'clock.

M. DE MENTHON: It might be preferable to adjourn, because M. Faure's brief which is going to be presented will last at least an hour. Perhaps it is better to adjourn until to-morrow morning. However, we will remain at the disposal of the Court.

THE PRESIDENT: When you said that the proof which will now be presented would take an hour, do you mean by that that it is an introductory statement or is it a part of the main case which you are presenting?

M. DE MENTHON: Your Honour, it is part of the general case.

THE PRESIDENT: Would it not be possible, then, to go on until 5 o'clock?

M. DE MENTHON: Yes, quite so.

THE PRESIDENT: We would prefer to go on until 5 o'clock.

M. DE MENTHON: All right, agreed.

M. FAURE: Mr. President and your Honours, I propose to submit to the Tribunal an introduction dealing with the first and the second part of the French case.

The first part relates to forced labour; the second part to economic looting. These two overall questions are complementary to each other and form a whole. Manpower on the one hand and material property on the other constitute the two aspects of the riches of a country and the living conditions in that country. Measures taken with regard to the one necessarily react on the other, and it is understandable that in the occupied countries German policy with regard to manpower and economic property was inspired, from the very beginning, by common directing principles.

For this reason the French Prosecution has deemed it logical to submit successively to the Tribunal those two briefs corresponding to the letters "H" and "E" of the Third Count of the Indictment. My present purpose is to define the initial directives covering the German procedure in regard to manpower and to material in the occupied territories.

When the Germans occupied the territories of Denmark, Norway, Holland, Belgium, Luxembourg, and, in part, continental France, they thereby assumed a material power of constraint with regard to the inhabitants and a material power of acquisition with regard to its property. They thus had, in fact, the possibility of utilising these dual resources on behalf of the war effort.

On the other hand, legally they were confronted with precise rules of International Law relating to the occupation of territories by the military forces of a belligerent

State. These rules very strictly limit the occupant, who may requisition property and services solely for the needs of the Army of Occupation. I here allude to the regulation annexed to the Convention Concerning the Laws and Customs of War signed at The Hague on 18th October, 1907, Section III, and in particular to Articles 46, 47, 49, 52 and 53. If it please the Tribunal, I shall merely cite the paragraph of Article 52 which defines in a perfectly exact manner the lawful conditions of requisition of persons and property:

> "Requisitions in kind and of services may be demanded of communities or of inhabitants only for the needs of the Army of Occupation. They will be proportionate to the resources of the country and of such a nature that they do not imply for the population the obligation of taking part in war operations against their native country."

These various articles must, moreover, be considered in the general spirit defined in the preamble of the Convention, from which I take the liberty of reading the last paragraph to the Tribunal:

> "Until such time as a more complete code of the laws of war can be enacted, the High Contracting Parties deem it opportune to state that in cases not included in the regulations adopted by them, populations remain under the safeguard and direction of the principles of the law of nations derived from the established usages among civilised nations, the laws of humanity and the requirements of public conscience."

From this point of view it is very evident that the total exploitation of the resources of occupied countries for the benefit of the enemy's war economy is absolutely contrary to the law of nations and to the requirements of public conscience.

Germany signed The Hague Convention, and it must be pointed out that she made no reservations at that time except with regard to Article 44, which relates to the supply of information to the belligerents. She made no reservation with regard to the articles which we have cited, nor with regard to the preamble. These articles and the preamble, moreover, reiterate the corresponding text of the previous Hague Convention of 28th July, 1899.

German official ratifications of the Conventions were given on 4th September, 1900, and 27th November, 1909. I have purposely recalled these well-known facts in order to emphasise that the Germans could not fail to recognise the constant principles of International Law to which they subscribed on two occasions, long before their defeat in 1918 and consequently outside the alleged pressure to which they referred in regard to the Treaty of Versailles.

While on this subject of juridical theory may I point out that in the agreement signed at Versailles on 28th June, 1919, in connection with the military occupation of the territories of the Rhine, reference is made, in Article 6, to The Hague Convention in the following terms:

> "The right of requisition in kind and in services as formulated by The Hague Convention of 1907 will be exercised by the Allied and associate armies of occupation."

Thus the governing principles of the rights of requisition by the occupiers is confirmed by a third International Agreement subscribed to by Germany, who in regard to the occupation of her own territory is here the beneficiary of this limitation.

What, then, will the conduct of the Germans be like in view of this factual situation, which involves power and temptation, and of the legal situation which involves a limitation?

The Tribunal is already aware, by virtue of the general presentation of the

American Prosecution, that the conduct of the Germans was to profit by the fact and to ignore the law.

The Germans systematically violated international rules and the law of nations, as far as we are concerned, both by forced labour and by spoliation. Detailed illustrations of these acts in the Western countries will be laid before you in the briefs which will follow my own. For my part I propose to concentrate for a moment on the actual concepts which the Germans had from the outset. In this connection I shall submit to the Tribunal three complementary propositions.

First proposition. From the very beginning of the occupation, the Germans decided, in the interests of their war effort, to seize in any way possible all the resources, both material and human, of the occupied countries. Their plan was not to take any account of legal limitations. It was not under the spur of occasional necessity that they subsequently perpetrated their illicit acts, but in pursuance of a deliberate intention.

Second proposition. However, the Germans took pains to mask their real intentions, they did not make known that they rejected international juridical rules. On the contrary, they gave assurance that they would respect them.

The reasons for this camouflage are easy to understand. The Germans were anxious from the beginning to spare public opinion in the occupied territory. Brutal proceedings would have aroused immediate resistance which would have hampered their actions. They also wished to deceive world opinion and more particularly American public opinion, since the United States of America had at that time not yet entered the war.

The third proposition which I lay before the Tribunal results from the first two. As the Germans contemplated achieving their aims and masking their intentions, they were of necessity bound to organise a system of roundabout means, whilst maintaining an appearance of legality. The complexity and the technical character of the procedure they used enabled them easily to conceal the real state of affairs from the uninitiated or the merely uninformed. These disguised means proved, in fact, just as efficient and perhaps even more so than would have been brutal seizure. They moreover enabled the Germans to have recourse to such brutal action whenever they deemed that this would yield them more advantages than disadvantages.

We are of the opinion that this analysis of the German intentions is of interest to the Tribunal for, on the one hand, it demonstrates that the illegal acts were premeditated, and that their authors were aware of their reprehensible character and, on the other hand, it enables one to understand the scope and extent of these acts, despite the precautions taken to mask them.

The evidence which the prosecution will submit to the Tribunal refers chiefly to the second and third propositions, for as regards the first, that is to say, the criminal intention and premeditation, it is demonstrated by the discrepancy between the facade and reality.

I say in the first place that the Germans at the time of the occupation made a pretence of observing the rules of International Law. Here is, by way of example, a proclamation to the French population, signed by the Commander-in-Chief of the German Army. This is a public document which is reproduced in the Official Journal containing the decrees issued by the military governor for occupied territories, No. 1, dated the 4th July, 1940.

I submit to the Tribunal this document, which will be Exhibit RF-1 of the French documentation, and from it I cite merely the following sentence:

"The troops have received the order to treat the population with regard and to respect private property provided the population remains calm."

The Germans proceeded in identical manner in all the occupied countries. I also submit to the Tribunal the text of the same proclamation, dated the 10th May, 1940, which was published in the Official Journal of the Commander-in- Chief in Belgium and in the North of France, No. 1, Page 1, under the title: "Proclamation to the Population of Belgium." The German text, as well as the Flemish text, bears the more complete title: "Proclamation to the Population of Holland and Belgium." In view of the identical nature of these texts, this copy may be considered as No. 1 of the French documentation.

I now submit another proclamation entitled: "To the Inhabitants of Occupied Countries," dated 20th June, 1940, and signed "The Military Governor of France." This is likewise published in the Official Journal of German decrees. This will be Document RF-2 of the French documentation. I will cite the first two paragraphs:

"The Commander-in-Chief of the German Army has given me authority to announce the following: First, the German Army guarantees the inhabitants full personal security and the safeguard of their property. Those who behave peacefully and quietly have nothing to fear."

I also quote passages from paragraphs V, VI and VII:

"V. The administrative authorities of the State, communities, the police and schools shall continue their activities. They therefore remain at the service of their own population.

VI. All enterprises, businesses and banks will continue their work in the interest of the population.

VII. (Finally.) Producers of goods of prime necessity, as well as, merchants, shall continue their activities and place their goods at the disposal of the public."

The passages which I have just quoted are not the literal reproduction of international conventions, but they reflect their spirit. Repetition of the terms: "At the service of the population," "In the interest of the population," "At the disposal of the public," must necessarily be construed as an especially firm assurance that the resources of the country and its manpower will be preserved for that country and not diverted in favour of the German war effort.

I now submit, as Exhibit RF-2, the text of the same statement signed by the Commander-in-Chief of the Army Group and published in the Official Journal of the Commander-in- Chief in Belgium, numbered as above, Page 3.

Finally, on 22nd June, 1940, an armistice convention was signed by the representatives of the German Government and by the representatives of the de facto authority which was at that time assuming the Government of France. This convention is likewise a public document. It will be submitted to the Tribunal at a later stage as Document L.D.F. Eco. I. At this stage I merely wish to cite the first sentence of paragraph 3, which reads as follows:

"In the occupied districts of France the German Reich exercises an the rights of an occupying Power."

This constitutes, then, a very definite reference to International Law. Moreover, the German plenipotentiaries gave in this respect complementary oral assurances. On this matter I submit to the Tribunal, in the form of French Document RF-3, an extract from the deposition made by Ambassador Leon Noel in the course of proceedings before the French High Court of Justice. This extract is reproduced from a book entitled "Transcript in extenso of the sessions of the trial of Marshal Petain," printed in Paris in 1945 at the printing office of the Official Journals, and constitutes a document acceptable in proof in accordance with the Charter of the Tribunal,

Article 21. This is the statement of M. Leon Neol, which I desire to cite to the Tribunal. M. Leon Noel was a member of the French Armistice Delegation.

THE PRESIDENT: Are you going to present this document to us?

M. FAURE: This document is presented to the Tribunal. We have given to the Tribunal the transcript of the proceedings, and in the book of documents the Tribunal will find the excerpt I am now quoting.

THE PRESIDENT: We are not in possession of it at present. I do not know where it is.

M. FAURE: I think that possibly this document was handed to the Secretariat of the Tribunal rather late, but it will be here immediately. May it please the Tribunal, I merely intend to read a short extract from this document to-day.

THE PRESIDENT: We will have it to-morrow, I hope?

M. FAURE: Certainly, Mr. President.

> "I have also obtained a certain number of replies from German generals which, I believe, could have been subsequently used; from General Jodl, who, in the month of May last, signed, at Rheims, the unconditional surrender of Germany and from General, subsequently Marshal, Keitel, who, a few weeks later, was to sign, in Berlin, the ratification of this surrender. In this way I got them to declare in the most categorical manner that in no event would they interfere with administration, that the rights which they claimed for themselves under the convention were purely and simply those which in similar circumstances International Law and international usage concede to occupation armies, that is to say, those indispensable for the maintenance of security, transportation and the food supply needs of these armies."

These assertions and promises on the part of the Germans were therefore formal. Now even at that time they were not sincere. Indeed, not only did the Germans subsequently violate them, but from the very beginning they organised a system whereby they were enabled to accomplish these violations in the most efficacious manner and at the same time in a manner which enabled them to some extent to mask them.

As far as economy and labour are concerned, this German system comes from a very simple idea. It consisted in supervising production at its beginning and its end.

On the one hand the Germans embarked immediately upon the general requisitioning of all raw materials and all goods in the occupied countries.

Thenceforth, it would depend upon them to supply or not to supply raw materials to national industries. They were thus in a position to develop one branch of production rather than another, to favour certain undertakings, and, conversely, to oblige other undertakings to close down. As events and opportunities demanded, they organised this appropriation of raw materials, principally with a view to facilitating their distribution in their own interest, but the principle was continuously maintained. They thus held, as it were, the key of entrance to production.

On the other hand, they also held the exit key, that is to say, of finance. By securing the financial means in the form of the money of an occupied country, the Germans were able to purchase products and to acquire, under the pretence of legality, the output of the economic activity of the country. In point of fact, the Germans obtained for themselves, from the outset, such considerable financial means that they were easily able to absorb the entire productive capacity of each country.

If the Tribunal finds it suitable, I will stop at this point.

(The Tribunal adjourned until 10.00 hours on 18th January, 1946.)

Thirty-Seventh Day: Friday, January 18th, 1946

M. EDGAR FAURE: Mr. President, your Honours. At yesterday's session I explained to the Tribunal the principles of the provisions made by the Germans to ensure the seizure of raw materials and the control of finance in the occupied countries.

These provisions will be demonstrated by numerous documents, which will be presented to the Tribunal in the course of the presentation of the case on economic spoliation and forced labour. I shall not quote these documents at this moment since, as I pointed out yesterday, the purpose of my introduction is limited to the initial concepts of the Germans in these matters. I shall only cite one document which reveals the true intentions of the Germans in the very first period. This document bears our No. 3-bis, and I offer it in evidence to the Tribunal.

It particularly relates to Norway. It consists of a photostatic copy, certified and authenticated, of a minute of a conference held in Oslo, 21st November, 1940.

THE PRESIDENT: Where shall we find it?

M. FAURE: I have just filed this document with the Tribunal, and in the book which has just been given to you you will find the text of the extract which I am about to quote in French:

"Oslo, 21st November, 1940."

THE PRESIDENT: Are the documents in our books marked in any way?

M. FAURE: As there are only five documents in this book, we have not numbered them. This is the fourth document in the book.

THE PRESIDENT: Is it headed "Conference under the presidency of the Reich Commissar"?

M. FAURE: Yes, that is the one.

THE PRESIDENT: Dated at Oslo the something of November, 1940?

M. FAURE: That is the one, yes, Sir.

THE PRESIDENT: One moment. When you file a document as an exhibit, it will be given a number, will it not?

M. FAURE: Yes.

THE PRESIDENT: What will be the number of this one?

M. FAURE: No. RF-3-bis.

THE PRESIDENT: Yes. What is the date? The date on mine is undecipherable.

M. FAURE: 21st November, 1940.

THE PRESIDENT: Very well.

M. FAURE: This document is the minute of a meeting held in Oslo under the presidency of the Reich Commissar. I would point out to the Tribunal that we file this document as particularly significant, because Norway is a country which was occupied at a very early date by the Germans. The date of 21st November, 1940, which you see, refers to the very earliest period of the German occupation, and moreover, in the text of the conference, there is an allusion to the situation of the seven months preceding.

You will find there exactly the psychology of the occupation as it existed in the period of April, 1940, to November, 1940, that is to say, at the same time as or even before the time when the Germans, while invading the other countries, made reassuring proclamations which I read to the Tribunal yesterday.

There were 40 personages present at the conference, among whom was the State Secretary, Dr. Landried, representing the Ministry of Reich Economy. The Reich Commissar expresses himself as follows:

> "To-day's conference is the continuation of a conference which was held in Berlin. On this occasion I should like, first of all, to stress and state definitely that the collaboration between the Wehrmacht and the Reich Commissar is exemplary. I must protest against the notion that the Wehrmacht carried out its financial task in a confused and irresponsible manner. We must also take into account the particular circumstances which were present in Norway and which are still partially present. Certain tasks were fixed by the Fuehrer which were to be carried out within a given time.
>
> At the time of the Berlin conference, the following points were fixed, which we can take as a guide for the conference of to-day. There is no doubt that the country of Norway has been utilised for the execution of the tasks of the Wehrmacht during the last seven months to such an extent that a further draining of the country without some compensation is no longer possible, if we wish to accomplish the future tasks of the Wehrmacht.
>
> I considered from the beginning that my obvious duty as Reich Commissar lay, first of all, in mobilising all the economic and material forces of the country to serve the cause of the Wehrmacht and not relying on the resources of the Reich, as long as I am in a position to organise the same resources in the country."

I will stop quoting the words of the Reich Commissar at this point, and I shall now cite the terms of the reply of Dr. Landfried, which you will find a little lower down in the document:

> "I am very grateful to be able to state that we have succeeded here in Norway in mobilising the economic forces of this country for German needs, and to an extent which it was not possible to attain in all the other occupied countries. I give you my cordial thanks in the name of the Minister of Economy. You have succeeded in getting the Norwegians to make the utmost effort."

I think the Tribunal will have observed the series of expressions which are used in this document and which are quite characteristic. The Reich Commissar says, "From the very beginning, my duty is to mobilise all the economic and material forces of the country for the cause of the Wehrmacht," and Dr. Landfried says, "We succeeded in mobilising the economic forces to an extent which Was not possible to attain in all the other occupied territories."

Thus, we see that Dr. Landfried does not say that the Germans had, in Norway, a particular concept of occupation and that in the other countries they used a different procedure. He says that it was not possible to do as well in the other countries. The only limitation he recognises is a limit of fact and opportunity, which will soon be overcome, but in no wise any limitation of law. The idea of a legal limitation never enters his mind, any more than it enters the mind of any of the 40 personages present.

There is no question here of an opinion or initiative of a regional administrative authority, but rather of the official doctrine of the Reich Cabinet and the High Command, since 40 high officials were present at this conference, and especially the representative of the Minister for Economy.

I should like to stress, at this point, that this German doctrine and these German methods for the mobilisation of the resources of the occupied countries necessarily extend to the labour of the inhabitants.

I said yesterday that the Germans ensured for themselves, from the very beginning, the two keys of production. By that very fact they had within their power the capital, which was labour. It depended on their decision whether labour worked or should not work, whether there should or should not be unemployment. This explains why, in a general way, the Germans took brutal measures, such as displacement and the mobilisation of workers, only after a certain time.

In the first period, that is to say as long as there existed in the occupied countries stocks and raw materials, it was more in the interests of the Germans to utilise labour locally, at least to a large extent. This labour permitted them to produce for their benefit, with the wealth of these countries, finished products which they seized. Thus, besides the ethical advantage of safeguarding appearances, they avoided the initial transportation of raw materials. The considerations or difficulties of transportation were always very important in the German war economy.

But when after a time - which was more or less long - the occupied countries were impoverished in their raw materials and truly ruined, at that moment the Germans no longer had any interest in permitting labour to work there. They would have had to furnish the raw materials themselves, and consequently that would have involved double transportation, that of raw material in one direction and that of the finished products in the other direction. At that moment it became more advantageous for them to export workmen. This consideration coincided, moreover, with the needs resulting from the economic situation of Germany at that time and with political considerations.

On the question of employment of labour, I shall read to the Tribunal a few sentences of a document which I offer as Exhibit RF-4. It is the same document from which I have just read and in the same document book. The note which you will find in the document book contains the sentence which concerns articles which appeared in the newspaper "Pariser Zeitung" on 17th July, 1942. I offer at the same time to the Tribunal a photostatic copy, which has been authenticated, of the page of the newspaper, from the collection in the Bibliotheque Nationale. This article is signed by Dr. Michel, who was the Chief of the Economic Administration in France. Its title is "Two Years of Directed Economy in France." It concerns an article written for the purpose of German propaganda since it appeared in a German newspaper which was published in Paris with one page in French. Naturally I wish to point out to the Tribunal that we shall in no way accept all the ideas which are presented in this article, but we should like to stress several sentences of Dr. Michel's as revealing the same sort of procedure about which I spoke a short time ago, which consisted of utilising labour first on the spot, as long as there was raw material, and then deporting this labour to Germany.

THE PRESIDENT: Have you given the exhibit a number?

M. FAURE: No. 4. I quote:

"The third phase is characterised by the transfer of orders from the Reich to France, in order to utilise the productive forces of French industry."

THE PRESIDENT: You were reading from "Afin D'utiliser," weren't you?

M. FAURE: Yes, "Afin D'utiliser."

THE PRESIDENT: Very well; I understand. You read another sentence, other than that which is set out in this book.

M. FAURE: Yes, it is a mistake in my brief. The first phrase is of no importance. I begin at:

> "In order to utilise the productive forces of French industry, the Reich began by transferring to France its orders for industrial articles which were of use to the war effort. One figure alone is adequate to show the success of the transfer of German orders: The value of the transactions made till to-day are expressed by a figure exceeding hundreds of billions of francs. A new blood circulates, flows in the veins of French economy, which works to the very limit of its capacities."

Some sentences which were in the original were omitted here, as they are not of interest, and I would like to read the following one:

> "When the stocks of raw materials tended to diminish as the war was prolonged, they began to hire available French labour."

Dr. Michel uses here very elegant formulas which cover the real intent, that is to say, the start of the transfer of women at the very moment when raw material, which the Germans had appropriated from the beginning of occupation, had begun to be exhausted.

The conclusion which I would now like to give to my presentation is the following: that the Germans have always considered labour, human labour, as a tool in their service. This consideration existed even before the official imposition of forced, or compulsory, labour, of which we will speak to you presently.

For Germans, the work of others has always been compulsory and for their profit; on the other hand, I should like to mention now that it was their intention that it should continue to be so even after the end of the war.

This is the last point that I would like to emphasise, but it shows the amplitude and the seriousness of the German conception and of the German projects. I shall quote in relation to this a document, which will be Exhibit RF-5 in our document book. Here is the document, which I file with the Tribunal, a work edited in French in Berlin in 1943, by Doctor Friedrich Didie, entitled " Workers for Europe." It is edited by the Central Publishing House of the National Socialist Party. It begins with a preface by the defendant Sauckel, and is stamped with his signature.

I shall cite to the Tribunal a paragraph from this work, which is the last page of my brief. This is Exhibit RF-5, and this paragraph is found on Page 23, I quote:

> "A great percentage of foreign workers will remain on our territory, even after victory and after being readapted to construction work, will complete what the War had prevented them from finishing, and carry out those projects which up to now had been no more than projects."

Thus, in a propaganda work, written consequently with great prudence and with intention to mislead, we find nevertheless this main admission by the Germans that they intended to keep, even after the war, the workmen of other countries, in order to ensure the greatness of Germany, without any limitation in time or objective. This, therefore, amounts to a policy of perpetual exploitation.

If it please the Tribunal, my introduction having come to an end, M. Herzog will present the brief relating to forced labour.

M. HERZOG: Mr. President and your Honours.

The National Socialist doctrine, by the high place which it gives to the idea of the State, by the contempt in which it holds individuals and personal rights, contains a conception of work which agrees with the principles of its general philosophy.

Work is not, in this philosophy, one of the forms of the manifestation of individual personalities, it is a duty imposed by the community on its members.

"The relationship of labour, according to National Socialist ideas," a German writer has said, "is not merely a judicial relationship between the worker and his employer; it is a living phenomenon in which the worker becomes a cog in the National Socialist machine for collective production." The conception of compulsory labour is thus, for National Socialism, necessarily complementary to the conception of work itself.

Compulsory Labour Service was first of all imposed on the German people. German Labour Service was instituted by a law of 26th June, 1935, which bears Hitler's signature and that of the defendant Frick, Minister of the Interior. This law was published in the "Reichsgesetzblatt," Part I, Page 769. I submit it to the Tribunal as Document RF-6.

From 1939 the mobilisation of workers was added to the compulsory labour service. Decrees were promulgated to that effect by the defendant Goering in his capacity as Plenipotentiary for the Four Year Plan. I do not stress this point; it arises from the conspiracy entered into by the accused to commit their Crime against Peace, and of which my American colleagues have already informed the Tribunal. I merely point out that the mobilisation of workers was applicable to foreigners resident in German territory, because I find in this fact the proof that the principle of compulsory recruitment of foreign workers existed prior to the war. Far from being the spontaneous result of the needs of German war industry, the compulsory recruitment of foreign workers is the putting into practice of a concerted policy. I lay before the Tribunal a document which proves this. It is Document 382 of the French classification, which I offer as Exhibit RF 7. This is a memorandum of the High Command of the German Armies of 1st October, 1938; the memorandum, drawn up in anticipation of the invasion of Czechoslovakia, contains a classification of possible violations of International Law; the explanation which the High Command of the Armed Forces thinks it possible to give appears in connection with each violation. The document appears in the form of a list in four columns; in the first is a statement of the violations of International Law; the second gives a concrete example; the third contains the points of view of International Law on the one hand and, on the other hand, the conclusions which can be drawn from them; the fourth column is reserved for the explanation of the Propaganda Ministry.

I read the passage which deals with the forced labour of civilians and prisoners of war, which is found on Page 6 of the German original, Page 7 of the French translation, the document which is referred to in my document book as Exhibit RF-7.

I read at the bottom of Page 7 of the French translation:

"Compulsory use of prisoners of war and civilians for war work, construction of roads, digging trenches, munition work, transport."

Second column:

"Captured Czech soldiers and civilians are detailed to construct roads and to load munitions."

Third column:

"Article 31 of an agreement signed 27th July, 1929, concerning the treatment of prisoners of war engaged on work which is directly connected with the War to force them to do such work is in any case contrary to International Law; prisoners of war and civilians can be used on highway construction but not on munition work."

Last column:

"The use of such measures can be justified by the necessity of war or by the assertion that the enemy acted in the same way first."

The compulsory recruitment of foreign workers is thus in accordance with National

Socialist doctrine, one of the elements of the policy of German domination. Hitler himself recognised this on several occasions. I quote in this connection his speech of 9th November, 1941, which was printed in the "Volkischer Beobachter" of 10th November, 1941, No. 314, Page 4, which I submit to the Tribunal as Exhibit RF 8. I read the extract of this speech, columns 1 and 2 and the first paragraph below, in the German original.

THE PRESIDENT: Exhibit RF 8, is it not?

M. HERZOG: Yes, your Honour.

"The territory which now works for us contains more than 250,000,000 men, but the territory in Europe which works indirectly for this struggle now includes more than 350,000,000. In so far as German territory is concerned, occupied territory, the domain which we have taken under our administration, it is certain that we shall succeed in harnessing the very last man to this work."

The recruitment of foreign workers thus proceeds in a systematic manner. It constitutes the putting into practice of the political principles applied to all the territories occupied by Germany. These principles, the concrete development of which in other departments of German criminal activity will be pointed out to you by my colleagues, are materially of two kinds: employment of all active forces of the occupied or dominated territories; extermination of all their non-productive forces.

These are the two justifications which the defendants have given for the establishment of the recruitment of foreign workers. There are many documents to this effect; I confine myself to the most explicit.

The justification for the recruitment of foreign workers, because of the necessity of associating the enslaved peoples with the German war effort, is primarily a result of the exposition of the motives of the decree of 21st March, 1942.

DR. STAHMER (Counsel for defendant Goering): Mr. President, I should like to point out that the translation into German is faulty. Whole sentences are omitted. This is apparently the result of the fact that the prosecutor is speaking too rapidly.

THE PRESIDENT: Will you go a little more slowly?

M. HERZOG: Yes.

The justification for the recruitment of foreign workers, on account of the necessity for associating the enslaved peoples with the German war effort, is primarily a result of the exposition of the motives of the decree of 21st March, 1942, appointing the defendant Sauckel as plenipotentiary for the employment of labour. The decree was published in the "Reichsgesetzblatt," 1942, Part 1, Page 179. I submit it and will read its complete text to the Tribunal as Exhibit RF 9.

"The decree of the Fuehrer concerning the creation of a plenipotentiary for the employment of labour, dated 21st March, 1942.

To assure to the whole of the war economy, and, in particular, the armament industry, necessary labour, it is important to establish a unified direction, which answers the needs of the war economy for the use of available labour, including hired foreigners and war prisoners, as well as the mobilisation of all labour still unemployed in the Greater German Reich, including the Protectorate as well as the Government General and the other occupied regions. This mission will be accomplished by Reichsstatthalter and Gauleiter Fritz Sauckel, in the capacity of general plenipotentiary for the employment of labour in the framework of the Four Year Plan. In this capacity he is directly responsible for the Four Year Plan."

I would like to point out here that the defendant Sauckel developed the same theme at the Congress of Gauleiter and Reichsleiter, held on 5th and 6th February, 1943, at Posen. He expressed himself in plain terms: he justified compulsory recruitment on the basis of National Socialist philosophy, and on the basis of the necessity of associating all the European peoples in the struggle carried on by Germany. His speech constitutes Document 1739-PS. I submit it as Exhibit RF 10, and I request the Court to accept the following passages in evidence against the defendant Sauckel. At first, Page 5 of the German text, fourth paragraph - this is found in the first page of the French translation:

> "The unprecedented violence of the war has forced me to mobilise in the name of the Fuehrer a great number of foreigners for labour in the domain of the German war economy, and to force them to large-scale production.
>
> The purpose of this is to insure in the labour domain the material means required by war in the struggle for the preservation of the life and liberty, in the first place, of our people, and also for the preservation of our Western culture for those peoples who, in contrast to the parasitical Jews and plutocrats, lead a life of work and endeavour and are honest and strong.
>
> Such is the enormous difference between, on the one hand, the work which was demanded at one period by the power and authority of the Jews in the Treaty of Versailles and the Dawes and Young Plans, work which took the form of slavery and tributary efforts, and, on the other' hand, the utilisation of labour which, in my capacity as a National Socialist, I have the honour to prefer and to carry out, and which represents a participation in the struggle by Germany for the liberty of Germany and for the liberty of friendly nations."

The compulsory recruitment of foreign workers did not have as its only object the maintenance of the level of German industrial production. There was also the conscious desire to weaken the human potential of the occupied countries.

The idea of extermination by work was familiar to the theorists of National Socialism and to the leaders of Germany; it constituted one of the bases of the policy of domination of the invaded territories. I lay before the Court the proof that the National Socialist conspirators envisaged the destruction by work of whole ethnical groups. A discussion which took place on 14th September, 1942, between Goebbels and Thierack is significant. It constitutes Document 682-PS, which I file with the Tribunal as Exhibit RF 11, from which I take the following passage:

> "Concerning the extermination of the social elements, Doctor Goebbels is of the opinion that the following groups must be exterminated: Jews and Gypsies, without discrimination; Poles who have still to serve three or four years' sentence; Czechoslovakians and Germans who have been condemned to death or to penal servitude for life or have been placed in protective custody for life. The idea to exterminate them by work is best."

The idea of extermination by work was not applied to ethnical groups alone, the disappearance of which was desired by the defendants; it also led to the employment of foreign manual labour in the German war industry to the extreme limit of the individual's strength. I will revert to this aspect of the policy of forced labour when I lay before the Tribunal the treatment of foreign workers in Germany: the cruelties to which they were subjected sprang from this main conception of National Socialism, that the human forces of the occupied countries must be utilised to the limit of extermination, which is the final goal.

The defendants have not only admitted the principle of compulsory recruitment of foreign workers; they have followed a consistent policy of putting their principle into practice, applying it in the same concrete manner in the various occupied territories.

To do this they resorted to identical methods of recruitment; they set up everywhere the same recruitment administration and promulgated the same orders.

In the first place, it was a question of urging the foreign workers to work in their own countries for the Army of Occupation and the services connected with it. The German military and civil authorities organised workyards in order to carry out on the spot work useful to their war policy. The workyards or shops of the Todt organisation, which, after the death of their founder, were under the direction of the defendant Speer, and those of the Wehrmacht, Luftwaffe, Kriegsmarine and the N.S.K.K. organisation, employed numerous foreign workers in all areas of Western Europe.

But the essential undertaking of the German labour services was the deportation of foreign workers to the munition factories of the Reich. The most varied means were used to this end. They were built up into a recruiting policy which can be analysed as follows:

In the beginning, this policy took on the cloak of legality. The use of labour took the form of requisition under the terms of Article 52 of the Appendix to the Fourth Hague Convention; it was also effected by means of voluntary recruitment of workers, to whom the German recruiting offices offered labour contracts.

I shall provide the Tribunal with proof that the labour requisitions effected by the National Socialist authorities were a deliberate misinterpretation of the letter and spirit of the international convention by virtue of which they were carried out. I shall show that the voluntary character of the recruitment of certain foreign workers was entirely fictitious; in reality their work contracts were made under the pressure which the occupation authorities brought to bear on their will.

The defendants lost no time in flinging aside their mask of legality. They compelled the prisoners of war to do work forbidden by international conventions. I shall show how the work of prisoners of war was incorporated in the general plan for the employment of labour from the occupied areas.

It was finally by force that the defendants brought to fruition their recruitment plans. They did not hesitate to resort to violent methods. Thus they established the compulsory labour service in the areas which they occupied. Sometimes they directly promulgated orders bearing the signature of military commanders or Reich Commissars; this is the case with Belgium and Holland. Sometimes they forced the de facto authorities themselves, whom they had set up in the occupied areas, to take legislative measures; this is particularly the case with France and Norway; sometimes they simply took direct action, that is, they transferred foreign workers to factories in Germany without providing a written order for this; this happened in Denmark. Finally in certain occupied areas where they began to carry out Germanisation, the defendants made the inhabitants of these territories a part of the labour service of the Reich. This was the case in the French provinces of Haut-Rhin, Bas-Rhin and Moselle, and in Luxembourg.

The policy of compulsory labour was asserted and systematised from the day when the defendant Sauckel was appointed General Plenipotentiary for the Employment of Labour.

Member of the National Socialist Party since its formation, member of the Diet of Thuringia and member of the Reichstag, Obergruppenfuehrer of the criminal organisations S.S. and S.A., the defendant Sauckel was Gauleiter and Reichsstatthalter of Thuringia. On 21st March, 1942, he was appointed General Plenipotentiary for the Employment of Labour by a decree of the Fuehrer. This decree was countersigned by Lammers, in his capacity as Reich Minister and Chief of the Chancellery and by the defendant Keitel; the responsibility of these latter is confirmed by this countersignature. The defendant Keitel has associated himself, by appointing Sauckel, with the policy of compulsory labour, the principle and the method of which he has approved.

I have already read this decree nominating Sauckel to the Tribunal. I would remind you that it placed Sauckel, in his capacity as General Plenipotentiary for the Employment of Labour, under the immediate orders of the Trustee for the Four Year Plan, the defendant Goering. The latter bears a direct responsibility in pursuing the plan for recruitment of compulsory labour. I shall produce numerous proofs of this. I ask the Tribunal to authorise me to produce, as first proof, the decree signed by the defendant Goering the day after the appointment of the defendant Sauckel. This decree, dated 27th March, 1942, was published in the "Reichsgesetzblatt," 1942, Part 1, Page 180. I file it with the Tribunal as Exhibit RF 12. Goering by this decree did away with all the administrative offices of the Four Year Plan which had been charged with the recruitment of labour, he transmitted their powers to Sauckel's department, thus confirming his appointment.

The powers of Sauckel between 1942 and 1944 were considerably reinforced by decrees of Hitler and Goering. These decrees gave full significance to the defendant Sauckel's title of Plenipotentiary. They gave him administrative autonomy and even legislative competency such as he could not aspire to, had he confined himself to executive tasks. The importance of the political part which he played during the last two years of the war increases in this measure the weight of the responsibility devolving upon him.

I would particularly draw the attention of the Tribunal to the decrees of the Fuehrer of 30th September, 1942, and of 14th March, 1943, and to the decree of the defendant Goering, of 25th May, 1942.

I will not read these decrees, which have been commented on by my American colleague, Mr. Dodd. I submit them in support of my contention.

I will first refer to the decree of the defendant Goering of 25th May, 1942. It was published in the "Reichsgesetzblatt," 1942, Part 1, Page 347. He delegates to Sauckel part of the powers relating to labour held by the Minister of Labour. I submit it to the Tribunal as Exhibit RF 13.

Hitler's decree of 30th September, 1942, gave Sauckel considerable power over the civil and military authorities of the territories occupied by the German Armed Forces. It made it possible for the defendant to introduce into the staffs of the occupying authorities personal representatives, to whom he gave his orders directly. The decree is countersigned by Lammers and by the defendant Keitel, and this appears in the collection of the directive decrees of 1942, second volume, Page 510, and I submit it as Exhibit RF 14.

In the carrying out of this decree representatives of Sauckel's department were in fact introduced into the Headquarters Staffs of the military commands. The interrogation of General von Falkenhausen, Military Governor of Belgium and Northern France, gives, in this connection, a proof which I would ask the Tribunal to be good enough to remember. General von Falkenhausen was interrogated on 27th November, 1945, by the head of the Investigation Section of the French delegation. I submit his evidence to the Tribunal as Exhibit RF 15. I read the following extract (Page 2, the seventh paragraph, of the French translation, and Page 2, the fifth paragraph, of the German translation):

"**Q.** Can the witness tell us what was the line of demarcation between his own powers and the powers of the Arbeitseinsatz?

A. Up to a certain time there existed in my department a labour service which dealt with the hiring of voluntary workers.

I no longer remember the exact date - perhaps autumn 1942-when this labour service was placed under the order of Sauckel, and the only thing I had to do was to carry out the orders which came through this way.

I do not remember, but Raeder, who is also in prison" - Raeder was a civilian official in the staff of General von Falkenhausen - "is very well informed about the dates and can undoubtedly give them better than I can.

Q. Before the question of labour was entirely entrusted to Sauckel's organisation, did there exist in the General Staff or in its services an officer who was in charge of this question? Afterwards, was there a delegate from Sauckel's service in this department?

A. Until Sauckel came into power there was, in my service, Raeder, who directed the Bureau of Labour in my office. This labour office functioned as an employment office in Germany, that is to say, it concerned itself with the requests for labour which would naturally be voluntary.

Q. What took place when this change happened?

A. After this change the office continued to exist, but the orders were given directly by Sauckel to the Arbeitseinsatz and passed through my office."

THE PRESIDENT: Would this be a convenient time to break off for 10 minutes?

Before the Tribunal adjourns I want to announce that the Tribunal will sit tomorrow, Saturday, until 1 o'clock.

(A recess was taken.)

M. HERZOG: I have just reminded the Tribunal of the legislative framework through which the activity of the defendant Sauckel was exercised. This framework was reinforced by the defendant's own decree. The first document attests that Sauckel deliberately assumed the responsibility of the general policy for the recruiting of foreign workers - the decree of the 22nd August, 1942, which appeared in the "Reichsgesetzblatt," 1942, Part I, Page 382. This decree lays down the principle of forced recruiting, and makes the necessary provisions for all the human potential of the occupied territories to be put in the service of the German war economy.

Sauckel forces the inhabitants of the conquered countries to participate in the war of Germany against their Fatherland. It is not only a violation of International Law, it is a crime against the rights of nations. I submit the decree to the Tribunal as Exhibit RF 17, and I shall read it:

"Ordinance No. 10 of the General Plenipotentiary for the Employment of Labour regarding the Arbeitseinsatz in the occupied territories under date of 22nd August, 1942.

In order to mobilise the labour of the occupied territories in the new organisation of the Arbeitseinsatz within the European framework, one must submit these forces to one central authority; it is necessary to assure a maximum return as well as a useful and rational distribution of this force, in order to satisfy the labour needs of the Reich and of the occupied territories. By virtue of the full powers which are conferred upon me, I order:

(1) By virtue of the decree of the Fuehrer, under date of 21st March, 1942, relative to the General Plenipotentiary for the Employment of Labour and by virtue of the ordinance of the Trustee for the Four Year Plan, under date of 27th March, 1942, relative to the application of this decree, I likewise have powers to employ, when necessary, the labour of occupied territories, as well as to take all the measures necessary to increase its production. Those German

offices which dealt with Arbeitseinsatz and for the policy of wages or my commissioners will, according to my directives, carry out this employment of labour and take all measures necessary to increase production.

(2) This ordinance extends to all the territories occupied during the war by the Wehrmacht, if they are under a German administration.

(3) The labour available in the occupied territories must be utilised in the first place to fulfil the primary war needs of Germany. This labour must be utilised in the occupied territories in the following order:

    (a) For the needs of the army, of the services of occupation and of the civilian services.

    (b) For the German armament needs.

    (c) For the food and agriculture.

    (d) For industrial needs other than those of armament, in which Germany is interested.

    (e) For industrial needs of the population of the territory in question."

A second document shows the willingness of the defendant Sauckel to take the responsibility for the treatment of foreign workers. It is an agreement concluded on 2nd June, 1943, with the Chief of the German Labour Front. I shall not read this document to the Tribunal. The document has been discussed by Mr. Dodd. I recall that it was published in the "Reichsarbeitsblatt" in 1943, Part 1, Page 588. I submit it in support of my brief as Exhibit RF 18.

Designated by Hitler and by the defendants Keitel and Goering, in order to pursue, under the control of the latter, the policy of recruitment of compulsory labour, the defendant Sauckel has consequently carried out his task in virtue of the responsibilities which he had assumed. I request that the Tribunal bear this in mind.

I request the Tribunal, likewise, to note that the policy of recruitment of foreign workers involves the responsibility of all German Ministers responsible for the economic and social life of the Reich. An interministerial office, or at any rate, an interadministrative office, the Central Planning Board for the Four Year Plan, has proceeded to formulate the programme for the recruitment of foreign workers.

All departments interested in the labour problem were represented at the meetings of the Central Office. General Milch presided at the meetings, in the name of the defendant Goering.

The defendant Sauckel and the defendant Speer took part, in person, and I shall submit to the Tribunal certain statements made by them. The defendant Funk also took part; he therefore knew of, and approved, the programme for the deportation of workers. He even collaborated in its formulation. As proof thereof I produce three documents inculpating him.

The first is a letter of 9th February, 1944, in which Funk is summoned to a meeting of the Central Planning Board. It is Document 674, which I submit to the Tribunal as Exhibit RF 19. I read:

"Sir: In the name of the Central Planning Board, I invite you to a meeting concerning the question of the utilisation of labour. It will take place on Wednesday, the 16th February, 1944, at 10 o'clock, in a board-room of the Secretaries of State at the Air Ministry, Leipziger Strasse, in Berlin.

In the Appendix I transmit to you some statistics on the subject of the development of the utilisation of labour. These statistics will serve as a basis for the discussion at the meeting."

Funk was unable personally to attend the meeting, but he arranged to be represented by Undersecretary of State Hayler. He received the minutes of the meeting and, on 7th March, 1944, he wrote to General Milch, in order to excuse his frequent absences from the meetings of the Board. I submit this document to the Tribunal. It is Document 675, which I submit as Exhibit RF 20. It is the report of the fifty-third meeting of the Planning Board. The Tribunal will note on Page 2 of the French translation that Minister Funk received a report of this meeting. He is mentioned on the second line of the distribution list: Reich Minister Speer first and on the second line Reich Minister Funk.

I now produce as Exhibit RF 21 the letter in which Funk excuses himself to Marshal Milch because of his inability to be present at the meeting.

> "Very honoured and very dear Field Marshal:
>
> Unfortunately the meetings of the Central Planning Board have always been set for dates on which I am already engaged by other important meetings. So it is to my great regret that I shall be unable to be present on Saturday at the meeting of the Central Planning Board, inasmuch as I have to speak on that day in Vienna in the course of a great demonstration in honour of the Anniversary of the day of the Anschluss.
>
> Secretary Hayler will likewise be in Vienna on Friday and Saturday, where there will be an important South- European Conference, in which foreign delegates will participate and at which I must also speak.
>
> Under these conditions I beg you to allow Ministerial Director and General of Police, Brigadefuehrer of S.S. Ohlendorf, who is the permanent deputy of State Secretary Hayler, to attend as my representative."

THE PRESIDENT: Does this document tell us anything more than that the defendant Funk was unable to be present?

M. HERZOG: This document, Mr. President, was given to me by my American colleagues, who asked me to use it in the case on compulsory labour, because they have not had time to use it in their charge against Funk. It is presented to the Tribunal to prove that Funk was following the meetings of the Central Planning Board and that he had permanent representatives there to represent him on all occasions who, by their report, kept him in touch with the work of the Central Planning Board. That is why we present to the Tribunal this document on defendant Funk.

I shall continue to quote:

> "Under these circumstances, I beg you to allow the Major- General of Police, Brigadefuehrer of the S.S., Ohlendorf, who is the permanent deputy of State Secretary Hayler, to attend as my representative. Herr Ohlendorf will have Ministerial Director Koelsen as a consultant for questions of consumer goods, and Counsellor of State Janke for questions concerning foreign trade."

The policy of the Central Planning Board for the Four Year Plan pursued by the defendant Sauckel is shown by the mass deportation of workers. The principle of this deportation is a criminal one, but the manner of its execution was even more criminal. I shall give the proof of this to the Tribunal by submitting, in succession, the methods of compulsory recruitment, its results and the conditions of deportation.

I wish here to thank the members of the French delegation and of the foreign delegations who have come to my aid in the preparation of my work, in particular, my colleague M. Pierre Portal, a Lyons barrister.

The brief which I have the honour of presenting to the Tribunal will be limited to the account of the recruiting of foreign labour in occupied territories of Western Europe, since the deportation of workers coming from Eastern Europe will be dealt with by my Soviet colleagues.

Throughout the occupation the local field commanders imposed requisitions of labour on the populations of the occupied territories. Fortification works considered necessary for the furtherance of military operations, and guard duties for the security of the occupation troops were carried out by the inhabitants of the occupied areas. The labour requisitions affected not only isolated individuals but entire groups.

In France, for instance, they affected, in turn, groups of Indo-Chinese workers, workers from North Africa, foreign workers, and Chantiers de Jeunesse (Youth workyards). I produce in evidence an extract from the report on forced labour and the deportation of workers drawn up by the Institute of Statistics of the French Government. This report bears the number 515 and I submit this to the Tribunal as Exhibit RF 22. This document, because of its size, has been taken out of the document book. I quote first of all Page 17 of the French text and 17, likewise, of the German translation.

I read the second paragraph before the end -

THE PRESIDENT: Is this it? *[indicating]*.

M. HERZOG: No, it is the document in the blue cover, on Page 17.

"Paragraph 6: The Forced Labour Recruitment of Constituted Groups: Finally, a last procedure adopted by the Germans on a number of occasions during the whole course of the occupations for direct forced labour, as well as for indirect forced labour: the 'requisition' of constituted groups already trained and disciplined and consequently an excellent contribution.

(a) Indo-Chinese Labour (M.O.I.): This formation of colonial workers had been intended from the beginning of the hostilities to satisfy the needs of French industry in non-specialised labour. Under the control of officers and non-commissioned officers of the French Army, transformed into civilian functionaries after the month of July, 1940, Indo-Chinese labour was, from 1945 on, obliged to do part-time forced labour, directly as well as indirectly."

I leave out the table on Page 16 and I read:

"(b) The North African work: Between 17th August and 6th November, 1942, the home country received two contingents of workers from North Africa; one was composed of 5,560 Algerians, the other of 1,825 Moroccans. These workers were immediately obliged to do direct forced labour which brought the number of North African workers enrolled in the Todt organisation to 17,582.

(c) Foreign labour: The law of 11th July, 1938, concerning the organisation of the nation in time of war provided for the cases of foreigners living in France, and obliged them to render services; under-officers and non-commissioned officers transformed into civilian functionaries by the law of the 9th October, 1940, the foreign labour was progressively subjected by the Germans to direct forced labour."

I leave out the table and I read:

"(d) Youth workyards (Chantiers de Jeunesse): On 29th January, 1943, the labour staff of the German Armistice Commission in Paris announced that the Commander-in-Chief 'West' was examining whether and in which way the formations of French workers might be called upon to perform tasks important for both countries. This resulted in partial recruiting and was followed by demands for young people from the workyards to supply direct labour."

Similar requisitions took place in all the other territories of Western Europe. These requisitions were illegal: they were carried out by virtue of Article 52 of the Appendix to the Fourth Hague Convention. In reality they systematically violated the letter and the spirit of this text of International Law.

What does Article 52 of the Appendix to the Fourth Hague Convention say? It is worded as follows:

> "Requisitions in kind and services shall not be demanded from municipalities or inhabitants except for the needs of the Army of Occupation. They shall be in proportion to the resources of the country and be of such a nature that the populations will not be obliged to take part in operations against their own country. These requisitions and services shall only be demanded on the authority of the commander of the locality occupied."

Thus the terms in which Article 52 authorises the requisition of services by an Army of Occupation are expressly formulated. These terms are four in number:

1. The rendering of services can be demanded only for the needs of the Army of Occupation. All requisitions made for the general economic needs of the occupying power are thus forbidden.

2. Services demanded by way of requisition must not entail an obligation to take part in military operations against the country of those rendering them. The rendering of any service exacted in the interests of the war economy of the occupying power, all guard duties or exercise of military control are forbidden.

3. Services rendered in a given area must be in proportion to its economic resources, the development of which must not be hampered. It follows that any requisitioning of labour is contrary to International Law if it results in the impeding or prevention of the normal utilisation of the riches of the occupied country.

4. Finally, labour requisitions must, under the provisions of the second paragraph of Article 52, be carried out in the area of the locality under the administration of the occupation authority who has signed the requisition order. The transfer of conscripted workers from one part of the occupied area to another and, especially, their deportation to the country of the occupied power are prohibited.

Labour requisitions exacted by German civilian and military authorities in the occupied areas did not conform to the spirit of Article 52. They were carried out to satisfy either the needs of German economy or even the needs of military strategy of the enemy forces. They deliberately refused to acknowledge the need of ensuring facilities for a reasonable utilisation of local resources; they finally took the form of migrations of workers. The case of those workers who were conscripted from all countries of Western Europe, and formed an integral part of the Todt organisation to help in building the system of fortifications known under the name of the "Atlantic Wall," may be taken as a typical example.

This violation of international agreements is a flagrant one; it called forth repeated protests from General Doyen, delegate of the French authorities with the German Armistice Commission. I ask the Tribunal to accept as evidence the letter of General Doyen, 25th May, 1941. This letter constitutes Document 283, and it is placed before the Tribunal as Exhibit RF 23. I read:

"Wiesbaden, 25th May, 1941. From the General de Corps d'Armee Doyen, President of the French delegation at the German Armistice Commission to Monsieur le General der Artillerie Vogl, President of the German Armistice Commission.

On several occasions, and notably in my letters No. 14,263/A.E. and 14,887/A.E.

of 26th February and 8th March, I respectfully protested to you against the use for which French labour has been employed within the framework of the Todt organisation in the execution of military work on the coast of Bretagne.

I have to-day the duty of calling your attention to other cases in which the occupation authorities have had recourse to the recruiting of French civilians to carry out services of a strictly military character, cases which are even more serious than those which I have already called to your attention.

If, indeed, in the case of the workers engaged by the Todt organisation, it could be argued that certain workers among them accepted voluntarily an employment for which they are being remunerated (although in practice most often they were not given the possibility of refusing this employment), this argument can by no means be invoked when the prefects themselves are obliged, at the expense of the departments and the communities, to set up guard services at important points, such as bridges, tunnels, works of art, telephone lines, munitions depots, and areas surrounding aviation fields.

The accompanying note furnishes some examples of the guard services which have been imposed upon Frenchmen in this way, services which before this were assumed by the German Army and which normally fall to the latter, since it is a question of participating in watches or of safe- guarding the German Army against risks arising from the state of war existing between Germany and Great Britain."

The occupying authorities, in face of the resistance which they encountered, were anxious that their orders regarding the requisitions of labour should be obeyed. The measures which they took to this end are just as illegal as the measures taken for the requisition itself. The National Socialist authorities in occupied France proceeded by legislative means. They promulgated ordinances by which sentence of death could be pronounced against persons disobeying requisition orders.

I submit two of these ordinances to the Tribunal as evidence. The first was given in the early months of the occupation, 10th October, 1940. It was published in the "Verordnungsblatt" of France on 17th October, 1940, Page 108.submit it to the Tribunal as Exhibit RF 24, and I read it:

"Ordinance relative to protection against acts of sabotage:

By virtue of the powers which have been conferred upon me by the Fuehrer and Supreme Commander of the Armed Forces, I decree the following:

"(1) Whoever intentionally does not fulfil or fulfils inadequately the tasks of supervision which are conferred upon him by the Chief of the Military Administration in France, or by a service undertaken by the latter, shall be condemned to death."

I will read paragraph 3:

"In less serious cases of infringements mentioned in paragraphs 1 and 2 of the present ordinance and in case of neglect, the offenders may be punished by solitary confinement with hard labour or imprisonment."

The second ordinance of the Military Commander in France to which I refer is dated 31st January, 1942. It was published in the "Verordnungsblatt" of France of 3rd February, 1942, Page 338.submit it to the Tribunal as Exhibit RF 25, and I read:

"Ordinance of 31st January, 1942, concerning the requisitioning of service and requisitioning in kind.

By virtue of the plenary powers which have been conferred on me by the Fuehrer and Supreme Commander of the Armed Forces, I order the following:

(1) Anyone who does not carry out these services or the requisitions in

kind which are imposed upon him by the Military Commander in France or by an authority designated by him, or who performs them in such a manner that the object of the services or requisitions is not fulfilled, shall be punishable by forced labour, imprisonment, or fine. A fine may be fixed in addition to a penalty of forced labour or imprisonment.

(2) In serious cases the death penalty may be inflicted."

These orders called forth a protest by the French authorities. General Doyen protested on several occasions against the first of them, without his protest having any effect.

I refer again to his letter of the 25th May, 1941, which I have just submitted to the Tribunal as Exhibit RF 23, and I read on page of the French translation, Page 4 of the German text:

" ... I have been asked to make a formal protest to you against such practices and to beg you to intervene so that an immediate end may be put to them.

From the 16th November, in letter No. 7843/AE, I have already protested against the ordinance that was decreed on the 10th October, 1940, by the Chief of the Military Administration in France, which laid down the death penalty for any person failing to carry out, or carrying out inadequately, the guard duties entrusted to him by the occupation authorities. I protested then that this requirement, as well as its penalty, was contrary to the spirit of the Armistice Convention, having as its object to relieve the French population from any participation in the hostilities.

I had limited myself to this protest in principle because at the time no concrete case of guard duties having been imposed had been called to my attention, but it was not possible to accept, as justifying the ordinance in question, the arguments which you proffered in your letter No. 1361 of 6th March. [Page 398] You pointed out in effect that, at Article 43 of The Hague Convention, the occupying power had the authority to legislate, but the authority to which you refer in this same article is subject to two restrictions: There can be legislation only to establish order, and to make public life secure in as far as possible. On the other hand, the ordinances decreed must" -

THE PRESIDENT: Is it not enough to show that General Doyen protested? It is not necessary to read all the argument which was put forward on the one side or the other.

M. HERZOG: I shall then stop this quotation, Mr. President.

The German ordinances which I have just read to the Tribunal thus contained formal violations of the general principles of the criminal legislation of civilised nations; they were made in contradiction to Article 102 of the Appendix to the Fourth Convention of The Hague and also in contradiction to Article 43, on which they were supposed to be based. They were, therefore, illegal and they were criminal, since they provided death sentences which no International Law or domestic law justifies.

The system of labour requisition furnishes the first example of the criminal character of the methods pursued by the defendants in the execution of their recruiting plan for foreign labour.

The National Socialist authorities then had recourse to a second procedure to give an appearance of legality to the recruiting of foreign workers. They called upon workers who were so-called volunteers. From 1940 on, the occupation authorities opened recruiting offices in all the large cities of the occupied territories. These offices were placed under the control of a special service instituted to this effect within the general staff of the Commanders-in-Chief of the occupation zones.

The Tribunal knows that these services from 1940 to 1942 functioned under the control of the generals. From 1942 on, and, more precisely, from the day when the defendant Sauckel became the Plenipotentiary of Labour they received their orders directly from the latter. General von Falkenhausen, Commander-in-Chief in Belgium and in the North of France, declared in the testimony which I have just read to the Tribunal that, from the summer of 1942 on, he had become the simple intermediary in charge of transmitting the instructions given by Sauckel to the Arbeitseinsatz.

Thus the policy of the German employment offices set up in the occupied areas was carried out on the sole responsibility of the defendant Sauckel from 1942, under the responsibility of the defendant Sauckel and his immediate superior, the Trustee for the Four Year Plan, the defendant Goering. I ask the Tribunal to take note of this.

The task of the employment offices was to organise the recruiting of workers for the factories and workshops set up in Europe by the Todt organisation and by the Wehrmacht, Kriegsmarine, Luftwaffe and other German organisations. It was also their task to obtain for the German munition factories the amount of foreign labour needed. Workers recruited in this way signed a labour contract; thus they had, theoretically, the status of free workers and were apparently volunteers.

The occupation authorities always made a point of the voluntary nature of the recruiting carried out by the employment offices, but the lines taken by their propaganda systematically took no account of what they were actually doing. In fact, the voluntary character of this recruiting was entirely fictitious: the workers of the areas who agreed to sign German labour contracts were subject to physical and moral pressure.

This pressure took several forms: it was sometimes collective and sometimes individual; in all its forms it was heavy enough to deprive the workers who suffered under it of their freedom of choice.

The nullity of contracts entered into under the reign of violence is a fundamental principle of the common law of civilised nations: it is found just as expressly stated in German law as in the laws of the powers represented in the Court or the States occupied by Germany. The German employment offices forced on the foreign workers labour contracts which had no legal significance, because they were tainted with violence. I make this as a definite statement and I will provide the Court with proof of my assertions.

First of all, I will show that the pressure was premeditated by the Germans. The pressure under which the foreign workers suffered was not the result of sporadic action on the part of subordinate authorities. It came from the deliberate intent, which the National Socialist leaders of Germany formulated into precise instructions.

I submit to the Tribunal Document 1183, which is the Exhibit RF 26; this is a directive dated 29th January, 1942, dealing with the recruiting of foreign workers. This directive comes from a section of the Arbeitseinsatz of the Commissariat for the Four Year Plan. It bears the signature of the Section Chief, Dr. Mansfeld, but it places the executive responsibility directly on the defendant Goering, the Trustee for the Four Year Plan. I read this circular:

"Berlin, S.W. 11, 29th January, 1942.
Saarlandstr. 96.
Subject: Increased mobilisation of manpower for the German Reich from the occupied territories and preparations for mobilisation by force.
The labour shortage which was rendered more acute by the draft for the

Wehrmacht and, on the other hand, the increased scope of the armament problem in the German Reich, render it necessary that manpower for service in the Reich be recruited from the occupied territories to a much greater extent than heretofore, in order to relieve the shortage of labour.

Therefore, any and all methods must be adopted which make possible the transportation, without exception and delay, for employment in the Reich of manpower in the occupied territories which is unemployed, or which can be replaced for use in Germany after most careful screening."

I read further on Page 2 of the German text:

"This mobilisation shall as heretofore be carried out on a voluntary basis. For this reason the recruiting effort for employment in the German Reich must be strengthened considerably, but, if satisfactory results are to be obtained, the German authorities who are functioning in the occupied territories must be able to exert any pressure necessary to support the voluntary recruiting of labour for employment in Germany.

Accordingly, to the extent that that may be necessary, the regulations in force in the occupied territories in regard to shifting employment, or concerning the ill will of those refusing work, must be tightened. Supplementary regulations concerning distribution of labour must above all insure that older personnel who are exempt will be exchanged for younger personnel, so that the latter may be made available for the Reich. A far-reaching decrease in the amount of relief granted by public welfare must also be effected, in order to induce labourers to accept employment in the Reich. Unemployment relief must be set so low that the amount in comparison with the average wages in the Reich, and the possibilities there for sending remittances home, may serve as an inducement to the workers to accept employment in Germany. When refusal to accept work in the Reich is not justified, the compensation must be reduced to an amount barely enough for subsistence, or even be cancelled. In this case partial withdrawal of ration cards and an assignment to particularly heavy, obligatory labour may be considered."

I here end the quotation, and. I call to the Tribunal's attention that this circular is addressed to all the services responsible for labour in the occupied areas. Its distribution in Western Europe was: the Reich Commissar for the occupied Norwegian Territories, the Reich Commissar for the occupied Dutch territories, the Chief of the Military Administration of Belgium and Northern France, the Chief of the Military Administration of France, the Chief of the Civilian Administration of Luxembourg, the Chief of the Civilian Administration at Metz, and the Chief of the Civilian Administration at Strasbourg.

It is thus proved that a general common plan existed with a view to compelling the workers of the occupied territories to work for Germany.

I have now to show how this plan was put into practice in the different occupation zones. The machinery of pressure which the National Socialist authorities exerted on the foreign workers can be analysed in the following manner: German labour offices organised intense propaganda in favour of the recruitment of foreign workers. This propaganda was intended to deceive the workers of the occupied areas with regard to the material advantage offered them by the German employment courts. It was carried out by the Press, the radio, and by every possible means of publicity.

It was also carried on as a side-line to official administrative duties by secret organisations which had been given the task of enticing foreign workers and thereby exercising illegal pressure.

These measures proved themselves to be insufficient. The occupation authorities then intervened in the social life of the occupied countries: they strove to produce artificial unemployment there, and at the same time they devoted their energies to making living conditions worse for the workers and the unemployed.

In spite of unemployment and the poverty with which they were threatened, the foreign workers showed themselves insensible to German propaganda. This is why the German authorities finally resorted to direct methods of pressure. They exercised pressure on the political authorities of the occupied countries to make them give support to the recruiting campaign. They compelled employers, especially the organisational committees in France, to encourage their workers to accept the labour contracts of the German employment offices. Finally, they took action by way of direct pressure on the workers, and gradually passed from so- called voluntary recruitment to compulsory enrolment.

The fiction of voluntary enrolment was dispelled when the people saw the individual arrests and collective raids of which the workers of the occupied areas rapidly became the victims.

There are innumerable documents capable of providing proof of the facts which I relate. I shall submit the most important of these to the Tribunal.

The documents which bring the proof of the publicity campaigns made in France by the German administration will be submitted to the Tribunal by Mr. Edgar Faure in the course of his brief on Germanisation and Nazification. By way of example I wish to draw upon a document which in the French classification bears the No. RF-516 and which I submit as Exhibit RF 27.

This is a report of the Prefect of the Department of the Nord to the Delegate of the Minister of the Interior in the General Delegation of the French Government in the occupied territories. This report points out that a German publicity car tours through the community of Lille in order to lure French workers to go to Germany. I quote the report:

"Lille, 25th March, 1942. Prefect of the Nord, Prefect of the Lille Region, to the Prefect, Delegate of the Minister of the Interior with the General Delegation of the French Government in the occupied territories.

Subject: German publicity car.

I have the honour of advising you that for some days a publicity car covered with posters urging French workers to sign up and go and work in Germany has been touring in the Lille area, while a loud speaker plays a whole repertoire of discs of French music, among which are featured the 'Marche Lorraine,' and the song 'Marchal, nous voila.'"

This is the end of my quotation.

THE PRESIDENT: I think we will adjourn until 2 o'clock.

(A recess was taken.)

M. HERZOG: Mr. President, your Honours. I wish this morning to show what the official propaganda was which was given out by the German offices in France in order to persuade volunteers to work in Germany. The effect of this official propaganda was reinforced by the clandestine bureaux of recruitment. Offices for clandestine recruiting were organised by the occupation authorities, apart from the administrative services, whose activities they completed. These employments bureaus were directed by German agents who often succeeded in acquiring local accomplices. In France these bureaus extended their ramifications in the non- occupied as well as in the occupied zone. Several documents attest to their existence. The first among them is a report transmitted on 7th March, 1942, by the Vice-President of the

Council of Ministers of the de facto Government of Vichy, to the General Delegate for Franco-German Economic Relations. It is Document 654 of the French archives.

This report is drawn up under the seal of Vice-President of the Council Darlan. It bears the signature of an officer of the latter's General Staff, Commander de Fontaine. I file this report as Exhibit RF 28 and I read it:

> "Vichy, 7th March, 1942. Your Honour, the General Delegate, I have the honour of transmitting to you in this letter, for your information, a report on the organisation of recruitment in France of workers for the German industry."

I now go to Page 2:

> "26th of February, 1942. Secret note on the organisation of the recruitment in France of workers for German industry. Excellent source: 1.Organisation of the recruitment of workers in France. One of the main organisations for the recruitment of workers in France for Germany was the Mechanical Society of the Seine, whose seat is in Puteaux, Seine, at 8 Quai Nationale, which was also known as A.M.S.
>
> This society was to function under the secret control of the Kommandantur, and of three engineers; one would have the capacity of chief engineer and the other two would be M. Meyer and M. Schronner. In addition to the work which it was to carry out, this society is particularly entrusted with the re-education of workers recruited in France and sent to Germany at the request of German industrial houses on premium payments. The A.M.S. society is assisted in these operations in the occupied zone by three centres of recruiting which function in Paris and are: the centre of Porte De Vincennes, the centre of Courbevoie, 200 Boulevard St. Denis and the centre of Avenue des Tourelles. These centres are also charged to co-operate with the operations of recruitment in the non-occupied zone. For this zone, the two principal centres are in Marseilles and Toulouse. A third centre will be at Tarbes.
>
>> (a) The centre at Marseilles is entrusted with the recruitment in the Mediterranean zone, under the direction of M. Meyer, who is mentioned above. The address of this engineer is not known, but one can get information about him in No. 24 Avenue Kleber, Paris, at the Militarbefehlshaber's.
>
> At Marseilles the A.M.S. office is situated at 85 Rue de Silvabelle. In his task M. Meyer is assisted by M. Ringo, residing in Madrague-Ville, 5 bis Boulevard Bernabo, near the slaughter house."

I here end my quotation. I submit to the Tribunal the correspondence exchanged between the months of December, 1941, and January, 1942, between the Prefect of the Alpes Maritimes and the authorities of the Vichy Government. This is Document 528,, which I file with the Tribunal as Exhibit RF 29. This correspondence emphasises the activity of the German agents in the clandestine recruiting, and particularly of M. Meyer, to whom the report of Commander Fontaine, which I just read, applies. I quote first the letter of the 10th December, 1941, in which the Prefect of the Alpes Maritimes confirmed the report which he had previously made on this question. It is the letter which is on the 5th page of the French text and the 7th page of the German text:

> "Nice, 10th December, 1941: The State Counsellor, Prefect of the Alpes Maritimes, to his Honour, the State Secretary of the Interior, General Secretariat of the Police Directorate for Home and Foreign Police. Object: The activity of foreign agents, attending to the enticing away of specialised

workers.

Reference: Your telegrams 12,402, and 12,426, of 28th November, 1941. My reports 955 and 986 of 24th November, 1941, and the 6th December, 1941. In my reports referred to I pointed out to you the activity of recruiting agents, who sought to have specialised workers discharged for the benefit of Germany.

I have the honour of giving you, below, some additional information gathered on this subject.

The German engineer Meyer and the French subject, M. Bentz, stopped on the 1st December, 1941, at the Hotel Splendid in Nice, coming from Marseilles."

Now, I go to the third paragraph before the end:

"I permit myself to draw your attention particularly to the fact that in Paris they hired workers to be sent to Germany."

Here I end the quotation.

These documents attest to the activity which the clandestine recruiting offices developed. I am not satisfied merely to point out their existence. I wish to show that these offices functioned under the initiative of the official administration and of the German Office for Labour.

The proof is furnished by a statement which the defendant Sauckel made on the first of March 1944, during the 54th conference of the central office for the Four Year Plan. The stenographic transcript of these conferences has been found. It forms Document R-124, to which my American colleagues have already referred. I submit it again to the Tribunal as Exhibit RF 30, and I shall read from an extract of the transcript of the session of the 1st March, 1944. This is Exhibit RF 30, in the French text, Page 2, second paragraph; in the German text, Pages 1770 and 1771. I quote the page numbers which are at the bottom and on the right of the German original. I read:

"The most abominable thing done by my adversaries" - this is a declaration of the defendant Sauckel - "is that they pretend that no executive measure has been foreseen in these sectors to recruit in a rational manner the French, the Belgians, and the Italians, and to send them to work. I therefore had begun to employ and train a whole group of French male and female agents who, for adequate remuneration, just as it was done in older times in Shanghai, would hunt for men, using liquor and persuasion...."

THE PRESIDENT: I am told that this has been read before by the Prosecutor of the United States.

M. HERZOG: I will not insist on it, Mr. President. I go on:

The propaganda of the official offices and that of the clandestine recruiting offices proved to be inefficacious. The National Socialist authorities then had to resort to methods of economic pressure. They tried to give to the workers, who were to go to Germany, the hope of material advantages. I cite in this respect an ordinance of the General Military Commandant in Belgium and in the North of France, which I submit to the Tribunal. It is an ordinance of 20th July, 1942, which appeared in the "Verordnungsblatt" of Belgium. It exempts from tax Belgian workers who work in German factories. I submit it to the Tribunal as Exhibit RF 31.

On the other hand, the occupation authorities sought to lower the living standard of workers who remained in the occupied territories. I said that they had made poverty a factor in their recruiting policy. I am going to prove it by showing how they went about creating artificial unemployment in the occupation zones and deteriorating the material situation of the unemployed.

I wish to recall that the German authorities also practised a policy of freezing salaries. This measure aided the recruiting campaign for labour to go to Germany and had also an economic bearing, and I would like to refer the Tribunal to the explanations which will be given it on this point by M. Gerthoffer.

Unemployment was produced by two complementary measures:

The first was the regulation of the legal length of work;

The second was the concentration and, if need be, the closing of industrial enterprises.

From 1940 the local Feldkommandanten concerned themselves with increasing the duration of work in their administrative zones. In France, initiative taken by the local authorities brought about reactions. The problem became general and was solved on a national plane. Long negotiations were imposed on the representatives of the pseudo-Government of Vichy.

Finally an ordinance of 22nd April, 1942, from the military command in France, reserved for the occupation authorities the right of fixing the duration of work in industrial enterprises. This ordinance appeared in their Verordnungsblatt for France, 1942. I submit it to the Tribunal as Exhibit RF 32 and I quote the first paragraph. First part:

> "For establishments and enterprises of all kinds, a minimum of working hours may be imposed. This minimum of the length of work will be decreed for a whole economic region, or for certain economic fields, or for individual enterprises."

In Belgium the length of work was fixed by an ordinance, by a directive, on the 6th October, 1942, which appeared in the "Verordnungsblatt" of Belgium. I submit this ordinance to the Tribunal as Exhibit RF 33. The regulation of the duration of work had not released a sufficient number of workers for the German factories; that is why the National Socialist authorities used a second method: under the pretext of rationalising production, they brought about a concentration of industrial and commercial enterprises, certain of which were closed at their instigation.

I cite in this relation the provisions which were taken or imposed by the Germans in France, in Belgium and in Holland. In France I would like to refer to two texts:

The first is the law of the Vichy Government of 17th December, 1941, which I submit to the Tribunal as Exhibit RF 34;

The second text to which I wish to draw the attention of the Tribunal is the ordinance of 25th February, 1942, issued by the Military Commandant in France. This ordinance appeared in the "Verordnungsblatt des Militarbefehlshabers" in France. I shall read from it to the Tribunal, because this ordinance seems particularly important, as the principle of compulsorily closing certain French enterprises is established by a legislative text of the occupying power. I shall read the first and second paragraphs. The first paragraph:

> "If the economic situation, notably the use of raw materials and secondary materials requires it, establishments and economic enterprises may be partly or completely closed."

Second paragraph:

> "The closing of these enterprises will be pronounced by the Feldkommandantur by means of a written notification addressed to the establishment or to the industrial enterprise."

THE PRESIDENT: That was Exhibit RF 35, was it not?

M. HERZOG: Yes, Mr. President.

In Belgium I refer to the ordinance of the Military Commandant, 30th March and 3rd October, 1942, which appeared in the "Verordnungsblatt" in Belgium. I submit to the Tribunal the ordinance of 30th March as Exhibit RF 36.

In Holland the regulating provisions of the occupying authorities were more stringent than elsewhere. I present an ordinance of the Reich Commissar for the territories of occupied Holland, 15th March, 1943.submit it to the Tribunal as Exhibit RF 37.

This ordinance presents a double interest: First it offers precise information which emphasises the method with which the German services executed their recruiting plan. It constitutes, on the other hand, the first document which I shall submit to the Tribunal, accusing the defendant Seyss- Inquart. The policy of Sauckel was carried out in Holland with the collaboration of Reich Commissar Seyss-Inquart. The ordinances regarding compulsory labour in Holland were all issued at the responsibility of Seyss-Inquart, whether they bear, directly or not, his signature. I ask the Tribunal to note this.

The increase of the legal length of work and the closing of industrial enterprises deprived thousands of workers of their jobs. The defendants did not hesitate to use material constraint to incite the unemployed to work on behalf of Germany. They threatened the unemployed that they would do away with their unemployment compensation. This threat was made on several occasions by the local Feldkommandants in Occupied France. I find proof in the protest made 8th March, 1941, by General Doyen, representing the French authorities with the German armistice commission. The document is 282, which I submit to the Tribunal as Exhibit RF 38.

I read the first page, third paragraph of the letter:

> "Moreover, the occupation authorities foresee that the workers who refuse the work offered them will see their right to unemployment compensation denied, and may be prosecuted by the war tribunal for sabotage of Franco- German collaboration."

Far from disavowing the initiative of their local authorities, the central office for labour gave them instructions to continue this policy. The proof is furnished by the directive of Dr. Mansfeld, dated 29th January, 1942, which I have just submitted to the Tribunal as Exhibit RF 26, in which instructions were given that the discontinuation of unemployment compensation should be utilised as a means of pressure against workers in foreign countries. The directive of Dr. Mansfeld shows that the blackmail by the National Socialist leaders was exercised not only over the control of unemployment compensation, but also in the issuing of ration cards.

Moreover, the defendants tried to force the inhabitants of the occupied territories to leave for Germany by increasing their difficulties in finding food. The proof of this desire is given in the transcript of the session of 1st March, 1944, of the Conference of the Four Year Plan. This document I referred to a short time ago as Exhibit RF 30. This is a passage which has not yet been read, which the Tribunal will please permit me to read. It is on Page 5 of the French translation.

THE PRESIDENT: Exhibit RF 30?

M. HERZOG: Yes, Pages 1814, 1815 and 1816 of the German text. The page numbers are at the bottom and on the right. I read on top of Page 5 of the French text. It should be Milch. It is General Milch.

> "Milch: 'Would not the following method be better? The German administration should concern itself with the feeding of Italians and say to them: " No one shall receive food unless he works in a protected factory or leaves for Germany.'"
>
> Sauckel: 'It is true that the French workman in France is better fed than the

German workman. The Italian workman, even if he does not work at all, is better fed in the part of Italy which we occupy than if he worked in Germany.'"

I end the quotation here.

I have shown the Tribunal that these measures were measures of an economic order - economic-social - which the National Socialist authorities took, to force workers in the occupied territory to accept labour contracts offered by the German authorities.

This indirect duress was strengthened by direct pressure which was simultaneously put on the local governments and the employers and on the workers themselves.

The National Socialist leaders knew that their recruiting policy could be facilitated by the local authorities. That is why they tried to make the pseudo-governments of the occupied territories guarantee or endorse the fiction of voluntary enrolments. I submit to the Tribunal an example of the pressure which the German Services placed on the Vichy Government for that purpose. They first arranged that the State Secretariat of Labour should issue a directive to all Prefects. It is the directive of 29th March, 1941. The German authorities were not satisfied with this directive; they were conscious of the illegality of their recruiting methods and they wished to justify them by an agreement with the de facto government of France. They required that this agreement be made known by public statement. The negotiations were carried out for this purpose in 1941 and 1942. The violence of the German pressure is substantiated by the letters concerning it addressed by Dr. Michel of the Administrative Staff to the General Delegate for Franco- German Economic Relations.

I refer especially to his letters of 3rd March, 1942, and 15th May, 1942, which constitute Exhibits RF 39 and 40. I read first to the Tribunal the letter of 15th May, which is RF 40:

"Paris, 15th May, 1942.

Purpose: The Recruiting of French Labour for Germany.

As the result of the conversations of 24th January, 1942, and after repeated appeals, the first draft of declarations of the French Government concerning recruiting was presented on the 27th; on the German side it was accepted with slight modifications and in written form on 3rd March, on the condition that attention should be directed, at the time of its transmission to the organisational committees, to the fact that the French Government approved expressly the acceptance of labour in Germany.

On 19th March it was recalled that a draft for a memorandum to the organisation committees should be submitted. The draft was afterwards submitted on 27th March. On the 30th March a proposal for modification was delivered to M. Terray, who should take it up with M. Bichelonne."

I omit the two following paragraphs, and I will read the last paragraph:

"Although no reason appears which explains the unaccustomed and incomprehensible delay, the draft was not presented until this day. More than two months having passed since the first request for the presentation of the memorandum, it is requested that this document be edited anew and presented on 19th May.

For the Military Commandant, Chief of the Administrative Staff.

Signed: Michel."

The Tribunal undoubtedly has observed that Dr. Michel demanded not only the circulation of a public declaration, but also required that the text of this statement be officially transmitted to the organisational committees. The pressure which occupation authorities put upon French industrial enterprises, to stimulate them to facilitate the departure of their workers to Germany, was brought about in fact through the medium of the organisational committees. The German offices for labour acted directly upon the organisational committees. They ordered conferences, in the course of which they dictated their will to the leaders of these committees. They also required that the organisational committees be informed of all the measures which the French authorities were led to take.

The committees might then be associated with these measures in the interests of German policy. The correspondence of Dr. Michel offers numerous examples of the constant efforts of the German authorities to act upon the organisational committees.

I have just offered an example of this to the Tribunal in the document which I read. I now offer another one. In 1941 the Germans requested especially that circulars, especially the directive of 29th March, 1942, addressed to the Prefects, regarding the recruiting of labourers for Germany, should be officially transmitted to the organisational committees. The occupation authorities obtained satisfaction through a circular of 25th April, which I submit to the Tribunal as Exhibit RF 41.

But the terms of this circular did not receive the approval of the German authorities, and on 28th May, 1941, Dr. Michel protested in violent terms to the General Delegate for Franco-German Economic Relations. This protest constitutes Document 522 in the French Archives. I submit it to the Tribunal as Exhibit RF 42, and I shall read:

"Paris, 28th May, 1941.

Purpose: Recruiting of Workers for Germany.

Reference: Your letter No. 192 of 29th April, 1941.

From your explanations I gather that even before my letter of the 23rd April was received, a circular for the organisational committees had been drafted and sent on 25th April.

This circular, nevertheless, does not seem to me adequate to support, in an efficacious manner, the recruiting of workers carried out by Germany. That is why I consider that it is necessary that, in another directive, attention may be drawn to the points which were particularly mentioned by me on 23rd April, and request that you submit to me as soon as possible the appropriate draft.

On the German side an impressive contribution toward the creating of a favourable atmosphere has been made by means of the intended release of an additional large number of prisoners of war, which was considered by you at the time of our conversation of 24th May as a necessary condition for the success of a reinforced recruiting of workers for Germany.

I therefore am probably not wrong in expecting that you will send to the economic organisations a communication so designed that the attitude of waiting, maintained by French economy up to now, will develop also, in the field of the release of labour, into a constructive co- operation. I then expect that you will submit to me your proposals with all possible promptness."

And, finally, the German Services placed direct pressure upon the workers themselves.

THE PRESIDENT: Are you reading from the document now?

M. HERZOG: No. I am resuming the text of the brief.

Moral pressure at first, the "operation de la releve" (prisoner exchange plan), tried in France in the Spring of 1942, is characteristic. The occupation authorities promised to compensate for the sending of French workers to Germany by a liberation of prisoners of war. The return of a prisoner was to take place upon the departure of a worker. This promise was fallacious, and reality was quite different.

I quote in this connection the report on compulsory labour and the deportation of workers, which I submitted this morning to the Tribunal as Exhibit RF 42.

I quote Page 51, both in the French original and in the German translation. In the French original it is the third paragraph of Page 51 and in the German translation the first paragraph:

> "If the Press, inspired by the occupying power, pretends in its commentaries to applaud the replacement plan of one prisoner for one worker, it is undoubtedly done upon order and based on calculation. Also this is the case, it seems, because until 20th June, 1942, two days before the speech cited before" - it was a speech of the chief of the de facto government of France - "it was indeed this proportion which the Germans Michel and Ritter had pretended to accept in their reports to the French administrative services.
>
> The proportion, in fact, of one to five, appears to have been a last minute surprise of which the Press never spoke."

Here I end my quotation.

The pressure of which foreign workers were the victims was also a material pressure. I said that the fiction of voluntary enrolment could not hold water in view of the arrests. I wish to submit a document to the Tribunal which furnished a characteristic example of the German mentality and of the methods utilised by the National Socialist administrations. This is a document which in the French Archives is No. 527, which I submit to the Tribunal as Exhibit RF 43. This is a letter from the delegate of the Reich Labour Minister in the French department of Pas de Calais. This official enjoins a young French workman to depart for Germany as a free agent, under threat of unfavourable consequences. I read the document; this is Exhibit RF 43, third page:

> "Sir:
>
> The 26th of March last, in Marquise, I ordered, you to go to work in Germany in your profession. You were to leave with the convoy of the 1st of April for Germany. You took no notice of this summons. I warn you that you must present yourself, furnished with your baggage, next Monday, 28th April, before 19.00 hours, at 51, Rue de la Pomme d'Or in Calais. I call your attention to the fact that you leave for Germany as a free worker, that you will work there under the same conditions, and that you will earn there the same wages as German workers.
>
> In the event of your not presenting yourself, I must tell you that unfavourable consequences may very well follow.
>
> Delegate for the Labour Ministry of the Reich:
>
> Signed: Hannerann."

The proof of the constraint which the German authorities exercised on the workers of the occupied territories, to bring about their allegedly voluntary enrolment, may be continued. The National Socialist authorities did not merely impose labour contracts tainted with violence on foreign workers. They themselves deliberately failed to honour these contracts.

I find proof of this in the fact that they unilaterally prolonged the duration of the enrolments made by foreign workers. This proof is based on several documents. Some ordinances were issued by the defendant Goering in his capacity as Delegate for the Four Year Plan, others by the defendant Sauckel.

I now call the attention of the Tribunal to an order of Sauckel's, dated 22nd

March, 1943, which I submit to the Tribunal as Exhibit RF 44. It is an extract from the volume of decrees, Vol. V, Page 203:

"Extension of work contracts, fixed for a period of time, of foreign workers, who during the time of their contract have absented themselves from their work without proper excuse.

The General Plenipotentiary for Employment of Labour decrees: 'The regular carrying out of the clauses of a contract for a fixed period of time, concluded by a foreign worker, necessitates that the worker should put all his energy at the disposal of the enterprise for the whole duration of the contract.

Nevertheless, it happens that foreign workers, as the result of slackness, delay in their return to work from visits to their homes' - and I draw the Tribunal's attention to the following words - 'serving of prison terms, internment in a camp of correction ...'"

THE PRESIDENT: Will you read that again?

M. HERZOG:

"The regular carrying out of the clauses of a contract for a fixed period of time concluded by a foreign worker, necessitates that the worker should put all his energy at the disposal of the enterprise for the whole duration of the contract. Nevertheless, it happens that foreign workers as a result of idleness, delay in their return to work from visits to their homes, serving of prison terms, internment in a camp of correction, or for other reasons, remain absent from their work without just cause, for a longer or shorter period of time. In such cases the foreign workers cannot be authorised to return to their country when the period of time, for which they agreed to work voluntarily in Germany, has elapsed.

Such a procedure would not correspond to the spirit of a work contract for a fixed period of time, whose object is not only the presence of the foreign worker, but also the work accomplished by him."

Kept by force in the German factories which they had entered under force, the foreign workers were neither voluntary nor free workers. The expose of the methods of German recruiting will suffice to show the Tribunal the fictitious character of the voluntary enrolment, on which it was supposed to be based. The foreign workers who agreed to work in the factories of the National Socialist war industry did not act through free will. Their number, however, remained limited. The workers of the occupied territories had the physical courage, the ethical courage, to resist German pressure. This is proved in an admission of the defendant Sauckel, which I take from the minutes of the meeting of 3rd March, 1944, of the conference of the Four Year Plan.

This is from an extract which has already been read by my American colleague, Mr. Dodd, so I will not read it again to the Tribunal. I merely wish to recall that the defendant Sauckel admitted that, out of five million foreign workers who came to Germany, there were not even two hundred thousand who came voluntarily. The resistance of the foreign workers surprised the defendant Sauckel as much as it irritated him. One day he expressed his surprise to a German general, who replied:

"Our difficulties come from the fact that you address yourself to patriots who do not share our ideals."

Indeed, only force could constrain the patriots of the occupied territories to work on behalf of the enemy. The National Socialist authorities resorted to force.

The Germans had, from the first, the possibility of imposing their policy of force on that kind of labour whose particular status guaranteed recruitment and apparent submission: the prisoners of war.

From 1940 on, the German military authorities organised labour Commandos in prison camps. They constantly increased the importance of these Commandos, who were put at the disposal of agricultural economy and the war industry.

The importance of the work required from war prisoners is substantiated by the Report on Forced Labour and the Deportation of Workers which I have filed with the Tribunal as Exhibit RF 22. We find on Page 68 of the French and German texts the following estimates:

There were, at the end of 1942, 1,036,319 French prisoners of war in Germany, 987,687 had been assigned to the work Commandos. Only the surplus, that is, 48,632 prisoners, remained unemployed.

The utilisation of prisoners of war in German factories does not constitute a distinct phenomenon which can be disassociated from the general plan for the recruiting of foreign workers; it is, on the contrary, an integral part of this plan.

The National Socialists have always considered that the obligation to work applied as much to war prisoners as to the civilian workers of the occupied territories. They have on many occasions expressed such a belief. I refer especially to two documents.

The first is the decree of the appointment of the defendant Sauckel, which I have filed with the Tribunal at the beginning of my explanatory remarks.

The second document to which I wish to draw the attention of the Tribunal is the tenth decree of Sauckel, which I submitted sometime ago as Exhibit RF 17. This decree formulates the principle of the obligation to work and applies to war prisoners, according to the terms of its Article 8.

Finally, Sauckel had, in another document, affirmed that the prisoners of war were to be subject to work to the same degree as civilian workers. This is found in the letter which he wrote to the defendant Rosenberg on 24th April, 1942, some days after his appointment, to explain his project to the latter. This is Document 016-PS, which my American colleague, Mr. Dodd, has already submitted to the Tribunal. I present it as Exhibit RF 45. I shall not read from it, but I call to mind that on Page 11 of the German text the problem of compulsory labour is treated in the general heading, entitled: "Prisoners of War and Foreign Workers."

These documents bring a double proof to the Tribunal. First of all, they reveal the willingness of the National Socialists to force prisoners to work on behalf of the German war economy, within the general frame of their recruiting policy. In the second place, these documents establish that the utilisation of prisoners of war was not undertaken only by military authorities; this utilisation was ordered and systematised by a civilian organisation, that of the Arbeitseinsatz. As well as the responsibility of the defendants Sauckel and Keitel, it entails also that of the German leaders who conducted the labour policy: the defendant Sauckel, the defendant Speer, and the defendant Goering.

The Tribunal knows that International Law regulates the conditions under which prisoners of war may be forced to work. The Hague Conventions formulated rules which were clarified by the Geneva Convention in Articles 27, 31 and 32:

> "ARTICLE 27:- Belligerents may use as workers healthy war prisoners, according to their rank and their attitudes, with the exception of officers and assimilated ranks. Nevertheless, if officers, or those of assimilated rank, ask for suitable work, it will be procured for them as far as possible. The non-commissioned officers who are war prisoners can be forced to work as supervisors only if they expressly request a remunerative occupation.
>
> ARTICLE 31:- The work furnished by the prisoners of war -"

THE PRESIDENT: I think we will take judicial notice of these Articles.

M. HERZOG: These rules of International Law determine positively the legal powers of the nation having prisoners of war in its custody. It is legal to force prisoners of war to work during the duration of their captivity, but this includes three legal limits:

(1) It is forbidden to require non-commissioned officers, who are prisoners, to work, unless they have expressly requested to do so.

(2) War prisoners must not be used for work which is dangerous.

(3) Prisoners must not be associated with the enemy war effort.

The National Socialist authorities systematically neglected these imperative provisions; they have exercised violent constraint on non-commissioned officers held in captivity, to force them to join labour crews. They have integrated war prisoners as workers in their factories and in the work yards, without considering the nature of the work imposed upon them. The utilisation of war prisoners by National Socialist Germany took place under illegal and criminal conditions. This I declare, and I wish to prove this to the Tribunal.

THE PRESIDENT: We will take a recess for 10 minutes.

(A recess was taken.)

M. HERZOG: Mr. President, your Honours.

Dating from 1941, the Germans exercised direct pressure on non-commissioned officers to force them to engage in productive work for the Reich war economy. This pressure, after the failure of propaganda methods, took the form of reprisals. Non-commissioned officers who refused were the object of ill-treatment; they were sent to special camps, such as Coberczyn where they were subject to a disciplinary regime. Some incurred penal sentences because of their refusal to work. I file, as proof, the report of the Ministry of Prisoners, Deportees, and Refugees of the French Government, Document UK-78-2, which is, in my document book, RF 46. The document is in a white file. I shall read from Page 18 of the French original, Page 10 of the German translation, Page 18, at the bottom of the page:

"Work of the Non-Commissioned Officers.

On this subject the Geneva Convention was explicit: non-commissioned officers who are war prisoners cannot be subjected to work as supervisors, unless they make an express request for a remunerative occupation.

In conformity with this article a certain number of non-commissioned officers refused to work from the beginning of their captivity. The strength of imprisoned non-commissioned officers was, at the end of 1940, about 130,000, and represented later a very important source of labour for the Reich. The German authorities tried, therefore, by every means, to induce to work the greatest possible number of those refusing. To this effect, during the last months of 1941, the non-commissioned officers who did not volunteer for the work were, in most camps, subjected to an alternating regime. For a few days they were subjected to punishments such as the diminution of food rations, doing without beds, the obligation to undergo physical exercises for a number of hours, and particularly the 'pelote' (punishment drill). During another period they were promised work, in conformity with their wishes, and other material advantages, for example, special regulations of insurance, extra letter provisions and higher wages. These methods led a certain number of non-commissioned officers to accept work. The non-commissioned officers who persisted in their refusal to work, were subjected to a very severe disciplinary regime and to arduous physical exercises."

The National Socialist military authorities utilised the prisoners of war for dangerous work. The French, British, Belgian and Dutch prisoners were used to transport munitions, to load bombs or planes, to repair aviation camps, and to construct fortifications. The proof of the use of prisoners of war for the transportation of munitions and for the loading of bombs on planes, is furnished by the affidavits of repatriated French prisoners of war. These affidavits have been assembled in the report of the Ministry of Prisoners, which I have just quoted, and which I shall quote again.

I now quote Page 27 of the French document, Page 14 of the German translation. It is the same document from which I have just quoted, Exhibit RF 46, Page 27:

> "(b) The requisition of prisoners for the construction of fortifications and for the transport of munitions, occurs very often in the close vicinity of the line of fire.
>
> The war prisoners, Command 274 of Stalag 2-B, complained, December, 1944, of being employed on Sundays in the construction of anti-tank trenches.
>
> On 2nd February, 1945, the prisoners of Stalag 2-B, evacuated before the advance of the Russian Army, worked, as soon as they arrived at Sassnity, at fortification works and anti-tank works, in particular around the city.
>
> After falling back from Stalag 3-B, the war prisoners were engaged, to the end of April, in doing ditch work, digging trenches, and in transporting aviation bombs.
>
> Kommando 553 at Lebus was obliged to carry out work in the front lines under the fire of Russian artillery.
>
> Numerous comrades, drawn back at Furstenwalde, were employed in loading bombs on German bombers.
>
> In spite of their protests to the International Committee of the Red Cross in Geneva and to the colonel commanding Stalag 3-B, about billeting in barns, very bad hygiene and insufficient food, the latter answered that he was obeying superior orders of the O.K.W., ordering the prisoners to dig trenches."

The National Socialist leaders, for that matter, admitted that they used French and British prisoners of war for military work on aerodromes exposed to allied bombardment.

I offer in proof two notes, the first addressed by the O.K.H. to the War Prisoners Section of the Wehrmacht, and the second by Wilhelmstrasse to the German representative at the Wiesbaden Armistice Commission.

The memorandum of the O.K.H., dated 7th October, 1940, constitutes Document 549. I submit it to the Tribunal as Exhibit RF 47, and I read it in full:

> "The protest of the French delegation shall be considered unfounded. The lodging of war prisoners in camps situated in the vicinity of aviation fields is not in contradiction to the rules of the rights of nations.
>
> According to Articles 9 and 4 of the Convention on the Treatment of War Prisoners - of 27th July, 1929 - no prisoners of war shall be exposed to the fire of a combat zone. Combat zones in this sense must be understood as the space in which normally a battle between two armies is carried on, thus extending to a distance of about 20 kilometres from the advance line. On the other hand it is possible that the areas exposed to aerial attacks do not belong to combat zones. At this period of air war there no longer exists any sure shelter. The fact of using war prisoners for the construction of a camp and for the repairing of

destroyed runways does not seem to lend itself to any controversy.

According to Article 31 of the Convention quoted here above, war prisoners must not be used in works directly related to war activity. The construction of shelters, houses, and camps is not directly a war act. It is recognised that war prisoners may be employed in the construction of roads. Accordingly their utilisation for the reconstruction of aviation camps that have been destroyed is permissible: on the roads, trucks, tanks, ammunition cars, etc. are driven, and on the aviation fields there are planes. It is all the same.

On the other hand, it would be illegal to use war prisoners in loading bombs, munitions, etc. on bombers. Here a work directly related to war activity would be involved.

By reason of the juridical situation expounded here above, the O.K.H. has rejected the idea of withdrawing French prisoners of war employed in work in the aviation camps."

I draw the attention of the Tribunal to this document. It emphasises the ill faith of the leaders of National Socialist Germany, which was two-fold: In the first place, the note of 7th October, 1940, which I have read, acknowledges that it is forbidden by International Law to use prisoners of war for the loading of bombs and ammunition on bombers. But I have just brought proof to the Tribunal that the French prisoners of war were used for this purpose. In the second place, the note of the O.K.H. contests the dangerous character of the work carried out on the aviation fields.

Now, the note of Wilhelmstrasse, to which I shall now refer, and which I submit to the Tribunal as Exhibit RF 48 - this note recognises, on the contrary, that prisoners submitted to work on an aviation field incur grave danger because of the military purpose of this work.

I will read to the Tribunal a note of the German Foreign Office dated 14th February, 1941, Exhibit RF 48:

"Article 87 of the Agreement of 1929 on Prisoners of War provides that, in case of difference of opinion on the subject of the interpretation of the Agreement, the protecting powers shall offer their services to settle the dispute. To accomplish this, any protecting power may propose a meeting of representatives of the belligerent powers. In the relation between Germany and France, protecting powers no longer exist. France herself assumes the responsibilities of a protecting power in questions on prisoners of war."

I shall pass on from this quotation to Page 2 of the same document:

"As to the point in dispute, it is well to call attention to the following:

The French conception, according to which prisoners of war may not be quartered near air fields and may not be employed in repairing plane runways, cannot be based on the exact content of Articles 9 and 31; but, on the other hand, it is certain that French prisoners of war quartered and employed under these conditions are in a particularly dangerous situation, because the air fields in occupied territories are used exclusively for German military purposes and thus constitute a special objective for enemy aerial attacks.

The American Embassy in Berlin has likewise made a protest against a similar use of British prisoners of war in Germany. Thus far no answer has been made, because a rejection of this protest might result in German prisoners being employed in similar work in England."

The utilisation of war prisoners for the construction of fortifications is substantiated by Document 828-PS, which I file with the Tribunal as Exhibit RF 49. It is a letter of 29th September, 1944, addressed by the Chief of the First Army Corps to the

O.K.W., to give an account of work on fortifications accomplished by eighty Belgian prisoners of war. I quote:

"According to the teletype referred to, it is reported that in the territory of Stalag 1-A, Stablack, Einsatzbereich 2-213, Tilsit-Loten, near Ragnitz, there are forty Belgian prisoners of war, and in Lindbach, near Neusiedel, forty Belgian prisoners of war who were employed in fortification labour."

There remains the task of proving that Allied prisoners, forced to work in Reich armament factories, were associated with the enemy war effort. To this end I first offer Document 1206-PS. This document is a memorandum dated 11th November, 1941. It is a resumé of a report made 7th November, 1941, to the Aviation Minister by the Reichsmarshal. The document, consequently, establishes the direct responsibility of the defendant Goering. The use of Russian war prisoners is treated in a general way in this document, but it deals also with the use of war prisoners of Western European countries. I submit this document to the Tribunal as Exhibit RF 50, and I read:

"Berlin, 11th November, 1941.

Notes on statements made by the Reichsmarshal in a meeting of 7th November, 1941, in the Reich Ministry of Air.

Subject: Employment of Russian labour in the war economy."

THE PRESIDENT: Has that already been put in by the United States?

M. HERZOG: Yes.

THE PRESIDENT: Then perhaps you could summarise it.

M. HERZOG: I think, Mr. President, that it was presented by the United States Prosecution. I shall, therefore, simply quote an extract, the fifth and sixth paragraphs of the first page, concerning the employment of French and Belgian war prisoners as individuals in the economy of armament. This use of war prisoners in the Reich munitions factories corresponded to a common plan. It is the result of a systematic policy. The administrative offices for labour deliberately assigned to armament factories all war prisoners who seemed capable of carrying out specialised work. I quote, in this connection, Document 3005-PS. It is a directive addressed, in 1941, by the Ministry of Labour to the Directors of Personnel Procurement concerning the respective use of French and Russian prisoners of war. The document has been submitted and commented upon by my American colleague, Mr. Dodd, shall, therefore, not read it. I simply point out that this circular deals with the employment of all French war prisoners in the armament factories of the Reich.

After the capitulation of Italy, Italian soldiers who had fallen into the hands of the Germans - they were not called prisoners of war, but rather "military internees" - were forced to work. I offer in this connection a directive of the defendant Bormann, of 28th September, 1943, Document 657- PS, which I submit to the Tribunal as Exhibit RV 52.

The Italian military internees are placed in three categories: some ask to continue the struggle on the side of the German Army; others desire to keep a neutral attitude; others have turned their arms against their former allies. The military internees of the second and third categories must, in the terms of the circular, be forced to work. I read:

"Circular No. 55/43 G.R.S., Top secret. Concerns the treatment and putting to work of Italian military internees.

The O.K.W., in connection with the General Plenipotentiary for the Employment of Labour, has regulated the treatment and the putting to work of Italian military internees. The most important general lines of the ordinances of the O.K.W. are the following."

I shall omit the rest of the first page and proceed to Page 2 of the French translation:

"The Italian internees who, when investigated, do not declare themselves ready to continue the struggle under German command, are put at the disposal of the General Plenipotentiary for the Employment of Labour who has already given the necessary instructions for their employment, to the Chiefs of the Regional Labour Offices.

It is to be noted that Italian military internees must not be utilised together with the British and American prisoners of war."

The prisoners of war offered passive resistance to German force. The National Socialist authorities intervened again and again, to attempt to increase their output. I refer to Document 233-PS, which I file with the Tribunal as Exhibit RF 53. It is a directive of the O.K.W. of 17th October, 1944. The purpose is to point out to the war prisoner bureaux, measures capable of increasing the productivity of the prisoners. I read from the document:

"Subject: Treatment of War Prisoners - Increase in Production.

The measures taken until now, in regard to the treatment of war prisoners and the increasing of their productivity, have not given the results that had been hoped for. The offices of the Party, and those of economy, continually complain of the poor labour output of all the war prisoners. Therefore the following directives for prisoners of war are made known, in agreement with all interested offices of the Party and State. Accordingly, all guard companies and their auxiliaries are to be given detailed instructions.

Collaboration with the bearers of sovereignty of the N.S.D.A.P. The co-operation of all officers in charge of war prisoners with the bearers of sovereignty of the Party must be strengthened to an even greater extent. To this end the commanders of the war-prisoner camps shall immediately detail, for all the Kreise in their command, an energetic officer acquainted with all questions concerning prisoners of war, to act as liaison officer to the Kreisleiter. This officer shall have the duty of treating in closest collaboration with the Kreisleiter, according to the instructions of the camp commander, all questions concerning prisoners of war which might become public knowledge. The aim of this collaboration should be:

(a) To increase the labour output of war prisoners;
(b) To solve all difficulties quickly and on the spot;
(c) To organise the employment of war prisoners in the Kreise in such a way that it fulfils the political, military and economic requirements.

The Chancellery of the Party will give the necessary orders to the Gauleiter and the Kreisleiter.

(2) Treatment of the prisoners of war. The treatment of prisoners of war shall be dictated within limits compatible with security, with the sole purpose of increasing, as far as possible, the labour output. In addition to just treatment, the providing of the prisoners with the food due to them according to stipulations, and with proper billets, the supervising of the labour output is necessary to achieve the highest possible results.

Available means must be employed with extreme rigour as regards the lazy and the rebellious."

I shall stop my quotation here. The resistance of war prisoners caused the German Labour Bureaux to use a subterfuge to force them to work. I refer to the operation called the transformation of war prisoners into free workers. It consisted in transforming prisoners of war into so-called free workers, to whom a labour contract was offered. The operation was perfected by the defendant Sauckel in the course of one of his trips to Paris on 9th April, 1943. To Germany it offered the advantage of permitting the use of transformed prisoners in armament factories, without directly violating the Geneva Convention. For the prisoners it presented only a seeming advantage, the decrease of the surveillance to which they were subject. In reality the length and the nature of the work imposed upon them was in no way changed; their housing conditions and the quality of their rations remained unchanged. Moreover, this operation, presented by German propaganda as a measure favourable to war prisoners, brought about a deterioration of their juridical status.

The prisoners of war were not fooled; in most cases they refused to cooperate with this German manoeuvre; some agreed to do it, but a number of these took advantage of the first leave granted them because of their change in status, and fled. The report of the Statistical Institute on Forced Labour which I submitted to the Tribunal this morning as Exhibit RF 22, gives in this connection the following information. I quote it, Page 70 of the French text, Page 70 of the German translation. I shall read the second paragraph:

"The transformation of prisoners into 'free' workers, which was realised or carried out as the second Sauckel act, and which, because of this fact, must be counted in the present list as dating from the 25th of April, 1942, was decided by Sauckel, in the course of a trip to Paris on 9th April, 1943, It was to involve, after the prisoner had signed his contract as a labourer, a leave to go to France - depending on the return of the men who had gone on leave before. Two attempts were made to carry out this plan. On the 24th of April, 1943, out of 1,000 on leave, 43 did not return. In the month of August following, 2,000 out of 8,000 did not return. A last appeal directed to them was published in the Press of 17th August without result. There is no third experiment, and the transformation in practice limited itself to the removal of sentinels and of camp guards, but did not change either the nature or the duration of the work, or the housing conditions or the rations. On the other hand, it entailed loss of rights to receive packages from the International Red Cross and loss of diplomatic protection for prisoners of war."

The forced utilisation of war prisoners did not permit the German authorities to solve the labour problem of the war economy. That is why they applied their policy of force to the civilian populations of the occupied territories.

The National Socialist authorities systematised their policy of force from 1942 on by establishing the Bureau of Compulsory Labour in the different occupied territories. From the end of 1941 it has been verified, that neither the recruiting of voluntary workers nor the utilisation of prisoners, permitted a solution of the problem of labour required for the war economy. The Germans then decided to proceed to the forced enrolment of civilian workers. They decreed a veritable civilian mobilisation, the execution of which characterises their criminal activity.

I refer to a directive of 29th January, 1942, given by Dr. Mansfeld under authorisation of the defendant Goering. I remind the Tribunal that I have filed this document already as Exhibit RF 26. I read the passage from the document where I stopped this morning, Page 2, last paragraph of the French translation, Page 2, last paragraph also of the German original:

"In order to avoid a damaging of the armament industry, all misgivings must yield to the necessity of filling in, at any rate, the gaps in the labour employment caused by extensive drafting into the Wehrmacht. To this end the forced mobilisation of workers from the occupied territories must not be neglected, if the voluntary recruitment remains unsuccessful. The mere factor of a compulsory mobilisation will, in many cases, make recruiting easier.

Therefore, I ask you to take immediate measures in your district to promote the employment of workers in the German Reich on a voluntary basis. I herewith request you to prepare for publication, regulations making possible the forced mobilisation of labour from your territory for Germany, so that they may be decreed at once in case recruiting on a voluntary basis remains without the success necessary to relieve labour employment in the Reich."

The appointment of the defendant Sauckel may be considered a preparatory measure for the establishment of the Bureau of Compulsory Labour. It was necessary that a central authority be set up in order to co-ordinate the activity of the different labour departments and in order to proceed to the mobilisation of civilian workers. The terms of the exposition of the motives of the decree of appointment are explicit: the mission of the Plenipotentiary for Labour consists in satisfying the labour needs of the German economy through the recruiting of foreign workers and the utilisation of war prisoners. The decree of Sauckel, dated 22nd August, 1942, which I have filed with the Tribunal as Exhibit RF 17, expresses, moreover, the will of the defendant to go about recruiting by means of coercion.

The institution of the office of compulsory labour represents deliberate violation of international conventions. The deportation of workers is forbidden by several contractual regulations which have the value of positive law. I shall quote, first of all, Article 52 of the Annex to the Fourth Convention of The Hague. I have already given a commentary on it to the Tribunal, to demonstrate that the requisitioning of labour effected by the authorities of the occupation was illegal.

All the more, the institution of compulsory labour was prohibited by Article 52, Compulsory labour was imposed upon foreign workers in the interest of the war economy; it was carried out in armament factories of National Socialist Germany; it deprived the occupied territories of labour necessary for the rational exploitation of their wealth, it therefore is not within the framework of that labour requisition which Article 52 of The Hague Convention authorises.

The prohibition of forced labour is, moreover, affirmed by another international convention. It is a question of the Convention of the 25th of September, 1926, on slavery, of which Germany is a signatory. This treaty makes forced labour equivalent to slavery, in its Article 5.ask the Tribunal to refer to it.

Deportation of workers is the object of a formal prohibition. Forced labour in German war factories was, therefore, instituted in flagrant violation of International Law and of all pledges subscribed to by Germany. The National Socialist authorities transgressed positive International Law; they likewise violated the rights of nations.

The latter guarantees individual liberty, on which the principle of forced recruitment is a characteristic attack.

The violation of treaties and contempt for the rights of individuals are the tenets of National Socialist doctrine. Therefore the defendants proceeded not merely to the mobilisation of foreign workers; they proclaimed the necessity and the legitimacy of forced labour. I shall, first of all, indicate to the Tribunal certain declarations made by the defendants which have the strength of confessions. I shall thereupon indicate how the occupation authorities introduced the service of compulsory work in the different occupied territories. I shall demonstrate, finally, that the Germans took measures of violent coercion in an attempt to assure the execution of the civilian mobilisation, which had been decreed.

The legitimacy of forced enrolment has been upheld by Hitler. The proof of this can be found in the report of the Four Year Plan Conference held on the 10th, 11th and 12th of August, 1942. It is contained in Document R-124, which I presented this morning as Exhibit RF 30.shall not read it to the Tribunal, because my American colleague, Mr. Dodd, has done so during his presentation on forced labour. I recall that the document to which I refer indicates that the Fuehrer agreed to exercise all the necessary constraint in the East as well as in the West, if the question of recruiting foreign labourers could not be regulated on a voluntary basis.

The necessity of the utilisation of compulsory labour was expressed in identical terms by certain of the defendants.

I shall not stress the numerous statements of the defendant Sauckel to which I have already drawn the attention of the Tribunal. The exposition of the motives of his decree of 22nd August, 1942, the programme included in his letter of 24th April, 1942, and the policy advocated in his speech at Posen in February, 1943, reproduce faithfully the determination of the defendant to justify the principle of forced recruiting. I shall not revert to this. I present to the Tribunal the declaration of the defendant Jodl. This declaration is an extract from a long speech made by Jodl on 7th November, 1943, at Munich, before an audience of Gauleiters. This speech is Document L-172. I offer it in evidence to the Tribunal as Exhibit RF 54.I shall read Page 2 of the French translation, second paragraph, Pages 38-39 of the German original:

"This dilemma of manpower shortage has led to the idea of making more thorough use of the manpower reserves in the territories occupied by us. Here, right thinking and wrong thinking are mixed up together. I believe that, in so far as it concerns labour, everything has been done that could be done; but where this is not yet the case, it appeared preferable, from the political point of view, not to have recourse to measures of compulsion, but rather to aim at order and economic relief. In my opinion, however, the time has now come to take steps with remorseless vigour and resolution in Denmark, Holland, France and Belgium, and also to compel thousands of idle persons to carry out the fortification work, which is more important than any other work. The necessary orders for this have already been given."

The German Labour Service had not waited for the appeal of General Jodl to decree the mobilisation of civilian foreign workers. I am going to show the Tribunal how the Bureau of Compulsory Labour was established and organised in France, in Norway, in Belgium, and in Holland.

I should like to remind the Tribunal that in Denmark there was never any legal regulation for forced labour, and that this was carried out as a simple de facto measure.

I also wish to remind the Tribunal that the Bureau of Forced Labour was introduced in a special form in Luxembourg and in the French departments of Alsace and Lorraine. The occupation authorities incorporated the citizens of Luxembourg and the French citizens residing in the departments of Bas-Rhin, Haut-Rhin and Moselle, in the Labour Service of the Reich. This incorporation was carried out by ordinances of Gauleiter Simon and Gauleiter Wagner. The ordinances constitute an integral part of the Germanisation plan for territories of Luxembourg, Alsace and Lorraine. Their consequences surpass those of the measures of forced enrolment which were taken in other occupied territories. That is why I refer the Tribunal, on this point, to the explanation which will be given in the prosecution brief of M. Edgar Faure.

Two German texts of a general nature serve as a foundation for the legislation on forced labour in the occupied territories of Western Europe.

The first is the decree of Sauckel of 22nd August, 1942, to which I have drawn the attention of the Tribunal on several occasions. This decree prescribes the mobilisation of all civilian workers in the service of the war economy. Article 2 - of which I remind the Tribunal - prescribes that this decree is applicable to occupied territories. This decree of 22nd August, 1942, thus constitutes the legal charter of the civilian mobilisation of foreign workers. This mobilisation was confirmed by an order of the Fuehrer of 8th September, 1942. It is Document 556-PS-2, which I file with the Tribunal as Exhibit RF 55, and from which I shall read:

"The Fuehrer and Supreme Commander of the Wehrmacht. General Headquarters of the Fuehrer, 8th September, 1942.

The extensive coastal fortification, which I have ordered to be erected in the area of Army Group West, makes it necessary that, in the occupied territory, all available workers work to the fullest extent of their production capacity. The previous allotment of labour for this work is absolutely insufficient. In order to increase it, I order the introduction of compulsory labour and the prohibition of changing the place of employment without permission of the authorities in the occupied territories.

Furthermore, in the future, the distribution of food and clothing ration cards to those subject to labour draft shall depend on the possession of a certificate of employment. Refusal to accept an assigned job, as well as abandoning the place of work without the consent of the authorities in charge, will result in the withdrawal of the food and clothing ration cards.

The G.B.A., that is, the office of the defendant Sauckel, in agreement with the military commander or the Reich Commissar, will issue the appropriate decrees for execution."

The forced enrolment of foreign workers was preceded by preliminary measures, to which the order of 8th September, 1942, which I just read, refers. I am speaking of the freezing of labour. To carry out the mobilisation of workers it was necessary that the public services exercise strict control over their use in the industrial enterprises of occupied territories. This control had a double purpose: it was to facilitate the census of workers suitable for work in Germany; and also to prevent workers from avoiding the German requisition by alleging a real or fictitious employment.

The National Socialist authorities exercised this control by restricting the liberty of hiring and of discharging, which they had given over to the authorities of the Labour Bureau.

In France, the freezing of labour was brought about by the law of 4th September, 1942.shall shortly expose to the Tribunal the conditions under which, this law was formulated. I shall, for the moment, simply supply it to the Tribunal as Exhibit RF 56 and ask the Tribunal to take judicial notice of it.

In Belgium the freezing of labour was carried out by the ordinance of the military commandant of the 6th of October, 1942.submit to the Tribunal Exhibit RF 57, of which I ask the Tribunal to take judicial notice.

Finally, in Holland, where the Bureau of Compulsory Labour was established early in 1941, an ordinance of the Reich Commissar dated 28th February, 1941, which I offer to the Tribunal as Exhibit RF 58, organised the freezing of labour.

The immobilisation of labour was brought about under an economic pretext in all countries. In reality it constituted a preliminary measure for the mobilisation of workers, which the National Socialists immediately proceeded to carry out.

In France, the Bureau of Compulsory Labour was established by the legislation of the pseudo-Government of Vichy, but this legislation was imposed upon the de facto French authorities by the defendants, and especially by Sauckel. The action which Sauckel brought against the Government of Vichy, to force it to favour the deportation of workers into Germany, was exercised in four phases: I shall briefly review for the Tribunal the history of these four Sauckel actions.

The first Sauckel action was initiated in the Spring of 1942, soon after the appointment of the defendant as Plenipotentiary for Labour. The German armament industry had an urgent need for workers. The service of the Arbeitseinsatz had decided to recruit 150,000 specialists in France. Sauckel came to Paris in the month of June, 1942. He had several conversations with French ministers. Otto Abetz, German Ambassador in Paris, presided over these meetings. They brought about the following results:

In view of the reluctance of French authorities to establish forced labour it was decided that the recruiting of the 150,000 specialists would be carried out by a pseudo-voluntary enrolment. This was the beginning of the so-called exchange operation, to which I have already drawn the attention of the Tribunal.

But the Tribunal knows that the exchange operation was a failure and that, despite an intensification of German propaganda, the number of voluntary enrolments remained at a minimum. The German authorities then put the Vichy Government in a position to proceed to forced enrolment. I offer in evidence the threatening letter of 26th August, 1942, addressed by the German, Dr. Michel, Chief of the Administrative Staff, to the General Delegate for Franco- German economic relations. This is French Document 530, which I shall submit to the Tribunal as Exhibit RF 59:

"Paris, 25th August, 1942.

Military Commandant in France, Economic Section, to M. Barnaud, General Delegate for Franco-German Relations, Paris.

President Laval promised Gauleiter Sauckel, General Plenipotentiary for the Employment of Labour, to make every effort to send to Germany, in order to reinforce the German armament economy, 350,000 workers, among them 150,000 metal workers.

The French Government proposed originally to solve this problem by recruitment, in particular of the 'affectes speciaux.' This method has been abandoned and that of voluntary enrolment has been attempted with a view to the liberation of prisoners. The months which have passed have demonstrated that the end in view cannot be achieved by means of voluntary recruiting.

In France, German armament orders have increased in volume and assumed a more marked and urgent character. Besides, the accomplishment of special tasks has been requested, which can be successfully carried only by having a very considerable number of available workers.

In order to assure the realisation of the tasks for which France is responsible in the domain of labour supply, the French Government must be asked, henceforth, to put into execution the following measures:

(1) The publication of a decree, relative to the change of place of work. By virtue of this decree the place of work cannot be changed and labour cannot

be hired without the approval of certain specified services.

(2) The institution of a compulsory registration of all persons out of work, as well as of those who do not work during the whole working day, or are not permanently employed.

This compulsory registration will make it possible to determine, as fully as possible, the reserves that are still available.

(3) The publication of a decree for the mobilisation of workers for important tasks, relating to the policy of State. This decree is to furnish:

(a) the necessary labour for Germany;

(b) the workers necessary in France for the carrying out of orders which have been transferred here for special tasks.

(4) Publication of a decree protecting young specialists. This decree must impose upon French enterprise the obligation of turning out, by means of apprenticeship and systematic education, young workers possessing sufficient qualifications.

For the Military Commandant, the Chief of the Administrative Staff.

(Signed) Dr. Michel."

Dr. Michel's letter forms the basis for the law relative to the utilisation and the orientation of labour. It is the law of 4th September, 1942, which I have filed with the Tribunal as Exhibit RF 56.

In the application of the law all Frenchmen between 18 and 50, who did not have employment for more than 30 hours a week, were forced to state this at their local city hall. A decree of 19th September, 1942, and an enabling directive of 22nd September, provided regulations for the different phases of the statement.

Sauckel's first action was achieved through a legislative plan; the defendant had merely to dip into the labour resources which were established by it. But the resistance of the French workers caused his recruiting plan to fail. This is why Sauckel undertook his second action, beginning in January, 1943.

The second Sauckel action is marked by the setting up of the Service of Compulsory Labour, properly speaking. Until then workers had been the only victims of the policy of force of the defendants. The latter understood the demagogic argument which they could derive from this de facto situation. They explained that it was inadmissible that the working classes of the occupied territory be the only ones to participate in the German war effort. They required that the basis of forced labour be enlarged by the establishment of the Bureau of Compulsory Labour.

This was established by two measures. A directive of 2nd February, 1943, prescribed a general census of all French of masculine sex born between the 1st of January, 1912, and the 1st of January, 1921. The census took place between the 15th and 23rd of February. It had just been put in force when the law and decree of 16th February, 1943, appeared. These regulations established the Bureau of Compulsory Labour for all young men born between the 1st of January, 1920, and 31st of December, 1922. I file them with the Tribunal as Exhibits RF 60 and RF 61, and I ask the Court to take judicial notice of them.

The action carried out by the defendant, to impose the legislation which was not in the domain of common law, is substantiated by numerous documents. I particularly draw the attention of the Tribunal to four of these, which permit us to retrace the activities of the defendant Sauckel during the months of January and February, 1943. On 5th January, 1943, Sauckel transmitted to the different departments of his administration an order of the Fuehrer which the defendant Speer had communicated to him. This is Document 556-PS-13, which I file with the Tribunal as

Exhibit RF 62. I shall read its first paragraph:

"(1) On 4th January, 1943, at 8 o'clock in the evening, Minister Speer telephones from the General Headquarters of the Fuehrer to give the information that, according to a decision of the Fuehrer it will no longer be necessary, when recruiting specialists and assistants in France, to have any particular regard for the French. One may likewise in the said country exercise pressure and use more severe measures to the end of procuring the necessary labour."

On 11th January, 1943, the defendant Sauckel was in Paris. He attended a meeting which brought together, at the Military Commandant's, all responsible officials of the Labour Service. He announced to them that new measures of constraint were to be taken in France. I refer you to the minutes of the meeting which constitutes Document 1342-PS, which I file with the Tribunal as Exhibit RF 63. I shall read from Page 2 of the French translation, Page 1, fourth line of the second paragraph of the German original:

"Gauleiter Sauckel likewise thanks the various services for the successful carrying out of the first action. Now already, at the beginning of the new year, he sees himself obliged to announce new severe measures. There is a great new need of labour for the front as well as for the Reich armament industry."

I pass to the end of the paragraph. I shall read from the next paragraph:

"The situation at the front calls for 700,000 soldiers fit for front line service. The armament industry would have to lose 200,000 key workers by the middle of March. I have received an order from the Fuehrer to find 200,000 foreign specialised workers as replacements, and I shall need for this 150,000 French specialists, while the other 50,000 can be drawn from Holland, Belgium and other occupied countries.

In addition, 100,000 unskilled French workers are necessary for the Reich. The second action of recruitment in France makes it necessary that, by the middle of March, 150,000 skilled workers and 100,000 unskilled workers and women be transferred to Germany."

The defendant Sauckel went back to Germany a few days later. On 15th February he was in Berlin at the meeting of the Central Office of the Four Year Plan. He gave a commentary on the law, which was to appear that very day, and revealed that he was the instigator of it.

I refer once more to the minutes of the conference of the Four Year Plan, included under R-124, which I submitted this morning to the Tribunal as Exhibit RF 30. I shall read an extract from this document, which my American colleagues have not mentioned. It is Page 7 of the French translation of the document, Pages 284-5 of the German original:

"This is the situation in France. Since my collaborators and I succeeded, after difficult discussions, in persuading Laval to establish the law of compulsory labour, this law has been extended, thanks to our pressure, so successfully, that since yesterday three French age-groups have already been called. This is why we are now legally qualified to recruit in France, with the assistance of the French Government, workers of three age-groups, whom we shall be able to employ henceforth in French factories, but among whom we shall be able to choose some for our own needs in Germany, and send them there."

In fact, the defendant Sauckel returned to France on 24th February. I offer in evidence to the Tribunal the letter which he addressed to Hitler before his departure to inform him of his trip. It proves the continuity of the action of Sauckel. The letter constitutes Document 556-PS-25, which I submit to the Tribunal as Exhibit RF 64, and I shall read it:

"General Plenipotentiary for the Employment of Labour to the Fuehrer General Headquarters of the Fuehrer.

My Fuehrer:

I allow myself herewith to take leave of you before undertaking my official trip to France which has already been arranged. The objective of my trip is:

(1) To put at the disposal of the Reich, within the anticipated time, workers replacing German workers of key industries, for the benefit of the Wehrmacht.

May I add that Marshal Keitel and General von Unruh received a communication from me yesterday to the effect that half of these workers intended to replace German workers in the key industries, that is, 125,000 French qualified specialists, have already arrived in the Reich on 1st January, 1943, and that a corresponding number of soldiers has already been drafted. I shall now make sure, in France, that the second half shall arrive in the Reich by the end of March, or earlier if possible. The first French programme was executed by the end of December.

(2) To assure the necessary labour for the French wharves in order to permit the carrying out of the programme undertaken there by Grand Admiral Donitz and Gauleiter Kauffmann.

(3) To assure the necessary labour for the programme of the Luftwaffe.

(4) To assure the necessary labour for the other German armament programmes which are in process in France.

(5) To prepare supplementary labour in agreement with State Secretary Backe, in view of intensifying French agricultural production.

(6) To have conversations, if necessary, with the French Government on the subject of the carrying out of the labour service, the calling up of age groups, and so forth, with, a view to activating the recruitment of labour for the benefit of the German war economy."

(The Tribunal adjourned until 19th January, 1946, at 10.00 hours.)

Thirty-Eighth Day: Saturday, January 19th, 1946

M. HERZOG: Mr. President, your Honours.

At the end of yesterday's session I was expounding to the Tribunal the conditions under which the Compulsory Labour Service was progressively imposed in France. I reached the second action of the defendant Sauckel as set out in the laws of 16th February, 1943.

Sauckel's second action precipitated the enforced enrolment of Frenchmen during the months of February and March, 1943. Several tens of thousands of young men of the 1940 and 1942 classes were deported to Germany by the application of the law of 16th February. The tempo of these deportations slowed down in the month of April, but the Arbeitseinsatz immediately formulated fresh requirements. On 9th April, 1943, the defendant Sauckel asked the French authorities to furnish him with 120,000 workers during the month of May, and 100,000 during the month of June. In June he made it known that he wished to effect the transfer of 500,000 workers up to 31st December.

Sauckel's third action was about to begin. It was to be marked, on 5th June, 1943, by the total mobilisation of the 1942 class. All exemptions provided by the law of 16th February and subsequent texts were withdrawn, and the young men of the 1942 class were hunted all through France.

In reality, Sauckel's third action was especially manifested by a violent pressure on the part of the defendant, envisaging wholesale deportation by forced recruiting. I offer in evidence three documents, which testify to the action taken by Sauckel in the summer of 1943.

The first document is a letter from Sauckel to Hitler, dated 27th June, 1943. Drafted by the defendant upon his return from a trip to France, it contains an outlined plan for the recruiting of French workers for the second half of 1943. Its object was, on the one hand, to secure that one million workers be assigned, in France, to French armament factories and, on the other hand, that 500,000 French workers be deported to Germany. This letter constitutes Document 556-PS- 39, which I submit to the Tribunal as Exhibit RF 65. I quote:

"Weimar, 27th June, 1943.

My Fuehrer:

With your permission I beg to report my return from my official trip to France. Inasmuch as the free labour reserves in the territories occupied by the German Armed Forces have been, numerically, absorbed to saturation point, I am now carefully examining the possibilities of mobilising additional labour reserves in the Reich and the occupied territories to work on German war production.

In my reports of 20th April, I was allowed to point out that intensive and careful utilisation must be made of European labour forces in territories submitted to direct German influence.

It was the precise purpose of my recent stay in Paris to investigate the possibilities still existing in France for the recruitment of labour (Arbeitseinsatz). My task was accomplished by extensive conferences and my own personal investigation. On the basis of a carefully established balance sheet I have come to the following decision:

(1) Assuming that war economy measures in France are carried out which would at least prove partially effective, or approximately approach, in efficacy, the measures carried out in Germany, then - until the 31st of December, 1943 - a further million workers, both men and women, could be assigned to the French war and armament industries for work on German orders and assignments. In this case it should prove possible to place additional German orders in France.

(2) In consideration of these measures, and given a careful study of the subject, together with the co-operation of our German Armament Services and the German Labour Recruiting Offices, it should be possible to transfer a further 500,000 workers, both men and women, from France to the Reich between now and the end of the year.

The prerequisites which I have established for the realisation of this programme are as follows:

(1) Closest possible collaboration between all German agencies, especially in dealing with the French agencies.

(2) A constant check on French economy by joint commissions, as already agreed upon by the Reich Minister of Armaments and Munitions, Party Member Speer and myself.

(3) Constant, skilful and successful propaganda against the cliques of de Gaulle and Giraud.

(4) The guarantee of adequate food supplies to the French population working for Germany.

(5) An emphatic insistence on this urgency before the French Government, in particular before Marshal Petain, who still represents the main obstacle to the further recruiting of French women for compulsory labour (Arbeitseinsatz).

(6) A pronounced increase in the programme which I have already introduced in France, for re-education in trades essential to war production."

I omit the next and read the last paragraph:

"I consequently beg you, my Fuehrer, to approve my suggestion of freeing one million Frenchmen and Frenchwomen for German war production in France proper, in the second half of 1943, and, in addition, of transferring 500,000 Frenchmen and Frenchwomen to the Reich before the end of the current year.

Yours faithfully and obediently,

(Signed) Fritz Sauckel."

The document to which I would now like to call the Tribunal's attention proves that the Fuehrer gave his approval to Sauckel's programme. A note drawn up on 28th July, 1943, by Dr. Stothfang, under the letter-heading of the Plenipotentiary General for Manpower Utilisation (Arbeitseinsatz), gives a report on a discussion between Sauckel and the Fuehrer. It is Document 556-PS-41, which I submit to the Tribunal as Exhibit RF 66. I shall limit myself to reading the last paragraph.

"(d) The transfer envisaged for the end of the year of 1,000,000 French workers to the war industries in France, and the transportation of 500,000 other French workers to the interior of the Reich has been approved by the Fuehrer."

A document finally establishes that the defendant Sauckel, on the strength of

Hitler's approval, attempted to realise his programme by working on the French Government. This document is a letter from Sauckel to Hitler. It is dated 13th August, 1943, upon the defendant's return from a trip to France, Belgium and Holland. It is Document 556-PS-43. I shall read it to the Tribunal. It is Exhibit RF 67:

"Weimar, 13th August, 1943.

My Fuehrer:

With your permission I beg to report my return from my official trip to France, Belgium and Holland. In the course of tough, difficult and tedious negotiations, I have imposed upon the occupied Western territories, for the last five months of 1943, the programme set forth below, and have prepared very detailed measures for realising it: in France - with the Military Commander, the German Embassy and the French Government; in Belgium - with the Military Commander, and in Holland with the offices of the Reich Commissar.

The programme provides:

(1) In France, the transfer of one million French workers, both men and women, from the civilian to the German war industries in France. This measure should render possible a new important shifting of work on German orders to France.

(2) Soliciting and recruiting of 500,000 French workers for work in Germany. This figure should not be made public abroad.

(3) In order to render void any passive resistance from large groups of French officials, I have ordered, in agreement with the Military Commander in France, the introduction of labour recruiting commissions for each two French departments, and placed them under the supervision and direction of the German Gau offices. Only in this manner can the complete recruitment of the French labour potential and its intensive utilisation be made possible. The French Government has given its approval."

If the Tribunal will allow me, I shall quote the rest of this letter; the following paragraphs concern Belgium and Holland. It will allow me to refer to this document later without reading it again.

"(4) A programme was secured in Belgium for the employment of 150,000 workers in the Reich, and with the approval of the Military Commander in Belgium an organisation for compulsory labour, corresponding to that in France, has been established."

I pass to the fifth paragraph.

"(5) A programme has likewise been prepared for Holland, providing for the transfer of 150,000 workers to Germany and of 100,000 workers, men and women, from Dutch civilian industries to German war production."

Such was Sauckel's programme in 1943. His plan was partly thwarted by the resistance of officials and patriotic workers. Proof of this is furnished by a statement of the defendant. I am referring to the report on a conference of the Central Office for the Four Year Plan held on 1st March, 1944. I submitted this document to the Tribunal yesterday as Exhibit RF 30. I shall read from the first page of the French translation, second paragraph-German text 1768-1769.

"Last autumn, as far as foreign manpower is concerned, the labour recruiting programme has been severely battered. I do not wish to elaborate the reasons here. They have been discussed at length; all I have to say is: the programme has been wrecked."

Sauckel, however, was not discouraged by the difficulties encountered in 1943. In 1944 he attempted to realise a new programme by the trick of the fourth action. The National Socialist authorities decided to secure, in 1944, the transfer of four million foreign workers to Germany. This decision was made on 4th January, 1944, during a conference at the Headquarters of the Fuehrer and in his presence. The report on this conference constitutes Document 1292-PS. I submit it herewith to the Tribunal as Exhibit RF 68, and I read from Page 3 of the French translation - Page 6 of the German original, last paragraph:

"Final results of the conference:
(1)The Plenipotentiary General for Manpower Utilisation shall produce at least four million new workers from the occupied territories."

The details concerning the contingents demanded from each occupied territory must have been determined on 16th February, 1944, during a conference of the Central Office for the Four Year Plan. Yesterday I submitted the report of this session at the outset of my explanations, under Exhibit RF 20. I am quoting the conclusions to-day. They will be found on the first page of the translation, second page of the German original:

"Results of the 53rd session of the Office for Central Planning."
Labour recruiting (Arbeitseinsatz) in 1944.
(1) About 500,000 new workers can be mobilised from among the German home reserves."

I omit the rest.

(2) Recruiting of Italian labour to the number of 1,500,000; of these - 1,000,000 at the rate of 250,000 per month from January to April and 500,000 from May to December.
(3) Recruiting of 1,000,000 French workers at equal monthly rates from 1st February to 31st December, 1944 (approximately 9 1,000 per month).
(4) Recruiting of 250,000 workers from Belgium.
(5) Recruiting of 250,000 workers from the Netherlands."

I abstain from quoting further, since the other paragraphs concern the Eastern European countries.

The Tribunal has seen that France was called upon to furnish a large contingent of workers. After the 15th of January Sauckel went to Paris to inflict his demands on the French authorities.

The fourth Sauckel action consisted of two distinct measures: the adoption of the procedure known as the combing of industries, and the publication of the law of 1st February, 1944, which widened the sphere of application of compulsory labour. The system of combing the industries led the labour administration to carry out direct recruiting in the industrial enterprises. Mixed Franco-German commissions were set up in each department. They determined the percentage of workers to be deported. They proceeded to requisition and transfer them.

The practice of combing the industries represents the realisation of the projects elaborated by defendant Sauckel since 1943. In the documents which I have read to the Tribunal Sauckel announced, in fact, his intention of creating mixed labour commissions.

The law of 1st February, 1944, marked the culminating point of Sauckel's actions in the field of legislation. It extends the scope of application of the law of 4th September, 1942. As from February, 1944, all men between the ages of 16 and 60, and all women between the ages of 18 and 45 were subject to compulsory labour.

I submit to the Tribunal the law of 1st February, 1944, as Exhibit RF 69, with the request to take judicial note of it.

The proof of the pressure that Sauckel exerted on the French authorities in order to impose on them the publication of this law is furnished by a report of the defendant to Hitler. This report is dated the 25th of January, 1944. It was, therefore, drafted during the negotiations which characterised the fourth Sauckel action. It constituted Document 556-PS-55, which I submit to the Tribunal as Exhibit RF 70. I shall read this document:

"My Fuehrer:

On the 22nd of January, 1944, the French Government, together with Marshal Petain, accepted the majority of my demands for increasing the working week from 40 to 48 hours, as well as for extending the compulsory labour law in France and utilising French manpower in Germany.

The Marshal did not agree to the compulsory work of women in the Reich, but he did agree to the compulsory work of women inside France, to be limited to women between the ages of 26 and 45. Women between 15 and 25 are to be employed only at their place of residence.

Since this, nevertheless, represents appreciable progress in comparison with the extremely difficult negotiations which I had to conduct in Paris, I approved this law, in order to save further loss of time, on condition that the German demands were energetically met and carried out.

The French Government likewise accepted my demand that French officials sabotaging the enforcement of the Compulsory Labour Law should be punished by severe penalties, including the death penalty. I have left them in no doubt that further and more rigid measures would be adopted, should the demands for the manpower required not be fulfilled.

Your ever obedient and faithful, Fritz Sauckel."

I draw the attention of the Tribunal to the problem of compulsory labour of women, referred to in the two preceding documents. For a long time the French authorities categorically opposed the introduction of female labour. The defendant Sauckel did not cease to exercise violent activity.

On the 27th June, 1943, in a letter to Hitler, he suggested that an energetic statement of German interests be made before the French Government. I have already quoted this letter to the Tribunal, Exhibit RF 65. I shall not revert to it, but I emphasise the fact that the law of 1st February did not satisfy Sauckel and did not in the least appease his demands. His dissatisfaction and his determination to pursue his policy of compulsion become apparent from a report of 26th April, 1944, bearing his signature; that the report was forwarded is certified by Berk, one of his assistants.

This report - there actually were four reports submitted jointly - constitutes Document 1289-PS. I submit them to the Tribunal as Exhibit RF 71, and I quote from the second page:

"France (1). The problem of women.

At the time of the promulgation of the French Compulsory Labour Law, the French authorities (Marshal Petain in particular) have urgently desired that women be exempted from performing compulsory labour in Germany. In spite of serious objections the G.B.A. approved of this exemption. The reservation was made, however, that the approval was given on condition that the contingencies imposed were met; or else the G.B.A. would retain the right of taking further measures. Inasmuch as the contingencies are far from being met, the demand must be addressed to the French Government of extending the compulsory labour service to women also."

The fourth Sauckel action, therefore, was directed in such a manner as to utilise all of France's manpower. The French resistance and the development of the military operations hindered the execution of the Sauckel plan. The defendant, in the meantime, had contemplated such extraordinary measures as would have to be taken on the day the Allied Armies landed. I quote again Document 1289-PS, Exhibit RF 71, and I read on Page 3:

"Measures concerning compulsory labour in the case of invasion:

To some extent precautions have been taken to evacuate the population of those areas invaded and to protect valuable manpower from being seized by our enemies. In view of the actual situation of labour utilisation in Germany, it is necessary to induct efficient workers to the greatest extent possible into efficacious employment within the Reich. Orders to this effect on the part of the Wehrmacht are indispensable for carrying out these measures.

The following text is proposed for an order by the Fuehrer... "

I shall not read the text of the order proposed by Sauckel.

The Allied victory, however, came so quickly that Sauckel did not have the chance to realise fully his plan of mass deportation. All the same, he started to carry it out, and deportations of workers went on up to the day of liberation of the territory. Several hundred thousand French workers were finally stationed in Germany as a result of the various Sauckel actions. Will the Tribunal, please, bear this in mind.

The compulsory labour service was introduced in Norway in the same manner as in France. The defendants imposed upon the Norwegian authorities the publication of a law instituting the compulsory registration of Norwegian citizens, and ordering their enrolment by force. I quote in this respect the preliminary report on the crimes of Germany against Norway, a report prepared by the Norwegian Government and submitted to the Tribunal as U.K. 79. I now submit it as Exhibit RF 72, and I quote from the first page, third paragraph:

"The result of Sauckel's order in Norway was the promulgation of the Quisling law of 3rd February, 1943, concerning the compulsory registration of Norwegian men and women for the so-called national labour effort.

Terboven and Quisling openly admitted that the law had been promulgated to enable the Norwegian people to utilise its manpower for the benefit of the German war effort.

In a speech of 2nd February Terboven incidentally declared that he himself and the German Reich supported this law with their authority, and he threatened to use force against any one attempting to oppose its application."

In Belgium and in the Netherlands the German authorities used a direct procedure. The compulsory labour service was organised by decrees of the occupying power.

In Belgium these were decrees of the Military Commander, and in the Netherlands decrees of the Reich Commissar. I remind the Tribunal of the fact that the authority of the Military Commander in Belgium extended to the North of France.

A decree of 6th March, 1942, established the principle of compulsory labour in Belgium. It was published in the Belgian "Verordnungsblatt" of 1942, Page 845. I submit it to the Tribunal as Exhibit RF 73, and I ask the Tribunal to take judicial notice of it.

The decree of 6th March excluded the possibility of forced deportation of workers to Germany. However, such deportation was ordered by a decree of 6th October, 1942, which was published in the Belgian "Verordnungsblatt" of 1942, Page 1060. I submitted it to the Tribunal as Exhibit RF 57 in the course of my explanations.

The German activities in Belgium gave rise to interventions and protests by leading Belgian personalities, among others the King of Belgium and Cardinal van Roey.

The decrees instituting compulsory labour in Belgium and the North of France bore the signature of General von Falkenhausen, but the latter proclaimed his decree of 6th October on the order of Sauckel. I refer once more to the testimony of General von Falkenhausen, which I submitted to the Tribunal yesterday as Exhibit RF 15. I ask your permission to quote the following passages, first page, fifth paragraph:

"Q. On 6th October, 1942, a decree was published which instituted compulsory labour in Belgium, and in the Departments of Northern France, for men between the ages of 18 and 50 years, and for single women between the ages of 21 and 25 years.

A. I was Commander-in-Chief for Northern France and Belgium.

Q. Does the witness recall having promulgated this decree?

A. I do not remember exactly the text of this decree because it was issued following a long dispute with the labour deputy Sauckel.

Q. Did you have any trouble with Sauckel?

A. I was fundamentally opposed to the establishment of compulsory labour, and consented to promulgating the decree only after receiving orders.

Q. Then this decree was not issued on the initiative of von Falkenhausen?

A. On the contrary.

Q. Who gave instruction in this matter?

A. I suppose that at that time Sauckel was already responsible for manpower and that at that time he gave me all instructions on Hitler's orders."

I take up the quotation again on Page 3 of the French translation, fourth paragraph:

"Q. Since you were opposed to the idea of compulsory labour, did you not protest when you received these instructions?

A. There were unending quarrels between Sauckel and myself. In the end this contributed greatly to my discharge."

The violence of the pressure exerted by the defendant Sauckel in Belgium, in order to impose his plan of recruitment by force, is also demonstrated by the document which I have just submitted to the Tribunal as Exhibit RF 67. The Tribunal will remember that it is the report addressed on the 13th August, 1943, by Sauckel to Hitler on his return from France, Belgium and Holland.

Finally, I have to deal with the introduction of compulsory labour in the Netherlands. I request the Tribunal to charge the defendant Seyss-Inquart, as well as the defendant Sauckel, with the institution of compulsory enrolment in the occupied Dutch territories.

As a matter of fact, the deportation of the Dutch workers was organised by decrees of the Reich Commissar. They established all the more the responsibility of the defendant, who, in his quality as Reich Commissar, derived his powers directly from the Fuehrer.

The defendant Seyss-Inquart introduced the compulsory labour service in the

Netherlands by a decree of 28th February, 1941, published in the Dutch "Verordnungsblatt" of 1941, No. 42. I referred to this decree as Exhibit RF 58 in the course of my explanation yesterday, and asked the Tribunal to take judicial notice of it.

As in Belgium the compulsory labour service could originally be enforced in the interior of the occupied countries only, but, just as in Belgium, it was soon extended in order to permit the deportation of workers to Germany. The extension was made effective by a decree of Seyss-Inquart of 23rd March, 1942, which appeared in No. 26 of the "Verordnungsblatt." I submit it to the Tribunal as Exhibit RF 74, and I ask the Tribunal to add it to the record.

The defendant Seyss-Inquart had thus paved the road on which the defendant Sauckel was to be enabled to proceed to action. Sauckel actually utilised all the human potential of the Netherlands. New measures were soon necessary, measures which Seyss-Inquart adopted.

A decree dated 6th May, 1943, "Verordnungsblatt," 1943, Page 173, ordered the mobilisation of all men from 18 to 35 years of age. I submit this decree to the Tribunal as Exhibit RF 75.

Moreover since the 19th of February, 1943, Seyss-Inquart had issued a decree which permitted his services to take all measures in the utilisation of manpower which he considered to be opportune.

This decree, which appeared in the "Verordnungsblatt" of 1943, has been submitted to the Tribunal as Exhibit RF 76.

The extent of deportation from Holland in 1943 is attested to by a letter of 16th June, 1943, from Sauckel's representative in the Netherlands. This letter, which bears the French document number 664, is submitted to the Tribunal as Exhibit RF 77. I quote:

"In conformity with the census decree of 7th May, the 1920 to 1924 classes have been registered on filing cards. Although this involved very much work it was nevertheless possible to send 22,986 workers to the Reich, and, in addition, the prisoners of war put at our disposal. During the month of June the deficiency of the month of May will be made up.

These classes include, according to the Statistical Service of the Kingdom of Holland, 80,000 each. It is from these classes that transfers to the Reich have been made so far. 446,493 persons have been transferred to the Reich up to 1st June, 1943, and a number of them have returned from there. The figures as per index are as follows:

1921 class, 43,331;
1922 class, 45,354;
1923 class, 47,593;
1924 class, 45,232.

As up to 80 per cent. have been deferred, it is now imperative to begin transporting entire classes to the Reich. The Reich Commissar has given his agreement to this action. The other authorities involved, of Economy, Armament, Agriculture, and the Armed Forces, pressed by necessity, have given their approval."

At the end of the year 1944, the German authorities increased their pressure on the Netherlands. During that period tens of thousands of persons were arrested within two days in Rotterdam. Systematic raids took place in all the larger cities of Holland, sometimes improvised, sometimes after the population had been publicly summoned to appear in places named. I submit to the Tribunal various proclamations of this kind. They form Document 1162-PS, and have already been submitted to the Tribunal by Mr. Dodd. I shall not read them again. I use them in support of my argument and submit them as Exhibit RF 78.

These documents do not reveal isolated facts; they show a systematic policy which the defendants were to pursue up to 5th May, 1945, when the capitulation of Germany brought liberation to the Netherlands.

I still owe the Tribunal a supplementary explanation. The defendants did not stop at introducing compulsory labour service in the occupied territories. I declare that they proceeded to criminal coercion in order to ensure that the mobilisation of foreign workers was carried out. I am going to prove this fact.

The measures taken by the National Socialist authorities to guarantee the forced enlistment of foreign workers cannot be dissociated from the procedures they applied to ensure the so-called voluntary enlistment. The pressure was more violent, but it sprang from the same spirit. The method was to deceive, and, where this proved unsuccessful, to use coercion. The defendants very soon realised that no kind of propaganda would lend the cloak of justice to compulsory labour in the eyes of its victims. If they had any doubts in this respect, these would have been dissipated by the reports of the occupation authorities. The latter were unanimous in their reports of the political trouble provoked by this compulsory enlistment and of the resistance encountered by them. That is why the defendants once again used force in their attempt to ensure that the civilian mobilisation decreed by them was carried out.

First in line among the coercive measures to which the Germans had recourse, I mention the withholding of the ration cards of defaulters. The Tribunal knows from the circular letter of Dr. Manfeld, submitted as Exhibit RF 26, that this measure had been proposed since January, 1942, and will recall that by decree of the Fuehrer of 8th September, 1942, which I submitted as Exhibit RF 55, this measure was put into effect. This order provided that food and clothing ration cards were not to be issued to persons incapable of proving that they were working, nor to those who refused to do compulsory work.

Hitler's order was put into effect in all occupied territories. In France, circulars by the occupation authorities prohibited the renewal of ration cards of those French people who had eluded the census of 16th February, 1943. In Belgium, the forfeiture of ration certificates was regulated by an order of the Military Commander. It is the order of 5th March, 1943, published in the "Verordnungsblatt" for Belgium, which I submit to the Tribunal as Exhibit RF 79.

General von Falkenhausen, the signatory of this order, admitted its grave significance during the interrogation, which I have submitted to the Tribunal as Exhibit RF 15, and to which I refer again. General von Falkenhausen declared that the defendant Sauckel was the originator of this order, and that he had refused to grant an amnesty proposed by the General. I quote, Page 4 of the French translation, fifth paragraph:

"**Q.** Does the witness remember an order of 5th March, 1943, by which those refusing to enter the compulsory labour service had their ration cards withdrawn?

A. I do not remember. At the time when the order was issued for men from 18 to 50 years old, the implementing orders were not given by myself but by my offices, and I am not conversant with the details of the application of reprisals. I was not the executive head of the administration. I was above it.

Q. But at that time you were informed of the means of pressure and manner of treatment which the authorities thought fit to employ?

A. I do not wish to deny my responsibility for everything for, after all, I was aware of many things. I remember in particular the order regarding ration cards, because on various occasions I proposed that an amnesty be declared for persons who were obliged to live illegally, and who did not have a ration card.

Q. To whom was this proposal made?

A. To Sauckel, with the consent of President Revert.

Q. What was the attitude taken by Sauckel at that time?

A. He refused to grant such an amnesty."

In Holland likewise the renewal of ration certificates which did not bear the stamp of the labour office was prohibited.

The defendants, however, used a method of coercion which was even more criminal than the forfeiture of ration cards. I refer to the persecution directed against the families of those who refused to do compulsory labour. I call this method criminal, because it is based on the concept of family responsibility, which is contrary to the fundamental principles of the penal law of civilised nations. It was, nevertheless, sanctioned by several legislative texts issued or imposed by the National Socialists.

In France, I quote the law of 11th June, 1943, which I submit to the Tribunal as Exhibit RF 80, with the request that it take judicial notice thereof.

In Belgium, I refer to the order of the Military Commander of 30th April, 1943, and particularly to paragraphs 8 and 9. I submit this order to the Tribunal as Exhibit RF 81, with the request that it take judicial notice thereof.

Judicial action by the defendants was likewise directed against the employers and against the officials of the employment bureaux. In France, the action was initiated by two laws of 1st February, 1944. I emphasise that these laws were issued on the same day as the Compulsory Labour Law, and I confirm that they were imposed at the same time. In support of my statement, I submit the admission of the defendant Sauckel, in his letter of 25th February, 1944, which I read a little while ago to the Tribunal as Exhibit RF 70. I submit to the Tribunal the laws of 1st February, 1944, as Exhibit RF 82, with the request that it be added to the record.

There were still other measures of coercion. One of these, for instance, was the closing of the faculties and schools to defaulting students. It was decreed in Belgium on 28th June, 1943; in France, on 15th July, 1943. In Holland the students were victims of a systematic deportation from February on. I quote in this connection a letter of 4th May, 1943, from the Higher Chief of the S.S. and Police. This is Document 665, which I produce as Exhibit RF 83.

THE PRESIDENT: Perhaps this is a good time to break off.

(A recess was taken.)

M. HERZOG: Mr. President, your Honours. At the suspension of the session I was about to read to the Tribunal the letter of 4th May, 1943, which gives evidence of the action taken in Holland towards a systematic deportation of the students. I quote Exhibit RF 83, Document 665 in the document book:

"Subject: Action against Students.

The action will start on Thursday morning. As it is now too late to have this published in the Press to-day, an announcement by the Higher Chief of the S.S. and Police will be made over the radio, beginning tomorrow at 7 o'clock; it will be published to-morrow in the morning and the evening papers. Besides that, we will follow the directives given in yesterday's telegram."

Following is the text of the proclamation:

"Ordinance on the Registration of Students."

I will omit the first paragraph and I quote:

"1. All persons of the male sex who have attended a Dutch university or academy during the years 1942-43, and have not yet finished their studies according to the curriculum (referred to below as 'students'), are to report between 10.00 and 15.00 hours on 6th May, 1943, to the commander of the sector of the S.S. and the Security Police competent for their respective residence, for the purpose of their induction into the compulsory labour service."

I omit paragraphs 2 and 3 and quote:

"4.(1) Persons violating this ordinance, or trying to circumvent it, particularly such persons who do not comply with their duty to register, or either intentionally or through negligence state any false data, will be punished by imprisonment and/or unlimited fines, unless other laws providing a more severe penalty are applicable.

(4) Those exercising paternal authority or guardianship over the students are co-responsible for their reporting as prescribed. They are subjected to the same penalties as the offenders themselves.

5. This ordinance becomes effective on promulgation.

(Signed) The Higher Chief of the S.S. and Police with the Reich Commissar for the Occupied Dutch Territories."

Since no measures whatsoever succeeded in intimidating the workers in the occupied territories, the defendants, finally, resorted to their police forces to ensure the arrest of those workers destined for deportation to Germany.

This intervention by the police had been demanded by the defendant Sauckel. I submit two documents in evidence. The first consists of the minutes of a conference which took place on 4th January, 1944, at the Headquarters of the Fuehrer. I have just submitted this document to the Tribunal as Exhibit RF 68. I quote, French translation, Page 2, last paragraph; German original, Page 4, in the middle of the page:

"The Plenipotentiary General for Manpower Utilisation (G.B.A.) Sauckel, declared that he would try with fanatical determination to obtain this manpower. Up to now he had always kept his promises regarding the number of workers to be provided; with the best will in the world, however, he was not in a position to make a definite promise for 1944. He would do everything possible to provide the manpower required for 1944. The success would depend mainly on the number of German police put at his disposal. If he had to rely on the police of the countries concerned his project could not be carried out."

I refer now to the statements made by Sauckel at the conference of the Central Office for the Four Year Plan on 1st March, 1944. It is Exhibit RF 30, to which I repeatedly have called the attention of the Tribunal. The passage which I am about to quote has not yet been referred to before the Tribunal. Page 3 of the French Translation - German text, Page 1775 ff. - 15th line from the bottom, Page 3 of the French translation:

"The term 'S-factory' (S-Betrieb) in France is actually nothing else but a protection against Sauckel's grasp. That is how the French look at it, and they certainly cannot be expected to think differently. They are Frenchmen, in the first place, who are faced with a German point of view and German actions different from theirs. It is not up to me to decide whether the protected factories (Schutzbetriebe) are useful and necessary. I have only described the situation from my point of view. Nevertheless, I still hope to succeed eventually by using my old organisation of agents on the one hand and, on the other hand, by those measures which I have fortunately been able to wrest from the French Government.

In the course of negotiations, lasting five to six hours, I obtained from M. Laval the concession that the death sentence may be imposed on officials who sabotage the recruitment of labour and other measures. Believe me, it was very difficult. I had to fight hard to succeed, but I did succeed. I am requesting, especially of the Armed Forces that, in case the French Government does not really put its mind to it, most drastic action now be taken by the Germans in France. Please do not resent my following remark: Several times, when in the company of my assistants, I have faced situations in France which caused me to ask: 'Is there no respect in France for the German Lieutenant and his ten men?' For months on end everything I said was paralysed by the reply: 'What do you want, Herr Gauleiter? Do you not know that we have no police forces at our disposal? We are powerless in France.' This was the reply given over and over again. How, in the face of these facts, am I to achieve labour recruitment in France? The German authorities must co-operate, and if the French, despite all their promises, do not remedy the situation, we Germans must make an example of one case, and on the provisions of this law, put some prefect or mayor against the wall if he does not co-operate, or else not a single Frenchman will go to Germany."

By such means, finally, the deportation of workers to Germany was achieved by arresting them, and by the threat of reprisals. It was a logical consequence of the National Socialist system, that the policy of recruiting foreign workers was accomplished by police terror.

I have told the Tribunal that the resistance offered by the prisoners of war and by the workers of the occupied territories, against the activities of the defendants, which were in turn insidious or brutal, wrecked the plan for the recruitment of foreign workers. The defendant Sauckel encountered the greatest difficulty in carrying out the programme which he had persuaded Hitler and the defendants Goering, Speer and Funk to accept.

From this it does not follow that Nazi Germany did not succeed in carrying out mass deportations of foreign workers. The number of native workers from the occupied territories of Western Europe who were deported into Germany was very high. More numerous still were those workers compelled to work at home in factories and workyards under the control of the occupation authorities.

I shall give the Tribunal statistical information which will enable it to verify my statements. These statistics are fragmentary. They are excerpts from reports compiled by the Governments of the occupied countries after their liberation, and from reports sent during the war by the Arbeitseinsatz office to its superiors.

These statistics of Allied origin are incomplete. The records on which they are based have been partially destroyed. Further, the administration of the occupied territories are in possession of second-hand information only, whenever the requisition of workers was made directly by the occupation authorities. As to the German statistics, they are also incomplete, since the Allied authorities have not yet discovered all the records of the enemy.

It is, however, possible to give to the Tribunal an exact evaluation of the extent of the deportations effected by Germany. This evaluation will furnish proof that the violations of International Law committed by the defendants did not remain in the tentative stage, characterised by a beginning only, though reprehensible even as such. They brought about such social disorder as, under penal law, constitutes the perpetration of the crime.

I shall first submit to the Tribunal the statistics furnished by the reports of the French Government. The French Government's report has been published by the Institute of Market Analysis. It contains numerous statistical tables from which I quote the total figures. The figures are as follows:

738,000 workers were pressed into compulsory labour service in France.

875,952 French workers were deported to German factories.

987,687 prisoners of war were utilised for the Reich war economy.

Thus, a total of 2,601,639 workers of French citizenship were pressed into work serving the war effort of National Socialist Germany.

From the official report of the Belgian Government it appears that 150,000 persons were pressed into compulsory labour; and the report of the Dutch Government gives a figure of 431,000 persons; but it should be noted that this figure does not take into account the systematic raids undertaken during November, 1944, nor the deportations carried out in 1945.

I am submitting to the Tribunal exact figures which cover all the stages of the policy of recruiting foreign labour. These figures are taken from the reports of the defendant Sauckel himself, or of various administrative offices concerned with the deportation of labour. The extent of labour utilised in the occupied territories is demonstrated by the statistics concerning workers who were used in constructing fortifications of the so-called Atlantic Wall, as part of the Organisation Todt, which I recall was directed by the defendant Speer after the death of its founder. These statistics are to be found in a teletype message sent to Hitler by the defendant Sauckel on 17th May, 1943. It is Document 556-PS-33, which I submit to the Tribunal as Exhibit RF 84. I quote:

"The Mandatory of the Four Year Plan - the Plenipotentiary General for Manpower Utilisation, Berlin, to the Fuehrer, Headquarters of the Fuehrer.

My Fuehrer! I beg to submit to you the following figures on the manpower employed in the Todt Organisation:

In addition to the manpower assigned to the entire German industry by the 'Manpower Utilisation' since I took office, fresh workers have also been constantly supplied to the Todt Organisation. The total figure of the workers employed by the Todt Organisation was as follows:

End of March, 1942-270,969.

End of March, 1943-696,003.

It should be noted that the 'Manpower Utilisation' has, with great speed and energy, assigned workers preferably to the Todt Organisation in the West for the purpose of completing the work on the Atlantic Wall. This is all the more remarkable because (1) in France, Belgium and Holland... "

I omit a few lines and quote from Page 2:

"Despite the difficulties involved, the manpower strength of the Todt Organisation in the West was increased from 66,701 workers at the end of March, 1942, to 248,200 workers at the end of March, 1943."

The number of foreign workers deported to Germany by 30th September, 1941, is furnished by a report which was found in the archives of the O.K.W. It is Document 1323-PS, which I submit as Exhibit RF 85. According to this document, 1,226,686 workers were employed in Germany on the 30th September,1941. Of that number, 483,842 came from the occupied Western territories. I quote from the document the number of labour deportees by country of origin. I shall confine myself to the columns of interest to the Western States, since the statistics of workers deported from the East of Europe come within the province of my Soviet colleague.

"Denmark, 63,309.
Holland, 134,093.
Belgium, 212,903.
France, 72,475.
Italy, 238,557."

Finally, on 7th July, 1944, Sauckel, in one of his last reports, informed the National Socialist Government of the results of his campaign during the first half of 1944. I quote the document, which bears the No. 208-PS, and which I submit to the Tribunal as Exhibit RF 86. I read from the second page -

"C. The foreigners came from:
France, except the North, 33,000.
Belgium, including the North of France, 16,000.
Netherlands, 15,000.
Italy, 37,000."

This is the fresh manpower put at the disposal of German industry during the period of 1st January to 30th June,1944.

I have furnished the proof I owed to the Tribunal. The Tribunal will, moreover, remember Sauckel's admission at the 43rd conference of the Four Year Plan, which I have read to you previously. Sauckel admitted that there were 5,000,000 foreign workers in Germany, of whom 200,000 were actually volunteers.

The enormity of the crime exposed is established by the circumstances of its perpetration, and by the multitude of the victims affected. To prove the gravity of its effect, I have but to recall the treatment to which foreign workers were subjected in Germany.

German propaganda always claimed that foreign workers deported to Germany were treated on an equal basis with German workers; the same living conditions, the same labour contracts and discipline. This contention, as such, is not conclusive. My American colleagues have furnished proof of the blows which the National Socialist conspirators have dealt to the dignity and decency of the life of the German worker. But the actual facts were different. Foreign workers did not enjoy the treatment in Germany to which they were entitled as human beings. I affirm this and I shall try to prove it to the Tribunal.

But, before going into that, I wish to call its attention to the significance of the next crime which I am denouncing. It does not only make the crime of deportation complete, but provides its true meaning also. I said that the policy of the defendants in the occupied territories could be summed up as follows:

Utilisation of the productive forces and extermination of the unproductive forces. This is the principle representing one of the favourite concepts of National Socialism, on the basis of which the treatment inflicted on foreign workers by the defendants should be judged. The Germans have exploited the human potential of the occupied countries to the extreme limit of the strength of the individuals concerned. They showed some consideration for foreign workers only in so far as they wished to increase their output. But as soon as their capacity for work decreased, the foreign workers shared the common lot of deportees.

I shall prove my argument by expounding to the Tribunal the working and living conditions and rules of discipline which were imposed on foreign workers deported to Germany.

I request the Tribunal to charge the defendant Sauckel with the acts I am going to denounce. He was put in charge of the working conditions for foreign workers, following an agreement to which he readily consented. The text of this agreement, made with Ley, the Chief of the German Labour Front, on 2nd June, 1943, was published in the "Reichsarbeitsblatt," 1943, Part 1, Page 588. I submitted this to the Tribunal at the beginning of my presentation as Exhibit RF 18.

This agreement shows that the treatment of foreign workers was subject to control by the inspection department of the "Manpower Utilisation" (Arbeitseinsatz). The defendant Sauckel could, therefore, not ignore the mistreatment to which foreign workers were subjected. If not prescribed, it was tolerated by him.

The working conditions of workers deported to Germany provided the first evidence of the determination of the defendants to exploit the human potential of the occupied territories to the extreme limit of its strength.

First, I call the attention of the Tribunal to the working hours imposed on foreign workers. The working hours were legally set at 54 hours per week by Sauckel's decree of 22nd August, 1942. Actually, most foreign workers were subjected to still longer working hours. Rush work, which necessitated overtime, was mostly assigned to foreign workers. It was not unusual for the latter to be forced to work 11 hours a day - that is, 66 hours a week - provided they had one day off per week.

For this purpose, I quote the report of the Minister for Prisoners, Deportees and Refugees, Document U.K. 783, which I submit as Exhibit RF 87:

"Working Hours." I quote paragraph 2:

The average number of working hours was 11 and sometimes 13 a day in certain factories, e.g. Maschinenfabrik, Berlin 31. In Berlin-Spandau, the Alkett factory, imposed 10 1/4 hours' work on dayshift and 12 hours on nightshift. At Konigsberg, the caterpillar treads factory, Krupp, imposed 12 hours a day."

The work of foreign workers was remunerated by wages identical with those of the German workers.

I call the attention of the Tribunal to the illusory character of this equality. The policy of freezing wages was a permanent element of the wage and price policy pursued by the National Socialist Government; consequently, the wages of the workers employed in Germany remained limited. They were, moreover, heavily burdened with rates and taxes. Finally, they were encroached upon by fines which the German employers had the right to impose upon their workers. These fines could reach the amount of the weekly wage for slight breaches of discipline.

I submit in evidence Document D-182. These are two drafts of speeches to foreign civilian workers. One of them is intended for Russian and Polish workers. I leave this to be dealt with by my Soviet colleagues. I submit the other to the Tribunal as Exhibit RF 88, and I quote:

"Draft of an address to foreign civilian workers: Maintenance of Labour Discipline, January, 1944. I must inform you of the following: The increase in lack of punctuality and in absenteeism has caused the competent authorities to issue stricter regulations to ensure labour discipline, whereby the competence of the employers to impose penalties has been extended. Violations of labour discipline, such as repeated unpunctuality, being absent without cause or excuse, leaving a job without authorisation, will in future be punished by fines up to the average daily wage. In more serious cases - e.g., repeated absences without cause or excuse, or insubordination, fines up to the average weekly salary will be imposed. In such cases, moreover, the additional ration cards may be taken away for a period up to four weeks.... "

The precariousness of wages, which, after these various cuts, were actually received by the foreign workers, did not allow them to raise their standard of living in the places to which they had been deported. I maintain that this standard was insufficient, and that the attitude of the Arbeitseinsatz in this matter constitutes a characteristic violation of the elementary principles of the rights of man. I will confirm this by submitting to the Tribunal proof of the inadequacy of food and medical care to which the foreign workers were entitled.

The German Propaganda Services issued, in France, illustrated pamphlets in which the accommodation for foreign workers were represented as being comfortable. It was quite different in reality.

I will not dwell on this point. Mr. Dodd, my American colleague, has already submitted and commented upon Document D-288, an affidavit by Dr. Jaeger, chief medical officer in charge of the working camps in the Krupp factories. I will not read this document again to the Tribunal, but I would like to repeat that in it Dr. Jaeger stated that French prisoners of war working in the Krupp factories had been billeted for more than half a year in kennels, urinals, unused ovens; the kennels were three feet high, nine feet long and six feet wide, and the men had to sleep there, five in a kennel. I submit this document, in support of my argument, as Exhibit RF 89.

Often to this unsanitary accommodation, inadequate food was added. In this respect I wish to explain the following to the Tribunal:

I do not claim that the foreign workers deported to Germany were systematically exposed to starvation; but I do maintain that the leading principle of National Socialism found its expression in the food regulations for foreign workers. They were decently fed only in so far as the "Manpower Utilisation" wished to maintain or to increase their capacity for work. They were put on a starvation diet the moment when, for any reason whatsoever, their industrial output diminished. They then entered that category of unproductive forces, which National Socialism sought to destroy.

On 10th September, 1942, the defendant Sauckel declared, to the First Congress of the Labour Administration of Greater Germany: "Food and remuneration of foreign workers should be in proportion to their output and their good will." He developed this point of view in documents which I am offering in evidence to the Tribunal.

I refer, in the first place, to the letter from Sauckel to Rosenberg, which is Document 016-PS, and which I shall not read since it has already been read to the Tribunal by my American colleagues. I wish, however, to draw the Tribunal's attention to the second paragraph, Page 20 of this document, which concerns the work of prisoners of war and foreign workers:

"All these people must be fed, lodged and treated in such a way that they may be exploited to the maximum with a minimum of expense."

I ask the Tribunal to remember this formula. The aim to exploit the foreign manpower to the maximum at a minimum of expense. It is the same concept which I find in a letter of Sauckel of 14th March, 1943, addressed to all Gauleiter. It is Document 633-PS, which I submit to the Tribunal as Exhibit RF 90.

"Subject: Treatment and Care of Foreign Labour.

Not only our honour and reputation and, still more than that, our National Socialist ideology, which is opposed to the methods of plutocrats and Bolshevists, but also cool common sense in the first place demand proper treatment of foreign labour, including even Soviet- Russians. Slaves who are underfed, diseased, resentful, despairing and filled with hate, will never yield that maximum of output, which they might achieve under normal conditions."

I pass now to the next to the last paragraph:

"But since we will need foreign labour for many years, and the possibility of replacing it is very limited, I cannot exploit them on a short-term policy nor can I waste their working capacity."

The criminal concept revealed by these documents is particularly manifest in the establishment of the food sanctions which were inflicted on the deported workers. I refer to Document D-182, which I have just submitted as Exhibit RF 88, and I remind the Tribunal that it provides the possibility of inflicting on recalcitrant workers the penalty of a partial suppression of food rations. Moreover, the foreign workers, who were all the more exposed to diseases and epidemics, since they were poorly lodged and fed, did not enjoy proper medical care.

I submit in evidence a report made on 15th June, 1944, by Dr. Fevrier, Head of the Health Service of the French Delegation with the German Labour Front. It is Document 536. I submit it as Exhibit RF 91, and I quote from Page 15 of the French original, Page 13 of the German translation, the last paragraph at Page 15 of the French original:

"At Auschwitz, in a very fine camp of 2,000 workers, we find, going about free, tubercular people, who were recognised as such by the local German doctor of the Arbeitsamt, but this doctor, out of hostile indifference, neglects to repatriate them. I am now taking steps to obtain their repatriation.

In Berlin, in a clean hospital, well lighted and ventilated, where the chief doctor, a German, makes the rounds only once in three weeks, and a female Russian doctor every morning distributes uniformly the same calming drops to every patient, I have seen a dozen tuberculars, three of them transformed prisoners. All of them except one have passed beyond the extreme limit at which treatment might still have had some chance of proving effective."

No statistics have been made of foreign workers who died during their deportation. Professor Henri Desaille, Medical Inspector General of the Labour Ministry, estimates that 25,000 French workers died in Germany during their deportation. But not all of them died of diseases. To slow extermination was added swift extermination in concentration camps.

The disciplinary regime over the foreign workers was, in fact, of a severity contrary to the rights of man. I have already given some examples of penalties to which the deported workers were exposed. There were still more. The workers who were deemed recalcitrant by their supervisors were sent to special reprisal camps, the "Straflager"; some disappeared in political concentration camps.

I remind the Tribunal that I have already, indirectly, proved this fact. In the course of my presentation I submitted as Exhibit RF 44, the ordinance of Sauckel of 22nd March, 1943, which extends the term of the labour contracts by the length of time which the workers spent in prison or in internment camps.

I will not dwell on this point. Mr. Dodd, my American colleague, has submitted to the Tribunal the documents which prove the shipment of labour deportees to concentration camps. For the rest, I take the liberty of referring the Tribunal to the presentation which M. Dubost will deliver to the Tribunal within a few days.

I emphasise, however, the significance of this persecution of foreign workers. It completes the crime of their deportation and renders proof of the coherence of the German policy of extermination.

I have already reported to the Tribunal the events which marked the civilian mobilisation of foreign workers for the service of National Socialist Germany. I have shown how the device of compulsory labour was inserted into the general framework of the policy of German domination. I have denounced the methods employed by the defendants to enforce the recruitment of foreign manpower. I have emphasised the importance of the deportations undertaken by the Arbeitseinsatz, and I have recalled how the deported workers were treated and ill-treated.

The policy of compulsory labour encompasses all the infractions under the jurisdiction of the Tribunal: Violation of international conventions, violation of the rights of man and crimes against Common Law.

All the defendants bear official responsibility for these infractions. It was the Reich Cabinet which set up the principles of the policy of enforced recruitment; the High Command of the German Armed Forces tried to carry them out in the workshops of the Wehrmacht, the Navy, and the Air Force; the civilian administration made use of it to support the German War production.

I recall more particularly the guilt of certain of the defendants: Goering, Plenipotentiary for the Four Year Plan, co-ordinated the planning and the execution of the plans for the recruitment of foreign workers. Keitel, Commander-in-Chief of the Armed Forces, co-signatory of Hitler's decrees, integrated compulsory labour with his manpower policy. Funk, Reich Minister of Economics, and Speer, Minister of Armament, based their programme of war production on compulsory labour. Sauckel, finally, Plenipotentiary General for the Utilisation of Manpower, proved to be the resolute and fanatical agent - to use his own words - of the policy of compulsory enrolment which, in Holland, was promoted and carried out by Seyss-Inquart.

The Tribunal will appreciate their respective responsibility; I demand the Tribunal to condemn the crime of mobilisation of foreign workers. I ask the Tribunal to restore the dignity of human labour which the defendants have attempted to destroy.

M. GERTHOFER: Mr. President, your Honours. The French Prosecution is in charge of that part of the Indictment concerning the deeds charged to the defendants which were perpetrated in the countries of Western Europe, as provided for by Article 6 (b) of the Charter of 8th August, 1945.

This article provides for violations of the laws and customs of war which concern, on the one hand persons, and on the other hand, private and public property.

The part of the Indictment concerning persons - i.e., ill-treatment inflicted on prisoners of war and on civilians, torture, murder, deportation as well as devastations not justified by military exigencies - were presented to you, and will be presented to you by my colleagues. M. Delpech and I will have the honour to present to you the pillage of private and public property.

The Tribunal will have to be informed of the most and part of the presentation of the French Prosecution. We shall strive to present it as briefly as possible, to shorten the quotation of the numerous documents submitted to the Tribunal, and to avoid, whenever possible, statistical material in order to bring only the principal facts to light. Nevertheless, sometimes we will go into detail in order that the Tribunal may appreciate certain characteristic facts now charged to the defendants, facts which are customarily designated as "economic looting."

Before approaching this subject, I should like to ask the Tribunal's permission to express the sincere gratitude of the Prosecutors of the Economic Section of the French Delegation to their colleagues of the other Allied Delegations, and particularly to those of the American Section of the Economic Case, who have been kind enough to put at our disposal a great number of German documents discovered by the United States Army, and considerable material means for their reproduction in a sufficient number of copies.

I shall have the honour of presenting in succession to the Tribunal:

(1) General remarks on the economic looting of the occupied countries of Western Europe;

(2) the special case of Denmark;

(3) that of Norway;

(4) that of Holland.

My colleague, M. Delpech, will present a fifth part covering Belgium and the Grand Duchy of Luxembourg. I shall have the honour of presenting to you the sixth part relating to France, and also the conclusion. Finally, M. Delpech, in a special presentation, will give you specific information on the looting of works of art in the occupied countries of Western Europe.

In the course of the presentation, we shall submit a certain number of documents. We shall quote only the passages which seem to us the most important. When the same document relates to several different questions, we shall quote those excerpts concerning each question when it is presented, indicating each time the reference in the document book, since it is impossible to make known to you all the excerpts at the same time, because of the complexity of facts.

In his speeches and in his writings, Hitler never concealed the economic aims of the aggression of which Germany was to become guilty. The theories of race and living space increased the envy of the Germans at the same time as they stimulated their belligerent instincts.

After having conquered Austria and Czechoslovakia without bloodshed, they turned against Poland, and prepared to attack the countries of Western Europe, where they hoped to find what was lacking to assure their hegemony.

This fact is revealed in particular by Document EC-606, discovered by the United States Army, which I submit to the Tribunal as Exhibit RF 92. This is the minutes of a conference held by the defendant Goering on 30th January, 1940, with Lieutenant-Colonel Conrath and Director Lange of the Machine Constructing Group attending. The following is the principal passage of the minutes:

"Field Marshal Goering told me at the beginning that he had to inform me of the intentions of the Fuehrer and of the economic measures resulting therefrom.

He stated:

The Fuehrer is firmly convinced that it would be possible to bring the war to a decisive conclusion by making a great attack in the West in 1940. He assumes that Belgium, Holland and Northern France will fall into our possession; he, the Fuehrer, forms his opinion on the calculation that the industrial areas of Douai and Lens, of Luxembourg, of Longwy and Briey might, as far as raw materials are concerned, replace the deliveries from Sweden.

Therefore, the Fuehrer has decided, regardless of the future, to utilise fully our reserves of raw materials, at the expense of possible later years of war. He feels that this decision is justified, since it is supported by the view that the best stocks are not stocks of raw materials but stocks of finished war materials. Moreover, when the aerial war begins, it must be taken into account that our finishing factories may be destroyed. The Fuehrer is also of the opinion that the maximum output must be achieved in 1940, and consequently that long-range production programmes should be put aside, in order to accelerate those which can be terminated in 1940."

When the invasion of the countries of Western Europe began there was an abundance of products of every kind; but after four years of the methodical looting and the enslavement of production, these countries were ruined, and their entire population was physically weakened as the result of rigorous restrictions.

To achieve these results, the Germans used every method, particularly violence, trickery and blackmail.

The purpose of the present statement will be to specify the main spoliations ordered by the German leaders in the countries of Western Europe, and to show that they constitute, as far as these countries are concerned, War Crimes which come under the jurisdiction of the International Military Tribunal for Major War Criminals.

It is not possible to draw an exact balance sheet of the German looting and the profit derived by them as a result of the enslavement of production in the occupied countries. On the one hand, we have not enough time. On the other hand, we find ourselves faced with actual impotence, resulting from the secret nature of certain operations and the destruction of archives through acts of war, or deliberate destruction at the time of the German rout.

Nevertheless, the documents now collected and the information gathered make it possible to give a minimum estimate of the extent of spoliation. However, I shall ask the Tribunal's permission to make three preliminary remarks:

(1) The numerous acts of individual looting committed by the Germans will not be referred to in this presentation, since they come under the competence of a different jurisdiction.

(2) We shall only mention for the record the incalculable economic results of German atrocities; for instance, the financial loss experienced by the immediate relatives of breadwinners murdered, or the loss suffered by certain victims of ill-treatment, who are totally or partially, temporarily or permanently incapacitated for work; or the damage resulting from the destruction of localities or buildings for the purpose of vengeance or intimidation.

(3) Finally, gentlemen, we shall not discuss the damage resulting from purely military operations, which cannot be considered as economic results of war crimes. When damage caused by military operations is referred to, some discussion will be necessary.

With the permission of the Tribunal, I shall make a few general remarks on the economic looting of Western Europe. Economic looting is to be understood as the removal of wealth of every kind, as well as the enslavement of the production of the various countries.

To reach such results in countries which were generally highly industrialised, and where numerous stocks of manufactured products and abundant reserves of agricultural products existed, the German project was faced with real difficulties.

At first, although the Germans had used this procedure to its maximum extent, requisitions were not adequate. In fact, they had to find the opportunities for ferreting out all sorts of things, which were sometimes hidden by the inhabitants and, on the other hand, they had to maintain, for their own profit, the economic activity of these countries.

The simplest way of becoming masters of the distribution of existing products and of production was to take possession of almost all means of payment, and, if necessary, to enforce their distribution in exchange for products or services, at the same time combating the rise of prices.

Faced with starvation, the populations were thus, naturally, forced to work, directly or indirectly, for the benefit of Germany.

The first part of this presentation will be divided into five chapters:

(1) Seizure of currency by the Germans;

(2) Enslavement of the production of the occupied territories;

(3) Individual purchases, which should not be confused with individual acts of looting;

(4) The black market, organised by and for the profit of Germany;

(5) Examination of the question of economic looting from the view point of International Law and in particular of The Hague Convention;

First chapter, seizure of currency by the Germans.

To have at their disposal all means of payment, the Germans used almost identical methods in the various occupied countries. First, they took two principal measures. One was the issue of paper money, by ordinance of 9th May, 1940, published in the "Verordnungsblatt fur die besetzten franzosischen Gebiete," official German gazette, which will subsequently be referred to by its official abbreviation V.O.B.I.F., which I submit to the Tribunal as Exhibit RF 93; this ordinance concerned Denmark and Norway, and on 19th May, 1940, was rendered applicable to the occupied territories of Belgium, Holland, Luxembourg and France. The Germans proceeded to issue bank notes of the Reichskreditkasse, which were legal tender only in the respective occupied countries.

The Germans then took a second measure: the blocking of existing currency within the occupied countries as a result of the ordinance of 10th May, 1940, published in V.O.B.I.F., Page 38, which I submit as Exhibit RF 94. In regard to Holland these ordinances are those of 24th June, 7th August, 16th August and 17th September, 1940, which have been submitted as Exhibits RF 95, 96, 97 and 98; in regard to Belgium, these ordinances are those of 17th June and 2nd July, 1940, submitted as Exhibits RF 99 and 100.

These measures, notably the issuing of paper money, left exclusively to the whim of the Germans, without any possible control on the part of the financial administration of the occupied countries, were to serve, as we shall see, as powerful means of pressure to impose the payment of enormous war tributes under the pretext of maintaining occupation troops, as well as alleged payment agreements known as "clearings," which functioned almost exclusively to the benefit of the Occupying Power.

The latter thus procured for itself, under false pretences, means of payment from which it profited by realising considerable sums for its sole benefit.

All agricultural and industrial products, raw materials, goods of every kind, or services, for which Germany apparently made regular payment by means of either notes of the Reichskreditkasse or by so-called clearing agreements, or by war tributes known as indemnities for the maintenance of occupation troops, were exacted with full knowledge that no consideration would be forthcoming. Thus we can be sure that, as a rule, such regulations were purely fictitious and were the most used fraudulent procedure to effect the economic looting of the occupied countries of Western Europe.

These questions will be examined in a more exact manner later on. I shall limit myself for the moment to pointing out to the Tribunal that, to effect the economic looting of occupied countries with their own money, it was necessary that this money should preserve an appreciable purchasing power. Therefore, the efforts of the Germans were directed toward stabilisation of prices. A severe regulation prohibiting rises in prices was subsequently promulgated by several decrees - V.O.B.I.F., Pages 8, 60 and 535, submitted as Exhibit RF 101. Nevertheless, the application of such measures could not prevent economic laws from acting. The payment of tributes, which were excessive, considering the resources of the invaded countries and the mass purchases made in these countries by the Occupying Power, could not but have as their principal result a continuous rise of prices. The leaders of the Reich were perfectly aware of the situation, and watched very attentively this rise in prices, which they were attempting to moderate.

This we know principally from the secret reports of Hemmen, President of the Armistice Commission for German economic questions; which we will discuss when we examine the particular case of France.

Chapter 2, Enslavement of the production of the occupied countries.

When the Germans invaded the countries of Western Europe, great disorder was created as the result. The population fled before the advance of the enemy. Industries were at a standstill. German troops guarded the factories and prevented anyone from entering.

I am not able to give you a list of the factories affected by this situation, since there was almost no exception.

Nevertheless, as an example, we will present to the Tribunal the original of one of the numerous posters exhibited in industrial plants in France. I submit this poster as Exhibit RF 102. It is dated Paris, 28th June, 1940. One text is in German, and the other is in French. Here is the French text:

> "By an order of General Field Marshal Goering of 28th June, 1940, the Generalluftzeugmeister took possession of this factory as trustee. Only persons having special permits from the Generalluftzeugmeister, Verbindungsstelle, Paris, may enter."

Hardly had the factories been occupied by the military, when German technicians, at the heel of the troops, proceeded methodically to remove the best machines.

This is revealed by a secret report of Colonel Helder, dated December, 1940, and emanating from the Economic Section of the O.K.W., Pages 77 and 78, that the removal of thousands of machines from the occupied territories was to be organised, in violation of the terms of Article 53 of The Hague Convention.

This document is submitted as Exhibit RF 103.

On the other hand, immediately after the invasion, the working population - their resources being exhausted - naturally gravitated around these factories in the hope of securing a means of subsistence. Problems of an identical nature arose in all the occupied countries: to stop the looting of machinery, which was taking place at an alarming rate, and to keep the workers employed.

The Germans for their part forced the factories to resume work under the pretext of assuring subsistence to the population. The ordinance of 20th May, 1940, published in the V.O.B.I.F., Page 31, which we submit as Exhibit RF 104, applicable to the Netherlands, Belgium, Luxembourg and France, orders that work should be resumed in all stores and industries of food supply or agriculture. The same text provided for the appointment of temporary administrators, in case of absence of the directors or in other cases of emergency.

(The Tribunal adjourned until 21st January, 1946, at 10.00 hours.)

About Coda Books

Most Coda books are edited and endorsed by Emmy Award winning film maker and military historian Bob Carruthers, producer of Discovery Channel's Line of Fire and Weapons of War and BBC's Both Sides of the Line. Long experience and strong editorial control gives the military history enthusiast the ability to buy with confidence.

The series advisor is David McWhinnie, producer of the acclaimed Battlefield series for Discovery Channel. David and Bob have co-produced books and films with a wide variety of the UK's leading historians including Professor John Erickson and Dr David Chandler.

Where possible the books draw on rare primary sources to give the military enthusiast new insights into a fascinating subject.

The English Civil Wars

The Zulu Wars

Into Battle with Napoleon 1812

Waterloo 1815

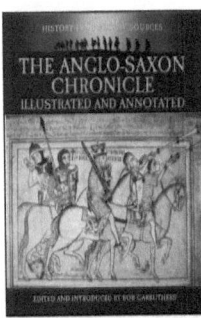
The Anglo-Saxon Chronicle

The Battle of the Bulge

The Normandy Campaign 1944

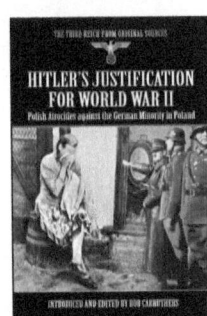
Hitler's Justification for WWII

Hitler's Mein Kampf - The Roots of Evil

I Knew Hitler

Mein Kampf - The 1939 Illustrated Edition

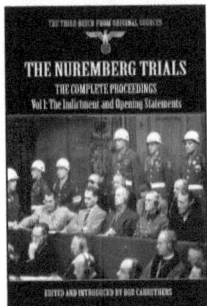
The Nuremberg Trials Volume 1

For more information, visit codahistory.com

 Tiger I in Combat
 Tiger I Crew Manual
 Panzers at War 1939-1942
 Panzers at War 1943-1945
 Wolf Pack - the U boats
 Poland 1939
 Luftwaffe Combat Reports
 Eastern Front Night Combat
 Eastern Front Encirclement
 Panzer Combat Reports
 The Panther V in Combat
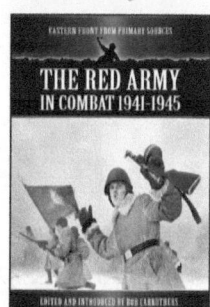 The Red Army in Combat
 Barbarossa - Hitler Turns East
 The Russian Front
 The Wehrmacht in Russia
 Servants of Evil

www.ingramcontent.com/pod-product-compliance
Lightning Source LLC
Chambersburg PA
CBHW030515230426
43665CB00010B/618